The Economics of the Environment

Peter Berck

*Department of Agricultural and
Resource Economics
University of California, Berkeley*

Gloria Helfand

Addison-Wesley

Boston   Columbus   Indianapolis
New York   San Francisco   Upper Saddle River
Amsterdam   Cape Town   Dubai   London
Madrid   Milan   Munich   Paris   Montréal   Toronto
Delhi   Mexico City   São Paulo   Sydney
Hong Kong   Seoul   Singapore   Taipei   Tokyo

If you purchased this book within the United States or Canada you should be aware that it has been imported without the approval of the Publisher or the Author.

Editorial Director: Sally Yagan
Editor in Chief: Donna Battista
Acquisitions Editor: Adrienne D'Ambrosio
Assistant Editor: Jill Kolongowski
Director of Marketing: Patrice Jones
Executive Marketing Manager: Lori DeShazo
Managing Editor: Nancy Fenton
Senior Manufacturing Buyer: Carol Melville
Manager, Rights and Permissions: Michael Joyce
Cover Designer: Bernadette Travis
Manager, Cover Visual Research &
   Permissions: Karen Sanatar

Chapter Opener Image: © Galyna
   Andrushko/Shutterstock
Supplements Editor: Alison Eusden
Full-Service Project Management
   and Text Design: Elm Street
   Publishing Services
Composition: Integra Software Services
   Pvt. Ltd.
Printer/Binder: Courier Westford

Text Font: Meridien Roman

Credits and acknowledgments borrowed from other sources and reproduced, with permission, in this textbook appear on appropriate page within text.

10 9 8 7 6 5 4 3 2 1

Addison-Wesley
is an imprint of

ISBN 10: 0-321-75264-3
ISBN 13: 978-0-321-75264-2

Brief Table of Contents

Table of Contents

Preface

The first word that comes to many people's minds when they hear the word "economics" is money. The environment conjures visions of majestic landscapes, not the commercial system. Yet environment and economics are inextricably linked, primarily through the concept of scarcity. In economics, things have value because they are limited in availability. Environmental resources, from clean air to fish stocks, are damaged by economic exploitation. Scarcity is the underlying theme of both economics and environmental studies.

This book explains how both markets and market failures affect the environment. Environmental economics is a powerful lens through which to view both economics and environmental issues. This book's goal is to explain how to measure the value of environmental goods; how to use these measurements to weigh environmental costs against the benefits of economic activity; and how to implement policies to correct market failures. For example, if gasoline prices accounted for the environmental harm of driving, welfare would improve. Students of both economics and environmental science will benefit from understanding these relationships.

This text is written with an eye primarily to students who have already taken a principles of economics class. Students without a principles class may nevertheless find the text accessible with some extra attention in some of the early chapters. Students who are taking introductory economics in an agricultural or environmental program are likely to appreciate seeing economic examples in contexts directly relevant to their interests.

This text includes all of the graphical economic tools necessary to understand the application of microeconomic principles to environmental problems. For instance, technology-based effluent standards are a key element in the U.S. Clean Water Act. We explain them with isoquants and show graphically the difference between standards and price-based measures. Grandfathering, which permitted polluting power plants to operate 40 years after the U.S. Clean Air Act was passed, motivates our discussion of long-run and short-run market equilibria. Readers of this text will, we hope, appreciate the breadth and richness of the applications of economics tools, as well as the implications of market behaviors for our world.

Why This Book?

Why should there be another environmental and resource economics book? Why is this text different from other texts? Its unique or otherwise useful features include:

- Accessible treatment of environmental economics using graphical tools;
- Reality-based cases, mostly numerical, that motivate each chapter;
- Additional boxed examples of classic and contemporary environmental issues;

- Summaries of key lessons after major sections of chapters as well as at the ends of chapters;
- Numerical and conceptual exercises for students and supplemental materials for instructors associated with each chapter.

THE ORGANIZATION OF THIS BOOK

This textbook teaches environmental and resource economics through the core models of economics. It integrates the two topics completely. The book begins with the demand-supply framework and immediately puts it to work to explore the efficacy of taxes in lowering energy use and the effect of agricultural subsidies on land use. These explorations are based on real numerical estimates. Chapter 3 explains market failures affecting the environment. The theory of demand and an extended example on the demand for energy are in "Consumer Behavior and the Environment" (Chapter 4). This provides firm grounding for "Measuring Benefits to Consumers" (Chapter 5), where the concepts of consumer surplus, equivalent and compensating variation, willingness to pay, and willingness to accept are analyzed. In turn, these are the basis for a discussion of nonmarket valuation (Chapters 6 and 7), where we provide up-to-date explication of the major methods of stated and revealed preference. These chapters explain what economists do with real data to get real estimates. Next, we move to the topic of producer behavior in "From Production to Pollution" and "Production, Pollution, Output, and Prices" (Chapters 8 and 9). The first of these chapters uses isoquants and isopollution curves to show the relation between emissions and cost minimization. The second examines supply in the long and short run, including grandfathering, to show how the cost of pollution control can be passed forward to the consumer.

Market equilibrium (Chapter 10) is shown not always to be the efficient equilibrium. This chapter shows how to go from basic microeconomic concepts to marginal cost of abatement. This approach demonstrates how economic tools are very useful for explaining the role of markets in environmental problems and the ways people's decisions affect the environment.

With this foundation, the text provides extended applications of economic tools to environmental problems. Chapter 11 takes on the Coase theorem from both the perspective of environmental economics and the perspective of law and economics. It uses the illustration of marginal cost of abatement curves from Chapter 10 to show the cost of extreme legal regimes for sulfur oxide emissions. Market based instruments and command and control instruments are the subjects of Chapter 12, while Chapter 13 looks at political economy and enforcement issues in environmental policy.

To build toward sustainability, the text introduces dynamic analysis, starting with discounting and the effect of the discount rate on energy conservation in Chapter 14. This leads to a detailed examination of benefit-cost analysis (Chapter 15), which is central to such issues as the building of Tellico Dam and the choice between nuclear and conventional power. In Chapter 16, nonrenewable resource theory—with old-growth redwood trees as the example—shows how capital market equilibrium is important for ecosystem preservation. Chapter 17 explores the sorry state of fisheries and the market failure of open access. With these examples of natural capital, the text moves to the macroeconomic level and discusses how natural capital functions and is accounted for in nations (Chapter 18). Chapter 19 concludes the text with an economic accounting for sustainability. Throughout, environmental topics are integrally linked with economic modeling.

We have sought to combine thorough economics with clear exposition, well-demonstrated examples, and straightforward graphs. The presentation is primarily verbal and graphical, with some simple algebra and an occasional area of a triangle or trapezoid; additional math is not required, though there are occasional hints about using more advanced math for these topics.

REAL-WORLD CASES

A unique feature of this text is the extended use of one core example per chapter, based in actual data. Immediately after a short introduction, each chapter begins with the description of the example. The rest of the chapter then draws on that example. For example, Chapter 4 uses data on consumer tradeoffs between electricity and other goods, from a study of electricity prices in Montana, to examine indifference curves, budget constraints, and demand curves. In Chapter 8, data on lettuce production using water and fertilizer motivate the study of isoquants. Chapter 16's discussion of nonrenewable resource management is based on exhaustible old-growth redwoods. Chapter 17 exploits research on North Sea herring to explore fisheries management. This lack of widgets makes the topics more than theoretical curiosities; they come from real work and highlight real issues.

The motivating cases include agriculture, energy, air and water quality, wildlife protection, land management, and climate change. These examples introduce students to active research in environmental economics. It shows how economists "put price tags" on environmental goods and how we measure trade-offs. It also shows what environmental economists do for a living. The concepts and cases the students learn are not just academic exercises, but also contributions to environmental policy.

MULTIPLE EXAMPLES

If we used only one example per chapter, students might not look beyond it; they might see the concept of indifference curves, for instance, only as it applies to electricity in Montana. To show that indifference curves apply equally to trade-offs between endangered species and development or to factors weighed in buying a car, the chapters include numerous boxed examples that apply the same concepts to completely new situations. These introductions to multiple issues will reinforce the concepts and show how widely applicable they are.

Each chapter ends with yet another short example. These final cases are typically more suggestive than conclusive. They aim to leave students thinking about how to apply the chapter's teachings to the new setting.

REINFORCING KEY LESSONS

To help keep students focused, each major chapter heading concludes with bullet points that bring the students back to the major lessons, and each chapter ends with a higher-level set of lessons.

END-OF-CHAPTER EXERCISES AND SUPPLEMENTS

Each chapter concludes with a number of exercises to give the students hands-on experience with the topics covered. These include numerical examples as well as qualitative questions intended to get students to apply the issues beyond the familiar cases.

Solutions to the end-of-chapter exercises and an online instructor's manual with teaching tips are available for download at the Instructor's Resource Center (www.pearsonhighered.com/irc) on the catalog page for *The Economics of the Environment*. The book's Companion Web site, www.pearsonhighered.com/berck_helfand features Web links to additional readings and economic data.

Those to Whom We Owe Many, Many Thanks

Students of Environmental Economics and Policy at the University of California at Berkeley (Peter), Agricultural and Resource Economics at the University of California at Davis (Gloria), and both Economics and Environment at the University of Michigan (Gloria) have been the primary source of inspiration for this book. Those who took our classes helped us hone our logic and come up with the right stories. Thank you for all the opportunities both to teach and to learn.

Probably the individual who heads the list of People for Whom We Are Grateful is Adrienne D'Ambrosio of Pearson Higher Education. She has been the constant contact, critic, source of encouragement and feedback, and manager of logistics since we first started talking with Pearson. Her insights into the textbook market, suggestions for packaging the material, and continual support along the way have greatly improved the book and definitely helped keep the authors going. The team at Pearson—primarily Nancy Fenton, Jennifer Jefferson, Jill Kolongowski, and Peg Monahan—has edited, suggested, dealt with reviewers, and helped us integrate reviewer comments through many drafts and much polishing. Allison Campbell at Elm Street Publishing Services, who has coordinated the production and final design of the text, has had the heroic duty of making this book look and read as well as it does.

The reviewers of this textbook deserve great credit for making us present the material even more clearly and rigorously. They challenged us, forced us to rethink our presentation, and sometimes even let us feel good for a few minutes. We humbly thank:

Amy W. Ando, *University of Illinois at Urbana-Champaign*

Lori Bennear, *Duke University*

Darrell Bosch, *Virginia Tech*

Nancy Brooks, *Cornell University*

Smita Brunnermeier, *Princeton University*

Linda T. M. Bui, *Brandeis University*

Dr. James O. Bukenya, *Alabama A&M University*

Christopher Burkart, *University of West Florida*

Mary A. Burke, *Florida State University*

Louis Cain, *Loyola University Chicago*

Richard Carson, *University of California, San Diego*

Ariaster B. Chimeli, *Ohio University*

Bentley Coffey, *Clemson University*

Surendra Devkota, *University at Albany, State University of New York*

Mitchell R. Dudley, *College of William & Mary*

K. William Easter, *University of Minnesota*

Tisha L. N. Emerson, *Baylor University*

Molly Espey, *Clemson University*

George Frisvold, *University of Arizona*

Kristine M. Grimsrud, *University of New Mexico*

Jahn K. Hakes, *Albion College*

John Halsted, *University of New Hampshire*

Diane Hite, *Auburn University*

Richard D. Horan, *Michigan State University*

John K. Horowitz, *University of Maryland*

Paul C. Huszar, *Colorado State University*

Debra Israel, *Indiana State University*

Andy Keeler, *The Ohio State University*

Derek Kellenberg, *University of Montana*

Neha Khanna, *Binghamton University*

Robert Kling, *Colorado State University*

Josh Kneifel, *University of Florida*

Janet Kohlhase, *University of Houston*

Stephan Kroll, *Colorado State University*

Mark Leonard, *University of Nebraska*

Gabriel A. Lozada, *University of Utah*

John Mackenzie, *University of Delaware*

Wade Martin, *California State University, Long Beach*

Laura McCann, *University of Missouri*

Robert Mendelsohn, *Yale University*

Olivier F. Morand, *University of Connecticut*

Darek Nalle, *University of Idaho*

Michael O'Hara, *Colgate University*

Lars Olson, *University of Maryland*

David Popp, *Syracuse University*

Reza Ramazani, *Saint Michael's College*

Doug Reynolds, *University of Alaska Fairbanks*

Tom Rhoads, *Towson University*

Mark Roberts, *Pennsylvania State University*

Duane Rosa, *West Texas A&M University*

James Roumasset, *University of Hawaii*

Caroliniana M. Sandifer, *University of Georgia*

Peter M. Schwarz, *University of North Carolina Charlotte*

Sabina Shaikh, *University of Chicago*

Gerald E. Shively, *Purdue University*

William Shobe, *University of Virginia*

Hilary Sigman, *Rutgers University*

Benjamin Simon, *George Washington University*

Katharine Sims, *Amherst College*

Kevin Siqueira, *University of Texas at Dallas*

Arthur Small, *Columbia University/Pennsylvania State University*

Jeremy Blair Smith, *Boston University*

Martin D. Smith, *Duke University*

Zachary A. Smith, *Northern Arizona University*

Scott Templeton, *Clemson University*

Mariano Torras, *Adelphi University*

Christian Vossler, *The University of Tennessee, Knoxville*

Jeffrey Wagner, *Rochester Institue of Technology*

John E. Wagner, *State University of New York– College of Environmental Science and Forestry*

Michael Wetzstein, *University of Georgia*

Jeff Williams, *Kansas State University*

Mark Witte, *Northwestern University*

Jinhua Zhao, *Michigan State University*

Some other reviewers did not explicitly allow us to include their names here. You know who you are, and we're glad to have had your comments, too.

Jacqueline Geoghegan at Clark University, Richard Woodward at Texas A&M University, and Jeff Perloff at University of California at Berkeley all used prepublication versions of this text and made many, many suggestions for its improvements.

Camille Kustin and Janelle (Kinkor) St. Pierre, while University of Michigan graduate students, provided much appreciated research for some of the examples in the book.

Cyndi Spindell Berck, a writer and lawyer, worked with us on the third draft, contributing her experience in public policy and teaching as well as her editorial skills. She contributed examples and greatly improved the clarity of the text. We will get credit for many logically flowing arguments and turns of phrase that rightfully belong to her. Because she is wife of one coauthor, at least she will share in the royalties.

Our families have lived with this project as long as we have. Gloria is grateful to Harvey, David, and Miriam Michaels, not to mention numerous Helfands, for humoring her periodic lectures and tirades about economics, the environment, and teaching. Peter is grateful to Cyndi, David, Michelle, and Joseph Berck for their support. In addition, we wish to thank those who taught us. Peter's teachers include Paul Samuelson, Marty Weitzman, and particularly Bob Solow, who taught that pollution is gunk, not emissions. Gloria owes her conversion to environmental economics to Harold Barnett, Tom Barlow, Peter Emerson, and Peter, who is a mentor and friend as well as coauthor.

Peter Berck
Gloria Helfand

Economics and the Environment

Environmental and resource issues have the public's attention. Extinction of species, toxic spills, depletion of tropical rainforests, and climate change regularly make the front pages of newspapers. People's activities are regularly harming the functions of the natural world. We cut down forests to clear the land for farming and housing developments; we pollute the air to produce electricity, cars, and other goods that support our lifestyles. At the same time, people work hard to protect wilderness areas from destruction, to improve air and water quality, and to find cleaner energy sources. Economics, as a social science that studies how people behave in market situations, provides a great deal of insight into the nature of environmental problems and what we can do about them. This chapter will examine:

- A definition of environmental and resource economics;
- Why understanding market forces is necessary for understanding environmental problems;
- Why understanding that markets fail is necessary for understanding economic problems.

Climate Change

According to the Intergovernmental Panel on Climate Change, an international panel of top scientists, people are changing the climate of our planet. Driving, using electricity, producing and using consumer goods, and other everyday activities produce "greenhouse gases" (GHG) that accumulate in the atmosphere and trap heat. As greenhouse gases increase in our atmosphere, ocean levels will rise and flood coastal lands, while other areas will experience droughts. Mass migrations will occur as people seek to avoid these changes. Agricultural production zones will shift. Pests and diseases from the tropics will migrate into areas where they currently are not found. Ecosystems will face new stresses, and many species will go extinct.

If the potential effects of climate change are so dire, why do we emit green-house gases? How will people respond to climate change? How can we change people's behavior to reduce the damages?

Addressing climate change will involve great social and technological changes. Reducing emissions will require large investments in energy efficiency, changes in individual behavior, and research and development into methods to keep GHGs out of the atmosphere. Likely adaptations to climate change include changing where crops are grown, finding new crop varieties, providing flood defenses for areas previously not prone to flooding, and relocating some major cities. Can human society rise to these challenges?

In fact, people are already doing these things, and more, to prepare ourselves for the future. Electricity generators are investing in emissions-free wind power and are conducting research in solar energy. As gasoline prices increase, people buy more fuel-efficient cars and try to live closer to where they work. Farmers seek new drought-tolerant varieties and change what they grow in response to long-range weather forecasts. These changes in behavior result in part from expected changes in the prices associated with GHG generation and the markets for agricultural goods.

At the same time, people are reluctant to take more extreme measures to reduce our GHG emissions. Driving less to reduce gasoline consumption is difficult for people who need to get to jobs, school, stores, or social activities. Letting our homes and businesses be colder in the winter and warmer in the summer would affect our health, comfort, and productivity. People in developing countries want improved standards of living, and increased energy consumption is necessary for the businesses that would improve their well-being. Changing behavior to reduce climate change–related activities is costly, and people want to avoid those costs.

Environmental economics provides insights into why people act as they do in the face of environmental problems. Markets provide powerful signals that influence our decisions about producing and consuming goods. But what about resources such as clean air and water? These environmental goods are not normally bought and sold in markets. The lack of market signals influences people's use of these goods, leading to excess use. This relationship between the importance of markets and the lack of markets for environmental goods is the subject of this text.

Environmental and Resource Economics

Environmental and resource economics is the application of the tools of economics to the topic of environmental and resource issues. Let's look at these terms separately.

A common definition of **economics** is the study of the allocation of scarce resources. When there is not enough of something—housing, food, energy, forests—so that anyone can have as much as desired, some process must develop for determining who gets how much of the goods. Processes can include standing in line, government mandates, war, or markets. As we will see, economics focuses on markets as a means to allocate goods: markets typically waste less time than standing in lines, involve less bureaucracy than government mandates, and are less bloody than wars.

Environmental and resource issues involve the interaction between people and the natural world. People get tremendous benefits from the natural world: clean air and water, forests that provide us with opportunities for recreation as well as wood products, minerals and metals that we use in production of many goods, plant and animal species that provide us with food, medicine, and pleasure. We also have great influence on the health of the natural world: our activities affect the quality of the air and water, and the quantity and quality of minerals, metals, and habitats. Conflicts over environmental issues arise when human activities lead to degradation of the natural world, such as pollution, destruction of habitat, species extinction, and changes in our climate. With careful resource management, we can make use of some of nature's bounty without excessive harm to the availability of those goods for future generations.

Environmental and resource economics examines human behavior in using and abusing environmental resources. We do not have infinite supplies of clean air and water, oil, or plant and animal species; any of these can be depleted through heavy use. The tools of economics can help us understand both why people tend to deplete these resources and why depletion is not to our advantage.

IN SUMMARY

- Economics studies the allocation of scarce resources, especially but not only through market processes.
- Environmental and resource issues arise from human interaction with the natural world.
- Environmental and resource economics uses the tools of economics to analyze environmental and resource issues.

The Power of Markets

Markets provide opportunities to watch people make choices. Where people live, what schools they attend, what jobs they take, and what goods they buy require choices involving prices. How do farmers decide what crops to grow? Will people commute by car, take public transportation, or live close enough to work that they can walk? Will people increase the heating in their homes during the winter, or wear sweaters? All these decisions require people to consider how much money they would spend or receive for the different options. If prices change, then people's choices will change. For instance, suppose that the price of gasoline increases. In response, people are likely to immediately reduce their driving on discretionary trips, by such actions as combining errands or carpooling. Over time, if the price stays high, they will take additional actions, such as finding alternative transportation methods, buying more fuel-efficient cars, or even moving closer to frequent destinations. While people can become fixed in their habits, they are also adaptable, and responding to changes in prices is one source of behavior change.

Many market activities have environmental consequences. Less expensive gasoline, for instance, increases the amount of gasoline that people use. Using gasoline, however, contributes to both climate change and health problems. Burning gasoline emits greenhouse gases, including carbon dioxide and nitrous oxide. It also produces pollutants that affect health, including nitrogen oxides, carbon monoxide, hydrocarbons, and particulate matter. In addition, inexpensive gasoline makes living far away from work relatively easy: people pay more for commuting in exchange for less expensive housing. As a result, housing and other land development moves out of central cities into previously rural areas, disrupting wildlife habitat and paving over land that previously absorbed rainfall. If gasoline becomes more expensive, the air pollution, climate change, and land use effects associated with gasoline use will decrease.

Prices can be a very effective way to change human behavior toward the environment. Other means of changing behavior exist. Environmental psychologists, for instance, have found that some methods, such as asking people to give written or verbal commitments, can induce behavior changes. Similarly, communications researchers emphasize the importance of targeting the intended audience and appealing to people's existing values in order to get people to respond to new information. Using markets to influence environmental behavior is an additional tool. Even people who are not interested in environmentalist values will respond to changes in prices by buying different combinations of goods.

The power of markets can either benefit or harm the environment. Low prices for gasoline lead to high use and, thus, high damage; high prices reduce those damages. High demand for goods from rare species, such as the traditional Asian medicines derived from tigers' body parts, can drive those species toward extinction. People and organizations have purchased environmentally sensitive lands to protect them from development. The common feature in these and many other examples is that markets influence the quality of the natural environment. Understanding market forces, then, is critical for addressing environmental issues.

IN SUMMARY

- Markets provide people with the opportunity to make choices in response to prices. Changes in prices lead to changes in those choices.
- Market choices influence the natural environment, in both positive and negative ways. Because of this influence, prices can be used to change people's behavior toward the environment.

Problems with Markets

Markets are very effective means of making goods and services available to consumers, and market prices provide important information about these goods and services. High prices typically indicate that a good is not readily available. In response, consumers will be more cautious in their use of the good. In addition, the high price gives producers an incentive to provide more of the good; as they provide more, the good becomes more available, and the price is likely to drop. Prices, then, provide signals to both consumers and producers about the availability of goods.

Many environmental goods, however, are not bought and sold in markets. Individuals do not buy and sell the air they breathe or the quality of the water in the lakes, rivers, and oceans around them. At the same time, each individual's actions affect everyone's air and water quality. One person driving a car makes everyone's air slightly dirtier. Fertilizers and pesticides applied to farms or individuals' gardens often end up seeping into nearby rivers and lakes. The dirty air and water impose real costs on people, by damaging people's health, harming the area flora and fauna, and making the area less pleasant as a place to live. If the individuals creating the harm do not have to pay those costs, though, they do not get a market signal to reduce the damaging behaviors.

While markets are very powerful, they do not always work effectively. Environmental goods are a classic case of market failure. A market has failed if there are missed opportunities for everyone involved in the market to be better off by moving goods from one use to another; the market has left some people worse off than they could be. When environmental goods are not traded in markets, consumers have no signal to reduce their consumption, and producers have no signal to make more of the good available. People with different plans for the good (for instance, factories that want to use air and water as ways to dispose of waste, and people who want to breathe air and drink water) each claim to have the right to the resource. The absence of markets for environmental goods thus leads to conflicts and abuse of those resources.

Markets also fail for goods other than environmental goods. For instance, monopolies (producers that can manipulate prices) impose great costs on consumers. Research into new technologies and medicines frequently suffers from market failures: who should pay the high costs of discovery if, once the new product is discovered, anyone can produce it? Market failures are not limited to specific sectors of the economy, either: a problem in the market for gasoline will influence housing and car markets, as gasoline prices influence people's decisions on where to live and what to drive. Because markets are intricately interconnected, most markets are influenced by shortcomings in other markets.

The fact that markets are such powerful organizing influences in our society does not mean that markets are left to their own devices. A large number of government policies influence markets. Examples include the income tax code, agricultural commodity programs, and worker health and safety regulation. Some of these policies are meant to address market failures; other policies redirect otherwise functional markets to benefit some people at the expense of others. Completely free markets—that is, markets completely free from government interference and market failures—are quite unusual. One reason for this is that markets are highly interconnected; policy makers are not willing to leave a market unregulated if it is going to have undesirable effects throughout the whole economy. Understanding that markets do not always work effectively, and that those problems are likely to spill over into markets that are otherwise very effective, is also necessary for addressing environmental problems.

IN SUMMARY

- Markets often do not exist for environmental goods. This failure of markets may be the basis of conflicts over environmental goods.
- Markets may not work effectively for other goods and situations. A problem in one market is likely to cause difficulties in other markets connected to it. Because markets are highly interconnected, problems in provision of environmental resources affect and are affected by many other markets.

CHAPTER SUMMARY

Here are the key lessons from this chapter:

- Environmental and resource economics applies the tools of economics to the subject of environmental and resource issues. Economics is the study of the allocation of scarce goods. Conflicts arise over the use of environmental goods because there is not enough available for people to have them in their pristine state and also to use them for production or waste disposal. Because environmental goods are scarce, economics offers important insights into their management and abuse.
- Markets are very powerful ways of allocating goods. Market signals, usually prices, affect what people produce and buy, as well as how those goods are produced; they can have strong effects on the environment, both for good and for ill. Understanding how markets work contributes greatly to understanding environmental controversies.
- While markets have desirable properties as ways to allocate goods, they often do not operate perfectly. Markets often fail for environmental goods, as well as other goods. Understanding that markets fail contributes greatly to understanding the role of economic analysis in public policy; understanding how they fail gives further insight into environmental problems.

KEY TERMS

economics *(p. 2)*
environmental and resource
  economics *(p. 2)*

environmental and resource
  issues *(p. 3)*

EXERCISES

1. Consider the following environmental issues. For each of them, describe someone who benefits from environmental protection and someone who bears the cost of environmental protection. Describe those benefits and costs.
   (a) Reducing water pollution from livestock production
   (b) Protecting endangered species whose habitat is affected by human settlements
   (c) Harvesting fish from a lake so much that the fish population might die out

(d) Extracting coal by stripping away the soil and forests overlying it, leading to disturbed landscapes and water pollution

(e) Using up the world's supply of petroleum

2. Do people respond to market incentives? Consider the following policies. How do you expect people to respond to them? What environmental impacts might arise?

   (a) Many places require that "brownfields"—places that previously received contamination, usually from industrial use—be cleaned up before they can be put to new uses. Brownfields are commonly in urban areas. Suburban and rural areas are sometimes known as "greenfields" because they lack contamination concerns. Where would new businesses want to locate?

   (b) In the western United States, a great deal of land is owned by the federal government, which does not pay local property taxes. The federal government does, though, give a share of the proceeds of sales of wood products from its lands to support local government purposes, such as schools. How might the local governments view wilderness protections that reduced wood harvests?

   (c) Many developing countries seek to develop export markets because people in wealthier countries have more ability to buy products than people in their own countries. They can produce goods more cheaply, due to lower labor costs and, often, fewer environmental restrictions on production. What factors would a company consider in deciding where to locate its production? What factors would a developing country consider in deciding whether to increase environmental protections?

   (d) When gasoline prices hit record levels in the summer of 2008, some U.S. presidential candidates proposed a "gas tax holiday"—reducing the federal gasoline tax—to ease the cost increase. These same presidential candidates expressed concern over the consequences of climate change, to which burning fossil fuels such as gasoline is a contributor. What effects, if any, would a "gas tax holiday" have on climate change?

2 | Supply and Demand
Market Forces and the Environment

People drive cars, even though driving produces pollutants. Manufacturers emit pollutants into land, air, and water because avoiding pollution would increase their costs. Prices have a great influence on both of these decisions. When gasoline prices are high, people switch to public transportation, use carpools, or take fewer trips; when polluting is expensive, producers look for less-polluting ways to make their goods. The market forces of supply and demand have an enormous effect on the environment. By determining the quantities of goods and services produced and consumed, market forces also determine how much pollution is produced and how many resources are used up. This chapter will examine:

- Supply and how producers decide how much to produce;
- Consumer demand;
- Market equilibrium;
- How to use supply and demand to understand the electricity market;
- How to use supply and demand to study government policies affecting agricultural land.

An Energy Crisis

Governments used to regulate electric utilities heavily. In recent years, though, a trend both in the United States and in Europe has allowed the market, rather than the government, to determine the price consumers pay for electricity. In 1998, California adopted a deregulation policy to allow a competitive market for electricity. The following *New York Times* article describes what happened next:

> But in recent weeks, the California Independent System Operator, the nonprofit group that manages the state's power grid, has been forced to scramble daily for as much as one-third of the electricity the utility companies need to keep lights on in the state.

Electricity prices for peak hours have soared to $1,400 per megawatt per hour, a more than 20-fold increase from last year. The Independent System Operator has been spending an additional $50 million to $100 million a day for electricity, costs that are passed onto utility companies and ultimately consumers. (*New York Times,* December 16, 2000)

Deregulation was intended to produce power from the cheapest source and lower the price to its consumers. Instead, the prices of power went way up. In the aftermath of the California energy crisis, much research has focused on how the crisis came to be. One view is that factors such as warm weather and economic growth increased the amount of power people wanted to buy without anyone building more plants to produce the electricity. A fundamentally different view is that the producers and sellers of power intentionally idled their plants, so that there would be less electricity produced and the price would go up. This chapter uses the concepts of supply and demand to understand these arguments and to assess the environmental impacts of electricity production and consumption.

Supply

The production of electricity has huge environmental consequences. Most energy production in the United States comes from burning fossil fuels, such as coal and natural gas. Burning these fuels leads to production of greenhouse gases (GHG). Greenhouse gases collect in the atmosphere and act like a blanket on the earth to hold heat. As a result, the earth's climate is warming. This warming has increasingly large effects on agriculture (through changes in climate and thus growing regions), shorelines (as icecaps melt and increase ocean volume, thus causing coastlines to go under water), weather (due to disruptions in existing systems), and entire ecosystems (due to all of the factors mentioned previously). Understanding the market for electricity, then, is a first step in applying economics to the problem of climate change.

First, let's think about the price of electricity. This book focuses on prices in a *competitive market*. A **competitive market** is one where both producers and consumers are *price takers*. **Price takers** have no control over the market price; they simply respond to it. Individuals at the grocery store decide how much of various goods to buy, but they buy at the posted price. They are acting as price takers. The purpose of the electricity reform was to get the producers of electricity to act as price takers. As price takers, they would be expected to sell as much electricity as would increase their profits without concern for how their actions might change the price. Let's see how things were supposed to work.

The basics of supply and demand are these: **Producers** make and sell goods that **consumers** buy. The amount sold is called the **quantity supplied**, and the amount bought the **quantity demanded**. As price changes, producers change the amount that they make. Price increases lead producers to provide more of the good, and, as price decreases, producers provide less of the good, all other things being equal. This relationship between the quantity supplied and price is called the **supply curve**, or simply **supply**. The supply curve can answer a number of "what if" questions. For instance, how much electricity would be supplied if the price were $20 per megawatt hour? (A megawatt hour, or MWH, is a million watts for an hour). More generally, how much electricity will be supplied if the price were $P/MWH? Similarly, the relationship between the quantity demanded and price is called the **demand curve**, or **demand**. As price changes, the amount that consumers buy changes. Generally, as price decreases, consumers buy more of the good, and as price increases, consumers buy less of the good. Finally, the intersection of supply and demand determines the market price and quantity. Let's first look at supply, then demand, and then their interaction.

THE SUPPLY CURVE FOR ELECTRICITY IN CALIFORNIA

Like most supply curves, the supply curve for electricity in California slopes upward because suppliers provide a greater quantity when the price is higher. The higher price gives producers, who typically seek to increase their profits, an incentive to make more product. The upward-sloping curve, labeled S_0 in Figure 2.1, is a supply curve for fossil-fueled electricity in California. The vertical axis is price (in this case, dollars per MWH), and the horizontal axis is quantity (in gigawatt hours, or GWH, which are 1,000 MWH).

To see how this supply curve works, choose a price on the vertical axis, for instance, $30/MWH. Drawing a horizontal line from that price to the supply curve, and then a vertical line down to the horizontal axis, reveals that generators are expected to produce 13 GWH (or 13,000 MWH) each hour when the price is $30/MWH.

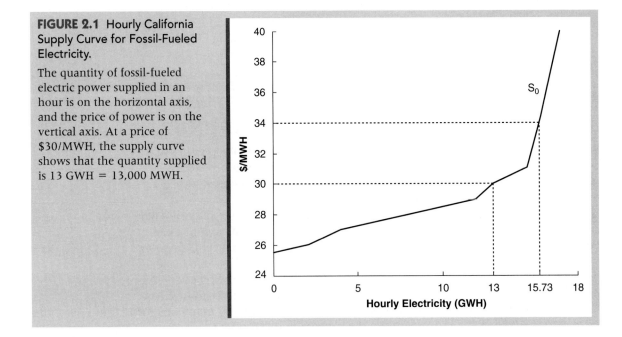

FIGURE 2.1 Hourly California Supply Curve for Fossil-Fueled Electricity.

The quantity of fossil-fueled electric power supplied in an hour is on the horizontal axis, and the price of power is on the vertical axis. At a price of $30/MWH, the supply curve shows that the quantity supplied is 13 GWH = 13,000 MWH.

The supply curve in Figure 2.1 is based on a study of electricity supply in California. The researchers used a list of fossil-fueled plants that included the costs per megawatt hour for each plant to produce electricity. Plants that burn fuel efficiently have lower costs of production than plants that burn fuel less efficiently. They get more electricity output per unit of fuel input. When the price of electricity is low, only those firms with the lowest costs find it profitable to operate. Thus, at low prices, the electricity comes only from efficient plants. At higher prices, less efficient plants also find it profitable to operate, and electricity comes from these plants as well. The supply curve, then, reflects the costs of producing the good. At higher prices, more plants with higher costs operate, and more electricity is produced. As a result, the supply curve in Figure 2.1 slopes upward. Note that it is a market supply curve. It indicates the total amount of electricity made by all of the firms at different prices. Although supply curves describe how quantity responds to price, the standard graph draws them the opposite way, with price responding to quantity—price on the vertical axis and quantity on the horizontal axis.

A change in the price causes a change in the quantity supplied. For example, Figure 2.1 shows that an increase in the price of electricity to \$34/MWH would cause a change in quantity supplied to 15,734 MWH. The new combination of price and quantity will be a different point on the same curve. A change in quantity supplied as price changes is called a **movement along the supply curve**.

SUPPLY SHIFTERS

Figure 2.1 shows quantity supplied as a function of **own price**, the price of electricity itself. As well as own price, other factors determine the quantity of electric power that producers make available. While own price determines which point is chosen on the supply curve, these other factors determine where the supply curve itself lies on the graph. A change in the cost of production is an example of a *supply shifter*. **Supply shifters** are factors other than own price that affect the supply curve. Instead of causing a movement along the supply curve, they shift the location of the supply curve.

For example, most electricity in California is made from natural gas; natural gas is an input to production of electricity. When the price of natural gas increases, even while the own price of electricity is held constant, every gas-fired plant will see its costs increase. Those plants that were just barely worth running will now lose money if they produce electricity. They will not choose to operate under these conditions. In this situation, the supply curve for electricity has shifted to the left. A shift to the left means that less electricity is produced at any given market price for electricity. Similarly, a decrease in the cost of natural gas would cause the supply curve for electricity to shift right, so that more electricity is produced at any price.

Line S_1 in Figure 2.2 shows a supply curve for electricity that has shifted to the left. On the old supply curve, S_0, 13 GWH would be produced at a price of \$30/MWH. On the new supply curve, S_1, only 4 GWH would be produced at \$30/MWH.

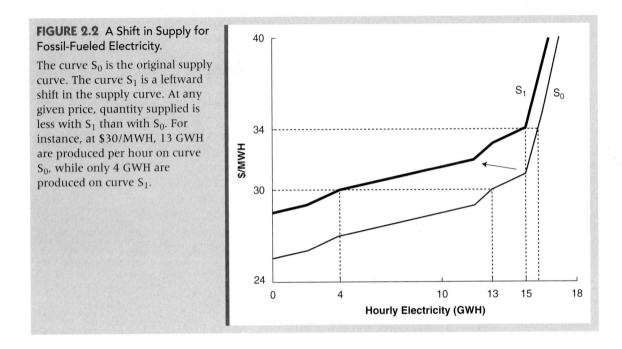

FIGURE 2.2 A Shift in Supply for Fossil-Fueled Electricity.

The curve S_0 is the original supply curve. The curve S_1 is a leftward shift in the supply curve. At any given price, quantity supplied is less with S_1 than with S_0. For instance, at \$30/MWH, 13 GWH are produced per hour on curve S_0, while only 4 GWH are produced on curve S_1.

Several factors can cause the supply curve to shift. First, as in the example, a change in the price of an input to production can shift the supply curve. Second, a change in technology can shift the curve. Developing more efficient gas-burning plants has led to a rightward shift of the supply curve for electricity, so that more electricity will be produced at a given price. Third, a change in the number of producers can also shift the supply curve. Building more power plants will shift the supply curve for electricity to the right, so that more electricity will be produced at a given price. Finally, circumstances outside the market system, such as weather, natural disasters, or human-made disasters, can shift the supply curve. For instance, a fire or earthquake that disables a production plant would reduce the quantity of electricity supplied at any given price, thus shifting the supply curve to the left.

IN SUMMARY

- A price-taking supplier decides how much to produce based upon the observed price. She believes that her own supply decision will not change the price.
- The supply curve is the relationship between quantity and price that shows how much of a good producers will make as a function of the price.
- The supply curve, which is based on the costs of producing the good, usually slopes upward, to indicate that producers will supply a greater quantity of the good if the price is higher. A change in price leads to a movement along the supply curve, as suppliers provide a larger or smaller quantity of the good.

- The supply curve can shift either to the left or the right in response to changes in the prices of inputs to production, changes in technology, changes in the number of producers, or events such as weather and disasters.
- A shift in the supply curve means an increase or decrease in the quantity that producers will supply at any given price.

Demand

Supply is one side of the market. Demand is the other. The amount of electricity that consumers buy is the quantity demanded. The demand curve, or demand, is the relationship between the price of electricity and the quantity demanded. For every price P (such as $30/MWH), the demand curve answers the question, "How much would people buy if the price were P?"

A consumer has many choices concerning how much electricity to use. Should she use incandescent or more energy-efficient compact fluorescent lights? Turn the lights off when she leaves the room? Air condition the home to 82°F or 78°F? Price is one determinant of those decisions. Usually, a higher price of electricity leads consumers to turn down the air conditioning, turn off the lights, and replace the light bulbs. A higher electricity price creates greater savings to all these activities. As a result, consumers will use less electricity as the price of electricity rises. Most individuals' demand curves for electricity will slope downward. Adding up the quantity demanded from each consumer produces the market demand curve. Because the individual demand curves slope down, so does the market demand curve.

THE DEMAND FOR ELECTRICITY IN CALIFORNIA

The downward-sloping line, labeled D_0, in Figure 2.3 is an estimate of the market demand curve for electricity in California. The quantity of electricity is on the horizontal axis, and the price is on the vertical axis. It is read the same way as the supply curve: start with the price, trace a line from the vertical axis to the demand curve, and then trace a line straight down to the horizontal axis to determine the quantity that people will purchase at that price. At a price of $30/MWH, consumers will buy 15.3 GWH of electricity. When the price is $34/MWH, consumers will purchase just over 15.1 GWH. When the price of electricity changes, the quantity demanded changes. This change in quantity demanded is a **movement along the demand curve**. If the price of electricity increases, consumers demand a smaller quantity. For this reason, the demand curve for electricity slopes down, like most demand curves.

The steepness of the demand curve reflects how much people change their consumption when the price changes. In the case of electricity, people do not respond strongly to price changes, at least in the short run. The demand curve is relatively steep. For other goods, though, a proportionally small price change leads to a large change in quantity demanded, and the demand curve is relatively flat. Box 2.1 discusses another way to describe how quantity changes in response to price changes.

FIGURE 2.3 California's Hourly Demand for Electricity.

The demand curve D_0 is the demand in California for fossil-fueled electricity produced in-state. At a price of $30/MWH, the curve shows that consumers will demand 15.3 GWH. When the price is $34/MWH, consumers will purchase 15.1 GWHs.

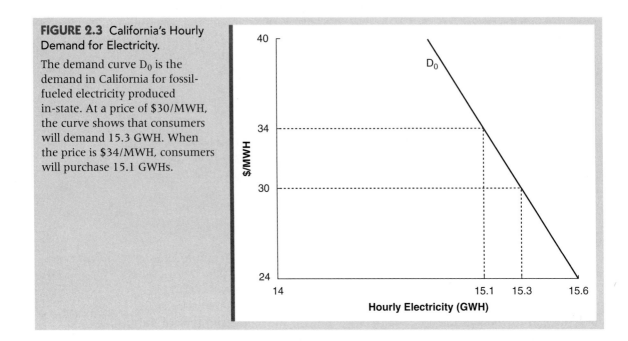

BOX 2.1

Elasticity

The response of demand or supply to price is often stated in percentage terms. The **price elasticity of demand** is the percent change in quantity demanded caused by a 1 percent change in price. Using the two points on the demand curve shown in Figure 2.3, we can calculate the price elasticity of demand. When the price of electricity increases from $30/MWH to $34/MWH, it increases by $\frac{34 - 30}{30} = 13.33\%$. As a result, quantity demanded decreases from 15.3 to 15.1 GWH, which is $\frac{15.1 - 15.3}{15.3} = -1.31\%$. The percent change in quantity divided by the percent change in price is $-1.31/13.33 = -0.098$. Therefore, the elasticity of demand calculated between the two points on the demand curve is -0.098. As with most calculations of percentage changes, it is equally acceptable to divide by the new price (34) or the average of the two prices (32), even when they give slightly different values. It is also possible to compute elasticity at a point, rather than between two points.

   Although the elasticity of demand is -0.098, economists often assume their readers know the sign is negative and just say 0.098 when they mean -0.098.

DEMAND SHIFTERS

Like the supply curve, the demand curve can shift. If something causes consumers to demand a greater quantity of electricity at any price, the demand curve for electricity shifts to the right. Similarly, if consumers demand a smaller quantity of electricity at any price, the demand curve shifts left. The curve D_1 in Figure 2.4 shows the old demand curve, D_0, shifted right to reflect a larger quantity of electricity demanded at a given price.

A number of factors can shift the demand curve for electricity. First, a consumer's income is likely to affect the demand curve. Richer consumers are likely to have larger refrigerators, larger homes, and more swimming pools than poorer consumers. All these things lead to people using more electricity at any given price when their income increases.

Electricity is a *normal good.* **Normal goods** are goods whose demand curves shift right as income increases. At any given price for the normal good, people demand a greater quantity when their income increases. With increased income, the demand curve for electricity shifts to the right. Increased income led to a rightward shift in the demand curve for electricity in California in the twentieth century. A similar effect is taking place with the increase in income in twenty-first-century China.

Changes in the prices of related goods can also shift the demand curve for electricity. Let's consider two types of relationships between goods: goods that *substitute* for electricity and goods that *complement* electricity.

Two goods are **substitutes** if an *increase* in the price of the first good leads to a rightward shift in the demand curve of the second good. Fossil-fueled electric

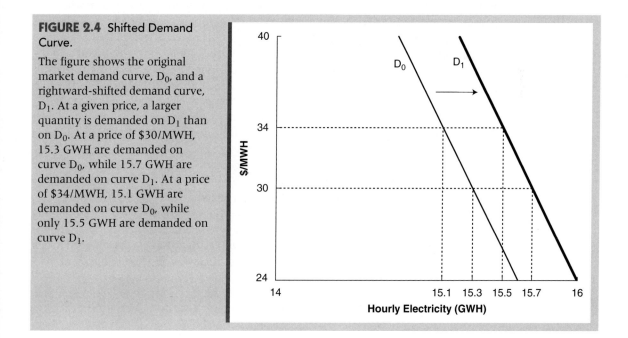

FIGURE 2.4 Shifted Demand Curve.

The figure shows the original market demand curve, D_0, and a rightward-shifted demand curve, D_1. At a given price, a larger quantity is demanded on D_1 than on D_0. At a price of \$30/MWH, 15.3 GWH are demanded on curve D_0, while 15.7 GWH are demanded on curve D_1. At a price of \$34/MWH, 15.1 GWH are demanded on curve D_0, while only 15.5 GWH are demanded on curve D_1.

power and solar panels are substitutes. When the price of fossil-fueled power goes up, the demand for solar panels shifts to the right.

In contrast, a *decrease* in the price of air conditioners leads to a rightward shift in the demand for electricity. That's because people will need more electricity to run the increased number of air conditioners. Air conditioners and electricity are **complements**: a decrease in the price of one good leads to an increase in the quantity demanded for the other, at any given price for the second good. In other words, the demand curve for the second good shifts to the right. Goods consumed together, such as laptops and electricity, are complements.

A third factor that shifts the demand curve for electricity is a change in a consumer's characteristics, which economists typically refer to as **tastes and preferences**. For instance, some families put up large Christmas light displays that use a great deal of electricity, while other people with the same income and facing the same electricity prices do not put up displays at all. These families are displaying different tastes and preferences. If some families scaled back the wattage of their displays because of concern about climate change, the demand curve for electricity would have shifted leftward because of a change in tastes.

BOX 2.2

When Less Is Better

The opposite of a normal good is an *inferior good*. The demand curve for an **inferior good** shifts leftward when income rises. Indoor air pollution is a serious problem in less-developed countries. A major source of pollutants is cooking and heating. The indoor air pollution problem decreases as people become richer. Increased income leads to a leftward shift in the demand for the dirtiest fuels, like wood, and a rightward shift in the demand for cleaner fuels, like bottled gas. So wood is an inferior good, and bottled gas is a normal good. The process of shifting fuels from dirty ones, like wood, through intermediate fuels, like kerosene, to clean fuels, like bottled gas, is described as the fuel ladder. One development strategy to decrease the incidence of disease from indoor air pollution is to subsidize the purchase of stoves and speed the process of fuel switching to cleaner fuels.

Subcompact, non-sporty cars were inferior goods for a long time. Larger cars were normal goods. As people's incomes grew, they bought more large and fewer subcompact cars. This empirical regularity underlay the view of automobile companies that making people buy smaller cars would be a disservice to them. It would be making them act as if they were poorer than they really were. Others argue that demand for cars is heavily influenced by advertising. If, instead of advertising how "tough" a truck was, the auto companies advertised how hard the truck was on the environment, perhaps subcompact, non-sporty vehicles would no longer be inferior goods.

A fourth set of factors that affect demand for electricity is events largely outside the economic system. Just as a natural disaster can shift the supply curve, natural or human activity can shift the demand curve. The demand curve for air conditioning, and hence for electricity, shifts rightward in hot weather because more electricity is consumed at any given price for electricity.

The final factor that affects the demand curve is, not surprisingly, the total number of people in the market—the population. Because the market demand is the sum of the individual demands, the market demand will shift to the right when there are more individuals.

For goods that can be stored, unlike electricity, expectations of future prices may shift the demand curve. If, for instance, concerns arise over access to oil from the Middle East in coming months, the demand for oil may increase immediately as importers seek to purchase oil while they can.

Our examples so far have focused on the reasons for a rightward shift in demand. The same is true in reverse for a leftward shift. For a normal good, demand shifts left if income decreases, population decreases, the price of a substitute decreases, or the price of a complement increases. Similarly, changes in tastes and preferences, and events such as natural disasters, can shift demand to the left.

In California's electricity market, the most important demand shifters have been the increase in population and the increase in income. Both of these factors led to the demand curve for power in California shifting to the right. Were these enough to produce the very high prices in 2000?

IN SUMMARY

- A demand curve shows how much of a good will be bought in response to its price. An individual demand curve is the demand curve for a single consumer. The market demand curve, the sum of the individual demand curves, is the demand from all consumers.
- The demand curve slopes downward, to indicate that consumers buy less of a good if the price increases.
- A shift in the demand curve means an increase or decrease in the quantity that consumers demand at any given price. The demand curve can shift either to the left or the right in response to changes in consumers' income, the prices of substitutes and complements, tastes and preferences, noneconomic factors, and population.

Market Equilibrium

Taken together, the decisions of producers and consumers in response to price determine the quantity of electricity produced and consumed. Let's look now at how the price and quantity of electricity come about.

EQUILIBRIUM IN CALIFORNIA'S ELECTRICITY MARKET

In a competitive market, both consumers and producers respond to the market price. So far, however, we have not considered where the market price comes from. To do so, let's examine both the supply curve and the demand curve on the same diagram, as shown in Figure 2.5. A **market equilibrium** occurs when the quantity supplied at a given price equals the quantity demanded at that price. The equilibrium occurs at the intersection of the demand curve, D_0, and the supply curve, S_0. The demand curve, D_0, contains all necessary information about consumers and no information at all about producers. Similarly, the supply curve contains all necessary information about producers and no information about consumers. It is only when they are put together that it is possible to find the equilibrium, which consists of one combination of price and quantity. At a price of $32/MWH, producers generate 15.2 GWH, exactly the amount consumers will buy. The producers and the consumers made independent decisions on how much to produce and consume. At the *equilibrium price*, their independent decisions led them to produce and consume the same amounts. The **equilibrium price**, also called the **market price**, is the price that leads the quantity supplied to equal the quantity demanded. In this example, the equilibrium price is $32/MWH. Put another way, the market **clears** at $32/MWH.

How does this equilibrium change when something shifts the supply curve? Perhaps there is an increase in the price of the fossil fuel needed to generate electricity, so that less electricity is produced at any price. In other words, the supply curve for electricity shifts left. Figure 2.6 shows what happens to price and quantity when the supply curve shifts left from S_0 to S_1. The old equilibrium price and

FIGURE 2.5 Equilibrium.

At the price $32/MWH, the quantity of electricity supplied and the quantity demanded are equal. Both the quantity demanded and the quantity supplied are 15.2 GWH for an hour.

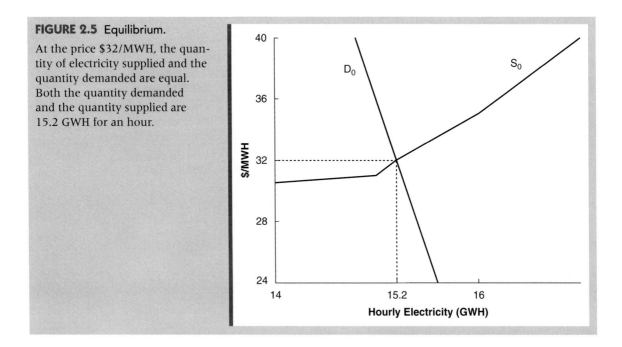

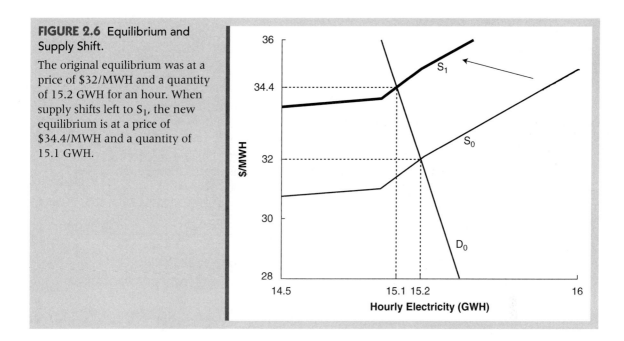

FIGURE 2.6 Equilibrium and Supply Shift.

The original equilibrium was at a price of $32/MWH and a quantity of 15.2 GWH for an hour. When supply shifts left to S_1, the new equilibrium is at a price of $34.4/MWH and a quantity of 15.1 GWH.

quantity were $32/MWH and 15.2 GWH. The new equilibrium price and quantity are $34.4/MWH and 15.1 GWH. This new equilibrium price and quantity occurs where the shifted supply curve, S_1, intersects the demand curve, D_0. Notice that, while the supply curve has shifted, the demand curve has not. The change in price has led to a movement along the demand curve to a new equilibrium.

DISEQUILIBRIUM

Figure 2.7 shows a market out of equilibrium. Suppose that a regulator sets a *price ceiling* for electricity at $30/MWH. A **price ceiling** is a maximum price that can be charged for a good. The supply curve says that, at a price of $30/MWH, 13 GWH would be produced. The demand curve indicates that, at a price of $30/MWH, consumers want 15.3 GWH. At a price of $30/MWH, then, consumers want more electricity than producers are generating; there is unmet or *excess demand*. **Excess demand** for electricity occurs when consumers want more at a given price than producers are willing to produce at that price.

Figure 2.7 also shows what happens if the price is set at $38/MWH. At that price, the quantity supplied is 16.6 GWH, but the quantity demanded is only 14.9 GWH. Now producers are generating more electricity than consumers are willing to buy at that price; *excess supply* exists. **Excess supply** of electricity occurs when producers supply more at a given price than consumers will buy at that price.

In both of these cases, the electricity market is out of equilibrium, or in *disequilibrium*. **Disequilibrium** is the name for market outcomes where the quantity supplied does not equal the quantity demanded.

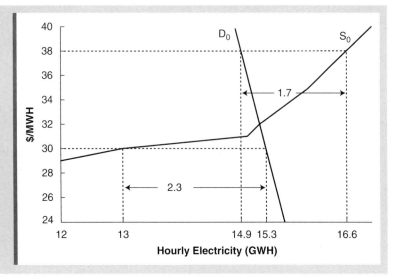

FIGURE 2.7 Disequilibrium.

If the price of electricity is set at $30/MWH, the quantity demanded, 15.3 GWH, exceeds the quantity supplied, 13 GWH, by 2.3 GWH. If, on the other hand, the price is set at $38/MWH, the quantity supplied, 16.6 GWH, exceeds the quantity demanded, 14.9 GWH, by 1.7 GWH.

MARKET FORCES TENDING TOWARD EQUILIBRIUM

When a market is in disequilibrium, economic forces encourage market prices to tend toward their equilibrium values, to restore equilibrium. When the price is below the equilibrium price, quantity demanded exceeds quantity supplied. Some consumers would like to purchase more of the good at the current price but cannot obtain it. They might be willing to bid up the price of the good, either to encourage producers to make more of the good, or to buy some of the good from other consumers who had less desire for it. As a result, there is pressure to increase the market price, which increases the quantity supplied and reduces the quantity demanded, and brings the market toward equilibrium.

Governments are often under pressure to provide desirable goods at low price; as a result, markets for government-provided goods are often in disequilibrium. Wilderness permits for popular areas have more people requesting them than there are permits. If the permits were priced higher, the permit market would tend toward equilibrium. More extremely, the old Soviet Union priced soap below the equilibrium price. There was often no soap, but it was cheap.

A similar process occurs in reverse. When price is above the equilibrium price, quantity demanded is less than quantity supplied. Some producers do not get to sell their product at all. As a result, they may slow or stop producing the good. They may also offer their excess product at a lower price. The lower price leads consumers who did not want to pay high prices into the market, and market forces again prod consumers and producers toward equilibrium. The fashion industry provides an excellent example of this sort of corrective tendency in markets. Near the end of a clothing season, prices are reduced drastically. Consumers who can think a year ahead get very good deals on clothing that will be one year out of style by the time they wear it, and producers can empty their shelves.

When consumers and producers can adjust quickly to shifts in supply and demand, new market equilibria form quickly. That was not the case during the electricity crisis in California. Let's see how that market disequilibrium came to be.

THE ENERGY CRISIS REVISITED

Figure 2.5 offers a good approximation of the market equilibrium in California in August of 1999. By early 2001, however, the electricity market was clearly out of equilibrium. Consumers wanted more electricity than producers were making available. Blackouts resulted because the quantity demanded exceeded the quantity supplied. In a competitive market, the price of electricity should rise in this circumstance. The higher price would induce consumers to conserve, for instance, by turning off appliances not in use, using those appliances less, and buying more energy-efficient appliances over time. The higher price would also encourage more electricity generation from less efficient plants. Why did this not happen? The answers are still not entirely clear, and they are the subject of lawsuits and speculation. Here are several pieces of the explanation.

First, consumers were not getting the right price signals. Electricity is billed by the month and reflects the cost to the utility of providing power for that month. The very high prices and the blackouts only occurred on a few days each month when the temperature was very hot. The price charged for the month was the average of a lot of normal prices and just a very few high prices. As a result, on the very hot hours of very hot days, consumers were still paying only mildly elevated prices. On the other hand, the utilities transporting the power to them were paying prices hundreds of times higher. For instance, the average cost of power for the month of March was $32/MWH, while the cost to generate electricity on March 20 was closer to $200/MWH. With the price of electricity averaged over the month, the consumers who turned off their air conditioners on March 20 and saved a MWH would only see their bills go down by $32, even though the utility saved $200. Because the consumers were never exposed to the very high prices, they never responded to them.

Second, major producers each had more than one power plant. When demand was very high (shifted to the right) because of warm weather, some of the producers chose not to use all of their available capacity to produce power. With fewer plants producing power at any given price, the supply curve shifted left, as in Figure 2.6. As a result, the quantity supplied decreased and the price increased. Some say that the plants that were not used were down for maintenance. Others say that the owners of the plants shut them down to raise prices and increase their profits. It is clear that, even though prices went up quite a bit, there was still not enough power to meet the quantity demanded.

IN SUMMARY

- In a competitive market, equilibrium occurs where quantity demanded equals quantity supplied, where the demand curve and the supply curve intersect. The price at the equilibrium is the market-clearing price.
- A change in the equilibrium occurs when either the supply curve or the demand curve shifts. A shift of the supply curve causes a movement along

the demand curve, which is a change in quantity demanded. A shift of the demand curve leads to a movement along the supply curve, which is a change in quantity supplied.
- Disequilibrium occurs when quantity supplied does not equal quantity demanded.
- Market forces tend to lead price to adjust toward an equilibrium price.

Using Supply and Demand for Energy Policy

Because burning fossil fuels is unavoidably linked to emissions of GHG and their harmful effects, it is in society's interest to reduce fossil fuel use. How will people reduce these emissions? What can be done to avoid some of the worst effects of climate change? The economics of supply and demand provides tremendous insight into addressing such environmental problems and will help explain the effects of two different policies for reducing fossil fuel use and GHG: *quotas* and *taxes*. *Quotas* and *taxes* represent the two fundamental classes of regulatory instruments: the **command and control (CAC)** approach and the **market-based incentives (MBI)** approach.

In a CAC approach, the regulator requires an action or outcome. *Quotas* are an example of the CAC approach. A **quota** is a limit, such as a limit on outputs (goods produced), inputs (material used in making outputs), or effluents (discharged waste products). A quota can also be a mandate to make a product in a certain way. In this example, the quota will be a limit on outputs—a requirement not to produce more than a certain amount of electricity.

By contrast, *taxes* offer an example of MBI. A **specific tax** is an amount of money paid to the government for each unit of an item sold. Taxes per gallon on gasoline, per segment on aircraft flights, and per MWH on electricity sold are all specific taxes. Taxes can be on effluents, inputs, or outputs. Taxes are a MBI because they provide incentives to reduce emissions through the operations of markets, rather than by prohibiting behaviors.

Both CAC and MBI are used to limit pollution to a level below what would occur in an unregulated marketplace. In simplified form, the following example shows one of the major differences between quotas and taxes.

QUOTAS

Let's examine the effects of an **output quota**, a limit on the quantity of output a firm produces, for the electricity market. In this case, the government will not allow the market to determine the output of electricity but rather will require firms to produce less than the equilibrium output. Because electricity uses fossil fuel, a government might want to limit the use of electricity as a way of reducing GHG emissions.

Figure 2.8 shows the same supply and demand curves for fossil-fueled electricity in California that this chapter has been using. The demand curve for electric power consumption is drawn very steeply; this is the graphical way of showing that consumers do not change their electricity consumption very much when the price changes. That is a good assumption for an analysis of a relatively short time period, like a few months.

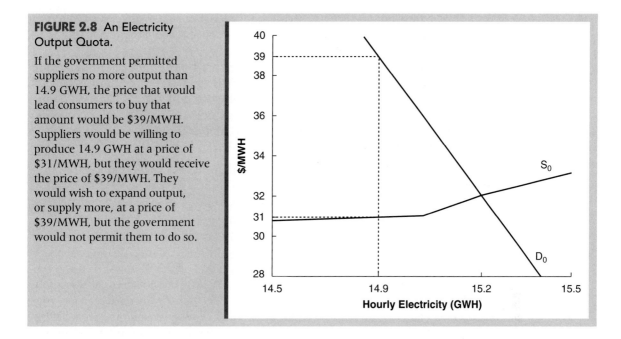

FIGURE 2.8 An Electricity Output Quota.

If the government permitted suppliers no more output than 14.9 GWH, the price that would lead consumers to buy that amount would be $39/MWH. Suppliers would be willing to produce 14.9 GWH at a price of $31/MWH, but they would receive the price of $39/MWH. They would wish to expand output, or supply more, at a price of $39/MWH, but the government would not permit them to do so.

The demand for electricity is considerably flatter when the time period is longer. In a longer time period, consumers can adjust by buying more efficient appliances; in a short period, all they can do is use their appliances and air conditioners less.

In Figure 2.8, the supply curve for fossil-fueled electricity generation starts off very flat, reflecting the existence of many low-cost fossil fuel–based power generators. Once these low-cost generators are all producing, the supply curve becomes steeper, reflecting the necessity of bringing older, less efficient, more expensive plants into production.

As in Figure 2.5, the market equilibrium is at a quantity of 15.2 GWH and at a price of $32/MWH. Now suppose that the California state government wants to reduce GHG emissions from fossil-fueled plants, and it decides to set a quota on electricity generation.

The vertical line in Figure 2.8 shows a quota of 14.9 GWH. As a fixed quantity, unresponsive to price, it is a vertical line starting from 14.9 GWH on the horizontal axis. It would come from a rule saying that producers could not supply more than this amount of power. To see what price would lead consumers to consume just this quantity of power—that is, to have the quantity demanded be 14.9 GWH—trace the vertical line up from the quantity axis to the demand curve and then over to the price axis. When the price to consumers is $39/MWH, they purchase 14.9 GWH.

Faced with a price of $39/MWH, producers would like to supply considerably more power than 14.9 GWH. In fact, they would like to produce so much more electricity that it does not fit on this figure. On the larger Figure 2.1, based on the same data, it is possible to follow a price of $39/MWH over to the supply curve and then down to the horizontal axis to see that producers would like to generate 17 GWH at that price. Nevertheless, in this case, the government prevents them from doing so. It only allows an output of the quota, 14.9 GWH.

If the price stayed at $31/MWH, the price that leads producers to make 14.9 GWH, consumers would want to use 15.15 GWH, more than producers would be willing to supply at that price. Blackouts probably would result, as happened in the California energy crisis. Therefore, the quota succeeds in lowering output quantity and thus emissions, but it results in a higher price to consumers than if the market equilibrium were allowed to occur.

TAXES

A tax on consumption of electricity, by making it more expensive, would also succeed in lowering output. Let's consider a specific tax of $8/MWH. The effect of this tax is to create an $8 gap between the price that a consumer pays and the price that a producer gets; that $8/MWH tax goes to the government. For instance, in Figure 2.9, at 14.9 GWH of consumption, the price on the demand curve is $39/MWH. If the consumers pay $39/MWH and the government takes $8/MWH, only $31/MWH is left for the electricity producers. From the producers' perspective, the tax reduces every price on the demand curve by $8/MWH. In other words, it looks to the producers like the demand curve has shifted down by the amount of the tax because the price the producer gets equals the price the consumer pays, minus the $8/MWH tax.

For a specific tax, then, the **after-tax demand curve** shows how much money per unit the producer receives from the consumer as a function of market quantity after subtracting the tax. It is found by vertically shifting the demand curve down by the amount of the tax. This is curve $D - t$ in Figure 2.9.

The equilibrium after tax is found at the intersection of the after-tax demand curve and the supply curve. It is at a price of $31/MWH for producers and quantity of 14.9 GWH. Consumers pay the producer a price of $31/MWH plus the tax of

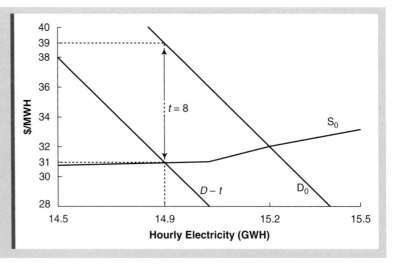

FIGURE 2.9 A Tax on Electricity.

The figure shows the results of a tax of $8/MWH. When consumers buy a quantity of 14.9 GWH in an hour, the price they pay is $39/MWH. The price that they pay, less the tax, is the curve $D - t$. It shows the amount producers receive—the amount consumers pay less the tax—as a function of the quantity demanded. The intersection of the supply curve and $D - t$ gives the after-tax equilibrium. Price is $31/MWH, and quantity is 14.9 GWH.

$8/MWH, or $39/MWH total, while producers receive $31/MWH, and the government earns $8/MWH.

It makes no difference whether it is the consumer or the producer who hands the money over to the government. If the consumer pays the tax, then she gives the government $8 and the producer $31 per unit. If the producer pays the tax, then it takes $39 from the consumer, gives $8 to the government, and keeps the other $31 for itself. The economic outcome is the same either way: $31 to the producer, $8 to the government, and the consumer lays out $39.

In the usual situation, when demand slopes down and supply slopes up, a tax results in the price that consumers pay going up and the price that producers receive going down, compared with not having the tax.

BOX 2.3

An Algebraic View of Taxes

Let's write the formula for the demand curve the way it is drawn. Price, on the vertical axis, is a function of quantity, on the horizontal axis. It gives the price the consumer pays, P^d, as a function, DP, of the quantity in the market, Q. The equation is $P^d = DP(Q)$.

Now look at the supply side, and write the price that producers receive as a function of output. Again, this is just the formula for the supply curve the way it is drawn on the diagram. Let P^s be the price the producer actually receives. The equation for the supply curve is $P^s = SP(Q)$, the amount that one would need to pay producers per unit to induce them to produce output Q.

If consumers pay P^d and the government exacts a tax of t/MWH ($t = $8 in the example), then the producers are paid $(P^d - t)$/MWH. Therefore, the price paid to producers as a function of market quantity is $P^s = DP(Q) - t$. It is the price consumers are willing to pay, less the tax. It is the leftward-shifted demand curve in Figure 2.9, the demand curve displaced down by t. The producer gets what the consumer pays, less the tax.

After-tax equilibrium requires the intersection of the supply and demand-less-tax curves, or $SP(Q) = DP(Q) - t$. The quantity where the demand-less-tax curve and the supply curve intersect is the after-tax equilibrium quantity. Let's call that quantity Q_t. The price on the supply curve at the quantity Q_t is the price producers receive. The price on the demand curve at the quantity Q_t is the price that consumers pay. The difference between these two prices is the tax.

The equation $SP(Q) = DP(Q) - t$ can be used to solve the tax problem another way. Add t to both sides of the equation and get $SP(Q) + t = DP(Q)$. This equation adds t to the supply curve and then finds the intersection with demand. It gives the same answer for Q_t as before because it is the same equation being solved. Here the consumer pays what the producer gets plus tax. The effects of a tax on quantity and price do not depend on whether the consumer or the producer pays the tax.

COMPARING THE QUOTA AND THE TAX

For both the quota and the tax, the output of electricity is the same, 14.9 GWH. The price for the consumer is also the same, $39/MWH. What is different is the price for the producer. In the case of a quota, the generator receives the price the consumer pays, $39/MWH. In the case of a tax, the generator receives the price the consumer pays less the tax, or $31/MWH. Figure 2.10 has the same curves as Figure 2.9 and adds a shaded box. The shaded box shows the tax revenue that the government receives. Its height is the tax ($8/MWH), and its width is output (14.9 GWH). The area ($t/MWH times MWH = $) is the amount of money the government receives with a tax: 14.9 GWH * 1,000 * MWH/GWH * $8/MWH = $119,200.

Faced with a choice between a tax and a quota that achieves the same level of output, a producer will always prefer a quota. With a quota, the producer receives a higher price. In this example, the producer is $119,200 richer. If, instead, a tax were used, the $119,200 would go to the government, which could use it to provide additional services or to reduce the other taxes that people pay.

Many environmental laws are, however, based on quotas, perhaps in part because producers prefer the higher prices and not having to pay the tax. As we explore more tools later in this book, more sophisticated types of quotas and taxes will appear. In many cases, MBI approaches control pollution at a lower cost than CAC. Understanding that taxes and quotas can achieve the same environmental goals, but that they have very different effects on producer profits, is a valuable insight for environmental policy. While the economic analysis of environmental

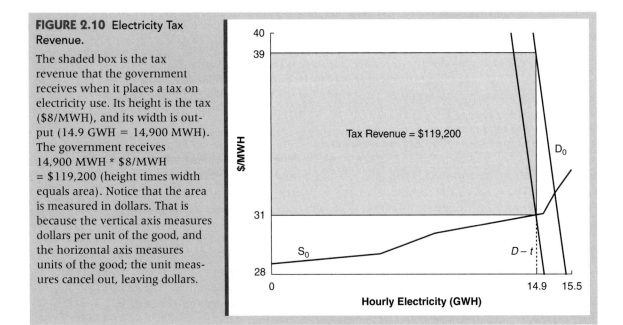

FIGURE 2.10 Electricity Tax Revenue.

The shaded box is the tax revenue that the government receives when it places a tax on electricity use. Its height is the tax ($8/MWH), and its width is output (14.9 GWH = 14,900 MWH). The government receives 14,900 MWH * $8/MWH = $119,200 (height times width equals area). Notice that the area is measured in dollars. That is because the vertical axis measures dollars per unit of the good, and the horizontal axis measures units of the good; the unit measures cancel out, leaving dollars.

programs can play a major role in their enactment and success, the effects of policies on various producers and consumers can affect the politics of these efforts.

IN SUMMARY

- Market-based incentives (MBI) include taxes on effluents, production, or inputs. Command and control (CAC) includes quotas on effluents, production, and inputs.
- It is possible to reduce a polluting activity by limiting production. A production quota mandates how much output a producer may supply. Under a quota, the price to consumers goes up to reduce quantity demanded to the level of the quota.
- It is also possible to reduce a polluting activity by taxing the activity. The tax increases the amount that consumers pay, but producers receive that price less the tax payment, which goes to the government, and thus producers will get less than they would under the quota.
- Both the tax and the quota can achieve the same environmental target, but they result in very different prices for producers.

Using Supply and Demand to Understand Land Use

Supply and demand can be used to explore many other environmental issues. Habitat preservation, perhaps the most important element in the preservation of species and certainly of whole ecosystems, is one such issue.

The Midwestern United States used to be covered with long- and short-grass prairies. Buffalo, prairie chickens, deer, and elk were abundant. Prairie dogs and black-footed ferrets were commonplace. Today, a visitor will mostly see soybeans, corn, and hogs in the eastern prairie, and wheat and cattle in the west. While economic incentives have played a major role in this vast ecological transformation, and continue to do so, the government has had a major hand in setting those incentives. It is therefore useful to know whether the government has made the loss of prairie ecosystems worse than it would otherwise be, or whether government policies have helped to protect prairies.

Throughout American history, the U.S. government has been very active in encouraging the settlement of the American West. Among its important policies were the Homestead Act, the subsidization of railroads, and the land banks. The Homestead Act of 1862 gave away 160 acres of public lands—those the United States owned through conquest or purchase—to anyone who would pay $18 and live on and work that land for five years. The subsidies to railroads, which included grants of land to the railroads on alternating sides of the railroad right of way, gave the railroads large amounts of land. They sold that land into the private land market and also promoted transportation for the grain that could be grown there. The land bank was a government-sponsored bank that made loans to farmers that commercial banks were not at that time willing to make. These and other government programs sped up the settlement of the American West. Put differently, these and other government programs sped up the destruction of prairie habitat through its conversion to farmland.

THE FARM PROGRAMS

The interaction of agricultural policy and conservation policy has a long history. In the United States, modern agricultural policy begins with the Agricultural Adjustment Act (AAA) of 1933. The AAA was a response to the Great Depression, in which prices for farm products fell dramatically. Both the low farm prices and the depression itself were worldwide phenomena. One purpose of the AAA was to raise prices to farmers. That act was declared unconstitutional by the U.S. Supreme Court because the court did not accept that the United States could make laws whose purpose was to control prices. To reinstate the provisions of the 1933 act, Congress amended the Soil Conservation and Domestic Allotment Act of 1935, the successor to the Agricultural Adjustment Act, to state that the goal of the act was to decrease soil erosion, which had contributed to the losses suffered by farmers during the depression. To receive payments under the act, farmers had to take measures to preserve and restore soil.

The dual goals of financially supporting farmers and conserving farm land remain to this day. Financially supporting farmers contributed to the loss of prairie ecosystems, but the conservation programs have had positive environmental effects. Determining whether the dominant effect of the past 75 years of agricultural policies has been habitat loss or soil conservation requires measuring how farmers have responded to the economic incentives created by these policies.

This section examines a type of financial support for farmers known as a **price support** program, a policy designed to raise prices to farmers. This particular price support is called a **marketing loan**, a loan using crop as collateral that could be repaid either with money or with the collateral. The marketing loan program was responsible for very large surpluses of wheat, corn, and soybeans in the late 1950s. At the same time, the program was coupled with a requirement to set aside some land and not use it for agricultural production.

RAISING PRICES AND CONSERVING LAND

With the supply and demand framework, let's estimate how much additional farmland the marketing loan program brought into production for one year, 1960. The amount of land brought into production can then be compared with the amount of land protected by conservation programs.

In 1960, the U.S. government, via its Department of Agriculture (USDA), offered to "loan" farmers $1.78 per bushel (bu) of wheat, with the wheat as the collateral for the loan. Under this agreement, farmers could choose to give the USDA their wheat in total satisfaction of their loan obligations, even if the market price of wheat was less than $1.78/bu. If the price of wheat rose above the loan rate, farmers could ask for their wheat back and sell it at the market price. In 1960, the market price was less than the loan rate, as it had been for several previous years. The farmers dutifully gave their wheat to the USDA in satisfaction of their "loans." Because farmers had the option to pay back their loans using wheat valued at $1.78/bu, instead of selling it to consumers, they effectively faced a price of $1.78/bu.

Figure 2.11 shows an approximation of the supply and demand diagram for wheat in 1960. The figure indicates the equilibrium quantity of wheat without any government interference. Output would have been 1,308 million bushels at a price of $1.70/bu.

Figure 2.12 adds the government loan program into the picture. The price the suppliers see is the loan rate of $1.78/bu. The quantity supplied at the loan price of $1.78/bu comes from following the dashed horizontal line to the intersection with the supply curve. Quantity supplied is 1,357 million bushels. Because farmers had no reason to offer wheat for a price below that level—the federal government would take as much wheat as the farmers wished—consumers also faced that price.

The quantity consumers demanded is found by following the dashed line leading from the loan price of $1.78/bu to the intersection with the demand curve, at 1,276 million bushels. Of the 1,357 million bushels supplied, consumers were willing to buy only 1,276 million bushels. The USDA effectively bought the excess supply of 81 million bushels of wheat for $1.78/bu, for a total cost of $144 million.

In economic terms, the loan rate was a **price floor**, a price below which the government would not permit sales. The USDA enforced the price floor by buying the excess wheat and either storing it or giving it away. In 1960, total storage had accumulated over many years to 1.3 billion bushels, roughly equal to one year's production.

To see the effect of the loan program on land use, let's compare the amount of land that would be used for wheat production without the loan program to the actual land

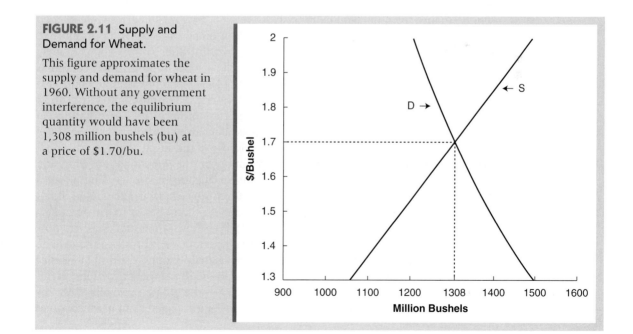

FIGURE 2.11 Supply and Demand for Wheat.

This figure approximates the supply and demand for wheat in 1960. Without any government interference, the equilibrium quantity would have been 1,308 million bushels (bu) at a price of $1.70/bu.

FIGURE 2.12 The Government Loan Program for Wheat.

This figure shows the effect of the marketing loan program. Farmers faced a price of $1.78/bu, the loan rate, which was higher than the price that would obtain in the free market, $1.70/bu. The amount they produced is found where the dashed line leading from $1.78/bu intersects the supply curve, at 1,357 million bushels. The quantity demanded is found where the dashed line leading from $1.78/bu intersects the demand curve, at 1,276 million bushels. Of the 1,357 million bushels supplied, consumers were willing to buy only 1,276 million bushels. The government bought the remaining 81 million bushels.

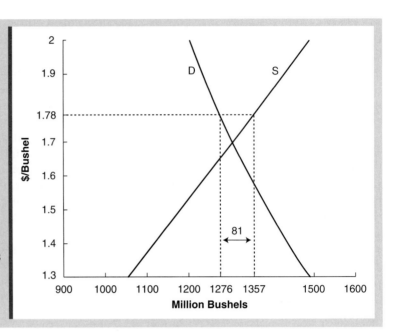

used with the program. Without the program, the equilibrium quantity of wheat supplied would have been 1,308 million bushels. With the program, farmers supplied 1,357 million bushels. Thus, 49 million extra bushels were produced. If each acre produced roughly the same amount of wheat, then 49/1,357 of the wheat-growing acreage was used to produce the 49 million extra bushels. In 1960, 54.9 million acres were planted to wheat. So the percent of extra acres times the number of acres is the number of extra acres: 49/1,357 * 54.9 million = 1.98 million. In other words, approximately 1.98 million extra acres—almost the area of Yellowstone National Park (which is 2.2 million acres)—were devoted to wheat because of the marketing loan program.

Although there have been many modifications of the farm programs from 1933 to present, the programs still exist, and they still raise farm prices. There have been three major objections to price supports and similar farm subsidy programs. In the 1960s, the objection arose due to the need to dispose of the surplus wheat. Although some of the surplus was given away to poor nations in the Food for Peace program, by 1960 the government had a whole year of production in storage. The political embarrassment of storing food while people were hungry both in the United States and abroad was an impetus for change. The second objection has been the program's cost to the federal government and, thus, to taxpayers. Each time that one farm program has been changed to reduce the cost of that program, new programs have been introduced that make total costs at least as much as the old ones. Currently, disaster payments and heavily subsidized crop insurance add to the taxpayer burden.

The final objection is to the environmental cost of the programs. While programs that raise prices and thus encourage the use of more land and water can hardly be good for the ecosystems that previously inhabited the land, the current agricultural programs of the United States are a mix of conservation and production-oriented programs. For instance, in 1986 the United States first introduced the Conservation Reserve Program. Through this program, the United States rents land from farmers for 10–15 years. As a condition of the rental, the farmers must plant a conservation cover, such as grass, that reduces erosion and requires little chemical use. The land then serves as habitat for wildlife. Conservation reserves totaled 34 million acres as of November 2008, roughly the area of the state of Illinois. There is reserve land in every state. This may be the single most important conservation program in the United States.

While agricultural policies are heavily geared toward increasing income to farmers, over time the policies have become more accommodating of conservation aims. It is hard to measure whether, in the aggregate, farm programs are a net loss or benefit to the environment.

◤ IN SUMMARY

- Government intervention in markets can lead to a disequilibrium, where quantity supplied does not equal quantity demanded.
- The U.S. government has been heavily involved in agricultural markets throughout its history. These policies have often involved price floors, intended to increase farmers' incomes, combined with measures to reduce soil erosion and other adverse effects of farming.

Energy and Agriculture

Energy and agriculture are linked in two important ways. First, the fossil fuels that provide most of our energy are important inputs to agricultural production. Oil provides energy in the form of diesel fuel for pumping water, plowing fields, and harvesting crops. Oil also is used in making fertilizers. If the price of oil increases, as it did in 2008, an input to agriculture becomes more expensive, and the supply curve for food crops shifts to the left.

Second, when the price of oil is high enough relative to the price of food crops, food crops are turned into energy. Currently, sugar cane and corn are distilled to ethanol and are used as additives to gasoline. American lawmakers representing farming communities have promoted ethanol and other biofuels as environmentally friendly alternatives to fossil fuels, though there is debate about the existence of these environmental benefits. It is clear, however, that ethanol production shifts the demand curve for food crops right: demand for food crops grows when they are also used to make fuel.

In 2008, several factors, including the increase in oil prices and the production of ethanol, combined to drive up the prices of staple food grains such as corn. Corn prices reached $6 per bushel by April 2008, after hovering between $2 and $3/bu for the previous 10 years. Poor people in Mexico and other developing countries protested in the streets because they could not afford food.

The ongoing debate about ethanol asks whether it provides environmental benefits that are worth the impact on hungry people. Supply and demand provide us with powerful tools for analyzing the problems of meeting human needs while preserving the environment.

CHAPTER SUMMARY

Here are the key lessons from this chapter:

- The supply curve represents how much producers of a good provide in response to a market price. It typically slopes upward, indicating that a higher price induces greater production. It can shift due to changes in the prices of inputs to production, changes in technology, changes in the number of producers, or the effects of outside forces such as the weather.
- The demand curve represents how much consumers purchase of a good when they face the market price. It almost always slopes downward, indicating that a higher price reduces the quantity demanded. It can shift because of changes in consumer income, changes in prices of substitute and complementary goods, changes in tastes and preferences, outside forces such as weather, or changes in population.
- Market equilibrium occurs when the price in the market induces the quantity supplied by producers to equal the quantity demanded by consumers. If the market price leads to either excess demand or excess supply, in a competitive market the price tends to head back to the price that provides equilibrium. The equilibrium price and quantity change if either the supply curve shifts, causing a movement along the demand curve, or the demand curve shifts, causing a movement along the supply curve.
- Government programs can change the market equilibrium and affect the environment as well. Government can restrict production via a quota, or it can tax production. While these two policies can achieve the same quantity (or environmental) goals, they lead to different effects on producer profits and government revenues.
- In agriculture, governments often set a price floor—ensuring a minimum price to producers—that can create excess supply at the same time that they create programs to reduce soil erosion and other damages from farming. The net effect of these programs on the environment is an area of continuing study.

KEY TERMS

after-tax demand curve *(p. 24)*

clears *(p. 18)*

command and control (CAC) *(p. 22)*

competitive market *(p. 9)*

complements *(p. 16)*

consumers *(p. 9)*

demand *(p. 10)*

demand curve *(p. 10)*

disequilibrium *(p. 19)*

equilibrium price *(p. 18)*

excess demand *(p. 19)*

excess supply *(p. 19)*

inferior good *(p. 16)*

market equilibrium *(p. 18)*

market price *(p. 18)*
market-based incentives (MBI) *(p. 22)*
marketing loan *(p. 28)*
movement along the demand
  curve *(p. 13)*
movement along the supply curve *(p. 11)*
normal goods *(p. 15)*
output quota *(p. 22)*
own price *(p. 11)*
price ceiling *(p. 19)*
price elasticity of demand *(p. 14)*
price floor *(p. 29)*

price support *(p. 28)*
price takers *(p. 9)*
producers *(p. 9)*
quantity demanded *(p. 9)*
quantity supplied *(p. 9)*
quota *(p. 22)*
specific tax *(p. 22)*
substitutes *(p. 15)*
supply *(p. 9)*
supply curve *(p. 9)*
supply shifters *(p. 11)*
tastes and preferences *(p. 16)*

NOTES

The story about California's electricity crisis comes from Laura M. Holson, "Government Acts to Calm California's Energy Market," *New York Times* [Late Edition (East Coast)], December 16, 2000, sec. A.14.

The supply curve for the electricity example comes from Severin Borenstein, James Bushnell, and Frank Wolak, "Measuring Market Inefficiencies in California's Restructured Wholesale Electricity Market" (Center for the Study of Energy Markets, Berkeley, California, June 2002). The diagram does not account for purchases of electricity from out of state, or purchases from nuclear or hydroelectric plants. Thus, while this provides a realistic example of supply and demand, it is not a complete picture of California electricity production.

The Agricultural Adjustment Act was declared unconstitutional in *United States v. Butler*, 297 United States Supreme Court Reports 1 (1936) (the "Hoosac Mills" case).

The agricultural example was constructed by the authors using the actual price and quantity numbers for 1960 and Bruce Gardner's estimate in "North American Agricultural Policies and Effects on Western Hemisphere Markets Since 1995, with a Focus on Grains and Oilseeds" (WP 02-12, Department of Agricultural and Resource Economics, University of Maryland, College Park, Maryland). Gardner examines the effects of policy with a number of assumptions about elasticities, including −0.5 as an estimate of the one-year time-frame demand elasticity. The effect of price supports on wheat production is based on Mark A. Krause, Jung-Hee Lee, and Won W. Koo, "Program and Nonprogram Wheat Acreage Responses to Prices and Risk," *Journal of Agricultural and Resource Economics* 20 (1995): 96–107.

EXERCISES

1. Consider the market for purchase of new cars.
   (a) What factors likely influence the demand for cars? That is, either for an individual or in the aggregate, what factors will cause either movements along the demand curve for cars or shifts of the demand curve for cars? Identify at least four factors.

(b) If you were to draw a demand curve for cars, how would you label the axes—that is, what are you measuring along each axis? Would this demand curve slope up or down, be vertical, or be horizontal? Why?

(c) What factors likely affect the supply of cars? Identify at least three factors.

(d) If you were to graph the supply of cars, would it slope up or down, be vertical, or be horizontal? Why?

(e) If the cost of steel goes up, which (if either) of these curves might be affected? How? What will happen to the equilibrium price and quantity of cars? Why?

(f) If the cost of parking goes up, which (if either) of these curves might be affected? How? What will happen to the equilibrium price and quantity of cars? Why?

(g) The U.S. Environmental Protection Agency will require new light trucks and sport utility vehicles (SUVs) to install new pollution control devices that will increase their cost. For the purposes of this question, and from the perspective of federal rules, these are not cars, even though people use them in the same way as they use cars. Which (if either) of the supply or demand curves for cars might be affected? How and why? What will happen to the equilibrium price and quantity of cars?

(h) Consider the difference between the short run of a few days or weeks and the long run of a few months or years. Suppose that the price of gasoline goes up. Which, if either, curve do you expect to be affected in the short run? How and why? What will happen to the equilibrium price and quantity of cars? Why?

(i) In the long run, do you expect additional changes beyond those you identified in (h)? If so, what are they, and why?

2. Look again at Figure 2.2. Trace it onto a piece of scrap paper. Now draw two demand curves on your figure. Draw one that is horizontal at $P = \$32/\text{MWH}$ and one that is vertical at quantity $= 15$ GWH.

(a) What happens to the equilibrium price when the supply curve shifts from S_0 to S_1 in each case?

(b) A horizontal demand curve means that consumers will buy any amount produced at a price of $32/MWH or less, but they will buy none if the price goes higher. A vertical demand curve means that consumers do not respond at all to price—they will buy the same quantity regardless of how much it costs. Which do you think is closer to how consumers buy electricity? That is, do consumers pay a lot of attention to price (the horizontal curve), or do they ignore price (the vertical curve)?

(c) Compare your answer in (b) to the true demand curve in Figure 2.3. When the price shifted, did the quantity demanded change a lot or a little?

3. This chapter explained one of the two main ways that money was transferred to farmers. Another method was called a target price-deficiency payment program. Let's use Figure 2.12 to examine that program as well, although the actual program operated a decade later and with higher prices. In the target price

program, the government would set a price that it guaranteed to farmers, $1.78/bu in the example. Instead of buying wheat until the price reached the target price, the government would allow all of it to be purchased by consumers.

(a) Assuming that the producers decide how much wheat to grow based on the supply curve, find the quantity supplied. Now use that quantity and the demand curve to find the price that consumers would pay if they were to buy that much wheat.

(b) The government paid farmers the difference between the target price and the price that consumers paid. Find the amount that the government paid per bushel by subtracting the consumer price from the target price. Now find the total amount the government would have had to pay by multiplying the number of bushels by the government payment per bushel.

(c) Compare your answer from (b) to the government's cost under the loan program. Your comparison should explain why the government never used the target price program without other programs in place to limit production.

(d) Compare the target price-deficiency payment plan to the tax on energy. In both cases, government creates a gap between the price consumers pay and the price producers receive. Does quantity supplied equal quantity demanded under these programs?

(e) To address environmental problems, the government may tax pollution or subsidize a reduction in pollution. Based on what you have seen about a tax compared with a target price-deficiency payment scheme, which do you think that a producer would prefer? Which is more expensive for the government, and why?

4. A chemical factory has leaked a toxic substance into the ground because fixing the leak was more expensive than the small amount of toxic substance was worth to them. Once it was discovered that the substance was contaminating local water supplies, though, the factory agreed to fix the leak.

(a) Draw supply and demand curves for the chemicals produced by the factory before the contamination was discovered.

(b) Which, if either, of these curves will be affected by the decision to fix the leak? Adjust your diagram to reflect this change. What, if anything, has happened to the equilibrium price and quantity?

(c) How have the buyers of chemicals from the factory (who live far away from the contamination) been affected by the decision to fix the leak? Why do they feel that effect? Do you think that this effect is appropriate? Why or why not?

3 Markets and Market Failure
A Cause of Environmental Degradation

Is clean air free or beyond value? Breathing it costs nothing, but having it is a necessity for life. The absence of a market for clean air leads people to treat it as though it is infinitely available at no cost. Polluting costs the same amount as breathing. The environmental consequences are, however, very different.

When markets work well, they are effective tools for producing and distributing goods, including natural resources. When markets do not work well, the results can harm both people and the environment. Understanding how effective markets are when they work well, and how dangerous they can be when they do not, is critical for protecting the environment. This chapter will examine:

- How a market protects scarce resources;
- How environmental goods are economic goods;
- The advantages markets provide;
- Five reasons why some markets do not work well: market failures.

Protecting Wolves Through Markets

Wolves have long been an object of fear and hatred to many people. Within what is now the United States, about 400,000 wolves roamed freely at the time of European settlement. European settlers colonizing North America viewed the wolf, like much of the natural landscape, as a symbol of the wild America that had to be subdued and conquered in the name of civilization. Movement into the American West by those settlers, and settlers' subsequent vigorous hunting of bison, deer, elk, and moose, led to a decline in wolves' sources of food. As a consequence, wolves began to hunt homesteaders' sheep, cattle, and other livestock.

In response to the threat to livestock and personal safety, ranchers and government agencies initiated aggressive campaigns to eliminate wolf populations. Bounty programs began in the eighteenth century and continued until 1965, offering $20–$50 per wolf. By 1925, few wolves were left in the lower 48 states.

The Endangered Species Preservation Act of 1966, later amended to the Endangered Species Act of 1973, brought protection to the gray wolf in 1967. However, because of low numbers of breeding populations, it was doubtful that wolves would successfully establish new colonies in the lower 48 states without additional efforts. A combination of increased scientific research on wolf ecology and behavior; changing public perceptions of wolves; environmentalist movements; and other social, economic, and demographic factors made wolf restoration a political issue. The late 1980s saw several wolf reintroduction bills presented to Congress, but they were vehemently opposed by ranchers and state governments.

In 1994, after years of study, research, and organized public input, and despite continued opposition, the Secretary of the Interior approved the Northern Rocky Mountain Wolf Recovery Plan. As part of the plan, 14 wolves in two packs from Canada were transported to Yellowstone National Park in 1995.

One factor that may have helped reintroduce wolves in Yellowstone was an innovative program from Defenders of Wildlife, a nonprofit wildlife protection organization. In 1987, Defenders created what is now known as the Bailey Wildlife Foundation Wolf Compensation Trust to pay ranchers for any livestock killed by a wolf. In 2008, the fund paid $161,000 for 429 animals killed by wolves.

With the shift of the financial burden of wolf recovery from the livestock owners to those who support wolf reintroduction, ranchers had less of a financial incentive to object to wolf reintroduction. The financial compensation is not complete. Ranchers still must protect children and pets from wolves, and sheep must expend energy to avoid wolves. Still, local residents have come to support and expect the compensation.

Now, more than 170 wolves in 14 packs have claimed Yellowstone as their home. As a result, a more balanced ecosystem is returning to the area. Elk numbers, which had been very high, have begun to decline due to hunting by wolves. This allows aspen, willow, and cottonwood saplings, previously overgrazed by elk, to mature. In addition, beaver populations, which rely on those saplings, are rebounding. Beaver dams cause river systems to slow, allowing vegetation to anchor the banks; the vegetation attracts small mammals and migratory birds. Wolf populations in the west have risen enough that the wolves may no longer need some of the protections under the Endangered Species Act. Some in Wyoming still consider the wolf a predator that should be shot on sight.

Private Goods and Public Goods

Why are some goods traded in markets and others are not? Historically, people have not bought and sold most environmental goods; they have fallen outside the realm of markets. Indeed, the very idea of buying and selling wilderness preservation, protection of endangered species, or clean air may seem strange to most people. Let's examine the factors that affect the creation or absence of markets.

Economists use the word **utility** for a person's well-being. An economic **good** is anything that can change someone's utility, either directly or indirectly. A good can either increase or decrease a person's utility. Chocolate, for example, is a good that increases most people's utility. Polluted water is a good that decreases utility.

Goods do not have to be physical things. Economists' use of the word "good" is quite encompassing and includes both tangible and intangible items. Intangible goods are also called **services**. Examples include all types of labor services, such as accounting, factory work, and legal services.

Things that indirectly increase utility are also goods. For instance, coal is used to make electricity, and electricity increases utility. Therefore, coal is also a good. So, goods are tangible or intangible things that can change utility directly or indirectly.

Chocolate and electricity are two very ordinary goods. Quantities are easily measured, producers are paid for the quantities they supply, and consumers are charged for the quantities they consume. There are markets for these goods, and the interaction of supply, demand, and sometimes government regulation results in observable prices and quantities.

Chocolate and electricity are both examples of *private goods*. A **private good** is both *rival* and *excludable*. A good is **rival in consumption** when the use by one person precludes the use by another person. If one person eats a chocolate, nobody else can have it. When one consumer turns on an air conditioner, the electricity used to cool his room is not available to cool someone else's room. Also, a consumer cannot just take electricity, at least not legally; people pay for what they use. Consumers who do not pay are *excluded* from using the good. A good is **excludable** when consumers can be prevented from using the good.

Not all goods, though, are private goods. Anyone can harvest fish on the high seas, so they are not excludable. However, because a fish can only be taken once from the sea—one fisher's use of the fish precludes another fisher from using the same fish—they are rival. A fishery thus has one of the characteristics of a private good, rivalry, but lacks the other characteristic, exclusion. A good that is rival but not excludable is a good for which there is **open access**.

Club goods are excludable but not rival. Clubs can decide who can belong to them; once someone is a member, though, he has access to the services of the club. Pay television is a club good. Watching it does not stop others from watching it, but it is available only to those who pay the fees.

Finally, some goods can be used or enjoyed by anyone, and one person's use does not prevent another from using it. Anyone can enjoy gazing at the moon, and watching it does not diminish it. Goods like the moon that are both nonrival and nonexcludable are called **public goods**.

Rivalry and excludability are matters of degree, not absolutes. Goods can be partially rival—for instance, a library may put limits on the number of books a customer may borrow. Goods may also be partially excludable—the library may be free to all who live in a community but costly to those outside the community. Many goods fall into the spectrum between pure public and pure private goods.

ENVIRONMENTAL SERVICES AND ENVIRONMENTAL GOODS

Environmental economists are interested in services provided by the environment. The atmosphere provides services by absorbing wastes from industrial plants, providing protection from ultraviolet light, and supplying oxygen and carbon dioxide. Services provided by clean water include sustaining aquatic life and absorbing sewage. Each of these intangible services—clean air services and clean water services—is a good. Services provided by the environment are **environmental services**. Because services are a type of good, and because environmental quality affects people's utility, environmental services are economic goods.

The existence of wolves is a good because it affects many people's utility. Some consumers—environmentalists—are happier if there are wolves in the world. Other consumers, especially ranchers, are less happy with wolves in the world. Either way, the existence of wolves affects their utilities. Therefore, wolf existence is a good. The efforts of Defenders of Wildlife to promote wolf preservation resulted in an increase in wolf existence services.

For environmentalists, wolf existence services offer an example of an *existence service*. An **existence service** is a good from which people benefit even if they have no direct experience or contact with it; the mere fact that the good exists makes them better off. This type of good was first recognized by economist John Krutilla in 1967 when he observed that "[t]here are many persons who obtain satisfaction from the mere knowledge that part of the wilderness of North America remains even though they would be appalled at the prospect of being exposed to it." In this sentence, he invented the "armchair environmentalist," a person who enjoys nature without ever having to see it.

Some goods, such as the air pollutants termed nitrogen oxides (NO_x), decrease everybody's utility. For goods that always decrease utility, it will sometimes be easier to define the absence of the good as a new good that always increases utility. In this case, reduction of NO_x increases utility. "Reduction of NO_x" is equivalent to "cleaner air." The term **abatement** is used to refer to pollution reduction. Whether the good is abatement of NO_x or cleaner air, it is a good that increases utility. This redefinition means that the goods in this text will typically increase utility.

Most environmental goods have one or both of the characteristics of public goods. Many of the services provided by clean air, for example, are nonrival and nonexcludable: the amount of air is not diminished when one person breathes, and no one can be excluded from breathing. Fisheries are an open access good: no one can be excluded but one person's consumption prevents another from consuming the goods.

SCARCE GOODS

Economics is especially interested in *scarce* goods. An item is **scarce** if people want more of the good than is available at a price of zero—in other words, more is demanded than is supplied when the good is available for free. Figure 3.1 shows the

FIGURE 3.1 Scarce Electricity.

At the price of zero, no electricity is produced, and 16.8 GWH are demanded.

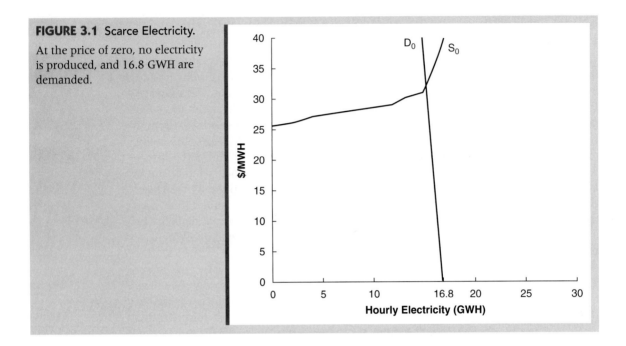

supply and demand for electricity again. Notice that, at a price of zero, 16.8 gigawatt hours, or GWH (1 GWH = 1,000 megawatt hours, or MWH), are demanded, but nothing is supplied. The fact that a greater quantity is demanded than supplied at a price of zero means that electricity is a scarce good.

One way to tell whether a good is scarce is to see if its price is above zero. If it is scarce, it will have more quantity demanded than supplied at zero. As price increases, quantity supplied goes up, and quantity demanded goes down. At a high enough price, quantity supplied and demanded are equal at a positive price. For instance, in eighteenth-century New York, oysters were so plentiful in the harbor that they were the food of the poor. They were available for free; anyone could harvest as many as he could eat, and there were still oysters left. The quantity demanded was less than the seemingly limitless quantity supplied by the ocean. Oysters were not a scarce good. Now, oysters are an expensive delicacy. A restaurant offering free oysters would have to turn people away. Because quantity demanded exceeds quantity supplied at a price of zero, oysters are now scarce. The fact that the price is greater than zero signals their scarcity.

If a good is scarce, then some people will not get all they want of it. There must be some way to allocate the limited quantity. Price is the way that a market system allocates scarce goods. A later section in this chapter considers other ways to allocate scarce goods.

What about environmental goods for which there is no observable market price? The absence of a market price does not change the definition of whether a good is scarce. For instance, more clean air services are demanded than supplied at a price of zero. No one enjoys breathing polluted air; everyone wants clean air at all times and in all places. If they did not have to pay for cleaning the air, people would surely want the air to be cleaner. Clean air is a scarce good. However, clean air is not usually bought and traded in markets. Except for some market-based environmental policies, which appear later in this book, there is no observable price for clean air. Still, clean air services, and most other environmental goods, are scarce goods.

OPPORTUNITY COST

If a person helps out in his parents' business or around the house but doesn't get paid, is his labor worth nothing? The **opportunity cost** of a good is its value in its next best use. In the case of working in a parents' business or around the house, the opportunity cost of labor is what a person would be paid if he worked in the best job he could get. For the same reason, when students study, the time is not without economic value; the opportunity cost is what could have been earned if they were working instead of studying. Labor is a scarce good. The opportunity cost of labor is much greater than zero. If the price were zero, far more labor would be demanded than would be supplied. The fact that a good has a positive opportunity cost is another signal that the good is scarce. People are willing to give up something—the opportunity cost—to get the good.

WOLF EXISTENCE AS A GOOD

Let's apply these concepts to the wolf example. The armchair environmentalists who contribute money to Defenders of Wildlife or the Wolf Compensation Trust are buyers of wolf existence. The ranchers historically opposed the existence of wolves and thus reduced their supply. Now, in exchange for money paid for dead livestock, ranchers reduce their opposition to wolf preservation policies and thus allow, or provide, wolves. In a sense, ranchers "sell" wolf existence to environmentalist consumers. Wolf existence is a scarce good, signaled by the fact that the price of wolf existence is greater than zero.

In the 1960s, there was no market for wolf existence. Because nobody offered to pay the ranchers any money to let wolves exist, the "price" for tolerating wolves was zero. Armchair environmentalists wanted a quantity of wolves when the price was zero, and the quantity demanded exceeded the quantity that ranchers were willing to supply at a price of zero. Wolf existence was a scarce good. Ranchers did not accept wolf existence; instead, they lobbied against legislation that would reintroduce wolves. Then Defenders of Wildlife offered to pay for wolf damage—in effect, it created a market for wolf existence. Today there is a price greater than zero for this scarce good. As a result, wolves are loose on the range in Wyoming.

IN SUMMARY

- A good is anything that directly or indirectly affects a person's well-being, or utility.
- Services are intangible goods. Environmental services are goods.
- Private goods are rival and excludable. Rival means that one person's consumption of the good prevents another person from consuming it. Excludable means that people can be excluded from consuming the good.
- Goods that are nonrival and nonexcludable are called public goods. Goods that are nonexcludable but rival are open access goods. Club goods are rival but nonexcludable. Most environmental goods are public goods or open access goods.
- A good is scarce if quantity demanded exceeds quantity supplied when the price of the good is zero. A price greater than zero is one signal that a good is scarce.
- A good that does not have a market price still has a value measured by its price in the good's next best use. That value is called opportunity cost.

The Advantages of Markets

A **market** is an opportunity for exchange between two or more willing participants. Market exchanges involve sellers and buyers. For example, the local coffee shop is happy to offer a caffeine fix for $1.50, and, before an 8:30 a.m. exam, many students are happy to pay for it. Money is not necessary in a market. If a student works for the campus food service, part of the compensation might be free meals and coffee. However, a major advantage of conducting transactions with money is that a person doesn't have to work specifically for whoever is offering food, or to have exactly the right combination of goods to exchange. Instead, people can earn money at any job and use it to purchase the goods and services they desire.

PARETO IMPROVEMENT

The participants in a market exchange their goods voluntarily. If the cup of coffee is not worth $1.50 to someone, that person walks away from the coffee shop. As a result, market exchanges only happen if each party is better off, or at least no worse off, than before. So markets do not make one person better off at the expense of another. In this way, the price of the good allocates it among consumers.

If a party is better off than before the exchange, his utility has increased. Such a mutually advantageous exchange is called *Pareto improving*, named for the nineteenth-century economist Vilfredo Pareto, who invented this concept. A **Pareto improvement** results when an action makes at least one party better off and nobody worse off. In many market situations, both parties benefit, nobody in the rest of the world is hurt, and a Pareto improvement results. The allocation of goods that results after a voluntary trade is **Pareto preferred** to the allocation that existed before. When the exchange affects only the participants in a market, market exchanges are Pareto improving: people buy or sell only if they are better off.

Look at Figure 3.2, a more detailed demand and supply diagram for electricity. The equilibrium price and quantity are $P = \$32/\text{MWH}$ and $Q = 15.2$ GWH. Suppose that only 15 GWH were produced. To get consumers to buy only that amount, the price would have to be about $36/MWH. Is there a way to make both the consumers and the producer better off? Suppose the producer then sold the consumers an additional 200 MWH (0.2 GWH) at a price of $32/MWH. The demand curve shows that the consumers will voluntarily buy up to 15.2 GWH at $32/MWH. People only do voluntary things if they make them better off. So the consumers will buy the extra 200 MWH and be better off. What of the producers? They are willing to sell up to 15.2 GWH at a price of $32/MWH, so they will voluntarily sell the extra 200 MWH and be better off. Because both parties are better off, the equilibrium is Pareto preferred to the hypothetical production of 15 GWH.

There was nothing special about our starting point of 15 GWH. The same argument could be made for any starting point below the equilibrium. What of starting points above the equilibrium, like 15.4 GWH? If that quantity were produced, producers would insist on a price of $32.75/MWH, but consumers would buy only about 15.15 GWH at that price. Is there a way to make both the consumers and producers better off? Producers would prefer to stop making some of the electricity than to have excess electricity without being able to sell it; reducing production reduces their cost and lowers the price. If the price goes down, consumers are willing to buy a little more, until they are back at the equilibrium of $Q = 15.2$ GWH and $P = \$32/\text{MWH}$. Therefore, both the consumers and producers will be better off. The same argument

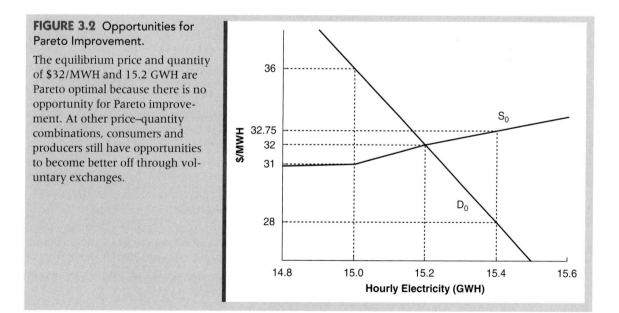

FIGURE 3.2 Opportunities for Pareto Improvement.

The equilibrium price and quantity of $32/MWH and 15.2 GWH are Pareto optimal because there is no opportunity for Pareto improvement. At other price–quantity combinations, consumers and producers still have opportunities to become better off through voluntary exchanges.

can be made for any starting point above the equilibrium. Because there is a way to make the consumers and producers both better off from any point other than the equilibrium, the equilibrium is Pareto preferred to all other outputs.

At the equilibrium price and quantity, the buyers are not willing to buy any more than they have already bought, and the sellers are not willing to sell any more than they have already sold. No further opportunity exists for buyers and sellers to engage in a trade that makes at least one of them better off and leaves the other no worse off. At that point, the only way to make one person better off is to make another person worse off. An outcome where there are no further possible trades that make at least one party better off and no one worse off is called a **Pareto optimum**; it is also described as **Pareto optimal**. The equilibrium in Figure 3.2 is Pareto optimal. When a market system permits voluntary trades,

---

BOX 3.1

Rationing and Black Markets

During wars, many goods that are readily available in peacetime may become scarcer. Some imported goods may come more infrequently, either because the goods come from enemy countries or because international transport is vulnerable to attacks. Domestically produced goods may be diverted to the war effort and thus be less available for civilian use. If markets operate freely, the prices of all these goods will rise, sometimes dramatically. Wartime governments would prefer not to pay high prices, though, and neither do civilians. One remedy, used for various wars in various countries, has been rationing.

Under rationing, consumers are each given a limited quantity at a price lower than the market-clearing price. In World War II, the United States rationed gasoline, nylon stockings, sugar, and automobile tires, among other goods; England rationed a number of foods. The allocations could be based on need, on per-capita consumption, or on political access; important government officials sometimes got higher rations than others.

Regardless how goods are rationed, people may not end up with the quantities that best suit their needs. Someone who wanted to make a birthday cake might not get enough butter, sugar, or eggs for it; other people might be willing to sell them— for a sufficient price.

Rationing often leads to the development of black (illegal) markets, in which consumers resell rationed goods to each other at prices above the rationed price. Let's focus on the trades among consumers. Is it wrong for the person with extra sugar to sell it at a price above the rationed price to the family with a birthday? Both the buyer and the seller are participating in a voluntary exchange; each will enter into it only if each is better off from it. So long as nobody outside the transaction is harmed, these black-market exchanges are therefore Pareto improving.

participants exhaust all the trades that are Pareto improving. As a result, the equilibrium in a market system that has none of the imperfections described in this chapter is Pareto optimal.

ALLOCATION OF GOODS

If a good is scarce, not everyone can have as much as he wants for free. How should the good be distributed among the people who want it? A variety of means exist to allocate scarce goods. One method is standing in line. In many wilderness areas in the United States, camping permits are given out free on a first-come, first-served basis; those who are late may not get them. Another method is rationing. During World War II, for example, the U.S. government rationed gasoline, sugar, and other goods to citizens. During the 2008 Olympics, to reduce air pollution, Beijing allowed drivers to use their cars only every other day. Similarly, drivers in Mexico City are not allowed to use their cars one day a week. "Might makes right" is yet another allocation system: fights and wars are often fought to get goods. In market-based economies, however, goods are typically allocated by price. London, Oslo, and Stockholm charge a price to drive into the city, and New York may soon follow. People willing and able to pay the market price purchase the good—in this case, the right to drive into the city.

Markets are highly effective at allocating goods. The market decides who will make the goods and who will get the goods. The equilibrium price ensures that the amount that consumers want to buy matches the amount that producers want to sell. If quantity supplied does not equal quantity demanded, price can adjust up or down to bring the two together again so that the market clears.

Consider, again, wolves in Yellowstone. In the absence of the trust fund established by Defenders of Wildlife, the ranchers who thought they would lose livestock to wolves had little incentive to give up their lobbying effort to keep wolves out of the park. Once environmentalists offered to pay for damages, rancher opposition was reduced. The creation of a market, with Defenders of Wildlife paying for livestock killed by wolves, contributed to a viable wolf population in Yellowstone for the first time since the early twentieth century. The compensation program allocated the scarce good, wolf existence, in a Pareto-improving manner: environmentalists were better off, and ranchers were no worse off.

Suppose that, instead, the U.S. Department of the Interior decided to reintroduce wolves over the ranchers' objections and that the compensation program was not in place. Environmentalists would be better off having the wolves than not having the wolves, but ranchers would be worse off. Their utility would be reduced both when wolves ate their livestock and when they would need to take care to keep their pets and children safe. Because someone would be made worse off, the policy would not be Pareto improving. It is likely that ranchers would have continually pressured the Department of the Interior to change its decision, and the wolves might not have been introduced, or only a smaller number might have been permitted. In this situation, a market mechanism produced a Pareto-improving result.

Markets do not necessarily result in equitable allocations of goods. A market may allocate goods in a Pareto-improving manner yet result in great inequities between richer and poorer people. Consider a person who has little in the way of possessions and whose labor, because of lack of skills, is not very valuable. No amount of free exchange will make this individual rich. Indeed, this individual's ability to work for a living may not yield enough money for rent and food, much less support for a family. Nevertheless, because all opportunities for mutual exchange may be exhausted, extreme poverty can exist in a Pareto-optimal allocation. Markets are not designed to address issues of distribution of wealth.

IN SUMMARY

- A Pareto-improving exchange makes at least one party to the trade better off and leaves no one worse off. When there are no further Pareto-improving trades to make, the allocation of goods is Pareto optimal. When the outcome is Pareto optimal, any further trade that would make one person better off would make another person worse off.
- Markets are one means to allocate goods. Other methods to allocate goods include standing in line, rationing, and violence.
- Exchanges in a market only happen if all participants in the trade are made better off, or at least not worse off. As long as nobody else is affected by the exchange, markets exhaust the Pareto-improving trades. This is a key advantage of markets relative to other allocation methods.
- Pareto optimality does not guarantee equity.

Market Failure

Many goods of interest to environmental and resource economists are not allocated in perfectly functioning, Pareto-improving markets. A **market failure** occurs when markets do not allocate goods in a Pareto-optimal manner. When a market fails, potential Pareto-improving exchanges do not or cannot happen. Without these exchanges, markets cannot work in the effective ways just described. These exchanges may be limited because of characteristics of the good or because of institutional settings. Breakdowns in markets for environmental goods are commonly described with the following categories. They are not mutually exclusive; a good may fall into multiple categories. These terms are very common in both economics and environmental studies.

1. *Lack of ownership or transferability.* It is hard to trade a good that no one can own or whose purchase is illegal. Lack of ownership of a natural resource also means that no one can be excluded from using it.
2. *Open access.* Open access is the term for a good that is rival but from which it is impossible to exclude people.

3. *Externality.* An effect, other than a change in prices, of a market transaction on a nonparticipant in that market is an externality. The effect is called an externality because it is external to the market.
4. *Public goods.* Because a public good is both nonrival and nonexcludable, use of it by one person does not limit others' use of it.
5. *Providing for the future.* If people put inadequate weight on the effects of present activities for the future, the future may end up without sufficient resources.
6. *Government-caused failure.* Government activities can reduce the efficiency of markets.

Markets, including natural resource markets, also fail for other reasons, including imperfect competition and asymmetric information. Competition is imperfect when producers are able to set the price higher than it would be in a competitive market. Asymmetric information means that one party to a transaction knows more than the other about the good. For instance, a seller of a used car knows the faults with that particular car, while the buyer only knows the faults for an average car of that type. These topics must be left to other courses, to allow focus on these six environmentally oriented failures.

LACK OF OWNERSHIP AND TRANSFERABILITY

At a minimum, the requirements for market transactions are ownership and transferability. That is, exchange can happen only if it is clear that one person can own the good and that the ownership can be transferred to another person. In order to own a good, the good must be excludable. Nonexcludable goods aren't meaningfully owned because anyone can take what he or she wishes.

That cup of coffee before an 8:30 a.m. exam is an example of a good that can be owned and transferred. Markets for coffee exist, and people sell coffee for money all the time. For other goods, though, establishing ownership rights that can be exchanged can be physically or legally difficult.

Some goods can be difficult, if not impossible, to own and transfer because they are not divisible into marketable portions. Public goods such as clean air, the diversity of species in the world, and scenic vistas cannot easily be subdivided into pieces that can be bought and sold. As a result, as future discussions in this book will elaborate, markets by themselves do not provide incentives for Pareto-optimal amounts of these goods.

Water provides an example of a good whose ownership and transfer are often legally limited. **Appropriative water rights**, common in the western United States, have three characteristics: (1) They allow a person to take a specific amount of water from a watercourse. (2) The person must take the water from the watercourse and use it for a beneficial purpose, usually for irrigated agriculture. Otherwise, the person loses his right to the water. (3) When there is insufficient water to meet all claims, water is allocated first to those who filed their claims first. Until very recently, appropriative water rights could not be bought or sold independently of the land on which the water was located because the rights specified that the water had to be used on that land. Driven by an increase in urban water demand, legislators, particularly in California and Colorado, have changed the laws to permit water transfers so that water previously earmarked for farms can be used in cities. Now there are water markets in the western United States. Legal change permitted the rights to be transferable.

Appropriative rights, however, are not secure property rights. Ownership is secure when it can be taken away only with legal process and for predictable reasons. For instance, unless someone has unpaid debts, the money in that person's bank account will not be taken away. Even if someone does have unpaid debts, specific legal proceedings are required to take money away. Ownership security is imperfect when ownership can be taken away or diminished. For instance, laws and policies can change appropriative water rights. The U.S. federal courts have required the government to maintain a minimum flow of water for salmon in Oregon's Klamath River, even if, as a result, farmers get less water for irrigating crops in the Klamath basin; the legal decision reduced the security of the farmers' rights to water. Thus, water rights provide an example of a good that has been nontransferable and, even when transferable, has imperfect security of ownership.

The absence of security or transferability can play a major role in slowing economic development in poor places. In Ethiopia, agricultural land cannot be sold and can only be rented for limited times. As a result, people who are good at farming may not be able to buy farmland. People who own land but would prefer to work in other occupations cannot sell their farms and use the proceeds to start a business or train in a profession. The destructive effects of imperfect ownership rights on the development process cannot be overestimated.

OPEN ACCESS

A key aspect of ownership is the ability to exclude others. For many natural resources, such as grasslands, forests, and the ocean, it is very difficult to limit access; these are open-access resources. Everybody and nobody owns an open-access resource. Most of the world's fisheries, especially in open oceans, are open-access resources. There are no limits to the number of fishers. As a result, from an individual fisher's point of view, it makes no sense to preserve breeding stock of fish to ensure fish supplies for the future. The fisher reasons that, if he were to stop fishing and go home, then other fishers would catch the fish that he had spared. Most fishers are likely to reason in the same way and not show any restraint. As a result, as soon as the fishing technology exists to deplete a fishery profitably, it is depleted. Although all fishers would be better off by restraining themselves, the market does not provide that restraint.

Lack of property rights in general, and open access in particular, result in overuse of resources. They also reduce investment to maintain or improve resources because potential investors will not be able to profit if they cannot keep others away from the venture in which they are investing. Lack of transferability also traps resources in uses that are not their most productive ones. For all these reasons, markets fail in the absence of ownership and transferability.

BOX 3.2

A Tale of Two Fisheries

Lobster harvesters in the United States face diminishing catches and intense competition due to open access to the fishery. "Right now, my only incentive is to go out and kill as many fish as I can," said a New England lobster fisher quoted in the *New York Times*. "I have no incentive to conserve the fishery because any fish I leave is just going to be picked by the next guy."

In contrast, Australia and New Zealand have placed a limit on the total number of lobster traps (also called pots). The two governments assigned permits to working lobster fishers. "From then on," according to the *New York Times*, "any newcomer who wanted to set a trap in those waters had to buy a license from someone already in the business." The limited number of traps meant that more lobsters could stay in the ocean to breed, and the stock levels stayed higher. Higher stock levels meant more lobsters caught per pot and higher profits. To protect the value of their licenses, the lobster fishers of Australia and New Zealand have become conservationists. One Australian bought a license for $2,000 per pot in 1984; the market price of a pot climbed to $35,000 by 2000. "It's my retirement fund," he explained. "No one's going to pay me $35,000 a pot if there are no lobsters left."

EXTERNALITY

Trades between willing people make each party better off. But what happens when a transaction has a side effect? Suppose that growing the coffee beans for that morning cup involves clearing forests and damaging habitats for species that other people want to protect. Now, people not party to the coffee purchase may suffer from others' desire for caffeine, and the exchange is no longer Pareto improving. All transactions have a **pecuniary effect**, an effect on the price of the item purchased. A rightward shift in demand for coffee in Europe, for instance, raises the price of coffee everywhere, and coffee drinkers everywhere suffer from the pecuniary effect of higher prices. An externality, on the other hand, results when growing coffee causes losses of tropical forests that many people would prefer to see preserved. The nonpecuniary effect of a transaction on a third party is an **externality**. Higher prices are not an externality, but loss of habitat is.

Externalities make up much of the subject matter of environmental economics. Although the market allocates electricity, for example, electricity generation often produces air pollution that makes breathing difficult, even for people who are not using the electricity. People buy and sell paper, but neither the buyer nor seller pays for all the damage caused by bleach released from paper plants into streams and lakes. Externalities are common. They are, however, unlikely to be addressed adequately by private markets: the participants in the market decision have no reason to think about the effects of their activities on third parties, even if the third parties suffer from their exchange.

Externalities can be either negative or positive. Negative externalities, such as pollution, impose harm on third parties. Because the market participants can ignore the harm, they have no incentive to reduce the harm: negative externalities tend to be over-provided. Positive externalities occur when a third party receives unintended benefits from someone else's action. For instance, one person may have a lovely garden that a neighbor enjoys tremendously without doing any of the work himself. Unlike negative externalities, which are provided more generously than the recipients would like, positive externalities tend not to be provided in as large a quantity as the recipients would like. The gardener, for instance, might not put quite as much work into his garden as the neighbor would like.

PUBLIC GOODS

Public goods are nonrival and nonexcludable. Existence services fit that description perfectly. One person's enjoyment of the existence of wolves does not affect any other person's enjoyment, and no one can be stopped from enjoying the existence of wolves. Clean air is a public good; the sun and the climate are public goods; public television and radio and national defense are public goods. The provision of public goods is at the heart of many environmental problems.

The market does not provide enough of public goods. Consider two neighbors who live in a duplex and share a small rose garden. The rose garden is a public good: neither neighbor can exclude the other from enjoying the garden, and one neighbor's enjoyment of the sight and scent of the garden does not diminish the other neighbor's ability to enjoy it. Imagine that a local gardener offers a pruning service for a flat fee of $20 a week. Both neighbors want to have the roses pruned, but neither neighbor is willing to pay more than $10 for the service. Each hopes the other will pay the full amount. If one neighbor pays it, the other neighbor will share all the benefits without paying anything. Because neither is willing to pay the gardener's price, however, the market outcome is that the rose garden does not get pruned. Table 3.1 summarizes this situation.

Suppose, now, that the neighbors agree to each contribute $10 to share a visit from the gardener. Now, both neighbors are better off: each receives a pruned garden in exchange for $10. The gardener is better off because he willingly exchanges

TABLE 3.1 Supply and Demand for Gardening.

	PRICE FOR PRUNING	
	$20	$10
WILL THE GARDENER WORK?	YES	NO
WILL A NEIGHBOR PAY?	NO	YES

his labor for $20. Because they all make this exchange willingly, they are all better off. This Pareto-improving exchange, however, did not come about through market mechanisms. Instead, it required collective action outside of the market. Thus, the market failed to provide a Pareto improvement where one was available.

Because no one can be excluded from using a public good, people can pay nothing and still enjoy the good. One who receives benefits and does not pay for them is a **free rider**. Suppose that there are three neighbors, each willing to pay no more than $10 for a gardener. If two of them get together and pay the gardener, the one who enjoys the garden without paying is a free rider.

An **imperfect public good** is partially, but not wholly, diminished by use and may or may not be excludable. A work of art is partly a public good: viewing the Mona Lisa alone is better than viewing it with 50 other people standing in front of it, but the other 50 people are not directly damaging the picture and the potential of others to view it. Similarly, a book can be privately owned and thus excludable, but it can be shared among many people.

Many environmental goods are imperfect public goods. While the existence value conveyed by a wild area is wholly nonexcludable and nonrival, the value from visitation of natural areas, on the other hand, is subject to crowding. Most prefer to see natural areas without hordes of other viewers.

Protecting wolves in Yellowstone is a public good. Not all people who care about wolves in Yellowstone are dues-paying members of Defenders of Wildlife or contributors to the Wolf Compensation Fund. Those who don't contribute are free riders who benefit from the efforts of those who have put up the money to reintroduce wolves. If all people who cared about wolf protection contributed to the fund, wolves might be reintroduced not only in Yellowstone but in other parts of their historical range as well. Without a mechanism to require the free riders to contribute, however, the quantity of wolf protection services is smaller than it might be.

BOX 3.3

Preventing Free Riders

California property owners in flood-prone areas are concerned with maintaining levees, which keep back flood waters. If a levee collapses, the river floods all the low-lying property. If the people who care most about levee collapse maintain the levees, they confer a benefit also upon those who do not contribute to maintenance.

California law provides a way around the free rider problem. Citizens in a local area can vote to create an assessment district, a local area in which property taxes are collected and earmarked specifically for a local problem, such as levee maintenance. A minority that does not vote in favor of creating the assessment district still has to pay taxes if the ballot measure passes, so that there will be no free riders. In this way, the levees are maintained, everyone benefits, and everyone has to pay.

PROVIDING FOR THE FUTURE

Many activities that individuals or groups undertake, such as building electricity-generating facilities, preserving wilderness, driving species to extinction, and increasing the national debt, have significant consequences for future generations. Those who conduct these activities in the present rarely ignore the future completely. After all, the benefits and costs of major investments will come over time, and current generations hope to reap the benefits during their lifetimes. They also think about providing for future generations, such as when parents save money to pay for their children's college educations, or when governments build schools and parks for children yet unborn. When the present generation makes these decisions, though, two main problems may arise.

First, people now make decisions based on what they think future generations will want. It is probably fair to say that people in the present would change some of the decisions that people in the past made, in part because some of those previous actions led to irreversible changes that limit current choices. Seeking to eliminate wolves from the United States might not have been a priority in the early twentieth century if people in the present had their way. Would current generations have so completely eliminated the American prairie ecosystem in favor of farming? Today, in the Conservation Reserve Program, the American government pays farmers to keep about as much land as the state of Illinois planted with a semi-permanent conservation cover, to provide some of those ecological functions. If the policy makers of the late 1800s had known that later generations were interested in conserving the prairie, might they have set aside a large prairie wilderness area with the original flora and fauna? If so, current generations would have the choice between farming the last of the prairie or preserving it. Every generation faces decisions that will affect the future. Because, without time machines, people in the present cannot discover the wants of people in the future, this problem cannot be overcome completely. It does suggest, though, that current decision makers may want to leave some options open for the future rather than commit to irreversible decisions in the present.

Second, when people face tradeoffs between the present and the future, how much weight should they place on the future? Consider, for instance, the current generation's willingness to reduce its consumption of fossil fuels to reduce the problem of climate change. Some people argue that the present generation has an obligation to reduce heating, driving, and electricity use to help avoid future climate damages. Others look at the poor conditions in which many people currently live and want to improve their welfare, in part through better access to relatively inexpensive fossil fuel–fired energy. The choice over how much to reduce fossil fuel use to reduce the damages from greenhouse gases depends heavily on the importance people put on present well-being relative to the future.

It is clear that people do not ignore the future in their day-to-day activities. Whether they pay adequate attention to the future, though, and how much weight the future should have in these decisions, are open questions.

GOVERNMENT-CAUSED FAILURE

Governments intervene in our lives in many ways: through tax policies, regulations on polluters, land ownership, international relations, agricultural policies, and countless other actions. Government decision makers assure us that they act in the best interests of the public. They make that claim whether they are elected figures, brutal dictators, corrupt officials, lazy paper-pushers, or hard-working public servants. It is probably fair to say, though, that politicians and bureaucrats likely have their own agendas in addition to the public interest, whether those agendas include reelection, increased budgets for their agencies, greater political power, their individual views of the public good, or a desire to enhance their own private good.

One classic role for government, in economic theory, is to correct market failures such as negative externalities, open access, and inadequate provision of public goods. If government does not intervene in markets to correct these problems, negative externalities can be overprovided, open access resources abused, and public goods underprovided. If government does intervene in markets, though, will it act in ways that enhance public welfare? Like beauty, the answer often lies in the eye of the beholder. Are the agricultural programs described in Chapter 2 worth their cost because they help increase farmers' incomes and support agricultural production, or do they impose unjustified burdens on the general public for the benefit of one narrow sector? Will an international treaty to reduce greenhouse gases, and thus climate change, protect society from warming, drought, greater storm activity, and social dislocation, or will it decrease jobs and wealth for society, limit people's activities, and cause serious social dislocation? While economists typically recommend how government should intervene in markets, government decision makers do not always follow such recommendations. In fact, they rarely follow the suggestions exactly. If government intervenes, will it make things better or worse than if it had stayed out?

Government-caused failure occurs when government intervenes in ways that decrease rather than increase social welfare. It is not a classic market failure because governments are not classic market actors. Nevertheless, in the world of public policy, government failure is always a possibility. Governments can greatly improve people's lives, but they can also make lives miserable. Sometimes the same public policy does both, affecting different groups in different ways. For example, increased cigarette taxes protect young people from the serious health risks of smoking, but these taxes also create a hardship for sellers and consumers of cigarettes.

IN SUMMARY

- If a market fails, then some Pareto-improving exchanges won't happen.
- Lack of ownership and transferability, open access, externalities, providing for public goods, and failure to give adequate weight to future impacts are common forms of market failures for environmental goods.
- When governments intervene, they might increase social welfare by reducing market failures, or they might decrease social welfare by creating new problems. The possibility of government failure in public policy should always be considered.

Transcontinental Pollution

Everyone has access to the atmosphere. It provides garbage collection services for all the waste gases from transport, agriculture, and industry. Some of these waste gases can travel surprisingly long distances. Hogbin Yu and his colleagues measured the trans-Pacific flow of pollution in teragrams, a unit of measurement of the mass of pollution aerosol (1 teragram is about 2.2 billion pounds). Satellite data confirmed 18 teragrams of pollution aerosol was exported from East Asia to the northwestern Pacific Ocean, and 4.5 teragrams reached North America annually from East Asia over the study period.

Because the atmosphere is a global public good and the potential pollutants are many, keeping the atmosphere clean requires agreement among a large group of its users. These agreements take the form of treaties among countries. For example, the Kyoto Protocol aims to limit greenhouse gas emissions, and the Montreal Protocol limited chlorofluorocarbons, the cause of the atmosphere's ozone hole.

International treaties suffer from the difficulties associated with addressing open-access resources. Each country would like every other country to control its pollution, but no country wants to have pollution limits imposed on it. While the same is true for individual polluters as for countries, a notable difference is that polluters within a country are legally subject to the laws of the country. In contrast, each country is sovereign, subject only to restrictions that it agrees to accept. It cannot be forced to sign a treaty, except perhaps through war. As a result, a country is likely to agree to a treaty only if it is better off by joining than by staying away. Because countries often benefit if every other country participates in a treaty, but they stay out, it is perhaps surprising that so many treaties get enacted.

CHAPTER SUMMARY

Here are the key lessons from this chapter:

- An economic good is anything that affects someone's well-being, or utility.
- A good is scarce if quantity demanded is greater than quantity supplied at a price of zero. A price greater than zero is one signal that a good is scarce. Scarce goods can be allocated by price, among other methods.
- Environmental goods are both economic goods and scarce goods.
- A Pareto-improving exchange leaves everyone better off or no worse off. Pareto optimality occurs when there are no more exchanges to be made that would make one person better off and no one worse off. At that point, the only way to make one person better off would make at least one other person worse off.
- A market failure is the failure of a market to allocate goods in a Pareto-optimal way.
- Market failures are caused by lack of ownership and transferability, open access externalities, public goods, inability to predict the future, and government failure. Markets typically fail for environmental goods.
- Government intervention in markets can make society better or worse off. It must therefore be invoked carefully.

KEY TERMS

abatement *(p. 39)*
appropriative water rights *(p. 47)*
club goods *(p. 38)*
environmental services *(p. 39)*
excludable *(p. 38)*
existence service *(p. 39)*
externality *(p. 49)*
free rider *(p. 51)*
good *(p. 38)*
government-caused failure *(p. 53)*
imperfect public good *(p. 51)*
market *(p. 42)*
market failure *(p. 46)*

open access *(p. 38)*
opportunity cost *(p. 41)*
Pareto improvement *(p. 42)*
Pareto optimal *(p. 44)*
Pareto optimum *(p. 44)*
Pareto preferred *(p. 42)*
pecuniary effect *(p. 49)*
private good *(p. 38)*
public goods *(p. 38)*
rival in consumption *(p. 38)*
scarce *(p. 39)*
services *(p. 38)*
utility *(p. 38)*

NOTES

The sources for the wolf story are "Wolves of North America," http://www.defenders.org/wildlife/wolf/regions/new.html, last visited September 30, 2004; "Gray Wolf," http://www.fws.gov/endangered/i/A03.html, U.S. Fish and Wildlife Service, last visited January 30, 2008; Steven H. Fritts et al., "Planning and Implementing a Reintroduction of Wolves to Yellowstone National Park and Central Idaho," *Restoration Ecology* 5 (1997): 7–27; Lisa Naughton-Treves, Rebecca Grossberg, and Adrian Treves, "Paying for Tolerance: Rural Citizens' Attitudes toward Wolf Depredation and Compensation," *Conservation Biology* 17 (2003): 1500–1511; and Ken Kostel, "A Top Predator Roars Back," *OnEarth* 26 (2004): 6–7. John Krutilla's discussion of the armchair environmentalist can be found in "Conservation Reconsidered," *American Economic Review* 57 (1967): 777–786. The contrasting fisheries story is from John Tierney, "A Tale of Two Fisheries," *New York Times Magazine,* August 27, 2000. The story on long-range pollution transport can be found in Hogbin Yu et al., "A Satellite-Based Assessment of Transpacific Transport of Pollution Aerosol," *Journal of Geophysical Research* 113 (2008): D14S12 et seq.

EXERCISES

1. In each of the following situations, discuss whether free markets are likely to provide Pareto-optimal levels of the goods or whether a market failure distorts the markets.
   (a) Although a restaurant has a separate smoking section, the smoke from that section spreads to the nonsmoking part of the dining area. As a result, some of the nonsmokers leave before they have finished their dinners.
   (b) A restaurant owner decides on his own to separate, both physically and through ventilation systems, the smoking and nonsmoking sections of his restaurant. Both smokers and nonsmokers find the arrangement acceptable.
   (c) Radon, a naturally occurring gas, increases the risk of cancer in poorly ventilated basements in areas with particular geologic characteristics. For

purposes of this question, assume that radon affects only homeowners living in the house, and the homeowner can easily find out radon levels in the house. Ventilating the radon out of a home costs about $1,000.

(d) If a homeowner takes care of the radon in his home, he may reduce radon levels in neighbors' houses as well.

2. Describe the role of opportunity cost in the following scenarios. In particular, explain how opportunity cost can help assign values to goods in these examples.
   (a) Instead of working this weekend and earning $100, a student decides to go hiking.
   (b) A student decides to go to a private university with tuition of $25,000 per year, though he also was accepted into a state university with in-state tuition of $6,500 per year.
   (c) Another student, faced with the same choice, decided to go to the state university.
   (d) The first student decided to work in the cafeteria for $8 per hour and therefore take five years instead of four years to finish at the private university. The second student made the same decision at the state university.

3. Are the following decisions Pareto improving? Pareto optimal? Explain why or why not.
   (a) The restaurant owner in 1(b) spent $10,000 to install the separate ventilation systems but felt it was worth it in terms of improved customer satisfaction and resulting increase in visits.
   (b) The restaurant in 1(b) has employees as well as customers. The owner requires the employees, regardless of whether they like cigarette smoke, to work in both the smoking and nonsmoking parts of the restaurant.
   (c) The homeowner in 1(d) decided not to install a radon ventilation system because he was unwilling to pay more than $500 (the cost to him of the additional risk due to radon exposure) to eliminate the radon in his house.
   (d) Because 10 neighbors of the homeowner in 1(d) would benefit $100 each from reduced health risks due to radon if the homeowner put in the ventilation system, the homeowners' association for the neighborhood required the homeowner to install the abatement system.

4. Provide an example of:
   (a) Goods that are (i) private, (ii) public, (iii) nonexcludable and rival, (iv) excludable and nonrival.
   (b) A situation where people have lost part of the value of their property to the government and not been compensated. The higher the percentage of the value lost, the better the example.
   (c) An externality that affects not only the market that produces the externality but another market as well.
   (d) A public good (i) provided by a government and (ii) provided by a private party.

5. Consider a group of students who share a bathroom, and there are no janitorial services provided. Some of the students prefer a clean bathroom; others have a high tolerance for messiness.

(a) Explain why, using concepts in this chapter, there is a good chance that the bathroom will end up a mess.

(b) Are there circumstances in which the mess is Pareto optimal? Are there circumstances where the mess is a market failure?

(c) Consider several ways to reduce the mess:

   (i) The students work out a cleaning schedule among themselves. Each student is honor-bound to comply, but nobody keeps track.

   (ii) Students work out a cleaning schedule among themselves. Each student who cleans knows who the previous cleaner was and grades that student on her performance.

   (iii) The building manager institutes a fee for all building residents to pay for a custodian.

   Which is likely to be easiest to get started? What outcome do you expect for each of these options? Which is most likely to lead to peaceful relations among the students?

4 | Consumer Behavior and the Environment

Shopping, for some people, is a way of showing their environmental interest. They choose products made with recycled content, look for organic
content, buy more energy-efficient goods, or simply buy less. Consumer
decisions about which goods to purchase and how much of a good to purchase affect the environment in a number of ways. This chapter explores how
prices and income interact with consumers' preferences to determine demand
for a good, and how demand in turn affects the environment. This chapter will
examine:

- How a consumer decides how to allocate her budget among the various
  goods she might buy;
- What factors affect a consumer's choices;
- How individual consumer choices add up to market demand.

Electricity's Role in Generating Greenhouse Gases

Every time someone turns on a light or a computer, she consumes electricity and
contributes to the impact of electric power generation on the environment. The
electricity generation industry is a major source of greenhouse gases (GHGs), which
contribute to climate change, and other emissions. In 2003, electricity producers
in the United States generated 3.2 million megawatt hours (MWHs) and emitted
2.4 billion metric tons of carbon dioxide (CO_2), a GHG, and 10.6 million metric
tons of sulfur dioxide, a source of acid rain.

In the United States, many fuels produce electricity. Coal accounts for 51 percent of the electricity, nuclear energy 20 percent, natural gas 17 percent, and
hydropower 7 percent. The remainder comes from petroleum and other fuels. Each
of these major fuel sources has associated environmental problems. Burning coal
produces the air pollutants sulfur dioxide and nitrogen oxides, as well as toxics,
including mercury, which can cause nerve damage. Coal also causes water pollution, and coal mining has drastically changed many landscapes. Natural gas and

petroleum also produce air pollutants, although less than coal. All three fossil fuels—coal, natural gas, and petroleum—produce CO_2 when burned. Hydropower, from dams, comes at the expense of free-flowing streams and their fisheries and is particularly hard on salmon. Nuclear power carries a small probability of very big accidents: the 1986 Chernobyl disaster in the Ukraine, for instance, spread a cloud of radioactive material around the world and created a highly hazardous zone around the reactor. In addition, there is as yet no satisfactory way to dispose of used nuclear fuel, which remains hazardous for a very long time, and reactors produce material that can be used in nuclear weapons. There is no electricity generation method currently in large-scale use that does not have adverse environmental consequences.

The quantity of sulfur dioxide and nitrogen oxides in the air has been regulated in the United States since the 1970 Clean Air Act Amendments. However, the political recognition of the need to control GHG emissions is of much more recent origin. Most developed countries, with the notable exception of the United States, signed the 1997 Kyoto Protocol, whose purpose is to reduce GHG emissions. The original 15 members of the European Union (EU), for instance, agreed to reduce their carbon dioxide emissions by 8 percent from their 1990 levels sometime between 2008 and 2012.

One way these countries plan to meet their Kyoto targets is through taxes. Because a tax on a good reduces the quantity sold, a tax on GHG-producing energy sources would reduce the quantity sold and GHG emissions. Seven European countries now use carbon taxes to reduce CO_2 emissions in the electricity sector. The highest reported carbon tax for household electricity users is 97 Euro ($115) per MWH in Denmark. Germany charges 21 Euro ($25). For comparison, the residential price of electricity in the United States averaged $115 per MWH in 2009. From the perspective of a consumer in Europe, the carbon tax is a price increase and will affect the quantity of electricity that consumers demand.

Even though the United States did not sign the Kyoto treaty, it is possible to estimate what would happen if a high electricity tax were used in the United States. Because consumers of electricity are largely unaware of the hourly price variations that occur, the quantity of electricity they use does not change in response to hourly changes. On a yearly basis, however, consumers do respond to changes in their electric rates. This chapter uses data on electricity demand for the state of Montana, which regulates its electricity market, to examine the effects, both on demand and on emissions, of a large electricity tax.

Why Consumers Buy What They Buy

According to the basics of the theory of demand, consumers consider the prices of goods on the market and, given their incomes, buy the combinations of goods that best suit their needs and desires. These goods provide them with utility, the economists' term for happiness or well-being. This section discusses the pieces of this problem: choices among bundles of goods, the role of budgets, and how to describe individual preferences.

GOODS AND BUNDLES OF GOODS

A consumer does not buy individual goods in isolation. Instead, she allocates income among a number of goods, and the amount of a particular good a consumer buys is affected by the amounts of other goods the consumer buys. A consumption **bundle** is a list showing the quantities of each good purchased. Because modern consumers buy thousands of different goods, it is common, rather than estimating demand curves for each good, to focus only on the goods related to the question at hand. For instance, studying the costs of GHG regulations requires an understanding of what consumers will buy if they buy less gasoline. For these purposes, a bundle might be defined in terms of the quantities of five aggregate goods that affect gasoline demand: gasoline, shelter (where a person lives), food, public transportation, and everything else. When there is only interest in one good, such as electricity, it is possible to analyze demand with just two categories: electricity and everything else.

THE BUDGET CONSTRAINT

"Had we but world enough, and time," the bundles of goods that a person might consume would be very large—she would take as much of any good as she would like, until she is satiated. Lack of money deters people from buying many of the goods that they desire, and it forces people to make tradeoffs among the goods they seek. In many cases, these limits pose significant hardships; poor families, for instance, may have to choose between medicine and food. On the other hand, it is fortunate for the earth that there are budgetary limits on the quantities of electricity and gasoline that people can consume. A **budget constraint** is the set of all bundles that the consumer can afford with no income left over.

Consider a consumer who has an income of Y and spends it on two goods. One good is electricity (E). The other good is everything else: a composite good, called stuff (S), which includes all nonelectricity goods. For simplicity, this example focuses on the decision of a consumer in one year. Her income simply appears at the beginning of the year. She then decides how much of her money to spend on electricity and how much stuff to buy. Because she is focusing only on this one year, there is no reason for saving, and she will spend all the income either on electricity or on stuff.

In this two-good economy, a bundle consists of units of stuff S and megawatt hours (MWH) of electricity E. She considers the prices of these two items, P_S and P_E, to be fixed and outside her control. Income is Y. The budget constraint is an equation expressing that a consumer's income must equal the sum of what she spends on the goods in her consumption bundle. Here, the budget constraint says that the amount of money the consumer spends on electricity (the price of electricity times the number of MWH she buys) plus the amount she spends on stuff (the price of stuff times the number of units of stuff she buys) must equal her income:

$$Y = P_S S + P_E E$$

The budget constraint defines all possible bundles of S and E that cost exactly Y. Recall that each bundle is a combination of some number of units of E and some number of units of S. The consumer does not have enough money to purchase any bundle that costs more than Y. She can afford any combination of S and E that costs less than Y or exactly Y. Because she has no reason to spend less than Y, she will use up all her money between stuff and electricity. Thus, she will purchase a bundle that costs exactly Y.

Figure 4.1 shows the budget constraint in the form of a graph, with S on the vertical axis and E on the horizontal axis. Each possible quantity of S that the consumer might choose to buy is a point on the vertical axis. Each possible quantity of E that the consumer might purchase is a point on the horizontal axis. Each possible pair (S, E) that the consumer could afford, given her income, is a point on the budget constraint. The graph is based on data for an average person in Montana in the United States.

Drawing this graph requires an equation that shows how much S the consumer can buy as she changes how much E she buys. Doing so involves solving the budget constraint equation for S as follows. Rearranging the equation happens in the following steps:

$Y = P_S S + P_E E$ can be rewritten as

$P_S S = Y - P_E E$. Dividing through by P_S then yields

$S = Y/P_S - (P_E/P_S)E$

This equation shows the quantity of S that the consumer can buy as a function of E—in other words, how much stuff the consumer can buy if she buys quantity E of electricity.

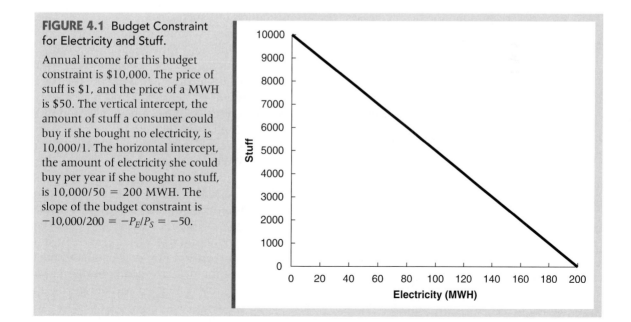

FIGURE 4.1 Budget Constraint for Electricity and Stuff.

Annual income for this budget constraint is $10,000. The price of stuff is $1, and the price of a MWH is $50. The vertical intercept, the amount of stuff a consumer could buy if she bought no electricity, is 10,000/1. The horizontal intercept, the amount of electricity she could buy per year if she bought no stuff, is 10,000/50 = 200 MWH. The slope of the budget constraint is $-10,000/200 = -P_E/P_S = -50$.

Graphing a straight line requires finding only two points on the line and connecting them. The easiest two points to find are the points where the consumer spends all her income on one good and none of her income on another. These are the points where the budget constraint intersects each of the axes.

If the consumer spends all her money on stuff, and none on electricity, then $Y = P_S S$. Rearranging this equation to isolate S on the left shows that the consumer can buy $S = Y/P_S$. If the consumer does not buy any electricity, she can buy an amount of stuff equal to her income, Y, divided by the price of stuff, P_S. In the example, if her income is $10,000 and each unit of stuff costs $1, she can buy 10,000 units of stuff if she does not buy any electricity. This point, $(0, Y/P_S)$, is at the top left corner of Figure 4.1: the quantity of electricity consumed is 0, and the quantity of stuff consumed is 10,000 units.

If the consumer instead spends all the money on electricity, the same steps show that $E = Y/P_E$. If the consumer buys no stuff, she can buy an amount of electricity, E, equal to her income, Y, divided by the price per MWH. Connecting these two points yields the budget constraint, a straight line between the points $(0, Y/P_S)$ and $(Y/P_E, 0)$. All the points between these two show possible combinations of electricity and stuff that the consumer can buy within the limitations of her budget.

Also useful to know about the budget constraint is its slope, the amount of stuff that the consumer must give up if she increases the amount of electricity she used by 1 MWH. Calculating the slope of a straight line starts with choosing two points on the line. Just as in drawing the budget constraint, the intercept on the vertical axis and the intercept on the horizontal axis are convenient points to use. Dividing the change in vertical distance (stuff), $-Y/P_S$, by the change in horizontal distance (electricity), Y/P_E, produces the slope, $-(P_E/P_S)$. The negative sign indicates that consumption of S decreases when consumption of E increases.

The equation $S = Y/P_S - (P_E/P_S)E$ also provides the slope. In the standard slope-intercept equation, the first term on the right-hand side of the equation is height of the intercept on the vertical axis, and the term multiplying E is the slope, $-(P_E/P_S)$.

The budget constraint in Figure 4.1 is based on income Y of $10,000, the price of electricity at $50/MWH, and the price of stuff as $1 per unit. Thus, if all money were spent on stuff, the consumer could buy $Y/P_S = 10,000$ units of it, and one point on the budget constraint is (MWH = 0, Stuff = 10,000). If, instead, the consumer spent all her money on electricity, she could get $Y/P_E = 200$ MWH, and another point on the budget constraint is (MWH = 200, Stuff = 0). The budget constraint connects these two points.

The slope of the budget constraint is the vertical distance between these two points ($-10,000$) divided by the horizontal distance (200): the slope is -50. If the slope is calculated as $-P_E/P_S$, with $P_S = 1$ and $P_E = 50$, then $-P_E/P_S = -50$. The consumer has to give up 50 units of stuff to get another MWH of electricity. Put another way, the consumer has to give up $50 worth of one-dollar units to purchase one $50 unit of electricity. Remember that the negative sign indicates that it is impossible, along the constraint, to have more than one good without giving up some of the other good.

BOX 4.1

Trading Off Between Gas and Food

When consumers have to spend more to fill up their gas tanks, they have to spend less on something else to stay within their budget constraints. Researchers found that consumers changed their expenditures on food when gasoline prices rose. From 2000 to 2005, gas prices in the United States varied from $1.50 to $3.00 per gallon. Even when gas prices doubled, the quantity of gas purchased changed very little because people chose not to change how they went to work or where they went on vacation. As a result, an increase in gas prices translated into a decrease in the amount of money available for other purchases. For instance, when gas prices increased by 100 percent, expenditures on food eaten away from home declined by roughly 50 percent. Instead of eating out, consumers spent 15–19 percent more on groceries. They also changed their behavior at the grocery store. Supermarket scanner data show that when gas prices were high, consumers were more likely than usual to choose the brand of cereal, juice, or yogurt that was on sale. They also bought a lot of chicken cuts that were on sale, possibly because chicken is cheaper than beef. These effects were especially noticeable at stores that serve lower-income neighborhoods. In this way, consumers were able to offset about 70 percent of the effect of a doubling of gasoline prices on their budgets.

PREFERENCES

A budget constraint defines the set of affordable bundles, but it says nothing about which of those bundles the consumer purchases. The choice of a bundle, among the affordable bundles, is a matter of individual preference.

Economists assume that each person has preferences about consumption bundles. Preferences tell us how a person makes tradeoffs between goods. Preferences describe the happiness consumers get from consuming goods, not the monetary costs they pay to get those goods. Any two bundles can be ranked in one of three ways:

The chooser prefers bundle A to bundle B.

The chooser prefers bundle B to bundle A.

The chooser is indifferent between bundle A and bundle B. That is, the consumer is equally happy consuming bundle A or bundle B.

No two people have the same preferences. For example, one consumer may prefer a bundle with 7,500 units of stuff and 50 MWH of electricity to a bundle with 2,500 units of stuff and 150 MWH. Another consumer may prefer the second bundle to the first. Yet another may be indifferent between the two bundles. Preferences are specific to individual people.

Economists make several assumptions regarding consumer preferences. First, each consumer is consistent in her preferences. That is, if a consumer prefers bundle A to bundle B, then she won't also prefer bundle B to bundle A. Second, preferences are transitive; if she prefers bundle A to bundle B, and bundle B to bundle C, then she prefers A to C.

Third, "more is better." A consumer's happiness is increased if she receives more of at least one good and not less of any other good. Figure 4.2 illustrates this principle. Bundle A has 5 MWH and 9,700 units of stuff. Every consumer is expected to prefer every bundle that has at least as many MWH as bundle A and also has more stuff than bundle A. Similarly, each consumer prefers every bundle that has as much stuff as bundle A and also has more MWH than bundle A.

Look at the area above and to the right of A in Figure 4.2. It is the area to the right of and above the two dashed lines. Every point in that area has more of at least one of the goods than bundle A and also has no less of the other good than bundle A. All consumers should prefer every point in that area to A. Two such points are B and C. Everyone should prefer bundle C, with $9,773 of stuff and 8 MWH, to bundle A, with $9,700 of stuff and 5 MWH. Similarly, all consumers prefer bundle B (5 MWH, $9,800 stuff) to bundle A. Notice that Bundle B has more stuff but the same amount of electricity.

Fourth and finally, economists assume that people choose the bundles that they prefer. If a consumer prefers bundle A to bundle B and she can afford either bundle, then she will choose bundle A. This assumption is economists' definition of a person behaving rationally.

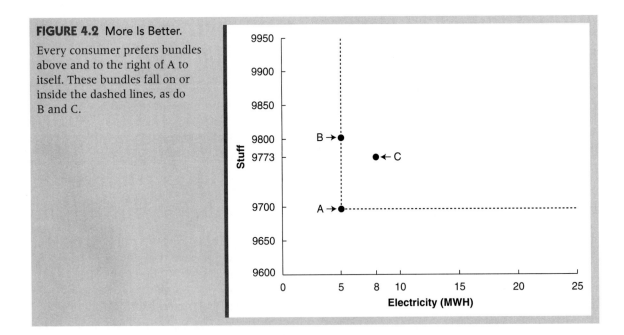

FIGURE 4.2 More Is Better.

Every consumer prefers bundles above and to the right of A to itself. These bundles fall on or inside the dashed lines, as do B and C.

The economists' assumption of rational behavior provides the link between observable choice and unobservable preferences. If an economist observes a consumer buying bundle C and the consumer can afford both bundles B and C, then the economist will conclude that bundle C is preferred or indifferent to bundle B. So by observing purchases, economists can learn about underlying preferences that otherwise may not be observable.

INDIFFERENCE CURVES

Discussion of consumer choice may appear abstract, but it leads to a practical method of graphing preferences, using the idea of indifference. An **indifference curve** is the set of all bundles that produce the same utility—satisfaction or well-being—as any other point on the curve. It is a graphical representation of preferences. Figure 4.3 shows two indifference curves in the same kind of graph used for the budget constraint, with stuff on the vertical axis and electricity on the horizontal axis. The indifference curve that goes through bundle A shows the set of all bundles that are indifferent to A—that is, the person making the choice is equally happy with A and with any other point on that indifference curve, such as D. An individual has the same utility at any point on that indifference curve.

Now look at the indifference curve through C. Points B and E lie on that indifference curve, which means that the consumer gets the same utility from bundles B, C, and E. Does the consumer get more utility on the higher or lower

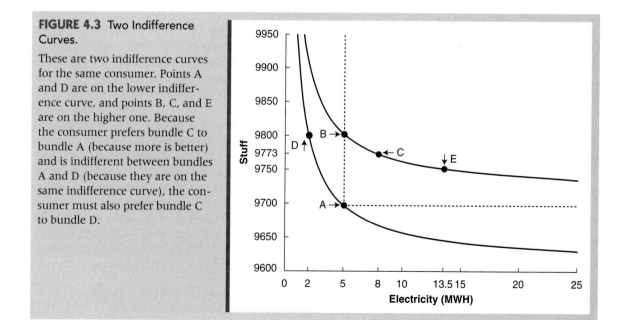

FIGURE 4.3 Two Indifference Curves.

These are two indifference curves for the same consumer. Points A and D are on the lower indifference curve, and points B, C, and E are on the higher one. Because the consumer prefers bundle C to bundle A (because more is better) and is indifferent between bundles A and D (because they are on the same indifference curve), the consumer must also prefer bundle C to bundle D.

indifference curve? The higher indifference curve includes bundles like C that have both more electricity and more stuff than bundle A on the lower indifference curve. Because the consumer prefers bundle C to bundle A under the assumption that more is better, the higher indifference curve represents more utility than the lower indifference curve. All points on the higher curve give the same utility, so the consumer prefers every point on the higher curve (for instance, B or E) to every point on the lower curve (for instance, A or D). Utility is therefore higher on higher indifference curves.

Two other properties of indifference curves come from the properties of preferences. First, indifference curves slope down. Consider a bundle like A. If a little stuff were added to bundle A, it would create a new bundle, B, that was preferred to A because more is better. To create a bundle that has more stuff than A and is indifferent to A, it is necessary to take away some electricity. Otherwise, if the new bundle added stuff but didn't take away electricity, the consumer would prefer the new bundle, rather than being indifferent between the bundles. D is the new bundle that adds stuff, subtracts electricity, and is indifferent to A. So, any new bundle with the same level of utility as a given bundle (like A) must have more of one good (for instance, stuff) and less of the other good (here, electricity). Because electricity use must decrease when stuff increases in order to keep the bundles indifferent, the curve slopes down, showing that consumption of one good decreases when consumption of the other increases and utility does not change.

The second property is that indifference curves don't cross. If they crossed, then, at the point of intersection, the same bundle would be on two indifference curves. To the right of the intersection, one of these curves would be higher than the other one. Hence, a single bundle would be on both a higher and lower indifference curve and would have two different levels of utility. Because one bundle can't have different levels of utility, indifference curves can't cross.

Indifference curves have one final property: they are usually shaped like a crescent moon, as in Figure 4.3. This shape relates to how much stuff the consumer must give up to get one more unit of electricity, if the utility level stays constant. Suppose the consumer has a lot of stuff and only a little electricity, such as bundle D in Figure 4.3. At that point, she might be a little sick of stuff, but she would really like more electricity. She would willingly give up a lot of stuff to get more electricity. That implies a steep drop down the indifference curve. The steepness indicates that the consumer is willing to give up a large amount of one good to get more of the other good. At bundle A, though, the consumer has more electricity than she did at bundle D, so getting even more electricity is not as important. As a result, she won't give up as much stuff to get more electricity as she did when she started at bundle D. Now the drop along the indifference curve is smaller than it was at bundle A. As the consumer gains more electricity, she willingly gives up less stuff to get still more electricity. The indifference curve's crescent shape is a result of the changing relative preference for the goods in the bundle. In other words, the slope of the indifference curve commonly gets less steep for points farther right on the curve.

BOX 4.2

Decisions, Decisions: Buying a Car

The electricity market is relatively easy to describe because there is only one kind of electricity. Usually the only decision that people face is how much to use. For other goods, the decision is more complex. Consider the market for automobiles. Unlike electricity, a car purchase involves a large number of choices. First, a car is one very large element in a bundle of goods a consumer might buy. In addition, a consumer has to choose among a wide variety of car characteristics, including its size, styling, acceleration, and safety features. It is impossible to put all these features into a two-dimensional figure. Instead, preferences for these different characteristics show up in multidimensional versions of indifference curves that allow for multiple tradeoffs at once.

One study of car choice by Pinelopi Goldberg used the Consumer Expenditure Survey of the Bureau of Labor Statistics, which has data on about 32,000 Americans. The people surveyed bought about 200 different types of cars. The researcher set up a mathematical model with more than 200 different goods. For each of these 200 types of cars, the researcher collected information about price and characteristics. People choose among characteristics such as horsepower, power steering, and fuel efficiency when they buy cars. At the time the data were collected, fuel prices were low, and Goldberg was interested in how much people valued fuel efficiency. The study found that fuel efficiency was important for the choice of small cars: people were more likely to buy more fuel-efficient small cars. Fuel efficiency did not affect the choices among large cars, however; for people who wanted large cars, horsepower mattered.

Goldberg's study on car choices was published in 1995. By 2008, gasoline prices were much higher. Increased public consciousness about climate change also may have affected consumers' preferences. Purchases of sport utility vehicles (SUVs) fell; purchases of small, fuel-efficient cars increased. In response, in 2008 Toyota announced its decision to switch an entire plant's production from the Highlander SUV to the Prius hybrid.

Cars are responsible for 17 percent of greenhouse gas emissions in the United States. In California, the most populous state, cars contribute 40 percent of GHGs produced in the state. Because cars play a major role in production of GHGs, understanding the factors that affect the vehicles that people purchase is an important consideration in making climate change policy.

IN SUMMARY

- Consumers do not choose what goods to purchase independent of all their other purchases. A bundle of goods is a listing of the quantities of all the goods a consumer purchases.
- The budget constraint identifies all the bundles that the consumer can afford if she spends all her income on them. The budget constraint is a straight line

whose slope measures the number of units of one good that a consumer must give up to be able to buy a unit of the other good.

- Consumers have preferences over bundles of goods. A consumer can prefer bundle A to bundle B, or she can prefer bundle B to bundle A, or she can be indifferent between them. Economists assume the following: (1) People are consistent in their preferences. They cannot prefer A to B and also prefer B to A. (2) If consumers prefer A to B, and B to C, then they prefer A to C. (3) People behave as if more is always better than less. (4) People are rational; they will choose the bundles they prefer.

- An indifference curve is a set of bundles of goods that give the same level of utility. Indifference curves slope downward because a person will only stay indifferent if getting more of one good involves getting less of the other good. Higher indifference curves are more desirable than lower indifference curves because some points on a higher indifference curve have more of all goods than some points on the lower indifference curve, and more is better. Indifference curves do not cross because crossing indifference curves indicate contradictions in preferences. Indifference curves are typically crescent-shaped because, when a consumer has a great deal of a good, getting more of that good is not worth as much to her as it was when she had very little.

Deciding How Much to Consume

The underlying assumption of the theory of choice is that people choose the bundle that makes them happiest among the bundles they can afford. The budget constraint represents the affordable bundles. The indifference curves identify which bundles people prefer. This section puts the indifference curves and the budget constraint on the same diagram to show which bundle the consumer will choose. Figure 4.4 shows a budget constraint, three indifference curves, and four bundles. The budget constraint is the bold, straight, diagonal line. It defines the bundles the consumer can afford. The curved lines are the indifference curves.

Bundle G is special. Bundle G is located where an indifference curve just touches, but does not cross, the budget constraint. Let's consider a bundle that a consumer prefers to G. Bundle F is such a bundle; it is on the highest indifference curve. The consumer prefers bundle F to bundle G, but she cannot afford it. Because it falls above the budget constraint, she cannot choose it. Bundle G, on the middle indifference curve, is affordable.

Now let's consider other bundles the consumer can afford. Bundles under the budget constraint, like bundle H, are affordable. But bundle G is preferable to bundle H because bundle G is on a higher indifference curve. The consumer will therefore choose bundle G in preference to bundles under the budget constraint. What about bundle E, which is on the budget constraint? It too is on a lower indifference curve than is bundle G. The bundles the consumer prefers to G, like F,

FIGURE 4.4 The Chosen Bundle.

The figure shows three indifference curves and a budget constraint (the bold, straight, diagonal line). The consumer would choose bundle G because she prefers it to all other bundles, such as H and E, that she can afford. Note that she cannot afford bundle F.

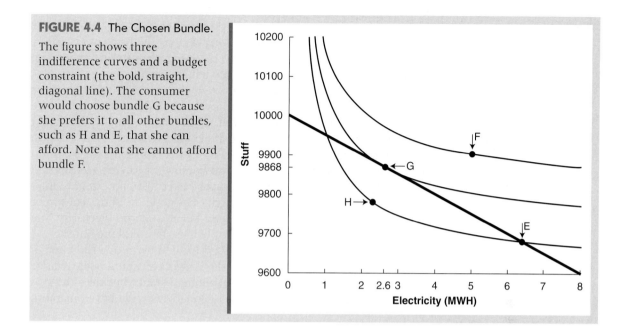

are not affordable. Bundles that she can afford, like E and H, are less desirable than G. Thus, bundle G provides the most utility of all the bundles the consumer can afford.

Notice that the indifference curve touches the budget constraint at G and is otherwise above it. The tangency, or point of touching, between the budget constraint and an indifference curve defines the highest utility bundle that the consumer can purchase with her available income.

It is important to note a few things about this selected bundle. First, it identifies exactly how much of each good the consumer will purchase—found by identifying the coordinates of the point. Recall that the horizontal axis measure is the amount of electricity, and the vertical axis measure is the amount of stuff. The coordinates of the point tell how much electricity and how much stuff the consumer can buy while finding the highest affordable utility level. In other words, that point identifies the quantities demanded of both stuff and electricity. The selected point G has 2.64 MWH and $9,868 worth of stuff. Because the budget constraint is the same one as in Figure 4.1, the price of electricity is still $50, and the price of stuff is still $1. Thus, with an income of $10,000 and a price of $50/MWH, the consumer will choose to buy 2.64 MWH.

Second, if any of the factors that determine the budget constraint or the indifference curves change, then the chosen bundle changes. The factors that can shift the chosen bundle include the price of the electricity, income, the price of stuff, or the preferences of the consumer. Let's see how each of these factors changes the selected bundle and thus affects consumer demand for electricity.

CHANGING PRICE OF ELECTRICITY

Figure 4.5 shows what happens to the budget constraint as the price of electricity increases. The bold line on the right shows the old budget constraint, when the price of electricity was \$50/MWH. The line on the left shows the new budget constraint, now that the price of electricity is \$100/MWH. The way to tell that the price of electricity has gone up is that the electricity intercept, Y/P_E, is different in the new budget constraint. If she now spent all her money on electricity, she could only buy 100 MWH, instead of the 200 MWH she could previously have bought. The stuff intercept, Y/P_s, is still in the same place because it represents the point on both budget constraints where the consumer purchases no electricity, and she can still purchase the same amount of stuff. Notice that the old constraint is higher than the new constraint. Now that the price of electricity has gone up, if the consumer chose to purchase zero units of stuff and spend all her income on electricity, she would not be able to buy as many MWH with \$10,000 as she could previously.

The information in this figure can also be used to see how much the price of electricity has increased. Recall that the slope of the budget constraint is the change in vertical distance divided by the change in horizontal distance between the two points where the budget constraint hits the axes. For the new budget constraint,

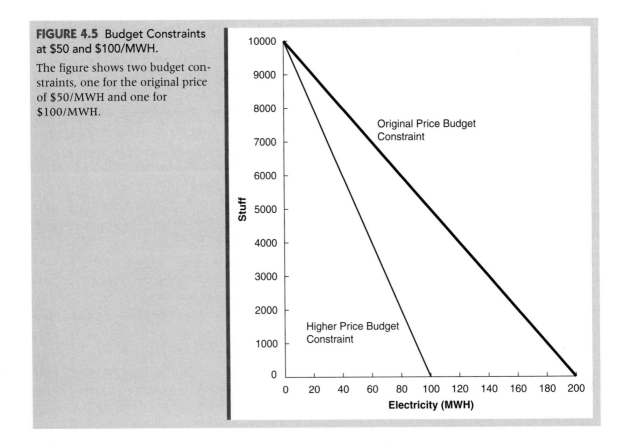

FIGURE 4.5 Budget Constraints at \$50 and \$100/MWH.

The figure shows two budget constraints, one for the original price of \$50/MWH and one for \$100/MWH.

the vertical change is −10,000, and the horizontal change is 100, making the slope −10,000/100 = −100. Also recall that the slope of the budget constraint is given by $-P_E/P_S$. Because $P_S = 1$, and the slope on the new budget constraint is −100, then $-P_E = -100$ and $P_E = 100$. The price of electricity, then, is twice as high on this budget constraint as on the original budget constraint.

Figure 4.6 shows the upper corner of Figure 4.5 and adds two indifference curves for a typical consumer. This enlarged picture makes it easier to see the points of tangency. The point of tangency, or touching, between the budget constraint and the indifference curve identifies the bundle of goods that will provide the highest utility while not exceeding the budget constraint. The tangency of the new budget constraint, with $P_E = \$100/MWH$, and the indifference curve is at the point where the consumer buys 1.81 MWH of electricity and 9,819 units of stuff. Compare this to the chosen bundle on the older and higher budget constraint. When the price of electricity is $50/MWH, the old budget constraint is tangent to an indifference curve at the point where the consumer buys 2.64 MWH of electricity and 9,868 units of stuff.

It's also useful to consider the proportion of the consumer's income that is devoted to each good under different budget constraints. At the old price, consumer expenditures on electricity were $50/MWH * 2.64 MWH = $132. With the higher price, they are now $100/MWH * 1.81 MWH = $181, an increase of about one-third, even though the price of electricity doubled. The higher price discouraged use of electricity so that expenditures went up less than the price increase. With either price, though, the expenditure on electricity is between 1 and 2 percent of total income. Even though the amount spent on electricity is a small part of the consumer's budget, the price increase is still enough to have an effect on the quantity demanded.

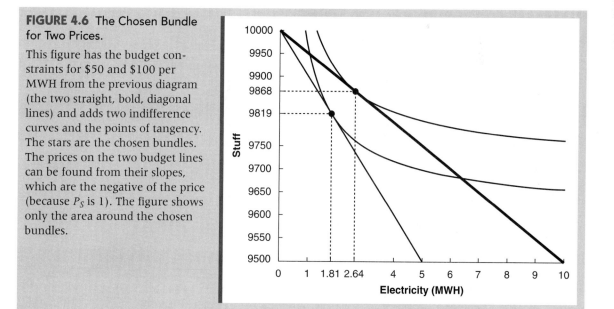

FIGURE 4.6 The Chosen Bundle for Two Prices.

This figure has the budget constraints for $50 and $100 per MWH from the previous diagram (the two straight, bold, diagonal lines) and adds two indifference curves and the points of tangency. The stars are the chosen bundles. The prices on the two budget lines can be found from their slopes, which are the negative of the price (because P_S is 1). The figure shows only the area around the chosen bundles.

Let's recap the steps needed to find the quantity purchased as a function of price when this information is presented in a diagram:

1. Graph the budget constraint. The intercepts represent the maximum amount of each good that a consumer buys if she spends all the money on one good. The slope is the ratio of the prices of the goods.
2. Find the tangency between indifference curve and budget constraint. The tangency identifies the chosen bundle of goods that will provide the highest utility without exceeding the budget constraint.
3. Find the quantity of each good purchased at the tangency. This is the chosen bundle.

This information can be used to draw a demand curve. The demand curve shows how much a consumer will purchase at different prices. This example has produced the quantity demanded for electricity at two different prices: a price of $100/MWH produces a demand of 1.81 MWH, while a price of $50/MWH produces a demand of 2.64 MWH. Figure 4.7 plots the demand curve showing these two points. The rest of the graph comes from repeating this exercise with different prices and indifference curves.

A change in the quantity of electricity consumed due to a change in its price is a movement along the demand curve for electricity. Comparing Figures 4.6 and 4.7 shows that the movement along that demand curve corresponds to a movement from the point of tangency on the higher budget constraint to the point of tangency on the lower budget constraint.

Suppose, now, that this price increase came about because a tax of $50/MWH was imposed on electricity. In this case, a tax less than Denmark charges and

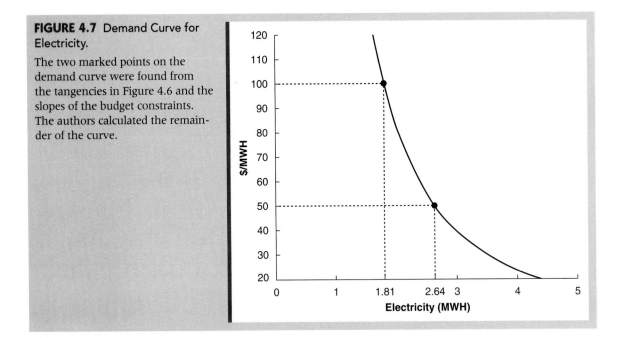

FIGURE 4.7 Demand Curve for Electricity.

The two marked points on the demand curve were found from the tangencies in Figure 4.6 and the slopes of the budget constraints. The authors calculated the remainder of the curve.

greater than Germany charges would save 0.84 MWH per household. This is 32 percent of household electricity use. While this tax would certainly save power and reduce carbon dioxide emissions, the households would be quite unhappy at the roughly one-third increase in their electricity bills.

Notice that the change in the price of electricity led not only to a change in the quantity of electricity demanded but also to a change in the quantity of stuff demanded. Figure 4.6 shows that the quantity of stuff went down from 9,868 to 9,819. Because the change in the quantity of stuff was not caused by a change in the price of stuff, the observed change in quantity is due to a shift in the demand curve for stuff. A change in the price of electricity shifts the demand curve for stuff.

CHANGING INCOME

A change in income shifts the demand curve because a change in income shifts the budget constraint. Figure 4.8 shows an upward shift of the budget constraint of 20 percent, or $2,000. When income (Y) increases, the budget constraint hits the vertical axis, Y/P_S, and the horizontal axis, Y/P_E, at higher values. Notice that the

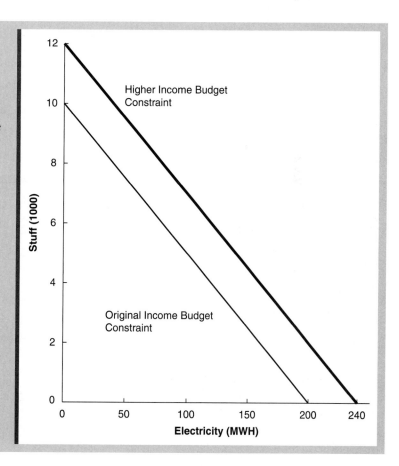

FIGURE 4.8 Two Budget Constraints with Different Incomes.

The figure shows the original budget constraint and a new budget constraint, in bold, with $2,000 more in income. Because the prices remain the same, the two budget lines have the same slope.

new budget constraint is parallel to the old; the slope, $-P_E/P_S$, remains the same. This is because the prices of the two goods haven't changed.

Figure 4.9 shows both budget constraints and indifference curves. It only shows the upper left corner of the graph, to show the tangencies accurately. Before the increase in income, the chosen electricity consumption was 2.64 MWH. The new quantity is 2.91 MWH. In this case, the quantity of electricity demanded has increased. Because demand increases when income increases, electricity is a normal good. The demand curve for electricity shifts right with an increase in income.

People have generally gotten richer over time. In the United States, average real income (adjusted for inflation) increased by more than 20 percent between the years 1998 and 2004. The exercise just completed with the electricity demand curve predicts that electricity usage would have increased by 10 percent as a result of the income growth of 20 percent. Rapidly developing nations such as China and India are consuming more electricity due to economic growth, contributing to significant pollution problems in the process. Although electricity use doesn't grow as fast as the economy as a whole, it does grow substantially over time. Therefore, the natural trend, if not countered by regulation, is for growth in carbon emissions and other pollutants.

DIFFERING PREFERENCES

People with different preferences will have different indifference curves. For instance, electricity is used for heating. Northern California is noticeably warmer in the winter and cooler in the summer than Montana. It would not be surprising to

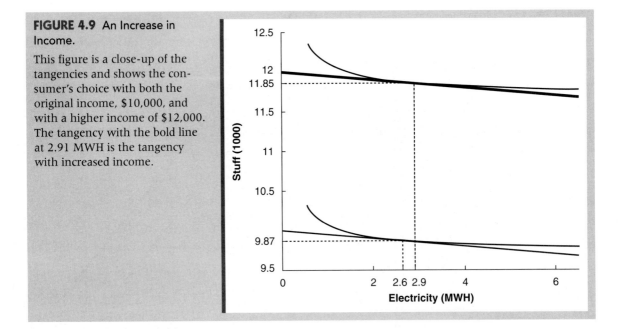

FIGURE 4.9 An Increase in Income.

This figure is a close-up of the tangencies and shows the consumer's choice with both the original income, $10,000, and with a higher income of $12,000. The tangency with the bold line at 2.91 MWH is the tangency with increased income.

find that a Berkeley consumer, faced with the same price and same income as a Montana consumer, would choose to purchase less electricity. It must be that a Northern California consumer would have indifference curves that are tangent to the budget constraint at a point closer to the vertical axis than those of a Montana consumer. Many other cases exist where individuals have different preferences and therefore buy different items, even facing the same prices and income.

IN SUMMARY

- A consumer chooses the bundle that she most prefers and that still is affordable. The bundle where the indifference curve and the budget constraint are tangent gives her the highest utility of all affordable bundles.
- The resulting bundle identifies the quantities demanded of each good. If the price of the good on the vertical axis is $1, the slope of the demand curve is the negative of the price of the good on the horizontal axis. The quantity demanded and the price are a point on the demand curve.
- A change in the price of one good leads to a pivot of the budget constraint and a new tangency. The new quantity, at the tangency, of the good whose price changed, combined with the new price, gives a second point on the same demand curve.
- An increase in income results in a parallel shift upwards in the budget constraint. Because prices are not changed, the quantity at the new tangency and the old price are a point on a shifted demand curve.
- People with different preferences will buy different bundles of goods.

Adding Up Demand for All Consumers

So far this analysis has looked at the demand curve for only one individual. Many questions of interest, though, require understanding the total response of all consumers. For instance, determining how a policy to reduce GHGs affects the demand for electricity involves the effects for a large group of people. A demand curve for a group of people is called an **aggregate demand** or **total demand curve**. Let's add the demand curves for two individuals; the process is the same for many individuals.

Algebraically, if the demand curve for the first individual is $Q_1(P)$ and the demand curve for the second individual is $Q_2(P)$, then the total demand for both individuals is $Q_T(P) = Q_1(P) + Q_2(P)$. To do this graphically, consider two consumers, each of whom has the same non-bolded demand curve, as shown in Figure 4.10. At a price of $50/MWH, each consumer buys 2.64 MWH; a price of $50/MWH therefore leads to total consumption of $2 * 2.64 = 5.28$ MWH. When the price is $100/MWH, each consumer buys 1.81 MWH. Total consumption for that price is $2 * 1.81 = 3.62$ MWH. Figure 4.10 shows this adding up. For a specified price, the aggregate quantity demanded results from summing the individual quantities. This process is called **horizontal addition** because quantities are added horizontally at a fixed vertical elevation, the price.

FIGURE 4.10 Adding Up Demand Curves.

The figure shows the demand curve for one person, the curve closest to the vertical axis, and the demand curve for two people who have the same individual demand curve; the aggregate demand is twice the demand curve for one person and is shown in bold. One person demands 2.64 MWH at $50/MWH, and two people demand 5.28 MWH at that same price.

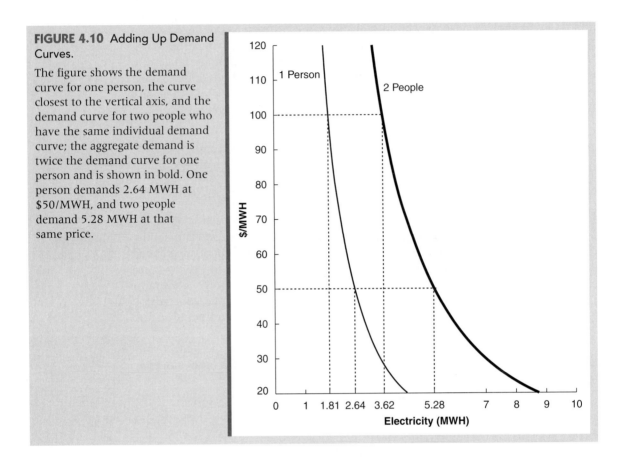

When consumers have different demand curves, the process is the same: find the quantity that each consumes for a specified price, and add those quantities. For instance, a consumer with income of $10,000 facing a price of $50/MWH consumes 2.64 MWH, while a consumer with income of $12,000 facing that same price consumes 2.91 MWH. At a price of $50/MWH, then, the aggregate demand is 2.64 + 2.91 = 5.55 MWH. The combination of $50/MWH and 5.55 MWH becomes one point on the aggregate demand curve. Other points come from adding up the quantities demanded at different prices.

For more than two consumers, the procedure is the same. For a specified price, the sum of the quantities demanded becomes a point on the aggregate demand curve. The aggregate demand curve is often more useful than individual demand curves. It permits statements about the general effects of changes in prices, income, or preferences on quantities. For instance, Montana has about 950,000 people. Because the individual demand curve in Figure 4.10 is an average of all Montanans' behavior, then total electricity consumption in Montana at a price of $50/MWH is about 950,000 * 2.64 MWH = 2,508,000 MWH per year. At a price of $100/MWH, electricity usage will drop to 950,000 * 1.81 = 1,719,500 MWH. The reduction in consumption, 788,500 MWH, is about one-tenth the size of a typical nuclear power plant. All else the same, increasing the price of electricity in Montana, then, would reduce the need for new power plants.

IN SUMMARY

- The aggregate or total demand curve is the total of all consumers' purchases of a good at various prices. It comes from summing the quantities that each consumer purchases for a specified price and then repeating the procedure for other prices.
- The aggregate demand curve is used to estimate the overall effects of a change in the factors that determine consumer demand.

Demand for Electricity and Greenhouse Gases

Greenhouse gas emissions have decreased in European Union countries that have imposed carbon taxes on households and industries and have taken other steps to reduce energy consumption. In Denmark, for instance, GHG emissions from energy industries fell 1.7 percent between 1990 (the benchmark year for GHG reduction) and 2004. GHG from energy industries fell 18.9 percent from 2003 to 2004 alone. For residential and commercial energy use in Denmark, emissions fell 19.1 percent from the baseline year, due to carbon taxes and other energy taxes. These taxes raised the price of electricity; as a result, people consumed less.

The picture is more complicated, though. GHG emissions from energy industries fluctuated up and down between 1990 and 1996, before declining since 1997. The United Nations researchers who studied these data explained that Denmark generates electricity from fossil fuels and sells it to neighboring countries. These neighboring countries produce their own electricity from hydropower. When they have less hydropower available, they demand a greater quantity of electricity from Denmark. So, the demand curve for fossil-fuel electricity generated in Denmark for export shifts up when hydropower falls short in other countries. When this happens, carbon emissions from electricity generation in Denmark increase. Demand shifts, then, have an impact on climate change.

CHAPTER SUMMARY

Here are the key lessons from this chapter:

- People's consumption of goods affects the environment. Consumers choose among bundles of goods based on their incomes, the prices of the goods, and their preferences. Once a consumer knows her income and the prices of the goods, she can identify which bundles are affordable. She decides among the affordable bundles based on her personal characteristics, tastes, and preferences.

- The consumer decides the quantity demanded of a particular good as part of a bundle. As a result, the demand curve for that good does not depend only on the price of the good itself; it also depends on the prices of other goods and on income. The budget constraint summarizes the relationship between income and prices. Finally, the quantity demanded depends on the consumer's tastes and preferences for different goods. Indifference curves summarize the consumer's individual preferences.
- Changes in the price of a good result in a movement along the demand curve (a change in the quantity demanded), while changes in prices of related goods, income, or tastes and preferences result in a shift of the demand curve.
- The aggregate demand curve measures the total response of consumers to changes in prices or other factors that affect demand. It comes from horizontal summation of individuals' demand curves.

KEY TERMS

aggregate demand *(p. 75)*

budget constraint *(p. 60)*

bundle *(p. 60)*

horizontal addition *(p. 75)*

indifference curve *(p. 65)*

total demand curve *(p. 75)*

NOTES

"Had we but world enough, and time," is the first line of Andrew Marvell's poem "To His Coy Mistress," in Marvel, Andrew (ed.), *Complete Poetry* (London: J.M. Dent & Sons Ltd., 1984). Marvell's poem may also be found at http://www.luminarium.org/sevenlit/marvell/coy.htm.

The electricity demand example in this chapter is from an unpublished study of electricity demand in Montana in 1986 by Professor Jeffrey Lafrance. We have engaged in very slight rounding of income and prices for the purposes of exposition.

The research on gas prices and food expenditure is found in Dora Gicheva, Justine Hastings, and Sofia Villas-Boas, "Revisiting the Income Effect: Gasoline Prices and Grocery Purchases," *National Bureau of Economic Research*, Working Paper 13614 (November 2007). It can be found at http://www.nber.org/papers/w13614.

The study of car purchasing decisions is found in Pinelopi Koujianou Goldberg, "Product Differentiation and Oligopoly in International Markets: The Case of the U.S. Automobile Industry," *Econometrica* 63 (1995): 891–951.

To know more about U.S. energy use, visit the website of the U.S. Energy Information Administration, http://www.eia.doe.gov/fuelelectric.html.

The information about GHG from energy production in Denmark is from the United Nations Framework Convention on Climate Change, "Report of the Centralized In-Depth Review of the Fourth National Communication of Denmark" (February 1, 2007), Table 2, Greenhouse Gas Emissions by Sector for Denmark, 1990–2004, p. 5; paragraph 12, p. 5; and paragraph 23, p. 8. http://unfccc.int/resource/docs/2007/idr/dnk04.pdf. In the broad category called the energy "sector," GHG actually *increased* 2.7 percent from 1990 to 2004. However, the energy sector includes manufacturing, construction, and transportation as well as "energy industries" and "other" activities. "Other activities" include residential and commercial energy use. GHG emissions declined between 1990 and 2004 for "energy industries" and "other." The increase in emissions from the energy sector was due largely to transportation, but fluctuating demand for electricity for export was one factor in the increase of GHG in the energy sector.

EXERCISES

1. Put a piece of paper over Figure 4.6 and trace the axes, the higher priced budget constraint, and both indifference curves. Now consider what happens when the price of stuff increases from 1 to 100/99 (about 1.1) while the price of electricity is $100/MWH. Where does this new budget constraint intersect each axis? (This will take a little work—to calculate the horizontal intercept, you'll need to figure out how much electricity it is possible to purchase when the consumer buys 9,500 units of stuff because that is the bottom of the vertical axis.) Now draw this new budget constraint on your diagram. Draw a new indifference curve on your figure that is tangent to your new budget constraint. Given the information at hand, any indifference curve you draw that follows the rules (slopes down, doesn't cross, is crescent shaped) is an acceptable answer. Now use your figure to find two points on the demand curve for stuff.

2. Let's say that the demand curve for gasoline is $Q_D = 10 * I * P_E/P$, where Q_D is the amount of gasoline consumed (in gallons), I is per-capita income (in thousands of dollars), P_E is the price of ethanol, and P is the price of gasoline. The following questions are based on this demand curve.
   (a) Does gasoline consumption increase or decrease when price increases, holding everything else constant? How do you know? (Hint: Try using different values of P.)
   (b) Is gasoline a normal good or an inferior good, according to this demand curve? That is, if people become wealthier, does gasoline consumption go up or down? How do you know? (Hint: Try using different values of I.)
   (c) Is ethanol a substitute or a complement to gasoline? That is, does gasoline consumption go up or down when the price of ethanol increases? How do you know? (Hint: Try using different values of P_E.)
   (d) If this demand curve represents the aggregate demand for 20 people in a community with identical income and preferences, what is each individual's demand curve for gasoline?
   (e) The price of both gasoline and ethanol is $2.40/gallon, and per-capita income is $10,000. (Keep careful track of units!) How much gasoline is consumed? What is each individual's consumption?
   (f) Continue using the prices and income from (e). The government considers imposing a tax of $0.60/gallon on gasoline. What will the new consumption level be? How much revenue will the government collect?

(g) A news reporter notes that the government revenue will be $0.60 times the consumption in (e). Is the reporter right, or should she be sent back to study more economics? Why?

(h) As an alternative to the gasoline tax, the government is considering subsidizing ethanol consumption. What would the subsidy per gallon on ethanol have to be to achieve the same consumption level? If consumers increase their consumption of ethanol by exactly as much as they reduce their consumption of gasoline, how much will the subsidy cost the government?

(i) Which policy, the gas tax or the ethanol subsidy, would consumers prefer (if they don't think about the effects on government revenues)? Which policy would farmers who produce the ingredients for ethanol prefer? Which policy would gasoline producers prefer? Why?

(j) What are the opportunity costs associated with using the subsidy? What are the opportunity costs associated with using the tax?

3. Emissions are the product of these numbers: emissions/energy use, energy use/output, output/capita, number of people. In countries like the United States, energy use per unit of output decreases over time. What effects over time might you expect for these other numbers? As a result, what do you think happens over time to emissions, and why? What might be different in a rapidly developing country like India or China?

4. Environmental education activities seek to change consumers' behavior to be more environmentally friendly, even when prices and income are constant. What in this model of consumer demand are the environmental educators trying to change? (Hint: Does environmental education change the budget constraint?) Suppose that an environmental educator encouraged people to reduce their electricity consumption in order to reduce greenhouse gas emissions. Draw a diagram showing how a consumer's chosen bundle might change if the education initiative were successful.

5. Do environmental goods have demand curves? Consider drinking water. In many places in the world, water supplies carry some risk to those who drink it, due to both natural and anthropogenic (human-caused) effects. The water can be made safer to drink by such actions as filtering, boiling, and use of chemical decontaminants.

(a) Do you expect the cleanliness of drinking water to be affected by income? Do you expect it to be a normal or an inferior good? Why?

(b) Do you expect the cleanliness of drinking water to be affected by the cost of decontamination? For instance, do you think the number of people with access to cleaner water is affected by the availability and price of fuel to boil water?

(c) Does cleaner drinking water have substitutes or complements? Provide one example of each, or explain why you don't think an example exists.

(d) What factors, if any, might affect people's preferences for cleaner drinking water? Provide one example of something that might change people's preferences, or explain why you don't think an example exists.

Measuring Benefits to Consumers

When a government is considering undertaking activities that affect private markets, such as regulating pesticides or improving air quality, it typically examines whether the benefits exceed the costs. Doing this comparison requires an estimate of the benefits associated with the activity. Because costs are expressed in monetary terms, benefits must be measured in money. Measures of benefits come from consumer preferences. While the demand curve signals how much a consumer will purchase when faced with a market price, additional steps are necessary to get at the monetary value that the consumer places on the good. This chapter uses the relationship between a consumer's preferences and a consumer's demand curve to provide estimates of the benefit of a good to that consumer.

Important environmental resources are not traded in markets. The estimation of these benefits is especially important because policy makers want to know why they should protect environmental resources. If people value these resources, the argument for their protection is clear; if that value is larger than the costs associated with protection, the argument is even stronger. This chapter will examine:

- How to estimate a money measure of the value of a good—a consumer's total willingness to pay—from the demand curve for that good;
- How to add up individual benefits to get total benefits for a group of people, both for public goods and for private goods;
- Two other methods for estimating a money measure of the value—compensating variation and equivalent variation—that estimate the change in income equivalent to the difference between indifference curves.

Electric Power in India

Farmers in India make extensive use of pumped groundwater. Electricity runs those pumps. The electricity is heavily subsidized; the subsidy is about 89 percent of the costs of producing the electricity. As India moves toward a more market-oriented economy, the state governments are trying to move away from subsidizing power. If power is not subsidized, then the price of power to individual consumers will have to increase.

Agriculture in the state of Andhra Pradesh is heavily dependent upon pumped water. A survey of 449 farmers found that the average farmer was using 2 pumps 7 hours per day for 273 days per year. The farmers' incentives for water conservation are not as they would be in most other places. In Andhra Pradesh and much of India, a farmer pays according to the size of his pumps. A 5-horsepower pump pays one price; a 10-horsepower pump pays a higher price. The price paid is independent of how much the pumps are used. The use of the pumps is limited by the number of hours a day the pumps have electricity. Typically, farmers in this region receive electricity for one 6-hour and one 3-hour block of time each day. This combination of the availability of electricity and the size of the pump determine total energy use. From a farmer's point of view, the payment made per pump is a fixed amount, based on the size of the pump. The price of electricity does not determine how much the pump is used, but it does affect how many pumps the farmer has.

Calculated on a U.S. dollar per MWH basis, the price of electricity to the farmers is between \$3.86/MWH and \$9.32/MWH. Those having smaller pumps pay the lower rate per MWH. They are likely to be the poorest farmers. Those with the largest pumps, likely the farmers with the most income, pay the highest rate. The allocation of the lowest price to the poorest farmer was intentional in the current policy.

The current policy is very expensive to carry out because it requires large subsidies to the price of electricity. The subsidy for those with the smallest pumps is 93 percent, while the subsidy for those with the largest pumps is 84 percent. The choice for the state is whether to find money to pay those subsidies or to reduce the subsidies.

The market answer would be to meter the power and charge all users the same price. Letting the market work will produce a Pareto-optimal allocation of electricity, in the absence of market failures. Not all farmers, though, can afford an increase in the price of electricity. Many farmers live on about \$2 per person per day. The state is reluctant to raise prices for these farmers. How can the state raise more money from selling power and yet not harm the well-being of the poorest purchasers?

One practical solution is to raise the price for only the largest users. Charging different prices for different quantities of a good is called **price discrimination**. Price discrimination, besides being a practical way to raise revenue, opens the door to the measurement of how much people are willing to pay for a good, a concept quite distinct from how much they actually pay.

Total Willingness to Pay and Consumer Surplus

When consumers respond to prices by changing the bundles that they choose, they reveal information about the value that they place on what they purchase. This section discusses the difference between how much something is worth to a consumer and how much he pays for it; it also discusses a way to use the market demand curve to estimate that value.

TOTAL WILLINGNESS TO PAY

How much is additional electricity worth to consumers? The value of a good to someone should be reflected in what he would give up to get it.

Consider a single consumer and a good, electricity. Suppose that the price for electricity is $55/MWH and the consumer uses about 2.5 MWH per year. Do these numbers indicate that the value he places on electricity is 2.5 MWH * $55/MWH = $137.50? In other words, does the amount spent—the cost to the consumer—equal the value to the consumer?

The answer is no. If expenditure were a good measure of his value of electricity, then he would be indifferent between paying $55/MWH and buying 2.5 MWH, or paying $2.50/MWH and buying 55 MWH because both these choices require expenditures of $137.50. If any real-life consumer is given this choice, though, the principle of "more is better" indicates that the preferred combination is 55 MWH at a price of $2.50/MWH. Therefore, the same expenditure does not lead to the same level of utility, and expenditure is not an adequate measure of value to the consumer.

Now consider the choice between using electricity and a candle for lighting. A single 100W light bulb burning 8 hours a day, using 0.29 MWH in a year, will cost $15.95 for a whole year at $55/MWH plus $1 for the light bulb itself. Is that all the electricity is worth to the consumer? Suppose, instead, that the consumer had no electricity and had only two choices: candles or darkness. Candles produce a dimmer and smokier light and cost much more than electricity: 365 eight-hour candles cost $294. Yet a consumer would probably pay that amount rather than sit in the dark. Because the consumer is willing to pay $294 per year for lighting, and would prefer even more to have electricity instead of candles, the consumer would probably be willing to pay at least as much as the cost of the candles to have 0.29 MWH of electricity each year. The price of the good is not a good measure of the total value of the good to a consumer.

If expenditure and price are not good measures, then, what alternative measures exist? A consumer's demand curve comes from making choices between goods when faced with a limited budget. The demand curve might thus provide information about what a consumer is willing to give up to get more of a good.

Let's examine household electric purchases. The curve (above the bars) in Figure 5.1 is the demand curve. Suppose that a consumer buys electricity in increments of half MWH. A half MWH is about the electricity use of a refrigerator and a light bulb for a year. If the price of electricity is as high as $470/MWH, the consumer would consume only one half MWH per year. If the price drops, though, he would buy additional units of electricity. The next unit, at a price of $294/MWH, will be used for purposes that are less important to him, perhaps a computer. If the price decreases even more, the amount of electricity used increases, again for purposes that are less valuable to him than the original half MWH.

For each unit of electricity, then, the demand curve tells us the maximum amount that someone would pay for that particular unit. A consumer's **marginal willingness to pay** for the Qth unit of a good is the price that the consumer would be willing to pay for one more unit of the good, if he has already purchased $Q - 1$ units of it.

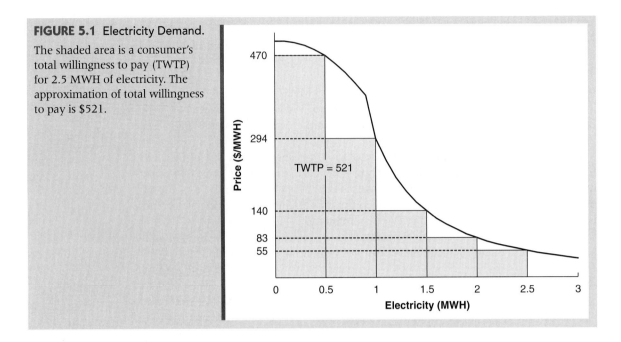

FIGURE 5.1 Electricity Demand.
The shaded area is a consumer's total willingness to pay (TWTP) for 2.5 MWH of electricity. The approximation of total willingness to pay is $521.

(In economics, the term "marginal" refers to someone's response to a one-unit change. In mathematics, it means the first derivative, or the slope of a line at that point.) On the demand curve, marginal willingness to pay is the point associated with the Qth unit of a good. In Figure 5.1, for instance, the consumer's willingness to pay for the first unit of electricity is $470. Thus, the demand curve identifies the marginal willingness to pay for each unit of a good.

Total willingness to pay (TWTP) for Q units of a good is the total amount that a consumer would be willing to pay to get Q units. TWTP comes from summing up the marginal willingness to pay for each unit to get the total value of the purchased goods. Thus, in Figure 5.1, where each unit is one half MWH, the marginal willingness to pay for the first unit is 0.5 MWH * $470/MWH = $235. It is the area of the leftmost bar in Figure 5.1. The marginal willingness to pay for the second unit is the area of the second bar from the left, 0.5 MWH * $294/MWH = $147. Therefore, the approximate total willingness to pay for 1 MWH is $235 + $147 = $382.

It was arbitrary that quantity is measured in half MWH units. Suppose that a unit is actually smaller. In Figure 5.2, the size of the purchases is only 0.2 MWH. In this case, the approximation of total willingness to pay for 1.0 MWH is the area of the bars on the chart between zero and 1.0. TWTP for 1 MWH is now approximately 0.2 * 498 + 0.2 * 483 + 0.2 * 454 + 0.2 * 412 + 0.2 * 294 = $428. Continuing this process yields TWTP for 2.6 MWH as $600. If the units were even smaller, the areas of the bars would come ever closer to being the entire area under the demand curve. For this reason, the precise measurement of TWTP is the area under the demand curve up to the number of units purchased.

FIGURE 5.2 A Better Approximation.

Total willingness to pay is here approximated in increments of 0.2 MWH. Compare the area in the bars up to 1 MWH in this diagram to the previous diagram. In this diagram, the area is closer to the whole area under the demand curve. The total willingness to pay for 1 MWH is $428; for 2.6 MWH, it is $600.

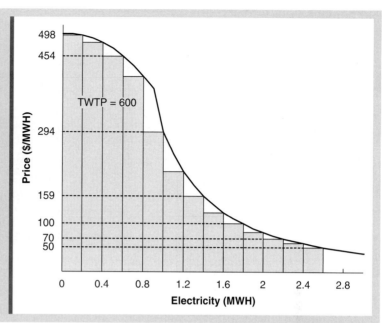

CONSUMER SURPLUS

When a consumer buys goods, the goods are worth something to him; one measure of that value is TWTP. However, TWTP does not account for the amount that the consumer spends to get the goods. *Consumer surplus* provides the net gain—the surplus—that the consumer gets from purchasing the goods. **Consumer surplus** is total willingness to pay—the total value of the good—less the amount paid. Figure 5.3 again shows the demand curve for electricity. The light shaded box plus the shaded area under demand and above $50 is TWTP, the area under the demand curve between zero and 2.6 MWH (the amount purchased when the price is $50/MWH). Adding up the boxes in the previous figure produced the estimate of TWTP as $600.

Consumer surplus is the area below the demand curve and above the price the consumer pays. Getting to consumer surplus requires subtracting the amount paid for the electricity from TWTP. The light shaded rectangle in the diagram represents this expenditure: 2.6 MWH * $50/MWH = $130. Subtracting the expenditure (the rectangle) from TWTP (the entire shaded area) gives consumer surplus, the darker shaded area. This consumer surplus area is $470. In other words, by purchasing 2.6 MWH of electricity, the consumer experiences a net benefit of $470—the difference between his TWTP and the amount he must pay. The value of the electricity is clearly more than the amount paid for it, and consumer surplus is an estimate of that value.

An increase in price makes consumers worse off because a consumer will buy less when the price is higher. But how much worse off? The change in consumer surplus is a money measure of how much a price increase harms consumers.

FIGURE 5.3 Consumer Surplus.

Total willingness to pay for 2.6 MWH is both shaded areas on the diagram. The amount paid (price times quantity) is the lighter shaded rectangle. Consumer surplus (TWTP less the amount paid) is the area below the demand curve and above the price the consumer pays; this area is in the darker shade.

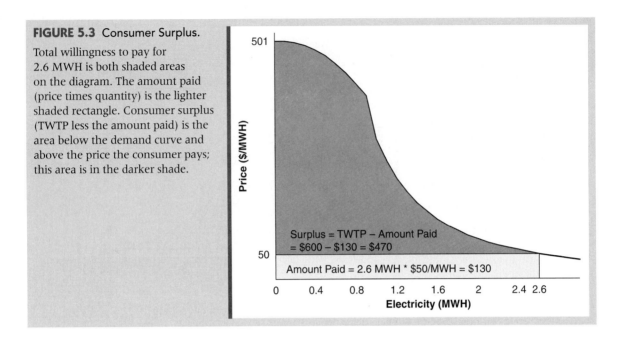

Surplus = TWTP – Amount Paid
= $600 – $130 = $470

Amount Paid = 2.6 MWH * $50/MWH = $130

Figure 5.4 shows the demand for electricity again. The original price and quantity are $50 and 2.6 MWH. When the price is increased to $100, the quantity is 1.8 MWH. The original consumer surplus is both shaded areas (it continues above the part of the graph shown). Consumer surplus when price is $1.8/MWH is the light shaded area above the line where price equals $100. Therefore, the change in consumer surplus is the area bounded by the two price lines, the vertical axis, and the demand curve. It is the darker shaded area. The trapezoid rule provides an approximation of this area: the change in consumer surplus is about $\frac{1}{2} * (100 - 50) * (1.8 + 2.6) = \$110$.

To recap: The consumer used to get electricity for $50/MWH and now must buy it at $100/MWH. The consumer used to spend $130 on electricity and now spends $180 on electricity. The consumer spends $50 more on electricity. But that is not the amount the consumer is harmed. The consumer gives up $107.80 in consumer surplus. So the harm to the consumer is not the same as the change in consumer outlay.

IN SUMMARY

- The value of a good to a consumer is different from the amount spent on the good. Otherwise, paying $10 per unit to get one unit would provide the same utility as paying $1 per unit to get 10 units. The expenditure on a purchase does not measure its value to the consumer.
- The demand curve for a good gives the marginal willingness to pay—what the consumer is willing to give up in order to get one more unit of the good.

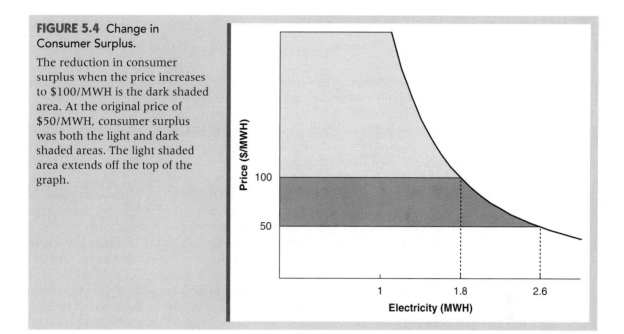

FIGURE 5.4 Change in Consumer Surplus.

The reduction in consumer surplus when the price increases to $100/MWH is the dark shaded area. At the original price of $50/MWH, consumer surplus was both the light and dark shaded areas. The light shaded area extends off the top of the graph.

Summing up the marginal willingness to pay (or, more accurately, calculating the area under the demand curve up to the quantity purchased) gives the total willingness to pay (TWTP) for the total quantity purchased.

- TWTP is a measure of how much money a person is willing to give up in order to get a quantity of goods. It takes into account that the first units a person buys of a good are more valuable than the subsequent units.
- Consumer surplus is the difference between total willingness to pay and actual expenditures. It is an approximation of the net gain to the consumer from purchase of a good.
- On a price–quantity graph, consumer surplus is the area below the demand curve and above the price the consumer pays.
- When the price of a good changes, the change in consumer surplus is a money measure of how much better or worse off the consumer is due to the change.

Adding Up and Consumers' Surplus

So far the analysis of consumer surplus has been for a single consumer. However, many times policy makers want to know the total social benefits associated with a change in price, quantity, or other market-related activity. Doing so is actually fairly simple: either individual benefits can be summed, or aggregate demands can be used to estimate aggregate benefits.

BOX 5.1

Water Scarcity in Tunisia

Worldwide, the percentage of rural populations with access to a reliable source of water has increased from only 30 percent in 1980 to 70 percent by 1994. Bringing water into remote rural communities requires expensive infrastructure and management. When these investments are provided by government agencies, water prices and quantities are not set through market processes. Instead, these agencies set prices and quantity at levels intended to keep water affordable and recover costs.

In rural Tunisia, the price for water is 0.18 dinars (approximately $0.13) per cubic meter ($m^3$), and a consumer consumes about 66 m^3 per year. Four liters, which is 0.004 m^3 of water, is the amount a person needs to consume every day, in drink or food, to stay alive. Researchers Zekri and Dinar constructed a demand curve for water in rural Tunisia. They found that, if the price is as high as 0.38 dinar/m^3, a family would consume only one 6 m^3 unit per year. This consumption rate, about 16 liters per day per family, is very close to a subsistence level. At that price, they would give up other uses of water and buy only the biologically necessary units. If the price drops, though, they would buy more. The next unit, at a price of 0.36 dinar, would be used for purposes that are important, but not absolutely required, such as bathing or cooking. If the price decreases even more, the amount of water used would increase, again for purposes that are less valuable—perhaps laundry or washing floors.

Researchers used their demand curve results to show that total willingness to pay less costs—consumer surplus—would increase if water distribution was expanded.

ADDING UP FOR MARKETED GOODS

Paul Samuelson, a Nobel Laureate in Economics, was fond of reminding his students that the apostrophe in consumers' surplus is after the s. As used, consumers' surplus is almost always about the surplus of a group of people, not just about an individual. Just as adding individual demand curves gives aggregate market demand, adding the consumer surplus for individual consumers gives aggregate consumer surplus.

An additional way of calculating consumers' surplus is to calculate it directly from the market demand curve. Consumers' surplus for the market demand curve is the area under the market demand curve, just as it was for the individual demand curve.

There is an important implicit assumption in this adding-up exercise: because all that matters is the sum of individual consumer surplus, it is just as good to give an additional dollar to one person as another. In other words, additional money given to a poor person or to a rich person has the same degree of social desirability. Two alternatives to simply adding up individuals' consumer's surplus to get consumers' surplus are to produce a weighted sum of consumer's surplus, or to separately consider the surplus of different types of individuals. For the first, there is no agreement at all on what those weights would be. How much should a dollar be worth to a poor person compared with a dollar to a wealthy person—the same, more, or less? Because there is no consensus as to how to weight different consumers, what is left is to consider subgroups of the population. In general, this process is called a distributional analysis; in environmental analysis, considering the effects of a project on the poor or on minority groups is termed an environmental justice analysis. It is a practical solution to the undesirability of treating all people alike and simply adding up all surpluses, regardless of who gets that surplus.

ADDING UP FOR A PUBLIC GOOD

Adding up demand curves for marketed goods starts with every person's quantity demanded for a specific price and then sums them; this process is repeated to get all the points on the market demand curve. This method, however, does not work for public goods. No one can be excluded from using a public good, and one person's use does not diminish another person's ability to use it. In other words, individuals can benefit from public goods without actually purchasing them.

Nevertheless, people do have demand curves for environmental goods. The next two chapters will explain methods for estimating these demand curves; for now, the lesson is how to estimate the sum of consumer benefits from them. The key to the economics of public goods is that everyone experiences the same amount of the public good, regardless of how much of it each person "buys."

Figure 5.5 has hypothetical demand curves for wolves in Yellowstone for two individuals, plus the vertical sum of the two demand curves. When the quantity of

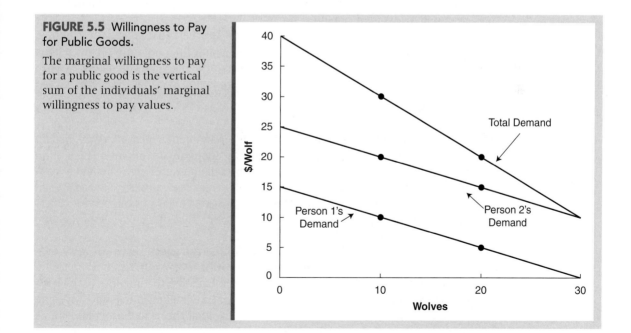

FIGURE 5.5 Willingness to Pay for Public Goods.

The marginal willingness to pay for a public good is the vertical sum of the individuals' marginal willingness to pay values.

wolves is 10, one person is willing to pay $10 for the tenth wolf, while the other person is willing to pay $20/wolf. Because each person gets a benefit from the same wolves, the rule for getting total willingness to pay for all consumers is to add up the values for individual willingness to pay. Thus, the marginal willingness to pay of the two people for 10 wolves is the vertical sum of these two values, or $30/wolf. When the quantity of wolves rises to 20, the marginal willingness to pay now is $5/wolf + $15/wolf = $20/wolf. When the quantity gets to 30 wolves, the first person no longer is willing to pay for additional wolves; the second person's marginal willingness to pay now becomes the demand curve.

In other words, because many people benefit from the same public goods, the total demand curve comes from adding the marginal willingness to pay curves vertically, rather than horizontally. In contrast to the procedure with market demand curves, where quantities demanded for a specified *price* are summed, values for marginal willingness to pay for a specified *quantity* are summed. The total willingness to pay is the area under the summed marginal willingness to pay curve for a public good.

IN SUMMARY

- Total of willingness to pay comes either from summing the values for each individual consumer's willingness to pay or by finding the area under the summed marginal WTP curve. Similarly, total consumers' surplus can be calculated either by adding up each individual consumer's consumer surplus or by calculating the area under the market demand curve and subtracting total expenditures.
- Using consumers' surplus as a measure of social benefits assumes that it does not matter who gets benefits—a dollar to a wealthy person is worth the same as a dollar to a poor person.
- Unlike summing individual demand curves for marketed goods, the summed demand curve for public goods comes from holding quantity constant and adding vertically the values for each individual consumer's marginal willingness to pay.

Exact Money Measures

While consumer surplus may seem like the appropriate money measure of the benefit that consumers get from a good, it is in fact only an approximate measure. This section explores why that is the case, and it presents two exact measures of the benefit to consumers from a good. For most marketed goods, consumer surplus is a very good approximation of the exact measures. However, the exact measures can be very different from consumer surplus and from each other in the case of *publicly provided* goods, including most environmental goods.

Many public goods, including many environmental goods, have an additional characteristic: they are *publicly provided*. The term **publicly provided goods** refers to a good where the individual consumer does not get to choose the quantity of the good that is provided. Public education is publicly provided. Individual families do not get to choose the class size; they must accept the class size that the school provides. Not all publicly provided goods are public goods, though. While public education is a publicly provided good, it is an imperfect public good. Every additional student increases the class size and decreases the teacher time per student; education is thus at least partially rival and partially excludable. Environmental goods are usually both nonrival in consumption and publicly provided. Nobody individually gets to choose how clean the air is, nor does any one person's breathing interfere with the breathing of others.

Consumers of publicly provided goods do not choose their individual quantities of the goods in response to price because the total quantity from which they get benefits depends on how much others provide. A consumer does not individually buy and keep wolves. Instead, an individual or organization "provides" the good, and everyone benefits, without having to pay. For instance, Defenders of Wildlife "provides" wolves, and everyone who appreciates wolves benefits from the whole wolf population, whether or not they make a contribution to Defenders of Wildlife.

The ability to control the quantity of the good that's purchased contributes to consumer surplus being a good approximation of a consumer's welfare for private goods. If the consumer wants more of a good, he can buy it. The lack of control in the quantity of a public good, on the other hand, can have a significant effect on the measured value of that quantity to a consumer. Because he cannot provide more of the good for himself alone, his valuation of loss of the good may be very high.

CONSUMER SURPLUS IS APPROXIMATE

The motivation for total willingness to pay is that the consumer is willing to pay a high price for the first unit of the good and only a lower price for the next and subsequent units of the good. Suppose that a good were really sold this way. Figure 5.6

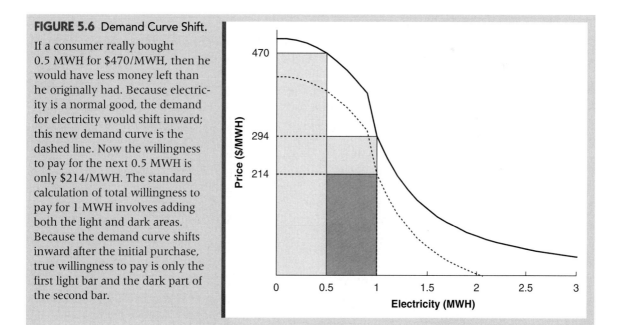

FIGURE 5.6 Demand Curve Shift.

If a consumer really bought 0.5 MWH for $470/MWH, then he would have less money left than he originally had. Because electricity is a normal good, the demand for electricity would shift inward; this new demand curve is the dashed line. Now the willingness to pay for the next 0.5 MWH is only $214/MWH. The standard calculation of total willingness to pay for 1 MWH involves adding both the light and dark areas. Because the demand curve shifts inward after the initial purchase, true willingness to pay is only the first light bar and the dark part of the second bar.

shows what would happen. The solid line is the same demand curve as in the previous figures. If the consumer bought 0.5 MWH, he would be willing to pay $470/MWH for it. Once he made that transaction, he would be $235 poorer. Because he now has less money than he had before, his demand curve would shift inward: because electricity is a normal good, he would buy less of it at any price when income decreases. The dashed line in Figure 5.6 shows what the demand curve might be after his initial purchase. Now his marginal willingness to pay for the next 0.5 MWH, found from his shifted demand curve, is $214/MWH. It is less than the $294/MWH that was used to calculate total willingness to pay. So the amount of money that a consumer would pay if he had to buy electricity a little bit at a time is less than the area under the original demand curve. Because the demand curve would shift with every unit of the good purchased, the original demand curve will not provide an accurate measurement of TWTP, and the resulting measure of consumer surplus is only an approximation to the value of a good; it is not an exact value. While an ideal measure of the change in utility would calculate the effect of only one factor changing, consumer surplus includes changes in both price and income.

Constructing exact money measures requires working with the indifference curves and budget constraints that underlie the demand curve. Let's think of a specific policy, a price increase for electricity. A price increase decreases utility. Policy makers want to know the value of that utility decrease in dollar terms. There turn out to be two ways to make that measurement. The next section discusses why there are two different measures; the following sections work through a market example, the demand for electricity, for the two measures. The final section shows how the analysis is adapted for environmental goods.

DOES UTILITY CHANGE HAPPEN?

The demand for electricity provides a terrific laboratory to examine price changes. In the last chapter, a consumer had a choice of buying electricity *(E)* or other stuff *(S)*. Figure 5.7 is the same as Figure 4.6, except that it has one additional line on it. To recap the analysis of demand: the initial price of electricity is $50/MWH, while a unit of stuff is the exact size that costs $1/unit. In Figure 5.7, there are two indifference curves (i and ii) and three budget constraints (I, II, and III). The analysis starts with the budget constraints labeled I and II. The budget constraint associated with the initial price, $50/MWH for electricity, is the top budget constraint in the figure, labeled I, and is tangent to (touches) the top indifference curve, i, at the point where $E = 2.64$ and $S = 9,868$. This point identifies how much electricity and how much stuff the consumer will buy.

Suppose that the price of electricity doubles to $100/MWH. Budget constraint II has the price of electricity at $100/MWH. Like constraint I, it intersects the vertical axis at $10,000 because income has not changed: if the consumer spent all his money on stuff, he would still be able to buy $10,000 worth of it. When the price increases from $50/MWH to $100/MWH, though, the new budget constraint is rotated in: if the consumer spent all his money on electricity, he could only buy half as much. With this new budget constraint, the consumer can only achieve the utility level of

FIGURE 5.7 Equivalent Variation.
Budget constraint I's tangency
with indifference curve i is the
original equilibrium. Budget
constraint II's tangency with
indifference curve ii shows that a
doubling of price leads to the new
and lower level of utility. Budget
constraint III, which has the original price and a new lower income
of $9,892.94, is also tangent to
indifference curve ii, so it also
leads to the lower level of utility.
Equivalent variation is the
amount of income given up in
place of the price increase to get to
the new lower level of utility. It is
$10,000 − $9,892.94 = $107.06.

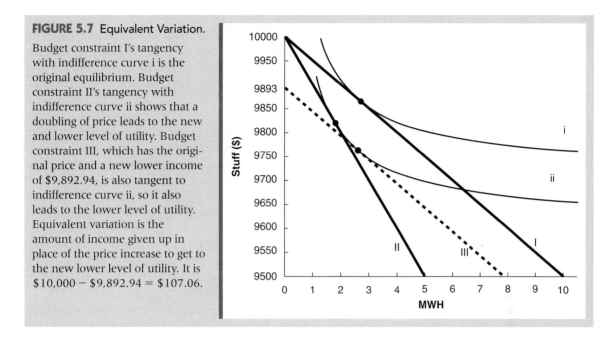

indifference curve ii, a lower indifference curve, and he'll purchase 1.8 MWH of E
and 9,819 units of S.

So far, this analysis is exactly the same as deriving the demand curve for electricity. Now, however, rather than looking at the change in the quantity of electricity
purchased, let's look at the change in utility levels. The consumer, before the price
increase, is on indifference curve i; after the price increase, he is on the lower indifference curve, ii. Is there a way to measure the difference in utility between difference curves i and ii in monetary terms?

In fact, there are two money measures of the difference. Both measures are
the result of thought experiments—asking what would happen to the consumer if the
consumer's income were to change. One measure, equivalent variation, is the amount
of money that needs be taken from the consumer, at the original prices, to move the
consumer from indifference curve i to curve ii. The other, compensating variation, is
the amount of money that needs be given to the consumer to return the consumer to
indifference curve i, given that the price increase decreased his utility to indifference
curve ii. So one difference between these two measures is whether the consumer, at
the end of our thought experiment of adding or subtracting money, is on the new or
the old indifference curve. One measure looks at a situation where a change in utility
happens. The other measure looks at the situation where the consumer remains at the
same utility level.

Let's start with the situation in which a change in utility happens. This example
looks at a decrease in utility caused by an increase in price. When price increases,
the consumer is clearly less happy and is on the lower indifference curve, ii. There

are two ways in which the consumer's utility can decrease from indifference curve i to indifference curve ii. One is a price increase; this is what really happens. In Figure 5.7, the price increase causes the movement from the tangency of budget constraint I and indifference curve i to budget constraint II and indifference curve ii.

There is another way to reduce a consumer's utility from indifference curve i to ii: by taking away money, or reducing income. Starting again from the tangency of i and I, imagine a new budget constraint III that is parallel to the original budget constraint, I, but is tangent to indifference curve ii. This new budget constraint keeps the original prices because it is parallel to the original budget constraint. The new budget constraint has lower income because it has a lower vertical intercept.

The two ways to get from indifference curve i to indifference curve ii are thus either to raise prices (which is what really happens) or to take money away (a thought experiment). When a price change results in a change in utility level from i to ii, the **equivalent variation (EV)** is the amount of money that would have to be taken away from the consumer in order to have the same effect as the price increase: that of reducing the consumer's utility level from i to ii. Both the price increase and the taking of his money leave him on the new, lower indifference curve, ii.

The second measure of the utility change is called **compensating variation (CV)**. As shown in Figure 5.8, the price change reduces the consumer's utility to the level on indifference curve ii. Now, consider the thought experiment of giving him money to get him back to indifference curve i. He is hurt by the increased price and

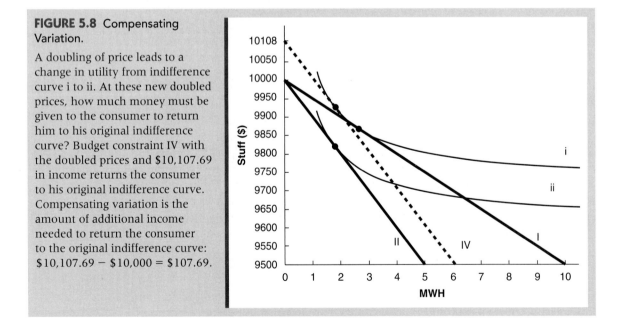

FIGURE 5.8 Compensating Variation.

A doubling of price leads to a change in utility from indifference curve i to ii. At these new doubled prices, how much money must be given to the consumer to return him to his original indifference curve? Budget constraint IV with the doubled prices and $10,107.69 in income returns the consumer to his original indifference curve. Compensating variation is the amount of additional income needed to return the consumer to the original indifference curve: $10,107.69 − $10,000 = $107.69.

helped by a gift of money. The money compensates for the price change, so that he is returned to his original utility level, i. When a price change results in a change in utility level from i to ii, the compensating variation (CV) is the amount of money that, if given to the consumer, would return the consumer's utility level to i. In other words, CV is the change in income that compensates exactly for the price change. In this thought experiment, change in utility does *not* happen because the higher price is offset by the gift of money.

Equivalent variation (EV) assumes that there will be a new utility level. Compensating variation (CV) assumes the old utility level will be maintained. They are both exact money measures of the value to a consumer of a price change. They both can also be used as exact money measures for the change in the quantity of a publicly provided good.

In the case of a publicly provided good, such as an environmental good, there may be no market and no price. However, both CV and EV can be computed in this case too. Just as an increase in the price of a marketed good leads to the consumer purchasing a smaller quantity, a decrease in the quantity of a publicly provided good means that the consumer "consumes" a smaller quantity of the publicly provided good; how much would that be worth in monetary terms?

Let's consider an increase in the number of wolves in Yellowstone and see how the analysis differs for a publicly provided good compared with a private good. Our armchair environmentalist's utility will go up if there are more wolves, even though he does not change his market behavior at all. Measuring EV requires finding out how much his utility would increase if there were added wolves, and then finding the amount of money that provides the same utility increase. Money and wolves are two equivalent ways of increasing his utility. The EV measure assumes that he has changed utility.

In contrast, CV requires a measure of the income he would give up in order to increase the number of wolves. The wolves increase the consumer's utility. Taking money from him returns him to his original level of utility. The amount of money that is taken from him is CV. The taking of money compensates for the adding of wolves. The CV measure assumes that his initial utility is unchanged.

Another way to compare EV and CV is to think about entitlement. Suppose that this environmentalist has a right to the increased wolves. To stop him from exercising his right to increase the wolf population would cost at least EV; for less than that amount, he is unwilling to give up the increase in the wolf population. Suppose, instead, that he had no such right. Now he would be willing to pay up to CV in order to pay for that wolf increase. The difference between EV and CV is that, in one case (EV), he is entitled to the increase in wolf numbers and must be paid if it does not happen; in the other case (CV), he must pay to get the change in wolf numbers.

CV and EV are well-defined concepts, and every economist will understand these terms. There are two other terms that are also used, particularly in the discussion of the valuation of nonmarket goods (like the Yellowstone wolves). The term **willingness to pay (WTP)** refers to the situation where a consumer is offered

BOX 5.2

Does an Endangered Species Have the Right to Exist?

The 1973 Endangered Species Act (ESA) is intended to protect species of both plants and animals from extinction. The law in essence gives the species the right to exist. In addition to prohibiting anyone from harming these species, the law requires protection of their habitats because the species is not likely to continue to exist if its habitat vanishes. The requirement for habitat protection has led to a number of conflicts between development activities, such as housing or dam construction, and species protection. Those who want the jobs or economic activity associated with development resent the limitations on their opportunities due to such species as the Furbish's lousewort or the cactus ferruginous pygmy owl (whose names may not help their cause).

Should those who lose jobs or development opportunities be compensated for these losses? If the species indeed have the right to exist, then the initial utility for environmentalists includes species protection. If a developer wants to disrupt the species' habitat, it would have to provide compensation (for instance, habitat in another location). This payment would be compensating variation: environmentalists can either prevent development or receive compensation to allow the development. The money or other compensation (such as habitat elsewhere) would flow from developers to environmentalists. As a result, the environmentalists' utility would stay at the initial, high level.

In the case of the northern spotted owl, though, forest industry workers received compensation. The owl lives in old-growth forests in the Pacific Northwest; protecting its habitat required great reductions in timber harvests. Those in the logging industry protested vigorously, claiming that their livelihoods were more important than the owl. Implicitly they claimed that they had the right to maintain their utility by continuing to log the forests and that environmentalists were entitled only to the utility associated with harvested forests.

If environmentalists were entitled only to harvested forests, they would have two choices: they could live with harvested forests, or they could offer to pay to keep the forests in their pristine state. They would pay up to their equivalent variation. Either choice would give them the new, lower utility level.

In the compromise plan developed to protect the northern spotted owl and its habitat, money from the U.S. government (that is, from the general public) provided forest workers with job retraining funds. Because owl protection is a public good, collecting the payment from the general public approximately collects the funding from people who benefit from the owl's protection.

Why would environmentalists agree to pay forest workers when the workers had no right to log because the Endangered Species Act gave the spotted owl the right to exist? Environmentalists may not have been sure that the legal protections of the ESA would survive the political process. It may have been better to pay the loggers an amount less than equivalent variation to be sure of the habitat's protection.

something desirable, like an increase in the number of wolves, and is asked, "how much would you be willing to pay" to get the thing. The term **willingness to accept (WTA)** refers to the situation where a consumer must give up something, such as some wolves in Yellowstone, and is asked how much he would have to be paid to accept the loss.

Whether a WTP or WTA question elicits CV or EV as an answer depends upon how the question is asked. The key issue is whether the consumer will end up with the same or changed utility. Consider these common cases:

1. "What is the most money that you would be willing to pay to have more wolves in Yellowstone?" This WTP question elicits CV because getting the wolves requires giving up money until there is no utility gain.
2. "What is the most money you would be willing to pay so that ranchers will not kill Yellowstone wolves?" Here utility is going to go down, either because wolves die or because he must pay money. This WTP question elicits EV.
3. "What is the least amount of money you would you be willing to accept instead of having an increase in Yellowstone wolves?" This WTA question elicits EV. Here there are two alternatives, both of which make the consumer better off: either getting more wolves or getting more money.
4. "What is the least amount of money you would be willing to accept to allow ranchers to kill Yellowstone wolves?" This WTA question elicits CV. Though wolves die, the consumer gets enough money to return to the original utility level.

By far the most common type of question is the WTP question phrased as in case (1) to elicit CV. It is often the easiest question for a survey respondent to understand. The implicit assumption in asking this willingness-to-pay question is that an environmental gain is not an entitlement; consumers must pay to get it.

IN SUMMARY

- Consumer surplus is not an exact measure of the effects of a price change to a consumer because the price change implicitly includes a change in purchasing power—income—along with it. The alternatives are two exact money measures—measures that estimate the money value of the change in utility from a change in price or quantity, especially in estimating the benefits from changing environmental quality. These measures are equivalent and compensating variation.
- Equivalent variation (EV) is the most money that a consumer would pay instead of having an increased price or a decreased quantity of a good. It assumes that the utility change will happen. Compensating variation (CV) is the least amount of money a consumer would accept to allow an increased price or a decreased quantity. The money received plus the change in price or quantity leave him no worse off than before. Utility change does not happen.
- Which measure is appropriate depends on whether the change is considered inevitable unless action is taken to stop it (in which case EV is the right

measure), or whether nothing is expected to happen unless action is taken to make it happen (in which case CV is more appropriate).

• In studies that seek to estimate the value of nonmarket goods, such as environmental goods, economists often use the terms "willingness to pay" and "willingness to accept." They refer to paying money to get an environmental benefit or being paid money to accept an environmental degradation. Depending on how the question is phrased, the answer can refer to CV or EV.

EQUIVALENT VARIATION FOR ELECTRICITY DEMAND

Both EV and CV can be measured using indifference curves. To explore the difference between EV and CV, let's continue with the example of electricity demand in Montana because it has indifference curves.

The beginning of the last section used Figure 5.7 to show the effects of doubling the price of electricity from $50/MWH to $100/MWH. Let's walk through the steps in calculating EV as an exact money measure of the consumer's utility loss resulting from a doubling in the price of electricity. First, in Figure 5.7, line III is a third budget constraint that is parallel to but lower than the original budget constraint, I. It achieves the level of utility of indifference curve ii because budget constraint III is tangent to (touches) indifference curve ii.

Notice that budget constraint III is parallel to budget constraint I. Recall that budget constraint I is based on the original price of $50/MWH for electricity and the price of $1 per unit of stuff. If two budget constraints are parallel, their slopes are the same. The slope of the budget constraint is the ratio of the prices of electricity and stuff, and the price of stuff never changes—it is $1 per unit. If the slopes are the same, the ratio of the prices is the same. If the ratio of the prices is the same, and if the price of stuff hasn't changed, then the price of the other good—electricity—must be the same. Thus, budget constraint III has the same prices as budget constraint I: $50/MWH for electricity and $1 per unit of stuff.

The income on a budget constraint can be found from the intersection of the budget constraint with the vertical axis. This is because the budget constraint intercepts the vertical axis at the point where the consumer is consuming no electricity and spending all his income on stuff. This point is Y/P_S, where Y is income and P_S is the price of stuff; in other words, the budget constraint hits the vertical axis where the quantity of electricity consumed is 0 and the quantity of stuff consumed is total income. Knowing the intercept and knowing P_S (which is $1/unit of stuff) allows calculation of income. Budget constraint III has a lower income than budget constraint I because it is closer to the origin and has a smaller intercept. From the graph, the new intercept is a little less than $9,893. Nongraphical methods allowed the authors to calculate it much more exactly to be $9,892.94.

The consumer has now reached this new, lower indifference curve both because of a higher price and a lower income. On the diagram, the change in the vertical intercepts from budget constraint I to budget constraint III is $107.06. Because the price of stuff is $1, the change in income between the two parallel budget constraints is $107.06. This is the equivalent variation. The consumer is indifferent between giving up $107.06 and having prices double. Either way, his utility is less than it was before the price increase. The EV amount tells us how much less.

COMPENSATING VARIATION FOR ELECTRICITY DEMAND

Now let's turn to compensating variation (CV), shown in Figure 5.8. Again, price increases from $50/MWH to $100/MWH. Budget constraints I and II are just as in Figure 5.7, and the increase in price again results in the consumer choosing a bundle on the lower indifference curve ii.

For compensating variation, however, the goal is to measure the income that will get the consumer back to the original, higher indifference curve, i. Remember that CV is appropriate when the consumer's utility does not change; in other words, he ends up on the original indifference curve.

In Figure 5.8, budget constraint IV is parallel to budget constraint II. Again, if two budget constraints are parallel, and if the price of one good (stuff) is unchanged, then the price of the other good is also unchanged. Budget constraint IV, like II, represents the new price for electricity of $100/MWH, and it is tangent to indifference curve i. Therefore, the consumer will be returned to his original level of utility. Budget constraint IV has a higher vertical intercept than II, though, which means that it represents more income: it brings the consumer back to the original indifference curve (i) and leaves him as well off as originally, but with the higher price and higher income.

The next step is to calculate the amount of money (the CV) that leaves the consumer as well off as he was before the price change. The vertical intercept for budget constraint IV is the point at which he spends all his money on stuff at $1 a unit and buys no electricity. That vertical intercept indicates what his total income has to be to compensate for the loss of utility due to the increased price of electricity—in other words, what his new income must be for his new budget constraint to be tangent to the original indifference curve, i. The graph shows that the vertical intercept for budget constraint IV—the total income—is a little more than $10,100. Again, other methods provide it more exactly, $10,107.69. The change in income between budget constraints II and IV is the compensating variation. In our diagram, it is $107.69.

The increase in the price of electricity has made the consumer worse off. To make him as well off as before the price increase, either the price must go back to the original values, or the consumer must receive a higher income. Compensating variation measures how much he would have to be compensated to make him as well off as he was before the price increase, by estimating the amount of money associated with the new prices that would bring him back to his original indifference curve.

COMPARING CV, EV, AND CONSUMER SURPLUS
FOR MARKETED GOODS

The difference between CV and EV is quite small in the electricity example: EV is $107.06, while CV is $107.69, a difference of less than 1 percent. This is a common outcome for marketed goods. As discussed, the difference between them is due to the different "entitlements" associated with them. For this example, under EV, the change in utility is measured starting from the lower, reduced indifference curve. For CV, the change in utility is measured from the higher, initial indifference curve. Because a higher indifference curve can only be achieved with higher income, EV and CV differ in the practical income level—that is, the purchasing power—that the consumer is assumed to have. Because consumers choose different bundles and have different utility levels for different income levels, it is no surprise that CV and EV are different.

For most consumer goods, as in the electricity example, the difference in practice is hard to notice. The change in purchasing power associated with price changes as a percentage of someone's income is typically very small. Does, for instance, a $2 increase in the price of a whole pizza lead to an appreciable effect on a student's over-all purchasing power, even if the student is on a tight budget? Even if pizza is a significant part of a student's diet, the student's ability to consume goods in general is not affected too much because he can substitute other types of food and buy less pizza to adjust to the price increase.

Economist Robert Willig showed the approximate relationships among consumer surplus, CV, and EV. He found that, when consumer surplus for a good is not a large part of income, and when demand for a good is not much affected by income, then the error in using consumer surplus instead of CV or EV is small enough that it can be ignored. In other words, for most goods, consumer surplus is a fine approximation to either of the other measures. For marketed goods, then, even though consumer surplus is not an exact measure of consumer well-being, it is usually close enough.

COMPARING CV AND EV FOR PUBLICLY PROVIDED GOODS

One trait that nonmarket environmental goods have in common with marketed goods is that the amounts people want of these goods depend on the amounts they have to pay for them. It is usually expensive to increase the supply of environmental goods. For example, improving air quality will require new pollution-control devices on cars and electric utilities; more wolves will mean more livestock kills and thus more compensation to ranchers. How much environmental quality are people willing to purchase? Most evidence suggests that people are willing to pay for easy improvements but are less willing to make huge sacrifices for small additional gains. If improving air quality requires higher utility bills and more expensive cars, many of us might accept small changes but resist big changes. Some people don't want to pay for any wolf protection, and even many armchair environmentalists will not want so many wolves that the animals start appearing in their backyards. Thus, even though people are not accustomed to thinking about demand curves for environmental goods, we do appear to have them.

However, markets are not very successful at providing most environmental goods. If goods are not provided by markets, then the usual market process—consumers observing a market price and deciding how much of the good to buy—does not apply. Environmental goods are often provided without the consumer spending anything; activities by others (such as Defenders of Wildlife or the National Park Service) change the quantity of the environmental good, possibly without any direct expenditures of their own. They are publicly provided goods: the consumer does not decide how much of the good is available.

To estimate the value of these goods, it is more useful to look at changes in their quantities than changes in price. If the air gets cleaner, everyone experiences an improvement in well-being, but this change in utility is not due to a change in the price for clean air because there is no market price for it. Thus, for environmental goods, it makes more sense to talk about the effect on utility from changes in quantities rather than changes in price.

Another, less obvious, way in which environmental goods differ substantially from marketed goods is the ease with which people can substitute between environmental goods and marketed goods. Some goods can be substituted easily for each other (margarine for butter, for example). While people may be able to breathe dirty air if necessary, nobody can do without air entirely; having more of other goods will not compensate for loss of clean air. The evidence of most of the twentieth century indicates that there was not an adequate substitute for wolves in the Yellowstone ecosystem; people who care about the wolves would not readily accept more marketed goods (such as snowmobiles) in exchange. If there are not useful substitutes for a good, which may often be true for environmental resources, then CV and EV can differ by quite a lot.

To see this point, let's examine a consumer who has extreme preferences; in particular, he is completely inflexible in his consumption patterns. He likes two goods, stuff and wolves. Figure 5.9 shows his indifference curves. These L-shaped

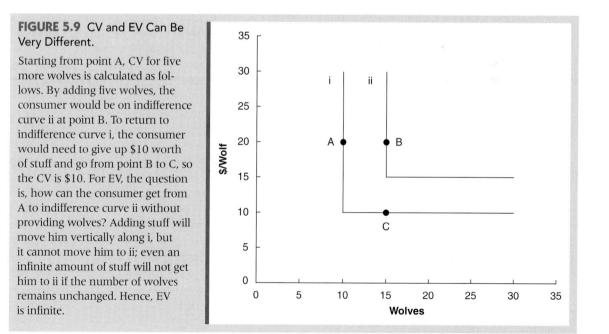

FIGURE 5.9 CV and EV Can Be Very Different.

Starting from point A, CV for five more wolves is calculated as follows. By adding five wolves, the consumer would be on indifference curve ii at point B. To return to indifference curve i, the consumer would need to give up $10 worth of stuff and go from point B to C, so the CV is $10. For EV, the question is, how can the consumer get from A to indifference curve ii without providing wolves? Adding stuff will move him vertically along i, but it cannot move him to ii; even an infinite amount of stuff will not get him to ii if the number of wolves remains unchanged. Hence, EV is infinite.

indifference curves apply when two goods are perfect complements (or nonsubstitutes). Two goods are complements if they are consumed together. Shoes and socks are complements. Two goods are **perfect complements** if they are always consumed together in a specific ratio. Right and left shoes are perfect complements. If the two goods in Figure 5.9 were right and left shoes, for instance, almost all people would want to have the same number of each. Having 12 right shoes but only 10 left shoes would not increase utility compared with having 10 of each (matched, one hopes). In this case, the "more is better" assumption only holds for pairs of shoes, not individual shoes, because shoes are useful only in pairs; there are no substitution possibilities.

For the consumer in Figure 5.9, stuff and wolves are like right shoes and left shoes: more stuff won't increase utility for this consumer unless more wolves appear as well. For this consumer, who has very strong preferences for biodiversity, wolves and stuff are perfect complements. Wild wolves are like the air he breathes; just as stuff does no good if he cannot breathe, stuff does no good in a world without wolves.

This consumer does not get to choose the quantity of wolves in Yellowstone, and he does not face a price for wolves. Instead, the quantity of wolves is determined by Defenders of Wildlife (of which he is not a member).

In Figure 5.9, let's say the consumer is at point A on indifference curve i, with 20 units of stuff and 10 wolves. Because of his inflexible preferences, getting more stuff without another wolf appearing in Yellowstone will not make him better off; he cannot be happier unless there are more wolves. As a result, he stays on the same indifference curve even if he gets more stuff. On the other hand, if more wolves appear in Yellowstone, he can move horizontally to indifference curve ii and increase his utility.

Suppose that five more wolves appear in Yellowstone. Because the consumer doesn't have to pay for the wolves, his consumption bundle moves horizontally across to bundle B from its original bundle A because he can continue to spend all his own money on stuff. He is now on the higher indifference curve, ii.

Now let's look at CV and EV when the quantity of wolves changes. Measuring CV requires figuring out how much stuff he would have to give up if the wolves stayed in Yellowstone, but he had to get back to his original indifference curve, i. If he gave up $10 worth of stuff, he would then be at bundle C, with five more wolves but less stuff than at A. Because bundles A and C are on the same indifference curve i, he would be just as well off as he was at the beginning. The amount of stuff he gave up is worth $10. This is the compensating variation for the wolves, $10.

For EV, the consumer is entitled to be on the higher indifference curve, ii. EV is the amount of money that he would have to be paid if the new wolves were not added, in order to leave him as well off as he would be if the new wolves were added. In other words, EV is the amount of money that would leave the number of wolves the same as they were at point A on indifference curve i but still move his utility up to indifference curve ii. Is there any amount of money we can give him, holding the number of wolves constant at the original level, that will get him to the higher indifference curve ii from curve i? No, there is not because the only way he can get to a higher indifference curve is for there to be more wolves in Yellowstone. Adding stuff just moves him up along indifference curve i. In this case, EV is infinite!

Why do we now see a huge difference between CV and EV? There are two key factors: (1) the environmentalist was not able to influence the number of wolves but had to accept what was publicly provided, and (2) the environmentalist was unwilling to accept any stuff in exchange for wolves.

This extreme example also shows one other difference between using EV and CV to measure the value of increasing the quantity of a nonmarketed good. CV asks how much income the consumer would give up in order to get the good. The answer is limited by the consumer's income. EV asks how much money the consumer would take instead of getting an environmental improvement. The answer is not limited by income. EV can be a really big number!

These results hold for a publicly provided good any time a consumer is inflexible about substituting goods for environmental quality, although the results are not as extreme if a consumer's preferences are more flexible than those used here. As the willingness to substitute goods for environmental quality goes down, the difference between CV and EV will go up.

For marketed goods, even if a consumer has inflexible preferences between two marketed goods, EV will not become infinite because the consumer can reach the higher indifference curve with a finite amount of money just by buying the goods. The fundamental problem with the publicly provided good is that, in this extreme case, no matter how much money the consumer has, he himself cannot purchase an additional wolf. Without an additional wolf, he cannot be made better off.

ADDING UP CV AND EV

Compensating and equivalent variation are defined for individual consumers. Finding CV or EV for a group of consumers involves adding up the CV or EV for each. What about the more common situation when this information isn't available for individual consumers, but there are data for the whole market? This is the case with the electricity data. In this case, the market CV or EV comes from dividing the market data by the number of consumers to create an average, or representative, consumer. Next, the data from that representative person are used to calculate CV and EV. Finally, total CV or EV for the whole market comes from multiplying the CV or EV for the representative consumer times the number of consumers. An estimate of market CV or EV, then, is the sum of the CV or EV for the individuals who make up that market.

 IN SUMMARY

- Equivalent variation (EV) considers different ways to get to a new indifference curve. If a decrease in environmental quality or an increase in price decreases utility, then EV is the change in income that would decrease utility by the same amount. If an increase in environmental quality or a decrease in price increases utility, the EV is the change in income that would produce the same increase in utility.

- EV is measured by finding the income level associated with the old price levels but the new indifference curve. The difference in income between the original budget constraint and the new, parallel budget constraint is the EV.
- Compensating variation (CV) considers a change in income that offsets a change in price or environmental quality so that the consumer stays on the original indifference curve. In the case of a utility decrease, CV measures the amount that the consumer would need to be paid to be willing to accept the loss. If the change increases utility, compensating variation estimates how much the consumer would pay to ensure that the change happens.
- CV is measured by finding the income associated with the new prices but the original indifference curve. The difference in income between the new budget constraint and the parallel budget constraint on the old indifference curve is the CV.
- Because the effect of different income levels on the demand curve is very small for most marketed goods, EV and CV are quite similar for private goods. As a result, consumer surplus is likely to be a good approximation of an exact money measure of the change in utility due to a change in the price of marketed goods.
- Publicly provided goods, including most environmental goods, differ from marketed goods in that consumers have little control over the quantity of the goods available. As a result, it is usually more important to look at the effects of changes in the quantity of environmental goods than at the role of price changes.
- EV and CV may be very different when consumers are relatively unwilling to accept compensation for a reduction in the environmental good. A consumer's CV measures what he would be willing to pay to get an environmental improvement; it will be affected by the consumer's income. EV, on the other hand, measures what he would have to be compensated if the environmental good is not provided or is taken away. EV is therefore not limited by a consumer's income. If he is unwilling to substitute marketed goods for the environmental good, EV can in theory be infinite.
- As the willingness to substitute goods for environmental quality goes down, the difference between CV and EV goes up.
- CV or EV for a group of consumers is the sum of the CV or EV for individuals.

Electricity Price

Andra Pradesh is not the only place where electricity pricing is discriminatory. Discriminatory pricing schemes for power are common throughout the world. In California, Pacific Gas and Electric is a regulated utility. Its rate schedule has 85

BOX 5.3

How Different Are WTP and WTA?

The theory here predicts that CV and EV will be different. This difference can be due to income effects—a person is slightly poorer after buying a good and slightly wealthier after being paid for a good—and to lack of substitutes for a good. Are they always different, though?

Coursey and coauthors wondered whether people's lack of familiarity with either the good under study or the methods used to estimate CV or EV might affect people's bids. To investigate this question, they ran an experiment using students recruited from undergraduate business classes at the University of Wyoming. The students were asked to taste sucrose octa-acetate (SOA)—a bitter, unpleasant, non-toxic substance—for 20 seconds. Students in the CV experiment started with the assumption that they were not required to taste the SOA (that is, to stay on their initial indifference curve); they were offered money (compensation) if they would taste it. Students in the EV experiment were expected to taste the SOA (that is, to move to a new, lower indifference curve); they had to pay (from a credit they were given) not to taste SOA. The experiments ran in three stages. First, students in the CV experiment were asked how much they would have to be paid (their willingness to accept, WTA) to taste the SOA; in the EV experiment, they were asked how much they would pay (their willingness to pay, WTP) not to taste it. Next, they were given a few drops of the SOA so that they were familiar with it, and then they were asked for the WTA or WTP again. Finally, groups of eight students had to bid their WTP or WTA values; the four students with the lowest WTA or the highest WTP had to taste the SOA. The auctions were repeated at least four times, so that students got familiar with the method, before the final round determined who had to taste the SOA.

Initially, WTA values were significantly higher than WTP values. As the bidding process repeated, though, the WTA values fell, until they were not statistically distinguishable from the WTP values. The WTP values were much more stable than the WTA values across the experiments. These results suggest that familiarity with the good and with prices for the good may reduce the differences between WTP and WTA.

different parts. In one part, residential rates vary from $115 to $410/MWH. The pricing scheme allocates a baseline quantity of electricity to each residential unit depending on factors such as climate. The lowest rate applies to baseline usage. The next lowest rate applies to 101–130 percent of baseline usage, and so on, until the price is $410/MWH at 300 percent of baseline. This is called an increasing block rate. Because of this structure, a consumer's average price is always less than the highest price he pays. The amount the consumer purchases, though, is found from the intersection of his demand curve and price of the highest block of electricity that he uses. If the consumer is purchasing 300 percent of baseline, the price of $410/MWH determines how much he purchases. In fact, he would purchase the same amount under block-rate pricing as he would if the price was a straight $410/MWH. With the block-rate program, this consumer's total payment is lower than it would be if every unit he consumed was charged $410/MWH.

Why would a utility price this way? The utility has to meet two goals: (1) charge smaller and presumably poorer consumers less and (2) discourage excessive use. A Pareto-optimal solution would be to charge the costs of the delivered power, about $200/MWH, to everyone. Then everyone would have the same incentive to conserve. With the current pricing system, consumers paying $410/MWH would like to buy some power from consumers paying $155, but they can't, so the pricing system is not efficient. On the other hand, the system transfers consumer surplus from larger to smaller users. So the political goal of transferring money is met, while some Pareto-improving exchanges do not happen.

Are there consequences to this decision? The users facing the $410/MWH rate find it attractive to buy solar systems. At present, solar systems are financially feasible in California only because of a combination of the higher-than-market rate for electricity and generous subsidies for photovoltaic systems. They are not an outcome that would occur in a market economy.

CHAPTER SUMMARY

Here are the key lessons from this chapter:

- The demand curve is an estimate of a consumer's marginal willingness to pay for one more unit of a good. The area under the demand curve from the origin to the quantity purchased sums up the marginal willingness to pay to provide an estimate of total willingness to pay.
- Consumer surplus is the amount that a consumer gains from a good over and above the amount paid for it. It is total willingness to pay less the amount paid (price times quantity).
- Consumer surplus is only an estimate of the value of a good to a consumer. There are two exact money measures of the value of a good to a consumer: compensating variation (CV) and equivalent variation (EV). Both compensating and equivalent variations measure in money terms the change in the utility level associated with a price (or quantity) change. They differ in the implied starting point: equivalent variation assumes that the starting point is the new utility level, while compensating variation starts with the original utility level.
- For marketed goods, compensating variation, equivalent variation, and consumer surplus are likely to be almost identical. In practice, the difference between them is related to the effects of the price/quantity change on purchasing power (that is, income). Because these effects are typically small, the three measures are not likely to differ by much.
- The analysis of changes in net benefits for environmental goods differs from that for marketed goods in several ways. First, because environmental goods

are typically public goods, the analysis is usually done for changes in quantities of those goods rather than changes in price. Secondly, consumers do not buy public goods by the unit; they benefit from a quantity of public goods even if they do not contribute to its provision, and they often have very little control over the quantity available. Finally, if consumers are unwilling to be compensated for reductions of environmental goods by getting more marketed goods, then the gap between compensating variation and equivalent variation may become very large.

- In environmental economics, willingness to pay (WTP) and willingness to accept (WTA) are used to describe situations where people are asked to pay for an environmental improvement or are offered payment for environmental degradation. Depending on how the questions are worded, either WTP or WTA questions can elicit CV or EV as answers.

- Summing up any of these changes in utility can be done by adding up all individuals' consumer surpluses, compensating variations, or equivalent variations. Alternatively, consumers' surplus for all consumers is the area under the market demand curve, and willingness to pay for a public good is the area under the vertically summed marginal willingness to pay curve.

KEY TERMS

compensating variation (CV) *(p. 94)*
consumer surplus *(p. 85)*
equivalent variation (EV) *(p. 94)*
marginal willingness to pay *(p. 83)*
perfect complements *(p. 102)*

price discrimination *(p. 82)*
publicly provided goods *(p. 90)*
total willingness to pay (TWTP) *(p. 84)*
willingness to accept (WTA) *(p. 97)*
willingness to pay (WTP) *(p. 95)*

NOTES

The discussion of power in India is from Rafiq Dossani and V. Ranganathan, "Farmers' Willingness to Pay for Power in India: Conceptual Issues, Survey Results, and Implications for Pricing," *Energy Economics* 26 (2004): 359–369.

The discussion of consumer surplus, EV, and CV is from Robert D. Willig, "Consumer's Surplus without Apology," *American Economic Review* 66(4) (September 1976): 589–597.

The study of Tunisian water is by Slim Zekri and Ariel Dinar, "Welfare Consequences of Water Supply Alternatives in Rural Tunisia," *Agricultural Economics* 28 (2003): 1–12.

The L shape in Figure 5.9 is called Leontief preferences, to honor Wassily Leontief, the first user of this functional form.

The analysis of the difference between EV and CV in the case of the consumer with inflexible preferences comes from W. Michael Hanemann, "Willingness to Pay and Willingness to Accept: How Much Can They Differ?" *American Economic Review* 81(3) (June 1991): 635–647.

EXERCISES

1. While price is a very effective way of allocating goods, governments sometimes like to keep the price of a good low for political reasons. Suppose, using Figure 5.1, that the utility decided to provide 1 MWH of electricity but only charge $83 per MWH.
   (a) What is total willingness to pay?
   (b) What is consumer surplus in this case? Remember that consumer surplus is the area under the demand curve but above the price paid, between the vertical axis and the quantity consumed.
   (c) If the utility sells the electricity at the market-clearing price of $294/MWH, what is the consumer surplus?
   (d) What happens to the difference in consumer surplus between these cases? Does it vanish?

2. Whether those who want environmental gains should pay for them, or whether they should be compensated if the gain does not happen, is closely related to rights for the goods. The University of Michigan owned a historic house in the city of Dexter, Michigan, a few miles from the university's campus. The university planned to sell the house to the highest bidder because it had no reason to keep it and could use the funds for other purposes. Some residents in Dexter wanted to keep the house as it is, rather than see it torn down. Did the university have the right to sell the house to the highest bidder, in which case the residents would have to purchase the property to keep it as it is (equivalent variation because their utility would go down with the destruction of the house), or did the residents have the right to expect the university to maintain the property in its current state, in which case the residents would have to be compensated if it were sold (compensating variation)?

   The answer depends on how laws are written. In this case, the residents raised sufficient funds to buy the property from the university. While the university had the right to sell, residents' equivalent variation was high enough that both sides were satisfied with the deal. How might a law be written so that residents would have to be compensated for a change in a property that affected them? When should laws give "veto" rights to affected residents, and when should the rights belong to the owners of the property?

3. Are expenditures ever a good measure of the gains to an individual from purchasing a good? First, try to think of a case where expenditures exactly measure total willingness to pay. (Hint: What is it about the slope of the demand curve that leads to the existence of consumer surplus?) Secondly, if total expenditures equal total willingness to pay, what is the consumer surplus for the good? Do expenditures measure benefits?

4. What do CV and EV look like for a publicly provided good if a consumer does not view them as perfect complements? To examine this case, draw a curved indifference curve, with Wolves on the horizontal axis and Stuff on the vertical axis. If the quantity of wolves is 5, the consumer's utility is the point on that

indifference curve associated with Wolves = 5. The consumer's income is the vertical coordinate for that point because Stuff costs $1 per unit. Suppose that Defenders of Wildlife now provides five more wolves. The consumer's income has not changed, but the number of wolves has. Identify this new point, and draw the indifference curve that goes through it. Is the consumer better off or worse off? How can you tell?

Now, let's figure out EV and CV. For EV, the consumer is entitled to be on the new indifference curve. Adding five wolves to get to the new point is one way to get to this indifference curve; another way is to stay at five wolves and add more income. Identify EV on your diagram.

For CV, the consumer must stay on the original indifference curve. How much money would have to be taken away if there are 10 wolves to get back to the original indifference curve? Identify CV on your diagram.

5. A major assumption underlying all these welfare measures is that each individual consumer is the best judge of what is better for himself. In addition, a consumer's actions reveal these preferences. Thus, if a consumer buys nonrecycled paper when recycled paper is available at the same price, the consumer reveals that he prefers the nonrecycled paper; in addition, he would be worse off if nonrecycled paper were not available.

(a) Suppose the price of recycled paper is higher than the price of nonrecycled paper. A consumer buys the nonrecycled paper. Would requiring that all paper be recycled make him worse off? Why or why not?

(b) Suppose the price of recycled paper is higher than the price of nonrecycled paper. A consumer buys the recycled paper anyway. Is this consumer irrational? Why or why not? Is he made worse off by the presence of nonrecycled paper? Why or why not?

(c) A university is considering requiring the use of recycled paper, although it is more expensive than nonrecycled paper. Students are either like the consumer in (a), and would buy cheaper nonrecycled paper if it is available, or like the consumer in (b), who buy more expensive recycled paper. What is the total effect on student well-being if recycled paper is required—that is, does consumers' surplus increase or decrease?

(d) What is the effect of greater availability of choices on consumer well-being? That is, in economic modeling, do additional choices make people better off or worse off? Why?

6 | Revealed Preference Methods

Clean rivers and lakes provide great benefits. Water supply, fish habitat, and recreational opportunities all improve when water quality improves. While few would contest that these benefits are real, some are surprised to learn that these are economic as well as ecological benefits. The fact that people are willing to trade other goods for clean water signals their economic desirability. Demand curves reflect those tradeoffs for marketed goods. Environmental goods, though, are not typically marketed. When there is no market for a good, such as improved water quality in a lake, visiting a beach, breathing clean air, or hiking in a wilderness area, economists use *nonmarket valuation* methods—methods to estimate the demand for goods that are not traded in markets and the value that people place on those goods. This chapter will examine:

- Valuation methods for nonmarket goods that people use;
- How to use regression analysis for organizing and analyzing data;
- How to estimate demand for recreation from data on visits: the travel cost method;
- How to use property values or wages to estimate environmental benefits: hedonic pricing;
- How observing people's efforts to avoid harm from pollution provides estimates of the costs of pollution: averting behavior.

New Bedford Harbor Superfund Site

The Comprehensive Environmental Response, Compensation, and Liability Act (CERCLA, also known as the Superfund law) allows the United States and the states to sue those responsible for hazardous waste sites for "natural resource damages." The Massachusetts New Bedford Harbor case was the first time that the National Oceanographic and Atmospheric Administration (NOAA) sought money not only to clean up a site but also to offset natural resources damages. NOAA provided the following background on the New Bedford case:

> New Bedford Harbor is a major commercial fishing port and industrial center in southeastern Massachusetts on Buzzards Bay. From the 1940s to the 1970s, electrical parts manufacturers discharged wastes containing PCBs and toxic metals into New Bedford Harbor, resulting in high levels of contamination throughout the waters, sediments and biota of the Harbor and parts of Buzzards Bay. Hundreds of acres of marine sediment were highly contaminated. One location contained the highest concentrations of PCBs ever documented in a marine environment.

> Biological effects of the contamination include reproductive impairment and death of marine life throughout the estuary, along with loss of marine biodiversity in areas of high contamination. The economic impact was severe, due to long-term fishing closures, lost beach use, diminished property values, and reduced opportunities for coastal development.

The five companies found to be responsible for the damages to New Bedford Harbor paid $109 million to the state and federal governments. Of that total, the amount attributed to damages to beach recreation and to fishing was $20.2 million. The larger share of the settlement was the cost of remediation, which is the cost to prevent further damage to people or ecosystems. The funds were and are still being used to remove contaminated sediments from the floor of the harbor and to improve fishing and recreation in New Bedford Harbor.

The costs associated with cleaning up environmental damages can be very large. In exchange for those costs, people get improved water quality, fish that are safer to eat, more recreational opportunities, and increased property prices. This chapter examines some of the ways to estimate the value of these environmental improvements.

Use Values Associated with Nonmarket Goods

Marketed goods clearly have value. Electricity powers many of the tools people use on a daily basis. Food provides nourishment. Housing provides shelter. A good does not have to be only for basic human needs. The arts, whether marketed or not, can provide greater understanding of and appreciation for our world.

Many environmental goods are of use as well. People benefit from clean air every time they breathe; they enjoy recreation, including the opportunity to hike, admire vistas, or spot wildlife in natural areas; and people live longer when they can avoid exposure to toxic substances.

For many reasons, it is very useful to know how valuable these environmental goods are. For instance, ignoring the value of clean water encourages manufacturers to emit pollutants. One way to make polluters pollute less is to make them pay for the environmental damage their pollution causes. The first step to making polluters pay is to estimate the value of the damage they have done to environmental goods. The design of environmental policy may also depend on estimates of value. Policy makers often want to compare the benefits of an activity, such as cleaning the air or protecting a park, with its costs. Knowing the values associated with protecting environmental goods contributes to better environmental policies.

Finding the values of marketed goods is relatively easy because the data for market demand curves and consumer surplus measures come from market transactions that are often observable. Nevertheless, economists can also find the values of goods that are not marketed. Those goods fall into two categories, those with and without *use value*. A good has **use value** when consumers take an action in order to benefit from the good. Purchasing a good is an action. But use value comes not only from goods that are purchased, like electricity. Goods with use value also include clean air, recreation, and toxic avoidance. Although these nonmarket goods are not purchased, people do take actions that determine how much of these goods they obtain. These actions include choosing to live in an area with better air quality, traveling to an area for recreation, and buying bottled water to avoid contaminated tap water. People also benefit from goods without taking action. Examples of goods with *non-use value* include remote ecosystems and endangered species. While these goods change people's utility, most people never visit these places or see these species. Goods that are obtained without action have **non-use value**. **Passive use value** is a synonym for non-use value. Some goods have only non-use values. The armchair environmentalist may not show her interest for an environmental good through use of the good, but the care and concern are real. Because goods must have value to somebody, all goods have either non-use value, use value, or both.

There are two types of methods that can be used to value nonmarket goods: *revealed preference methods* and *stated preference methods*. **Revealed preferences** are those preferences that an observer can infer from a person's action: people are putting their money or their time where their mouths are. Whenever alternative A costs at least as much as alternative B, and the consumer chooses alternative A, then alternative A is revealed preferred to B. For example, consider the choice of going to beach A or to beach B. Everything but the choice of beach is the same: the same things are taken for lunch, the same car is used to drive, and so on. Indeed, the only difference between the beaches is that beach B is polluted and beach A is not. If it costs $2 to go to beach A and $1 to go beach B, and the consumer goes to beach A, then going to beach A was revealed to be preferred to going to beach B, with that preference worth at least $1. Methods that expose underlying preferences from an action are **revealed preference methods**. Because revealed preference methods depend on an action, they can only be used on goods that have use values.

Stated preference methods expose preferences based on a statement and not on an action. Instead of observing beach-going behavior, a stated preference method would depend on the answer to a question, such as, Would you rather go to beach A or beach B? Because stated preference methods do not depend on an action, they can be used both on goods that have use values and goods that have non-use values. Stated preference methods are the subject of Chapter 7.

In the case of marketed goods, it is possible to estimate consumer benefits (consumer surplus, equivalent variation, or compensating variation) from the demand curve. The goal of nonmarket analysis, then, is to find a demand curve for a nonmarket good. The problem is that nonmarket goods are, well, nonmarket. People do not pay per cubic foot of clean air when they breathe, just as many beaches or parks do not charge admission. Because there is no market price, it is not possible to see how people vary their use of the good when the market price changes, and the demand curve cannot be directly estimated. However, for goods with use value, observations of people's behavior toward these resources can be used to estimate the monetary value that people place on these nonmarket goods.

Many marketed goods are closely associated with nonmarket goods. For instance, people who visit a recreation site face transportation costs, such as airplane tickets and gasoline. Someone who wants to live in an area with clean air must buy or rent a home in the neighborhood. One way to reduce exposure to toxics in drinking water is to buy bottled water.

These market actions can be used to infer the use value that people have for nonmarket goods. For instance, if traveling to a site becomes more expensive due to high gasoline prices, people are likely to travel less. The changed number of trips in response to changed travel costs provides information on how quantity demanded changes with price. With this information, it is possible to estimate the change in consumer surplus associated with a change in the environmental good.

The rest of the chapter outlines three commonly used revealed preference methods for estimating the demand curve for environmental quality: travel cost, hedonic pricing, and averting behavior.

IN SUMMARY

- Nonmarket goods, including environmental goods, have value. Estimating their value in monetary terms helps identify the benefits of environmental policies.
- Some nonmarket goods, including many environmental goods, have use value. Use value means that consumers take an action in order to benefit from the good.
- Other nonmarket goods have non-use value. Non-use value means that the consumer can benefit from the good without taking observable action.
- Revealed preference methods expose underlying preferences from observable action. If the first alternative costs no less than the second alternative, and the consumer chooses the first alternative, then the first alternative is revealed preferred to the second. Because revealed preference methods depend on observation of action, they can only be used on goods that have use values.

Using Data to Estimate Demand

For both marketed and nonmarket goods, economists collect prices, quantities, and related information with the goal of figuring out the relationship between price and quantity—the demand curve. The demand curve for a good depends on the price of the good, the prices of related goods, a consumer's income, and personal preferences.

Because all of these factors influence demand, any demand curve should include these factors. What is the process that turns these data into a demand curve that can be plotted on a graph or written as an equation? The usual method for using an equation to represent a relationship in observed data is *regression analysis*. **Regression analysis** is a tool to identify relationships between a *variable* that the researcher seeks to explain and other *variables* that provide some explanation. It is the most common method to turn data on the use of goods into demand curves for those goods.

Suppose a researcher has observed both the number of times that five people have visited a beach and the cost of their visits. Table 6.1 contains these hypothetical data. Each row of the table is called an observation and contains the data on a single person. In each row, first comes the person's identification (here, a letter), followed by what it costs to make a beach visit (the price). People who live farther from the beach have a higher price per visit. The third number in each row gives the number of visits that person makes to the beach. Figure 6.1 plots these five sets of data points, showing them as triangles. The task of *regression analysis* is to find a straight line that comes as close as possible to these data points. The equation for that line will relate price to quantity—that is, it will be the demand curve.

Let's call the quantity of visits Q and the cost of visits P. A straight-line relationship between Q and P can be written as $Q = a + bP$. In this equation, a and b represent two unknown numbers. The unknown numbers in a regression equation are called **parameters**. Notice that one of the parameters, b, is multiplied by price P. A **variable** is an observed piece of data, not an unknown. P, the cost of a trip to the beach for each consumer, and Q, the number of trips that the consumer takes, are variables that come from observation and measurement. A regression can be used to estimate the parameters a and b that explain how the amount of P affects the level of Q. More generally, a **regression** is a method to estimate the parameters of an equation that explains one variable in terms of other variables and those parameters.

TABLE 6.1   Hypothetical Data on the Cost and Number of Beach Visits.

The first column identifies five people. The second column shows how much it costs each person to travel to the beach. The third column shows the number of times each person visits the beach.

PERSON	COST (PRICE) TO VISIT	NUMBER OF VISITS
A	$0.9	28
B	$1.95	17
C	$3	14
D	$3.95	12
E	$5	5

In the equation $Q = a + bP$, b is the slope of the line. The slope indicates how quantity consumed responds to changes in price. Estimating the value for b reveals how travel cost affects the number of trips.

The other parameter, a, is the point where the line described by $Q = a + bP$ intersects the vertical axis. Because the plot has Q on the vertical axis, the place where the line intersects the vertical axis shows the quantity of beach trips consumed when the price is zero. The observed values of Q and P are used to estimate values for parameters a and b. That information then provides a typical individual's demand curve for beach trips.

The task at hand, then, is to estimate the parameters a and b. Figure 6.1 shows a solid line that comes very close to the data points. A line with a different slope or different vertical intercept would not fit as closely to the points. The estimate from this line is that a, the vertical intercept, has a value of 30, and b, the slope, has a value of 5. The equation for the line is thus $Q = 30 - 5 * P$. This is a *regression line*. It suggests that if the price of a trip to the beach is zero, a consumer will go 30 times. If the price is $6, a consumer will not make any trips. Putting a price of $0.90 into the equation produces an estimate—a *predicted value*—of 25.5 trips. A **predicted value** from a regression is the value of the variable on the left-hand side of the equation, when the values of the variables on the right-hand side of the equation are given.

The solid regression line does not go through the data points, but it is close to them. It is possible to see how close by comparing the actual data with the line. For instance, the first data point has a quantity of 28 trips and a price of $0.90. The predicted value at

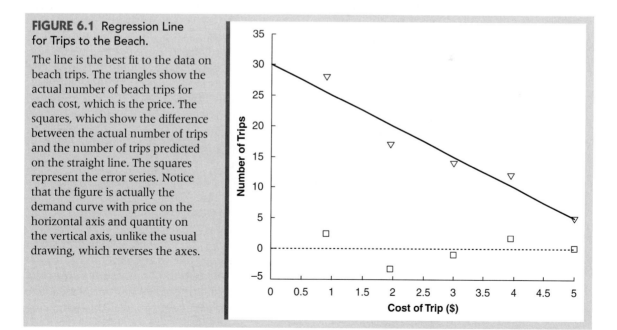

FIGURE 6.1 Regression Line for Trips to the Beach.

The line is the best fit to the data on beach trips. The triangles show the actual number of beach trips for each cost, which is the price. The squares, which show the difference between the actual number of trips and the number of trips predicted on the straight line. The squares represent the error series. Notice that the figure is actually the demand curve with price on the horizontal axis and quantity on the vertical axis, unlike the usual drawing, which reverses the axes.

$0.90 is only 25.5 trips. The error in the estimate is $28 - 25.5 = 2.5$ trips. The same method can be used to calculate the errors for each of the other four data points. The squares on the bottom of Figure 6.1 make up the **error series**: the difference between the predicted value and the actual value for each observation.

Suppose that different values were used for a and b, such as $a = 25$ and $b = -4$. Plotting $Q = 25 - 4 * P$ for the actual data would produce a new line much farther from the data points, and the error series would show much bigger errors.

The method to find the values of a and b that give the equation of the closest fitting line is called *least squares regression*. The rule is to choose the parameters (a and b) that minimize the summed squares of the errors between the actual and the predicted values of Q. Squaring the errors ensures they are positive. Minimizing the sum of the squared errors is one way of minimizing the distance, either positive or negative, between the data points and the line. A **least squares regression** gives the estimates of the parameters that minimize the sum of squared errors between the actual and predicted values.

Let's generalize this process. In many situations, researchers collect data on something they want to explain. The item that they want to explain—demand for beach trips, for instance—is the **dependent variable**. The factors that explain the dependent variable are **independent variables**. In the previous example, the number of beach trips is the dependent variable. Because the example included only one factor—price—that affected demand for beach trips, price was the only independent variable. A more complex analysis can include many different factors that affect the dependent variable, such as the price of travel, income, the price of substitute beaches, and weather.

The beach example has only two parameters: a, the vertical intercept (the quantity of beach trips demanded at a price of zero), and b, the slope (a measure of how much of an effect price has on quantity demanded). An analysis with more variables, such as income and cost to visit substitute sites, would include more parameters, one for each variable. Each observation—a person, in our example—will have associated with it the number of visits that person makes, her income, and her costs for visiting each substitute site. Each variable is multiplied by its associated parameter; the parameter is the slope associated with that variable. When these products are added up, they give a predicted value for the dependent variable. For instance, if income and travel cost to visit a substitute site are included, the equation becomes:

$$Q = a + bP + c * \text{Income} + d * \text{Cost of substitute site}$$

The estimation problem is to find a set of parameters (a, b, c, d) so that the predicted values of the dependent variable are as close as possible to the observed values of the dependent variable. Regression analysis, usually done by computer, finds the parameters that give that closest fit. The parameters (the letters) estimate the effect of the independent variables (the factors) on the dependent variable (the item being studied).

IN SUMMARY

- Regression analysis is used to find a line that best approximates the relationship between dependent and independent variables. It identifies parameters that relate the independent variables to the dependent variable. Each parameter indicates how much the dependent variable changes when the independent variable with which it is associated changes.
- One use of regression analysis is to estimate the demand curve for goods with use value.

Travel Cost: Estimating Recreational Demand from Visitation Data

How often do people visit an area for recreational use? If it is a neighborhood park, people may visit it frequently. If it is a regional attraction, they may go a few times a year. Other sites, such as Yellowstone National Park, Stonehenge, or the Great Wall of China, may be once-in-a-lifetime-at-best opportunities. A consumer's decision to visit these sites is likely based on how costly it is, both in time and money, to travel to these places—that is, it depends on the price of visiting them. The local parks cost little to visit; if the consumer has a dog, she may visit them several times a day. Attractions that are farther away, requiring more time and money, will draw her less often, even if she enjoys them much more. People who live close to Yellowstone, Stonehenge, or the Great Wall of China are likely to visit them much more often than those who live far away. The fact that people with a higher cost of visiting go to a place less often than people with a lower cost of visiting indicates that the price of a visit affects the quantity of visits. In other words, there is a relationship between the price of visiting an area and the quantity of visits to an area. This relationship is the demand curve for visiting the area. Using data on frequency of travel to estimate the demand curve for recreational use of an area is known as the **travel cost method (TCM)**.

TRAVEL COST EXPLAINED

The idea for the TCM dates back to 1947, when economist Harold Hotelling suggested to the National Park Service "that it is possible to set up appropriate measures for evaluating, with a reasonable degree of accuracy, the service of national parks to the public." He proposed that, if people visit a park, they must expect the value of the visit to equal or exceed the cost to them of visiting the area. By observing the distance, and thus the transportation costs, of people who visit a park, and then observing how often people visit, a researcher can observe different prices (travel costs) and different quantities (numbers of visits). These pieces of information are the start of data collection for a demand curve. Because the demand curve is affected by factors other than price, estimating the demand curve also requires demographic information (to get measures of income, as well as tastes and preferences) and cost of travel to sites that might be substitutes for the site being studied.

Let's return to the PCB-contaminated beaches in New Bedford. Economist K. E. McConnell set out to find out how much recreation was lost because of this contamination, and how much that recreation was worth. He started by writing a questionnaire to determine how often people used the beaches. A team of interviewers then administered his questionnaire to 499 people. Of those, 495 responses were usable. The questionnaire asked about the cost of visiting one of the affected beaches (Fort Point Beach), the cost of visiting other nearby beaches, and the number of trips to Fort Point Beach. McConnell calculated the cost of visiting Fort Point Beach as the sum of the actual cost of getting to the beach and back as well as the time cost of travel. For instance, a respondent who lived a five-mile roundtrip from the beach would have a cost for her automobile of 42 cents. She would also spend about six minutes to get to the beach. If her after-tax wage rate were $8 per hour, and it took 15 minutes to travel the five miles, then the opportunity cost of her time in commuting to the beach, measured using her wage, would be $2. Her total cost of traveling to Fort Point would then be $2.42. McConnell then performed the same calculations for her possible travel to the next nearest beach other than Fort Point, resulting in the cost for her travel to that other beach. Finally, the interviewers recorded the number of times she went to Fort Point. Table 6.2 shows the data from the study for five of the interviewees, numbered I through V.

This example has observations on quantity (number of trips to Fort Point), price (travel cost to Fort Point), and the prices of two related goods (the travel cost to the next two nearest beaches). These data can go in a regression to figure out the relationship between the quantity of trips and these different prices.

If the parameters of the regression are a, b, c, and d, the demand curve for trips to Fort Point is:

Number of trips = a + b * travel cost to Fort Point + c * travel cost to nearest other beach + d * travel cost to second nearest other beach

Using statistical analysis on the full data set will produce the four parameters (a, b, c, and d) that describe the line that comes closest to the data points.

TABLE 6.2 Five Observations on Costs of Travel to Fort Point and Other Beaches.

PERSON	NUMBER OF TRIPS TO FORT POINT	TRAVEL COST TO FORT POINT	TRAVEL COST TO NEAREST OTHER BEACH	TRAVEL COST TO SECOND NEAREST OTHER BEACH
I	12	2.06	2.30	3.34
II	15	2.95	3.45	5.28
III	15	1.53	4.66	4.68
IV	16	1.07	2.73	2.63
V	20	1.60	3.77	5.54

Note: Travel costs are roundtrip and are in 1986 dollars.

Table 6.3 shows the values for the estimated parameters. The equation for the demand for trips to Fort Point Beach becomes:

$$\text{Number of trips} = 12.43 - 5.48 * \text{travel cost to Fort Point}$$
$$+ 2.03 * \text{travel cost to nearest other beach}$$
$$+ 2.03 * \text{travel cost to second nearest other beach}$$

Notice that increased travel costs to Fort Point reduce the number of trips that someone takes. In other words, the demand curve slopes down. In particular, each $1 additional cost to travel to the beach reduces the number of trips by an average of 5.48. Trips to Fort Point go up when the cost of traveling to other beaches goes up. This means that the other beaches substitute for Fort Point.

McConnell made his estimates for his whole data set with a method called Tobit that accounts for the many people who took zero trips. He did the exercise twice. The first time, he asked people how many trips they made knowing that there were PCBs in the harbor. The second time, he asked how many trips they would make if there were no PCBs in the harbor. Now he had two demand curves for recreation, one with and one without PCBs in the harbor. Not surprisingly, the existence of PCBs shifted the demand curve for recreation to the left—that is, it reduced demand.

This example is not a pure example of revealed preference: while the data on people's visits to the polluted beaches were based on their actual visits, the information on visits to unpolluted beaches were based on their beliefs about their future actions, so they are stated preferences. The travel cost method can be used with either kind of data, though the revealed preference data are more reliable.

The benefits measure is consumer surplus, the area under the demand curve less the costs incurred to go to the beach. Consumer surplus was calculated with and without pollution; the difference was the lost consumer surplus for beach recreation from PCB contamination for the 495 people interviewed.

The last step was to estimate the total change in consumer surplus for residents of the area because this estimate was only from part of the population. To do so, McConnell divided his estimate by 495 to get consumer surplus per person, and he multiplied that value by the number of people in New Bedford, adjusted for those who did not go to the beach. This gave him an estimate of the losses in beach recreation for a single year. Thus, the local beach-goers revealed their preferences for consumption of beach trips at various prices.

Conducting a travel cost study in practice is quite complex. It involves careful construction of a method to collect data on visitation rates and other important variables, and it often involves complex statistical methods to estimate the demand curve from the data collected. Nevertheless, because of its usefulness for calculating

TABLE 6.3 Parameter Estimates for Trips to Fort Point Beach.

NAME	a (INTERCEPT)	b (COEFFICIENT ON TRAVEL COST)	c (COEFFICIENT ON TRAVEL COST TO NEAREST BEACH	d (COEFFICIENT ON TRAVEL COST TO SECOND NEAREST BEACH)
VALUE	12.43	−5.48	2.03	2.03

the value of recreational opportunities in a wide variety of settings, environmental economists conduct many travel cost studies every year.

BOX 6.1

Letter from Harold Hotelling to the Director of the National Park Service Proposing the Travel Cost Method

Harold Hotelling invented the travel cost method with this 1947 letter to the National Park Service. In the last paragraph of the letter he shows how to extend the analysis to competing parks, thus laying out the framework for more than fifty years of studies in travel cost:

> After a letter from Mr. A. E. Demaray, and a conference with Dr. Roy A. Pruitt of the National Park Service, I am convinced that it is possible to set up appropriate measures for evaluating, with a reasonable degree of accuracy, the service of national parks to the public . . .

> Let concentric zones be defined around each park so that the cost of travel to the park from all points in one of these zones is approximately constant. The persons entering the park in a year, or a suitably chosen sample of them, are to be listed according to the zone from which they come. The fact that they come means that they service of the park is at least worth the cost, and this cost can probably be estimated with fair accuracy. If we assume that the benefits are the same no matter what the distance, we have, for those living near the park, a consumers' surplus consisting of the differences in transportation costs. The comparison of the cost of coming from a zone with the number of people who do come from it, together with a count of the population of the zone, enables us to plot one point for each zone on a demand curve for the service of the park. By a judicious process of fitting it should be possible to get a good enough approximation to this demand curve to provide, through integration, a measure of the consumers surplus resulting from the availability of the park. It is this consumers surplus (calculated by the above process with deduction for the cost of operating the park) which measures the benefits to the public in the particular year. This, of course, might be capitalized to give a capital value for the park, or the annual measure of benefit might be compared directly with the estimated annual benefits on the hypothesis that the park area was used for some alternate purpose.

> The problem of relations between different parks can be treated along the same lines, though in a slightly more complicated manner, provided people entering the park will be asked which other national parks they have visited that year. In place of a demand curve, we have as a result of such an inquiry, a set of demand functions. The consumer surplus still has a defining meaning, as I have shown in various published articles, and may be used to evaluate the benefits from the park system.

> This approach through travel costs is one of several possible modes of attack on this problem. There are also others, which should be examined, though I think the method outlined above looks the most promising.

ISSUES IN USING THE TRAVEL COST METHOD

Any user of travel cost information must understand what the method does and what it does not do. Probably the most important idea to understand about TCM is that it estimates the value of recreational use of an area. Thus, it captures the use value associated with people hiking, hunting, swimming, sightseeing, and otherwise visiting an area. It does *not* include in its measurement the non-use values for people who do not visit an area. If the area is a regional park with no particularly remarkable features, this drawback is not important. The only people likely to have any interest in the park are those in the neighborhood who use it. However, for unique sites that attract visitors from around the world, such as Yellowstone, Stonehenge, or the Great Wall of China, those who visit the site may be a subset of people who care about the future of the area. People who cannot visit China may nevertheless read about or study the Great Wall and want to see it preserved. Similarly, many may care deeply about the future of wildlife in Yellowstone even if their preferred vacations are to cities or shorelines. While recreational use of many areas is likely to tell us about most of their value, the recreational value associated with unique sites may not reflect the total value people place on the site.

Economists are actively researching the travel cost method to improve its accuracy. First, researchers are examining methods to estimate the value of time in a travel cost model. The demand for visiting a place depends not only on the cost of getting there but also on the time required for visiting. Should a person's wage be used as an estimate of the value of time? Because many people use vacation time—meaning that they do not give up any wages—then wage may not offer a good estimate of how people value the time associated with travel. Indeed, some people may believe that getting there is half the fun and consider the journey to be a benefit rather than a cost. Thus, economists are studying different methods to identify ways to include the cost of time in travel cost models.

Another area of research involves estimating the value of visiting one site on a multidestination trip. For example, rarely does a visitor from another country go only to the Great Wall of China; the traveler is likely to visit other cities and sites in China as well. How, then, can the value of visiting the Great Wall be separated from the values of all the other aspects of the trip? Certainly the cost of traveling from Beijing to the Great Wall can be used, but should part of the airfare to Beijing also be counted in the cost? Sometimes the decision to visit one site is estimated jointly with the decision to visit other sites, to identify the relationships among visitation to these sites.

Third, researchers are examining how to incorporate the time spent at a site as part of the quantity side of the visitation model. For example, if Peter spends a day at Yellowstone, while Gloria spends a week at Yellowstone, has each of them consumed one visit? Has Gloria consumed seven times the number of visits that Peter has? If they started from the same place, is the same travel cost associated with different levels of consumption? Often the quantity measure is not visits but rather the number of "recreation visitor-days" (RVDs) associated with a site. The measure, RVDs, is the number of days spent visiting a place in a year or other fixed time period.

These issues associated with TCM do not invalidate the method. Rather, they suggest that there is room for refining the methods for understanding how people decide which sites to visit, as well as our methods for estimating the value of those sites. Although environmental economists have made tremendous advances in studying the recreational values associated with different areas, there is still work to be done. In the meantime, the travel cost method demonstrates that people are willing to pay for their use of environmental goods, and that their use of those goods depends on the price of using them.

IN SUMMARY

- The travel cost method starts with the assumption that the value someone puts on visiting a place is at least as high as the amount she spends on a trip to the area. The cost of a trip is the relevant price variable for a visit. The relationship between the number of trips and the cost of travel is the demand curve for visiting the area. The resulting demand curve is used to estimate the consumer surplus for the area.
- In a typical travel cost study, researchers collect information on the number of trips to an area, the time and money spent to get to the area, and the availability of substitute sites. Regression analysis is used to find how the number of trips changes as these other factors change.
- TCM estimates only the value of visits to a site. It does not include any values that non-users of the site may have.
- TCM can be methodologically complex due to such factors as the appropriate measure of the cost of time, how to estimate the value of a site when a person has multiple destinations, and how to measure a visit.
- Because TCM is based on actual human behavior, where people make real tradeoffs associated with their recreation choices, economists consider it a reliable way of measuring the benefits of recreation at a site.

Hedonic Pricing: Estimating Environmental Benefits from Property Values or Wages

The consumption of environmental goods is often determined by the use of market goods. When a family buys a house, it gets a package that includes the physical attributes as well as the local air quality. When a person takes a job, she gets a package that includes pay as well as the chance of being injured. Different houses cost different amounts, and different jobs pay different amounts. The idea of hedonic pricing is to use variation in the price of the purchased good to infer the value of the attached environmental good.

HEDONIC PRICING EXPLAINED: PROPERTY

Would a homebuyer rather have a house next to the sewage treatment plant in New Bedford or one a few miles up the coast, assuming the two houses were otherwise the same? Would she rather have a house with a view of a bay and three bridges or a view of the neighbor's kitchen window? Would she prefer a house near a freeway with both noise and increased level of small particulates in the air, or would she rather live a few miles away? Nearly everyone prefers the cleaner, prettier sights, yet some people do live with the view of their neighbor's house, the occasional smell of sewage, the noise, and the increased particulate matter. People live in these less desirable places because they cost less.

The *hedonic pricing method* is based on the idea that a good is made up of attributes. For instance, a house consists of the characteristics of the house itself (size, layout, age, number of bedrooms and baths, etc.) and the neighborhood in which it is located (access to stores, quality of the schools, crime rate, proximity to parks, views, pollution, noise, etc.). The value of the house and the levels of the attributes are variables; they are observed. The amount that each attribute contributes to the price of the house, however, can't be directly observed; it must be inferred. For instance, call the value of the house P, the number of square feet in the house S, and the distance to the bay D. The object is to find the unobserved prices for the attributes so that the sums of these attribute values explain the value of the house. That is, the goal is to find the parameters a and b so that $P = a * S + b * D$. The **hedonic pricing method** explains the price of an item as a function of that item's attributes. Let's take a real example to see how this works.

The Chesapeake Bay is a large estuary between the states of Maryland and Virginia through which many major rivers flow into the Atlantic Ocean. Access to the bay influences property prices in the area. However, the bay is surrounded by urban and agricultural users. Their runoff, including sewage and fertilizer, pollutes the bay. Water quality in the bay also influences property prices. So does the nature of specific locations, such as access to roads that lead to major cities.

For Chesapeake Bay, economists Christopher Leggett and Nancy Bockstael examined the relationship between property values and a measure of water quality, fecal coliform contamination. Fecal coliform is a health hazard; it also can make water look and smell bad. To find the relationship, Leggett and Bockstael had to decompose property values into their component parts. Table 6.4 presents one of their regressions. The parameters for the factors in the table indicate the effect on property price of changing that factor by one unit. For instance, a property one mile farther to Baltimore than an otherwise identical property will have its property value lowered by approximately $9,000.

Notice in Table 6.4 that the parameter for fecal coliform concentration is a negative number; an increase in coliform concentration of 100 (an increase with potentially serious health effects) leads to a decrease of about $6,500 in property value (100 * −0.0656 gives the change in property value in thousands of dollars). In fact, if all properties in the study area met the water quality standard for fecal coliform, the associated benefit is estimated to be up to $12 million for one county in Maryland. In other words, the price for housing would go up due to this water quality improvement. The increase in property value becomes an approximate measure of the benefit of improving water quality, or reducing fecal coliform contamination, in this area.

Property values or housing prices, as determined by the interaction of those who happen to be buyers and sellers at a given time, offer an estimate of the value of cleaner water both to those buying and selling and to those currently owning homes. A person who buys a house after a coliform cleanup pays more than she would have

TABLE 6.4   Hedonic Price Equation for Housing Near Chesapeake Bay (Leggett & Bockstael). Dependent Variable: Market Price Minus Value of Structure (in $1,000s).

VARIABLE	PARAMETER
INTERCEPT	4445.8358
LOT SIZE (ACRES)	131.0783
LOT SIZE SQUARED	−8.4342
DISTANCE TO BALTIMORE (MILES)	−9.0215
DISTANCE TO ANNAPOLIS (MILES)	−17.0269
DISTANCE TO BALTIMORE × DISTANCE TO ANNAPOLIS (MILES SQUARED)	0.5333
DISTANCE TO BALTIMORE × % OF RESIDENTS WHO COMMUTE OUT OF COUNTY	−13.2027
% OF NEARBY LAND DENSELY DEVELOPED	325.6553
% OF NEARBY LAND OF LOW DENSITY	59.7778
% OF NEARBY AREA THAT'S WATER OR WETLANDS	275.9341
% OF NEARBY AREA OPEN SPACE	20.5546
SERVED BY PUBLIC SEWER?	−0.8928
INVERSE OF DISTANCE TO SOURCE WITH WATER DISCHARGE PERMIT (1/MILES)	−149.4962
INVERSE OF DISTANCE TO MARINA (1/MILES)	0.1445
INVERSE OF DISTANCE TO SEWAGE TREATMENT PLANT (1/MILES)	5.9401
FECAL COLIFORM CONCENTRATION (COUNTS PER 100 ML)	−0.0656

before the cleanup. This transaction also affects the property values of those holding onto their homes; because they have the ability to sell their homes, the change in housing value affects the opportunity cost of staying in their homes. Homebuyers reveal through their actions the value that they place on cleaner water.

HEDONIC PRICING EXPLAINED: WAGES

Many environmental and occupational safety activities involve reducing risks—for instance, reducing the risk of cancer through reduced air pollution or exposure to toxic substances. The estimate of workplace wage required to compensate someone for having a higher risk on the job reveals how individuals trade off safety for money. These tradeoffs reveal people's preferences for risk and safety. Because the hedonic pricing method can decompose a wage into its constituent parts, it can measure this tradeoff.

Consider a job in a convenience store in a nice neighborhood compared with working the same job at the same kind of store in a dangerous neighborhood. The same job skills are required, and the job likely has the same requirements, but the job in the dangerous neighborhood has a greater risk of robbery and thus more risk to a person's safety. If the wages are the same between the two jobs, most people would prefer working in the nice neighborhood due to the lower risk. Getting people to take the job in the dangerous neighborhood requires some incentive, such as higher pay. The additional risk influences the price of labor. The difference in wages for the dangerous and safe jobs tells how much the employees need to be paid to accept the danger.

Suppose, for instance, that the job in a safe neighborhood has a small risk of death, 1 in $10,000(10^{-4})$ each year. That probability means that, if 10,000 people all experienced the same conditions, on average 1 of them would die per year; or, if 5,000 people faced the risk, 1 would die every two years; or, if 1,000 people faced the risk, 1 person would die, on average, every 10 years. In contrast, suppose the job in the unsafe neighborhood had three times the risk $(3 * 10^{-4})$ of death each year. The company can get people to work in the unsafe neighborhood only by paying an extra \$1,000/year. Thus, some people will accept a risk increase of $2 * 10^{-4}$ in exchange for \$1,000. This process reveals how people trade off between risk and income.

People reveal in many ways—by very fast driving or smoking cigarettes, for instance—that they are willing to accept some risks in exchange for the benefits associated with the risks. A number of methods are used to measure how much risk people are willing to bear. For instance, suppose a water pollutant poses a risk of death of 2 people out of 1 million $(2 * 10^{-6})$ people exposed to it. Now suppose a filter is available to cut the risk of death in half, to 10^{-6}, and the city government asks residents to vote on a tax of \$10 per person to install the filter. If people vote for the tax, then they reveal that reducing the risk of death by 10^{-6} is worth at least \$10 to them; if they vote against it, they are willing to accept the (very small) risk to keep the money.

The **value of a statistical life (VSL)** is the willingness to pay to avoid a risk that would result in one more death in the population. In the job example, \$1,000 per year was necessary to accept a risk of $2 * 10^{-4}$; the VSL in this case is $\$1,000/(2 * 10^{-4}) = \$5\,million$. In the pollution example, \$10 per person would reduce the risk by 10^{-6}; the VSL is $\$10/10^{-6} = \$10\,million$. While the VSL is sometimes called the value of a human life, it is a poor name for a more subtle concept, the willingness to pay for risk reduction.

The value of a statistical life associated with a risk reduction is often derived from hedonic wage models because these measure how people in practice trade off increased risk for increased wage. The fact that people reveal their wage–risk tradeoff from actual behavior, rather than from what people say that they might do, provides increased credibility to the results.

BOX 6.2

Mortality Risk by Industry and Age

There are very large differences in the chance of a fatal accident for workers of different occupations and ages. Transportation workers aged 55 to 64 have the highest chance of death; 25 are killed per million workers per year. Laborers, who include workers in construction, the most dangerous industry, are second, with a risk of death (for those ages 55 to 64) of 15 per million workers per year. Executives, clerical workers, professionals, and machine operators all have death risks below 5 per million per year. At age 20–24, the risk for transportation workers is only 12 per million, and for laborers only 6 per million. Clearly there is a significant difference in the risk of death by occupation and also by age.

Using this information on the differences in mortality and accidents by occupation, and information on wages, economists Joseph Aldy and Kip Viscusi used hedonic regression to find the value of a statistical life. The implied value of a statistical life for a 28-year-old was over $5 million, while the value for a 51-year-old was only $2.5 million. In general, they found that the value of a statistical life increased from age 18 to approximately 30 and declined afterward.

These figures represent the tradeoffs people make in their job choices; they indicate how much people with more risky jobs must be compensated to take those jobs. When people are older, they have less time left to live; the evidence here suggests that their willingness to pay for risk reduction may decrease as they get older. The results in other studies find a less straightforward relationship between age and the value of a statistical life.

In 2003, the U.S. Office of Management and Budget proposed that the value of a statistical life for people over 70 years old be lower than the value used for younger people. Public resistance to the "senior death discount," as the different value became known, led to withdrawal of that proposal.

ISSUES IN USING THE HEDONIC PRICING METHOD

Just as with the travel cost method, it is important to understand both the power and the limits of the hedonic pricing method. Both hedonic property price models and hedonic wage models must be interpreted with care. Supply and demand processes determine both property prices and wages. The regression models take into account the effects of both supply and demand. Not only are consumers willing to pay more for a house with better characteristics; producers also face greater expenses to make those houses. The higher price for a more desirable house thus includes both cost effects and demand effects. The changes in prices and wages predicted by changing an environmental quality or risk variable cannot identify exactly how consumers alone will trade off environmental quality and money because the estimates include both sides of the market. Nevertheless, these values can sometimes be interpreted as upper or lower bounds on the consumer benefit associated with a change in environmental quality.

Also, like travel cost, hedonic property price models do not include benefits to those not in the market being studied. For instance, recreational users of Chesapeake Bay who do not live in the area would also benefit from improved water quality, but the hedonic property price analysis does not measure those benefits. Additionally, as with travel cost, the estimate does not include non-users who benefit from the existence of the area without actually using it. If these other benefits are expected to be important for an area, then hedonic property price analysis likely provides an underestimate of the total benefit associated with an environmental improvement.

The use of hedonic wage analysis or any other methods to estimate the value of a statistical life feeds into morally and politically charged debates. Can protecting a human life, even if only from a probability of a risk, be converted into a dollar value? It is true that people behave as though there are amounts they would not be willing to pay to reduce risk. For instance, many people do not wear bicycle helmets, which reduce the risk associated with riders cracking open their skulls if they have accidents; they give a wide variety of reasons for this decision. Thus, people do not put infinite values on their own lives (or everyone would cover themselves in bubble wrap, or avoid getting out of bed). Nevertheless, the ethical implications of calculating the value associated with those tradeoffs are huge. If people willingly put themselves at risk to earn a higher salary, or to avoid some costs, should society accept that they are the best judges of those choices? In a society with finite resources, where it is impossible to reduce all risks, how do we decide which risks to reduce? Should voluntary risks, such as whether to wear a bicycle helmet, be viewed differently from involuntary risks, such as breathing dirty air? While there is no question that people face tradeoffs between money and risks all the time, and sometimes choose money over safety, how we use that information is more complex than the calculation itself.

IN SUMMARY

- The price of goods, particularly housing and labor, is explainable by the attributes of the good. Regression analysis is used to find the hedonic prices, the amount by which the value of a good increases when an attribute increases by one unit. The value of these attributes provides information about the value of environmental goods, including on-job risks, distance to recreation sites, and water quality.
- Hedonic property price analysis has been used to estimate a wide variety of characteristics of a neighborhood, including the value of improved air or water quality or proximity to parks.
- Hedonic wage analysis has been used to examine how people trade off job risks and wages. If people are willing to accept a higher wage in exchange for an increased risk, then it is possible to estimate the value of a statistical life, the value of reducing the likelihood of one death due to the risk.

- Like travel cost estimates, hedonic price estimates do not include the value of an environmental good to people who are not in the markets. Nevertheless, as revealed preference estimates, they also have the credibility associated with people paying real money for improved environmental quality.
- Although hedonic wage models estimate the value of a statistical life, what those estimates mean and how they are used involve complex moral and political issues. While economic methods allow estimation of these values, they are not the exclusive guides to how to use them.

Averting Behavior: Estimating Willingness to Pay for Avoiding Environmental Damages

Even if sewage or toxics leak into water, people can avoid getting sick from it. While a consumer would always prefer no contamination in the first place, she can still defend herself when there is contamination. In the case of drinking water, there are many technology choices. Buying bottled water or using a water filter to avoid contaminated tap water is an example of *averting behavior*. The water is polluted, but a person avoids getting sick by not drinking it. One way to find out how much people are willing to pay to have the water cleaned up is to see how much they pay to avoid the contaminated water. The **averting behavior** approach uses individual or household expenditures on risk reduction to estimate the value of environmental improvements to the households.

AVERTING BEHAVIOR EXPLAINED

The simplest case of averting behavior is the case above: there is harm, and there is a single action that averts the harm. Bad water's consequences are averted by bottled water. When a consumer uses bottled water, it must be worth at least the cost of the water to the consumer to avoid the risk, but it may be worth more than the value of the water. The amount that she spent avoiding the risk is only a lower bound on the harm; the cost of the harm may be greater.

What happens when the harm cannot be completely eliminated or when there are many possible ways to avoid the harm? Car accidents can be prevented in many ways. A driver can buckle up, buy a car with more than the required two airbags, drive carefully, drive *really* sober—the Swedish 0.02 blood alcohol, not the American 0.08—and so on. Each of these averting activities has a cost. How much cost is the driver willing to incur in order to avert harm?

The consumer will start with the least-cost practices, such as buckling her seat belt and driving sober; for those, the harm avoided is very likely to exceed the cost. As she considers more expensive steps, such as buying a new, safer car, the harm avoided is likely to be lower; she will think more carefully about whether the benefits in terms of risk reduction outweigh those costs. The last measure that she does will probably have benefits that barely outweigh the costs. Because she considered the earlier steps clearly worth doing, though, the total amount she spent on averting behavior is lower than the benefit she got for risk aversion. Thus, the cost of averting behavior is generally an underestimate of the value of the risk avoided. Nevertheless, it provides some information on the value of what is otherwise a nonmarket good.

In 1987, residents of Perkasie, Pennsylvania, faced contamination of their drinking water and exposure to vapor in their homes from trichloroethylene (TCE), a toxic chemical. The TCE was left by Stainless, Inc., and was part of its former industrial activities. In response, many of those residents bought bottled water or water filters, boiled their water, or hauled water from elsewhere. Economists Abdalla, Roach, and Epp found that the costs associated with these activities were estimated to average between $22 and $48 per household during the 21-month contamination period. Awareness of the risk appears to have played a role in their decision to undertake averting behavior but not in their decision of how much averting behavior to conduct; instead, the major determinant of how much people spent on averting behavior was whether they had young children in the house.

In another example, residents of the area around Pusan on the Nak-Dong River in Korea faced industrial pollutants in the early 1990s. Almost every person took steps to avoid drinking untreated river water. By 1996, water quality was greatly improved and met safety standards in all but about 2 percent of samples. Despite that improvement, people still undertook risk-avoidance measures. They did so for two reasons: (1) They believed the river water was still unsafe even though it wasn't. (2) They found the taste and amount of suspended solids unappealing. Mi-Jung Um, Seung-Jun Kwak, and Tai-Yoo Kim interviewed 256 households about their averting behavior and found that households were willing to pay $4.10 to $6.10 per household per month to improve water quality. This valuation was based on people's perceptions of how dangerous the river water was. When the interviewees were informed about the true state of the river, they said they would take fewer averting actions, and their willingness to pay fell to $0.70 to $1.70 per household per month. So averting behavior measures perceived harm and not necessarily actual harm.

In both Pusan and Pennsylvania, people perceived an environmental risk. Also in both cases, many people undertook actions to avoid the risk. Economists expect that, when people pay money for an environmental improvement, the improvement must be worth at least as much as the amount that they paid. If it is possible to estimate how expenditures change when the risk changes, the result estimates the value of avoiding risk. The benefit associated with averting expenditures typically provides a lower bound (a minimum) estimate on the benefit associated with avoiding a risk.

ISSUES IN USING THE AVERTING BEHAVIOR METHOD

Difficulties with the averting behavior method start with measurement. The method relies on comparing the costs of reducing a risk, or improving environmental quality, and the change in environmental quality. Both may be difficult to measure in practice. It may not be clear, for instance, how much of an increase in quality is associated with boiling water or installing a water filter. Additionally, as the Korean example suggests, people's views of the risk involved, as well as the reduction in risk, may not be scientifically accurate. It is a challenge to decide which estimate of the change in risk—what consumers believe or what scientists say is true—is appropriate to measuring the environmental change.

Additionally, some measures, such as purchasing water, involve time as well as money. As a result, how the cost of time should be added into the cost of the risk reduction can pose similar problems to those associated with the travel cost method.

Often, averting behaviors have a purpose in addition to reducing an environmental risk. Using an air conditioner, for example, both reduces exposure to outdoor air pollutants and cools a house. Researchers then have to decide how much of the use of the air conditioner to attribute to the desire to breathe cleaner air. Similarly, many people buy bottled water for convenience or taste, not because the water supply is unsafe. In that case, the challenge is to separate out the portion of the cost that is specific to reducing risk. Despite these issues, because people demonstrate a demand for the environmental benefit by paying to get it, this market activity provides a signal of the value of environmental quality.

IN SUMMARY

- The averting behavior method measures individual household response to an environmental risk. If a person undertakes a risk-reducing approach, the benefit associated with that action must exceed the cost. The cost of the risk-averting behavior is a lower bound estimate on the value of the environmental harm.
- Aversion is a response to perceived risk, which may be different from actual risk of harm.
- Difficulties with using this method center on problems in measuring both the change in the environmental risk and the price of the risk reduction activity.

Revealed Preference Methods in Perspective

Environmental policy debates very commonly use revealed preference methods. For instance, parks often collect information on the origins of visitors to their sites to demonstrate the importance (value) of their site. They can use that information to justify increased budgets for maintenance, park rangers, and other tourist support at the site. The U.S. Environmental Protection Agency uses hedonic wage models to estimate the benefits associated with reducing the risks to human life and health associated with improved air and water quality. These estimates of benefits are critical for assessing the net gains to society from various activities.

The revealed preference methods have the significant advantage that they are based on actual human behavior. People in these cases are actually showing their preferences by how they spend their money. Talk is cheap; other people may not put much credence in the intensity of concern for the environment if it is only in words. If, instead, money changes hands as a demonstration of environmental concern, the words are now backed with deeds, and those words are much harder to ignore.

At the same time, it is important to keep in mind what exactly the revealed preference methods measure. They are quite powerful for measuring use value—the value associated with recreation in an area or with a scenic vista from a home, for instance—even if methodological problems might arise. They only measure use values, though. If people care about environmental goods that they do not directly use—for instance, if they care about protection of ecosystems they never intend to visit because they are concerned about protection of biodiversity—the revealed preference methods will not capture those values. Those values and their measurement are the subject of the next chapter.

CHAPTER SUMMARY

Here are the key lessons from this chapter:

- Many environmental goods have use value; consumers undertake observable actions showing their interest in the environmental goods.
- Regression analysis finds the best fitting line to observed data. One of its uses is to estimate the parameters of demand curves for goods with use value.
- The travel cost method is based on finding an association between visitation to an area and the cost of getting to that area. That information can be used to trace out a demand curve for recreational activity at a site.
- Hedonic pricing finds how a market price—typically either property values or wages—is related to the attributes of the good. Attributes of housing include proximity to recreation, air quality, size of house, and so on. Attributes of work include location, risk of death, required skill level, and so on. How the good's price changes when an environmental attribute changes provides an estimate of the value of the environmental attribute.
- Expenditures on averting behavior provide direct evidence of people spending money to reduce environmental harm. These expenditures are used to estimate the benefits from harm reduction.
- Revealed preference approaches have the distinct advantage that they are based on actual behavior. They provide strong evidence of environmental concern because people are giving up their money and time for environmental protection. At the same time, they do not measure any benefits that are not associated with the specific uses that they measure.

KEY TERMS

averting behavior *(p. 128)*

dependent variable *(p. 116)*

error series *(p. 116)*

hedonic pricing method *(p. 123)*

independent variables *(p. 116)*

least squares regression *(p. 116)*

non-use value *(p. 112)*

parameters *(p. 114)*

passive use value *(p. 112)*

predicted value *(p. 115)*

regression *(p. 114)*

regression analysis *(p. 114)*

revealed preferences *(p. 112)*

revealed preference methods *(p. 112)*

stated preference methods *(p. 112)*

travel cost method (TCM) *(p. 117)*

use value *(p. 112)*

value of a statistical life (VSL) *(p. 125)*

variable *(p. 114)*

NOTES

The story on New Bedford Harbor is from the National Oceanographic and Atmospheric Administration, http://www.darp.noaa.gov/northeast/new_bedford/index.html. The settlement is described in "$21 Million Pact in Harbor PCB-Pollution Suit," *New York Times*, September 6, 1992, p. 28. The entire data set for beach use at Fort Point Beach can be found at http://www-agecon.ag.ohio-state.edu/people/haab.1/bookweb/newbedford_data.htm. A particularly observant reviewer might notice that this example does not actually use revealed preference data: McConnell asked people how they would respond to beach cleanup, not how they actually did respond. We used this example because of the simplicity of the example and the easy availability of the data.

Harold Hotelling of the Department of Mathematical Statistics, University of North Carolina, wrote his letter to Mr. Newton B. Drury, Director of the National Park Service, on June 18, 1947.

The effect of fecal coliform on property value is from Christopher Leggett and Nancy Bockstael, "Evidence of the Effects of Water Quality on Residential Land Prices," *Journal of Environmental Economics and Management* 39 (2000): 121–144. The role of age in the value of a statistical life is from Joseph E. Aldy and W. Kip Viscusi, "Age Variations in Workers' Value of Statistical Life," National Bureau of Economic Research, Inc., Working Paper 10199 (2004).

The story of TCE in Pennsylvania is from Charles W. Abdalla, Brian A. Roach, and Donald J. Epp, "Valuing Environmental Quality Changes Using Averting Expenditures: An Application to Groundwater Contamination," *Land Economics* 68(2) (May 1992): 163–169.

The example of water pollution in Korea is from Mi-Jung Um, Seung-Jun Kwak, and Tai-Yoo Kim, "Estimating Willingness to Pay for Improved Drinking Water Quality Using Averting Behavior Method with Perception Measure," *Environmental and Resource Economics* 21 (2002): 287–302.

EXERCISES

1. The methods of nonmarket valuation can be used for situations that do not involve environmental goods. For instance, consider pizza from different places. Prices differ, and the nature of the pizza differs as well—some have better-quality ingredients than others, crust styles differ, and the amount of sauce varies. Which of the methods described in this chapter might be used to look at the effects of different quality factors on the price of pizza?

2. The following table gives information on visitors to Jellybear Park:

CITY OF ORIGIN	POPULATION	DISTANCE (IN MILES)
ALABASTER	1,000	1
BEAUTIFUL	3,000	3
CORNUCOPIA	5,000	5
DELIGHT	7,000	7

   A researcher keeps careful track of visitors to Jellybear and learns that there is a total of 3,750 visits to the park in one year. The only cost of traveling to the park is mileage, at $1/mile. The researcher estimates the relationship between costs and number of visits per capita (per person) to be Visits per capita = 1 − 0.15 * One-way cost.
   (a) Add columns to this table identifying total costs of a visit from each place, visits per capita from each town, and the total number of visits from each town (the visits per capita multiplied by the population).
   (b) Why doesn't the researcher observe anyone coming from Delight to Jellybear?
   (c) If getting to the park is the only cost associated with a visit (there is no admission price), how many people in total visit Jellybear? Start a table with one column showing admission price (in this case, $0) and another showing total visits.
   (d) Because of management costs, park managers are considering charging for admission to Jellybear. They are considering prices ranging from $1/visit to $5/visit. For each whole dollar value between $1 and $5 per visit, figure out (i) the new cost of visiting for each town, (ii) the new number of visits per capita from each town, (iii) the new number of visits from each town, and (iv) the total visits (remember that negative visits do not exist; they count as zero).
   (e) Put the information on admission price and total visits in the table from (c). This table shows the relationship between admission price and total number of visits. What is it?
   (f) Estimate the consumer surplus associated with visiting Jellybear Park when the admission fee is $0. (It will be an approximate value because the relationship in (e) is not a straight line.)
   (g) What method did you use to estimate the value of visits to Jellybear Park? Why?

3. Two companies require identical skills and training from their workers. Both employ 10,000 people. On average, Safety First has one worker fatality per year, while Safety Second has two worker fatalities per year. Jobs at Safety First pay $50,000/year, while jobs at Safety Second pay $50,500/year.
   (a) Why do these jobs with identical requirements pay different salaries, based on the information presented here?

(b) What is the risk for a worker of a fatal accident at each company? What is the pay premium associated with the higher risk?

(c) The value of a statistical life is the difference in wage divided by the difference in risk. What is the value of a statistical life for workers with these skills and training?

(d) Do you expect this value of a statistical life to be appropriate for the population as a whole? Why or why not?

4. The effects of averting behavior can be complicated by the fact that the pollution is nonrival and nonexclusive (it affects everyone), while the averting behavior is typically private (only the person spending the money benefits). Suppose drinking water quality for everyone is improved (for instance, by cleaning up a toxic spill). Are averting expenditures on water filters likely to increase or decrease in response to the pollution cleanup? If the water filter continues to reduce risk by the same amount, will the benefit measured by the averting behavior method be the same as when water quality was worse? If the value changes, does this mean that the measured benefit is a highly variable number (and therefore more likely to be questioned), or is there a reason that we would expect expenditures to change when the risk is different?

5. Could a revealed preference method other than travel cost have been used in the Bedford Harbor case to estimate the effects of contamination? Explain how hedonic pricing or averting behavior approaches might have been used, or why they would not have worked.

Stated Preference Methods

Many people express great concern about protecting endangered species and their habitats without ever seeing the species or visiting the area. For example, many people who live outside the tropics and don't travel to the region want to protect tropical rainforests. Chapter 6 discussed one set of nonmarket valuation methods, those that rely on revealed preferences to estimate the value from using an environmental good. Those methods require that the environmental good be connected to a marketed good; a consumer's demand for that marketed good provides information about the consumer's preference for the environmental good. For many environmental goods, though, there may not be a connection to a market good. This chapter will examine:

- Non-use (also known as passive-use) values of environmental goods;
- Contingent valuation, a survey method used to estimate non-use and use values based on stated preferences;
- Conjoint analysis: another stated preference method;
- Experimental economics methods, which explore how people respond to market and nonmarket situations;
- Objections and responses to "assigning price tags" to the environment;
- Strengths and limitations of stated preference methods.

The Exxon Valdez and Prince William Sound

Prince William Sound is located in southern Alaska, east of Anchorage. Surrounded by the Chugach Mountains, it contains spectacular scenery, diverse habitats, glaciers, and a tremendous variety of wildlife, both terrestrial and marine. All of these natural resources attract tourists, who take cruises through the area. Prince William Sound also contains the port of Valdez, the southern end of a pipeline that carries oil from Prudhoe Bay, in northern Alaska. At the port of Valdez, the oil is transferred to tankers that then take it to the lower 48 states.

On March 24, 1989, a tanker called the Exxon Valdez hit a reef in Prince William Sound. The result was a spill of 11 million gallons of oil, the largest tanker spill to occur in the United States. The oil coated beaches and animals, resulting in the deaths of sea otters, birds, seals, killer whales, and fish eggs. The state of Alaska and the U.S. government not only required Exxon to clean up the spill, which cost the company more than $2 billion, but they also sued to recover the damages to natural resources. What were those damages? Certainly the fishing and tourism industries were hurt substantially by the spill. In addition, people around the country and the world watched pictures of the spill; did they have a stake in the outcome?

Non-Use Values of Environmental Goods

It is possible to estimate the use values of environmental goods (such as recreation or health) by looking at the effects on related markets of changing the environmental good. In many cases, though, people care deeply about environmental goods even when they do not intend to make use of them. In some of these situations, people's behavior provides information about their concern for the environment. For instance, people may write letters to policy makers, or they may send money to environmental organizations that promise to work for protection of the resources. However, in many cases, people may care even though they do not take action. They might, if asked, be willing to pay to protect the environment. Because these people do not make active use of the goods they seek to protect, these values are non-use values. Non-use values can take several forms.

In some cases, people clearly have no intention of making use of the resource. They may dislike going to remote areas, for instance, and thus have no interest at all in going to see Prince William Sound. Nevertheless, some of these people may place *existence value* on the resource: they care about its existence regardless of any potential use of the resource. They may care about an area out of appreciation for the intricacies of ecological systems, for instance, or they may feel that it is important to preserve all ecosystems and species because of a belief that all creations and creatures are here for a reason. **Existence value** is the term for preferences for environmental goods from which people never intend to experience a use value.

In other cases, someone not using a resource in the present may intend to use it in the future. He may be willing to pay to protect the possibility of future use. In other words, he wants the option to use the resource later. An **option** is the right, but not the obligation, to do something. For instance, a concert ticket conveys the right to attend a concert, but it does not obligate the owner to go to the concert if he becomes sick the day of the concert or reads an unfavorable review and decides not to go after all. In financial markets, options convey the right (but not the obligation) to buy something at a known price, such as the right to buy 1,000 barrels of oil for delivery next December at a price of $50/barrel. A person who is willing to pay to keep open the possibility of visiting a pristine Prince William Sound has option value for the area.

One reason to protect ecosystems, such as rainforests, is that they may be important sources for marketable products. Another reason is that the existence value of an ecosystem may become much greater in the future; for instance, few nonnative Americans valued the existence of prairie ecosystems during pioneer times, but many modern Americans place great value on the diminished amount of undisturbed prairie that remains. Preservation makes it possible at a future date to decide either to continue to preserve the habitat or to convert it to some other use. Thus, preservation has option value because it provides the option to have the resource in the future. Indeed, preservation provides the ability to decide the fate of the resource in the future, after time has allowed greater learning about the future value of the resource in both its protected and developed forms.

Finally, many people may place a *bequest value* on an environmental good. A bequest is a gift to a future generation; **bequest value** is the amount that someone would be willing to pay to be able to provide future generations with a good. While individuals of the present may not care about the resource directly, they may wish to keep it available as a bequest. In some ways, bequest value is a special case of existence value because it is protection for a good that the current generation does not intend to use. In other ways, it is a special case of option value because it preserves options for use (and non-use) values for future generations.

For most purposes, it is not important to distinguish which of these values people place on environmental goods. It *is* important to know that people who do not make direct or indirect use of an environmental good may nevertheless have demand for the good. Because there is unlikely to be any explicit market-related behavior for this armchair environmentalism, the revealed preference measures of Chapter 6 will not measure these values. Instead, economists have focused on, in essence, asking people about the values they place on these goods. Because these questions typically involve, not direct observation of people using the resource, but rather people's expressions of their desires, this approach is called stated preference: that is, people state their preferences for these goods.

IN SUMMARY

- Non-use or passive-use values for environmental goods are those desires for environmental protection that have no uses of the resource associated with them.
- These values include existence value (protecting a resource purely because a person believes it is worth protecting); option value (protecting a resource for the possibility of using it in the future); and bequest value (protecting a resource so that future generations can either use or preserve the resource).
- Stated preferences are the values that people say that they place on goods.

Measuring Stated Preferences Using the Contingent Valuation Method

At this point it should be clear that it is not necessary to use a resource to care about it. Indeed, many public opinion polls indicate that people have strong opinions about various environmental goods, such as the Arctic National Wildlife Refuge in far northern Alaska, or tropical rainforests in the Amazon Basin, that they are unlikely to use directly. To measure not only whether they care about the good but also how much they care about it, the important question is to estimate how much they are willing to give up to protect it. It is through that willingness to sacrifice other goods or other activities in order to protect the good that people signal the importance they place on the good. However, most people who have non-use values for environmental goods do not spend money to prevent wildlife in Prince William Sound being killed in an oil spill or to protect tropical rainforests. Is their desire for environmental protection "cheap talk," or would they "put their money where their mouths are" to increase protection?

Answering this question is difficult because people are not used to thinking about what they would give up to protect environmental resources. They may think that the money to protect these resources should come from those harming the resources or from government. (Indirectly, though, consumers are likely to pay these costs, either through increased costs of goods—for instance, gasoline prices might increase due to the higher costs of shipping oil in a manner that prevents spills—or higher taxes to pay for government expenditures.) Also, they are unlikely to have experience with paying for environmental protection because these are public goods and are not purchased in markets. As a result, it may be difficult for people to think in a meaningful way about what they would give up to protect a resource.

The *contingent valuation method (CVM)* has been developed, starting in the 1960s, specifically to tackle the problems involved in estimating non-use values. (It also can be used to estimate use values.) Because there is no market-related action to be observed for non-use values, the **contingent valuation method** uses surveys to ask people questions designed to identify what they are willing to give up to protect a resource. The surveys present at least two possible outcomes for the resource. One outcome is generally what would happen if no further conservation action were taken. The other outcomes are generally what might happen if a government or a private group were to undertake a program that would protect the resource. A CVM survey asks people if they would pay a particular price, or how much they would pay, to achieve one outcome rather than another. The responses to the survey are contingent on the hypothetical scenarios presented; that is what gives the method its name.

A CVM survey typically includes background information on the resource, so that people can make informed decisions about its future. For instance, Richard Carson and others conducted a CVM survey to estimate the damages from the Exxon Valdez. It began by describing Prince William Sound in a manner similar to the beginning of this chapter, but in more detail. The assumption is that people will understand the tradeoffs better if they understand all sides of the issue. The background information often includes questions about whether there might be too much or too little funding going to a variety of government programs, so that the person answering the survey is thinking consciously about real monetary expenditures.

Then the survey describes the possible outcomes. In the case of the Exxon Valdez survey, the outcomes were the status quo and a specific program to prevent future spills by escorting oil tankers with two ships that would be capable of containing spills. Box 7.1 contains a description of that survey and excerpts from it.

BOX 7.1

The Exxon Valdez Questionnaire

The survey questionnaire used to estimate damages in the Exxon Valdez contingent valuation study starts by asking if we should spend more or less money on programs such as foreign aid, crime, energy, and education. It also asks about the respondent's attitudes to general policy goals such as drug treatment, air pollution, taxes, and setting aside more land for wilderness areas. These questions seek to ensure that the respondent is thinking about uses of money other than stopping oil spills; in this way, the respondent is likely to keep budget tradeoffs in mind when answering the willingness-to-pay question.

Next, to acquaint the respondent with the area around the accident and with the facts of the accident itself, the questionnaire asks about oil spills. The interviewer reads a script that says 11 million gallons of oil were spilled in Prince William Sound. The interviewer then shows the respondent several maps of Alaska, the oil pipeline from Prudhoe Bay to Prince William Sound, and maps of the Sound. The interview continues with descriptions and pictures of the spill and its effects. The effects included 1,000 miles of shoreline covered in oil, 100,000 dead birds (including one of the area's 5,000 eagles), 580 dead otters, and 100 dead seals.

Only after the survey has encouraged the respondent to think about budget tradeoffs and has provided information about the oil spill does it describe the proposed safety program for tankers:

Here's how the program would work.

Two large Coast Guard ships specially designed for Alaskan waters will escort each tanker from Valdez all the way through Prince William Sound until they get to the open sea. These escort ships will do two things.

First, they will help prevent an accident in the Sound by making it very unlikely that a tanker will stray into dangerous waters. (PAUSE)

Second, if an accident does occur, the escort ships will carry the trained crew and special equipment necessary to keep even a very large spill from spreading beyond the tanker. (PAUSE)

The interviewer shows pictures of the safety apparatus and describes the safety program in more detail.

(Continued)

BOX 7.1

continued

Next, the interviewer explains the method of paying for the safety program. Half of the payment would come from industry profits, and half would come from a tax on individuals. The tax is the amount that the respondent should believe she is paying for the program.

To reduce any influence of the interviewer's manner on the respondent's answers, the interviewer reminds the respondent that there are good reasons to vote for and against the tax and protection scheme. Only after all these efforts to ensure that the respondent answers honestly is she finally asked the willingness-to-pay question:

> At present, government officials estimate the program will cost your household a total of $60. You would pay this in a special one time charge in addition to your regular federal taxes. This money would only be used for the program to prevent damage from another large oil spill in Prince William Sound. (PAUSE)

> If the program cost your household a total of $60, would you vote for the program or against it?

The interview continues with a set of questions to see how well the interviewee understood the program and the consequences of not having a safety program. This "debriefing section" is intended to see if the respondent really is answering the questions that the interviewer is asking.

Finally, the survey asks questions designed to see how much the respondent is involved with nature or with Alaska. Bird watchers, for instance, might be expected to place a higher value on the oil safety program than others would. These questions are used to explore how a person's preferences affect his answer to the willingness-to-pay question.

The whole Exxon Valdez questionnaire is available via a link from Richard Carson's home page at http://weber.ucsd.edu/~rcarson/.

In the aftermath of the accident, the United States did put in place a safety program much like that described in the questionnaire. In one case, an escort ship did steer a tanker away from the rocks and prevent a spill.

Respondents are then asked a question about their willingness to pay (WTP) for the described program to protect the resource. This question can be asked in several ways. First, it can be asked as an open-ended question, such as, "How much would you be willing to pay?" Respondents may also be asked to check off an amount from a list of values, often termed a payment card, or to give a yes or no response to a specific value, such as, "Would you be willing to pay $50 to protect the resource?" The last approach is considered the most reliable because the respondent has to make a clear choice about a specific payment. It is often referred to as the referendum format because the respondent might be asked, "If there were a vote on whether to pay $50 to protect the resource, would you vote YES or NO?" Different survey respondents are asked to pay different amounts, so that those conducting the survey can estimate how high the payment would have to be to get people to say "no"—that is, their maximum WTP. Box 7.2 shows some of the data for a different survey, on removing Argo Dam in Ann Arbor, Michigan.

BOX 7.2

Data from a Contingent Valuation Survey: Argo Dam and Pond in Ann Arbor, Michigan

The city of Ann Arbor, Michigan, has been discussing whether to remove Argo Dam on the Huron River. At this time, the only use of the dam is to create a pond actively used by rowers. While the rowers strongly want to keep the dam in place, local environmental groups are interested in removing it to improve riverine ecology and provide river-based recreational opportunities. A survey conducted by graduate students at the University of Michigan asked people's attitudes toward the dam. Following are some answers to the question, "Would you vote YES or NO on the Argo Dam removal proposal with an added cost to you of $XX per year in property taxes (or rent)?"

The columns of Table 7.1 are (1) the subject's identification number, (2) the amount the subject was asked to pay, and (3) whether the subject said yes or no to the "are you willing to pay" question. The amount that each subject was asked to pay was selected randomly from a set of possible values. Table 7.1 shows how people's answers to the willingness-to-pay question changed as the payment requested changed. See http://sitemaker.umich.edu/argoproject for further details.

TABLE 7.1 Argo Pond and Dam Survey.
This table shows a few of the data from the willingness-to-pay survey.

RESPONDENT #	PRICE ASKED	ANSWER
1	$ 70	yes
2	$450	no
3	$ 25	yes
4	$ 70	yes
5	$450	yes
6	$800	no
7	$150	no

A critical part of the question is how the payment is to be made. For instance, a person might be asked if he would be willing to contribute to a fund to protect the resource, or to face increased taxes or reductions in other government activities, or to pay an increase in the cost of a good related to the resource, such as an increase in the price of gasoline associated with reducing oil tanker spills. The method of payment is called a payment vehicle. Many people respond as much to the payment vehicle as they do to the amount to be paid; for instance, people may say "no" because they don't believe in increasing taxes. The choice of payment vehicle must be made very carefully to make the payment vehicle represent a realistic possibility.

Often the respondent is asked why he answered as he did. These debriefing questions help to ensure that he understood the question and to determine whether something unexpected is influencing his choice. Sometimes people reject the premise of the question: for instance, they may feel that Exxon should pay the full costs of cleaning up the spill from the Exxon Valdez, and they should not have to bear any expenses. Responses that indicate a rejection of the underlying premise of the survey are called protest responses. These "protest" responses do not mean that the person does not care about the resource but that he is responding to something else in the question.

Finally, the survey usually asks demographic questions about the person, such as his education level, family status, income, and attitude toward environmental and other issues. These personal characteristics may be associated with preferences, and they affect a person's decisions on WTP. They assist in determining how a person's characteristics affect his choices.

Now, the survey data provide information on respondents' WTP for the environmental good. The next step is to use those responses to estimate the overall value of the good, or the total benefits that the good provides. This process can happen in several ways. If an open-ended question or payment card is used, then it is possible to estimate the total benefit by the following steps: calculate the average WTP from the survey results and multiply that value by the total affected population. This method works well if the people sampled are considered representative of the entire affected population—that is, if the survey group has a mix of demographic factors such as income and education that is similar to the population from which the survey respondents were selected. If the people sampled are not necessarily representative, it may nevertheless be possible to use statistical methods to estimate the relationship between WTP and demographic characteristics; the survey data might show, for example, that people with a higher level of education or income are willing to pay a maximum amount that is greater, on average, than people with less education. The average WTP can then be adjusted for those characteristics.

The referendum format asks a person to respond yes or no to being willing to pay one specific value; that value is likely to be either higher or lower than his maximum WTP. With a large enough sample of people, though, methods outlined in the appendix to this chapter can provide an estimate of the average maximum WTP per person (or household), which can then be multiplied by the number of affected people (or households) to get the total WTP.

In the case of the Exxon Valdez, the contingent valuation survey initially estimated a median household WTP of $30: that is, of all the English-speaking households in the United States (from which they drew their sample), about half would be willing to pay more, and about half would be willing to pay less, than $30 to avoid future oil spills. (The median value—the number in the middle of the data—produced a lower value than the mean, or average, because of some very high values in the sample that affect the average more than the median.) However, some survey respondents misinterpreted the nature and effectiveness of the program proposed to reduce oil spills. After adjusting for these misunderstandings, as well as for protest votes, the median WTP was estimated at $48/household. When multiplied by the total number of English-speaking households, their most conservative median estimate of the damages associated with the Exxon Valdez oil spill ($30/household) was $4.9 billion. Using the average WTP instead of the median produced an estimated value of $7.2 billion.

IN SUMMARY

- Contingent valuation uses surveys to ask people's preferences on the tradeoff between a change in environmental quality and monetary payments. The goal is to determine, on average, the maximum amount that respondents are willing to pay for the environmental quality change.
- The surveys typically include background information on the environmental issue, possible outcomes if a change is made, a question that asks the survey respondent about willingness to pay for the environmental change, and demographic information about the respondent.
- Contingent valuation can be used in a wide variety of situations because of its hypothetical nature, and it is a primary method to capture non-use values as well as use values of environmental goods.

Conjoint Analysis

Suppose that researchers wanted to investigate different possible levels of risk reduction for oil transport in southeast Alaska, or the relative effects of reducing those risks in multiple locations. A contingent valuation study involves either/or scenarios: the respondent can vote in favor of the measure to reduce oil spills, or not. In contrast, **conjoint analysis** asks people to choose among several scenarios. The scenarios differ in characteristics or attributes. These attributes could include cost, level of cleanup, and risk reduction. Conjoint analysis has its origins in marketing research, where it is used to identify combinations of features that consumers want, and are willing to pay for, in new products. When a researcher wants to understand the tradeoffs someone might make among different levels of an attribute, or different combinations of attributes, conjoint analysis is an increasingly used method. In a conjoint analysis survey, the respondent is asked to rate each scenario, to rank the scenarios from most preferred to least preferred, or to choose the most desirable scenario. Statistical analysis can then estimate how consumers trade off one attribute for another.

For instance, if the Exxon Valdez researchers had wanted to examine willingness to pay for different levels of risk reduction, Consumer A may have been asked to choose between Scenario 1 (no risk reduction, no additional cost), Scenario 2 (some risk reduction, higher cost), and Scenario 3 (high risk reduction, highest cost). The scenario could be even more complex: each scenario might include different locations of the oil tankers, to see whether people's willingness to pay varied with location. As in contingent valuation, by varying the costs that different consumers face, it is possible to estimate how a consumer trades off money for oil spill risks or location.

Prairie gardens are an alternative for Midwest lawns that have ecological advantages. Gloria Helfand and others used conjoint analysis to estimate people's willingness to pay for different amounts of prairie gardens using native plants in a suburban-style yard and to see how people viewed these arrangements relative to more traditional lawns. Previous research showed that it was possible to design lawns with prairie gardens in ways that people found attractive; this study sought to estimate whether people liked these alternative designs enough to pay for them. People were shown simulations of a conventional yard, a yard with 50 percent prairie garden, a yard with 75 percent prairie garden, and a yard with 75 percent prairie garden plus trees and shrubs, each with a different price; they then ranked their choices. The analysis showed that willingness to pay was highest for the 75 percent prairie garden option and outweighed any additional costs over a conventional yard. The research concluded that people are willing to pay for carefully designed prairie gardens in their yards.

Conjoint analysis, even more than contingent valuation, shows the great flexibility of the stated preference approach. It allows researchers to use a single survey to examine tradeoffs between several different attributes at different levels. It can even be used to see how people trade off between nonmonetary attributes: for instance, how much increased recreational opportunity will people desire if that recreational use leads to environmental damage?

IN SUMMARY

- Conjoint analysis, another stated preference approach, allows researchers to look at how people make tradeoffs among different combinations of attributes and different levels of those attributes.
- As a survey-based method, it shares with contingent valuation great flexibility to examine hypothetical scenarios.

Stated Preference: An Appraisal

The validity and usefulness of stated preference, especially contingent valuation, have been questioned almost as long as the methods have been in use. Empirical evaluation of the suitability of stated preference revolves around two issues: *hypothetical bias,* and scope. In addition, for conjoint analysis, the potential complexity of the tradeoffs that people face make survey design a major concern.

Hypothetical bias is the most enduring of these criticisms. **Hypothetical bias** is the possibility that people respond differently to hypothetical situations than to having to pay real money. In stated preference methods, the consumers do not pay for the goods. Does this make a big difference? In some studies, researchers have conducted both a contingent valuation study and a revealed preference approach. When Richard Carson and others compared the results of a number of these studies, they found that contingent valuation estimates for the same environmental good were actually lower than those from revealed preference studies (about 89 percent of the revealed preference values), even though the contingent valuation studies included both use values and non-use values, while the revealed preference studies included only use values. This finding bolsters the reliability of contingent valuation by showing that survey respondents were fairly conservative in their statements of willingness to pay. On the other hand, some laboratory experiments have found that people's statements of their willingness to pay are several times higher than what they actually would pay when money changed hands. The hypothetical bias can be lessened by using the referendum format, where research subjects have to make a yes or no choice, and actually vote no when the price gets too high. Both research and debate on the hypothetical bias continue.

The problem of scope is that people report being willing to pay no more for a large project than for a small one. Nobel Laureate Daniel Kahneman showed an example where subjects were asked their willingness to pay to clean up lakes in a specific region of Ontario and then asked willingness to pay to clean up all lakes in Ontario. Kahneman characterized the results as their being willing to pay about the same for some or all lakes. To him, that meant the answers were not based on preferences for cleaning up lakes but rather based upon the "warm glow" of being in favor of the environment.

Professors Richard Carson and Robert Mitchell examined similar evidence for many other cases. For instance, the CVM estimate for Pittsburgh residents to improve the water quality of the Monongahela River from "boatable" to "fishable" was $26 per person. A CVM estimate for cleaning up all the water in the United States in the same way was $68 per household. To them, the evidence shows that people value water close to them more than water far away, and that the demand curve for clean water slopes down. It is worth less per marginal unit to clean up additional water, so cleaning up a whole country could be worth only a little more than double what cleaning up a local source was worth.

Carson and Mitchell examined many such examples and concluded that problems of scope that others report may be more a problem with the design of those surveys than a criticism of CVM itself. For example, economist William Desvouges asked subjects in Atlanta shopping malls what they would be willing to pay to save birds from oil ponds in the Rocky Mountain Flyway. Some were asked their willingness to pay for a project saving 2,000 birds, and others were asked about a project saving 200,000 birds. The survey characterized saving 2,000 birds as saving much less than 1 percent of the birds, while saving 200,000 birds was characterized as saving 2 percent of the birds. The respondents may well have interpreted the questions as saving twice as many birds in the big project as in the small one. The author meant them to interpret it as saving 100 times as many. When the WTP for the large project was about twice that of the small project, the author said there was a problem of scope. Carson and Mitchell, however, said there was a problem with the survey. It is very difficult to know if problems of scope are endemic to stated preference methods, as Kahneman and others believe, or whether problems of scope simply reflect problems in survey methods, as Carson and Mitchell believe.

Because of the magnitude of the Exxon Valdez oil spill, and because of the belief that non-use values would be large in this case, contingent valuation came under very close scrutiny in the early 1990s. The National Oceanographic and Atmospheric Administration (NOAA), a branch of the U.S. Department of Commerce, convened a panel of eminent economists, including two Nobel Prize winners, to review the method and make recommendations. The panel accepted the validity of the method and recommended that researchers use many of the features described earlier, such as providing background information, using the referendum format, and including debriefing questions, as best practices.

The same issues about hypothetical bias apply to conjoint analysis. The advantage and the disadvantage of conjoint analysis is that each respondent gives information about more than one alternative. The advantage is that it is possible to get more information from the respondent and to test for consistency of choices. The disadvantage is that it is much harder to convince the respondent that many alternatives are real than it is to convince him that only one alternative is real. Think again of the Exxon Valdez and all the effort made in the survey to convince the respondent that the two ships and Norwegian boom were a real alternative to the current state of affairs. If it were a conjoint analysis with three or more alternatives, why wouldn't the respondent think of all the alternatives as simply made-up policy proposals? There is a tradeoff between the greater information available from conjoint analysis and the relative simplicity of a well-done CVM study.

Stated preference methods have major advantages. They can be tailored to a wide variety of situations because the exercise is based on a survey created by researchers. Secondly, and perhaps most importantly, they capture both use and non-use values. People can express their support (or lack thereof) for protecting a resource for whatever reasons they have, including moral, religious, personal, altruistic, or selfish motivations. As useful as the revealed preference measures are, they cannot capture non-use value, while a stated preference method can measure non-use value.

Stated preference has been considered controversial primarily because it is based on people responding to hypothetical scenarios. The reduction in bias associated with use of the referendum format has lessened some of the controversy, and there is a large, continually growing body of research to assess stated preference methods' merits relative to the revealed preference approaches. Because of its versatility and its ability to encompass all values associated with environmental goods, stated preference is likely to continue in use.

IN SUMMARY

- Stated preference methods have been subject to criticism about hypothetical bias and scope. Hypothetical bias is the concern that people give different answers when real money changes hands than they do in a hypothetical setting. Scope is the concern that people say they are willing to pay the same amount of money in response to any environmental problem, no matter how large, just to experience the "warm glow" of being willing to help.

- Careful survey design for stated preference is necessary to get reliable results.
- Comparing the results of revealed preference methods to stated preference methods suggests that a well-designed stated preference survey can give accurate results despite concerns about hypothetical bias.
- Economists differ on whether the problem of scope can be solved by using improved survey methods.
- On balance, most economists believe stated preference methods provide useful information.

Experimental Economics and Stated Preference

Experimental economics refers to the practice of using experimental and laboratory methods to explore more deeply how people behave in market and non-market situations. The primary advantage of an experiment is the ability to control the factors to which a person responds. In the real world, a person making a purchase may be affected by what other commodities are also available for purchase, the setting for the purchase (a store or the Internet, for instance), who is with the purchaser at the time, whether other people are making purchases at the same time, how the price is displayed, and so forth. In a laboratory setting, researchers seek to control all these factors, so that they can focus on the effects of one particular aspect of the market.

Experiments can have elements of both revealed and stated preference methods: participants in the study may get only hypothetical scenarios, or they may face choices with consequences. Because of the ability to control the scenarios that participants face, experiments are being used to explore the differences in how people respond to different forms of nonmarket valuation studies.

One active area of research in experimental economics is hypothetical bias: whether people respond differently to hypothetical situations than to actual markets. If hypothetical bias is a significant factor, then results from stated preference studies may exaggerate people's willingness to pay for environmental improvements. If, on the other hand, it is possible to reduce or eliminate hypothetical bias in survey design, then there is support for the use of stated preference results in policy analysis.

One example of this approach used several forms of markets to investigate hypothetical bias using sports memorabilia. Because active markets for sports memorabilia are very common, it is a useful area for research because people understand the goods. It can be a useful arena for improving methods in stated preference studies.

In Landry and List's experiment, each participant was given $10. In the "real" scenario, participants (who were randomly chosen attendees at a memorabilia show) responded either yes or no to paying either $5 or $10 to get a ticket stub "dated October 12, 1997, which [was] issued for the game in which Barry Sanders passed Jim Brown for the number 2 spot in the NFL all-time rushing yardage." If a majority of participants said yes, everyone (including those who said no) paid and got the stub. Requiring everyone to pay and get the ticket made the tickets, a private good, have characteristics of a public good. In the "consequential" scenario, researchers tried to replicate a scenario where people are not sure whether their responses will in fact make any difference to public policy: participants faced the same question, but whether they paid and got the ticket stubs, or whether they kept the money with no ticket stub, was determined by chance (a coin flip) instead of by majority vote. This scenario was meant to mimic the effects of asking people about voting on policy issues (as in the referendum format of contingent valuation) when a vote might not actually take place. In the "cheap talk" scenario, the participants were told about hypothetical bias; they were then encouraged to act as though they faced a real scenario, even though they would not get the ticket stubs. Finally, the "hypothetical" scenario asked participants to say how they would respond, though again they would not get ticket stubs. The results suggest that hypothetical bias is real: the "hypothetical" scenario had much higher willingness to pay than the other scenarios. On the other hand, while the "cheap talk" scenario had higher values than the "consequential" or "real" scenarios, the results of these three scenarios were statistically close, an outcome that suggests that results are more reliable if respondents have some expectation that they will have to pay for the good in question.

IN SUMMARY

- Experimental economics creates scenarios to explore how people behave in market and nonmarket situations.
- One function of experimental economics is to see how people's responses differ in hypothetical situations, compared with situations where they actually will spend money and receive something of value.

Objections and Responses to "Assigning Price Tags" to the Environment

Calculating the benefits of environmental goods in dollars can greatly improve the quality of analysis used for making public policy decisions. Because the costs of environmental protection, such as those associated with escorts for oil tankers, are relatively easy to calculate in dollars, having the benefits of environmental goods in dollars provides an important counterweight to those costs. Nevertheless, two major concerns are often raised about this activity: that estimating market values for environmental goods is morally questionable and that income shouldn't play a role in protecting environmental goods.

ETHICAL CONCERNS WITH NONMARKET VALUATION

Many people consider environmental protection similar to goods such as friendship, religious belief, and patriotism that cannot and should not be considered in market terms. Associating these goods with dollar values implies that these goods might be traded for money or for other goods; in other words, that there are reasonable trade-offs that could be made for these goods. Many people reject that notion for environmental goods. Several specific ethical objections can be raised against the use of nonmarket valuation methods for environmental goods.

First, many argue that environmental goods have intrinsic value—that is, they have value independent of how people judge them. Because economics is centered on people and how people value things, it cannot possibly calculate the full value associated with environmental goods. Because these goods have value above and beyond the value people place on them, nonmarket valuation inherently underestimates their value.

Secondly, some people believe as strongly about protection of some environmental resources as others do about their religion or their country: they would be willing to die to save that resource. For instance, some people have lived for several months on a platform in an old-growth redwood tree to prevent its being chopped down. In their minds, there are no substitutes for these goods. Economic analysis is very well suited to examining the effects of tradeoffs, such as giving up some electricity to get more stuff. These tradeoffs assume some degree of substitutability of goods. However, if people cannot conceive of any exchange that they would accept for sacrifice of some of the resource—if there is no possible substitute for the environmental good—then there is no finite value at which these people will trade some of the good for a different good. In this case, it is not clear what nonmarket valuation has to offer to understanding the value of the good. Even more challenging are cases where people have vehement preferences directly opposed to each other: some people who hunt whales, for instance, consider it a critical part of their religious or cultural heritage, while others view whales as scarce species and intelligent beings deserving protection. While a social decision must be made, the economic approach to the decision may not contribute much insight.

A third objection is less about the principle of valuation than about the means by which the good is to be protected. The usual assumption in most nonmarket valuation work is that a positive action—a change in the status quo—is required to achieve environmental protection. In that case, it is reasonable to expect that people should have to give up resources for the sake of the good, and compensating variation (willingness to pay for an improvement) is a reasonable approach. Others, though, argue that environmental protection is an intrinsic right; if there is to be any diminution of the resource, they would suffer a loss that would need to be compensated. This view rejects the premise of valuation exercises: that the environmental good must, in some sense, be purchased. If environmental quality is a right that people already have and should not have to purchase, then the value of the resource could be determined by calculating the equivalent variation (willingness to accept environmental damages), instead of the WTP for environmental protection.

These approaches can lead to different welfare measures: among other factors, WTP is limited by a person's income, while WTA is unbounded. As a result, some respondents to nonmarket valuation studies protest the premise of the exercises and give WTP values of $0 even if they care intensely about the good. It is for this reason that contingent valuation surveys often use follow-up questions to try to determine whether someone opposes an action because his WTP is truly zero or because he objects to the survey process for other reasons.

Finally, the objection is sometimes raised that placing a monetary value on nonmarket goods, such as emotions or environmental resources, cheapens the good. Some people are offended that these resources might be viewed as commodities that can be traded because they view them as separate, apart, and superior compared to market goods. Finding a price tag for something with a spiritual or abstract value "commodifies" it and reduces its special nature.

In the face of these objections, why do economists persist in using valuation exercises? The fact remains that a society must make decisions involving the allocation of scarce environmental resources. Not everyone views these goods as inherently different from market goods. While some people would be willing to put down their lives to protect the wildlife of Prince William Sound, others care little for the ecosystem and prefer oil to be shipped as cheaply as possible, while still others would carefully weigh their tax burden against their concern with a clean environment. As a society, we must make decisions involving these goods.

Estimating the value that people put on these goods makes that value concrete. Rather than telling policy makers that people like Prince William Sound a great deal, economists can estimate that the benefits to people for avoiding future damage to the site are worth at least $2.8 billion to them. As economist John Loomis has said, nonmarket valuation takes a good with a value somewhere between zero and infinity, and narrows that range. Politically, that information can be very powerful.

Estimating these benefits is necessary for comparing the benefits and costs of an action. Because costs are often easily measured in dollars, accurate measurement of benefits is necessary for comparison. Nonmarket valuation can provide useful information by showing that people are willing to commit money and other resources toward environmental protection. Expressing support for protecting the environment when no sacrifice is involved does not reveal commitment; however, being willing to give up other goods to accomplish this goal is meaningful to policy makers.

THE ROLE OF INCOME CONSTRAINTS

When asked whether they would be willing to pay $100 per year for protection of Prince William Sound, some people (especially those with limited means) might express a conflict. On the one hand, they might strongly support protection of the Sound and would willingly give up a great deal to accomplish it. On the other hand, $100 is a large amount of money; that expenditure might hurt them tremendously. Should income—ability to pay—play a role in nonmarket valuation?

The key issue to an economist is to measure what people are willing to give up in order to protect an environmental resource. It is a fact of life, no matter how unfortunate, that many people are poor and cannot afford many goods that more wealthy people can easily get. Both as individuals and as a society, people face finite resources; protecting the environment will require reductions in expenditures for other programs or goods. People have to recognize the constraints within which they operate, both as individuals and as a society, and income is one of those constraints. Thus, income influences people's expressions of value for nonmarketed goods.

It is worth noting, nevertheless, that sacrifice need not be measured only in dollars. People indicate their concern for environmental goods through time and labor as well as by money. For instance, a person might spend a weekend as a volunteer in a beach cleanup project, even though he might instead have used that time to earn income. Time and labor are limited resources, and individuals and societies must be thoughtful about how they spend those goods, just as they are careful about how they spend money.

◢◣ IN SUMMARY

- Estimating market values for environmental goods has raised some ethical objections. First, economics does not incorporate any intrinsic values that environmental goods may have; second, the valuation exercise assumes that it is possible to substitute other goods for environmental goods; third, people may reject the assumption that they have to pay for environmental protection; and finally, they may reject the "commodification" of a good they consider of spiritual or other value.
- On the other hand, estimating these benefits allows them to be included in public policy debates in a more tangible and quantified fashion. It also allows for direct comparison with the costs of protection.
- Environmental protection is costly. When we as individuals or a society face decisions about protecting the environment, we must consider the limited resources that we have available to us. For that reason, economists expect income constraints to affect people's decisions on their willingness to pay for environmental protection.
- People can manifest support for environmental protection in ways other than spending money; they can spend time and energy as well.

Windmills in Spain: A Conjoint Analysis

Should windmills be built near Zaragoza in Spain? Wind is a renewable and very low-carbon way of generating electricity, but the windmills occupy land. The proposed site was in La Plana, a 600-meter-tall limestone plateau in the Ebro Valley. La Plana is the last of the tablelands not already covered with wind farms and second residences. It is ecologically important in supporting birds of prey. Wind farms would disrupt the birds' use of La Plana, either by killing them outright when they collide with the windmills or by denying them nesting sites in the cliffs or trees. Windmill farms also change the landscape; the windmills create a very different view.

Begoña Alvarez-Farizo and Nick Hanley set out to use to conjoint analysis to find out what was important about these areas. They showed their subjects choice cards and asked them to rate the options. A typical choice card showed options for protection of cliffs, habitat and flora, landscape, and cost. For example, one choice card was yes to protection of cliffs, no to protection of habitat, yes to protection of landscape, and a cost of 1,000 pesetas (about $7), to be paid in increased taxes. To make the choices seem real, they showed the respondents pictures of how the cliffs looked and how they would look with wind farms. The latter was done by altering the photos to add windmills and roads.

The researchers did their analysis in two ways. The first was a choice experiment. For one group of respondents, they showed each respondent three cards and asked for the one preferred. The second method was a contingent rating. Respondents were shown 10 cards and asked to rate their preferences on a scale of 1–10. In all, 488 people were interviewed in Zaragoza.

The results showed considerable willingness to pay for preserving cliffs, fauna and flora, and landscape. In the choice experiment, cliffs were valued at 3,580 pesetas/year, fauna at 6,290, and landscape at 6,161. The contingent rating experiment gave much lower values: 3,062, 3,978, and 3,378 pesetas for cliffs, fauna, and landscape, respectively.

There are two things to be learned here. First, the summed environmental values of La Plana are worth at least 10,000 pesetas, or about $60 per interviewee per year. There were about 600,000 persons in the area, so an estimate of the value per year would be 6 billion pesetas, or $36 million. A windmill farm would need to generate at least that much value for it to be an efficient choice. Second, the exact method of survey administration matters a great deal. The difference between these two methods for a stated preference survey is too big to be explained as a random occurrence. There is no way to tell which of the estimates is correct. Perhaps this highlights the strengths and weaknesses of stated preference in general: the method clearly shows non-use values of significant magnitudes, but the estimates can be imprecise and dependent upon the exact methods used.

CHAPTER SUMMARY

Here are the key lessons from this chapter:

- People can appreciate goods for any reason that they wish. For environmental goods, many people appear to have non-use (also known as passive-use) values—values for goods they do not use. These include option, existence, and bequest values.
- Stated preference methods are ways of measuring values for nonmarket goods based on responses to hypothetical scenarios, rather than people's behavior. While revealed preference methods based on actual behavior can estimate use values, stated preference methods are necessary to estimate the non-use values of environmental goods in addition to the use values. In addition, because these methods pose hypothetical scenarios, they are very

flexible and can be adapted to a wide range of circumstances. Because these methods are based on responses to hypothetical situations, great care needs to be taken in designing stated preference studies to ensure that the results are reliable.

- Contingent valuation studies seek to estimate people's willingness to pay for a change in environmental quality. An increasingly common way to elicit this information is to ask people whether they would support an action if it would cost a specified amount. By varying the specified amount, it is possible to estimate the maximum amount that people on average are willing to pay for the environmental change.

- Conjoint analysis looks at how people trade off different characteristics of a good with other characteristics (including cost). It allows a wider range of options than a standard contingent valuation study.

- Stated preference methods are subject to criticism about hypothetical bias and scope, or "warm glow." The first concern is that people may say they are willing to pay more than they would actually pay. However, comparing revealed preference and stated preference methods suggests that responses in a hypothetical situation can be similar to actual behavior. The second concern is that people say they are willing to pay the same amount whether an environmental problem is large or small, just to experience the warm glow of saying they support the environment. This concern might be real or might simply be a problem of how the questions are asked. Most economists believe that stated preference methods are useful despite these concerns.

- Experimental economics studies how people respond to market and nonmarket situations. For example, researchers create scenarios to see the different responses in hypothetical and real transactions.

- Objections are sometimes raised on moral and ethical grounds to nonmarket valuation efforts. Some of the objections include the lack of consideration of the intrinsic values of resources, the assumption that other goods can be substituted for environmental resources, the assumption that environmental protection must be bought, and the treatment of environmental goods as commodities that can be sold and bought.

- As a society, we often face difficult decisions involving tradeoffs between environmental goods and other goods. Economists argue that having a greater understanding of the tradeoffs that individuals are willing to make to protect environmental goods provides important information for making these decisions.

KEY TERMS

bequest value *(p. 137)*
conjoint analysis *(p. 143)*
contingent valuation method *(p. 138)*
existence value *(p. 136)*

experimental economics *(p. 147)*
hypothetical bias *(p. 144)*
option *(p. 136)*
random utility model (RUM) *(p. 157)*

NOTES

Much of the material in this chapter about the Exxon Valdez is taken from Richard Carson et al., "Contingent Valuation and Lost Passive Use: Damages from the Exxon Valdez Oil Spill," *Environmental and Resource Economics* 25 (2003): 257–286. The guidelines of the panel reviewing the validity of contingent valuation after the Exxon Valdez disaster were published in the *Federal Register* 58(10) (January 15, 1993): 4601–4614 and can be found at http://www.darp.noaa.gov/library/pdf/cvblue.pdf.

The Argo Dam example comes from Wendy M. Adams, Meghan Cauzillo, Kathleen Chiang, Sara Deuling and Attila Tislerics, "Investigating the Feasibility of River Restoration at Argo Pond on the Huron River, Ann Arbor, Michigan," Master's Project, School of Natural Resources and Environment, University of Michigan, August 2004, http://sitemaker.umich.edu/argoproject/home.

A comparison of revealed preference and contingent valuation was done in Richard T. Carson, Nicholas E. Flores, Kerry M. Martin, and Jennifer L. Wright, "Contingent Valuation and Revealed Preference Methodologies: Comparing Estimates for Quasi-Public Goods," *Land Economics* 72(1) (February 1996): 80–99.

The study of exaggerated willingness to pay when no real money changes hands is in John A. List and Jason F. Shogren, "Calibration of Willingness-to-Accept," *Journal of Environmental Economics and Management* 43(2) (March 2002): 219–233.

The conjoint analysis for native plants can be found in Gloria E. Helfand, Joon Sik Park, Joan I. Nassauer, and Sandra Kosek, "The Economics of Native Plants in Residential Landscape Designs," *Landscape and Urban Planning* 78(3) (November 2006): 229–240.

A good review of experimental environmental economics is Jason F. Shogren, "Experimental Methods and Valuation," in Karl-Göran Mäler and Jeffrey Vincent (eds.), *Handbook of Environmental Economics*, Volume 2 (Amsterdam: Elsevier, 2005), pp. 969–1027. The sports memorabilia example is from Craig E. Landry and John A. List, "Using *Ex Ante* Approaches to Obtain Credible Signals for Value in Contingent Markets: Evidence from the Field," *American Journal of Agricultural Economics* 89 (2007): 420–429.

Richard Carson and Robert Mitchell examined the scope question in "The Issue of Scope in Contingent Valuation Studies," *American Journal of Agricultural Economics* 75 (1993): 1263–1267. The comments of W. H. Desvouges et al. about scope are in a consulting report, *Measuring Nonuse Damages Using Contingent Valuation: An Experimental Evaluation of Accuracy*, Report to the Exxon Corporation, Research Triangle Institute Monograph 92-1 (1992). The case for scope effects being endemic to CVM is in Daniel Kahneman and Jack Knetsch, "Valuing Public Goods: The Purchase of Moral Satisfaction," *Journal of Environmental Economics and Management* 22 (1992): 55–70.

The final example is from Begoña Álvarez-Farizo and Nick Hanley, "Using Conjoint Analysis to Quantify Public Preferences over the Environmental Impacts of Wind Farms. An Example from Spain," *Energy Policy* 30 (2002): 107–116.

EXERCISES

1. Stated preference methods are closely related to those used in marketing studies trying to determine whether consumers will buy a new good not yet on the shelves. For instance, consider when personal mp3 players did not yet exist, but people had portable compact disc players. How might the methods of contingent valuation or conjoint analysis be used to determine whether people would buy a personal mp3 player? What, if anything, is different about using these methods for environmental goods compared with goods that can be marketed but are not yet on the market?

2. The Forest Service is deciding how to allocate its recreational funding. It can increase fishing opportunities in an area (for instance, by stocking), or it can build more hiking trails. It presents several options in a survey:

OPTION	FISH STOCKED (HUNDREDS OF FISH)	HIKING TRAILS (MILES)	COST
A	1	8	$ 50
B	4	2	$100
C	4	8	$125

   In the first round, the survey respondent was asked to rank each option without regard to cost; in the next round, the survey respondent was given the cost information and then asked to rank the options while considering those costs.

   (a) In the first round, one respondent ranked alternative C as best, and ranked A as tied with B. Plot the different combinations on a graph, with Fish Stocked on the horizontal axis and Miles of Hiking Trails on the vertical axis. Draw indifference curves that reflect this set of preferences. Do these indifference curves reflect free disposal, slope downward, and not cross, as indifference curves should?

   (b) Based on the comparison of alternatives A and B, how does this respondent trade off between fish stocking and hiking trails? In other words, if he were to give up 100 fish stocked, about how many miles of hiking trails would he need to get in compensation? What does this comparison tell you about how this respondent values fish stocking compared with hiking trails?

   (c) When the respondent was presented with the cost information, he changed his ranking so that A was best, C was second-best, and B was least preferred. Does the fact that A and B are no longer equally preferred mean that the respondent is inconsistent in his preferences? Why or why not?

   (d) Compare alternatives A and C. What can you say about how much the respondent is willing to pay for 300 additional fish stocked when there are already 100 stocked?

   (e) Now compare alternatives B and C. What can you say about how much the respondent is willing to pay for six additional miles of hiking trails when there are already two additional miles of trails?

3. In the Argo Dam study, about 62 percent of the survey population preferred to take down the dam, while 31 percent preferred to keep it, and 7 percent expressed no preference. For those who preferred keeping the dam, the estimated willingness to pay to keep it was $161/adult; those who wanted the dam removed would pay an estimated $135/adult to have it taken down. Ann Arbor has about 96,000 people.
    (a) Democracy is based on each person having one vote. If there were a vote in Ann Arbor on dam removal, what is the likely outcome, if a representative fraction of the population votes?
    (b) If willingness to pay is a measure of how strongly people care about an issue, which group felt more strongly about whether to remove Argo Dam, those who wanted to keep the dam or those who wanted to remove it? Who would be more likely to show up to vote?
    (c) Use the above values to estimate whether the aggregate willingness to pay for keeping the dam was larger or smaller than the aggregate willingness to pay for removing the dam. Would this calculation produce a recommendation different from the outcomes in (a) or (b)? If so, what are some advantages and disadvantages of a decision based on (i) seeking high voter turnout from a representative share of the population, (ii) those who feel most passionate encouraging those who think like them to vote, or (iii) having the city council decide based on an analysis of whether net benefits are larger for keeping or removing the dam?

4. Are there alternatives to "commodifying" environmental goods through non-market valuation? Imagine that you are a public policy decision maker—either a legislator or the head of a government agency. You must decide whether to support new regulations on oil tankers that will increase the price of gasoline to consumers or to leave in place the current regulations, which have a higher probability of another oil spill. What information would be helpful to you in making this decision? Would you like to have the benefits of avoiding an oil spill measured in monetary units, or do you think that this information would not help you in your decision?

5. You are an analyst in a state Department of Parks and Recreation. The state is famous for Dizzy Vista Mountain, which has a fabulous view of an eagle's nesting area. You are asked to analyze a proposal by a state lawmaker to impose an annual tax of $10 per household to maintain the ecological health of the nesting area. The lawmaker based his proposal on the response to an email survey, in which he asked his constituents if they would be willing to pay $10 a year for this purpose; 85 percent said yes. Your department head asks you to check whether there was hypothetical bias in the lawmaker's survey. She suggests you survey visitors to Dizzy Vista Mountain. She gives you some free coupons for the parking lot at Dizzy Vista Mountain, each worth $5.
    (a) Design four experiments, one each for real, hypothetical, consequential, and "cheap talk" scenarios. Discuss what you expect to learn from each experiment and how you can use your work to evaluate the WTP determined in the state lawmaker's survey.

(b) Comment on studying visitors to Dizzy Vista Mountain. Why is this a good group to study? Are there reasons that it might not be a good study sample?

6. Now imagine that a national lawmaker, inspired by the willingness to pay in the state lawmaker's survey, sent a similar email survey to the same group of voters, asking if they would be willing to pay $20 a year to preserve every eagle nesting area in the United States. The questionnaire did not discuss the relative size of the eagle population at Dizzy Mountain to the nationwide eagle population. In this case, 80 percent said yes. Discuss the scope and warm glow effects that might be present in the survey. What information might the national lawmaker have added to the questionnaire? How would you write the questions to avoid the warm glow or scope effect and to obtain a more accurate estimate of WTP?

Appendix: Interpreting Contingent Valuation Surveys Using the Random Utility Model

The referendum type of contingent valuation survey results in a table where each observation shows the amount of money that the respondent was asked to pay to make the environmental improvement and whether the respondent answered yes or no. Each observation is shown in Table 7.1 in Box 7.2. How do we go from this list of data to an estimate of willingness to pay?

In the Argo Dam case, there are exactly two alternatives: to leave things as they are and pay nothing, the "no" alternative, or to make a change and pay something for the change, the "yes" alternative. It is likely to be safe to assume that the respondent will say "yes" if the yes alternative gives the respondent more utility than the no alternative. A **random utility model (RUM)** estimates the relationship between the choice of the "yes" or the "no" to both observable factors (such as the price of the good or the respondent's age) and unobservable factors (such as the respondent's emotional ties to the resource); for reasons discussed later, the unobservable factors put "random" in the method's name. The RUM assumes that a person will say "yes" to paying for an environmental quality improvement if the improved environment is worth more to him than the income he would lose by paying, and will say "no" if the payment is too high to make that improvement worthwhile to him.

In the Argo Dam Survey in Box 7.2, two respondents, Numbers 2 and 5, faced the same price, $450 in property tax, to remove a dam and restore the river environment. One said yes and one said no. For these two respondents to give different answers, they must be different in some observable or unobservable way. Observable characteristics of respondents may include demographic factors—income, education, and family size, for example—that might affect a person's answers. Yet it is still common that two people with the same observable characteristics will give different answers. In that case, their decisions must be based on some individual factors that we can't observe; for instance, perhaps one has more strongly held environmentalist values than the other. The "random" part of the RUM comes from the fact that researchers can't observe all factors that affect preferences; the decision must be affected by unobservable characteristics of the respondents that seem random from the researcher's point of view. Because respondents differ in the unobservable characteristics, such as preferences for the environment, only a fraction of those people who have identical observed characteristics and are faced with an identical choice will say yes.

Let's look at one respondent's choice. The respondent has income I, and that income gives him utility. His utility in the "no" case, where things stay the way they are, is $U_{no} = b * I$, where b is a parameter (a number) that converts income (I) to utility (U). In the "yes" case, the respondent would pay price P for the environmental improvement, but in exchange he would get an environmental benefit that is worth "a" to him in terms of utility. Because he pays P, his income remaining after the payment is $I - P$. His utility is then $U_{yes} = a + b * (I - P)$, where a is another parameter measuring the increase in utility from the environmental good. He says "yes" when $U_{yes} > U_{no}$. The algebra for that decision is $a + b(I - P) > bI$, or $a - bP > 0$. That is, the respondent would say yes as long as the price is less than $P = a/b$; if the price is higher, he would say no.

Now let's expand the model to two types of people, those who value the environment a lot (type e people) and those who don't care too much about the environment (type d people). Because the e people like the environment more than the d people, the e people get a greater increase in utility from the yes alternative than the d people get: $a^e > a^d$. Now let's go through the same steps as in the last paragraph to find out at what price each type of person changes from saying yes to saying no. Because the e people say yes when $a^e - bP > 0$, the e people say yes for all P lower than a^e/b. The d type says yes for all P lower than a^d/b.

The simple RUM can now explain a more complicated pattern of yes and no answers. Everyone says yes to prices less than a^d/b. Only the e people say yes to prices between a^d/b and a^e/b. Finally, nobody says yes to prices higher than a^e/b. So a RUM can explain respondents with the same observable characteristic (income I in this case) giving different answers to a binary choice question.

Figure 7.1 approximates the percent of people who said yes in response to different prices for the Argo dam removal project. For instance, about 38 percent of people who were asked whether they would pay \$100/year said yes, while about 10 percent of those who faced a price of \$450/year said yes. Of course, the people willing to pay at \$450/year would also be willing to pay \$100/year, though the reverse might not be true.

How can this information be used to estimate how much people are willing to pay for the increase in environmental quality? Suppose that, initially, a person is happy to pay $P = \$40$ to eliminate the chance of an oil spill in Prince William Sound. His willingness to pay for the environmental improvement must be at least \$40. If the payment increased to $P = \$80$, he might still say "yes," but he would probably think about his answer more. U_{yes} is still bigger than U_{no}, but that difference is shrinking. Suppose that he said "yes" to all values through a payment of $P = \$100$ but said "no" to all prices above \$100. His maximum willingness to pay is thus \$100, the amount that changes his vote from "yes" to "no." If $P = \$100$ is exactly the point

FIGURE 7.1 Percent of People Who Say Yes to Various Prices for Removing Argo Dam.

The stars show the percent who said yes at each price. The solid line is the estimated relationship between price and an answer of yes.

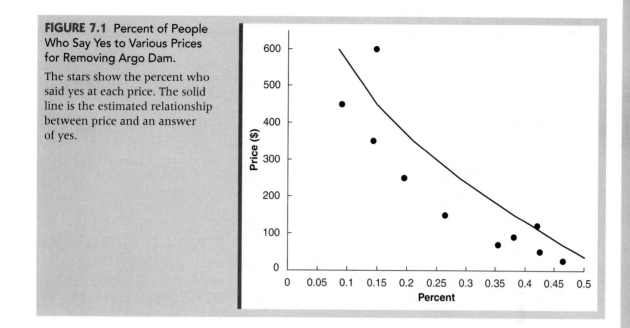

where he changed from "yes" to "no," then, at that point, he gets the same utility from "yes" and "no," which means that $U_{yes} = U_{no}$. In other words, $a = b * P$: the increased utility for the environmental improvement is equal to the utility he gains from income multiplied by the payment, which is income he gives up. At that point, then, $a - bP = 0$, which means that $P = a/b$: the willingness to pay for that specified difference in environmental quality is a/b. Using statistical analysis to find the parameters a and b provides a way to calculate a person's maximum willingness to pay for a change in environmental quality.

Because it is possible to estimate an individual's maximum WTP, it is then possible to estimate the average WTP for the surveyed people. Figure 7.2 shows an estimate of the proportion of people, out of the entire sample, who would be willing to pay at least the amount on the graph. For instance, about 15 percent are willing to pay at least $100, and perhaps 2 percent will pay as much as $450. If these were the only points, the average WTP would be 15% * $100 + 2% * $450 = $24. To get the average for all the points, it is necessary to add up, for each point on the curve, the proportion who answer yes times the value for that proportion; if there is a continuum of WTP values, the average becomes the area under the curve.

IN SUMMARY

- A random utility model (RUM) is a way to use "yes" and "no" answers about improving environmental quality for a price into an estimate of a willingness to pay for that change in environmental quality.

FIGURE 7.2 Proportion of People Who Would Be Willing to Pay at Least a Specified Price.

This figure shows the best estimate from statistical analysis of the proportion of people who would say yes to the specified amounts. The average willingness to pay in the sample is the sum of the proportion who would pay a price, times the price; more precisely, it is the area under this curve.

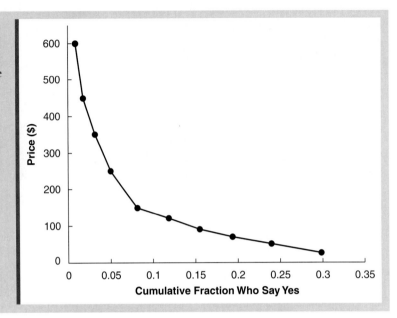

- The RUM assumes that a person will say "yes" to paying for an environmental quality improvement if the payment is worth less to him than the improved environment, and "no" if the payment is too high for that change. That decision provides information on how the respondent ranks the options and thus provides information on his utility levels.
- Once statistical methods have found the parameters that best predict when a person will say "yes" and when "no," those parameters can be used to estimate a person's maximum willingness to pay for the change in environmental quality.

From Production to Pollution

Paper can be produced with or without bleach. Crops can be grown with or without pesticides. Much environmental policy has focused on how to use production methods that are environmentally friendly. This chapter will examine:

- The environmental effects of inputs (goods needed to make other goods), technology (different methods for making goods), and production (using technology to turn inputs into goods for markets);
- How environmental policy can reduce pollution by changing the cost of inputs to production;
- The costs of alternative policies to reduce pollution.

Agricultural Pollution in California's Salinas Valley

The Salinas Valley of California is a very fertile area, producing highly valued crops, including strawberries, artichokes, broccoli, cauliflower, and lettuce. Two major inputs to production for all these crops are nitrogen fertilizer and water. Because there is little or no rain during the growing season, agriculture in the area is irrigated. One adverse consequence of the farming is that nitrogen fertilizer leaches out of the soil and seeps into the area's groundwater. This runoff is called nitrogen leachate, a very common water pollutant in agricultural areas around the world. Because the groundwater is a source of drinking water, such nitrogen contamination is a potentially serious problem. In the 1990s, California sought ways to reduce the amount of nitrogen leachate in groundwater. Gloria Helfand, Douglas Larson, and Brett House studied the nitrogen pollution problem in California's Salinas Valley; the numbers in this chapter are from their research.

Some pollution, such as that from factories, is termed **point source**, which means that it is easy to identify the source of the pollution and how much that source pollutes. It is often possible to point to the specific smokestack or effluent pipe from which the pollution flows. It is relatively easy for a pollution control agency to know who is polluting, to measure the pollution, and to determine if a polluter reduces its emissions.

Leachate from agriculture, in contrast, is hidden: the nitrogen dissolves into water and sinks into the soil. It enters groundwater or rivers through subsurface flows that cannot be observed. Additionally, because subsurface flows can travel, it is usually impossible to link the pollution to its sources. Pollution with uncertain origin is called **nonpoint source** pollution. Because it is very difficult to measure the pollution from each farm or other nonpoint source polluter, if regulators were to simply direct these producers to reduce pollution by a specific amount, it would be very hard to tell whether the producers have complied. For nonpoint sources, it is usually more practical for a regulator to take indirect actions, such as limiting the use of inputs that contribute to pollution.

While it may seem obvious that the application of nitrogen fertilizer causes the contamination of groundwater, irrigation water is also a major factor in causing leachate. Without the water, nitrogen would stay near the surface of the soil; excess water applications move the nitrogen from the root zones of plants down into groundwater. Reducing leachate, then, may involve reducing nitrogen use, reducing water applications, or both. In the case of lettuce production in the Salinas Valley, the most effective way to reduce nitrogen leachate is to reduce both water use and nitrogen application. However, reducing just water use works nearly as well. Leachate can be controlled by limiting applied water.

How a producer chooses inputs to production can have significant environmental effects. Knowing what factors influence a producer's decision will provide ideas on how to change those decisions if they lead to environmentally damaging impacts.

Inputs, Outputs, Technology, and the Environment

Production is the term for taking goods and converting them into something that will enter a market. A produced good that enters a market is an **output**. Lettuce, for example, is an output. Making an output typically requires **inputs**, the goods needed to make the output. Growing crops, for instance, uses inputs of land, water, nitrogen, farming equipment, and labor. An output of one market may be an input to another. Fertilizer, for instance, is an output of the chemical industry and an input to agriculture.

One way to produce 3.300 metric tons (abbreviated as t), dry weight, of lettuce is to use one hectare (10,000 square meters, abbreviated as ha) of land in the Salinas Valley, 78.48 kilograms (kg) of nitrogen, 673.8 millimeter-hectares of water (mm-ha, or the volume that covers a hectare one millimeter deep, which is 10 meters cubed of water), and other inputs including labor and the use of machinery. The recipe to produce an output is a called a **technique**; it is a list of inputs with instructions on how to combine those inputs to get the final product.

There is more than one technique to produce 3.300 tons of lettuce. For instance, it is possible to get 3.300 tons of lettuce with a little more nitrogen and a little less water. The set of all techniques that will produce a specified amount of an output is called the **technology** for producing that output. For now, let's consider the choice a lettuce farmer might make as to how much water and how much nitrogen to apply to her land. For simplicity, the quantity of land (one hectare) and the quantity of all other inputs will be constant. This allows examination of production as if there were only two inputs.

Figure 8.1 is a graph with these two inputs, nitrogen and water, on the axes. Nitrogen is measured in kg/ha. Water is measured in mm-ha per hectare, or

FIGURE 8.1 Lettuce Isoquants.

The figure shows three isoquants for lettuce. Points D and B both are input bundles that yield 3.300 t/ha and so are on the same isoquant. If point C also yields 3.300 t/ha then it is inefficient, as it uses more nitrogen and the same water as D to produce the same yield.

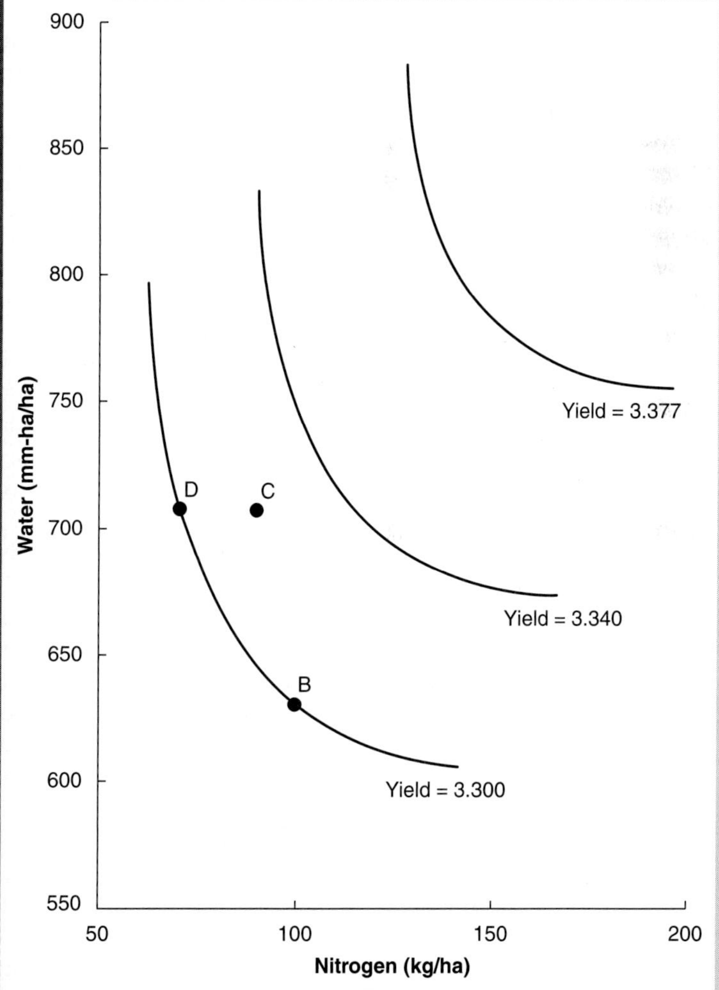

mm-ha/ha. Points D and B on Figure 8.1 are the inputs for two different techniques that produce 3.300 tons of lettuce on a hectare of land.

There are three points marked on Figure 8.1: D, B, and C. Each point represents a different combination of nitrogen and water that will produce 3.300 t/ha lettuce. There are also three curves. The curves are *isoquants*. All input combinations on an isoquant produce the same output. Other input combinations, such as C, may also be capable of producing that amount, but C is not on an isoquant. Let's see why not.

Let's look first at points D and B. Because points D and B are on the same isoquant, they produce the same output. However, because they use different combinations of nitrogen and water, they represent different techniques.

Now consider point C. Point C is an *inefficient* technique because it uses the same water as point D, but more nitrogen. If point C could produce the same output as D or B, would a farmer ever choose to use it? A technique is **inefficient** if there is another technique that makes the same output but uses less of at least one input and not more of any input. As long as nitrogen costs money, there is no reason for the farmer to choose combination C because producing 3.300 t/ha using technique C costs more than using technique D. So technique C is inefficient. Technique D, however, is *efficient*. A technique is **efficient** if there is no other technique that produces the same output and uses less of at least one input while using the same amount of the other inputs. In other words, any point below or to the left of technique D cannot produce 3.300 t/ha.

It is possible for multiple techniques to be efficient. One way to maintain the same level of production while reducing water use is to increase fertilizer use. Technique D uses more water than technique B, but it uses less nitrogen; both produce 3.300 t/ha. So techniques B and D are on the same isoquant. The **isoquant** is the set of all the efficient techniques that make a particular quantity of output. "Iso" comes from a Greek root meaning equal, or the same. "Quant" is a shortening of quantity. An isoquant thus shows how to produce the same quantity of output in many different ways.

As Figure 8.1 shows, there is a different isoquant for each quantity of output. Each isoquant is labeled with the output that is produced by any of the input combinations on that isoquant. The input combinations on the lowest isoquant produce 3.300 t/ha. The isoquant that is above (to the right of) the 3.300 isoquant is the 3.340 t/ha isoquant; the one at the top is the 3.377 t/ha isoquant.

An isoquant that is above another isoquant has a higher output. Consider a point on the higher isoquant, such as a point directly above B but on the 3.34 t/ha isoquant. Such a point uses more inputs than a point on the lower isoquant. Because isoquants only include efficient techniques, the higher point must produce more than the lower point. If it produced less or the same, it would be using more inputs for the same or lower output and be inefficient. The point directly above B has the same nitrogen and more water. If it is efficient it must produce more.

Now, let's consider the shapes that isoquants may take. Isoquants must slope down. To see why, consider an upward-sloping curve that has techniques to make the same output. Points higher up the curve use more of both inputs yet make the same output. Such techniques are inefficient. Isoquants include only efficient techniques. Such a curve cannot be an isoquant. Therefore, isoquants must slope down.

Like indifference curves, most isoquants are shaped like a crescent moon. (For an exception, see Box 8.1.) To illustrate, let's look again at points D and B in Figure 8.1. Point D uses less nitrogen and more water than point B. At point D, adding a little nitrogen allows the reduction of quite a bit of water, while holding output constant. At point B, adding a little nitrogen does not allow the reduction of nearly as much water. In other words, the slope of the isoquant (the change in water for a one-unit change in nitrogen) is steep when nitrogen use is low and water use is high. In contrast, for the nitrogen-intensive combination B, taking away a little nitrogen leads to a much smaller loss in production; keeping production the same (staying on the isoquant) will require a much smaller addition of water. At point B, when water is low and nitrogen is high, the slope of the isoquant is shallow. The result is the convex shape of Figure 8.1.

BOX 8.1

Algal Blooms and the Shape of Isoquants

The crescent shape of an isoquant suggests that it is possible to reduce use of one input by increasing use of the other—that is, that one input can substitute for the other. Is this a good assumption? In the case of plants (including agricultural crops), some scientists argue for what is called the limiting-nutrient hypothesis. This hypothesis says that plants require fixed proportions of nutrients, such as nitrogen, phosphorus, and water, to grow. Adding an excess of one of the inputs will not increase output if the plant's growth is limited by the available amount of a different nutrient. The isoquants for these inputs are L-shaped, indicating that they are perfect complements; in other words, the nutrients cannot substitute for each other at all.

The limiting nutrient hypothesis can be used to control pollution. Algae in lakes can grow very rapidly if the right amounts of nitrogen and phosphorus are present. These "algae blooms" suck oxygen out of the water and kill fish in the lake in a process known as eutrophication. If, however, it is possible to reduce the amount of phosphorus in the lake, the algae cannot grow.

In the 1970s, the Great Lakes suffered from eutrophication in a number of places. The state of Michigan imposed a ban on phosphorus in laundry detergents to reduce the amount of phosphorus going into the lakes. The algae blooms in the Great Lakes were reduced, and water quality in the Great Lakes improved. Because nitrogen and phosphorus are complements rather than substitutes for algae growth, it was necessary to control only one of those inputs to reduce eutrophication.

> ▰▰ IN SUMMARY
>
> - Production is a process that uses inputs to make outputs. Techniques are the recipes for making outputs using inputs. Technology for an output is a collection of techniques that make the same amount of output.
> - A technique is inefficient if there is another technique that makes the same output but uses less of at least one input and not more of any input. A technique is efficient if there is no other technique that produces the same output and uses less of at least one input while using the same amount of the other inputs.
> - An isoquant is the set of efficient techniques that produces a certain output. It represents different combinations of inputs that produce the same amount of output.
> - Isoquants slope downward and typically are crescent shaped. An isoquant above another isoquant has a higher level of output.

Isoquants, Input Costs, and Environmental Policy

So far in this analysis, producers will choose efficient techniques or input combinations over inefficient ones. Not yet explored is the producer's choice among the efficient techniques. Which point on the 3.300-ton isoquant will the lettuce producer choose? And why?

CHOOSING INPUTS

The farmer has many ways to produce lettuce. Production can be water intensive or nitrogen intensive; lettuce can be grown using different irrigation technologies, with different harvest methods, with or without the use of pesticides. How does a producer decide what technique to use?

Producers want to keep the cost of production as low as possible in order to keep *profits* as high as possible. The cost-minimizing combination of inputs may produce pollution as well as output, if the producer does not consider environmental effects. One way to influence the choice of inputs, and thus pollution, is using taxes or subsidies to change the prices of inputs. This section first examines the producer's input and output decisions in the absence of environmental policy; then it looks at how these decisions change in response to a tax on an input.

The cost of production for a technique comes from multiplying the price of each input by the quantity of that input, and then adding up the results for all inputs. Let's take the case with only two inputs, nitrogen fertilizer and water. The quantity of nitrogen fertilizer is N, the price of nitrogen fertilizer P_N, the quantity of water W, the price of water P_W, and the total cost of production TC. Then $TC = P_N N + P_W W$. Let's say that our farmer wants to produce 3.377 tons of lettuce on one hectare of land. For simplicity, this example holds constant all the other inputs of production; the farmer won't change the amounts of labor, machinery, or pesticide, but she can vary the amounts of water and nitrogen. The objective is to produce 3.377 t/ha of lettuce at the lowest possible cost. What would be the best amounts of nitrogen and water to achieve this goal?

Finding the amounts of nitrogen and water that will solve this problem requires rearranging the cost equation so that it can be graphed on the isoquant diagram. In Figure 8.2, water is on the vertical axis. To graph water consumption as a function of nitrogen, rewrite the equation for cost of production as follows:

$$TC = P_N N + P_W W \text{ becomes}$$

$$P_W W = TC - P_N N, \text{which becomes}$$

$$W = (TC/P_W) - (P_N/P_W)N$$

The last equation is an **isocost line**: a line that represents all the combinations of the inputs that cost the same. The slope of the isocost line is $-(P_N/P_W)$, the ratio of the price per unit of one input to the price per unit of the other input. The vertical intercept of the isocost line is (TC/P_W). TC/P_W is the ratio of the total cost of production to the price of the input that's on the vertical axis. In this case, water is on the vertical axis, so TC/P_W, the vertical intercept, is the ratio of total production cost to the price of water.

Figure 8.2 shows three isocost lines. The lines each have the same input prices, which means that they have the same slopes, but they have different intercepts on the vertical axis, which means they have different costs. A higher intercept means higher cost. The goal, once again, is to find the lowest-cost way of producing a fixed amount of lettuce, represented by the isoquant for 3.377 t/ha.

In Figure 8.2, the low-cost line hits the vertical axis at 1,142 mm-ha/ha of water. That's the point where the farmer uses no nitrogen at all. The price of water is $0.23/mm-ha. Having the price of water makes it possible to figure out the cost of the input bundle. The cost of the input bundle ($N = 0$, $W = 1,142$) on the low-cost line is $TC = P_W * W + 0 * P_N = \$0.23 * 1,142 = \$262.66/ha$. Because every point on the low-cost isocost line has the same cost, every point on that line costs $262.66/ha.

Now let's look at the medium-cost line. It intersects the vertical axis at ($N = 0$, $W = 1,229$). The cost of that input bundle is $\$0.23 * 1,229 = \$282.67/ha$, so every input bundle on the medium-cost line costs $282.67/ha. Finally, let's look at the high-cost line. Because the high-cost line has a vertical intercept of ($N = 0$, $W = 1,316$), every input bundle on that line costs $\$0.23 * 1,316 = \$302.68/ha$.

How does the farmer grow 3.377 t/ha of lettuce at the lowest possible cost? Let's look at a picture with both isocosts and the 3.377 t/ha isoquant, Figure 8.3 on page 169. On the low-cost line, there is no point that is also on the isoquant for 3.377 t/ha. Because the lowest isocost line does not reach the isoquant, there is no way to produce 3.377 t/ha at a cost of $262.66/ha.

On the medium-cost isocost line, point A touches the isoquant for 3.377 t/ha. In fact, Point A is the only point on that isocost that touches that isoquant—it is tangent to the isoquant. Reading across to the vertical axis and down to the horizontal

FIGURE 8.2 Three Isocost Lines.

The figure shows three isocost lines. The price of water is $0.23/mm-ha. The cost of every input bundle on the low-cost line is the same and is therefore the same as the cost of the bundle that is the vertical intercept. For instance, the cost on the low-cost line is $TC = 1,142\,\text{mm-ha/ha} * \$0.23/\text{mm-ha} = \$262.66/\text{ha}$.

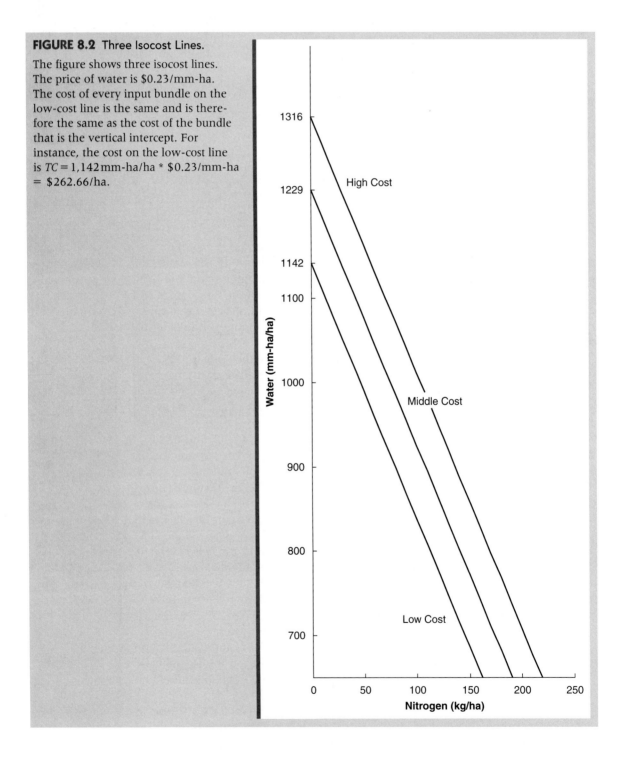

FIGURE 8.3 The Least-Cost Input Bundle.

Point A is the tangency between the isoquant for 3.377 t/ha of lettuce and middle cost isocost line. The input bundle at A is 139.05 kg/ha of nitrogen (rounded to 139 kg/ha) and 805.80 mm-ha/ha of water (rounded to 806 mm-ha/ha). Point E is also on the isoquant and so produces the same output as point A. However, because it is on the high isocost line, it costs more than point A. No input bundle on the low isocost is capable of making 3.377 tons/ha.

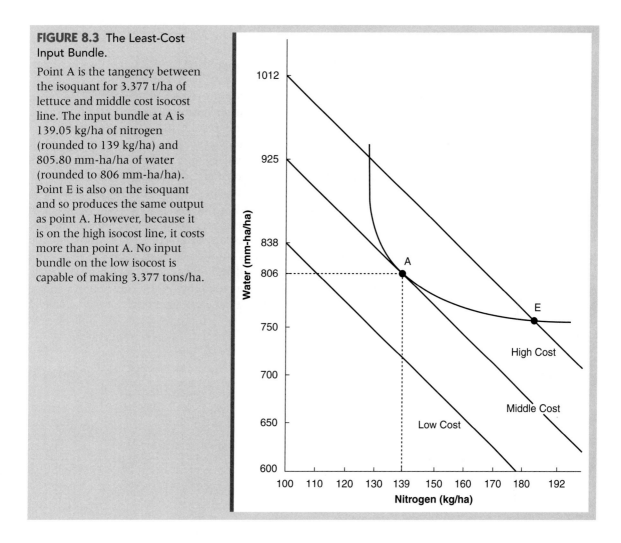

axis shows that Point A is 139.05 kg of nitrogen per hectare and 805.80 mm-ha of water per hectare. The cost at that point is $282.67/ha because the cost at every point on medium-cost line is $282.67/ha.

Finally, every point on the high isocost line, including point E, costs $302.68/ha. This is more than point A costs because every point of the high-cost isocost line costs more than A. So, although point E and point A make the same output, point E costs more and so is not the least-cost input bundle. Therefore, the cheapest way to grow 3.377 t/ha of lettuce is at point A, where the isocost line and isoquant are tangent.

BOX 8.2

Conservation Supply Curve

How much energy can be saved in a production process? Saving energy, one input to production, requires using more of other inputs to production if output is to be held constant. It is customary to display the results of such an analysis as a **conservation supply curve**, a graph of energy saved on the horizontal axis and cost of the other inputs needed to save that energy on the vertical axis. That is, all of the non-energy inputs are added together and treated as a single composite input. Like an isoquant, a conservation supply curve shows the tradeoff between two types of inputs, with output held constant. Unlike an isoquant, a conservation supply curve graphs energy saved instead of energy used on the horizontal axis. This gives the conservation supply curve its upwards slope, in contrast to the downward slope of an isoquant. Figure 8.4 shows a conservation curve for the paper industry, courtesy of a study by Worrell and others. They made the figure by considering a large number of techniques that could be used to save energy in the paper industry. The figure shows that considerable energy savings are available at low cost.

FIGURE 8.4 Energy Conservation Supply Curve for U.S. Pulp and Paper Industry.

This figure shows the cost of other inputs necessary to keep production constant but reduce energy use. The figure shows that many energy-conservation measures cost very little: 6.5 gigajoules (GJ) could be saved per ton at the then-current cost of energy of $3/GJ.

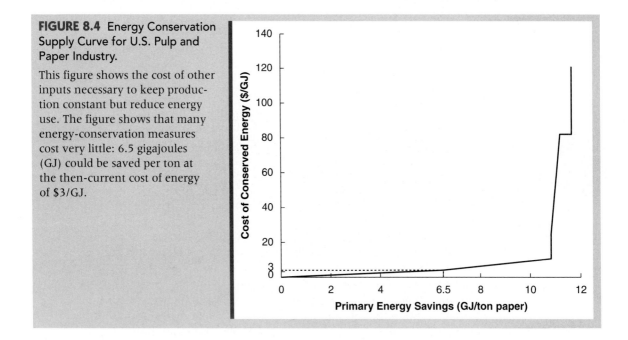

CHANGING OUTPUT

The cost of producing output has a pivotal role in determining how much output a producer will make and, therefore, a pivotal role in determining how much environmental damage results from production. The relationship between cost of production and the quantity produced comes from the choice of inputs.

Figure 8.5 shows three isoquants and three isocost lines, with each isocost line tangent to an isoquant. The isoquant representing 3.300 t/ha of lettuce is tangent to the lowest line in the figure at bundle G; that is, bundle G is the lowest-cost combination of nitrogen and water that will produce 3.300 t/ha. Similarly, bundles F and A

FIGURE 8.5 Three Points on a Cost Curve.

This figure shows how input choices, and thus costs, change as production increases.
The isoquants are marked with their lettuce yields in tons per hectare. See Table 8.1 for the calculation of costs.

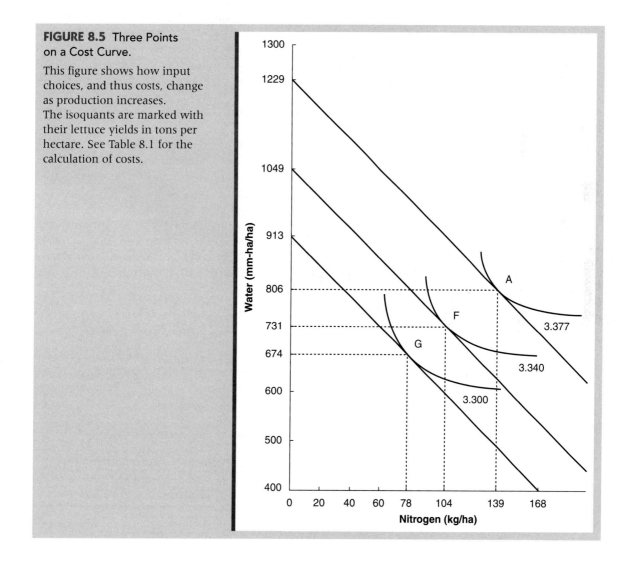

are the points of tangency representing the lowest cost for producing 3.340 and 3.377 tons/ha, respectively.

Each bundle is described by the coordinates for the point of tangency. The coordinates are the quantity of water and the quantity of nitrogen. Table 8.1 gives the coordinates of the points of tangency for the three curves, along with the costs associated with the three isocost lines. The cost of input bundle G is the price of water ($0.23/mm-ha) times the quantity of water (673.800 mm-ha/ha) plus the price of nitrogen ($0.70/kg) times the quantity of nitrogen (78.480 kg/ha); the costs for bundles A and F are calculated the same way.

Now let's consider different output quantities. The last column of Table 8.1 (with the heading Quantity) shows the different quantities produced. For each output quantity, there is a different cost of production. The second-to-last column of Table 8.1 (with the heading Cost) shows the different costs of production for each quantity produced. The numbers from these two columns—the quantity produced and the cost of production for the quantity produced—are graphed in Figure 8.6. In Figure 8.6, the cost of production is on the vertical axis, and the quantity produced is on the horizontal axis. The **cost curve**, $C(Q)$, describes the least amount of money needed to produce exactly output Q. Thus, the numbers in the last two columns in Table 8.1 identify three points on the cost curve in Figure 8.6. The cost curve is $C(Q)$ because it graphs the cost of production, C, for each quantity of production, Q. This cost curve to grow lettuce shows the relationship between output and the lowest cost to produce that output.

Both Table 8.1 and the upward-sloping cost curve in Figure 8.6 show that the cost of production increases as production increases. In this example, both nitrogen and water use increase as production increases. It is not always true that use of all inputs increases as output increases. However, the total cost of production always increases as the quantity produced increases. The cost curve will appear a great deal in the next chapter.

CHANGING AN INPUT PRICE

In the case of growing lettuce in the Salinas Valley, not only do water and nitrogen produce lettuce, but they also produce a negative externality, a polluting leachate. How does a change in the price for one of the inputs affect this effluent problem?

TABLE 8.1   Three Points on the Cost Function for Producing Lettuce.

POINT	NITROGEN (KG/HA)	WATER (MM-HA/HA)	COST ($/HA)	QUANTITY Q (T/HA)
A	139.05	805.80	$282.67	3.377
F	104.46	731.40	$241.34	3.340
G	78.48	673.80	$209.91	3.300

Note: The price of nitrogen is $0.70/kg and the price of water is $0.23/mm-ha.

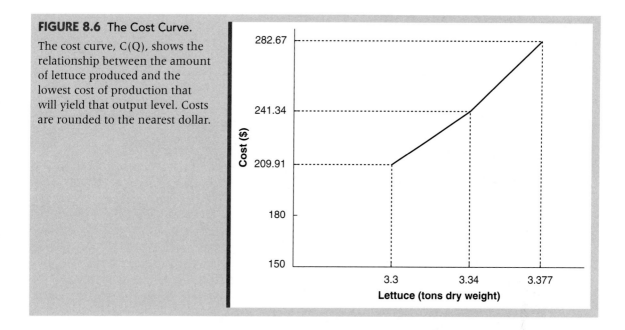

FIGURE 8.6 The Cost Curve.

The cost curve, C(Q), shows the relationship between the amount of lettuce produced and the lowest cost of production that will yield that output level. Costs are rounded to the nearest dollar.

For now let's think about the effects of a price increase for water, leaving the price of nitrogen unchanged. The first step is to revise the isocost lines with the new information about relative prices, and then consider the relationship of the revised isocost lines to the isoquant, to evaluate how the change in relative prices affects the cost of production and the mix of inputs.

Figures 8.7a and 8.7b show a single isoquant (output = 3.377 t/ha) with two isocost lines in a big-picture and a close-up view. Notice that they have very different axes: the intersection of the axes in Figure 8.7b is at (120 kg/ha, 700 mm-ha/ha), not (0 kg/ha, 600 mm-ha/ha), to permit the close-up view. As we are about to see, the two isocost lines reflect two different prices for water, which is on the vertical axis. Because the slope of the isocost line is the ratio of the input prices, isoquants with different water prices have different slopes and, therefore, are tangent to the isoquant at different points. In other words, a change in the price of water results in a change in the combination of water and nitrogen that will produce 3.377 t/ha of lettuce at the lowest cost. Because the price and the chosen input bundle change, the costs will also change.

First, recall the formula for an isocost line:

$$W = (TC/P_W) - (P_N/P_W)N.$$

The formula says that an isocost line has a vertical axis intercept of TC/P_W and a slope of $-(P_N/P_W)$. The slope, $-(P_N/P_W)$, is the negative of the ratio of the price of nitrogen to the price of water. If the price of one input changes while the price of the other input stays the same, the ratio of the prices changes, and therefore the two isocost lines have different slopes. The diagram indicates only that the slope of

FIGURE 8.7A The Effects of an Input Price Change.

The original isocost intersects the water axis at 1,229 mm-ha/ha and the nitrogen axis at 207 kg/ha. The high-price isocost line's intersection is at 959 mm-ha/ha on the water axis and 303 kg/ha on the nitrogen axis. Notice: the water axis starts at 600, not at zero.

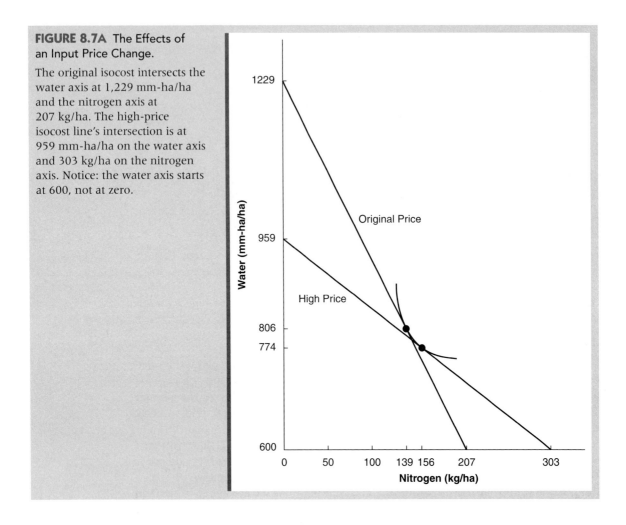

the isocost line, $-P_N/P_W$, has changed: it is shallower, which means that either P_N has decreased or P_W has increased. In this example, the change in the slope of the line comes only from a change—an increase, in this case—in the price of water, while the price of nitrogen is the original price of $0.70/kg.

Although an economist often has information about prices, the process of determining prices from a graph provides valuable insights about the relationships among prices, quantities, and total cost. Let's examine the figure to find out the old and new prices of water.

Figure 8.7a allows calculation of the slopes of each isocost line from the two points where each line intersects the two axes. The line with original prices intersects the vertical axis at ($N = 0$, $W = 1,229$), where zero nitrogen and 1,229 mm-ha of water are used. The original price line intersects the horizontal axis at ($N = 207$, $W = 600$), where 207 kg of nitrogen and 600 mm-ha of water are used per hectare. The slope of the line is rise/run = $(600 - 1,229)/(207 - 0) = -629/207 = -3.04$. Because

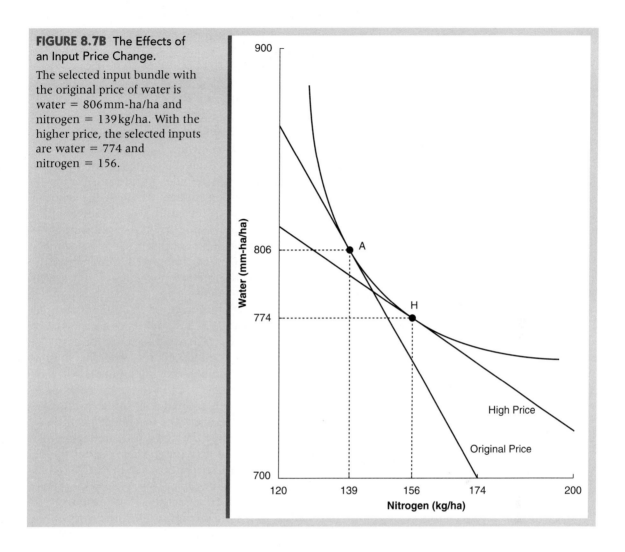

FIGURE 8.7B The Effects of an Input Price Change.

The selected input bundle with the original price of water is water = 806 mm-ha/ha and nitrogen = 139 kg/ha. With the higher price, the selected inputs are water = 774 and nitrogen = 156.

the slope of the isocost line is $-(P_N/P_W)$, then $-(P_N/P_W) = -3.04$, or $P_N/P_W = 3.04$. Solving for P_W produces $P_W = P_N/3.04$. Because $P_N = 0.70$ (the original price of nitrogen), the equation becomes $P_W = 0.70/3.04$. Therefore, the price of water, P_W, must be $(0.70)/3.04 = \$0.23$. This is as it should be, since our original price for water was \$0.23/mm-ha.

Now let's calculate the price of water on the line with the new, higher price for water. The new vertical intercept is 959, while the new horizontal intercept is 303; the slope of that line, which equals $-(P_N/P_W)$, is thus $-(959 - 600)/303 = -1.18$. Through use of the same formula as before, the price of water, P_W, $= (0.7)/1.18 = \$0.59$. The price of water increased by \$0.36/mm-ha.

Now let's look at the relationship between the isocost lines and the isoquant. The isocost lines in Figure 8.7a are tangent to the isoquant at different points. Keep in mind that each isocost line represents all the possible bundles of inputs that can be purchased for the same total cost, while the point of tangency between the iso-cost line and the isoquant represents the lowest-cost bundle. Thus, the fact that the isocost lines in Figure 8.7a are tangent to the isoquant at different points means that a change in the price of water results in a change in the lowest-cost combina-tion of nitrogen and water to produce 3.377 t/ha of lettuce.

Next, let's turn to Figure 8.7b, where the points of tangency are clearer. Point A is the tangency of the 3.377 isoquant with the original price line. Point H is the new tangency of the high price ($P_W = \$0.59$) isocost line with the 3.377 isoquant.

Table 8.2 shows the input bundles for points A and H, as well as the prices for each input and the cost of production for each bundle. As the price of water increases, with output held constant, the efficient bundle changes: the quantity of water decreases, while the quantity of nitrogen increases. For the new point of tangency, the amount of water decreases to 773.60 mm-ha. This result should not be a surprise: if water becomes more expensive, a producer seeks to avoid some of that expense and reduces the amount of water used. To maintain production and stay on the isoquant, though, the producer must increase the amount of nitrogen. Here, the amount of nitrogen has increased to 156.48 kg.

What happens, then, to the total cost of production when the price of an input increases? First, let's think about what to expect. When the price of water increases, the producer is likely to substitute nitrogen for water to avoid the price increase. The farmer can substitute nitrogen for water to some extent, but it's impossible to grow crops without any water at all. So the new cost-minimizing input bundle will have some nitrogen and some water. Does this new bundle cost more than the old bundle? Almost always, yes. The least-cost bundle at the old prices costs less than the new bundle at the old prices. (That's because it was the only least-cost bundle! Our draw-ings have only one least-cost bundle.) Now, because the new prices are higher than the old prices, the new bundle costs more at the new prices than it did at the old prices. As a result, the new bundle costs more at the new prices than the old bundle did at the old prices. Cost does go up when input prices go up. It's not surprising, then, that the total cost of producing 3.377 tons of lettuce has increased to $565.96/ha.

If an input price drops, the analysis works the same way. The producer will use more of the input with the lowered price, and total cost of production will drop.

TABLE 8.2 Costs and Changes in Input Price.

When the price of water increases, a farmer changes the amounts of both water and fertilizer used in order to minimize costs while keeping production constant.

TANGENCY	NITROGEN (KG/HA)	WATER (MM-HA/HA)	NITROGEN PRICE $/KG	WATER PRICE ($/MM-HA)	COST ($)
ORIGINAL (POINT A ON FIGURE 8.7B)	139.05	805.80	0.70	0.23	282.67
HIGH PRICE (POINT H ON FIGURE 8.7B)	156.48	773.60	0.70	0.59	565.96

NEW TECHNIQUES

The techniques are recipes that convert the inputs into the output. Techniques affect the location and shape of the isoquant. A new technique is typically an improved way of doing things. For instance, agronomic research might identify a superior irrigation method or better timing for application of fertilizer. A better technique is one that produces the same quantity of output with a decreased quantity of at least one input, and with no increase in any input.

How would a change in the technique available show up in the isoquant diagram? Figure 8.8 shows a new, improved technology for production. The higher isoquant is the original isoquant for producing 3.377 t/ha of lettuce, with a production cost of $282.67/ha and input levels $N = 139.05$ kg/ha and $W = 805.800$ mm-ha/ha. If no inputs increase, and if at least one input decreases, then the new isoquant must shift

FIGURE 8.8 Technical Progress.

In this figure, both isoquants produce 3.377 t/ha of lettuce. The lower isoquant uses a new technique that requires fewer inputs and thus can produce the same amount at lower cost. The move from the old to the new isoquant is technical progress.

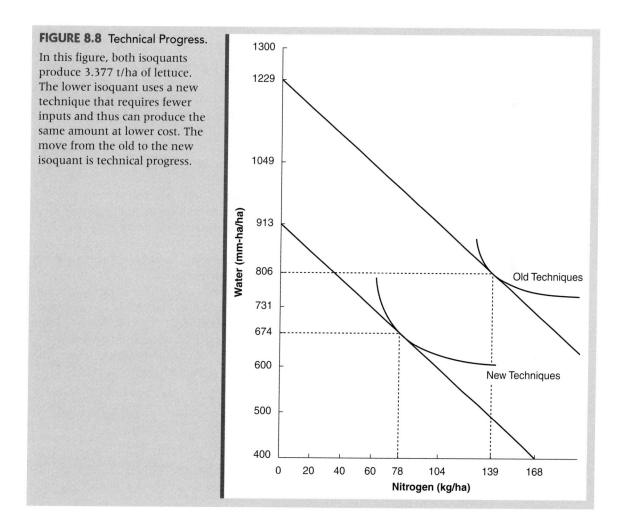

downward. An improved technology, represented by the lower isoquant, is closer to the origin but produces the same level of output, 3.377 t/ha. With the lower isoquant, though, the production cost is now $209.91/ha, which is less than the cost with the old technique. Input levels $N = 78$ kg/ha and $W = 674$ mm-ha/ha are also both less than the original levels.

In most situations, techniques should only improve: after all, if a producer has a choice between a higher-cost and a lower-cost way of producing goods, why would the producer ever choose the higher-cost method? Sometimes, though, a producer may be required to use a more costly method to meet other goals—perhaps environmental protection, perhaps pressure from interest groups, or perhaps restrictions placed on the use of the new technology. In those cases, the process reverses direction: a producer may be required to use the techniques represented by the higher isoquant even though she would prefer to use the newer techniques on the lower isoquant. Limiting technology in this way will increase the cost of production.

IN SUMMARY

- Isoquants define different techniques (input combinations and recipes for producing output) that produce the same amount of output. Isocost lines define the different combinations of inputs that have the same total cost.
- Producers seek the least-cost way of producing the level of output they have decided to make. To do so, the producer finds the lowest isocost line that touches the desired isoquant. The lowest isocost line that touches the isoquant defines the amount of each input necessary to produce a given quantity of output at the lowest possible cost.
- An increase in the price of an input leads to less use of that input and to a higher total cost of production. A decrease in the price of an input leads to an increase in use of that input and to a lower total cost of production.
- A new technique shifts the isoquant downward. Usually producers will only adopt new techniques that lead to less input use, and therefore to a lower cost of production, than the older production methods.
- The cost curve $C(Q)$ is the least amount of money needed to buy the inputs that produce output Q. The cost curve summarizes the relationship between the cost of production and the quantity produced. The cost of production increases if production increases, or if the price of an input increases, or if a less efficient technology is mandated. The cost of production decreases with improved technologies or a lower price for an input.

Costs and the Environment

Understanding why producers behave as they do is critical for getting to the root of most environmental problems. In discussing how the farmer decides on the amount of nitrogen and water, it is time to consider the environmental effects of using those inputs for growing lettuce.

Just as the isoquant shows the different combinations of nitrogen and water that produce the same amount of lettuce per hectare, it is possible to graph an *isopollution* curve that shows the different combinations of water and nitrogen that lead to the same groundwater pollution. An **isopollution curve** represents different combinations of inputs that produce the same level of pollution.

The isopollution curve for Salinas is shown as the dashed line in Figure 8.9. There is no general shape for isopollution curves. In this farming example, the isopollution curves slope down because, if water application increases, pollution will increase if the same amount of nitrogen is applied. The curve here corresponds to 121 kg/ha of leachate, the amount that results from the cost-minimizing technique in Figure 8.9. (There is no way to know this from the diagram; it is calculated from a model of agricultural runoff.)

There is no tangency for this line. This is because, in the absence of any regulation, the farmer has no economic reason to be aware of the pollution that she causes. She is interested only in finding the least expensive way to produce 3.377 tons of lettuce per hectare. The pollution level happens as a result of that choice. If she personally cares about pollution and has knowledge of the complexities of nitrate

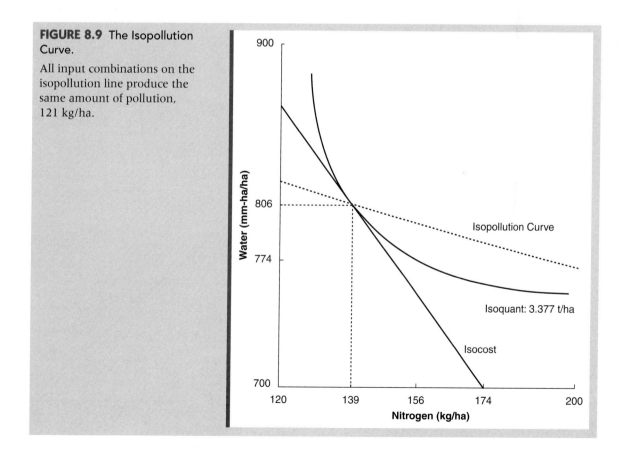

FIGURE 8.9 The Isopollution Curve.

All input combinations on the isopollution line produce the same amount of pollution, 121 kg/ha.

leachate, then she can produce her lettuce in a less polluting manner, but it will cost her more to produce this way. The least-cost way to produce is usually not the least-polluting way to produce.

This is an example of a very general problem. Recall from Chapter 3 that an externality happens when a market activity affects someone not involved in the transaction. Pollution is an unintended and often unrecognized side effect of production. As long as the least-cost input choice is not the lowest-pollution choice, avoiding the pollution will increase the cost of production.

For this reason, pollution control policies focus on the relationship between costs and pollution. Putting isoquants and isopollution lines on the same diagram makes it possible to look at this relationship. Figure 8.10 repeats all the elements of

FIGURE 8.10 Leachate and an Input Price Change.

The original level of leachate was 121.0 kg/ha. When the price of water is increased and output is held constant, the chosen input bundle changes from A to H. The new least-cost input bundle is on a lower isopollution curve than the original bundle. The level of leachate for the new bundle is 116.4 kg/ha.

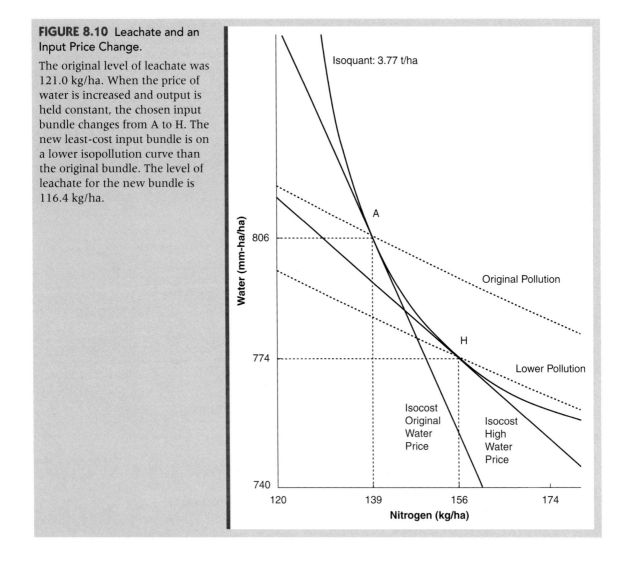

the price change diagram, Figure 8.7b, and adds two isopollution lines. The line labeled "Original Pollution" is the isopollution line from Figure 8.9, for 121 kg/ha of leachate. The line labeled "Lower Pollution" is new. It shows all the combinations of water and nitrogen that will result in 116.4 kg/ha of leachate.

The regulator's goal is to reduce leachate from 121 to 116.4 kg/ha. There are two basic ways to do this: either tell the producer how much pollution she can cause, or change the price of a polluting input. Let's begin with price.

There is one isoquant in Figure 8.10 because the quantity of lettuce is staying constant. There are two isocost lines. The line that includes point A is the isocost line for the original price of water. At the original price of water, point A is the chosen bundle because it is the tangency of the isoquant and the isocost line. Point A is also on the Original Pollution line: producing 3.377 t/ha of lettuce using 806 mm-ha of water and 139 kg-ha of nitrogen causes 121 kg/ha of leachate.

Now suppose that the price of water is increased by imposing a tax of $0.36/mm-ha. From the farmer's point of view, this is an increase in the price of water from $0.23 to $0.59/mm-ha. If the price of water increases, holding output constant, the farmer will shift her input choices from point A to point H. The line that includes point H is the isocost line for the new price of water. At the new price of water, point H is the chosen bundle because it is the tangency of the isoquant and the new isocost line. In other words, the farmer will change the mix of water and nitrogen, decreasing the amount of water from 806 to 774 mm-ha, and increasing the amount of nitrogen from 139 to 156 kg per hectare. The isopollution line through bundle H has 116.4 kg/ha of pollution. Thus, when the farmer responds to the change in the price of water by changing the input mix, the level of pollution will fall from 121.0 to 116.4 kg/ha. In general, raising the price of a polluting input has the effect of decreasing pollution.

A tax, then, is one pollution control policy. Now let's consider an alternative: an *effluent standard*. Effluent means emissions, or pollution. An **effluent standard** is a requirement to produce no more than a specified level of effluent. Assuming for now that the farmer is not going to change the quantity of lettuce she produces, a regulator could require that the farmer produce no more than the amount of leachate on the lower isopollution curve, 116.4 kg/ha. Which input bundle will the farmer choose in response to this requirement? When there was no tax or standard, her chosen bundle was point A, which happened to be on the original isopollution line. Looking again at Figure 8.10 shows that the lower isopollution line crosses the isoquant at point H. The mix of inputs at point H will satisfy the regulator, and so will any mix found at a point to the right of H, because any of those choices will result in 116.4 kg/ha or less of pollution. But the points to the right are higher-cost options than the bundle on the isoquant at point H. So the efficient bundle of nitrogen and water with the effluent standard is at H. This is exactly the same as the efficient bundle with a tax increase.

Faced with either the tax increase or the effluent standard, the farmer will choose the same amount of nitrogen and water, produce the same 3.377 t/ha of lettuce, and cause the same amount of pollution. The difference is in the cost of production. Under the standard, the price of water does not change. Under a tax, the price of water increases for every unit of water—not just on the units of water that the regulator would like the farmer not to use. The last column of Table 8.3 shows that the cost of meeting the effluent standard is $287.46/ha. This is a slightly higher cost of production than the original $282.67/ha, but nowhere near as sharp an increase as the $565.96/ha cost of production under a tax. So, when output is held constant, an effluent standard leads to lower pollution and higher cost than no standard, whereas a tax can lead to the same reduction in pollution and a greater increase in the cost of production than the standard.

The first two rows of Table 8.3 show the information for this price change. The last column of the table suggests why farmers resist policies to reduce pollution by raising the price of water. The farmer's cost of production is about double!

Although there are cost advantages to using an effluent standard to reduce the amount of nitrogen leaching into the groundwater, an effluent standard is often impractical for nonpoint sources such as agriculture. Because it's not easy to measure how much pollution comes from each field, it is very difficult to enforce an effluent standard for agricultural runoff. Imposing a tax gets around this problem, but it raises the price of every unit of water that the farmer uses.

Is there an alternative to taxes and effluent standards? One possibility is a restriction on what technology can be used. A **technology standard** is a requirement to use a particular technique in making a good. Building codes that require double-paned windows to save energy are a good example of a technology standard. In the case of lettuce, a technology standard might be to require the farmer to use the input combination of point H. This form of standard would have the same effect as the effluent standard, but it is based on use of inputs that a regulator can observe.

In this example, a technology standard requiring input combination H would result in 3.377 t/ha of lettuce and also achieve the environmental goal of 116.5 kg/ha of pollution. It is in no way certain, however, that a government will choose a technology standard that satisfies production and pollution goals. Without the farmer's specific knowledge of soil conditions, which affect both crop growth and pollution

TABLE 8.3   Costs with Price and Quantity Controls.

The original quantities of nitrogen and water, tangency A, are in the first row. The second row, tangency H, shows the new quantities of nitrogen and water that the farmer will use if the price of water increases due to a tax increase; the cost of production will roughly double. The third row shows an alternative policy, an effluent standard, that achieves the same reduction in water use, same nitrogen use, and the same reduction in leachate. The leachate reduction requires only a slight increase in cost of production.

TANGENCIES	N (KG/HA)	W (MM-HA/HA)	N PRICE ($/KG)	W PRICE ($/MM-HA)	COST ($/HA)
A	139.05	805.80	0.70	0.23	282.67
H (WITH TAX ON WATER)	156.48	773.60	0.70	0.59	565.96
H (WITH STANDARD)	156.48	773.60	0.70	0.23	287.46

levels, a regulator could easily set a technology standard for the farmer that would not achieve one or the other of these goals. This issue, of what type of policy to use, returns in Chapter 12.

So far, output has been constant. In fact, a change in production costs will have consequences for how much output is produced. Taxes and standards both result in a lower quantity of output and higher prices for consumers. However, they do not result in the same change in quantity and prices because taxes cost the firm more than standards do for the same pollution reduction. How they differ is a subject for the next chapter.

IN SUMMARY

- An isopollution curve represents different combinations of inputs that produce the same level of pollution.
- Because pollution is an externality, producers have no reason to consider environmental effects in their decision on how much of different inputs to use in their production processes.
- Pollution happens when the least-cost combination of inputs contributes to pollution; in other words, producers pollute when it is less expensive to pollute than not to pollute.
- One way to reduce pollution is to change the relative prices of the inputs, for instance, by taxing a polluting input, so that a cost-minimizing producer will choose a less-polluting input combination.
- Pollution also can be reduced by using regulatory standards, such as an effluent standard that limits pollution. If output remains the same, the effluent standard results in the same level of pollution and the same input mix as a tax, but the cost of production does not increase as much under an effluent standard as it does under a tax.
- A technology standard regulates the technique used in production. It can result in the same level of pollution and the same input mix as an effluent standard or a tax, if output is held constant.

Inputs to Electricity Production

Of the many possible inputs to electricity production, some produce more greenhouse gases than others. Oil produces less carbon dioxide (CO_2, a greenhouse gas) than coal, and natural gas produces less carbon dioxide than oil. In the United States, CO_2 emissions from electric power production increased from 2.08 trillion tons in 1995 to 2.51 trillion tons in 2005. Then, in response to increasing petroleum prices, power plants started using more natural gas. As a result, greenhouse gas emissions from electric power plants fell to 2.46 trillion tons in 2006.

In Denmark, between 1990 and 2004, GHG emissions from energy production fell 1.7 percent. This was mostly the result of a shift from coal to natural gas and the increasing use of renewable energy sources, such as wind power. Between 1997 and 2004, Denmark imposed carbon taxes on producers as well as consumers. Carbon taxes increased the cost to producers of using higher-emission inputs such as coal and oil relative to lower-emission inputs such as natural gas and wind.

In both of these cases, an increase in the price of a polluting input led producers to change production techniques to less-polluting alternatives. The only difference is that one was a deliberate choice to use a tax to accomplish an environmental goal.

CHAPTER SUMMARY

Here are the key lessons from this chapter:

- Producers make output from inputs. A production technique is the recipe that describes how the inputs are combined to make the output. A technique is efficient if there is no other technique that produces the same output and uses less of at least one input while using the same amount of the other inputs.
- An isoquant describes the combinations of inputs that all produce the same quantity. Isoquants slope downward: with production held constant, decreasing one input requires the other input to increase. If they sloped upward, then the isoquants would not describe an efficient production technique because more inputs than necessary would be used to produce the same output.
- An isocost line represents different combinations of inputs that have the same cost. A producer who wants to minimize the cost of producing a specified level of output will find the lowest isocost line that touches the isoquant for that output level. The resulting tangency identifies the combination of inputs that minimizes the cost of producing that level of output; it also identifies the minimum cost of production.
- The least-cost combination of inputs will change if input prices, technology, or the level of output changes. If an input price goes up, the cost of production will either go up or stay unchanged. If an input price drops, the cost of production will either drop or stay unchanged. Improved technologies reduce the cost of production; producers are unlikely to choose worse technologies unless they are required to do so by government regulation or other pressure.
- A cost curve shows the relationship between the amount produced and the minimum cost of producing at a given level. Increased output results in a higher total cost of production.
- An isopollution curve represents different combinations of inputs that produce the same level of pollution.
- A producer's decisions will have environmental implications, but price signals alone typically give producers no incentive to consider those environmental effects. Pollution and other environmental harm occur when the least-cost method of production leads to those results.

- By taxing or regulating environmentally damaging behavior, the government can give producers incentives to reduce environmental damage. Producers will respond to these incentives by changing the input combination to achieve the lowest cost of production.

KEY TERMS

conservation supply curve *(p. 170)*

cost curve *(p. 172)*

efficient *(p. 164)*

effluent standard *(p. 181)*

inefficient *(p. 164)*

inputs *(p. 162)*

isocost line *(p. 167)*

isopollution curve *(p. 179)*

isoquant *(p. 164)*

nonpoint source *(p. 162)*

output *(p. 162)*

point source *(p. 161)*

production *(p. 162)*

technique *(p. 162)*

technology *(p. 163)*

technology standard *(p. 182)*

NOTES

The information on reducing nitrogen leachate by reducing water use is from Gloria E. Helfand, "Alternative Pollution Standards for Regulating Nonpoint Source Pollution," *Journal of Environmental Management* 45 (1995): 231–241. Douglas Larson and Brett House helped develop the example.

Agricultural yield functions are covered in Sadi S. Grimm, Quirino Paris, and William A. Williams, "A von Liebig Model for Water and Nitrogen Crop Response," *Western Journal of Agricultural Economics* 12 (1987): 182–192.

The algal bloom story comes from Gloria Helfand and John Wolfe, "Michigan's Environment," Chapter 20 in Charles Ballard, Paul Courant, Douglas Drake, and Elizabeth Gerber (eds.), *Michigan at the Millennium* (Lansing: Michigan State University Press, 2003).

The conservation supply curve is from Ernst Worrell et al., "Opportunities to Improve Energy Efficiency in the U.S. Pulp and Paper Industry," Lawrence Berkeley National Laboratory Paper # 48354, 2001.

The information on emissions from U.S. power plants is from the U.S. Energy Information Administration, "Emissions from Energy Consumption at Conventional Power Plants and Combined-Heat-and-Power Plants, 1995 through 2006," *Electric Power Annual*, Table 5.1 October 22, 2007. To learn more about U.S. energy use, visit the website of the U.S. Energy Information Administration, http://www.eia.doe.gov/fuelelectric.html.

The information on emissions from energy production in Denmark is from the U.N. Framework Convention on Climate Change, "Report of the centralized in-depth review of the fourth national communication of Denmark" (February 1, 2007), paragraph 23, p. 7 and paragraph 67, p. 16. http://unfccc.int/resource/docs/2007/idr/dnk04.pdf.

EXERCISES

1. Ground-level ozone produces an interesting example of the consequence of isopollution curves that do not always slope downward. Ozone is an air pollutant that results from a chemical reaction involving hydrocarbons (HC) and nitrogen oxides (NO_x), both pollutants in their own rights, in the presence of sunlight. The isopollution curves for ozone production mostly slope downward but then bend up at one end. Consider Figure 8.11. It shows two isopollution curves, one with a higher level of ozone than the other. Thus, point A represents higher ozone levels than point B. In practice, air pollution regulators typically reduce ozone by requiring reductions in both NO_x and HC. Suppose, however, that ozone levels are at point B and that a regulator proposes to

FIGURE 8.11 Isopollution Lines for Ozone Production.

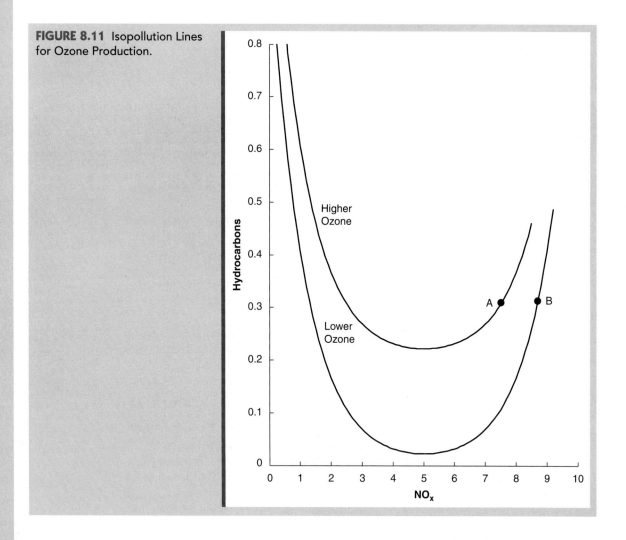

reduce only NO_x levels because NO_x itself causes damages. This phenomenon is known as NO_x disbenefit. What happens to ozone levels?

2. Automakers can produce cars using machinery and labor. In particular, 50 cars can be produced using the following combinations of machinery and labor:

MACHINERY	LABOR
5	2
4	3
3	5

(a) If you were to graph these points on a figure with machinery on the horizontal axis and labor on the vertical axis, what would you be graphing? In other words, what do these different combinations of inputs represent?
(b) Suppose machinery costs $30/machine, while labor costs $40/worker. How much would each of these combinations cost? Perform a similar calculation if machinery costs $50 and labor $40; and if machinery costs $70 and labor $40.
(c) What is the lowest-cost combination of machinery and labor when the price of machinery is $30 and the price of labor is $40? When machinery costs $50 and labor costs $40? When machinery costs $70 and labor costs $40?
(d) As the price of machinery rises relative to the price of labor, what happens to the relative amounts of machinery and labor that minimize cost?
(e) As the price of machinery increases, while the price of labor stays constant, what happens to the minimum possible total cost of producing 50 cars?
(f) Suppose that the use of machinery causes pollution, while the use of labor does not. Machinery costs $30/machine if environmental costs are not considered, but each machine causes $20/machine of environmental damage; labor still costs $40. The environmental damage does not harm the manufacturer. If there is no regulation concerning pollution, what input combination would the automaker use, and what would be the automaker's costs?
(g) If automakers had to pay for the damages associated with machine use, what input combination would they use, and what would be their costs?
(h) If the government instead used a standard to limit machine use to four machines, what input combination would automakers use, and what would be their costs?

3. From Table 8.2, the chosen input mix for the lettuce farmer is ($N = 139.05$, $W = 805.80$) when the prices are $P_N = \$0.70/kg$ and $P_W = \$0.23/mm\text{-}ha$. Suppose that the prices of both of these inputs double. Does the chosen input mix change? Why or why not? What happens to cost?

4. Let's consider the case where there are many inputs, two of which function exactly the same in the production process. For instance, suppose that red apples with and without white spots can be used interchangeably to make identical-tasting apple pie. Is there a unique cost-minimizing way to make

apple pies? Suppose that both types of apples initially have the same price; then, the price of the spotted ones increases. Which apples will be used after the price increase? Will the cost curve shift upward as a result of this price increase? How might the relationship between the two types of apples in the apple pie-making process be described?

5. The idea underlying "pollution prevention" is that, rather than reduce pollution after it is created, businesses should avoid creation of pollution in the first place, by using less polluting inputs and by changing production processes.

   (a) One of the arguments for pollution prevention is that pollution is waste, and reducing waste should reduce costs. For instance, in some cases, businesses are able to recapture and make use of compounds that would otherwise have been emitted into the air or water. Why would a firm produce waste if it could make use of those compounds?

   (b) In some cases, businesses have been able to reduce costs and increase profits through pollution prevention. One explanation is that the businesses were operating inefficiently before instituting pollution prevention. Are there any other explanations?

Production, Pollution, Output, and Prices

Total emissions are the product of emissions per unit of output times the number of units of output that each firm makes, times the number of firms making that product. This chapter focuses on the second and third parts of that equation: how pollution control measures affect output per firm and the number of firms in an industry, in both the short and the long run. Examining the amount of output a firm decides to make uses the cost curve, which shows the relationship between the cost of production and the amount of output. We will also see how the cost of pollution control is passed on to consumers in the form of higher prices, and how higher prices reduce pollution by decreasing consumption.

While there are many models of firm behavior, this chapter focuses on a very useful baseline model, that of price-taking firms: firms that respond to market prices for both inputs and outputs and cannot change those prices. This chapter will examine:

- Costs of production and the concept of marginal cost;
- The role of profits in an individual firm's decision on how much to produce and to pollute;
- How regulating pollution reduces output and increases consumer prices in an industry.

Emissions from Paper Production

Paper, although a vital input to a student's academic process, rarely merits much attention, and even less thought is given to its origins. It is therefore unlikely that users of paper consider the byproducts of its production: air pollution, water pollution, and changes to forest ecosystems.

Paper production usually begins with harvesting wood from forests. Unlike lumber production, where the size of a tree matters for the size of boards that can come from it, the size of a tree is not important in the production of paper; all that matters is the volume of pulp that can be gotten from an area of trees. As a result, forests used for pulp production will have younger trees and different ecological characteristics than forests grown for lumber or forests left as wilderness.

Once the wood is harvested, paper mills combine the wood with chemicals to make pulp. The process often results in significant emissions to water and air. Water pollutants include biological and chemical oxygen demand—compounds that reduce the oxygen in water and therefore kill many forms of aquatic life. Air pollutants include greenhouse gases, nitrogen oxides and hydrocarbons (which contribute to smog), and sulfur dioxide (which can cause acid rain and snow). The leaking to the air of bleach used to whiten paper is particularly noticeable to anyone within smelling distance. The pulp is then made into paper.

The European Union (EU) required pollution-control measures for its paper industry that increased costs by about 2 percent in 1999. The law allowed eight years for existing plants to comply but required new plants to comply immediately. Permitting existing plants to operate under less stringent rules than new plants is called grandfathering. Grandfathered firms have lower costs of production than firms that are subject to regulation. Let's use the example of paper production to examine the relationship between production costs and pollution.

Costs of Production

The technology that a firm uses is summarized in isoquants. The cost curve, $C(Q)$, is built up from input prices and isoquants. The convention in economics is to include the costs of all of the inputs, whether the firm's owner has had to pay for them or not. Inputs that the firm uses but does not pay for are valued at their opportunity cost, the value that they would have in their best use other than at the firm. For instance, if a firm's owners had a building that the firm used without paying for it, economists would count the market rent on that building as a cost of production. From the cost curve, we derive *fixed and variable costs, average fixed and average variable costs,* and *marginal costs.* These curves are the building blocks needed to explore a firm's choice of output and its profits.

FIXED AND VARIABLE COSTS OF INPUTS TO PRODUCTION

Production costs are the cost of the inputs to production. The inputs for making paper and other products can be organized into three categories: plant and equipment, labor, and energy and materials. The plant and equipment are **capital**; the money invested in them is the **capital cost**, or **capital investment**. In a study of the Swedish paper industry, Per-Olov Marklund and Eva Samakovlis found that capital's share of cost was 20 percent, labor's share of cost was 56 percent, and the rest went to energy and materials. The cost curves in this chapter take their work as a starting point.

In the decision on how much paper to produce, one consideration is how quickly the firm can change the inputs to achieve a different production level. If the paper mill's manager wants to increase production, he can buy more wood and chemicals and hire more workers. The capital investment, on the other hand, takes quite a while to change: the plant might have to be expanded or a new mill built. The inputs that can be changed quickly are **variable inputs**. The inputs that take considerable time to change—plant and equipment—are **fixed inputs**. The time span that is just long enough to change the variable inputs, but too short to change the fixed inputs, is called the **short run**. The **long run** is a time span so long that all inputs can be changed.

Now let's think about the cost of these inputs. First, what are the paper mill's costs if the paper mill produces nothing at all? If production is zero, the owners of that mill do not have to pay for wood, chemicals, or other variable inputs. However, they do have to keep making loan payments on the mill and equipment. The capital costs, then, are *fixed costs*. **Fixed costs, FC**, are the cost of producing nothing: $FC = C(0)$.

The *variable costs* of producing quantity Q, written $VC(Q)$, are the costs of the variable inputs: labor, material, and energy. **Variable costs, VC**, are all those costs that are not fixed: $VC(Q) = C(Q) - FC$.

A firm's manager also needs to know how much it costs on average to produce paper. **Average cost**, written **AC(Q)**, is the cost divided by the number of units made: $AC(Q) = C(Q)/Q$. **Average variable cost, AVC(Q)**, is the variable cost of making a certain quantity of units, divided by the quantity of units produced. Thus, $AVC(Q) = VC(Q)/Q$. **Average fixed cost, AFC(Q)**, comes from dividing fixed cost by all Q units: $AFC(Q) = FC/Q$. While FC stays the same no matter how many units are produced, AFC decreases as Q increases. Table 9.1 shows Q, C, AC, FC, AFC, VC, and AVC for the paper mill. Quantity is in thousands of metric tons, abbreviated kt. With $C(Q)$ and FC based on Marklund and Samakovlis, all the other columns were derived using the formulas discussed previously.

Let's graph AC, AVC, and AFC. All of the average cost measures are in dollars per ton. So our graph, like a supply and demand graph, has quantity on the horizontal axis and dollars per unit on the vertical axis.

The easiest curve to graph is average fixed cost. As shown in Figure 9.1, this curve starts very high and falls rapidly, as the fixed cost is spread among an increasing number of units. All average fixed cost curves have this shape because all of them take a fixed number of dollars and divide it by an increasing quantity of output.

To consider the shape of the average variable cost curve, let's consider the paper mill. The mill has a specified amount of machinery (fixed inputs) but a changeable number of workers (a variable input). When production levels are very low, adding workers may speed up production quite a bit, as the machinery can be used more efficiently. When production levels are high, adding workers still will increase production but not as much. That's because, when production is high, the machinery is being used almost to its capacity, and more workers will not be able to get much more production out of the machinery. In other words, for

TABLE 9.1   Costs for a Paper Mill.

Q (KT)	C(Q) (1,000$)	AC(Q) $/T	FC (1,000$)	AFC(Q) ($/T)	VC(Q) (1,000$)	AVC(Q) ($/T)
20	104881	5244.05	78660	3933.00	26221	1311.05
50	104937	2098.74	78660	1573.20	26277	525.54
100	105910	1059.10	78660	786.60	27250	272.50
150	110460	736.40	78660	524.40	31800	212.00
200	123380	616.90	78660	393.30	44720	223.60
268	167511	625.04	78660	293.51	88851	331.53
268.5	167999	625.69	78660	292.96	89339	332.73
269	168490	626.36	78660	292.42	89830	333.94
269.5	168984	627.03	78660	291.87	90324	335.15
270	169481	627.71	78660	291.33	90821	336.37
270.5	169981	628.40	78660	290.79	91321	337.60
271	170484	629.09	78660	290.26	91824	338.83
271.5	170990	629.80	78660	289.72	92330	340.07
272	171498	630.51	78660	289.19	92838	341.32
272.5	172010	631.23	78660	288.66	93350	342.57
273	172525	631.96	78660	288.13	93865	343.83
300	205087	683.62	78660	262.20	126427	421.42
350	295356	843.87	78660	224.74	216696	619.13
400	437137	1092.84	78660	196.65	358477	896.19

low levels of quantity, it is likely that output will go up faster than variable cost; this means that average variable cost will decrease as quantity increases from a low level. As quantity gets high, though, variable cost will go up faster than quantity, which means that average variable cost will increase. As quantity increases, average variable cost often first falls and then rises: the curve is shaped like a U, as shown in Figure 9.1.

Finally, let's think about the shape of the average cost curve. Because cost is the sum of fixed cost and variable cost, AC is the sum of AVC and AFC. AFC is very

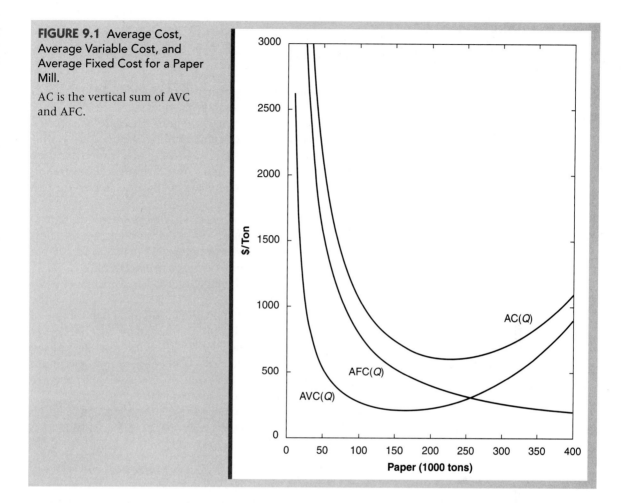

FIGURE 9.1 Average Cost, Average Variable Cost, and Average Fixed Cost for a Paper Mill.

AC is the vertical sum of AVC and AFC.

large when quantity is close to zero. Additionally, for a U-shaped AVC curve, AVC is also very large when quantity is close to zero. The sum of AFC and AVC must also be very large when quantity is close to zero. Both AVC and AFC decrease initially as quantity increases; as a result, AC also decreases initially as quantity increases.

As quantity gets larger, AFC becomes very small, but AVC increases. As quantity gets large, then, the fact that AVC becomes large means that AC also becomes large. Because AC decreases when quantity is small and increases when quantity is large, AC is also in the shape of a U. Because AC = AVC + AFC, AC(Q) is always above AVC(Q) by the amount AFC(Q).

MARGINAL COST

Our mill manager's output decision, with all its effects on the environment, can be summarized by asking, "Should I produce one more thousand-ton unit of

---

BOX 9.1

Environmental Costs for Refineries

Oil refineries are a heavily regulated industry. They must comply with standards that limit their emissions of such pollutants as sulfur oxides, and their products must meet strict requirements. The Clean Air Act Amendments of 1990 required refineries to produce cleaner fuels, including gasoline with oxygenates, low-sulfur diesel fuel, and reformulated gasoline in 1995. To make these products, they needed to invest in their refineries. The U.S. Energy Information Administration collected data on the costs of environmental compliance. These costs were of two types, operating costs and investments.

In 1995, the refineries spent $0.49 per barrel (42 U.S. gallons) on environmental operating costs. These costs included keeping emissions out of the air and extra refining to make gasoline and diesel fuels cleaner. With the other AVC equal to $26.49 per barrel, variable costs attributable to the environment were 1.8 percent of AVC.

In the early 1990s, refineries invested $10 billion over five years to meet environmental standards. To find a yearly cost, we need to consider how much of the investment is used up each year, called depreciation, and also how much the use of a dollar for a year is worth, called interest. If the environmental investment depreciated at a normal rate of approximately 5 percent, and the interest rate on the money invested was 10 percent, then the yearly cost of the investment was about $1.5 billion. In 1995, production was 5.8 billion barrels, so the increase in average fixed costs caused by environmental compliance was about $0.26 per barrel.

In 1995, the price per barrel of refined product was $27.04, and the total of the environmental average fixed and variable costs were $0.75. So environmental average costs were 2.8 percent of price.

---

paper?" That brings us to *marginal cost*. **Marginal cost**, or **MC(Q)**, is approximated as the cost of producing one additional unit beyond Q. In symbols, $MC(Q) = C(Q + 1) - C(Q)$. Marginal cost depends on quantity. In our mill example, the cost of producing one more ton of paper is very high when the plant is already producing near its capacity.

A better approximation of marginal cost is obtained by considering smaller amounts of additional output—for instance, a half kt instead of a whole kt. To approximate marginal cost with an amount other than one unit of additional output, the approximation is the difference in cost divided by the difference in quantity. Look at the first column of Table 9.2. For outputs between 268 and 273 kt, the table includes values for every 1/2 kt (that is, 500 tons) of output. Marginal cost evaluated at 268 kt, for instance, is $[C(268.5) - C(268)]/(0.5) = (167999 - 167511)/(0.5) = 976$. The line labeled MC($Q$) in Figure 9.2 on page 196 was calculated just this way.

When graphed, marginal cost always goes through the lowest point on the average cost curve. This is a general property of marginal and average. Think of grades as an example. Average grade is a grade point average. Marginal grade is the

TABLE 9.2 Cost and Marginal Cost for a Paper Mill.

Q	C	MC
20	104881	0.27
50	104937	5
100	105910	43
150	110460	156
200	123380	387
268	167511	976
268.5	167999	982
269	168490	988
269.5	168984	994
270	169481	1000
270.5	169981	1006
271	170484	1012
271.5	170990	1016
272	171498	1024
272.5	172010	1030
273	172525	1036
300	205087	1394
350	295356	2274
400	437137	3454

Note: Marginal cost is calculated in increments of ½ kt. Only the MC values for quantities between 268 and 272.5 can be replicated using the information in this table; the other values are derived using information not presented here.

grade in a course not yet included in the grade point average. If the marginal grade is higher than the average, the average goes up; if lower, it goes down. An average increases if a new member of the group is larger than the average of the previous members. So when the costs of a new unit are bigger than the average of the costs of the previous units, the average of the costs increases. By the same logic, if the

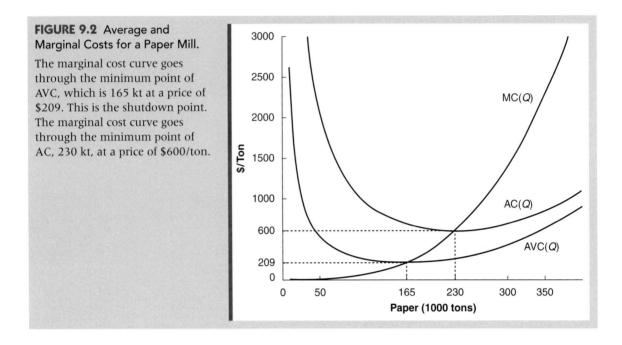

FIGURE 9.2 Average and Marginal Costs for a Paper Mill.

The marginal cost curve goes through the minimum point of AVC, which is 165 kt at a price of $209. This is the shutdown point. The marginal cost curve goes through the minimum point of AC, 230 kt, at a price of $600/ton.

marginal cost of producing the next increment is less than the average cost, it will pull the average cost down. Therefore, average cost rises whenever marginal cost is greater than average cost, and average cost falls whenever marginal cost is less than average cost. So when MC = AC, then AC must be at the bottom of the U where it neither rises nor falls. Figure 9.2 shows AC, AVC, and MC for the paper mill. The bottom of the U for average cost is 230 kt, where MC intersects AC. The same argument holds for average variable cost: marginal cost goes through the bottom of average variable costs. For the paper mill, the minimum is at 165 kt of paper.

IN SUMMARY

- The cost of production is the sum of fixed cost and variable cost.
- Fixed cost comes from inputs that can only be changed over time, such as factories and machinery; it does not change in the short run as production changes. This cost must be paid even if there is no output produced.
- Variable cost, such as the amount of energy or chemicals, can be changed quickly as production levels change. Variable costs increase as production increases because the firm must have more of the raw materials and labor to produce more output.
- Average fixed cost is equal to fixed cost divided by quantity (AFC = FC/Q). The graph of AFC is a downward-sloping curve because it is a fixed value divided by an ever-larger quantity.
- Average variable cost is equal to variable cost divided by quantity (AVC = VC/Q). The graph of average variable cost is typically U-shaped.

- Average cost equals average variable cost plus average fixed cost (AC = AVC + AFC). Because average cost is a vertical sum of the average variable cost and average fixed cost curves, the graph of average cost is always above average variable cost and average fixed cost and typically is U-shaped.
- Marginal cost, the cost of the next unit of production, is approximately the change in cost divided by a small change in output. The marginal cost curve goes through the bottoms of U-shaped average and average variable cost curves.

Supply, Profits, and Pollution in a Single Firm

Our U-shaped cost curve diagram lets us find the supply curve of the firm. Identifying it starts with the firm's objective, which is to make profits.

Let's assume that the mill can sell a unit of paper in the market for price P and that the mill can't influence the price of paper. When the paper mill sells Q units, it will receive price times quantity, PQ, in income. This total amount that the firm receives is called its **revenue**. **Profit** is revenue less cost. Profit is often abbreviated π (the Greek letter pi, since price is usually P). The profit for a quantity, $\pi(Q) = PQ - C(Q)$, is the amount that the mill owner earns from selling Q units of paper after paying for the production costs.

MAXIMIZING PROFITS BY CHOOSING QUANTITY

How can a price-taking firm maximize profits? One decision is the mix of inputs, accounted for in the cost curve. The remaining choice is the quantity of output. There are two steps to getting this answer: (1) determining whether the firm should make anything at all and (2) determining how much output to make, if any.

SHUTDOWN

Is it always a good idea to produce? Let's compare what happens in the short run if a firm produces something to what happens if it produces nothing.

If a firm does operate, profits are $\pi(Q)$ = revenue − variable cost − fixed cost = $PQ - VC(Q) - FC$. Because AVC is VC/Q, VC = Q * AVC. Substituting this expression for VC gives us:

$$\pi(Q) = PQ - Q * AVC(Q) - FC, \text{ which we can rewrite as}$$

$$\pi(Q) = Q[P - AVC(Q)] - FC.$$

If, on the other hand, the firm shuts down, it has no revenue, but it must still pay its fixed costs. That is, if it produces nothing, its profit is $\pi(0) = P * (0) - FC - VC(0) = -FC$. The negative number means that the firm loses money in the amount of the fixed costs; the firm experiences a negative profit, or loss.

If profits from producing a quantity of goods are greater than profits from producing nothing—in other words, if $\pi(Q) > \pi(0)$—then the firm will keep producing. The difference between profits when producing and profits when not producing is:

$$\pi(Q) - \pi(0) = \{Q[P - \text{AVC}(Q)] - \text{FC}\} - (-\text{FC}) = Q[P - \text{AVC}(Q)]$$

That is, $\pi(Q)$ is higher than $\pi(0)$ if $P > \text{AVC}(Q)$. The firm should produce if price is greater than the minimum point of AVC. If $P < \text{AVC}(Q)$, the firm does better by shutting down, and the firm will produce nothing. Fixed costs don't affect the decision whether to produce anything at all in the short run; only variable costs do. That's because the firm has to pay the fixed costs whether or not it operates.

Look again at Figure 9.2. At the minimum point of the average variable cost curve, average variable cost and marginal cost intersect where the price of paper is $209. When the price is below $209, the firm maximizes profit by producing nothing. This is the *shutdown point*. The **shutdown point** is where price equals the minimum of average variable cost; at lower prices, the firm will stop producing.

HOW MUCH TO MAKE

Once a firm has made the decision to produce, the remaining question is how much it will make. If price is greater than the minimum of average variable cost, a profit-maximizing firm will choose the level of output so that price equals marginal cost. Why? Let's turn to Figure 9.3, which highlights the decision making of our paper producer.

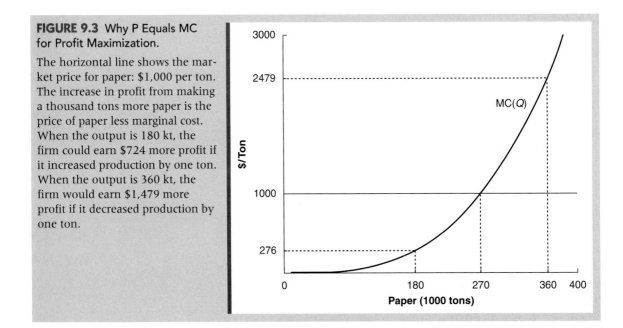

FIGURE 9.3 Why P Equals MC for Profit Maximization.

The horizontal line shows the market price for paper: $1,000 per ton. The increase in profit from making a thousand tons more paper is the price of paper less marginal cost. When the output is 180 kt, the firm could earn $724 more profit if it increased production by one ton. When the output is 360 kt, the firm would earn $1,479 more profit if it decreased production by one ton.

Figure 9.3 has an upward-sloping marginal cost curve and a straight horizontal line showing that the price of paper, P, is $1,000 per ton. What quantity of paper will the firm produce? As the figure shows, there are three possibilities: a quantity (for instance, 180 kt) for which marginal cost is lower than the market price for paper; a quantity for which marginal cost is higher than the price of paper, such as 360 kt; or a quantity for which marginal cost is equal to price. Because these are the only three possibilities, if we can eliminate two of these choices as possible places to maximize profits, the third is where profits are highest.

Suppose the firm is producing 180 kt of paper. If it made one more unit of output, it would get P = $1,000/ton for the unit, and it would incur a marginal cost of the 180,001st ton. In Figure 9.3, for Q = 180 kt, the marginal cost is $276/ton. Because P = 1,000 is greater than MC, the firm would get more revenue from selling the 180,001st ton than it would incur in costs. Therefore, its profits, revenue less costs, would rise by $724 for that ton. So the output 180 kt can't be output that maximizes profits because the firm can increase profits by selling one more unit. When marginal cost is less than price, more profit can be made by making more output.

Next, consider 360 kt, a quantity where price is lower than marginal cost. Figure 9.3 shows that $2,479 is the marginal cost associated with that quantity. By selling one unit less than 360 kt, the firm reduces costs by MC(360,000) = $2,479. Its revenues also go down, by P = $1,000. Because the avoided cost ($2,479) is greater than the foregone revenue ($1,000) for that unit, the firm has more profit ($2,479 − $1,000 = $1,479 more) if it doesn't produce that 360,000th unit. So it can't be right to produce Q = 360 kt, either. When marginal cost is higher than price, more profit can be made by making less output.

That leaves only the possibility that MC(Q) = P. A firm that chooses to make anything at all chooses its output Q so that MC(Q) = P. The marginal cost curve above the average variable cost curve is the supply curve for a firm.

PROFITS IN PICTURES

The firm's profits are revenue less cost, $\pi = PQ − C(Q)$. Because $C(Q) = AC(Q) * Q$, profits $= \pi = Q * [P − AC(Q)]$. There are three steps to finding a firm's profits, graphically shown in Figure 9.4.

Step 1: Find the quantity of output. The firm chooses to produce the quantity where $P = MC(Q)$. The dashed lines show that, when price = $1,000/ton, the quantity chosen is 270 kt.

Step 2: Determine AC(Q). The figure shows that, at Q = 270 kt, the firm's average costs are $628/ton.

Step 3: Draw the profits box. Profits = $Q * [P − AC(Q)]$. At Q = 270 kt, AC(Q) = $628/ton, and P = $1,000/ton. The height of the shaded box is $P − AC = $(1,000 − 628)/ton. The length is Q = 270 kt. Profits, the area of the shaded box, are $(1,000 − 628) * (270,000) = $100,440,000.

FIGURE 9.4 Three Steps to Profits.

The first part of this figure shows that the firm will produce 270 kt when price = $1,000/ton. The second part shows the average cost when production is 270 kt. The third part of the figure shows profit = $Q * [P - AC(270,000)]$.

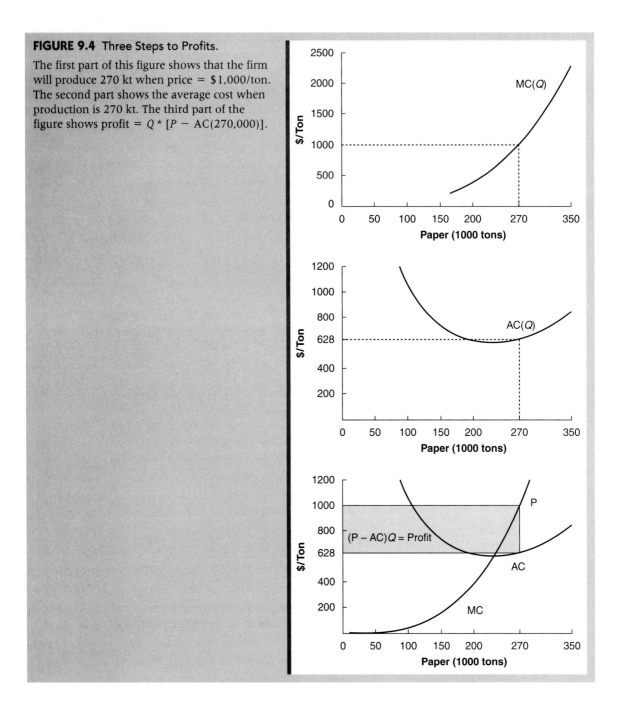

THE EFFECT OF POLLUTION CONTROL ON A FIRM'S SUPPLY CURVE

How does environmental regulation affect a firm's costs? Cost shouldn't decrease with regulation because firms are expected to make their output in the least-cost manner from the start. Fixed costs increase when the firm is forced to add capital equipment, such as bleach recycling for a paper mill or a scrubber for a coal-fired power plant. Variable costs increase when the plant must use a more costly input, such as a power plant using low-sulfur coal. Figure 9.5 shows the original cost curves and new cost curves with a 20 percent increase in fixed costs. Because fixed costs contribute nothing to variable or marginal costs, none of the marginal cost curve, the shutdown point, or the supply curve changes. Because AC is AVC plus AFC and AFC increases, AC increases. In the picture, AC increased by $69/ton.

Figure 9.6 shows the average cost curves and supply curves for a paper firm whose marginal and average variable costs increase by 50 percent because a regulation requires a more costly input. As a result of regulation, the quantity supplied drops from 271 to 238 kt. Pollution control regulations that increase marginal costs have two effects on plants. First, they cause the output to be made in a less polluting way. Second, because the new systems raise marginal costs, the plant will produce less. So the plant will produce with lower emissions per unit output and will produce less output. Both effects reduce pollution.

FIGURE 9.5 Firm Supply and Increased Fixed Costs.

The firm's supply curve, MC above AVC, does not change when fixed costs change.

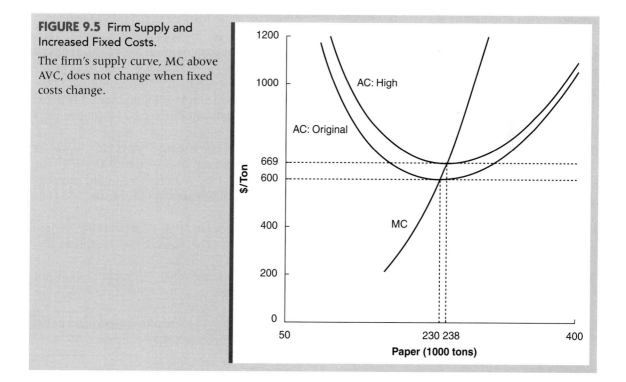

FIGURE 9.6 The Effect of Regulation on Output.

Regulation that increases marginal costs decreases output. The dashed lines are the original cost curves, and the solid lines the higher cost curves.

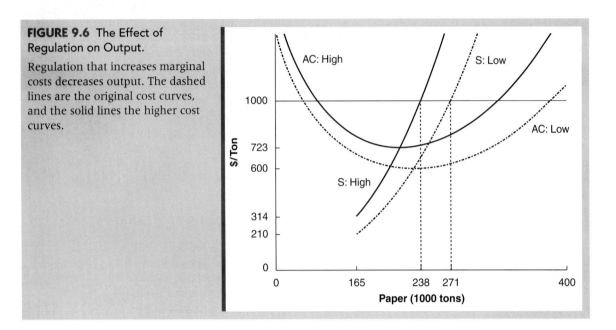

BOX 9.2

Reducing Agricultural Emissions by Changing the Price of Water

Let's return to our lettuce example from the previous chapter. A farmer gets more output by using more water and fertilizer. Her marginal costs are the cost of the additional water and fertilizer she needs to produce more lettuce. Increasing the price of water, with output held constant, reduces the level of pollution (nitrogen leachate) by reducing the use of water. In addition, her marginal cost curve shifts up because it is now more expensive to produce lettuce.

The price of lettuce is $1,429/ton. With the original price for water at $0.23/mm-ha, the price of lettuce equals the marginal cost of production when the farmer produces 3.377 tons of lettuce. When the price of water increases to $0.59/mm-ha, the supply curve shifts inward, and the new profit-maximizing yield is 3.326 tons of lettuce.

Both the change in the input mix and the change in production affect the amount of nitrogen leachate. First, holding output constant in response to the change in water price, the farmer moves along her isoquant to use less water. This shift reduces pollution, from the original 121 kg of leachate per hectare to 116.5 kg/ha. Second, the farmer reduces her output from 3.377 to 3.326 tons/ha as the price of water goes up. This adjustment in production causes pollution to drop even more, to 90.3 kg/ha. Most of the reduction of leachate for the lettuce system comes from cutting back output, rather than by adjusting the input mix while holding output constant.

IN SUMMARY

- Economists assume that firms maximize profits. Profit equals revenue minus costs. Revenue equals the quantity produced times the market price for each unit of the good. Profit $= PQ - C(Q) = [P - AC(Q)]Q$. It is a rectangle with width of Q and height of $P - AC(Q)$.
- To maximize profit, a firm chooses either zero output or output so that $MC(Q) = P$. $P - MC(Q)$ is the increment to profit from making one more unit. Units with a marginal cost greater than price are not made because they decrease profit. Units with a marginal cost less than price are made because they increase profit.
- When the minimum point of AVC, which is the shutdown point, is greater than P, a firm will produce nothing. Its profits will be $-FC < 0$ because it must pay its fixed costs even if it produces nothing at all.
- The marginal cost curve above average variable cost is the supply curve. The supply curve can be shifted by changes in input prices or changes in technology.
- Pollution control raises either variable costs, marginal costs, or both. When pollution control increases variable costs, it leads to lower firm output and lower emissions of pollutants.

Supply, Price, and Pollution Control in an Industry

The third part of the pollution control problem is the number of firms producing output because that determines total output and total pollution. Let's look first at the number of firms in an *industry* in both the long and the short run. An **industry** is all of the firms producing the same good. The short run in this model of firm and industry is the time period so short that the number of firms cannot change because that would require changes in fixed costs, while the output per firm can change. In the long run, a firm can close and sell the plant and equipment, or let them rust. The Rust Belt in Michigan and Ohio got its name when industrial plants did just that. And in the long run, new plants can be built.

The distinction between short run and long run matters in the production decision: in the short run, a firm keeps producing even if it's losing money, as long as price is above average variable cost. In the long run, though, when all costs are variable, a firm losing money will close permanently. Examining these effects begins with the industry supply curve, in the short run and long run.

THE SUPPLY CURVE IN THE SHORT RUN

The short-run industry supply curve is the sum of the supply curves of the firms in the industry. Let's say that our industry is made up of a fixed number (N) of identical firms. On the left of Figure 9.7 are the average cost curve and supply curve of a typical firm in the paper industry. At the price $P = \$250$/ton, our typical firm will choose the quantity associated with that price and produce 175 kt of paper. If there

FIGURE 9.7 Adding Up Supply Curves.

The figure shows the supply curve for a typical firm and the industry supply with two or three identical firms in the industry. The industry supply for two firms is twice the supply of the typical firm; the industry supply for three firms is three times the supply of the typical firm.

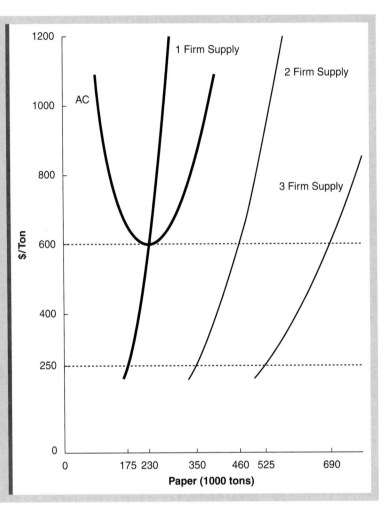

is a second, identical paper plant, it will produce the same amount. As a result, the industry of two firms will produce 2 * 175 = 350 kt of paper at a price of $250/ton. This point ($Q = 350$ kt, $P = \$250$) is on the line labeled "2 Firm Supply."

Next, look at the price $P = \$600$/ton of paper. At that price, each paper plant will produce 230 kt of paper, for total production in the two-firm industry of 460 kt. The point ($Q = 460$ kt, $P = \$600$) is on the same "2 Firm Supply" line.

This process of adding quantities for a specified price—that is, adding individual supply curves horizontally—gives the industry supply curve. The line labeled "2 Firm Supply" shows how much this industry will produce in response to different prices.

If there were three identical firms in the industry, we would multiply the quantity produced at each price by 3. At a price of $250/ton, quantity produced would be 3 * 175 = 525 kt; at a price of $600/ton, quantity would be 3 * 230 = 690 kt.

These points, and other points on the supply curve, are shown on the line labeled "3 Firm Supply" in Figure 9.7.

In more general terms, if there are N identical firms in an industry, the short-run quantity supplied from N firms at any given price, P, is N times the quantity supplied for one firm. Let's call the industry supply curve for N firms in the industry $S_N(P)$, and the supply curve for the typical firm $S^1(P)$. Then $S_N(P) = N * S^1(P)$. That is, the supply for N firms comes from multiplying the supply for a single firm by N.

What if producers are not identical? Perhaps they have different costs, resulting in different supply curves. The procedure is similar: for a specified price, the market supply curve comes from adding the quantities that each firm will produce at that price. Now, if $S^1(P)$, $S^2(P)$, and $S^3(P)$ are the individual supply curves for three different producers, then the three-firm supply curve is $S_3(P) = S^1(P) + S^2(P) + S^3(P)$. The industry short-run supply curve is the horizontal sum of the supply curves of the firms in the industry.

EQUILIBRIUM IN THE SHORT RUN

A market equilibrium requires that quantity supplied equal quantity demanded. The relevant supply curve is the market supply curve, the total amount produced by all firms in an industry. Let's now look in more detail at a short-run market equilibrium.

Three things define a **short-run equilibrium**: (1) the number of firms is fixed, (2) the quantity supplied by industry equals the quantity demanded, and (3) each firm produces according to its supply curve.

Figure 9.8 shows a possible short-run equilibrium in the paper industry. The downward-sloping line is the demand curve (in this case, drawn to make a clear example rather than based on actual data). The supply curve for a five-firm industry is the upward-sloping line.

The five-firm supply curve intersects the demand curve at a price of $747/ton and a quantity of 1,232.5 kt. Let's compare this outcome with our criteria for a short-run equilibrium: (1) the number of firms is fixed at five, (2) the quantity supplied equals the quantity demanded, and (3) each of the five firms produces 246.5 kt, which is where price equals marginal cost. We can verify the last condition by dividing the total output of the five identical firms, 1,232.5 kt, by the number of firms: 1,232.5 kt/5 = 246.5 kt. Therefore, this is a short-run equilibrium.

Now let's look in more detail at the situation for a typical firm, as shown in Figure 9.9 on page 207. Because the price of $747/ton is above the minimum point of AC, this firm will make profits. The profits box is shaded. With the assumption that all the firms are the same, then all the firms are operating with the same output and facing the same price, and they are all making profits.

What happens to the short-run equilibrium if environmental regulations shift the supply curve up? Figure 9.10 on page 208 shows the single-firm supply curve, a 10-firm industry supply curve, and the demand curve. The new supply curves show an increase of $248/ton in production costs when output is 216.5 kt tons per firm. In the new market equilibrium, price goes up: although firms must bear the increased costs, the firms pass some of these costs along to consumers. The higher price to consumers reduces their use of paper and thus reduces the environmental

FIGURE 9.8 Quantity Demanded Equals Short-Run Quantity Supplied.

The demand and supply curves for paper intersect at a quantity of 1,232.5 kt when price is $747/ton. Each of five identical firms is producing 246.5 kt.

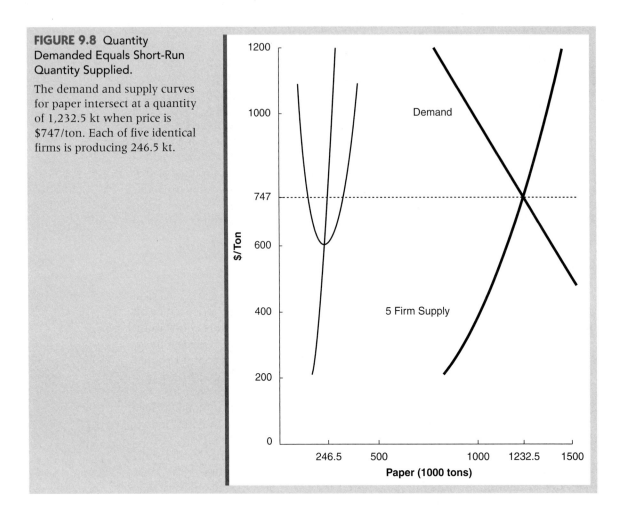

impact of paper production. Notice, though, that price does not go up by as much as costs do: price increases from $600/ton only to $743/ton. The higher price reduces the amount that consumers are willing to buy; to avoid even greater reductions in sales, producers will bear a reduction in profits. Thus, in the short run, producers and consumers share the effects of an increase in production costs.

These firms would stay in operation in the short run even if their profits were negative, as long as price is above the minimum of average variable costs. In the long run, however, firms do not stay in business with negative profits. We will look next at the long run.

AN INDUSTRY IN THE LONG RUN

The difference between the short run and the long run is that the capital investments that create fixed costs can change. In this context, it means that new producers can

FIGURE 9.9 Profits with Short-Run Supply.

At a price of $747/ton, quantity supplied and quantity demanded for paper are equal. The shaded box shows profit for a typical firm.

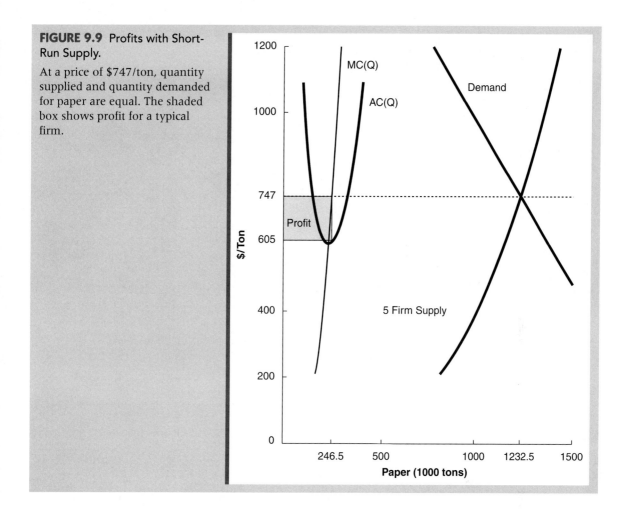

enter the industry, or existing producers can decide to shut down. What will persuade a producer either to enter or exit an industry? Profits!

The term profits refers to **economic profits**: revenue less all costs, including opportunity costs. Opportunity costs include the opportunity cost of the capital invested in the business. In the five-firm industry example, all the producers are making profits. Zero economic profits are enough to satisfy a business owner because investors are able to pay off their opportunity costs; they are earning in that industry just what they would earn in any other industry. The positive profits in the paper industry mean that each firm is earning more than firms in other industries are making. Because there is more to be earned in this industry, investors looking to make money will decide that the paper industry is a good place to operate. They will invest in paper-making plants and machinery and will enter the industry.

Figure 9.11 on page 209 shows what happens when another firm enters. The new short-run supply curve is the six-firm supply curve. Now, with another firm

FIGURE 9.10 Increased Costs in the Industry.

When costs increase due to, for instance, environmental cleanup, in the short run, price typically increases less than the increase in cost. Consumers and producers share the costs associated with cleanup.

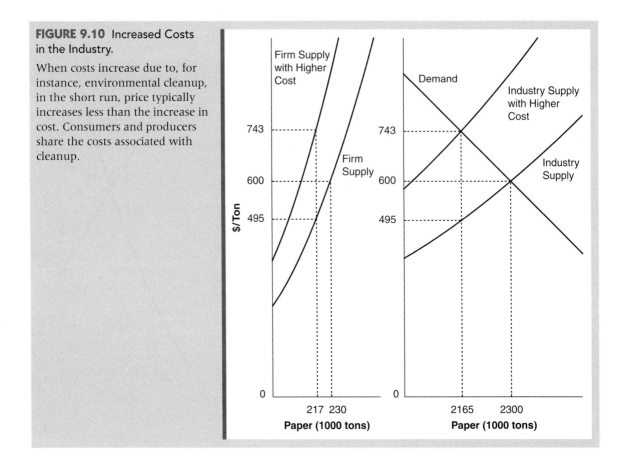

producing 246.5 kt when price is $747/ton, the industry supply curve shifts rightward from the five-firm supply curve. Because the supply curve shifts right, the demand curve no longer intersects the supply curve at $747/ton. The figure shows that a short-run equilibrium with six firms would have a lower price of $600/ton and a higher quantity of 1,380 kt.

Let's now look at profits. A price of $600/ton equals marginal cost where the marginal cost curve intersects the average cost curve, at the minimum point on the average cost curve. Because each firm produces the quantity of paper for which marginal cost equals price, then price, average cost, and marginal cost are all equal to each other at $600/ton. Profits $= PQ - C(Q) = Q * (P - AC)$. Because price is equal to average cost, $P - AC = 0$, which means that profits $= Q * 0$, and profits are zero.

Now the paper industry is paying all its costs, including its opportunity costs, exactly. It is making as much money as other industries—no more and no less. If the paper industry was earning less profit than other industries, investors would move their capital from the paper industry to other industries, and the number of

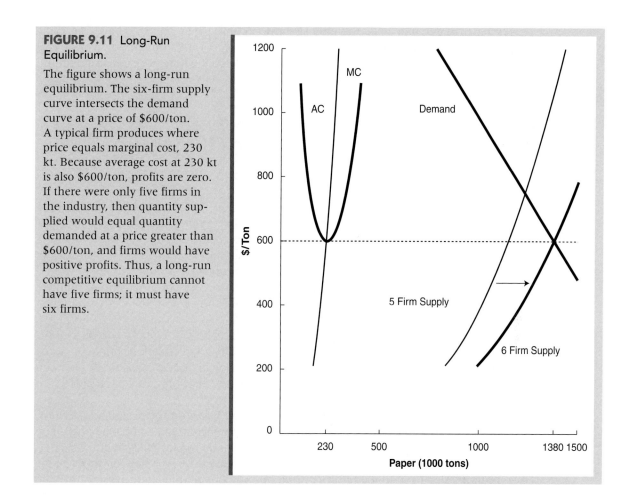

FIGURE 9.11 Long-Run Equilibrium.

The figure shows a long-run equilibrium. The six-firm supply curve intersects the demand curve at a price of $600/ton. A typical firm produces where price equals marginal cost, 230 kt. Because average cost at 230 kt is also $600/ton, profits are zero. If there were only five firms in the industry, then quantity supplied would equal quantity demanded at a price greater than $600/ton, and firms would have positive profits. Thus, a long-run competitive equilibrium cannot have five firms; it must have six firms.

firms making paper would decrease. If the paper industry was making more profit than other industries, investors would move their capital from other industries to the paper industry, and the number of firms making paper would increase. However, because there are zero profits with six firms, there is no incentive for investors to make new paper plants; there will be no further entry of firms and no exit of firms.

The **long-run equilibrium** also includes three elements: (1) the quantity supplied by industry equals the quantity demanded; (2) each firm produces on its supply curve (where $P = \text{MC}$ and $P \geq \text{AVC}$); and (3) all producers are making zero profits ($P = \text{AC}$). The key difference between the short-run and long-run equilibrium is that, in the short run, the number of producers in an industry is fixed and producers can make or lose money. In the long run, however, the number of producers in an industry will change until producers make zero profits. The **long-run supply curve** shows the relationship between price and quantity when firms have time to enter and exit. Because all firms in this paper industry have the same minimum average cost and because all firms will produce at minimum average cost in the long run, the long-run supply curve is a flat line where price equals minimum average cost.

COMPETITIVE MARKETS AND POLLUTION

Over time, a competitive market will encourage producers with low costs and punish those with high costs. In a form of "survival of the fittest," only the lowest-cost producers will continue in business. Lower costs produce lower prices, which consumers prefer.

On the other hand, this competitiveness means that it is hard for a producer to behave well toward the environment if there is no general requirement for environmentally good behavior. Environmental protection usually increases costs for a business; after all, if producing in an environmentally friendly way is cheaper than polluting, it is unlikely there would be any pollution. If a producer operates in a way that improves the environment but increases its costs, it cannot compete against producers who have lower costs because they ignore their environmental impacts.

One way around this obstacle is for a producer to argue that its product is different from the product that's made using a dirty, lower-cost technology. Some consumers may be willing to pay a premium for a "green" product. If so, then producers with different costs can all survive because they are, in essence, not producing the same good.

Other products cannot command a premium based on the production process. For instance, copier paper with 20 percent recycled content can be made by many different processes, including newer processes that do not leak bleach into the environment. A student who buys paper may choose to pay extra for the "green" product. However, in a photocopy shop, the student is unlikely to ask whether the paper in the machine was made without bleach. As a result, the shop owner will be at a competitive disadvantage if he buys the higher-priced paper as an input to photocopy services.

Because a single firm will be at a competitive disadvantage if it uses cleaner methods that cost more, governmental action is needed to require all firms to clean up. Pollution-control regulations add to the cost of production. Who pays these costs? Our model of costs in the long run provides the answer.

Reducing pollution causes average costs to increase for an industry. The increase in average costs causes the long-run supply curve for the industry to shift up. Figure 9.12 shows two long-run industry supply curves, one with lower average costs before pollution control and one with higher average costs after pollution is regulated.

In the short run, the increased costs lead to a price increase: producers pass some of the costs along to consumers. Price does not increase by the full amount of the upward shift in the short run, as the producers absorb some of the cost increase to keep selling. Absorbing the cost means, though, that they are losing money.

FIGURE 9.12 Long-Run Equilibrium: High- and Low-Cost Firms Compared.

The dashed lines are the long-run supply curves for the industry. LRS: High is the long run supply curve for firms with high costs, such as the cost of pollution control. LRS: Low is the long-run supply curve for firms with lower costs, such as firms not required to pay for pollution control. The U-shaped curves are the high-and low-cost average cost curves. For firms with high costs, minimum average cost is $69/ton greater than for the low-cost firm. In the long run, consumer price increases by the entire amount of the cost increase. Demand decreases from 2,600 to 2,535 kt.

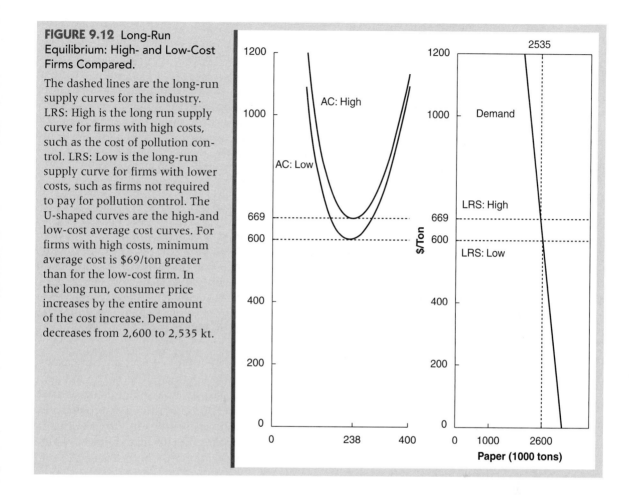

The new average cost curve has a minimum at $669/ton, representing an increase in fixed costs of about 20 percent. The higher dashed line is the new long-run supply curve, $69 higher than the long-run supply curve in Figure 9.12. The new equilibrium is the intersection of the new long-run supply curve with the demand curve at a price of $669/ton and a quantity of 2,535 kt.

There are three things to notice about the new equilibrium. One is the higher price. Because producers operate with zero profits both before and after the regulation, average costs increase by exactly the additional costs of pollution control. In other words, 100 percent of the costs of pollution control are passed on to the consumer! The second effect is that, because the new equilibrium price is higher, consumers buy less paper. At the old equilibrium, consumers bought 2,600 kt of paper at $600/ton; at the new equilibrium, consumers buy 2,535 kt of paper at $669/ton. The third thing to notice is that some producers will leave the market because consumers buy less paper.

The long-run supply curve is not always horizontal. It is possible for some firms to be lower cost than others due to limits on some aspect of production. For instance, if one firm is closer to the final market for a good than another, and there are no additional options for building nearby, then the closer firm will have a cost advantage in the long run as well as in the short run. If so, then the lower-cost producers will, as in the short-run case, not pass along all of the cost increase, and producers and consumers will again share the higher costs.

All of the policy's effects—higher prices, lower output, and fewer firms in the industry—are more pronounced with a tax on pollution than with an effluent standard. Chapter 8 showed that a tax is more expensive for a firm than a standard that causes it to produce the same amount of pollution per unit of output. A tax works by changing prices: it makes polluting inputs or pollution more expensive. The firm ends up paying the higher price on any polluting inputs or pollution it still has. A standard, on the other hand, requires changing production practices, but it does not change prices. The firm may use the same inputs and produce the same pollution under a standard as under a tax, but with lower prices. As a result, average costs are higher with a tax than with a standard. Because average costs are higher with a tax, in the long run there will be fewer firms in the industry. A tax therefore has greater impact in reducing pollution for the same effect on a single firm's emissions because it has greater effect in reducing output and consumption.

The "polluter pays" principle, a popular policy premise especially in Europe, says that the polluter should pay for the damages it causes. Notice, though, that polluters in a competitive market are likely to pass at least some of the damage costs along to consumers. Consumers contribute to environmental problems by buying goods associated with pollution; polluters share not only their costs but also their responsibility for damages with consumers. The higher prices in the market signal to consumers that polluting goods are costly both financially and environmentally.

GRANDFATHERING AND BARRIERS TO THE ENTRY OF CLEANER PLANTS

What happens if the costs of strict environmental regulation apply only to new plants and not to existing plants? This process, called grandfathering, is intended to ease the burden for facilities designed before the new requirements. Figure 9.12 had two types of firms, one with high costs and one with low costs. Now we have one explanation for the difference in costs: the low-cost firms might have been grandfathered in and allowed to use older, dirtier production technology, while the high-cost firms are strictly regulated. The new firms have $669/ton as the minimum of their average cost curve, while the old firms have $600/ton as their minimum. Let's assume the environmental regulation affected only fixed costs, and the two types of firms have the same MC curves.

If there is easy entry and exit, and if all firms are allowed to use the same low-cost technology, the equilibrium in both the long and short run will be a price of $600/ton. In Figure 9.13, this equilibrium is the intersection of the curve labeled Original Demand with the curve labeled Long-Run Supply, which is based on 10 identical firms in the industry. Suppose that demand shifts up, perhaps because of growth in population or income, which will increase demand for paper. The curve labeled New Demand represents demand after the shift.

What will firms do in response to this increase in demand? In a world of unrestricted entry and exit, if all firms were allowed to use the same low-cost technology, more low-cost producers would enter, and a new long-run equilibrium would occur at a price of $600/ton. However, because of the environmental requirements for new firms, any new plant that enters the industry will have $669/ton as its minimum average cost. As long as the price is below $669/ton, no new firms will enter because they would lose money on each ton produced.

FIGURE 9.13 Grandfathering.

Ten grandfathered firms have the lower AC; any new entrants have the higher AC. As long as the price is below $669/ton, no new firms enter. For production up to 10 * 230 kt = 2,300 kt, the supply curve is based only on production from the 10 grandfathered firms. Between prices of $600/ton and $669/ton, the supply curve follows the short-run supply curve of the grandfathered firms. The equilibrium between the original demand curve and long-run supply is at the beginning of this upward-sloping portion. When demand increases, the new long-run equilibrium is at the intersection of the long-run supply curve and the new demand curve, at a price of $669/ton and a quantity of 2,535 kt.

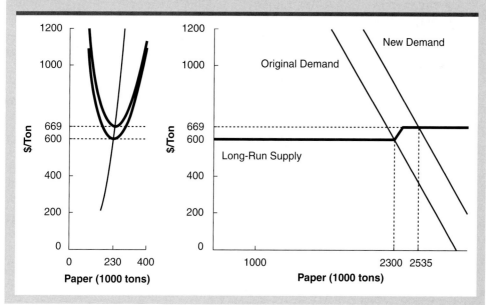

The existing firms will, of course, continue to produce at any price at or above $600/ton. As a result, the industry supply curve for prices greater than $600 but less than $669 is not horizontal; in both the long and short run, it is the upward-sloping 10-firm short-run supply curve. Only when the price reaches $669/ton will the new firms enter.

The long-run industry supply curve, then, follows the upward-sloping 10-firm supply curve from $600/ton to $669/ton at a quantity of 2,380 kt. At $669, as higher-cost firms enter the industry in response to the increased demand, the long-run industry supply curve becomes horizontal again. In Figure 9.13, it is the bold line labeled Long-Run Supply.

The long-run equilibrium has a price of $669/ton, but the minimum average cost for the grandfathered firms is still $600/ton. Because price is greater than minimum average cost for the grandfathered firms, they make profits. The new plants, however, are making zero profits. By limiting competition, the regulation allows existing plants to make positive profits, even in the long run. Indeed, these positive profits create the incentive for these old plants to stay in business as long as possible, which allows them to continue their polluting ways. This effect was almost certainly not what lawmakers had in mind when they first began adopting pollution regulations. Later environmental policies have tried to avoid these unintended consequences.

IN SUMMARY

- An industry consists of all producers who make the same good. The short-run market supply curve comes from adding horizontally the supply curves of the firms in the industry.
- A short-run equilibrium occurs when the number of firms in an industry is constant, the industry quantity supplied equals the quantity demanded, and each firm is producing a quantity where price equals marginal cost above the minimum of average variable cost. In the short run, firms are willing to operate with negative profits, as long as price is above the minimum of average variable cost. If costs increase due to environmental regulation, some or all of the new costs are likely to be passed along to consumers.
- In the long run, new firms can enter and exit the market because producers can change their fixed investments. If an industry is making positive profits, firms will enter; if an industry is making negative profits, existing firms will shut down and leave the industry.
- A long-run equilibrium has three requirements: (1) industry quantity supplied equals quantity demanded, (2) individual producers operate with their own supply curves, and (3) all producers make zero profits.
- If demand increases, price will increase in the short-run equilibrium. As a result of the demand shift, producers in the industry initially make positive profits. In the long run, though, the number of producers in an industry will adjust until profits are once again zero. The long-run supply

curve is horizontal at the zero-profits level when an industry consists of identical firms.

- In the short run, producers with different cost structures can stay in the market together. In the long run, though, producers with lower costs will drive producers with higher costs out of the market. If environmentally friendly behavior is more costly than environmentally damaging behavior, it is very difficult in a competitive market for an environmentally friendly producer to survive.
- If a regulation makes producers' costs go up, then the prices faced by consumers increase. Because producers were making zero profits in the long run without the regulation, they pass costs on to consumers in response to the regulation. Pollution control thus results in lower output and fewer firms in the industry. Because a tax is more expensive than a standard for a firm, a tax leads to less pollution in the long run than a standard that achieves the same pollution reduction per unit of output.
- If existing producers are "grandfathered," they face different, less costly rules than new entrants. As a result, they have the opportunity to make positive profits, even in the long run. Regulations that allow old, dirtier producers to operate at lower cost than new, cleaner producers may actually be profitable for polluting firms.

Grandfathering Under the Clean Air Act

The Clean Air Act (CAA) of 1970 is the primary law in the United States to protect and improve air quality. It covers both stationary sources (things that pollute the air and don't move, such as factories) and mobile sources (things that move and pollute, including cars, trucks, lawnmowers, and construction equipment).

The act splits responsibilities between the federal government and the states. The federal government sets standards that specify the maximum ambient concentration of key pollutants. Each state, in turn, writes a plan that explains how much the *existing* emitters in the state must reduce their emissions so that the state's air is sufficiently clean. The federal government regulates mobile sources, with the exception that California. which regulated vehicles before the federal government. can set its own standards.

Any new stationary source must meet stringent "New Source Performance Standards" required by the federal government. The idea was that these new plants should find it easier to meet stringent abatement requirements than existing plants, which were built before air quality was a major issue; life was supposed to be a little easier for existing plants, while any new plants faced high standards. Legislators expected the existing plants gradually to be retired, to be replaced by the cleaner plants.

Even today, though, many old plants—especially coal-fired power plants—are still operating. Electricity-generating companies keep these plants going rather than replace them. As a result, air quality gains have been slower than expected.

BOX 9.3

Major Provisions in the Clean Air Act

- *National Ambient Air Quality Standards (NAAQS).*   The U.S Environmental Protection Agency (EPA) sets ambient standards (concentration of pollutant allowed) for six major "criteria" pollutants. The standards are set primarily to protect human health. The states must regulate stationary sources so that these standards are met.
- *New Source Pollution Standards (NSPS).*   The EPA sets standards for new stationary sources, based on what can be accomplished by changing to a less polluting technology. A stationary source is subject to both state regulations and to NSPS.
- *National Emissions Standards for Hazardous Air Pollutants (NESHAPs).*   For hazardous air pollutants other than the "criteria" pollutants, the EPA standards are based on technological feasibility. They are meant to protect health.
- *Mobile sources.*   The EPA sets vehicle emission standards and regulates fuel. California may also make such regulations; if it does and if the EPA approves them, then other states may choose the California regulations.
- *Acid rain.*   There is an allowance-trading program for the precursors to acid rain. Power plants get emissions allowances; they may either emit sulfur oxides up to their allowance limit, sell some of the allowances to another plant, or buy allowances.

CHAPTER SUMMARY

Here are the key lessons from this chapter:

- Cost depends on the quantity produced. Fixed costs must be paid even if nothing is produced. All costs that are not fixed are variable. Average cost, AC, is cost divided by quantity; average variable cost, AVC, is variable cost divided by quantity. Marginal cost, MC, is the cost of making the next unit. AVC and AC are commonly U-shaped; MC intersects both AVC and AC at their minimum points.
- Firms choose the level of output that maximizes profits. If price is less than the minimum point of AVC, the profit-maximizing output is zero. Otherwise, the quantity where $MC(Q) = P$ maximizes profit.
- Pollution reduction increases costs. When it increases variable costs, the supply curve shifts to the left, and the AC and AVC curves both shift upwards. When it increases FC, the marginal cost curve and AVC curves do not shift, though the AC curve shifts upwards.
- A market supply curve comes from adding up the quantities that individual producers provide at a set price. It is the horizontal sum of individual supply curves.

- A short-run equilibrium occurs when (1) the number of producers in an industry is constant, (2) quantity supplied by the industry equals quantity demanded, and (3) each producer chooses its output based on its supply curve. In the short run, a producer may make either positive or negative profits.
- In the short run, pollution reduction that raises variable costs causes the industry supply curve to shift inwards and prices to increase. The price increase is less than the cost increase.
- In the long run, the number of firms in an industry can change. A long-run equilibrium occurs when (1) quantity supplied by the industry equals quantity demanded, (2) each producer chooses its output based on its supply curve, and (3) all producers make zero profits. Only producers with low costs will survive the competition because they are able to produce at lower prices than higher-cost producers.
- In the long run, pollution reduction that raises any costs shifts the long-run supply curve upwards, leading to an increase in price, a reduction in quantity, and therefore a reduction in pollution. When the industry is made up of identical firms, the price increase is exactly the increase in AC.
- Grandfathering, which treats existing producers differently than potential entrants to an industry, allows high-cost producers to make and keep profits, even in the long run. Such regulations also create an incentive for older, dirtier plants to stay in operation much longer than they otherwise might.

KEY TERMS

average cost, AC(Q) *(p. 191)*
average fixed cost, AFC(Q) *(p. 191)*
average variable cost,
  AVC(Q) *(p. 191)*
capital *(p. 190)*
capital cost *(p. 190)*
capital investment *(p. 190)*
economic profits *(p. 207)*
fixed costs, FC *(p. 191)*
fixed inputs *(p. 191)*
industry *(p. 203)*

long run *(p. 191)*
long-run equilibrium *(p. 209)*
long-run supply curve *(p. 209)*
marginal cost, MC(Q) *(p. 194)*
profit *(p. 197)*
revenue *(p. 197)*
short run *(p. 191)*
short-run equilibrium *(p. 205)*
shutdown point *(p. 198)*
variable costs, VC *(p. 191)*
variable inputs *(p. 191)*

NOTES

Information on emissions from paper production is from Lauren Blum, Richard A. Denison, and John F. Ruston, "A Life-Cycle Approach to Purchasing and Using Environmentally Preferable Paper," *Journal of Industrial Ecology* 1(3) (1998): 15–46.

    The variable and fixed costs of a paper mill in Sweden are from Per-Olov Marklund and Eva Samakovlis, "Reuse or Burn? Evaluating the Producer Responsibility of Waste," *Journal of Environmental Planning and Management* 46(3)

(May 2003): 381–398. We have adjusted the costs in several ways to make the issues in the text clearer. A greater percent of the costs are designated as fixed costs than is likely true. Additionally, we have made the marginal costs of the first few units quite large, while preserving the overall level of costs.

Information on emissions controls on paper production in Europe is from "EU Paper Industry Fears Pollution Control Costs," *Reuters*, May 21, 1999.

The diagram in Figure 9.13 exaggerates the effects of grandfathering so that it is easy to see. Actual production was about 2,500 kt of newsprint and was produced by about 20 plants of varying sizes; the real effects of the regulations were on the order of 2 percent of cost. We have drawn the figure as though the regulations were 20 percent of fixed cost, to make the effects visible on the graph.

More information about the Clean Air Act, including a link to the text of the law, is at http://www.epa.gov/lawsregs/laws/caa.html.

EXERCISES

1. As we've seen, environmental regulation affects the costs of producers, which affects the equilibrium through the long- and short-run supply curves. Let's look at another way that the paper industry, and its environmental effects, might get smaller.

   Figure 9.11 shows a long-run equilibrium with six firms in the industry. It also shows a short-run five-firm supply curve. If the five-firm supply curve stays as it is, what would have to change in this figure for five firms to be the long-run equilibrium number of firms? What might cause this change? Is government regulation the only way that the paper industry might produce less pollution?

2. In the Middle Ages, alchemists tried to convert various substances into gold. Barring advances in nuclear reactions, though, the amount of gold available in the world is fixed; unlike paper, producers cannot respond to changes in market conditions by creating new gold. Some gold deposits are easy to extract: for instance, the U.S. government stores a great deal of gold bullion near Fort Knox, Kentucky, and it could be "extracted" with only the effort required to pick it up. Other deposits, however, are very costly to extract: gold mining near Yellowstone National Park, for instance, involves digging huge piles of soil and using toxic chemicals to extract the gold. What effect does government storage of gold in Fort Knox have on the market price of gold? Does it encourage or discourage gold mining, including the environmental consequences of that mining? Which deposit/depository should be "extracted" first from a cost or an environmental perspective? (This question is inspired by Dale W. Henderson, Steven W. Salant, John S. Irons, and Sebastian Thomas, "The Benefits of Expediting Government Gold Sales," http://www-personal. umich.edu/~ssalant/ifdp.pdf.)

3. Sleeping bag production for the Sleepwell Company has cost $C(Q) = Q^3 - 10Q^2 + 35Q + 196$. The marginal cost curve for their production is $MC(Q) = 3Q^2 - 20Q + 35$.

(a) Identify both the shutdown point and the minimum average cost. (Hint: if you have access to a spreadsheet program, you may find it easier if you put into it the formulas for AVC, AC, and MC for values from $Q = 1$ to $Q = 10$.)

(b) The price of a sleeping bag is currently $67. How many sleeping bags will Sleepwell produce? What will be its profits?

(c) The market for sleeping bags is competitive, with multiple producers. Because sleeping bag technology is commonly known and there is no government rule against using that technology, all the producers operate with the same cost curves. The demand curve for sleeping bags is $Q_D = (1,001 - 3P)/25$. How many sleeping bags are people willing to buy at the current market price? How many producers do you estimate there are in the industry? Is the market in a long-run equilibrium? Why or why not?

(d) A new sleeping bag company enters the industry, and the price of sleeping bags drops to $42 per bag. How many sleeping bags are people willing to buy at the current market price? How many sleeping bags will each company make? Is the market in a long-run equilibrium? Why or why not?

(e) Regulators are concerned that the large number of people visiting parks and wilderness will cause damage to ecosystems. They decide that one way to keep people out is to limit the number of sleeping bags produced; without them, fewer people will stay overnight in the areas. They declare that no producer can make more than five sleeping bags, and no new sleeping bag plants may come into production. What price will lead to the quantity demanded equaling the quantity supplied under this rule?

(f) What will Sleepwell's profits be with this new price and a quantity of five sleeping bags produced?

(g) Does government regulation of sleeping bag production increase or reduce profits for sleeping bag producers? Why?

4. Some firms want to be environmentally friendly, even if "greener" production processes increase their costs. Consider two scenarios. In the first scenario, a "green" firm such as a renewable energy company is producing electricity. This is the same good that is being produced by a number of other, dirtier companies such as coal-fired power plants. It is impossible for consumers to determine whether the good that they are using, the electricity from their wall outlet, came from the green firm or the dirtier firms. In the second scenario, such as organic agriculture, it is possible for consumers to distinguish between the green firm and the dirtier firms. In which scenario is the green firm more likely to be successful? Why?

5. The Bureau of Reclamation is an agency of the U.S. government that manages many dams in the western United States. The water from its dams is used for irrigating agriculture. Let's assume that the Bureau is deciding what size dam to build. The water yield, which we will assume will sell at a fixed price P per unit to the farmers, increases linearly with the size of the dam. Let's assume as well that the costs, as a function of water yield, are U-shaped. Historically, the Bureau has been required to recover its costs rather than maximize profits in its water pricing. Recovering its costs means that it must

set its prices so that its revenues exactly equal its costs. Draw a U-shaped cost curve and a downward-sloping demand curve. Use this diagram to find the amount of water that the Bureau will produce. Compare it with the amount that a profit-maximizing, price-taking firm would produce. What is the opportunity cost to the federal government of this policy? In other words, if the Bureau maximized profits rather than recovered costs, what could it do with the additional money?

6. The cost curve for the city water supply is $C(Q) = 16 + \frac{1}{4}Q^2$, where Q is the amount of water supplied and $C(Q)$ is the cost of providing Q acre-feet of water. (An acre-foot is the amount of water that covers an acre of land to the depth of one foot.)

   (a) Provide the formulas for fixed costs (FC) and variable costs (VC). (Remember that FC are the costs of production when $Q = 0$.) Graph these, as well as the cost function, on the same diagram, with Q on the horizontal axis and $ on the vertical axis, from $Q = 0$ to $Q = 10$.

   (b) Provide the formulas for average fixed cost (AFC), average variable cost (AVC), and average cost (AC). (Remember that average cost of any kind is the corresponding cost divided by Q.) Graph all these on the same diagram, with Q on the horizontal axis and $/Q$ on the vertical axis, from $Q = 0$ to $Q = 10$.

   (c) The formula for marginal cost is $MC(Q) = Q/2$. Add this line to the diagram in (b).

   (d) What is the shutdown point—that is, the minimum of AVC? (Hint: Don't consider negative quantities. Negative water is not an appealing idea.) Does MC intersect AVC at its minimum? (To check, see if AVC and MC have the same value when Q is the amount at the shutdown point.)

   (e) What is the minimum value of AC? Does MC intersect AC at its minimum?

   (f) Identify the city's supply curve for water.

   (g) The price of water is $4/acre-foot. Add this information to the appropriate figure. Is this price above the shutdown point (the minimum value of AVC)? How much water will the city supply if it is operating to maximize profit? What will its profits be?

   (h) The city identifies a new way of treating water that is less expensive than the previous method. What do you expect to happen to the supply curve for water? If the price of water stays constant, what do you expect to happen to the quantity of water supplied?

   (i) Providing water to the city takes it out of the river. A biologist discovers that the reduced flows due to urban water use are harming the backstroking twiddler, an endangered species. If the city is required to account for the damage to the twiddler, what do you expect to happen to the supply curve for water? If the price of water stays constant, what do you expect to happen to the quantity of water supplied?

Maximizing Net Benefits in the Presence of Externalities

Gasoline prices broke the $4 per gallon barrier in the United States in 2008, the same year the polar bear was listed as an endangered species because of climate change associated with burning fossil fuels. Many Americans didn't have convenient public transit options, but, overall, Americans started driving less. It was an election year, and two presidential candidates proposed a "holiday" from federal gas taxes. (Barack Obama disagreed.) A gas tax holiday would have encouraged more driving, counter to the goal of reducing greenhouse gases, a concern of all the candidates.

The consumption of a marketed good such as gasoline provides benefits but also imposes external costs to the environment. How do we decide whether to pursue the benefits in the face of the costs? When a market failure such as an externality is present, does an unregulated market result in the right balance between production and pollution? This chapter will examine:

- The external costs of production and consumption;
- The concept of increasing net benefits to society, also known as increasing efficiency;
- The use of benefit-cost analysis to find the efficient level of production;
- Different ways of looking at the marginal costs and benefits of pollution and abatement.

The Benefits and Costs of Driving

Driving a car is expensive. Parking, insurance, depreciation (reduction in a car's value as it ages), maintenance, and gasoline are all part of the cost of driving. In 2006, the U.S. Internal Revenue Service (IRS) estimated the cost of driving a car at $0.485 per mile, not including parking, which can be significant; one of the authors of this book paid $1,440 per year for a parking permit, until he decided to start walking to work.

Let's look at what this cost per mile means for a typical driver. This typical driver goes 12,000 miles per year at an average of 20 miles per gallon, using about

600 gallons of gasoline. At the 2006 price of $3.00 per gallon, gasoline costs were $1,800, or 30 percent of a total cost of (12,000 miles * 0.485/mile) = $5,820.

The IRS cost estimate leaves out the cost of the time used in driving. At an average speed of 40 miles per hour, the typical driver spends 300 hours behind the wheel each year; at the 2006 California minimum wage of $6.75, this time was worth $2,025. If this cost is added to the IRS cost estimate, gasoline in 2006 accounted for just 23 percent of the total cost of $7,845 to drive a car for a year, without parking. (Residents of a college town might add the time spent looking for parking before getting the opportunity to pay for it.)

Why don't people choose buses or trains instead of driving? In most of the United States, it is difficult to travel to a job, shopping, childcare, and other stops using just public transit. Many of those who use public transit to commute to their jobs (such as the other author) end up driving some of the time.

Let's look at a morning routine. A parent takes a child five miles to school or child care and then travels 20 miles to work. One way to do this routine involves a stiff walk, three bus trips, and a train trip for just under $7 in about two hours. Let's say the parent earns $10 an hour. Counting the value of his time, the total cost is $27, assuming he could spend those two hours working for pay. Alternatively, driving the route takes 30 minutes for about $12 of driving cost (using the IRS value) and $5 of time, for a total of about $17. It is cheaper to drive. If the convenience of choosing when to leave for work (rather than leaving just in time for the bus) and not walking to the stop in inclement weather is worth anything, then it would be even clearer why people drive. Finally, because the value of time is a key component in the decision to drive, people who make higher wages have an even higher propensity to drive.

But what about the other costs of driving, those not borne by the driver? Are these costs so large that more people should be commuting some other way or just plain not driving at all? Table 10.1 presents estimates of the external costs.

At the U.S. fleet average of 20 miles per gallon, these external costs range from (0.13/mile * 20 miles/gallon) = $2.60/gallon, to (0.677/mile * 20 miles/gallon) = $13.54/gallon, in addition to the cost of the fuel!

Private Costs and External Costs

The analysis of consumers and producers so far in this book has focused on how each group behaves. Consumers allocate their limited income among goods that they want. Consumers are willing to pay for higher environmental quality, but often they are not able to purchase it through the market mechanism. Producers maximize profits and have no reason to account for environmental damage. The market equilibrium with an externality leads to a higher quantity of goods and a lower price for these goods than when firms and consumers have to pay for environmental damages. Consumers appreciate both the higher quantity and the lower prices of goods, but they dislike the environmental harm. The next step in the analysis is to quantify, in money terms, the benefits from making decisions that account for the

TABLE 10.1 Range of Reported External Costs in Costs-of-Driving Studies (Cents per Mile).

CATEGORY	LOW ESTIMATE	HIGH ESTIMATE
INFRASTRUCTURE	3.0	7.0
CONGESTION	4.0	15.0
AIR POLLUTION	1.0	14.0
CLIMATE CHANGE	0.3	1.1
NOISE	0.1	6.0
WATER	0.1	3.0
ACCIDENTS (EXTERNAL)	1.0	10.0
ENERGY SECURITY	1.5	2.6
PARKING	2.0	9.0
TOTAL	13.0	67.7

(*Source:* Harrington and McConnell, 2003.)

external costs. We are going to explore these costs in the context of the gasoline market, so we will start by laying out the supply and demand situation for gasoline.

In 2003, total gasoline sold in the United States was about 140 billion gallons, at a price of $2.30 per gallon. That is the equilibrium shown in Figure 10.1. The supply curve is drawn to have a price elasticity of 2.0, which is at the high end of what was found by Carol Dahl and Thomas Duggan. (With an elasticity of 2, if price increases by 10 percent, quantity supplied increases by 20 percent.) The demand curve was drawn with an elasticity of −0.7, in the middle of the estimates that Molly Espey found.

Included in the $2.30 price of gasoline is about $0.37/gallon of state and national taxes. That amount is somewhat less than the estimates of the costs of providing roads and bridges for cars. Thus, the current tax can be viewed as a user fee to pay at least part of the cost of the roads. It is not high enough to also include the environmental costs of gasoline described in Table 10.1.

Chapter 3 discussed the market failure called externalities: the non-pecuniary effect of a market transaction on parties outside the transaction. Externalities impose *external costs* on those who face their effects. **External costs** are the monetary values of the externalities, such as the value of adverse health effects and damage to ecosystems. These costs are not paid by a party to a market transaction but instead are borne by a third party, such as someone who bicycles to work while breathing air

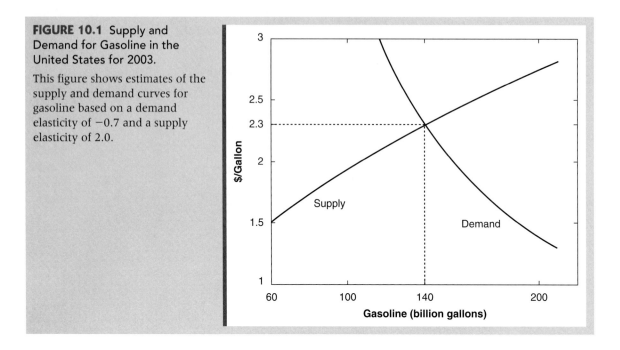

FIGURE 10.1 Supply and Demand for Gasoline in the United States for 2003.

This figure shows estimates of the supply and demand curves for gasoline based on a demand elasticity of −0.7 and a supply elasticity of 2.0.

polluted by cars. Nonmarket valuation methods are commonly used to estimate external costs that are incident upon consumers. For instance, the number and cost of asthma attacks increases when air pollution increases; air pollution increases when gasoline consumption increases. These facts and careful measurements give an upward-sloping external cost curve for the asthma-related externality of gasoline consumption External costs are estimated using the procedures in Chapters 6 and 7. Let's now examine the production and consumption of gasoline with and without consideration of external costs.

What would the market look like if the external costs of gasoline, estimated to range from $2.60/gallon to $13.54/gallon, were part of the price? The 2003 price of gas in the United States would have been almost double if the lowest estimate of external costs was added to the pump price and almost seven times higher if the highest estimate was used.

Between 2003 and 2008, market forces performed this experiment. In those five years, the price of gasoline in the United States almost doubled. Although this was not the result of an environmental policy decision, the effect on prices at the pump was the same. American consumers came to face gasoline prices similar to those of many European countries, which have long discouraged excessive driving by adding taxes to the price of gasoline. Gasoline consumption did indeed decrease in response.

Let's use the 2003 data to look at the effect of charging drivers for the low esti-mate of the external costs of driving. Figure 10.2 has three cost lines on it. The line labeled private MC is the original supply curve. The original supply curve reflects the

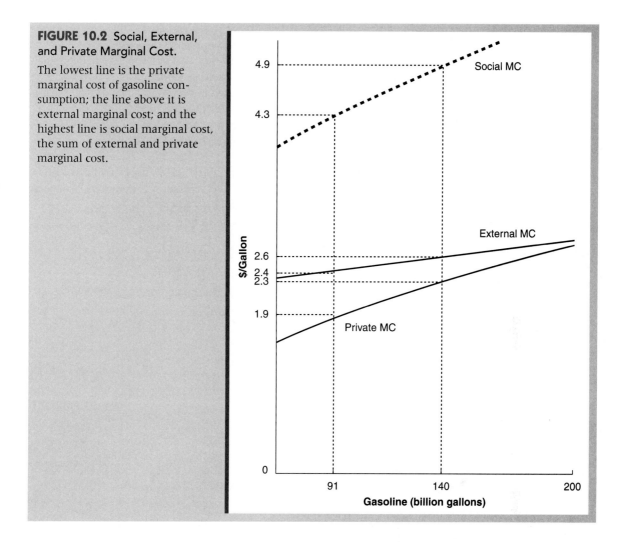

FIGURE 10.2 Social, External, and Private Marginal Cost.

The lowest line is the private marginal cost of gasoline consumption; the line above it is external marginal cost; and the highest line is social marginal cost, the sum of external and private marginal cost.

private costs of providing gasoline to motorists. **Private costs** are the costs to producers excluding external costs. The original supply curve is the private marginal cost curve or private supply curve.

The second curve on Figure 10.2 is an estimate of the external marginal costs. We use the lower end of the cost estimates, $2.60/gallon, as the estimate of external costs at 140 billion gallons. Because external marginal costs should be lower when quantity is lower, we take a lower figure, $2.40/gallon, to be the estimate of external costs at 91 billion gallons. The external costs in Figure 10.2 are a line through those two points.

The sum of external costs and private costs are **social costs**. The dashed line in the figure is the vertical sum of the external marginal cost curve and the private marginal cost curve; it is the *social marginal cost* curve. **Social marginal cost** is the sum of private and external marginal cost. When an additional gallon of gasoline is used, the total of its costs to everyone is the social marginal cost. For instance, at a quantity of 140 billion gallons, the social marginal cost is $2.60/gallon external marginal costs + $2.30/gallon private marginal costs = $4.90/gallon social marginal cost. At 91 billion gallons, it is $1.90/gallon private + $2.40/gallon external = $4.30/gallon social marginal cost. Repeating this exercise for different prices provides the entire social marginal cost curve, sometimes called the social supply curve. Because the social supply curve includes external costs, it lies above the private supply curve.

Figure 10.3 repeats the private and social marginal cost curves and also shows the demand curve. The social marginal cost curve intersects the demand curve at

FIGURE 10.3 Social Marginal Cost and Equilibrium.

The intersection of the demand curve and private marginal cost at 140 billion gallons is the equilibrium without government intervention. The intersection of the social marginal cost curve and the demand curve at 91 billion gallons is the equilibrium when the gasoline producers must pay the social marginal cost of production.

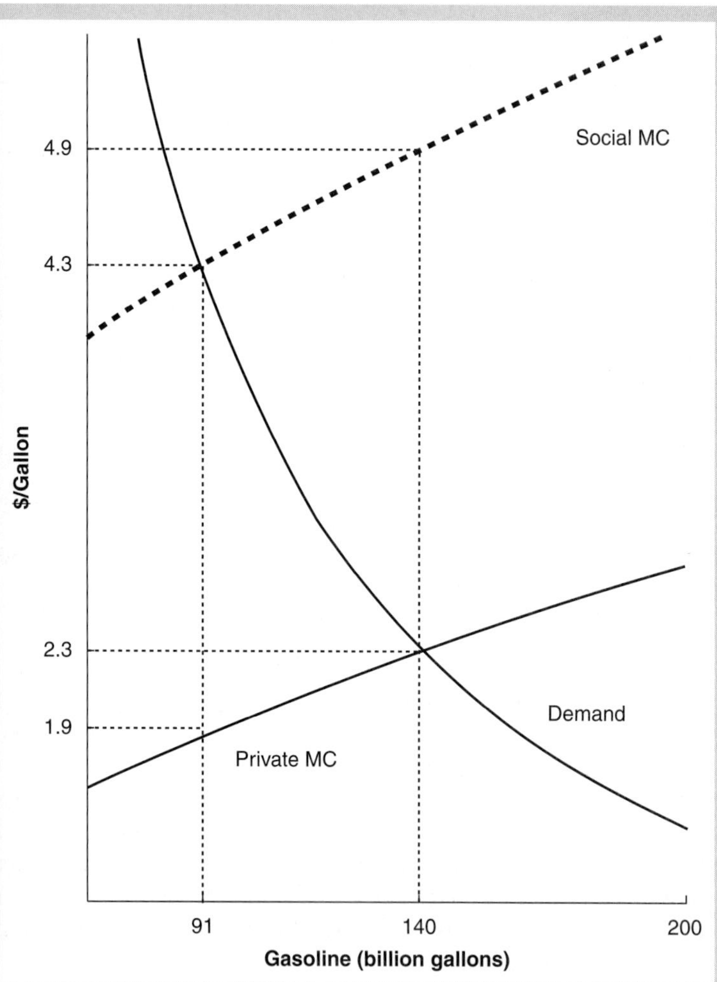

91 billion gallons and a price of $4.30/gallon. If the producers of gasoline had to pay the full external costs of gasoline use, the equilibrium would be at this new point with this much higher price.

How does increasing the price of gasoline help the environment? If the price of gasoline included these higher costs, consumers would not continue driving the same amount as in the past. Immediately, they would drive fewer miles in the same cars, perhaps by reducing the number of trips that they make, carpooling, or taking some trips on public transit. Over time, if the price of gasoline stayed high, they would be likely to buy more fuel-efficient cars. Additionally, when they chose new jobs or new places to live, commuting costs would affect those decisions. For instance, in Stockholm, Sweden, gasoline was more than $6 per gallon in 2003. As a result, families own fewer cars (often one per family) and drive less. Public transportation in Sweden is more extensive and reliable than in the United States. Because Swedes use public transit in greater numbers than do Americans, public transit companies can afford more frequent service. In addition, it is more important to live close to public transit; Swedish cities appear more compact than similarly sized American cities, with the added benefit of less urban sprawl onto undeveloped land. Thus, the full effects of increased gasoline prices, whether from environmental taxes or from increases in the price of gasoline, can take quite a long time to be seen but can positively affect not only air pollution and climate but also land use.

There are a few important things to note about the new equilibrium in Figure 10.3. First, although the external costs of driving were added to the price of gasoline, the price to consumers does not increase by $2.60, to $4.90/gallon. Because the increased price provides both firms and consumers with an incentive to change their behavior, gasoline consumption drops by 49 billion gallons. The new equilibrium price is $4.30/gallon for the consumers. Because the external costs are paid to the government and not the producer, the producer receives the price the consumer pays, $4.30, less the external costs, $2.40, which is only $1.90 per gallon. Additionally, although the producers pay the external costs, most of these costs are passed along to consumers, which gives them an incentive to reduce their gasoline consumption.

Including the external costs of gasoline consumption in the market price of gasoline leads to changed driving habits and much less gasoline consumption. Price is a strong signal, both to consumers and to producers, to alter behavior. Nevertheless, it is not a signal that consumers or producers like. An individual's calculation on how much to drive favors lower prices: the benefits to the individual of the time savings and convenience are large, and the damages that the individual's driving causes to himself are small. After all, much of the damage that he causes falls on other people. While this calculation makes sense for each individual, when all individuals decide that lots of driving is good for them, the total of all the damages caused by these individuals becomes huge. With damages at $2.60/gallon, consumption of 140 billion gallons at the original market equilibrium implies external damages of $364 billion annually.

IN SUMMARY

- External costs are costs of production and consumption that are not faced by the producer and consumer. Without regulation, the market-clearing price and quantity do not reflect the external costs of using the good.
- Environmental costs are real costs to human health and welfare. Because environmental costs are almost always external costs, private supply curves do not take into account external damages, such as the air or water pollution from an activity, because the producers do not have to pay those costs. An unregulated market equilibrium does not take these costs into account.
- Social marginal cost curves include external costs as well as private production costs. The social supply curve, because it includes additional costs, lies above the private supply curve.
- When the social supply curve intersects the demand curve, the resulting market equilibrium reflects a higher price to consumers, a lower price to producers, and a lower quantity of the good than does the private market equilibrium. It also results in reduced external damages

Finding the Right Level of Production

Gasoline suppliers are producing more gasoline at a lower price, and producing more pollution, than they would if drivers had to pay the social costs of driving. Drivers and shareholders in oil refineries will not want to change what they do because paying the social costs of environmental damages means higher prices for the drivers and lower profits for the refiners as sellers of gasoline. On the other hand, consumers (including drivers and shareholders in oil refineries) like breathing clean air and not facing road congestion. So how much output and pollution is the right amount? Is it better to make the drivers pay all the external costs, or is it better to leave things as they were?

PARETO IMPROVEMENT AND NET BENEFIT

Pareto improvement, discussed in Chapter 3, requires that nobody is harmed by an activity and at least one person benefits. Charging the external costs of gasoline is unlikely to be Pareto improving. Those who drive a great deal or own many shares in the stock of oil refineries are better off without the pollution charges. Those who live near freeways, which is where pollution is greatest, and drive little are better off with the pollution charges. Like charging for gasoline's external costs, most actions that affect the environment are not Pareto improvements. Actions that cause both gains and losses must be evaluated with criteria that consider the gains and losses of the proposed policy.

The common rule in economics for evaluating projects with losers and gainers is that the project should not be undertaken unless the net benefits, benefits less costs, including external costs, are positive. The **benefit-cost criterion** is that projects with positive net benefits should be done, while projects with negative net benefits should not be done. When markets have reached a situation where no changes to them can increase net benefits, those markets are **efficient**.

Charging drivers the external costs of gasoline increases net benefits if the reduction in damages from pollution exceeds the lost benefits from gasoline consumption. Even

---

BOX 10.1

Alternatives to Efficiency

What alternatives exist to efficiency as a criterion for deciding whether something is good? Here we will consider two of many: the Rawls *maximin principle* and a deep ecology perspective.

John Rawls (1921–2002), a political philosopher, has suggested that we as a society should behave to improve the lot of the worst-off person. In other words, if we could identify the person with the worst quality of life, or minimum utility, we should increase that person's well-being. Mathematically, we would maximize the minimum utility; hence, the idea is often called the **maximin principle**. If we made the worst-off person better off, eventually she would be as well off as the next-worse-off person; we would then need to improve both their lots in life. This process tends toward everyone having the same utility because the only way that there is not a worse-off person is for everyone to be equally well off. In contrast to efficiency, this criterion emphasizes distributional effects: what matters is making the worst-off person better off, rather than just increasing wealth. Efficiency can complement the Rawls maximin principle, though: if the pie is made bigger, the gains can be given to those who have the smallest pieces.

Deep ecology is a philosophical principle that moves away from a people-centered world to give more weight to nature. In this view, people are not the ultimate judges of value or well-being for the world; other living things and systems have values independent of what people think of them. Efficiency, in contrast, is human centered; it emphasizes benefits to people, and effects on the natural world matter only because people care about them. A deep ecology perspective might be described as seeking to minimize any adverse environmental impacts while allowing people to maintain a reasonable quality of life. People are only a part of the system in this view, rather than the primary focus of the system.

Economists have long wanted to participate in policy discussions and to be able to make judgments about the quality of alternative choices. The benefit-cost criterion is the most commonly used criterion in economics, but it is not the only one, and many people disagree with the recommendations of efficiency analysis. These two alternative criteria will create different recommendations than efficiency analysis will. Being aware of the advantages and limitations of efficiency, and of some alternative approaches, will increase your understanding of the economic approach to policy issues.

when there are positive net benefits, there can be losers. Even when the benefits from charging for external costs exceed the costs of doing so, there are people who are worse off. Those who drive a lot are worse off in the gasoline charge case. So projects that have positive net benefits are not necessarily Pareto improving.

When there are positive net benefits, it is possible in theory for the gainers from a program to compensate the losers to achieve a Pareto improvement. However, such compensation is often difficult if not impossible to arrange in practice. For instance, in the gasoline example, how could heavy gasoline users be compensated? Compensation that rewards them for driving, such as a tax rebate based on miles driven to work, would encourage driving, exactly opposite of the intended effect. The theoretical ability for losers to be compensated is usually just that, a theoretical possibility.

BENEFITS AND COSTS

The benefit-cost criterion requires measuring the benefits and costs of an action. Chapter 5 showed that total consumer benefits are measured as total willingness to pay (TWTP) for the good, the area under the demand curve. Now let's find a way to represent the cost side of our equation as an area on our diagram.

Costs are the social costs of the good, which include both private and external costs. Private costs, $C(Q)$, include fixed cost, FC, and variable cost, VC. Fixed costs are always the same. Can we calculate variable costs from the supply curve? In the same way that adding up the marginal willingness to pay gives total willingness to pay, adding up the marginal cost of a good gives variable cost.

Let's look at costs for making Q units of a good. They are FC + MC(1) + MC(2) + ... + MC(Q): the fixed costs, plus the cost of making the first unit, plus the cost of making the second unit, given that one unit was already made, and so on. Because $C(Q)$ is the sum of FC(Q) and VC(Q), subtracting fixed costs from both sides gives VC(Q) = MC(1) + ... + MC(Q). So variable cost is the sum of the marginal costs, or variable cost is the area under the marginal cost curve. In Figure 10.4, the variable costs of making 140 billion gallons of gasoline are darkly shaded. The same logic holds for social costs, private costs, or external costs. In all cases, variable costs are the area under a marginal cost curve. Thus, the area under the social marginal cost curve plus fixed costs is a measure of social costs.

Fixed costs are often left out of decisions because they can't be changed in the short run. In that case, it is common to speak of *producer surplus* instead of profits. **Producer surplus** is revenue less variable costs. In Figure 10.4, revenue (price times quantity) is the area of both shaded boxes, equal to $2.30/gallon times 140 billion gallons. Variable costs are the dark shaded area. The difference between revenue and variable costs is the light shaded area; it is the producer surplus. It is the area below price and above marginal cost.

Net private benefits, then, are TWTP less costs. Another way of measuring net benefits is that it is the sum of consumer plus producer surplus. Remember that consumer surplus is TWTP less the amount paid for the good (price times quantity). Producer surplus is revenue—price times quantity—less costs. Thus, consumer plus producer surplus is TWTP $- P * Q + P * Q - C(Q) =$ TWTP $- C(Q)$.

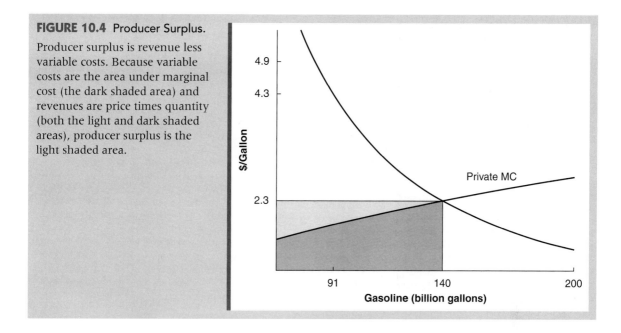

FIGURE 10.4 Producer Surplus.
Producer surplus is revenue less variable costs. Because variable costs are the area under marginal cost (the dark shaded area) and revenues are price times quantity (both the light and dark shaded areas), producer surplus is the light shaded area.

MAXIMIZING BENEFITS

The benefit-cost criterion seeks to maximize (or at least increase) the difference between total willingness to pay and social costs. We have two possible market equilibria to consider in our gasoline problem: the market equilibrium based on private costs, with a price of $2.30/gallon and a quantity of 140 billion gallons, and the equilibrium based on social costs, with a price of $4.30/gallon and a quantity of 91 billion gallons. To determine which has greater net benefits, let's consider the consumer question and the producer question.

Let's begin with consumers. Figure 10.5 shows the demand curve for gasoline. The TWTP for 140 billion gallons is the area under demand between zero and 140 billion gallons. The TWTP for 91 billion gallons is the area under demand between zero and 91 billion gallons. The difference in TWTP between these two equilibria is the shaded area, the area under the demand curve between those quantities. That is, the amount that consumers would be willing to pay to increase consumption from 91 billion to 140 billion gallons is the same as the amount that they would lose if the quantity instead decreased from 140 billion to 91 billion gallons. TWTP, the area between the curves, is about $154 billion. This is the benefit to the consumer of increased production or the loss from decreased production.

Now let's look at producers. Figure 10.6 on page 233 shows the social cost of changing production from 91 billion to 140 billion gallons. The cost of producing 140 billion gallons is the area under the social marginal cost curve between zero and 140 billion gallons, plus fixed costs. The cost of producing 91 billion gallons is the area under the social marginal cost curve between zero and 91 billion gallons, plus

FIGURE 10.5 Total Willingness to Pay Between 91 Billion and 140 Billion Gallons.

The shaded area is the total willingness to pay for an increase in consumption from 91 billion to 140 billion gallons.

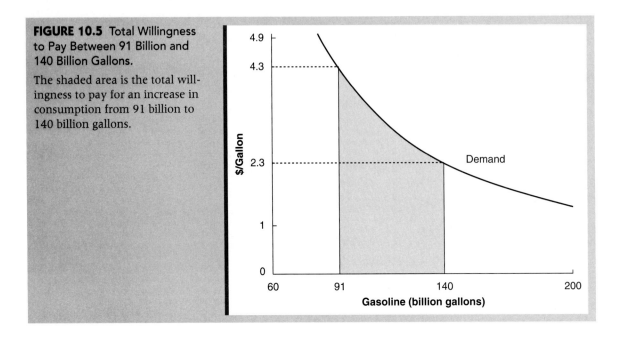

fixed costs. So the social cost of increasing production from 91 billion to 140 billion gallons is found by subtracting the area under the social marginal cost curve between zero and 91 billion gallons from the area under the social marginal cost curve between zero and 140 billion gallons. The fixed costs play no role in calculating the change in costs between two quantities because they won't change during this short-run change in production. Thus, the change in social cost is the area under the social marginal cost curve between these values. If production increases, not only will producers have higher production costs, but everyone who breathes will face increased damages from dirtier air. This cost difference is about $227 billion: that is, if production increases from 91 billion to 140 billion gallons, social costs increase by $227 billion. And if production decreases from 140 billion to 91 billion gallons, social costs decrease by $227 billion.

Now let's compare the benefits and costs of a change in gasoline consumption. Figure 10.7 on page 234 puts the demand curve together with the social marginal cost curve. Net benefits are the area between these two curves, shown as the dark shaded triangle in Figure 10.7. When quantity increases from 91 billion to 140 billion gallons, social costs increase by $227 billion, and TWTP increases by $153 billion. The net benefit, the difference between benefits and costs, of increasing consumption from 91 billion to 140 billion gallons is thus −$74 billion; the net benefit from decreasing consumption from 140 billion gallons to 91 billion gallons is $74 billion. In other words, net benefits are higher at 91 billion gallons, where social marginal cost intersects demand, than they are at 140 billion gallons.

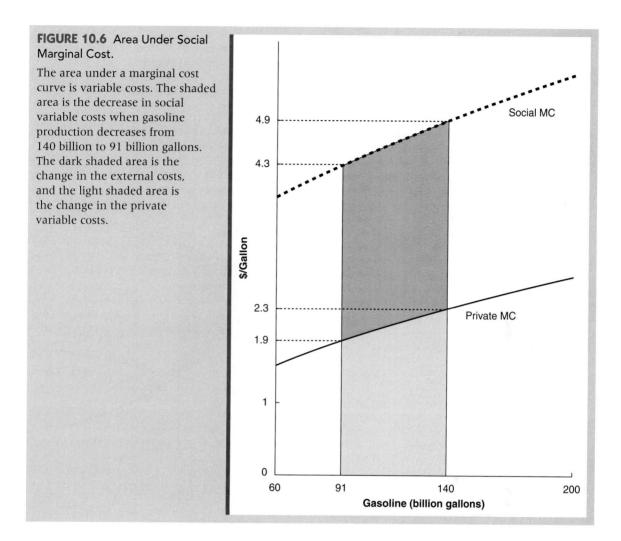

FIGURE 10.6 Area Under Social Marginal Cost.

The area under a marginal cost curve is variable costs. The shaded area is the decrease in social variable costs when gasoline production decreases from 140 billion to 91 billion gallons. The dark shaded area is the change in the external costs, and the light shaded area is the change in the private variable costs.

Is it a general rule that net benefits are highest where social marginal cost equals demand? Indeed it is. There are three cases to consider. First, let's look at the case where the price on the demand curve is above social marginal cost. This is true at any quantity below 91 billion gallons, such as the 70 billion gallons shown in Figure 10.8 on page 235. Increasing production by one unit would increase TWTP by an amount equal to the price on the demand curve. Increasing production also would increase social costs by the price on the social marginal cost curve. Because the price on the demand curve is a larger number than social marginal cost, net benefits would go up if one more unit of gasoline were produced. So, net benefits are not maximized where the price on the demand curve is greater than social marginal cost.

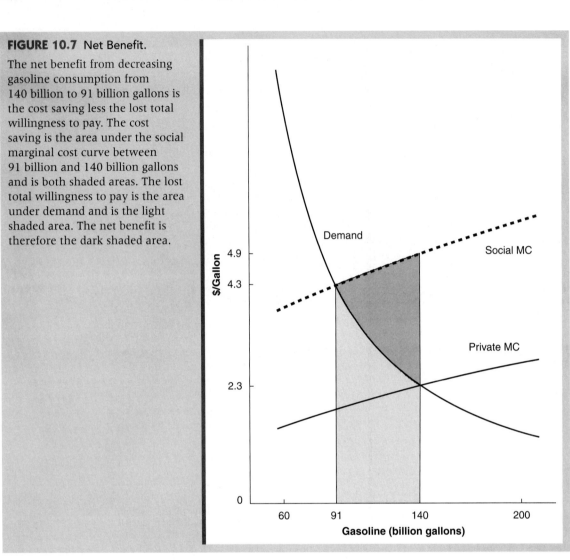

FIGURE 10.7 Net Benefit.

The net benefit from decreasing gasoline consumption from 140 billion to 91 billion gallons is the cost saving less the lost total willingness to pay. The cost saving is the area under the social marginal cost curve between 91 billion and 140 billion gallons and is both shaded areas. The lost total willingness to pay is the area under demand and is the light shaded area. The net benefit is therefore the dark shaded area.

Second is the case where the price on the demand curve is smaller than social marginal cost. This is true at a quantity of 140 billion gallons, as in Figure 10.7. This quantity represents the actual market equilibrium when external costs are not taken into account. Decreasing production by one unit decreases TWTP by the price on the demand curve. Decreasing production decreases social cost by the price on the social marginal cost curve. Because social marginal cost exceeds the price on the demand curve, net benefits are not at their highest at this level of gasoline production; if the quantity of gasoline decreased, net benefits would increase.

This leaves only the third case, where social marginal cost equals the price on the demand curve, as the situation where net benefits are maximized. In Figure 10.7,

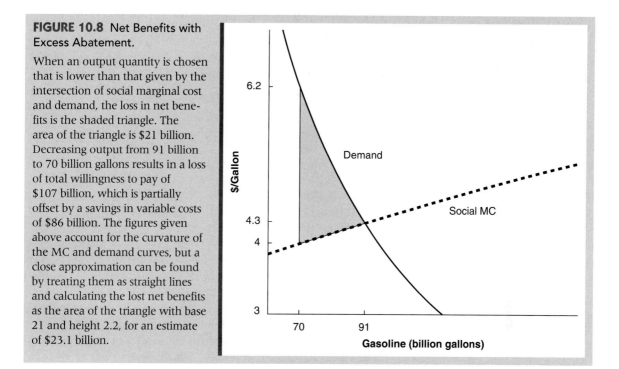

FIGURE 10.8 Net Benefits with Excess Abatement.

When an output quantity is chosen that is lower than that given by the intersection of social marginal cost and demand, the loss in net benefits is the shaded triangle. The area of the triangle is $21 billion. Decreasing output from 91 billion to 70 billion gallons results in a loss of total willingness to pay of $107 billion, which is partially offset by a savings in variable costs of $86 billion. The figures given above account for the curvature of the MC and demand curves, but a close approximation can be found by treating them as straight lines and calculating the lost net benefits as the area of the triangle with base 21 and height 2.2, for an estimate of $23.1 billion.

social marginal cost equals the price on the demand curve at a quantity of 91 billion gallons. So net benefits are maximized at 91 billion gallons, a considerably smaller quantity than the quantity where private quantity supplied equals quantity demanded. Thus, net benefits are largest when quantity is the level associated with marginal willingness to pay equaling social marginal cost.

If gasoline had no external costs, these same arguments would result in the efficient level of production occurring at the intersection of the demand curve and the private supply curve. This quantity is also the outcome that will result from market forces in an unregulated market. Economists' often-cited penchant for unregulated markets is because of the efficiency of these markets: they maximize net benefits if there are no external costs. The presence of external costs, however, makes a private market solution inefficient, and the support for unregulated markets is not justified in the presence of externalities or other market failures.

In other words, the private market equilibrium for gasoline does not lead to maximum net benefits because it does not take into consideration the environmental costs of gasoline use. The private market solution maximizes net benefits only if there are no external costs or other market failures. In the presence of external costs, the net benefit-maximizing level of gasoline production results from considering the effects on all parties, including worldwide habitats and communities affected by climate change.

DEADWEIGHT LOSS AND THE EFFICIENT LEVEL OF POLLUTION

There is a special name in economics for the cost associated with an inefficient situation: it is termed a **deadweight loss**. The private market solution for gasoline, with production of 140 billion gallons, is inefficient; it produces deadweight loss. Calculating a deadweight loss requires two outcomes, an efficient one and an inefficient one. The deadweight loss is equal to the difference between net benefits at the efficient outcome and net benefits at the inefficient outcome. In other words, it is the change in total willingness to pay less the change in social costs. The decrease in net benefits between 91 billion and 140 billion gallons, the dark shaded area in Figure 10.7, is the deadweight loss, $74 billion.

Deadweight loss also exists if too little gasoline is consumed. Suppose that environmentalists have been especially effective in their efforts to influence the pollution level, and gasoline use is driven to 70 billion gallons. For gasoline consumption below 91 billion gallons, the demand curve lies above the social marginal cost curve. The benefits of a little bit of driving—for instance, transporting people in ambulances or delivery of critical nutrition to people in desperate need in areas without other forms of transit—may be very high. The damages caused by a little gasoline use are low relative to these benefits. People are willing to put up with some environmental damages in order to gain the benefits from some gasoline use. In Figure 10.8, when gasoline consumption is reduced to 70 billion gallons, the deadweight loss is the area between the vertical line at 70 billion gallons and the demand and social marginal cost curves up to where they intersect; it is about $21 billion.

Does it make sense to talk about too little pollution being emitted? In many cases, the damage caused by a very small amount of pollution is, in fact, very small. For instance, a campfire produces sulfur dioxide, carbon monoxide, carbon dioxide, particulate matter, hydrocarbons known or suspected of causing cancer, and other pollutants. Sitting downwind of a campfire can make breathing very difficult, and the pollutants spread into the atmosphere to affect people elsewhere. Nevertheless, many people would regret, if not actively protest, a prohibition on campfires. Roasting marshmallows and telling ghost stories around campfires provide enough benefits that many people are willing to accept the emissions from an occasional campfire in a rural area. In other words, the demand for the polluting activity—campfires—exceeds the marginal costs of the activity—the pollution—for some campfires in some circumstances. The efficient level of pollution is unlikely to be zero in many cases.

The general steps to find deadweight loss in a supply and demand diagram are: (1) Find the quantity where net benefits are maximized. It is where the social marginal cost curve intersects the demand curve (in the example, 91 billion gallons). (2) Find the quantity associated with an alternative scenario (for example, where the private marginal cost curve intersects the demand curve, 140 billion gallons). (3) Find the triangle bounded by the social marginal cost curve, the demand curve, and the quantity associated with the alternative. That triangle is deadweight loss.

More generally, deadweight loss occurs whenever net benefits are not at their maximum. In this example, the social marginal cost curve lies above the demand curve for all gasoline production above 91 billion gallons. Deadweight loss is the triangle formed by the vertical line at the quantity produced (for instance, 140 billion gallons), the demand curve, and the social marginal cost curve, to the point where they inter-sect. This is the net cost—in this example, about $74 billion—imposed on society if the external costs of gasoline production are not included in the price of gasoline.

◢ IN SUMMARY

- Net benefits are benefits less costs. An action that increases net benefits may make some people worse off; if it does, it is not Pareto improving.
- The maximum of net benefits, the efficient level of production, occurs at the quantity where the demand curve intersects the social marginal cost curve.
- If there are no market failures, then private, unregulated markets are efficient. When a market failure is present, private market results are not efficient. Producers and consumers will ignore external costs for which they are not required to pay.
- Deadweight loss is the reduction in net benefits associated with either too much or too little of a good. It is the area between the demand curve and the social marginal cost curve.
- Just as too much pollution is inefficient, too little pollution, or, put another way, too much pollution reduction, can also be inefficient. A little bit of pollution may impose very few damages on people, while the costs of abating the last units of pollution may be very high.

Marginal Costs and Benefits of Pollution and Abatement

Because pollution imposes costs that are external to the private production process, we have added private marginal costs and external marginal costs to get social marginal costs. However, this is not the only way that economists talk about the pollution problem. There are two other common ways to arrange this information. The first way is to identify the marginal private benefits of polluting to both producers and consumers and compare them to the external costs of pollution. The second way is to discuss abating (having less pollution): instead of changing the quantity of the pollutant, gasoline, from 140 billion to 91 billion units, we might say that the pollution from 49 billion gallons of gasoline was abated. Because environmental economists and regulators may use any of these ways of describing the economics of externalities, it is useful to understand the connections among them.

MARGINAL BENEFIT AND COST OF POLLUTION

The demand curve gives the benefit to consumers of one more unit of gasoline, and the private marginal cost curve gives the cost to producers of producing that unit. Suppose that we subtract the private marginal cost curve for gasoline production from the demand curve for gasoline. The resulting curve is the **marginal benefit**

of polluting, the benefit to consumers less the private costs to producers of one more unit of pollution. Figure 10.9 shows this curve.

The marginal benefit of polluting line summarizes the private market solution for gasoline. The marginal benefit of polluting starts high because people are willing to pay a high price for the first units of gasoline and the marginal private costs of producing the first units of gasoline are low. As the marginal willingness to pay for gasoline use drops, and the marginal private costs of producing gasoline increase, the marginal benefit of polluting decreases, as shown in the downward-sloping shape of the marginal benefit of pollution curve. When the demand curve for gasoline use intersects the private marginal cost of production, the difference between these two curves is zero, and the marginal benefit of polluting curve hits

FIGURE 10.9 Marginal Benefit and Cost of Pollution.

The marginal benefit of polluting is the marginal willingness to pay less the marginal cost of one more unit of pollution. The marginal cost of polluting is the marginal external cost. The figure shows that the efficient level of output is 91 billion gallons.

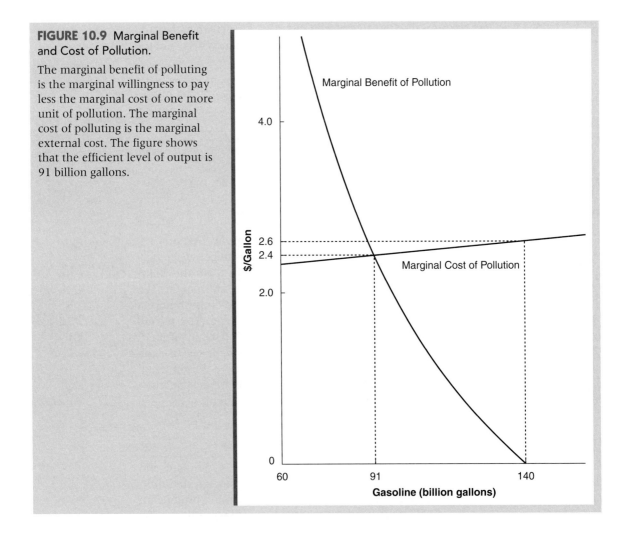

the horizontal axis, at a quantity of 140 billion gallons. Beyond 140 billion gallons, the marginal private costs of production exceed the marginal willingness to pay for additional gasoline consumption, and the marginal benefit of pollution becomes negative, even when external costs are not considered. The market equilibrium occurs when the net benefit of producing one more unit is zero; at that point, all gallons with positive net benefits, and no gallons with negative net benefits, are produced.

The private market solution does not consider external costs, though. The external cost associated with a polluting activity is the **marginal cost of polluting**. The marginal cost of polluting curve is also shown in Figure 10.9.

When the external cost of polluting is added in Figure 10.9, the efficient quantity of gasoline occurs when the marginal benefit of polluting equals the marginal cost of polluting. These two curves intersect at a price of $2.40 and a quantity of 91 billion gallons. The price of $2.40 is the external cost per gallon associated with production of 91 billion gallons. Thus, the marginal benefit and cost of polluting diagrams show exactly the same efficient quantity of gasoline production with and without external costs as in the supply and demand diagrams.

MARGINAL BENEFIT AND COST OF ABATING

Abatement is pollution reduction. The benefits of reducing pollution are the same as the costs of increasing pollution. The costs of reducing pollution are the same as the benefits of increasing pollution. What is the cost associated with pollution abatement? In our gasoline example, not reducing pollution at all—abating nothing—corresponds to the private-market equilibrium of 140 billion gallons. Giving up gasoline creates an opportunity cost, the forgone net benefits of that gallon of gasoline. People will face higher costs of transportation with less gasoline, as in the example of the commuting parent at the beginning of the chapter. The **marginal costs of abatement,** then, are the net marginal benefits to using gasoline that consumers and producers give up. Thus, the marginal costs of abatement are equal to the marginal benefits of pollution, though measured from a different starting point.

Let's create a marginal cost of abatement curve by plotting a few points on it. To begin, let's look at the relationship between pollution and abatement in Table 10.2. The first three rows show quantity abated, quantity used, and their sum. The quantity of gasoline produced is the measure of pollution. The reduction in gasoline use below the market equilibrium of 140 billion gallons is the measure of abatement. In each of the three columns in Table 10.2, the quantity of abatement in row one plus the quantity of production in row two add up to the market equilibrium quantity, 140 billion gallons, in row three. For any combination of pollution and abatement, the marginal cost of polluting in row four is the same as the marginal benefit of abating in row five, and the marginal benefit of polluting in row six is the same as the marginal cost of abating in row seven.

When there is no abatement, the private market equilibrium holds: 140 billion gallons of gasoline are used. At that usage, the private net benefits of polluting by

TABLE 10.2   Pollution Emitted and Abated.

This table shows that the marginal benefit of polluting is equal to the marginal cost of abatement when the sum of the quantity produced and the quantity abated is the unregulated amount of pollution.

	NO ABATEMENT	SMALL ABATEMENT	LARGE ABATEMENT
1. QUANTITY ABATED (BILLION GALLONS)	0	30	49
2. QUANTITY USED (BILLION GALLONS)	140	110	91
3. SUM OF Q PRODUCED AND Q ABATED (BILLION GALLONS)	140	140	140
4. MC POLLUTION ($/GALLON)	2.6	2.5	2.4
5. MB ABATEMENT ($/GALLON)	2.6	2.5	2.4
6. MB POLLUTION ($/GALLON)	0	1.2	2.4
7. MC ABATEMENT ($/GALLON)	0	1.2	2.4

using another gallon and the private net costs of abating by using one less gallon are both zero because private marginal benefits for a gallon of gas are exactly equal to private marginal cost when the market is in equilibrium without a pollution charge. Therefore, rows six and seven of the table are zero for the no-abatement alternative. With no abatement, row four shows the marginal cost of pollution, the external costs, $2.60/gallon. The benefit of abatement is the avoidance of the damages caused by pollution. In row five, the marginal benefit of abatement is also $2.60/gallon. With no abatement, the marginal benefit of abatement far exceeds the marginal cost of abatement; net benefits will increase with additional abatement.

Now let's look at an intermediate point, 30 billion gallons abated, or 110 billion gallons used. The marginal cost of pollution, in row four, $2.50/gallon, is equal to the marginal benefit of abatement in row five. The marginal benefit of pollution in row six, $1.20/gallon, is equal to the marginal benefit of pollution in row seven. Because the marginal benefit of abatement is still larger than the marginal cost of abatement, abatement should be increased further.

The last column of Table 10.2 has the marginal costs and benefits for 91 billion gallons produced and 49 billion gallons abated. Now the marginal benefit of abatement, which is the marginal cost of pollution, is $2.40/gallon. The marginal cost of abatement, which is the marginal benefit of pollution, is also $2.40/gallon. The marginal benefit of abatement equals the marginal cost of abatement at the same quantity where the marginal cost of pollution equaled the marginal benefit of pollution. This is the efficient level of pollution taking into account the externality of gasoline use.

The **marginal benefits of abatement** are the effects of the lessened pollution. The air will be cleaner, the climate will change less, and roads will be less crowded. In other words, the benefit from abatement is avoiding the damages from pollution, which are the external marginal costs of pollution. Thus, the marginal benefits of abatement are equal to the marginal costs of pollution, though measured from a different starting point.

Figure 10.10 plots the marginal cost of abatement and marginal benefit of abatement curves just derived. These curves are the mirror image of the marginal cost and benefit of polluting curves: they are reversed because 0 abatement = 140 billion gallons used, and 49 billion gallons of abatement = 91 billion gallons used.

The marginal benefit of abatement curve in Figure 10.10 starts at zero units abated. When there is no abatement, the marginal benefits of abating are very high

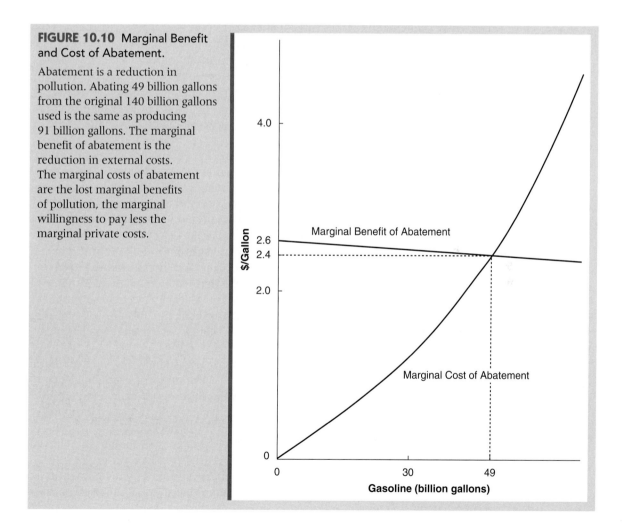

FIGURE 10.10 Marginal Benefit and Cost of Abatement.

Abatement is a reduction in pollution. Abating 49 billion gallons from the original 140 billion gallons used is the same as producing 91 billion gallons. The marginal benefit of abatement is the reduction in external costs. The marginal costs of abatement are the lost marginal benefits of pollution, the marginal willingness to pay less the marginal private costs.

because the uncontrolled pollution causes high damages. Similarly, the marginal costs of abatement are low when there is no abatement because it is easy to abate the first units. As more pollution is abated, the marginal benefits become lower as the damages are reduced, and the marginal cost becomes greater as people give up more desirable driving. The largest net benefit value in the diagram is at the efficient point where marginal benefit and cost from abating are equal, at 49 billion gallons of abatement, equivalent to 91 billion gallons uses.

WHEN ABATEMENT IS NOT JUST REDUCING OUTPUT

Reducing usage is the only way to abate pollution considered so far in this chapter. There are, however, other ways to reduce pollution. For auto emissions, the pollution can be reduced through changes in automobile design and gasoline formulation. For leachate from lettuce, less water can be applied. More generally, pollution can be reduced by changing the process used to make the good as well as by using less of the good. Thus, there are ways besides reducing consumption to reduce pollution.

It is a general rule that an increased number of options cannot make it more expensive to achieve a goal. If drivers can reduce pollution either by reducing their driving or by buying less-polluting cars or fuel, they cannot be worse off than if they could only reduce driving because reducing driving is still an option. Thus, additional options are likely to lower the costs associated with reducing pollution.

When there are ways of reducing pollution other than reducing the quantity of the good, measuring the quantity of the good no longer measures the quantity of pollution. Here and in Table 10.3, we revisit the example of nitrogen leachate from lettuce production. To recap, we considered the farmer's choice of how to grow lettuce in response to the price of water. Water is measured in millimeter-hectares, the quantity of water that is a millimeter deep on a hectare of land. If output stayed constant, increasing the price of water from \$0.23/mm-ha to \$0.59/mm-ha would lead the farmer to use less water and more nitrogen, and leachate would decrease. In addition, because the marginal cost of making lettuce increased when the price of water increased, the profit-maximizing amount of lettuce decreased. Now let's use these facts to find the marginal cost of abatement per hectare for reducing leachate, which is equivalent to the marginal benefit per hectare of producing leachate.

The first column of the table shows the values for production, water used and its price, nitrogen used and its price, profit, and leachate for the original price of water, \$0.23/mm-ha. Column two shows the values that result from a higher price for water, \$0.59/mm-ha, when output is held constant. Less water and more nitrogen are used per hectare, and both leachate and profit decline. The third column shows the values that result from a higher price of water with the output allowed to adjust in the profit-maximizing way. The increased price for water leads to an upward shift in marginal cost, and price equals marginal cost at a lower quantity of lettuce. Water used, nitrogen used, and leachate produced are all lower than they were originally, in column one.

TABLE 10.3 Lettuce Production Under Different Scenarios.

	ORIGINAL PRICES AND QUANTITY FOR LETTUCE AND WATER	NEW PRICE FOR WATER, OLD QUANTITY OF LETTUCE	NEW WATER PRICE, NEW QUANTITY OF LETTUCE
LETTUCE PRODUCED (T/HA)	3.377	3.377	3.326
WATER USED (MM)	806.8	774.8	670.20
PRICE OF WATER ($/MM-HA)	0.23	0.59	0.59
NITROGEN USED (KG)	138.77	155.53	115.12
PRICE OF NITROGEN ($/KG)	0.70	0.70	0.70
PROFIT[1] ($/HA)	4543.03	4259.73	4276.852
LEACHATE (KG/HA)	121	116.5	90.3

[1]This number is not actual profits because it does not include the costs of land, machinery, labor, or other inputs to the production process. It is the price of lettuce (1,429) times the quantity of lettuce, less the price of the each input times the quantity of each input. These numbers are most useful for comparing the three scenarios rather than for a literal statement of the profit from growing lettuce.

Column one, the original values, and column three, the abated values, have all the information needed to calculate the marginal cost of abatement for leachate. Because the lettuce-growing area where the leaching occurs is small, it is reasonable to assume that the price of lettuce will not change if production decreases just in this region. With a constant price, the change in total willingness to pay, the area under demand, is just the change in quantity times price. Change in TWTP = $P * (Q_{orig} - Q_{abate})$. The cost of abatement is the change in TWTP minus the change in costs. Thus, the cost of abatement is $P * (Q_{orig} - Q_{abate}) - (C_{orig} - C_{abate})$. Rearranging this gives $(P * Q_{orig} - C_{orig}) - (P * Q_{abate} - C_{abate})$: the cost of abatement is Profits$_{orig}$ − Profits$_{abate}$. From columns one and three, the change in profits is $4,543/ha − $4,277/ha = $266/ha.

There is one more detail. The farmer was induced to produce less leachate through a tax on the water she used. The tax increased the price of water from $0.23/mm-ha to $0.59/mm-ha. The tax revenue is the new water use times the difference in price: 670.20 mm * $.36/mm-ha = $241/ha. The tax revenue is a cost to the farmer, incorporated into her profits, but the tax revenue does not disappear; it provides a benefit to its recipient, who can provide more government services or reduce other taxes. The cost of abatement, then, is Profits$_{orig}$ − (Profits$_{abate}$ + Tax Revenue). The cost of abating from 121 to 90.3 kg/ha of leachate, then, is $4,543 − (4,277 + 241) = $25/ha. The marginal cost of abatement is the change in abatement costs divided by the quantity of leachate abated, or approximately ($25/ha)/(30.7 kg/ha) = $0.81/kg.

Notice that the marginal cost of abatement is measured in the volume of leachate, not the volume of lettuce. Because the leachate from lettuce can be reduced by either using less water to grow the lettuce or growing less lettuce, the marginal cost of abatement is not the same as the marginal cost of lettuce production. There are many possible quantities of leachate for each ton of lettuce because output alone does not determine leachate. Focusing on leachate rather than lettuce puts the emphasis on the environmental problem rather than on the lettuce.

Because the marginal cost of abatement is the same (but measured from a different starting point) as the marginal benefit of polluting, the marginal benefit of leachate production is $0.81/kg when 90.3 kg/ha of leachate are emitted. Polluting produces benefits—in this case, lettuce—that must be balanced against the environmental harm it causes. Focusing on the leachate rather than the lettuce production gives the farmer more options for reducing emissions and thus finding lower costs of abatement.

IN SUMMARY

- Three different methods can describe the efficient amount of pollution: demand and social marginal cost curves; marginal benefits and costs of polluting curves; and marginal benefits and costs of abatement curves. All three approaches give the same results for the efficient level of production and losses for producing other levels.
- The marginal benefits of polluting are the difference between the demand curve and the private marginal costs of production curve. The marginal costs of polluting are the external costs of production.
- Abatement is pollution reduction. The marginal benefits of abatement are the reduction in damages from pollution; they are the mirror image of the marginal costs of polluting. The marginal costs of abatement, lost willingness to pay or producer surplus, are the mirror image of the marginal costs of pollution.
- The marginal benefits and costs of pollution are graphed with pollution on the horizontal axis, while the marginal benefits and costs of abatement are graphed with abatement on the horizontal axis.
- The efficient amount of pollution is where the marginal cost of polluting equals the marginal benefit of polluting. The efficient amount of abatement is where the marginal cost of abatement equals the marginal benefit of abatement.
- When abatement can result from means other than reducing output, there can be multiple levels of pollution, and thus damages, for different output levels. The marginal benefits and costs of polluting and abating can include the additional possibilities for abatement in ways not possible with a focus on output. The costs of reducing pollution will almost always be lower than in the absence of these other options.

National Forest Timber Sales Below Cost

Now let's see how efficiency analysis can be applied to another environmental issue: the tradeoff between preservation and utilization in national forests. The U.S. Forest Service, an agency in the U.S. Department of Agriculture, manages about 190 million acres of government-owned land. In national forests, unlike national parks, resources such as minerals and lumber can be extracted for commercial uses. The U.S. Forest Service sells logging companies the right to harvest trees for wood products. The costs of harvesting-related activities, such as building roads and administering the sales, come from the agency's budget; most of the revenue from selling the trees goes to the U.S. Treasury. Because the agency accounted for revenues and costs separately, it rarely compared the two.

In the 1970s, economists and environmentalists looked at these accounts and found that the Forest Service, in many places, sold trees for much less than the costs associated with those sales. In other words, not only was the marginal benefit of wood (the market price) lower than social marginal cost; it was lower than the private marginal cost (the cost to the Forest Service). Environmentalists argued that this practice not only subsidized wood production in the national forests, leading to unfair competition with wood production from private forests, but it also encouraged environmentally damaging harvests. Loggers and communities whose existence depended on national forest harvesting argued for the importance of these sales to their continued livelihoods: even if the sales were inefficient, they gained benefits from them and wanted them to continue. Inefficient outcomes can be desirable to those who can gain benefits while putting the costs on others.

CHAPTER SUMMARY

Here are the key lessons from this chapter:

- Evaluating whether a policy improves or harms the world requires a way to measure how well off the world is. The appropriate measure depends on values; it is a question of individual and social ethics.
- Economists typically seek outcomes that increase net benefits. Efficiency involves maximizing total benefits minus total costs. It ignores the distribution of those net benefits, though. There may be individuals who lose due to an activity that has positive net benefits.
- The net gains from an activity are the difference between total willingness to pay and the social cost for the level of production. These gains are equivalent to the consumers' surplus plus the producers' surplus for that level.
- As long as marginal benefits (measured via the demand curve) exceed social marginal costs (the supply curve including external costs), it is efficient for production of a good to increase. Net gains are at a maximum when marginal benefits equal marginal costs. For any other level of production, either higher or lower, there is a deadweight loss.

- If there are no market failures, then unregulated markets in equilibrium are efficient, with no deadweight loss. If a failure exists in a market, then an unregulated market is not efficient; a deadweight loss results.
- The efficient level of a polluting activity can be found from the demand curve and social marginal cost curve, the marginal benefits and costs of pollution curves, or the marginal benefits and costs of abatement curves. They all contain the same information in rearranged ways.

KEY TERMS

benefit-cost criterion *(p. 228)*

deadweight loss *(p. 236)*

efficient *(p. 229)*

external costs *(p. 223)*

marginal benefit of polluting *(p. 237)*

marginal benefits of
   abatement *(p. 241)*

marginal cost of polluting *(p. 239)*

marginal costs of abatement *(p. 239)*

maximin principle *(p. 229)*

private costs *(p. 225)*

producer surplus *(p. 230)*

social costs *(p. 225)*

social marginal cost *(p. 226)*

NOTES

The candidates' positions on climate change and gasoline taxes were found on June 4, 2008, at johnmccain.com, BarackObama.com, and HillaryClinton.com, and in the *Wall Street Journal*, May 2, 2008 ("Clinton Introduces Gas-Tax Holiday Bill").

The external costs of driving listed in Table 10.1 are from Winston Harrington and Virginia McConnell, "Motor Vehicles and the Environment," *Resources for the Future Report* (April 2003), found at http://www.rff.org/rff/Documents/RFF-RPT-carsenviron.pdf. The data show average external cost per gallon. If we drew the cost curve using average costs, it would be a horizontal line because the external cost of producing one more gallon would be constant at all quantities of gasoline production. Instead, we use an upward-sloping marginal cost of pollution curve; this shows that each additional unit of gasoline creates greater external costs than the previous gallon. For the mirror image abatement graph, we use a downward-sloping marginal benefit of abatement curve, which shows that each additional unit of abatement provides fewer benefits than the previous unit.

The estimate of the demand elasticity for gasoline is the median estimate from Molly Espey, "Gasoline Demand Revisited: An International Meta-Analysis of Elasticities," *The Energy Journal* 20 (1998): 273–295. This number is not at all known with any precision despite its import for pollution policy. Carol Dahl and Thomas E. Duggan, "U.S. Energy Product Supply Elasticities: A Survey and Application to the U.S. Oil Market," *Resource and Energy Economics* 18 (1996): 243–263, surveys supply elasticities; the estimate used here for supply elasticity is on the higher end of those cited.

EXERCISES

1. Buchanan Industries receives profits from polluting according to the formula Profits $= \pi = 10Q - Q^2$, where $Q =$ pollution emitted (in tons), and profits are measured in dollars. Marginal benefits (MB) of polluting, derived from this function, are MB $= 10 - 2Q$. The damages associated with pollution from this facility are estimated as Damages $= D = Q^2 + 2Q$, where damages are measured in dollars. The marginal damages (costs) associated with that function are MD $= 2Q + 2$.

   (a) Draw a graph with the marginal benefits and marginal damage curves. Be sure to label the axes.

   (b) If Buchanan Industries could ignore the damages it caused, how much Q would it produce? How much profit would it earn at this level of production? How much would total damages be? What would be the net benefits, the difference between profits and damages?

   (c) What is the efficient Q for this industry? How much profit would Buchanan Industries earn at this level of production? How much would total damages be? What would be the net benefits, the difference between profits and damages?

   (d) Deadweight loss is the difference between the net benefits with the efficient level of pollution and net benefits with another level of pollution. What is the deadweight loss associated with Buchanan Industries ignoring damages that its production causes? Show the deadweight loss on your diagram. If Buchanan Industries would not on its own produce at the efficient Q, is it acting contrary to its own best interests by producing at the level in (c)?

   (e) Those who live near Buchanan Industries propose that Buchanan Industries produce no more than $Q = 1$. What is the deadweight loss associated with this level of production? If $Q = 1$ is an inefficient level of production, are those who live near the factory acting contrary to their own best interests by pushing for $Q = 1$?

   (f) Who benefits from reducing Q from the initial level in (a) to the efficient level in (b)? Who bears the costs? Is this change Pareto improving?

2. A policy maker decides that the government should build a dam across a river, even though the costs are greater than the benefits. Is the policy maker behaving irrationally? If not, why might the policy maker plan the project?

3. The demand for T-shirts is $Q = 20 - P/2$, where Q is the number of T-shirts and P is their price. The private cost of producing T-shirts is $C(Q) = Q^2$, with private marginal cost $MC_P = 2Q$. Washing and dyeing the T-shirts causes water pollution with total damages $C_E(Q) = Q^2/2$ and marginal external costs of $MC_E = Q$. Let's see how we can use this information to develop a social supply curve, marginal benefit and cost of pollution curves, and marginal benefit and cost of abatement curves.

   (a) First, let's figure out the market equilibrium when everyone ignores external costs. Remember that the supply curve is marginal cost above average variable costs. In this case it is the entire marginal cost curve. What is the private supply curve for T-shirts? Use that private supply curve plus the demand curve to find the equilibrium price and quantity. Draw a diagram showing the private supply, demand, and the equilibrium.

(b) Next, add the marginal external costs to your diagram. Then, calculate the social supply curve and add that to your diagram. Remember that, in this case, we first add (marginal) costs, not quantities, because these are the costs associated with each T-shirt. Finally, use the social supply curve and the demand curve to find the efficient price and quantity. Show these on your diagram.

(c) Calculate net benefits for each of the efficient and market solutions. These consist of the consumer surplus plus the profits less total damages for the relevant quantity; alternatively, it is total willingness to pay less both private and external costs. Which solution has higher net benefits? Do the two ways of calculating net benefits give the same answers? (They should!)

(d) Now we'll calculate the marginal benefits of polluting as the marginal profits to the T-shirt maker. Rewrite the demand curve so that P is a function of quantity; we do this so that we can subtract costs in dollars from benefits in dollars. Now, calculate marginal benefits of polluting $= P$ (from the demand curve) $-$ MC_P. On a fresh graph, draw this marginal benefit schedule. If the shirt producer can ignore external costs, how many T-shirts will it produce? Add the external costs of polluting, which are the marginal external costs to your diagram. What is the efficient quantity? Do you get the same answers as you did for (a) and (b)? (You should!)

(e) Finally, let's look at this from the abatement perspective. In this model, abatement is any reduction in production from the private-market equilibrium. First, provide a formula for abatement based on that description. Now, substitute that formula into the equations you have in (d) for the marginal benefit and marginal cost of polluting. If you do this substitution right, you will notice that what was the marginal benefit of polluting now increases as abatement increases; we'll call that the marginal cost of abatement. Similarly, the marginal cost of polluting now decreases as abatement increases; it's the marginal benefit of abatement. Which curve will the T-shirt producer use to decide its output? If the shirt producer can ignore external costs, how many T-shirts will he produce? If he has to take into account external costs, how much will he produce? Do you get the same answers as you did for (a) and (b), once you recognize that abatement is not the same as production? (You should!)

4. Welfare analysis can get complicated if there are multiple market failures. "The General Theory of the Second Best," by Lipsey and Lancaster [*Review of Economic Studies* 24 (1956–1957): 11–32] argues that, when there are multiple market failures, fixing only one market failure may make things worse than doing nothing. Two market failures may work in opposite directions, for instance; fixing one may have unintended consequences for the other.

For instance, consider a monopolist that pollutes. When a firm is a monopolist, it reduces its production so that it can increase price; although it sells fewer units, the higher price more than makes up for the reduced volume. Consumers lose, and total welfare is reduced, due to the higher price and lower quantity. The pollution problem, in contrast, is excess production.

(a) Draw a supply-demand figure for a firm with the demand curve $Q = 10 - P$, and marginal cost curve $MC = 2$ (based on total costs $C = 2 * Q$). If this were not a monopoly, what would be the equilibrium price and quantity? Calculate the firm's total revenue, total cost, and profit. Also calculate consumer surplus. Net benefits are consumer surplus plus producer surplus, which equals profit in this case; calculate that value.

(b) Suppose that, instead, the firm decided to act like a monopolist and restrict output. It produces 4 units and charges $6 for each unit. Calculate the firm's total revenue, total cost, and profit; consumer surplus; and net benefits. Are net benefits higher or lower? Is the firm better or worse off?

(c) Now let's consider the pollution problem. Suppose the firm produces marginal damages of $4/unit. For both (a) and (b), recalculate net benefits to account for the social damages.

(d) Find the new efficient equilibrium, now that social marginal costs are $6/unit. Calculate the firm's total revenue, total cost (including the pollution cost), and profit; consumer surplus; and net benefits.

(e) The monopolist, if forced to pay social marginal costs, will produce 2 units and charge $8 for each unit. Calculate the firm's total revenue, total cost (including the pollution cost), and profit; consumer surplus; and net benefits.

(f) Compare the results for (c), (d), and (e). Rank them, from the highest net benefits to the lowest.

(g) A regulator who can break up monopolies is examining this situation. Compare net benefits for the monopolist who pollutes [the recalculation for the monopolist in part (c)] with the competitive firm that pollutes [the recalculation for the competitive firm in part (c)]. Will the regulator improve net benefits by breaking up the monopoly?

(h) A regulator who addresses pollution separately examines the situation. Compare net benefits for the monopolist who pollutes [the recalculation for the monopolist in (c)] with net benefits for the monopolist who pays the full costs of pollution in (e). Will this regulator increase net benefits by taxing pollution?

(i) Does the "Theory of the Second Best" apply here? Does fixing a market failure always improve welfare compared with not fixing it?

CHAPTER 11

Private Markets and the Environment

The Coase Theorem

Tropical forests provide many ecological benefits from which people around the world gain benefits. They provide habitat for a huge variety of both plants and animals, not to mention many traditional human societies. They store large amounts of carbon dioxide that might otherwise be released into the atmosphere and increase global warming. They are sources of water for major cities around the world. Yet they are being depleted rapidly, sometimes for their wood products, sometimes to be converted into agricultural lands. Because people around the world care deeply about the benefits from intact tropical forests, why are they being lost? In fact, people in developed countries are making efforts to assist developing countries to protect these lands, though many environmentalists consider these efforts not to be sufficient.

Private markets will achieve efficiency in the absence of market failures. If a market fails, though, inefficiency will result: for instance, polluters will ignore the damages that they cause, and an inefficiently high amount of pollution will harm people. This chapter will consider one important approach to solving the problem of market failure: assigning ownership rights for goods that previously did not have rights and allowing a market to form. This chapter will examine:

- How rights can be defined for environmental goods;
- Using markets to address environmental problems;
- The limitations of markets for addressing environmental problems.

The Benefits and Costs of Sulfur Oxide Emissions

Sulfur oxides (SO_x, primarily sulfur dioxide, SO_2) are emitted by many industries, including coal-powered electric power generators. SO_x can significantly harm human health and ecosystems. They are a major source of acid rain; some lakes in the United States and Europe have become too acidic for fish because of SO_x emissions.

SO_x are also a source of particulate matter in the air, which is especially dangerous for people with breathing difficulties, such as asthma.

SO_x have been regulated under the U.S. Clean Air Act since 1970. Even so, under current rules, SO_x power plant emissions nationally are expected to be 9.1 million tons per year by 2010. This is considerably less than the 11.9 million tons emitted in 1995. However, during a similar period, Europe cut its emissions a great deal more: from 26.3 million tons to 15.2 million tons. Is 9.1 million tons the right amount of SO_x emissions for the United States? Let's look at some estimates of the efficient amount of emissions.

In the early 2000s, the administration of President George W. Bush and several lawmakers made varying proposals to further reduce these compounds. President Bush's Clear Skies proposal would reduce SO_x emissions by 6.1 million tons per year, resulting in emissions of 3 million tons per year by 2018. An alternative proposal, by Senator Jeffords, would reduce SO_x emissions by 6.85 million tons, resulting in emissions of 2.25 million tons per year by 2009. While the time difference is important, let's leave it aside and focus on the amount of emissions reductions.

A group of economists set out to estimate the efficient level of abatement. Figure 11.1 shows the amount of SO_x emissions abated—that is, the improvement in environmental quality—on the horizontal axis, measured in millions of tons abated. The vertical axis measures the cost per ton abated in dollars per ton. The marginal benefits of abatement curve (the demand curve for SO_x reduction) is flat; the flatness means that people are willing to pay a constant $3,500/ton to further

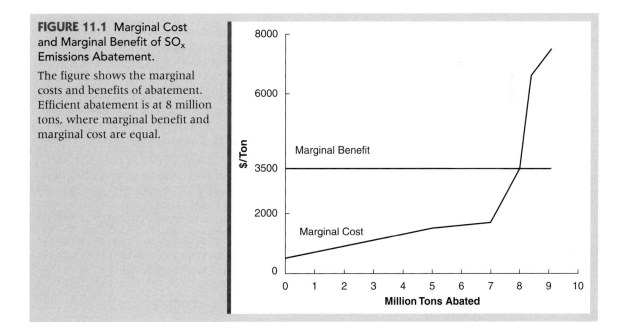

FIGURE 11.1 Marginal Cost and Marginal Benefit of SO_x Emissions Abatement.

The figure shows the marginal costs and benefits of abatement. Efficient abatement is at 8 million tons, where marginal benefit and marginal cost are equal.

reduce SO_x, regardless of the amount already cleaned up. The marginal cost of abatement measures how much power plants will have to spend to reduce SO_x emissions by one more ton. The marginal cost of abatement is less than $1,000/ton for the first million tons; it increases to $3,500/ton when 8 million tons are abated; and it is well over $7,000/ton for complete abatement, or elimination of all 9.1 million tons that power plants are expected to emit in 2010 if current rules aren't changed.

These researchers concluded that 8 million tons of SO_x is the efficient annual level of abatement, leaving 1.1 million tons of emissions. The efficient abatement of 8 million tons is a bit more than the Jeffords or Bush abatement proposals for between 6 and 7 million tons. For the first million tons, the marginal cost of abatement is less than $1,000/ton, while the marginal benefit of that first million tons of abatement is $3,500/ton; the marginal benefits exceed the costs. The marginal benefits of one more million tons of abatement continue to exceed the marginal costs up to 8 million tons of abatement. After that point, the marginal costs associated with reducing SO_x by one more million tons exceed the marginal benefits; the amount that consumers are willing to pay to reduce the adverse effects of SO_x is smaller than the increased costs that utility owners and ratepayers would bear through higher electricity costs.

How is it possible to achieve this efficient level of pollution? Can private markets achieve this goal?

Rights and the Coase Theorem

Chapter 3 discussed the lack of ownership and transferability as a source of market failure. One way to solve this market failure is by assigning property rights to non-market goods. This approach opens up some useful options for environmental policy.

What does it mean to have a right to something? Property rights bring to mind goods like land and personal possessions, tangible things that we bought or got as gifts, which we could give away or resell once we're through with them. Rights do not apply only to tangible goods, though. When a traffic light is green, a driver has the right to go through an intersection. In some places, people have the right to an environment free of cigarette and cigar smoke. The U.S. Declaration of Independence claims that people are "endowed by their Creator with certain unalienable Rights, that among these are Life, Liberty and the pursuit of Happiness." People can have rights to behaviors and intangible goods as well as to physical possessions.

Can rights to intangible goods or actions be bought and sold like rights to tangible goods? Let's start with an example from economist Ronald Coase. Suppose a rancher lives next to a farmer. Some of the rancher's cattle wander into the farmer's crops and destroy them. This destruction is a negative externality: the damage to the farmer's crops is not reflected in the rancher's cost of production. Because an externality is a market failure, this outcome is not efficient; there will be deadweight loss.

One solution to this externality problem is to regulate the rancher. The government could require the rancher to control her cattle and punish her if she did not do so. The rancher would control her cattle by building a costly fence. Coase, however, suggested solving this externality problem in a different way. His proposed solution was to make a clear assignment of a property right and then to let the rancher and the farmer bargain with each other. One possibility would be that the farmer could own the right to cattle-free crops. The farmer could either keep that right or sell his right to the rancher, in which case the rancher's cattle could wander onto the farmland. As an alternative, the rancher could own the right to let her cattle wander at will. She could then either keep that right or sell it to the farmer in exchange for keeping her cattle off the farmland. In Coase's view, as long as it was clear who owned the right to wandering cattle and it was possible to buy and sell those rights, the market would solve the market failure and come to the efficient solution. There would be no need for government regulation, although government would still have a role in enforcing ownership rights and agreements.

For instance, if the farmer owned the rights, he could charge a fee for wandering cattle, reflecting the damage that they did. The rancher could pay the fee and let her cattle wander, or she could maintain a fence between their lands and keep her cattle off, if fence maintenance were less expensive than paying the fee. If, on the other hand, the rancher owned the rights to let her cattle wander, the farmer could either live with the damage that the cattle caused or pay the rancher to stop her cattle from wandering into his field, which the rancher would do by maintaining a fence. In all these cases, the farmer and the rancher buy and sell the rights to wandering cattle. If it is possible to turn the externality (cattle wandering) into an ordinary good that is bought and sold in a market, then market forces can lead to an efficient outcome. In other words, the process of assigning and trading rights can solve the market failure.

A very important part of this example is that wandering cattle are easily traced to their owner and that crop damage from cattle is easy to observe and quantify. These characteristics of the cattle problem make it inexpensive to enforce the property rights to cattle-free crops: that is, this market has low *transaction costs*. A **transaction cost** is the cost of buying or selling a good, in addition to the price of the good. For example, someone who buys a house pays not only the price of the house but also the real estate agent's fee, financing costs, moving expenses, and so on. In the case of the wandering cattle, low transaction costs make it possible to solve the wandering cattle problem with markets. Coase suggested that rights assignment is a good way to solve externality problems, providing that the market for the rights has low transaction costs.

Let's now work these ideas out in the context of the rights to pollution.

RIGHTS TO THE ENVIRONMENTALIST

Suppose that one environmentalist represents all those who benefit from reduced SO_x, and one power plant is emitting all the SO_x. Further suppose that the environmentalist, by law, has unambiguous and saleable rights to a pristine environment. In that case, he can insist that the emitter reduce pollution to zero.

If emissions go to zero (abatement of 9.1 million tons), marginal costs of abating the last 1.1 million tons exceed the marginal benefits associated with that level of cleanup. Because it would be possible to increase the net benefits by allowing 1.1 million tons of emissions, the result is inefficient, and there is the possibility of both parties becoming better off through a Pareto-improving exchange. How might this happen?

To understand the Pareto-improving exchange, look at Figure 11.2, which is identical to Figure 11.1 except for some shading. That dark shading represents the deadweight loss associated with abating all 9.1 million tons instead of 8 million tons. The environmentalist gains $3.85 billion by the additional 1.1 million tons of abatement, but the emitter bears costs of $6.955 billion for those 1.1 million tons. The emitter, being a sensible businesswoman, asks the environmentalist to make a deal: she will pay him at least $3.85 billion (but no more than $6.955 billion) if she can avoid having to clean up those 1.1 million tons. Though the environmentalist is giving up $3.85 billion in air pollution benefits if he takes the deal, he can use the money from the emitter for any number of other purposes, including other environmental projects. As long as the emitter offers the environmentalist more in compensation than the environmentalist would get in benefits from the air pollution reduction, and as long as the compensation is less than the emitter would pay to clean up the pollution, both of them are better off from the deal.

The key to this deal is that the benefits to the environmentalist from the last units of abatement are small relative to the costs to achieve them. The environment has a capacity for absorbing and dealing with low amounts of pollution. The environmentalist can allow the emission of 1.1 million tons of SO_x, use some of the compensation

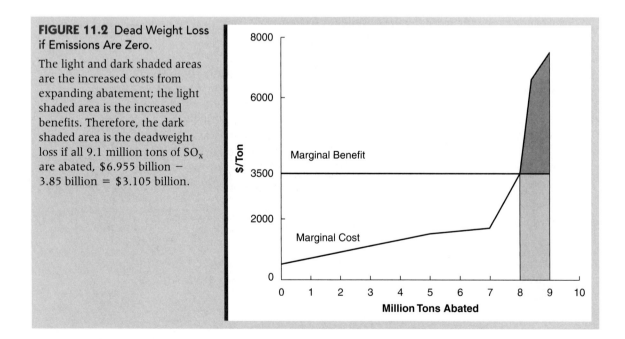

FIGURE 11.2 Dead Weight Loss if Emissions Are Zero.

The light and dark shaded areas are the increased costs from expanding abatement; the light shaded area is the increased benefits. Therefore, the dark shaded area is the deadweight loss if all 9.1 million tons of SO_x are abated, $6.955 billion − 3.85 billion = $3.105 billion.

to mitigate the effect of the 1.1 million tons, and use the rest of the money for other environmental purposes. Some could be spent, for instance, to aid in the recovery of lakes harmed by acid deposits, while the rest could be spent protecting habitat for endangered species. Meanwhile, the emitter is happy to pay any amount up to the abatement costs to avoid installing more pollution control equipment.

Would the deal end up producing the efficient level of 8 million tons? There are gains from allowing a little more pollution as long as the cost of one more unit of abatement exceeds the benefit of one more unit of abatement—in other words, as long as marginal cost (MC) exceeds marginal benefit (MB). At 8 million tons of abatement, MB = MC. For lower levels of abatement (higher levels of pollution), MB > MC. For the units of abatement less than 8 million tons (the units of pollution greater than 1.1 million tons), the cost of abating the pollution is less than the amount that the environmentalist would require in compensation, so the emitter would prefer cleaning up the pollution to paying the required compensation. In other words, the two will agree on pollution of 1.1 million tons but no more. This is the efficient equilibrium quantity because no further Pareto-improving trades can be made.

BOX 11.1

Rights to the Environmentalist: The Endangered Species Act

If a species is listed as endangered under the U.S. Endangered Species Act (ESA), strict rules apply to property that provides habitat for that species. In this case, the right is assigned to those who want species protection. A private landowner is not permitted to harm a member of the endangered species or its habitat. In some cases, landowners are not allowed to build on or otherwise develop their property. This has resulted in litigation and bitter political conflicts between landowners and public agencies.

These conflicts can be partly resolved through Habitat Conservation Plans (HCPs). An HCP is a bargain between the landowner and the public to protect a portion of private land as habitat for endangered species while allowing development on other parts. For instance, the owner of a four-acre lot that provides habitat for an endangered snake may agree to preserve half and build on the other half. The trading can involve another private landowner as well. If the owner of the four-acre lot wants to develop the entire lot, she can find someone who owns two acres of similar habitat and pay the second landowner to preserve the entire two acres. As Coase explained, if the value of building on the entire four-acre parcel is greater than the price the second landowner will charge to preserve the two-acre parcel, the deal will be made.

Under an HCP, a landowner receives an "incidental take permit" from the U.S. Fish and Wildlife Service, which allows a property owner to cause harm to an endangered animal's habitat. By allowing landowners alternative means to achieve their obligations to protect endangered species, HCPs reduce the cost of attaining the ESA's legal goals.

(Continued)

BOX 11.1

(continued)

To ensure that habitat conservation is permanent, these arrangements often use a permanent conservation easement. An easement, in this context, is a limitation on a landowner's right to use her property as she chooses. More commonly, an easement is a right to enter and cross over someone else's land. A permanent conservation easement is a permanent restriction on how land can be used; the land must be preserved as habitat for the endangered species.

HCPs have been put in place on a much larger scale. In San Diego County in Southern California, years of negotiations among developers, environmentalists, and public officials resulted in the San Diego Multiple-Species Conservation Program. This plan protects pieces of land that are mostly contiguous. This approach reflects a shift in Endangered Species Act enforcement, from protecting individual species on fragmented pieces of land to preserving biodiversity in a habitat large enough to be ecologically viable.

In San Diego, some owners gave up a portion of their land in exchange for being allowed to build in other areas. In other cases, public agencies paid for the land to be protected. It may seem surprising that the public, as the owner of the right to protect endangered species, ended up paying anything. However, a negotiated compromise such as this is often more widely accepted, and less costly, than a legal battle between government and landowners.

Like most compromises, the San Diego HCP left some environmentalists and some property owners dissatisfied. Nevertheless, the nonprofit Nature Conservancy has used the HCP as an opportunity to continue preservation efforts in San Diego County by acquiring rights to additional private land that connects to and buffers protected public land. As a result of these combined strategies, 2.7 million acres (4,261 square miles) is protected in San Diego County. For developers in that growing region, the plan clarifies their rights and obligations and streamlines the process of getting permission to build.

RIGHTS TO THE EMITTER

What happens if, instead, the law gives the emitter the right to emit and, in addition, allows her to sell that right? She can now pollute as much as she likes, which is 9.1 million tons of SO_x. Because abatement is costly, she will not bother to undertake any abatement. The environmentalist will suffer. As Figure 11.3 shows, the deadweight loss of not undertaking any abatement is the dark shaded area, $17.2 billion.

Is there any way now to achieve the efficient outcome? In the case where the environmentalist had the rights, the emitter offered to pay for some damages in exchange for not having to abate. Now, though, when the emitter has the rights, she has no reason to instigate a deal. The environmentalist, on the other hand, has reason to do so.

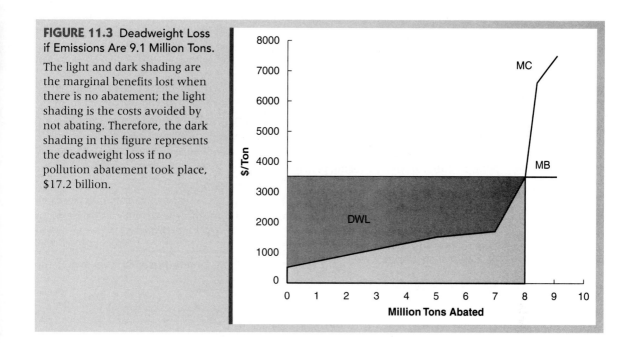

FIGURE 11.3 Deadweight Loss if Emissions Are 9.1 Million Tons.

The light and dark shading are the marginal benefits lost when there is no abatement; the light shading is the costs avoided by not abating. Therefore, the dark shading in this figure represents the deadweight loss if no pollution abatement took place, $17.2 billion.

The damage to the environmentalist is high, especially for the first tons of SO_x. Indeed, the environmentalist is willing to pay up to $3,500/ton for any abatement, while it costs the emitter only $500/ton to clean up the first million tons of abatement. The environmentalist would gain by paying for any abatement that the emitter is willing to undertake for $3,500/ton or less. In this case, the amount that the environmentalist is willing to pay for each additional unit of abatement exceeds the cost of abatement for up to 8 million tons of abatement; beyond that level, the marginal cost of abatement exceeds the marginal willingness to pay of the environmentalist. The emitter, for her part, will accept this deal because the amount paid to her exceeds the cost of abatement until the cost of abatement reaches $3,500 a ton, which happens at abatement of 8 million tons. This is exactly the same amount of abatement that would occur if the environmentalist had the rights.

THE COASE THEOREM

Two key points have been drawn from Coase's analysis. First, if it is clear who owns the rights, and if transaction costs are low, then market mechanisms or bargaining can solve many externality problems. Second, the efficient market outcome is often the same whether the rights are assigned to the person causing the externality or the person experiencing the damage; this is the case in both the wandering cattle example and the SO_x example. This pair of ideas is called the **Coase Theorem**. A bargain that follows this pattern is often called a **Coasian bargain**.

BOX 11.2

Rights to the Emitter: Permits to Emit SO$_x$

The U.S. Clean Air Act Amendments of 1990 provided that each electricity-generating plant over a certain size would receive an initial allocation of SO$_x$ emissions allowances. For each allowance, a plant could either emit one ton of SO$_x$ or sell the right to emit that ton to another plant. The initial allocations were given out free—in other words, rights were assigned to the emitters. Owners of new plants were required to buy permits, either from an existing permit holder or at a reserve auction conducted by the U.S. Environmental Protection Agency. The total amount of SO$_x$ that could be emitted was limited to about 50 percent of 1980 levels. It is also possible for individuals or organizations to buy SO$_x$ allowances and retire them, in order to increase abatement even further. As the Joint Economic Committee of the U.S. House of Representatives stated in a 1997 review of tradable SO$_x$ permits, "pollution problems are caused by a lack of clearly defined and enforced property rights" and "[e]stablishing ownership rights is the first step in taking advantage of market efficiencies."

The Coase Theorem is an application of the basic processes of supply and demand to nonmarket goods. In our example, demand for abatement of SO$_x$ comes from the environmentalist, and the emitter has an ability to supply abatement. As long as it is clear who owns and who buys abatement, a market equilibrium can result. What makes the Coase Theorem important is that it presents a private-market solution to some environmental problems. If the fundamental problem for many environmental goods is a lack of ownership or transferability, then provision of ownership and transferability should solve the market failure, and private markets will operate efficiently without government intervention, other than assigning rights and enforcing bargains.

IN SUMMARY

- Rights can be defined for goods, tangible or intangible, other than private property.
- If market failures arise due to lack of well-defined rights, assigning someone the rights to the goods and then allowing trading leads to the efficient quantity of a good. This works for environmental goods and other goods, as long as there are low transaction costs.
- The Coase Theorem says that when transaction costs are low, assigning rights and allowing trading will lead to two consequences. First, there will be an efficient outcome. Second, the efficient outcome will be the same regardless of who initially is assigned the right.

The Limits to Market Solutions

If private markets could be instituted for all environmental goods, there would be many fewer market failures and environmental problems could be handled efficiently. In fact, though, there are many environmental problems, and private markets do not appear to have worked to solve them. Why not?

There are at least four types of barriers to obtaining an efficient outcome through assigning and trading rights. The first is high transaction costs. Second, it may be difficult to define the right, divide the right into saleable units, and exclude people who don't participate in the transaction from enjoying the right. Third, one party may be able to manipulate the price of the rights being traded. Finally, there may be difficulties in enforcing the property rights and agreements to trade them.

TRANSACTION COSTS

The Coase essay itself discusses a major drawback to market solutions: the problem of transaction costs. Suppose, for instance, that the emitter has the right to pollute and that there are thousands of environmentalists. To negotiate a deal, the environmentalists need to coordinate among themselves to identify total willingness to pay and how much each individual will pay. Getting everyone to agree on a payment level and plan is likely to be very difficult. The emitter will probably not be willing to meet with each environmentalist singly. As a result, the difficulties involved in negotiating for cleaner air may lead to no deal, and abatement will continue to be zero, which is not efficient.

If, on the other hand, the thousands of environmentalists have the right to clean air, similar difficulties will arise in arranging a deal. Now the emitter has to meet with all the environmentalists and try to arrange deals with each of them. The costs of conducting the transaction may be higher than the costs of installing the abatement equipment. Once again, no deal is made. In this case, abatement will be complete, but abatement of all 9.1 million tons is not an efficient solution either.

When transaction costs are high enough, trading cannot take place. In this situation, it is impossible to use markets to get the efficient outcome. Instead, the initial allocation of rights is the same as the final outcome, and who gets the initial rights matters tremendously because it will determine both efficiency and distributional effects. If the emitter has the right to emit, for instance, then there will be 9.1 million tons of SO_x emitted, the air will be very dirty, the emitter will profit greatly, and deadweight loss will be \$17.2 billion. If, on the other hand, environmentalists have the right to clean air, then there will be no SO_x emitted, the air will be pristine, the emitter will face much higher costs, and deadweight loss will be \$3.11 billion. In this case, deadweight loss is lower if the rights are assigned to the environmentalist. In other situations, deadweight loss may be lower if the rights are assigned to the polluter. If transaction costs limit trading, then the initial allocation of the rights to the environmental good determines the outcome. In that case, it becomes very important to get that allocation correct.

One way to achieve the efficient outcome is for the emitter to be given the right to emit 1.1 million tons of SO_x, but no more. In that case, she will abate 8 million tons. This approach, though, requires a fairly sophisticated process of assigning rights: the agency that assigns rights must be able to do the analysis to determine the marginal benefits and costs associated with different levels of SO_x abatement. Because the rights assigner is likely to be some governmental body, the role of government in the presence of transaction costs becomes much larger than its role when those costs are zero. Government regulation, of course, is also expensive; many environmental economists are employed by government agencies to determine the efficient level of abatement. (The fact that neither the Bush nor the Jeffords SO_x proposal reached the efficient level reflects the give and take of political compromise.) In contrast, if transaction costs are low, all the rights assigner needs to do is say who has the rights and then let trading happen. Thus, transaction costs are one of the most significant barriers to using a system of assigning and trading rights to solve environmental problems.

BOX 11.3

Allemansrätt

Sveriges Grundlag: "Alla ska ha tillgång till naturen enligt allemansrätten."
(Sweden's Constitution: "All shall have access to nature according to all man's rights.")

In the United States, other people have no right to enter private land. Landowners can and do fence their property and post signs promising prosecution of those who trespass on their land to hunt or fish or just walk. Landowners can largely decide whether to admit the public and, if they admit them, what activities to allow. There are notable exceptions. For instance, California law assures access to the coast. Landowners seeking to develop coastal property must make available rights of way that allow visitors onto the beach. In general, however, private land in the United States is closed to use by others.

In Sweden and some other parts of Europe, the situation is entirely different. The right to roam about the countryside; to pick flowers, mushrooms, and berries; to camp for a night; to ski; to ride horses; to walk dogs; to swim; to boat; and so on has existed since medieval times. Owning property does not give the right to exclude visitors. The right to walk on other people's property is not unfettered. A visitor is not allowed to cut live trees, or walk through people's gardens, or ride horses through their crops. Still, in Sweden, it is perfectly normal to walk through another's land to a beach and picnic and swim where one chooses.

There is no way in the Swedish system for a landowner to buy the right to keep people off his land. In the United States, it's possible to buy and sell the right to pass over private property (an easement), but this is a complicated and expensive proposition. As a result, in both Sweden and the United States, the distribution of the right to pass over land is the same as the initial allocation of rights. The difference is that the initial allocation is to the public in Sweden and to the private landowner in the United States. The two situations have in common that it is difficult or impossible to make a trade. Where there is no assignment of private rights to start with (as in Sweden) or there are high transaction costs (as in the United States), the initial distribution of rights makes a tremendous difference.

DEFINING AND DIVIDING RIGHTS

There is a reason that rights do not exist for many environmental goods: such rights are difficult, if not impossible, to define. For instance, how should rights to clean air be defined? We cannot divide the air up into individual portions for everyone in the world to buy and sell as each sees fit. In the absence of the ability to divide it up, we all must share the same air resources. If the emitter pollutes her own air, she is polluting everyone else's air at the same time. If one environmentalist pays the emitter to reduce some pollution, all people benefit, even if they contribute nothing to help. Because clean air is a public good, there is no way to exclude people who are not parties to the transaction; they are free riders. When air is a public good, there isn't an obvious way to define each person's right to the good.

In some cases, such as SO_x allowances or damages from wolf attacks on livestock near Yellowstone, people have been able to define the environmental goods in ways that can be marketed. Even if rights can be defined, though, political and legal battles may still occur over the allocation of those rights. Because the rights are valuable, everybody wants to get them. If government allocates the rights, as in the case of SO_x permits, then interested parties will spend large amounts of time and money to get the rights; those investments in lobbying could serve other social purposes. In other cases, such as rights not to be harmed by wolf attacks on livestock near Yellowstone, the interested parties have to agree who has the rights before trading can take place. As Chapter 3 presented, Defenders of Wildlife ceded to ranchers the rights to have their livestock not be attacked by wolves. Instead, Defenders of Wildlife might have argued that wolves had the right to be in Yellowstone, and ranchers would have to accept the damages or undertake their own costly efforts to reduce the damages. If it had, legal battles may have delayed wolf introduction for a number of years. The difficulty of defining rights creates potentially large transaction costs, which pose an obstacle to the success of the Coase Theorem.

MARKET POWER

Suppose that the environmentalist owns the rights to clean air, but he is willing to let the emitter pay him to accept some pollution. The efficient price for him to charge would be $3,500/ton of SO_x. At that price, the emitter will buy the right to pollute 1.1 million tons. The environmentalist is willing to live with that much pollution, and he will receive a payment of $3,500/ton * 1.1 million tons = $3.85 billion. As the absolute owner of the rights over emissions, though, the environmentalist is not a price taker. A person who is not a price taker is said to have **market power**. He can set the price higher than $3,500, as Figure 11.4 shows. Suppose that he sets the price of pollution at $6,600/ton. The emitter is willing, at that price, to buy 0.7 million tons, for a total payment of $4.62 billion. The environmentalist faces less pollution and gets more money because of his ability to manipulate the market. While the environmentalist may like this outcome, the emitter is forced to reduce her activities more than is efficient, there are gains from trade that go unrealized, and net benefits are lower than if the price were $3,500/ton.

When there are very few agents in a market, one or more may try to manipulate the price, and efficiency will not happen. On the other hand, when there are many agents (either environmentalists or emitters) in the market, transaction costs may be high, and Pareto-improving market exchanges may not occur.

IMPERFECT INFORMATION AND IMPERFECT ENFORCEMENT

The legal system enforces rights and bargains. If, for instance, the emitter is legally responsible for compensating the environmentalist for damages but does not do so, the environmentalist may take legal action against the emitter to enforce his claim. Indeed, knowing that she might have to pay for environmental damages gives the emitter a strong incentive to reduce her emissions.

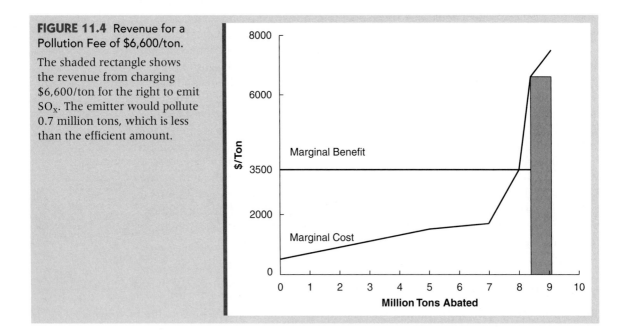

FIGURE 11.4 Revenue for a Pollution Fee of $6,600/ton.

The shaded rectangle shows the revenue from charging $6,600/ton for the right to emit SO_x. The emitter would pollute 0.7 million tons, which is less than the efficient amount.

Suppose that the environmentalist owns the rights to a clean environment, but the two sides never make a deal. The environmentalist might bring a lawsuit. If the lawsuit is successful, the court may award monetary damages equal to the benefits that the environmentalist lost from the emitter's failure to abate all 9.1 million tons. The damages will be measured as the benefits the environmentalist didn't receive because the abatement didn't happen. The award will be for damages for 9.1 million tons of pollution, not 8 million tons, because the environmentalist was entitled to complete abatement.

Rather than let this happen, the emitter will reduce her pollution by 8 million tons. Because the marginal benefits of abatement—the potential damages in a lawsuit—exceed the marginal costs of abatement up to 8 million tons abated, it is cheaper to pay the marginal costs of abatement for the first 8 million tons than to pay for the damages those tons cause. At the same time, it is cheaper to pay damages caused by the last 1.1 million tons than to clean them up.

For the legal system to work effectively, though, it must know not only who has the rights but also who violates the rights and by how much. For instance, if there were a hundred potential air polluters and only some of them polluted, it would be easy to tell that the air was polluted but hard to tell who did it. Sometimes those who breathe the pollution are not aware that they are damaging their health. Without the information that they are harmed, there will be no legal action. If it is difficult to identify the rights violations, the legal system may not be able to enforce the rights, and an efficient market outcome won't happen.

A major problem can arise, then, if enforcement is imperfect because information is incomplete. The emitter may claim that her emissions do not cause harm; any adverse effects to the environmentalist may be due to other causes. The environmentalist may claim that his damages are much higher than they actually are. One side may have a more effective lawyer presenting the information than the other side. The judge or jury may not understand all the arguments. A court, in sorting through conflicting assertions, may not find the underlying truth in the situation. The environmentalist may have the right to clean air, but, unless he can prove that the SO_x caused him damage, he may not have a means to get abatement and compensation from the emitter.

Imperfect information is not the only reason for imperfect enforcement. Another problem with the use of courts to enforce rights is that lawsuits can be expensive. The transaction costs involved in enforcing a right may be great enough that, regardless of the legality of the claim, the person with the right may not pursue his claim. For example, a person who wants to bring a lawsuit often must come up with tens of thousands of dollars in out-of-pocket expenses, even if a lawyer is willing to work without pay until successful resolution of the claim. If the claimant has only suffered a few thousand dollars in damage, it is not worthwhile to pursue the claim. This problem is sometimes solved when claimants band together in a class-action lawsuit, when a nonprofit organization pays the expenses, or when a government agency pursues the claim as a matter of public policy. Unless one of these solutions is available, an environmental right might not be enforced because of the transaction cost of enforcing it.

BOX 11.4

Liability for Pesticides

The pesticide DBCP kills fungus and nematodes, but it also causes low sperm counts in mammals, including humans. Farmers fumigated their fields with DBCP in the United States until 1979. The DBCP leached into the groundwater in aquifers (underground water deposits), which in some places serve as drinking water supplies. Water districts, which provide drinking water to consumers, then sought redress in the legal system; they sued the manufacturers of DBCP for the costs of making their water system safe again. From a legal perspective, the rights to clean water belonged to the consumers.

The lawsuits turned out to be difficult to prosecute. Who put the DBCP in the water? Many farmers had land over the aquifers in question. Many manufacturers made DBCP. Which ones affected a specific well, imposed on the consumers' rights to clean water, and therefore owed compensation for damages? If a DBCP producer knew how each farmer was likely to use its product, it could teach farmers the behavior that would lead them to apply DBCP safely. If each farmer knew how his application of DBCP would affect drinking water supplies, he would have an incentive to apply DBCP carefully and avoid well contamination. If, on the other hand, the farmers and the DBCP producers knew that it would be very hard to figure out each individual's contributions to the contamination of a particular well (indeed, they may not have known their contributions to contamination of particular wells), their incentive to abate was only as strong as the legal responsibility they were likely to face for the damages.

In California, the law allowed all manufacturers to be sued on the grounds that they all had a probability of causing the damage, even though it is possible that some guiltless manufacturers had to pay for the bad behavior of others. In this case, it is likely that all manufacturers who sell in the California market will take great precautions; indeed, they may not sell at all in the California market. On the other hand, if there had to be strong proof that a particular farmer or manufacturer polluted the water, many guilty parties might escape punishment because of the inability to prove that they caused the damage. In this situation, manufacturers are much less likely to exercise precaution. In other words, laws, by determining who has responsibility and rights in these cases, combined with imperfect information, will affect how much precaution polluters may take.

Yet another example of imperfect enforcement due to imperfect information occurs when the environmentalist will only know of the damages after they have occurred. If the emitter knows in advance of the damages that she will cause, she still has reason to abate. After all, if she does not abate, she will have to pay full compensation for the damages once they are discovered. As long as abatement is less expensive than paying compensation, she will abate.

If, however, there is a time lag between the time the emitter causes the harm and the time she faces paying the cost of the harm, she has a third option in some legal settings: she can emit, cause the damages, and, when required to pay compensation, she may declare bankruptcy and go out of business. Under bankruptcy law, she may not have to pay any compensation. For the time between her emissions and the damages, she gets the advantage of not having to pay for abatement. The cost savings from not paying for abatement and compensation, plus the gains from whatever new business she might enter, may be higher than the gains from keeping the current business going. In that case, the damage is done, and, despite the clear rights, efficiency does not result.

The damages from pollution can happen years after the initial emissions, due to circumstances such as long time lags in development of diseases such as cancer, slow accumulation of the adverse effects, or gradual failure of storage containers for toxic wastes. The lag between the time when abatement could be done and the time when the consequences happen may be long enough that even a responsible business may be long gone. Even more importantly, because this time lag may mean that an emitter will not have to be responsible for damages, the emitter has less incentive, if any, to abate and avoid causing the problems.

If the emitter has the right to pollute, those who face the damages still have an incentive to pay for abatement because they are likely to want to avoid future damages. They may not be willing to pay, though, if they do not know that there will be future damages or if they believe that they may move away or otherwise not have to face the damages themselves.

IN SUMMARY

- The efficiency of markets relies on a number of assumptions: low transaction costs, the ability to buy and sell units of the goods, price-taking buyers and sellers, perfect information, and effective enforcement of legal rights. These assumptions do not hold for many environmental goods.
- The presence of transaction costs in particular can lead to failure of markets for environmental goods. Because the initial allocation of rights may determine the final equilibrium, the efficiency of the policy will depend on who gets the initial allocation.
- Rights do not exist for many environmental goods because it is too difficult to define rights for public goods. Markets will fail as a remedy for pollution in this case because of the difficulty in assigning rights.
- If one participant in the negotiation has significantly more power than the other, then that agent may be able to manipulate the market to her benefit. While the existence of many market participants may lead to high transaction costs, the presence of few market participants may lead to inefficiency due to market manipulation.
- The ability to enforce rights is necessary for markets to work. However, enforcement of rights may fail in the face of imperfect information.

The Effect of Initial Assignment of Rights on Equilibrium Quantity

The second part of the Coase Theorem is that the initial assignment of rights will not have any effect on the amount of the externality that will result after trading. The same efficient output of SO_x results whether the consumer gets the right to clean air or the producer gets the rights to emit SO_x. The theorem is implicitly assuming that the income from the assignment of rights does not shift the marginal cost or marginal benefit curve in Figure 11.1. The assumption that changes in income are not important to the analysis at hand is a frequent assumption in economics. Analysis that makes this assumption is called **partial equilibrium** analysis.

Let's examine the consequences of not making the partial equilibrium assumption and of following the income stream. Suppose that the rights are shifted from the polluter to the environmentalist. Giving rights to the environmentalist increases his income. When consumers have more income, they demand a greater quantity of normal goods at any price; the demand curve—the marginal benefit curve in Figure 11.5—shifts up. When it shifts up, the intersection of marginal benefits and marginal cost of abatement moves upwards and to the right. Therefore, the efficient amount of abatement becomes larger. So the allocation of rights changes income, which changes the efficient level of abatement. If transaction costs were low enough, the actual level of abatement in the market would be this new efficient level of abatement.

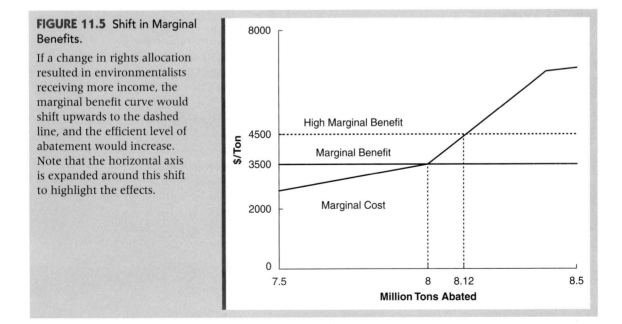

FIGURE 11.5 Shift in Marginal Benefits.

If a change in rights allocation resulted in environmentalists receiving more income, the marginal benefit curve would shift upwards to the dashed line, and the efficient level of abatement would increase. Note that the horizontal axis is expanded around this shift to highlight the effects.

Let's see what happens to the polluters. They lost the rights to pollute and are forced to pay money to pollute. When they pay the money, they make less profit. When they make less profit, they send less money to the firms' owners. The firms' owners are also people, and they may like cleaner air too. When they have less money, their demand for clean air shifts downward. If the upward shift in the marginal benefits curve from giving the rights to the environmentalists is bigger than the downward shift in the marginal benefits curve from the loss of income to the firms' owners, then the demand curve will still shift up, as in Figure 11.5. In one special case, the demand curve does not shift at all: when the firms' owners and the environmentalists are the same people. They have no change in income, and the rights allocation has no effect on the efficient outcome.

It is possible that a different equilibrium will result if the environmentalist has to pay for clean air rather than get paid to accept dirty air. Nevertheless, even if the equilibrium quantity of abatement is different because of the effect of income, the outcome will be efficient. For markets to result in Pareto improvements, it is necessary for rights to be assigned and exchangeable. How those rights are assigned can have great effects on the distribution of wealth in society, but any initial distribution can lead to an efficient outcome if transaction costs are low enough.

IN SUMMARY

- The quantity of abatement may be different depending on who receives the initial allocation of rights. This is because the initial allocation changes income, which changes the equilibrium.
- In practice, the extra income created by the assignment of rights is not likely to cause a great difference in the equilibrium quantity. Even if the equilibrium quantity is different, it will be efficient.

The Coase Theorem in Perspective

Two years after the Environmental Protection Agency accused the plant's owner, American Electric Power, of violating the Clean Air Act in this southeast Ohio hamlet, the company, which is contesting that accusation, is solving at least some of its problems by buying the town for $20 million.

Over the next few months, all 221 residents of Cheshire will pack up and leave. The 90 homeowners here will get checks for about three times the value of houses they probably could not have sold anyway. In return, they have signed pledges never to sue the power company for property damage or health problems.

The deal, announced April 16 [2002], is believed to be the first by a company to dissolve an entire town. It will help the company avoid the considerable expense and public-relations mess of individual lawsuits, legal and environmental experts said. (*New York Times*, May 13, 2002)

Can private markets solve environmental problems? In a variety of settings, environmentalists are paying money to achieve environmental goals, and private firms are participating in market trades of environmental goods. As well as buying land rights in San Diego, The Nature Conservancy has bought land rights in the tropical rainforests mentioned in the introduction to this chapter. Other examples include American Electric Power's purchase of Cheshire, Ohio; the trading of SO_x permits in the United States and fishery permits in New Zealand; donations to the Bailey Wildlife Compensation Trust to pay ranchers for stock losses caused by wolves; and the trading of carbon permits in Europe and the Northeastern United States, which show up in the next chapter. These efforts are sometimes considered evidence of the effectiveness of free market environmentalism, a view that environmental problems are better solved through definition of property rights, markets, and courts than through government action.

A major advantage of the Coase approach is that the only government machinery it requires is a legal system to enforce rights; it does not require regulatory agencies. It is costly and difficult to use the regulatory process to figure out the efficient quantity of an environmental good. Many people have a philosophical preference for less government regulation, and the experience of highly regulated economies, such as the former Soviet Union, suggests that private transactions often do a better job than government regulations in determining the efficient quantity of goods.

Are these private markets likely to achieve the efficient solution? For a variety of reasons, including high transaction costs, imperfect information, and market power, defining rights and allowing trades will not always lead to efficiency. In the Cheshire example, questions about the deal arose from people who lived outside town; others in town felt they could have gotten a better deal if they had negotiated further. The high transaction costs involved in coordinating the desires of many people, and the free riding problem associated with public goods, suggest that private markets will under-provide the public good. The Coase Theorem, then, can contribute to addressing environmental problems, but the circumstances where it is likely to achieve the efficient outcome are limited.

CHAPTER SUMMARY

Here are the key lessons from this chapter:

- Rights do not apply only to tangible goods; they can also apply to behaviors. If rights can be assigned to behaviors that affect the environment, so that market transactions can then occur, efficient outcomes can result.
- The Coase Theorem argues that efficient outcomes can result from assigning rights to goods or behaviors and then allowing trades, regardless of who gets the initial rights.
- The Coase Theorem will not solve externality problems in a number of settings, including the presence of high transaction costs, difficulties in defining and allocating rights, imperfect information, and the ability of rights violators to escape the consequences of their violations. If high transaction costs stops market exchanges, the result is an inefficient allocation, and the degree of inefficiency depends on the initial allocation of rights.

- The initial assignment of rights may affect the final outcome even in the absence of transaction costs because owning or selling rights increases wealth, while purchasing rights is costly. While the initial assignment can have a great effect on the distribution of wealth, it does not affect the efficiency of the solutions, as long as transaction costs are low.
- Sometimes the Coase Theorem has been used to achieve environmental gains. The fact that environmental goods are typically public goods, though, makes the Coase Theorem less useful because transactions costs are likely to be high and free riders may choose not to pay for the environmental good. As a result, other methods are necessary to deal with these market failures.

KEY TERMS

Coase Theorem *(p. 257)*

Coasian bargain *(p. 257)*

market power *(p. 262)*

partial equilibrium *(p. 266)*

transaction cost *(p. 253)*

NOTES

The efficient level of SO_x is discussed in H. Spencer Banzhaf, Dallas Burtraw, and Karen Palmer, "Efficient Emission Fees in the U.S. Electricity Sector," *Resource and Energy Economics* 26 (2004): 317–341.

Ronald Coase's article is "The Problem of Social Cost," *Journal of Law and Economics* 3 (October 1960): 1–44. In his paper, Coase presented several examples, including the farmer and rancher example in this chapter. Coase did not gather his examples up into a "theorem." George Stigler seems to be the first to call it the Coase Theorem in his textbook *The Theory of Price,* 3rd ed. (New York: MacMillan, 1966). A discussion of "free market environmentalism" by the Property and Environment Research Center was found at http://www.perc.org/about.php?id=700, accessed June 13, 2006.

Information about conservation easements and Habitat Conservation Plans, including the one in San Diego County, can be found in B. Drummond Ayres, Jr., "San Diego Council Approves 'Model' Nature Habitat Plan," *New York Times* (March 20, 1997); John H. Cushman, Jr., "The Endangered Species Act Gets a Makeover," *New York Times* (June 2, 1998); The Nature Conservancy's website, www.nature.org, specifically http://www.nature.org/wherewework/northamerica/states/california/preserves/art9761.html; and the U.S. Fish and Wildlife Service publication *Habitat Conservation Plans: Working Together for Endangered Species*, http://www.fws.gov/endangered/pubs/HCPBrochure/HCPsWorkingTogether5-2005web%20.pdf.

Information about SO_x permits can be found at http://www.epa.gov/air/caa/peg/acidrain.html. The 1997 congressional report on tradable permits is Hayden G. Bryan, Senior Economist, Joint Economic Committee of the U.S. House of Representatives (Jim Saxton, Chairman), *Joint Economic Committee Study: Tradable*

Emissions (July 1997). Note 4 of the report refers to Coase and "The Problem of Social Cost." The report can be found at http://www.house.gov/jec/cost-gov/regs/cost/emission.htm.

The story about American Electric Power buying the town of Cheshire is by Katharine Q. Seelye, "Utility Buys Town It Choked, Lock Stock and Blue Plume," *New York Times* (May 13, 2002), http://query.nytimes.com/gst/fullpage.html?res=9E00E7DF1439F930A25756C0A9649C8B63&sec=&spon=&pagewanted=1.

EXERCISES

1. A builder proposes a skyscraper that would block sunlight to the neighboring houses. The building would have net benefits to the builder of $100,000. The neighbors, who use some solar heating, would face reduced property values and increased heating costs totaling $80,000.
   (a) The law clearly stipulates that the neighbors have the right to solar access. Is a Pareto-improving exchange possible? What do you expect the outcome to be?
   (b) How, if at all, would the outcome be different if the builder had the right to construct the skyscraper, even if it blocked solar access?
   (c) Suppose again that the neighbors have the rights. Because there is a large number of neighbors, hiring an attorney to negotiate with all of them will be expensive, perhaps as much as $25,000. Is a Pareto-improving exchange possible? What do you expect the outcome to be?
   (d) Now suppose that the builder has the rights, and the costs of the lawyer (still $25,000) belong to the neighbors. Is a Pareto-improving exchange possible? What do you expect the outcome to be? Compare this scenario with those of the other parts of this problem. What has led to these different outcomes?

2. Profits associated with polluting for Friedman Inc. are $\pi = 40Q - 2Q^2$, where Q = pollution emitted (in tons), and profits are measured in dollars. Marginal benefits (MB) of polluting, derived from this function, are MB = $40 - 4Q$.
   (a) How much pollution do you expect Friedman to produce in the absence of pollution regulation?
   (b) The damages (costs) associated with pollution from Friedman are estimated as Damages = $D = 3Q^2$, where damages are measured in dollars. What are the damages (costs) associated with Friedman's unregulated level of pollution? What are the net benefits at this point?
   (c) The marginal damages (costs) associated with that function are MD = $6Q$. What is the efficient level of pollution? What are total benefits and costs at the efficient level of pollution? What is the level of net benefits at this point?
   (d) What are the marginal benefits and costs at the efficient level of pollution?
   (e) Suppose that the damages affect only one person, Samuelson, and Friedman has a clear right to emit as much as it likes. Samuelson and Friedman can negotiate at no cost. With no government regulatory programs, how much do you expect the firm to pollute? Why?

(f) Now suppose the damages affect only Samuelson, who has a clear right to be free of harm from pollution. Samuelson and Friedman can negotiate at no cost. With no government regulatory programs, how much do you expect the firm to pollute? Why?

(g) Suppose the damages affect only Samuelson, who has a clear right to be free of harm from pollution. Now, though, enforcing that right will require Samuelson to spend $500 in legal fees. With no government regulatory programs, how much do you expect Friedman to pollute, and why?

3. Consider how or if the Coase Theorem can be applied to the following scenarios. Specifically, think about the following issues for each of these questions:
   (i) Are property rights well defined?
   (ii) Will trading take place?
   (iii) Are any of the assumptions required for the Coase Theorem likely to be violated in an important way?
   (a) A tomato paste factory has been in a town for decades. During the summer, when tomatoes are ripe, it runs 24 hours a day, producing a lot of noise, a lot of truck traffic, and a distinct odor of tomato paste. A subdivision is proposed for vacant land next to the tomato paste factory. Those who would move into the subdivision may not like the noise, traffic, and odor produced by their neighbor.
   (b) Many urban and suburban people in Michigan are moving to rural areas to "get away from it all." They discover that farmers are not always desirable neighbors: their operations produce odors, they spray pesticides and fertilizers on their land, and they also can be noisy at some times of the year. The Michigan legislature passed a "right to farm" law that prohibits local communities from imposing restrictions on farming activities.
   (c) A number of places have prohibited smoking in public areas, including office buildings, restaurants, and bars.
   (d) Many hazardous waste sites were created decades ago, often before the harm associated with the waste was well known. The Comprehensive Environmental Response, Compensation, and Liability Act (CERCLA), also known as the Superfund law, states that the companies that generated the waste are responsible for the costs of its cleanup.

4. Simon owns land along the shore of Lake Michigan. The following table describes the marginal benefits to tourists of recreating along his property (per person who has access for a day), as well as the marginal costs to Simon of more people getting access to the shore (due to litter, noise, and seeing other people on the shore).

NO. PEOPLE	1	2	3	4	5	6	7	8	9	10
MB, PEOPLE	150	110	80	60	40	25	10	−10	−30	−60
MC, SIMON	10	20	30	40	50	60	70	80	100	125

(a) If Simon could not limit access across his property to the shore or otherwise limit or influence tourists' behavior, how many people would go to the seashore? (Fractions of people cannot exist. Give a whole-number answer.) Explain your answer.

(b) What is the efficient number of people to use Simon's shore? (Fractions of people still cannot exist. Give a whole-number answer.) Explain your answer.

(c) Now, Simon has the right and the ability to prevent people from using his property. In the absence of government programs to control seashore access, is there any way that the efficient solution might be achieved? If so, how? If not, why not?

Government Policies for Environmental Protection

The Upper Missouri River in Montana is designated as a National Wild and Scenic River. History and nature enthusiasts can enjoy the sight of deer, beaver, and eagles while paddling canoes along the route taken by Lewis and Clark during their exploration of the American West. Today, designation as a Wild and Scenic River protects the Upper Missouri from alterations to the waterway such as dams, but it does not protect the river from runoff coming from the cattle ranches and wheat farms that surround it. As a result, that stretch of river is so polluted with nitrates from agricultural runoff that boaters are advised to bring a supply of drinking water.

If environmental problems impose significant costs on society, and if private markets are unlikely to address these problems adequately, what can be done? Environmental problems are one of the classic reasons in economic theory for governments to intervene in markets. Unlike the case where all property rights are well defined and private markets lead to efficient allocations, government interference in markets is necessary to increase social benefits by requiring polluters to consider the effects of their activities. There are, though, many ways that governments can influence pollution generation, and they may lead to different outcomes. This chapter will examine:

- The complex nature of the pollution problem and the many ways that governments can address that problem;
- Some of the tools that a government agency can use to address externalities, including *standards* (also called *command and control regulation*);
- The alternative of *market-based incentives* as pollution-control tools;
- The advantages and disadvantages of these tools in different settings.

From Production to Damage

The purpose of environmental regulation is to limit damages from pollution. Understanding how to control pollution requires a grasp of the processes that create pollution, as well as the processes through which pollution causes damages. To do so, let's return to the problem of nitrate pollution in California's Salinas Valley. Applying fertilizer and water to the field produced lettuce but also caused nitrate runoff that contaminated groundwater. The contamination problem involves a number of decisions for both the farmer and the regulator. Let's explore those now.

Figure 12.1 shows all the steps that begin with production of goods and end with environmental damages. This example looks at damages from nitrates. Let's start at the top with the production process. Inputs to production produce goods. In this case, water and fertilizer produce lettuce but also result in nitrate runoff. Other agricultural producers, such as cattle ranchers, also create nitrate runoff. Emissions are the pollutants that are by-products of production.

A firm can emit less by reducing the amount of effluent created in the first place, or by cleaning up effluent at the source, before it gets into the environment. Let's look first at methods for reducing effluent. Two options appear in Figure 12.1: change inputs or change the production process. Either option can change the quantity of production. For example, if lettuce producers change the mix of inputs to use less water, the result is both a smaller quantity of lettuce and reduced nitrate runoff. Similarly, cattle feedlots can reduce nitrate by changing the mix of cattle feed.

Moving down Figure 12.1, we see that if emissions can't be completely prevented, they can be cleaned up. Farmers can use drainage pipes (underground pipes with holes to collect runoff), and cattle feedlots can use holding ponds (places to hold waste until it can be processed). These methods collect pollutants at the source, before they enter the environment.

However, not all nitrates are cleaned up. Moving down Figure 12.1 leads to the emissions that run off from irrigation or feedlots. It is usually very difficult to observe and measure the emissions from farming, while it is less difficult to observe and measure emissions from concentrated feeding operations. As we will see later in the chapter, this difference in observability strongly influences the choice of the type of regulation. This effluent gets into groundwater, lakes, and rivers, such as the Upper Missouri. There, the concentration of nitrates can be measured. The concentration of a pollutant in water, air, or soil (that is, in the environment) is called **ambient quality**, often measured in parts per million. At this point on the diagram, the emissions from all agricultural producers have combined. Now it is very difficult to pinpoint their source.

The presence of pollution in the environment, however, does not guarantee that it will cause harm. Further down the diagram, the link between ambient water quality and damages is exposure. Many pollutants pose relatively little danger at very low concentrations. Even at high concentrations, though, nitrates in water do not always cause damage because people can take action to avoid exposure to the pollution. People who canoe on the Upper Missouri carry jugs of water, for instance, to avoid ingesting nitrates.

FIGURE 12.1 From Inputs to Damage.

This figure shows the chain connecting inputs to production processes with environmental damages. Damages can be reduced at several points: by changing the quantity of inputs or the production process and, therefore, changing output; by cleaning up emissions at the source; by reducing exposure to pollutants in the environment; and by fixing the damage caused by the pollutants.

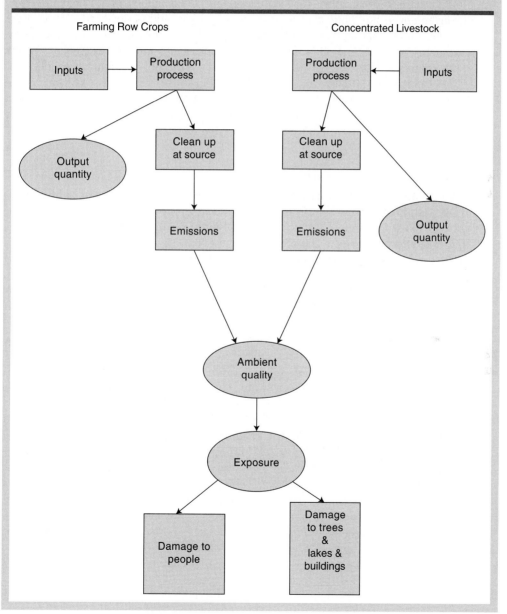

Even if there is exposure to a pollutant, the link between exposure and damages depends on who or what is exposed to the pollution. Some people, especially very young babies, are very sensitive to nitrates in water; nitrates can limit their ability to absorb oxygen. Older people do not suffer this sensitivity. Two people exposed to the same amount of pollution are likely to experience different damages.

Avoiding exposure to water pollution is easier in some cases than others. While it's not that hard to carry a three-day supply of water on a canoe trip, it is expensive and inconvenient to buy bottled water on a regular basis, and plastic bottles create their own environmental problems. Additionally, people are not the only victims of water pollution; the contaminated groundwater may move into surface water bodies, where it can contribute to growth of algae that suck oxygen out of water and thus kill fish.

Environmental policy can intervene at different places in this chain of events. Policy makers, then, have several choices to make as they decide whether and how to adopt pollution prevention policies, clean-up requirements, or efforts to reduce the harm from pollution. Let's now explore that decision-making process.

THE REGULATOR'S PROBLEM

Polluters are not likely to undertake abatement on their own because abatement is costly and produces few benefits for them. Private approaches to pollution problems, such as making polluters financially responsible for any damages that they cause, may take effect both at the end of the chain of events (by making a polluter pay compensation after the damage is done) and at the beginning (by creating an incentive to avoid polluting in the first place). For example, a person who suffered damages from pollution may have the right to file a lawsuit. The possibility of having to pay damages can persuade a firm to reduce pollution. This is an example of assigning the right to be free of pollution to a consumer or the general public; the "rights assigner" is the legal system rather than the regulatory arm of government. However, transactions costs, imperfect information, and other problems limit the usefulness of private rights. Even if a successful lawsuit deters future polluters, the damage that prompted the lawsuit has already been done. Because private rights aren't a complete solution, people often turn to government regulation to address environmental problems.

How should a regulator approach a pollution problem? The goal, of course, is to reduce the damage at the end of the chain of events, whether it's damage to people or ecosystems. Each link in the chain from inputs to damage is a potential place for action. How does a regulator choose where in that chain to require action? Each link is a source of uncertainty: it is not easy to tell how a change to an early link, such as inputs, affects a change to a later link, like damages. This uncertainty suggests that acting further along in the chain, toward damages, may be a better approach because it is more likely that damages will be reduced. On the other hand, the signals back to the polluters are subject to the same uncertainty: how does a farmer know what effect the runoff from his field is having many miles down the river?

Another factor for the regulator is the cost of abatement. Reducing pollution increases costs. Increased costs mean lower net benefits and greater political opposition, so the regulator has considerable incentive to consider costs. There are two issues for the regulator: (1) The tradeoff between higher cost and greater environmental benefit. Net benefits are maximized when the marginal benefits and costs of abatement are equal. (2) Finding the least-cost way to reach the environmental goal. Solving this issue requires each firm to use the right technique and produce the right amount of output as well as getting the right number of firms. Efficient government policy involves setting the right pollution-reduction goals and getting the reductions made in a cost-effective manner.

THE POLLUTION REDUCTION GOAL

A regulatory agency must choose what it wants to accomplish for the environmental quality goal. That choice will affect where abatement efforts should be concentrated. Pollution is not evenly spread out, due to physical geography, climate, and existing development plans. For instance, Figure 12.2 shows how the risk of nitrate contamination of groundwater varies across the United States. If the regulator's goal is to make all places achieve the same groundwater quality, the dark areas need more attention because pollution concerns are higher there. On the other hand, if the regulator's goal is to protect human health, the answer may not be as obvious. If, for instance, the dark areas are rural, with low population density, while the medium dark areas have more people (especially more people who are particularly sensitive to pollution), perhaps net benefits would increase more by reducing nitrate use there.

Regulations of different forms and at different places along the damages chain can significantly influence where damages happen. Reducing emissions, for instance, will affect ambient environmental quality where the emissions end up, which may not be where they are emitted. Bad water quality in the Gulf of Mexico comes from excess fertilizer applications in the upper Midwest that travel down the Mississippi River; damages from acid rain and snow in New England have their origins in emissions from power plants in the Ohio Valley. Regulating emissions near the Gulf of Mexico or

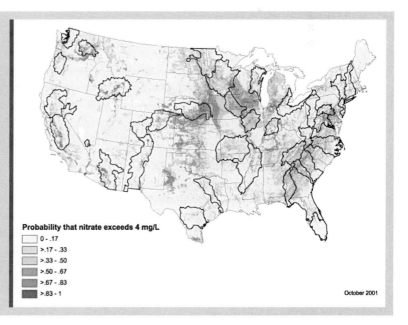

FIGURE 12.2 Spatial Variation in Pollution.

The amount of pollution in an area depends on the amount of emissions and the geologic, geographic, and atmospheric factors. This map shows groundwater nitrate contamination. As this figure demonstrates, the physical distribution of ambient pollution can vary greatly.

This map can be accessed at http://water.usgs.gov/nawqa/nutrients/pubs/est_v36_no10/est_v36_no10.html.

Probability that nitrate exceeds 4 mg/L
- 0 - .17
- >.17 - .33
- >.33 - .50
- >.50 - .67
- >.67 - .83
- >.83 - 1

October 2001

New England will not solve the pollution problems in these regions. Partly for this reason, much U.S. environmental regulation is controlled by the national, rather than state, government. Similarly, the European Union allows the European nations to coordinate their environmental policies. In other cases, international treaties may be necessary. Whether a regulator's objective is to achieve legally mandated ambient water quality levels, to provide the greatest public health benefit, or to achieve another environmental aim, a program to improve environmental quality must consider the location of both the polluting production process and the resulting damage.

COST AND FEASIBILITY OF REGULATION

Even when the source of a pollutant can easily be identified, the same method of abatement can't be used for all sources. Nitrogen oxides (NO_x) come from gasoline-fueled cars, diesel-powered trucks, coal-fired power plants, and many other sources. Even within a category, such as coal-fired power plants, there are significant differences in the effectiveness of different abatement methods. Nitrogen oxides result from nitrogen, a major component of air, burning in a combustion process. NO_x then interacts with hydrocarbons (another pollutant) to produce ozone, an oxygen compound that protects us from solar radiation when it's high in the atmosphere but is a pollutant when it's concentrated in the lower atmosphere. Because sources of NO_x vary widely in their production methods, including the type of fuel used and the heat of the combustion process, they need different technologies to reduce NO_x emissions. As a result, their costs of abatement are very different. Should all sources be required to abate the same amount? If not, what other rule might be used to decide how much different sources should abate?

Let's assume that a regulatory agency has already decided how much total abatement is needed. The agency must then consider the feasibility of any proposed rule for abatement. Feasibility includes two closely related considerations: what is the least costly way to meet an abatement target **(cost effectiveness)** and what is a technically practical way to abate **(technological feasibility)**. We will start with the question of cost.

Meredith Fowlie, Christopher Knittel, and Catherine Wolfram studied the marginal cost of abatement curves for two sources of nitrogen oxides: power plants and cars. Figure 12.3 shows the marginal cost of abatement for these two sources. The width of the figure is the total current abatement, 22.1 million tons. Any point on the horizontal axis represents a division of the total abatement into the amount that cars and power plants must each abate. For instance, if power plants abate 6.7 million tons, cars must abate $22.1 - 6.7 = 15.4$ million tons.

The power plants' marginal cost of abatement curve starts from the left and goes up, as usual, because it is more expensive for the power plant to abate the next ton of NO_x than the previous ton. However, the marginal cost of abatement curve for cars starts on the right and goes up toward the left. That's because cars have to abate whatever power plants do not abate; if power plants are required to abate less, cars will be required to abate more. Because the marginal cost of abatement for cars increases with every additional ton that cars have to abate, the

FIGURE 12.3 The Marginal Costs of Abating Nitrogen Oxides (NO_x).

This graph shows options for reducing NO_x from power plants and cars by a total of 22.1 million tons. The amount that power plants abate is measured from left to right; the amount that cars abate is measured from right to left, so that total abatement sums to 22.1 million tons. At the point where power plants abate 6.7 million tons and cars abate 15.4 million tons, the marginal cost of abatement is $0.43/pound for cars and $0.93/pound for power plants. The marginal costs of abatement for the two sources are the same—$0.45/pound—at the point where power plants abate 2.7 million tons and cars abate 19.4 million tons.

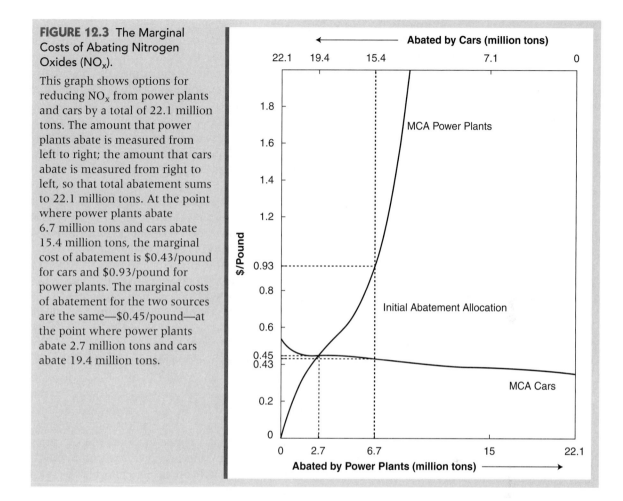

marginal cost of abatement curve for cars moves in the opposite direction of the marginal cost of abatement curve for power plants.

Suppose that 6.7 million tons for power plants and 15.4 million tons for cars is the current division of abatement. The marginal costs of abatement in Figure 12.3 at this point are quite different; for cars, the marginal abatement cost is $0.43 per pound, but it is $0.93 per pound for power plants. Is this efficient? Suppose that cars abated one more ton, while power plants abated one less ton. The marginal cost curves show that it is cheaper at this point for cars to abate one ton than for power plants to abate one ton. Therefore, if cars abate one more ton, and power plants abate one less ton, the same amount of abatement will happen, and the sum of the abatement costs for cars and power plants will be lower. As long as the marginal costs of abatement of the two sources of pollution are different, it is cheaper for one source to abate more than the other.

To continue with Figure 12.3, when power plants' abatement is 2.7 million tons and cars' abatement is 19.4 million tons, the marginal cost of abatement of both firms is equal at $0.45; there is no further way to reduce costs by reallocating pollution between the two sources. This result is called the **equimarginal principle**: the costs of abating a specified amount are at their minimum when all sources of pollution have equal marginal costs of abatement.

Equalizing marginal costs of abatement is necessary for cost effectiveness: that is, it minimizes the costs of achieving an abatement goal among pollution sources. Arranging to achieve pollution abatement with the lowest possible costs reduces the opposition to the abatement requirement and frees up resources to be put to other uses.

Notice that Figure 12.3 doesn't say anything about the marginal benefits of abatement. It may be that regulators used other information to decide that 22.1 million tons was the efficient level, where the marginal benefit of abatement equaled the marginal cost of abatement. Or it may be that regulators didn't have the information necessary to determine the efficient amount. In order to determine the efficient level of abatement, regulators would need to know the marginal benefit of abatement curve. Often this information is imprecise or changing, as ecologists and public health specialists continue to study the effects of pollutants. The abatement goal may be based instead on public health data, political considerations, or other criteria.

If regulators can't determine the efficient amount of abatement, achieving cost effectiveness may be a next best goal. This approach is used by the U.S. Acid Rain Program, which sets a goal for abatement of sulfur oxides (SO_x) and aims for the lowest cost in achieving it. Because polluters often know which methods of abating are less expensive than others, it is easier to achieve cost effectiveness than efficiency.

Reducing costs is not the only consideration for a regulator. Sometimes technological feasibility limits a regulator's choices. For instance, it is very difficult to measure the nitrate runoff that comes from a farm. It is much easier to observe and therefore regulate input use, such as the amount of fertilizer or irrigation water applied to a field. As an alternative, it is usually possible to measure the ambient water quality in the river, lake, or aquifer where the agricultural runoff ends up; a regulator could set a restriction on ambient water quality. If there is more than one farmer affecting the body of water, though, regulating ambient water quality may not give effective signals to farmers to reduce their emissions because each farmer will blame the others for any water quality problems. The ability to monitor a regulatory policy and to get behavioral changes from polluters varies with the pollution problem. A regulatory design needs to consider these factors.

IN SUMMARY

- Government regulation of pollution is necessary because private markets will not achieve the efficient level of pollution abatement.
- A regulator has many alternatives for how to reduce pollution. In deciding among these, the regulator usually considers environmental impacts, costs of achieving a policy, and technological feasibility of the alternatives.

- Location matters for pollution reduction because geography, climate, and human settlement patterns influence the damages that pollution causes. Regulators need to worry about where pollution reduction happens as well as how much abatement happens.
- Some forms of regulation are more costly than others. Reducing costs of abatement both reduces opposition to regulation and frees up resources that can be put to other social goals.
- For a specified amount of abatement, the sum of the costs of abatement for all sources is at the minimum if the marginal costs of abatement for all sources are the same. If the marginal costs are not equal, it is possible to reduce costs by rearranging how much each source abates.
- Some forms of regulation may be technically easier to achieve than others.

Pollution Standards Under a Command and Control Approach

Now let's examine some of the specific alternatives that a regulator has available. The regulatory agency can choose where to intervene in the sequence of events beginning with production and ending with damage. It also can decide what kinds of requirements to place on polluters. Almost all of the methods described here have been used somewhere at some time. The choices fall into two major categories: *command and control*, and *market-based instruments*.

The most straightforward way to reduce emissions is to require polluters to do things that result in less pollution. Because these are direct commands to firms and the firms are controlled to ensure compliance, they are sometimes called **command and control instruments**; as an alternative, because they specify standard behavior, they are sometimes called **standards**.

Standards can be placed on many points in the damages chain. *Input standards* address inputs; *technology standards* focus on the processes that a producer uses; *emissions* or *effluent standards* (often *technology-based emissions standards*) target the pollution when a source emits it; and *ambient standards* limit the concentration of pollution in the environment.

DIFFERENT FORMS OF STANDARDS

An **input standard** restricts the use of an input to production. In the United States, all agricultural pesticides are subject to safety restrictions, and some are banned completely. Another example is lead, a substance once commonly used in gasoline and paint; now, the use of lead in consumer products is strictly limited in the United States and more strictly limited in the European Union.

A **technology standard** or **process standard** directs producers to use a specific technology or process. A smokestack scrubber in a factory, which filters out particles and other contaminants on their way out of the smokestack, may be required under a technology standard. Some states require new electric power generators to install desulfurization technology. Another example is found in newer "green building codes," which require double-paned glass, reflective tile, and insulation in order to reduce energy consumption.

Emissions standards, also called **effluent standards**, require a source to emit no more than a given amount of effluent or a rate of effluent production. Under the U.S. Clean Air Act, for example, new sources of pollution must restrict the quantity of NO_x, SO_x, and other pollutants they emit. These standards are usually specific to an industry; the requirements may vary as well by other criteria, such as size or process. An emission standard doesn't restrict the firm's choice of inputs or process; a firm may use any approach that meets the emissions standard. Often, an emissions standard is a **technology-based emissions standard**, a standard that is set based on the effluent levels that would be emitted if a known technology were used. To set a technology-based effluent standard, a regulator starts by investigating technologies to control effluent. It estimates how much effluent would be emitted if a plant were to use these known technologies. Then the regulator sets that amount of effluent as the standard. The firm could meet the standard using the technology the regulator has investigated, but the firm could also meet the standard any other way. For instance, the U.S. Environmental Protection Agency (EPA) does not require automobiles sold in the United States to be equipped with catalytic converters. Instead, the agency has imposed automobile emissions standards in grams per mile of NO_x and hydrocarbons based on what catalytic converters are capable of doing, and cars typically have them as their way of meeting the standard. Using a technology-based emissions standard helps to ensure technological feasibility.

Ambient standards specify the concentration of pollution that is acceptable in the environment. These standards set requirements for pollution reduction, rather than specifying ways to achieve pollution reduction. The Clean Air Act requires everywhere in the country to achieve the National Ambient Air Quality Standards (see Table 12.1). In contrast, ambient standards for water quality vary; each state decides the level appropriate for its lakes and rivers. Abatement programs that target inputs, processes, or emissions are designed to achieve ambient quality goals.

EVALUATING POLLUTION CONTROL STANDARDS

Some criteria for evaluating any pollution policy are technological feasibility, cost effectiveness, and the incentives they provide for technological improvements. Let's evaluate input, technology, and emissions standards on these criteria.

The feasibility of using these standards depends on the ability to measure and monitor pollution. Emissions are relatively straightforward to observe in *point sources*, such as manufacturing plants. A **point source** emits its effluent from an identifiable point, such as a smokestack or discharge pipe. Because it's usually easy to observe the emissions, it is possible to use emissions standards; it is also usually possible to use process or input standards. For *nonpoint sources*, such as crop farming, on the other hand, the emissions may be hard to see or measure. **Nonpoint source pollution**

TABLE 12.1 National Ambient Air Quality Standards Under the U.S. Clean Air Act.

Primary standards are set to protect human health; secondary standards protect the environment. The level is the ambient standard, expressed either as parts per million (ppm) calculated by mass, or as milligrams per meter cubed (mg/m³), the mass of the pollutant in a m³ of air. The averaging time is how long a period is used to do the computation. A longer averaging time typically makes achieving a standard easier; a higher standard in a short time is intended to set maximum exposure.

	PRIMARY STANDARDS		SECONDARY STANDARDS	
POLLUTANT	LEVEL	AVERAGING TIME	LEVEL	AVERAGING TIME
CARBON MONOXIDE	9 ppm (10 mg/m³)	8-hour	None	
	35 ppm (40 mg/m³)	1-hour		
LEAD	1.5 µg/m³	Quarterly average		Same as Primary
NITROGEN DIOXIDE	0.053 ppm (100 µg/m³)	Annual (arithmetic mean)		Same as Primary
PARTICULATE MATTER (PM$_{10}$)	150 µg/m³	24-hour		Same as Primary
PARTICULATE MATTER (PM$_{2.5}$)	15.0 µg/m³	Annual (arithmetic mean)		Same as Primary
	35 µg/m³	24-hour		Same as Primary
OZONE	0.075 ppm (2008 std)	8-hour		Same as Primary
	0.08 ppm (1997 std)	8-hour		Same as Primary
	0.12 ppm	1-hour (applies only in limited areas)		Same as Primary
SULFUR DIOXIDE	0.03 ppm	Annual (arithmetic mean)	0.5 ppm (1,300 µg/m³)	3-hour
	0.14 ppm	24-hour		

occurs either when it's impossible to see the emissions or when the emissions travel a long way before they settle; in either case, the pollution cannot easily be traced to a specific source. For instance, the pesticides and fertilizers applied to fields migrate underground, where they may travel long distances, even across multiple farmers' fields, until they enter a river, lake, or other water body. Because it is impossible to observe the emissions, reducing nonpoint source pollution typically relies on the use of input and process standards, such as limits on the amount of fertilizer application or the method of pesticide application.

Input standards can be monitored if regulators can oversee use of the inputs; as occasional occurrences of illegal use of some pesticides suggests, monitoring input use is often difficult because regulators do not observe everything that producers do. Technology standards can be easy to monitor: it is easy to see if a company complies with a requirement to install a scrubber or if a city has a sewage treatment plant in place. Less certain is whether the technology will be used as expected: because it is possible to turn off a scrubber or a sewage treatment plant so that it is not in operation, having the technology is not a guarantee that it will be in operation. Some sewage treatment plants get overwhelmed during floods and may discharge raw sewage into lakes or rivers. The existence of the technology does not guarantee its effective use.

Next, let's consider the cost effectiveness of the standards. Setting a standard that requires the use of a known process helps to ensure that the requirement is technologically feasible. However, it does not allow a source to consider any alternatives. For instance, if all coal-fired electricity plants were required to use scrubbers, the sources would not be allowed to switch to the use of low-sulfur coal, which might be less expensive for many of them. Alternatively, requiring use of low-sulfur coal (an input standard) would not allow sources to consider installing a scrubber instead. In contrast, an emissions standard gives sources the flexibility to choose the option they prefer. Because sources will choose whichever method is cheaper, an emissions standard will not cost more than a technology standard or an input standard and may cost substantially less.

While effluent standards are likely to be lower cost than technology or input standards, they are nevertheless likely to be more costly than necessary to achieve a specified pollution reduction, since it is unlikely that the equimarginal principle will hold. Figure 12.4, a blowup of Figure 12.3, shows this problem. If the regulatory

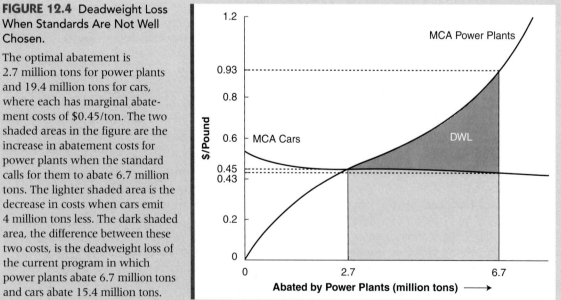

FIGURE 12.4 Deadweight Loss When Standards Are Not Well Chosen.

The optimal abatement is 2.7 million tons for power plants and 19.4 million tons for cars, where each has marginal abatement costs of $0.45/ton. The two shaded areas in the figure are the increase in abatement costs for power plants when the standard calls for them to abate 6.7 million tons. The lighter shaded area is the decrease in costs when cars emit 4 million tons less. The dark shaded area, the difference between these two costs, is the deadweight loss of the current program in which power plants abate 6.7 million tons and cars abate 15.4 million tons.

agency has enough information to choose different standards for each polluter, it can set those standards so that the marginal costs of abatement are the same for all sources. For instance, it could require abatement to be 2.7 million tons from the power plants and 19.4 million tons from cars, where both have marginal abatement costs of $0.45/pound. Alternatively, it could require the current state of affairs, a reduction of 6.7 million tons for power plants and only 15.4 million tons from cars. The deadweight loss for this allocation of abatement is the dark shaded area in Figure 12.4. It is the additional power plant costs, the area under the MCA Power Plants line between the two abatement levels, less the avoided cost for cars, the light shaded area under the MCA Cars curve. In practice, while regulators typically set different standards for different industries, all sources within an industry usually must meet the same standard. As a result, if two sources in the same industry have different abatement costs, then requiring them to meet the same standard leads to higher costs than necessary to meet the abatement requirement. Any requirement—input, technology, or emissions standard—that requires sources with different abatement costs to achieve the same standard is unlikely to minimize the costs of meeting the abatement target.

Another criterion by which standards are judged is the incentives that they provide to seek newer, cheaper, more effective abatement technologies. Emissions standards provide some of this encouragement: if a producer can come up with a new and less costly way to meet its effluent reduction target, the standard allows its use. An input standard may stimulate the search for alternatives to using that input. For instance, when chlorofluorocarbons (CFCs), once used as the propellant in aerosol cans, were banned due to concerns about their effect on the beneficial ozone layer high in the atmosphere, manufacturers soon found other propellants. It is possible, though, that the substitute may have undesirable characteristics. When lead was taken out of gasoline in the United States, one alternative was methyl tert-butyl ether, MTBE, until people found MTBE leaking out of storage tanks and contaminating groundwater. A technology standard, however, does not provide any incentive or ability for innovation, since it effectively locks in a particular abatement technology.

Table 12.2 summarizes the ability of different standards to achieve various criteria. As the table shows, no standard dominates on all criteria. Examples exist for all of them because each standard can be desirable for different circumstances.

IN SUMMARY

- Standards, also known as command and control regulation, mandate a certain level or type of environmental performance. Standards can be applied at different points in the damages chain, and they can take a variety of forms.
- Ambient quality standards regulate the concentration of pollutants in the environment. Effluent standards restrict emissions from each source. Input standards regulate the type and quantity of inputs to production. Technology standards require use of a specific pollution-control technology. Emissions or effluent standards require sources to achieve a level of emission reduction.

TABLE 12.2 Comparison of Command and Control Approaches.

	EMISSIONS STANDARD	INPUT STANDARD	TECHNOLOGY STANDARD
TECHNOLOGICAL FEASIBILITY OF MONITORING?	Usually feasible to monitor point sources, not nonpoint sources	Sometimes but not always easy to monitor	Can monitor equipment installation but not use
LEAST COST FOR SPECIFIED EMISSIONS (EQUIMARGINAL PRINCIPLE)?	No, unless sources are identical or each source has its own standard	No, unless sources are identical in how they use inputs or each source has its own standard	No, unless each source has its own standard or the standard achieves the same marginal abatement cost for all sources
ENCOURAGES INNOVATION?	Yes	Encourages substitutes for the input	No

- The technological feasibility of standards depends on the situation. Effluent standards are usually easy to monitor for point sources but not for nonpoint sources. Input standards are only as easy to monitor as the overall use of inputs. It can be easy to monitor the installation of technology standards, but their use may be more difficult to observe.
- An emissions standard, if feasible, allows more options and thus is likely to be less expensive than either an input or technology standard.
- While, in principle, a regulator can designate different standards for different polluters, in practice regulators use the same standard for a category of polluters (such as a specific industry). If different polluters in one category have different abatement costs, then it is unlikely that the equimarginal principle will apply, and emissions reduction may be more costly than is necessary.
- Emissions standards allow sources to find innovative ways of meeting the requirements. Input standards encourage the use of alternatives that may or may not be environmentally superior. Technology standards disallow the use of new technologies.

BOX 12.1

The Clean Water Act

Air and water pollution are both classic externalities. They have much in common in their origins and possible solutions, but their physical differences create different environmental problems. While air quality has natural variation, a species that can breathe the air in one part of the world can breathe the air in another part. In contrast, natural variation in water quality is great enough to have led to substantial ecological differences: species that live in naturally brackish water may not survive in fresh water. As a result, it is ecologically undesirable to have uniform ambient standards for all water bodies because it would change a number of ecosystems. In addition, a level of pollution that is dangerous for humans to drink may be safe enough for recreational use. States must identify "designated uses" for surface water bodies, such as recreation, aquatic habitat, or water supply. On the Upper Missouri River, for instance, the water is unfit for drinking but is safe for recreational boating. For these reasons, the Clean Water Act allows for differing levels of water quality.

The cornerstone of water pollution control is the National Pollutant Discharge Elimination System (NPDES), which requires every point source to have a permit that sets specific limits on its pollution. In most states, the states develop the permits for sources. The act uses technology-based effluent standards developed for categories of sources, and they are different for existing and new sources.

Point sources are not the only sources of water pollution, though. At this time in the United States, nonpoint sources, such as agricultural runoff and runoff from paved land and people's yards, are the leading cause of water quality problems. These sources are not well regulated because it is difficult to trace the pollution back to its source. Additionally, because sources of nonpoint pollution can be very small (such as each homeowner who fertilizes his yard or each car owner whose engine leaks a fluid), identifying and regulating each one would involve tremendous resources.

Instead of national ambient standards, each state is required to establish water quality standards for each of its bodies of water. The EPA must approve the states' setting of standards and may substitute its own if a state's standards are not acceptable. For waters that do not meet standards, the states must set Total Maximum Daily Load (TMDL), the maximum amount of pollution that may enter the water body. Setting TMDLs then requires developing a plan for the water body to achieve its standard. Developing these plans is a challenge. Because point source pollution is already well regulated through the NPDES permits, it is difficult to further reduce point source effluent. Further reductions might have to come from nonpoint sources, which are more difficult to regulate. Some economists and regulators have proposed trading between point and nonpoint sources of pollution as a way to improve water quality without explicitly regulating nonpoint sources.

The Clean Water Act in 1972 included provisions to fund construction of municipal wastewater treatment plants, urban plants that handle domestic sewage and sometimes industrial effluent. This *subsidy* program did not pay explicitly for effluent reductions and thus did not act in the same way as subsidies described later in this chapter. The program reduced the incentives of cities to find low-cost treatment options, and it did not ensure that adequate funds were available to run the plants. The program was changed into a loan program starting in the 1980s.

While it is unlikely that these programs achieve pollution abatement in the most efficient way possible, they have led to great water quality improvements.

Market-Based Instruments

Because ambient standards can be achieved in different ways, regulators aren't limited to command and control instruments. Instead of imposing a standard, a regulator can instead put a price on pollution to make polluting expensive. There are several ways to put a price on pollution, including a tax on emissions, a *subsidy* for abatement, or tradable pollution permits. These are often called *market-based instruments*, since polluters will respond to a price for pollution as they respond to prices for other goods. **Market-based instruments (MBIs)**, also called **market-based incentives** or **market mechanisms**, use incentives to encourage a change in behavior rather than requiring firms to undertake specific behavior. Some MBIs are a mix of standards and markets: they use markets to achieve efficient allocation of abatement among firms, though the regulator may set the maximum emissions. In a few cases, there is even a market where consumers can "buy" abatement; the U.S. acid rain program, for instance, lets consumers buy emission allowances and retire them. In most cases, though, there is no market for pollution transactions between polluters and the general population. To see how markets for pollution can work, let's first look at how a price for pollution affects polluters' behavior, and then we will discuss the different ways that a price can be put on pollution.

PRICING POLLUTION

Suppose that sources had to pay a price for each unit of pollution that they emitted. Figure 12.5 shows our two sources, cars and power plants, facing three hypothetical prices for their NO_x emissions. The highest price is \$0.60/pound of pollution; the middle price is \$0.45/pound; and the lowest price is \$0.20/pound. Suppose the middle price level, \$0.45/pound of pollution, is in place. The first ton of abatement for power plants has a marginal cost of less than \$0.20/pound. Because the cost of abatement is much lower than the price of \$0.45/pound, the power plants will abate rather than pay the price. The same is true for the second ton of abatement, and so on, until the marginal cost of abatement is \$0.45/pound, equal to the price. At that point, it becomes more expensive to abate than to pay the price. Figure 12.5 shows that power plants will abate a total of 2.7 million tons; they will pay the price on their remaining unabated emissions. Cars, similarly, will abate until their marginal costs of abatement equal \$0.45/pound, at an abatement level of 19.4 million tons. Total abatement is 22.1 million tons.

When faced with a price, each source will set its marginal cost of abatement equal to the price. If each source faces the same price, the price achieves the equimarginal principle: the marginal cost of abatement is the same for each source. This arrangement almost certainly is more cost effective than a standard that achieves the same amount of pollution: the amount that is spent on abatement is lower under the price than under the standard.

Now look at the higher price, at \$0.60/pound. Both sources abate more than at the original price because polluting has become more expensive; indeed, cars will stop driving or otherwise cease polluting entirely, while power plants will abate about 4.6 million tons. In contrast, under the lower price of \$0.20/pound, both sources abate

FIGURE 12.5 Using a Pollution Price to Reduce Pollution.

This figure (a blow-up of Figure 12.3) shows three pollution prices: one at $0.60/pound of pollution, one at $0.45/pound, and the third at $0.20/pound. At the low price, power plants abate 0.9 million tons, and cars none; the middle price leads to 22.1 million tons of abatement (2.7 million tons from power plants and 19.4 million tons from cars); and the high price leads to complete abatement from cars and 4.6 million from power plants.

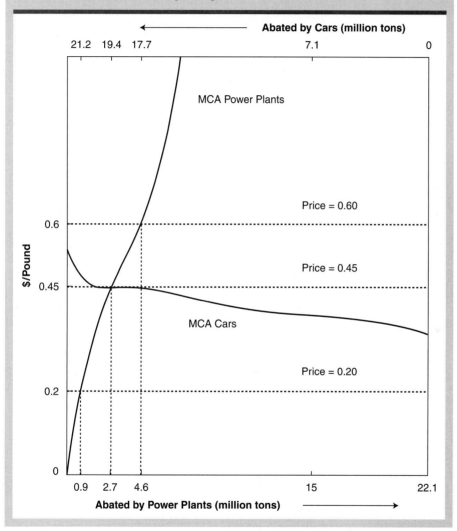

much less; cars will now not bother to abate at all, and power plants will abate only about 0.9 million tons. In other words, it is possible, using a price, to get any level of abatement, from none to 100 percent, by changing the level of the price. Polluters will not just pay the tax and keep polluting, as long as cleaning up is cheaper than polluting.

MARKET-BASED INSTRUMENTS

A **pollution tax**, a requirement to pay a set price for every unit of pollution that a source emits, is the most obvious way to set a price for pollution. Exactly as described previously, sources will prefer to abate as long as the tax exceeds their marginal abatement cost; for abatement that is more expensive than the tax, they will pay the tax.

Figure 12.6 shows the power plants in the original situation of abating 6.7 million tons. In the figure, the most they can abate is 13.4 million tons, which is an estimate of their total emissions. The area under the MCA curve—the dark shaded area—is their cost of abating, $7.2 billion. The tax revenue, the light shaded area, is $13.7 billion. In this case, the tax is much larger than the actual abatement costs.

There are ways to soften the costs to an industry facing a new pollution tax. For instance, the tax authority could return the money to the industry based on its performance before the institution of the tax. In this case, returning the money would have no effect on output or emissions. The tax rebate would arrive independent of the firm's abatement. If, on the other hand, the tax rebate depends on output after the tax

FIGURE 12.6 Taxing Power Plants.

This figure shows the original situation of power plants abating 6.7 million tons. The area under the MCA curve—the dark shaded area—is their cost of abating, $7.2 billion. The tax revenue, the light shaded area, is $13.7 billion.

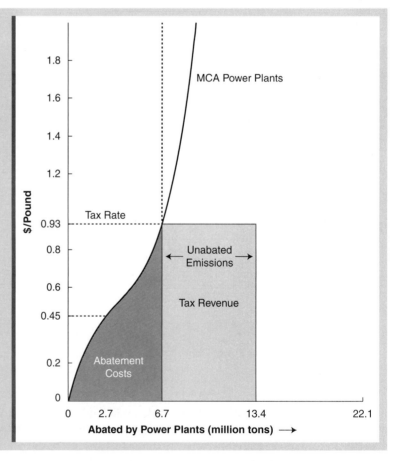

is instituted, the firm has an incentive to produce more output to earn more of the tax rebate. The second method will not produce an efficient quantity of output because it subsidizes output with the proceeds of the pollution tax! Because more output implies more pollution, it undoes part of the pollution-saving effect of the tax, too.

It is also possible to set a price by paying a source to reduce its emissions. A payment as an incentive to change behavior is called a **subsidy**. Suppose, in the Coasian world, that a source has the absolute right to pollute as much as it wants. A regulator could nevertheless offer to pay each source $0.93/pound of abatement that a source might conduct. Here, the opportunity cost of continuing to pollute serves the same function as a pollution tax: a firm has to weigh the cost of abatement against the offer of a subsidy. In Figure 12.7, sources have the option of getting $0.93/pound of abatement or continuing to pollute. This price per pound exceeds the marginal cost of abatement up to 2.7 million tons of abatement for power plants; in fact, power plants would profit from abatement up to 2.7 million tons. With a subsidy, power plants would have two profitable outputs: electricity

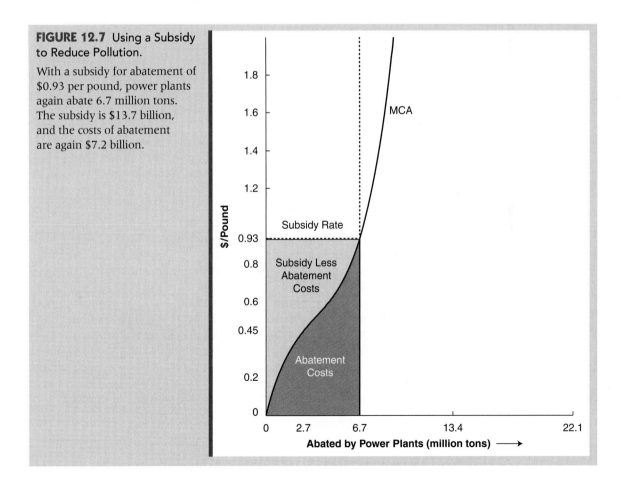

FIGURE 12.7 Using a Subsidy to Reduce Pollution.

With a subsidy for abatement of $0.93 per pound, power plants again abate 6.7 million tons. The subsidy is $13.7 billion, and the costs of abatement are again $7.2 billion.

and abatement. The profits from abatement would encourage more power plants to enter the industry; even if each plant is cleaner, now more plants are polluting.

A third, more subtle, way to achieve a price for pollution is to allow the buying and selling of pollution permits, known as a **marketable permit program**, a **tradable emissions permit program**, or a **cap and trade program**. In a marketable permit program, each permit represents a specified amount of emissions (for instance, one ton of NO_x). The regulator controls the total amount of pollution by capping the number of permits. The regulator then either assigns permits to sources—for instance, by setting standards that allow a specified amount of pollution—or sells permits at an auction. A source has to have a permit for each ton of pollution that it emits. If it wants to pollute more than the number of permits that it has, it must buy additional permits from other sources or at auction. On the other hand, if it pollutes less than the number of permits that it has, it can sell those permits to other sources.

Suppose that power plants and cars need to abate a total of 22.1 million tons of NO_x and that the current division is 6.7 million for power plants and 15.4 million for cars. At this allocation of abatement, abating is much more expensive for power plants than it is for cars. For that reason, power plants would be willing to pay cars to take over some of the abatement responsibility. The power plants would be willing to pay cars at least $0.43/pound (the amount that it would cost cars to abate another unit) but no more than $0.93/pound (the amount that it would cost power plants to abate another unit) if cars, instead of power plants, would abate another unit. The power plants could do this by buying emissions permits from cars. It continues to be worthwhile for power plants to buy permits from cars as long as power plants' marginal costs of abatement exceed those of cars. Buying and selling will stop when their marginal costs are equal at $0.45/pound, with power plants abating 2.7 million tons and cars abating 19.4 million tons. This equimarginal outcome is the same as occurs with a tax or a subsidy of $0.45/pound.

In Southern California, industrial plants that emit SO_x and NO_x are allowed to buy and sell emissions permits among themselves, as long as total emissions are reduced each year, in the Regional Clean Air Incentives Market (RECLAIM) program of the South Coast Area Quality Management District. As the program's website explains, "[b]ecause businesses are different, some can reduce emissions more easily and at less cost than others."

These MBIs—taxes, subsidies, and marketable permits—have in common a price for pollution. Because each source sets its marginal abatement cost equal to that price, these policies all achieve the equimarginal principle: that is, they have the desirable feature of attaining the desired pollution level with the least possible amount of money spent on abatement. For each source, there is only one abatement level where marginal abatement cost equals the price. As a result, a source abates the same amount under all three of these instruments when each instrument uses the same price.

EVALUATING MARKET-BASED INSTRUMENTS

The criteria we used to evaluate standards were technological feasibility, cost effectiveness, and the incentives they provide for technological improvements. For MBIs, cost effectiveness does not differ across sources because all achieve the equimarginal

---

BOX 12.2

Marketable Greenhouse Gas Permits

The Regional Greenhouse Gas Initiative (RGGI) is the first mandatory, market-based effort in the United States to reduce greenhouse gas emissions. Effective in 2008, 10 Northeastern and Mid-Atlantic states placed a cap on total CO_2 emissions from all electric power producers. This cap will be decreased 10 percent by 2018.

All electric power producers in these states are now required to hold a permit, or allowance, in order to emit CO_2. In 2008, the states began selling emission allowances in a series of auctions. In the first auction in September 2008, allowances for 12,565,387 short tons of CO_2 were offered for a minimum bid of $1.86 per short ton; all the allowances were sold for a clearing price of $3.07. RGGI plans to invest proceeds from the sales in carbon reduction strategies intended to benefit consumers; these include energy efficiency and renewable energy.

Producers can trade or sell their allowances within the 10-state region. A producer also can use *offsets* to stay within its allowance. An **offset** is an additional quantity of a pollutant that a firm is allowed to emit if the firm ensures that emissions outside its own operations are reduced by the same amount. RGGI allows an electric producer to plant trees, capture agricultural methane, develop energy-efficient buildings, or reduce emissions of other GHG to meet between 3.3 percent and 10 percent of its obligation.

RGGI is based on criteria of "flexibility," "consumer benefits," "predictable market signals," and "regulatory certainty." Economists are looking at this experiment with great interest to see if RGGI meets these criteria as it pursues its goal of reducing carbon emissions.

---

principle, as long as the instruments apply to abatement (or emissions) and not to inputs or other points of regulation. These sources differ a great deal on an additional dimension, though: who pays for the abatement. Because this dimension affects technological feasibility and incentives for technological improvement, let's start with who pays.

From a Coasian perspective, a pollution tax and a pollution subsidy reflect opposite principles on rights. A subsidy gives the right to pollute to sources; if the government or anyone else wants them to reduce their emissions, it pays them to do so. A tax, on the other hand, asserts that the general public, with the government as its agent, has the right to a pristine environment; any source that pollutes has to pay for the damages it causes. As a result, the two flows of money move in opposite directions. Under the tax, the polluters pay, not only for abatement, but also for any remaining pollution that they emit; as a result, a tax costs sources more money than a standard set at the same level, though it brings revenues to the government. Under the subsidy, in contrast, because the subsidy is higher than abatement cost for all but the last unit of abatement, sources make profits, while the general public, via the government, pays a great deal of money.

The profits from marketable permits go with whoever initially owns the permits. If the government auctions them, the government initially owns them, and they behave like a tax. If the government gives them away for free, then sources still have to pay for any abatement beyond the number of permits that they own; while this arrangement is much less expensive than buying the permits, it is still more expensive than being paid not to pollute. The permits do not have to be given to polluters; they could be given, for instance, to environmental groups. In some proposals to put a cap on greenhouse gas emissions, at least some of the permits might be given to countries in the developing world, as an enticement for them to participate in the cap; they would profit at the expense of the developed world. Many wealthy countries are, unsurprisingly, not enthusiastic about the idea. When permits are given out based on previous standards, they have the political advantages of not requiring major additional expenditures by either polluters or the government, while reducing costs of abatement relative to the standards. Whether new permits are given out to incumbent firms or auctioned, new entrants to the industry and those expanding production must buy permits for their emissions. For them, the permit system has the same incentives as a tax: the firms must pay to pollute.

Taxes, standards, and subsidies lead to different costs of compliance; these costs affect the long-run profitability of polluting sources, which in turn have different effects on the output and pollution of an industry. In the long run, a tax may lead some firms to exit the industry, as average costs shifts upward and those firms become unprofitable. A subsidy, in contrast, may actually lead to entry in the industry, as average costs shift down and firms see an opportunity for profit. Ethanol subsidies, for example, have caused an influx of firms into biofuel production. Because of exit and entry, over the long run a tax will result in less output and less pollution than a subsidy. An emissions standard, like the standard for NO_x emissions from cars, has incentives in between the tax and subsidy. Each new entrant gets limited rights to pollute at no cost. It thus costs less than being taxed on the pollution that does occur and more than being paid not to pollute even more. So an emissions standard has incentives for new entry between a tax and subsidy.

Finally, under some circumstances, a tradable emissions permit system can have the same incentives as a tax system; in general, though, its profitability depends on how the permits are distributed. If permits are auctioned, or if the owners of a business get free permits regardless of whether the firm stays in business, the firms will have the same entry/exit incentives as under a tax. On the other hand, if free permits only go to firms that are in operation, then the firms that get free permits have an added incentive to stay in business. Thus, tradable permit systems may or may not have the same ability as a pollution tax to make polluters bear the full cost of pollution and face the right incentives for entry and exit.

As these MBIs have been described, they all rely on measuring emissions; on that basis, technological feasibility does not differ among them. In practice, though, subsidies are rarely, if ever, used directly for abatement. Instead, subsidies have sometimes been provided for processes or technologies. For instance, in the United States, some agricultural programs pay subsidies to farmers if they plant buffer strips along water bodies to filter pollutants out of farm runoff. Ethanol subsidy programs encourage energy producers to shift their inputs from petroleum to corn, in the hope that carbon emissions will be reduced. These subsidies do not act like the abatement subsidies described previously because they do not focus on reducing emissions and are unlikely to satisfy the equimarginal principle. Nevertheless, like technology standards, subsidies for abatement technology may be easier to monitor than emissions standards, and subsidies make the technologies much more acceptable to the regulated groups.

Under all these scenarios, the market price for emissions provides an incentive for technological innovation. Because polluting is much more costly under a tax than under a subsidy system, and thus is more worth avoiding, taxes may provide a stronger boost than freely given permits, which provide a stronger incentive for innovation than do subsidies. Figure 12.8 shows the MCA curve for power plants in its original form and with a technical innovation that saves $0.20/lb on the costs of abatement.

If the industry were regulated by an emissions standard or an industry cap that required 6.7 million tons of abatement, then the original cost of abatement would be both shaded areas between 0 and 6.7 million tons, or $7.2 billion. With the innovation, the cost would be the lighter of the two shaded areas, $6.5 billion. Therefore, the innovation saves $0.7 billion, the darker of the two areas. If instead the industry were regulated with a tax of $0.93/lb, it would increase its abatement to 7.4 million tons. It would still save the darker of the two areas, $0.7 billion. In addition, it would incur extra costs of abatement, shown in the lightest area, of

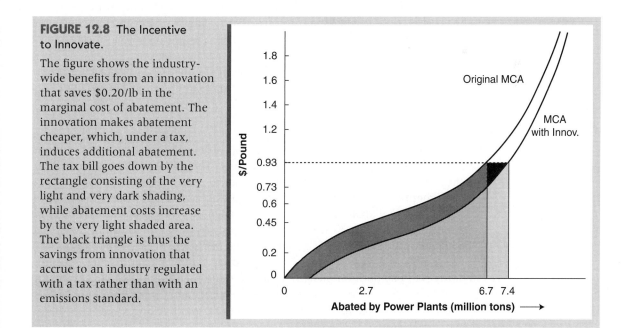

FIGURE 12.8 The Incentive to Innovate.

The figure shows the industry-wide benefits from an innovation that saves $0.20/lb in the marginal cost of abatement. The innovation makes abatement cheaper, which, under a tax, induces additional abatement. The tax bill goes down by the rectangle consisting of the very light and very dark shading, while abatement costs increase by the very light shaded area. The black triangle is thus the savings from innovation that accrue to an industry regulated with a tax rather than with an emissions standard.

TABLE 12.3   Comparison of MBI Approaches.

	POLLUTION TAX	SUBSIDY	MARKETABLE PERMITS
TECHNOLOGICAL FEASIBILITY?	If emissions are observable, yes.	If emissions are observable, yes; if the subsidies are applied to inputs or technologies, then feasibility depends on the ability to monitor those.	If emissions are observable, yes.
LEAST COST FOR SPECIFIED EMISSIONS (EQUIMARGINAL PRINCIPLE)?	Yes.	Yes, if applied to abatement.	Yes.
WHO (IMPLICITLY) HAS RIGHTS TO POLLUTION?	The government.	Pollution sources.	Whoever gets the permits.
EFFECTS ON POLLUTER PROFITS?	Most negative, as sources pay for abatement and for any remaining emissions.	Most positive. If applied to abatement, sources earn more in payments than they pay for abatement.	Dependent on how the permits are initially allocated.
ENCOURAGES INNOVATION?	Yes, perhaps most of these.	Yes, perhaps least of these.	Yes.

$1.3 billion; these would be more than offset by the $1.43 billion in taxes that it would no longer need to pay. The black area, $0.13 billion, is the extra savings that accrue to the innovators in a tax-based system that do not accrue in a standards-based system.

Table 12.3 summarizes the issues in choosing among taxes, subsidies, and marketable permits. Each has its desirable characteristics from various perspectives.

▰▰ IN SUMMARY

- Market-based incentives include the use of a pollution tax, an abatement subsidy, and marketable pollution permits. They all have in common that they result in a price for pollution. Because each source finds the level of abatement where marginal abatement cost equals the price, all sources have equal marginal abatement costs and thus achieve the minimum-cost way of abating pollution. If all three methods lead to the same pollution price, the total amount of abatement under all three MBIs will be the same.
- These policies differ in the ways that money flows. A pollution tax requires sources to pay both for abatement and for any pollution that it still emits. An abatement subsidy pays sources at least as much, and probably more, than it costs for the source to abate. With marketable permits, money flows to those who initially own the permits.
- All three provide strong incentives for technological innovation, but the incentives vary among the policies.

BOX 12.3

The Clean Air Act

"Laws are like sausages. It's better not to see them being made."

—Otto von Bismarck

The Clean Air Act of 1970 created the primary framework for improvements in air quality in the United States. It is a complex combination of flexibility and mandates, standards and markets, giving significant power to both the national and state governments.

The law establishes the National Ambient Air Quality Standards (NAAQS) for six pollutants, shown in Table 12.1. The primary standards are to protect human health; the secondary standards are to protect other aspects of human welfare, including effects on plants, visibility, and structures. Every area in the United States is expected to achieve these standards, though some areas (such as national parks) are expected to exceed them.

Each state decides how it will regulate sources within its boundaries to achieve the NAAQS. The states write State Implementation Plans (SIPs) that detail how sources will reduce their emissions. Because air pollution does not respect political borders, the EPA can step in if pollution from one state affects achievement of the NAAQS in another state.

In addition, any new source must meet federally specified New Source Performance Standards. Making these standards the same across the nation prevents states from trying to lure new industries by reducing standards on them (and possibly increasing standards on existing plants, which can't easily move). These standards are technology-based and are developed for different industrial categories.

Also regulated separately are mobile sources, such as cars, trucks, airplanes, construction equipment, boats, and even lawnmowers. Because these sources easily cross state boundaries, national regulation meant that people could not buy cheaper, more polluting vehicles and take them to places with poor air quality. The notable exception to national standards is California. Because California regulated vehicles before the 1970 Clean Air Act was passed, it continues to be able, with federal permission, to have more stringent vehicle emissions standards than the national level.

Most of these requirements have been written as various forms of standards. As early as the 1970s, though, the EPA allowed small forms of programs that acted like marketable permits. For instance, if a new source wanted to move into an area that had not yet achieved the NAAQS (and thus could not afford new air pollution), it could pay for abatement equipment on an existing source, as long as the abatement was more than the amount the new source would emit. In 1990, an amendment to the Clean Air Act set up a large-scale marketable permit program for sulfur dioxide emissions from power plants. The success of this program has led to proposals for trading in many additional contexts.

Though these multiple layers of laws and rules have been costly for many industries, they have also led to greatly improved air quality and reduced risks to human health and the environment. For instance, in 1995, power plants released 11,896,000 tons of SO_x and 7,855,000 tons of NO_x. In 2006, those figures were 9,524,000 tons of SO_x and 3,799,000 tons of NO_x.

Comparing Command and Control to Market-Based Incentives

Standards require polluters to undertake specified behavior. MBIs, by setting a price for pollution, provide an incentive to change behavior. Both can reduce pollution substantially. Is one form of pollution policy superior to others? Let's compare their effects on cost effectiveness, technological feasibility, and innovation.

Because MBIs allow all sources to equalize their marginal costs, they are at least as cost effective as standards. Indeed, the attractiveness of the use of MBIs is their ability to reduce abatement costs below those associated with standards.

MBIs are typically based on emissions. For that reason, if it is difficult to observe emissions, as in the case of nonpoint source emissions, MBIs may be more difficult to implement than technology or input standards. In recent years, proposals have arisen to allow point sources of water pollution to pay nonpoint sources to reduce their emissions, as a way to achieve greater water quality gains without explicitly regulating nonpoint sources (a politically unpopular move). These programs have not met with great success, partly because of the difficulty of measuring emissions reductions from nonpoint sources.

A standard requires uniform behavior, and thus abatement, from all sources to which the standard applies. In contrast, MBIs allow differences in the amount that sources abate. Because some sources will abate more under MBIs than under standards, and other sources will abate less under MBIs than under standards, the location of the sources can affect achievement of environmental goals. MBIs lead to the possibility of pollution "hot spots," places where emissions stay high because sources pay the pollution tax, or buy emissions permits, or forgo the subsidy, rather than abate. As a result, regulators should be cautious when switching from standards to a market-based scheme because pollution levels will go up in some places (and down in others) under the MBI.

Under an emissions standard and MBIs, sources face incentives to find new, cheaper technologies. Those incentives are likely to be stronger under MBIs, though. Standards provide no incentive to reduce emissions below the standard, while the price for pollution under MBIs gives an incentive both to reduce its abatement costs and to reduce its emissions.

These differences are summarized in Table 12.4. As the table shows, once again, neither of these categories of measures is always superior to the other.

◼◼ IN SUMMARY

- MBIs lead to the lowest possible abatement costs for a specified amount of emissions reductions. Standards are at least as expensive, and probably more expensive, than MBIs.
- MBIs are technologically feasible if emissions can be monitored. When emissions are not easy to monitor, technology or input standards may be more feasible.

TABLE 12.4 Comparison of Standards to Market-Based Incentives.

	STANDARDS	MBIs
LEAST COST FOR SPECIFIED EMISSIONS (EQUIMARGINAL PRINCIPLE)?	No.	Yes.
TECHNOLOGICAL FEASIBILITY?	Varies with kind of source and kind of standard.	Effective when emissions can be measured.
ASSURED REDUCTION FROM ALL SOURCES?	Yes.	No.
WHO HAS THE RIGHTS OVER EMISSIONS?	Source has right up to the standard.	Government has the right with a tax, polluter has the right with a subsidy. With permits, firms have the right up to the level of the permits.
DO SOURCES PAY MORE OR LESS THAN THE COSTS OF POLLUTION REDUCTION?	Sources pay pollution costs.	More with a tax, less with a subsidy, variable with permits.
EFFECTS ON SOURCE PROFITS?	Intermediate.	Most negative for tax, most positive for subsidy. Permits are cheaper than standard.
ENCOURAGES INNOVATION?	Probably less.	Probably more.

- Because MBI allow sources to choose their emissions levels in response to a price, they will achieve a different distribution of emissions among sources than will standards, which require all sources to behave the same. Because some sources will abate less than others, it is possible for pollution "hot spots"—places where pollution emissions are concentrated—to form.
- While standards and MBIs both provide some incentive for innovation, the incentive is likely to be stronger under MBIs.

Comparing the U.S. and European Approaches

Which environmental policies get implemented in practice depend on social, cultural, and political factors beyond economic efficiency and technological feasibility. To see this, let's compare U.S. and European approaches. While these areas have in common that they are affluent, democratic societies, their modes of addressing pollution are quite different.

In the United States, much of pollution policy starts with standards. European countries, on the other hand, have taxed emissions. People in European countries are accustomed to high taxes to support government social programs; taxing emissions is an extension of that pattern. In addition, this reflects the "polluter pays" principle, the idea that polluters are responsible for the damages they cause. The emissions taxes were often low enough that they provided little incentive to reduce emissions; on the other hand, the revenues from the taxes were used for pollution abatement equipment. The approach of charging low emissions taxes and using the revenue to subsidize abatement equipment does not guarantee efficient pollution control because it puts more emphasis on "end-of-pipe" abatement methods than on other approaches, but it has led to reductions. Over time, however, the tax revenues have become substantial: in the European Union, they average 2.5 percent of gross domestic product (GDP), compared with 1 percent in the United States. In Sweden, environmental tax revenues are 3 percent of GDP. The high energy taxes in Sweden have contributed to greenhouse gas emissions reductions beyond those required under the Kyoto Protocol.

The different policies arise from the political and cultural characters of these societies. Understanding these differences requires examining not only economic principles but also the nature of the societies in which they occur.

CHAPTER SUMMARY

Here are the key lessons from this chapter:

- The process that generates environmental damages involves a complex chain. The chain starts with inputs and technology to produce a product as well as emissions. The emissions contribute to ambient concentrations of pollution, to which people, ecosystems, structures, and other materials are exposed. The exposure causes damages to those who are susceptible.
- Environmental regulation happens at different and sometimes multiple places along this chain, depending on the nature of the pollutant and the feasibility of controlling the pollution at that stage.
- Using a regulatory tool that has lower abatement costs relative to alternatives reduces the political opposition to abatement and frees resources that can be put to more productive uses. The equimarginal principle—setting the marginal costs of abatement equal for all sources—minimizes the costs of achieving a specified amount of abatement. This property, while very desirable financially, may nevertheless allow emissions in some places to be higher than in others because sources differ in their total abatement costs.
- Pollution standards specify a behavior across all situations. These can vary from input or technology standards to effluent or ambient standards. For some pollutants, one form of standard may be more technologically or financially feasible than others.
- Market-based instruments (MBI) include a pollution tax, an abatement subsidy, and marketable pollution permits. Each allows sources to choose how

much to abate in response to a price for pollution. These instruments all achieve the equimarginal principle and thus have lower total abatement costs than standards. They are likely to lead to a different geographic arrangement of emissions than standards; that rearrangement leads to the potential for pollution to remain higher in some places than in others.

- A tax is at least as expensive for polluters as marketable permits, if the permits are distributed at no cost, because the tax requires payment for any pollution not abated, while the permits are free emissions. A permit system with free permits is also less expensive than effluent standards because sources have more choices under the permit system than with the standards. The subsidy is least expensive for polluters, though most expensive for whoever pays the subsidy.

- Incentives for improved abatement technologies are probably superior under MBIs, though standards also provide an incentive to seek improvements.

KEY TERMS

ambient quality *(p. 274)*

ambient standards *(p. 282)*

cap and trade program *(p. 292)*

command and control instruments *(p. 281)*

cost effectiveness *(p. 278)*

effluent standards *(p. 282)*

emissions standards *(p. 282)*

equimarginal principle *(p. 280)*

input standard *(p. 281)*

marketable permit program *(p. 292)*

market-based incentives *(p. 288)*

market-based instruments (MBIs) *(p. 288)*

market mechanisms *(p. 288)*

nonpoint source pollution *(p. 282)*

offset *(p. 293)*

point source *(p. 282)*

pollution tax *(p. 290)*

process standard *(p. 281)*

standards *(p. 281)*

subsidy *(p. 291)*

technological feasibility *(p. 278)*

technology-based emissions standard *(p. 282)*

technology standard *(p. 281)*

tradable emissions permit program *(p. 292)*

NOTES

The map of groundwater nitrate pollution was found at http://water.usgs.gov/nawqa/nutrients/pubs/est_v36_no10/est_v36_no10.html, accessed April 21, 2010.

Ambient air quality standards are listed at http://epa.gov/air/criteria.html, accessed December 9, 2008.

The example of marginal costs of abatement for power plants and cars is from Meredith Fowlie, Christopher R. Knittel, and Catherine Wolfram, *Optimal Regulation of Stationary and Non-stationary Pollution Sources*, Working Paper 14504 (Cambridge, MA: National Bureau of Economic Research, November 2008), http://www.nber.org/papers/w14504.

The RECLAIM program is described at http://www.aqmd.gov/reclaim/reclaim.html.

All of the information about the Regional Greenhouse Gas Initiative, and much more, can be found at www.rggi.org.

The quote about law and sausages is attributed to the nineteenth-century German Chancellor Otto von Bismarck at http://www.quotationspage.com/quote/27759.html.

The information about SO_x and NO_x emissions is from the U.S. Energy Information Administration, "Emissions from Energy Consumption at Conventional Power Plants and Combined-Heat-and-Power Plants, 1995 through 2006," *Electric Power Annual*, Table 5.1 October 22, 2007.

The comparison of American and European approaches is from Charles W. Howe, "Taxes versus Tradable Discharge Permits: A Review in the Light of U.S. and European Experience," *Environmental and Resource Economics* 4 (1994): 151–169 and Peter Berck and Runar Brännlund, "Green Regulations in California and Sweden," http://escholarship.org/uc/item/78x4r0z6.

EXERCISES

1. A pollution control agency is considering the following regulatory policies:
    (i) Taxing the use of one input that increases pollution. (Other inputs affect pollution too, both increasing and decreasing it.)
    (ii) Taxing the final goods that firms produce and sell on the market.
    (iii) Taxing pollution.

    For each of the following questions, explain why you have answered with the policy that you have, and explain why you have chosen that policy over the other two.
    (a) Which of these policies is most likely to reduce pollution?
    (b) Which of these policies might actually lead to an increase in pollution?
    (c) Which of these policies is most likely to be financially damaging to firms?
    (d) Which of these policies is most likely to encourage innovative methods of pollution reduction?

2. Q_A and Q_S are the pollution levels for Arrow and Solow Industries, respectively. Profits (benefits) associated with polluting activity, π_i (i = A,S), are $\pi_A = 10Q_A - Q_A^2/2$ and $\pi_S = 20Q_S - Q_S^2$. Marginal benefits (profits) for each firm are $MB_A = 10 - Q_A$, and $MB_S = 20 - 2Q_S$.
    (a) Unregulated, how much will each firm pollute? Why? What will total pollution be? What will each firm's profits be?
    (b) The Department of Environmental Quality (DEQ) would like to reduce pollution by 60 percent—that is, pollution levels will be only 40 percent of the initial level. Initially, it proposes a requirement that each firm roll back its emissions by 60 percent. How much will each firm pollute? What will total pollution be? What will each firm's marginal benefits be? What will each firm's profits be?
    (c) Someone in DEQ studied environmental economics and suggests a marketable permit system to achieve the 60 percent rollback, with each firm given

permits representing the level of its emissions in (b). Who (if either) will want to buy permits, and who will sell? How much will each firm pollute? What will be the equilibrium permit price? What will each firm's profits be?

(d) Next, someone in DEQ suggests a pollution tax. What level of tax will achieve the desired level of pollution? How much will each firm pollute? What will each firm's profits be?

(e) A third DEQ employee suggests subsidizing the pollution reduction from the initial levels identified in (a). What level of subsidy will achieve the desired level of pollution? How much will each firm pollute? What will each firm's profits be?

(f) Rank the four regulatory approaches (rollback, permits, tax, subsidy) from the firms' perspectives. Why do they have these rankings? Do they have the same rankings? Why or why not?

(g) Suppose that the DEQ wants to balance (i) its need to regulate pollution, (ii) effects of its regulation on polluters, and (iii) its desire to keep its budget under control. Which regulatory approach do you expect it to select? Why?

(h) There is a theory of agency behavior that suggests that one incentive of a public agency, or a division of a firm, is the desire to maximize its budget. Suppose that the DEQ, while wanting to achieve the specified pollution level, wants to maximize its budget. Which regulatory approach do you now expect it to select? Why?

(i) Arrow is located in a remote rural area with very low pollution levels (marginal damage = 6), while Solow is located in an urban area with other pollution sources and many more people exposed (marginal damage = 12). What is the efficient pollution allocation in this case?

(j) Are the incentive approaches (permit, tax, subsidy) more efficient than the standard under the conditions identified in (i)? Why or why not?

3. Two pollution sources are located in the same town, immediately next to each other. For every quantity of abatement, marginal costs of abatement for the first source are higher than marginal costs of abatement for the second source.

(a) If both the tax and standard achieve the same level of total emissions, is a uniform pollution tax more efficient than a uniform pollution standard (that is, a tax or a standard that is the same for both sources), less efficient than a uniform standard, or are you unable to tell? Why?

(b) Would the sources prefer to face a pollution subsidy or a marketable permit scheme, if permits are distributed at no cost based on the standard in (a), and both the subsidy and the permit scheme achieve the same level of total emissions? Why?

4. In the figure on the next page, MB1 is the marginal benefit that town 1 gets from abatement; MB2 is the marginal benefit for town 2. MC,A is the marginal cost of abatement for source A, and MC,B is the marginal cost of abatement to source B. Use this figure to answer the following questions.

(a) If source A is located in town 1, what is the efficient level of abatement for town 1? Why?

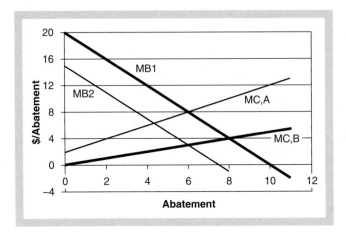

(b) If source A is located in town 1, what level of pollution tax will achieve the efficient level of abatement for town 1? Why will that level of tax achieve the efficient level?

(c) If source A is in town 1, and if source B is in town 2, is a uniform pollution tax or a uniform pollution standard (that is, a tax or a standard that is the same in both places) more efficient? Why?

Enforcement and Political Economy

Coal-fired power plants that were grandfathered in continue to produce sulfur oxides (SO_x) long after policy makers expected those plants to be retired. Government proposals to reduce SO_x don't even try to reach the efficient level of 9.1 million tons of abatement. Pollution policy in theory can be very different from pollution policy in reality. While the pollution sources in the previous chapters responded completely to the regulations that they faced, in reality they may not always comply. While the regulators in previous chapters sought to maximize net benefits to society, in reality they face political forces that often result in an inefficient amount of abatement. This chapter will examine:

- How government agencies monitor pollution and enforce environmental regulations;
- How sources decide whether, or how much, to comply with environmental policies, and options for regulators to influence *compliance*;
- Factors beyond the public good that influence regulatory behavior.

Enforcing Pollution Reductions from Diesel Trucks

On October 23, 1998, U.S. manufacturers of diesel truck engines agreed to pay $1.1 billion for environmental improvements and fines. The companies were accused of manufacturing the engines so that, although they would meet federal standards in the laboratory, nitrogen oxides (NO_x) emissions would increase above the standards when trucks were on the road at highway speeds. The extra pollution emitted by the trucks was thought to be annually about as much NO_x as would be emitted by 65 million cars, or 6 percent of total NO_x emissions from factories, automobiles, and power plants combined.

Complying with the federal standard would reduce fuel economy and thus increase costs for truckers. The desire to avoid these increased costs presented the engine manufacturers with an incentive to violate the standard because truckers would prefer to buy engines with lower costs of operation. It is not clear whether the truck manufacturers ultimately did benefit from these engines, however, when the penalty was added into the calculation.

Adopting an environmental regulation is only the first step in reducing pollution. The next step is *compliance*. **Compliance** means ensuring that producers obey the rule.

Compliance in Practice

Let's start with the process of compliance in practice before we look at more general principles. An effective program for ensuring compliance with environmental regulations has at least three parts: monitoring, enforcement action, and penalties.

Monitoring, the act of looking for violations, takes many forms and has varying degrees of effectiveness. Monitoring can be continuous or periodic. For an example of continuous monitoring, think about an electricity plant. The amount of SO_x it is allowed to emit is determined by a marketable permit system. These plants have continuous emissions monitoring devices that measure all the pollution that they generate. If a plant finds that it is emitting more SO_x than allowed by its permits, it is obligated to report its emissions and buy more permits.

Another type of continuous monitoring can be used for water pollution. Sewage treatment plants monitor for toxics, such as lab chemicals that don't belong in the drain, from companies that send their waste to the plants. However, some companies treat their own waste; in that case, the sewage treatment plant doesn't have a chance to test the waste.

Continuous emissions monitoring is very expensive and used only for large facilities. More commonly, monitoring is periodic. This is especially true for small sources. For instance, many dry cleaners use perchloroethylene, a toxic substance that can contribute to air or water pollution. Detecting violations of requirements requires visiting each shop. Another example is pollution from cars. Car emissions are very difficult to measure while cars are in use; instead, states with serious air pollution problems require cars to have smog tests that measure their emissions of pollutants per mile before they can be registered.

Finally, it is almost impossible to directly monitor nonpoint water pollution sources such as agricultural runoff, especially if some of the farms are located uphill and away from the rivers and lakes that they affect. In this case, local water resource agencies have to monitor streams and beaches for pollution.

Without monitoring, violations of environmental standards are almost certain to go undetected. Even with monitoring, though, it can be hard to find violators. For instance, California recently sent one of its licensed smog testers to jail for falsifying test reports; he was charged with six counts of computer fraud. It is unclear how long the tester had successfully avoided detection.

One advantage of monitoring is that a monitored firm can prove that it is compliant. That enables it to advertise itself as environmentally friendly and thus to compete successfully against firms that keep their costs lower by avoiding compliance.

The next step in compliance is to do something about a violation. An enforcement action is government action to make a polluter obey the law. Regulators have a variety of options for enforcement action, ranging from requests for correction to legal action. An informal enforcement action is most likely for a small source, such as a dry cleaner or a car that is found in violation. The regulator issues a notice of violation, and the shop or the car owner has to bring the equipment into compliance; there is often no penalty if the source complies promptly. In other situations, regulators may impose fines or pursue lawsuits. For the diesel engine manufacturers, there was substantial legal disagreement over whether the manufacturers' actions were a violation. The EPA asked a federal court to decide the issue. Before the court ruled, the manufacturers decided that they would be better off settling with the EPA than to have a court make a determination. Taking legal action is neither easy nor free, either for the regulator or for the polluter; suing a major manufacturer can involve many years and many millions of dollars in costs.

The last step, which is not always taken, is to impose a penalty. There are many types of penalties. Regulatory agencies can impose fines. The law often requires polluters to clean up their pollution and restore the environment. The government and private parties can sue the polluter for restitution for the damage done by the pollution. The plaintiff in lawsuits can ask for punitive damages, which are payments beyond the value of the damage caused, meant to deter future pollution. Finally, the government can criminally prosecute both corporations and individuals for their role in polluting. Penalties and jury awards for damages can be enormous. After the tanker Exxon Valdez spilled 11 million gallons of oil in Alaska's Prince William Sound in 1989, the Exxon Corporation eventually paid almost $3.4 billion in fines, cleanup expenses, damages, and other costs, and an additional $507 million in punitive damages. The last significant legal action in the Exxon Valdez spill was the decision of the U.S. Supreme Court on June 25, 2008, to reduce the punitive damages to $507 million; they had been set at $5 billion by a jury and reduced to $2.5 billion by a lower court. These penalties provide a significant deterrence to willful violation of the laws, but they do take significant time and legal resources to pursue; the Supreme Court decision came 19 years after the accident.

IN SUMMARY

- Ensuring compliance with pollution control requirements involves monitoring sources for violations, enforcement actions, and penalties for violations.
- Because monitoring costs may be large, regulators pursue different levels of monitoring actions for different sizes or types of sources.
- Enforcement actions may be as simple as telling a violator to correct violations, or they may involve complex lawsuits lasting many years. In some cases, regulators and polluters negotiate enforcement actions in order to avoid litigation.
- Penalties are typically monetary fines, though sometimes individuals may face criminal charges. The threat of penalties provides the incentive for sources to comply with pollution requirements.

BOX 13.1

Green Cleaners

The Environmental Protection Agency, more accustomed to going after large-scale polluters like smoke-belching factories, is cracking down on neighborhood mom-and-pop dry cleaners, forcing them to switch to greener cleaning agents instead of relying on a powerful stain remover linked to various health risks, including cancer. Last month the EPA announced that many dry cleaners in urban areas must phase out the use of perchloroethylene, a heavy-duty solvent that removes dirt and grease from suits and jackets and sometimes leaves the familiar chemical smell on newly dry-cleaned clothes. *(Boston Globe,* August 26, 2006)

Some dry cleaners didn't wait for EPA regulations. Zoots, a dry cleaning chain, uses a "perc-free" process and advertises itself as a "green" business.

The Economics of Enforcement

If sources pollute because polluting is cheaper than abating, then pollution policies are going to increase costs to sources. Once a pollution policy is enacted, sources will seek ways to avoid those cost increases. These methods may include finding cheaper abatement strategies, restructuring their production processes, and reducing production. In addition, sources may consider reducing costs by not fully complying with the policy, through exceptions or loopholes, or through deliberate violation of the law.

Why do some sources violate pollution policies, and how do regulators seek to achieve compliance? In a world where achieving, monitoring, and enforcing policies are all costly, answering these questions requires a closer look at the behavior of both sources and regulators.

COMPLIANCE BY SOURCES

Sources sometimes exceed their allowable emissions. They may discharge more effluent than allowed by standards, or they may under-report their emissions under a permit system. These violations arise because of accidents, lack of attention and caution, or willful violation. Most of the violations could be avoided if a source were willing to spend enough money on precautionary activities, but the costs of perfect prevention can be very high. A source may discover only in an accident that it had not taken enough precaution, or it might make an explicit decision to avoid some of the costs of compliance, as the EPA claimed about the diesel manufacturers.

Let's consider how a source might decide how much precaution to undertake when it faces a pollution standard. Note that the analysis is no different for a market-based incentive if the source is considering under-reporting its emissions.

Figure 13.1 is an estimate of the marginal benefits of polluting for a representative power plant. For small amounts of emissions, the benefits of one more unit of pollution are positive and large: the plant increases profits by increasing pollution. The gains from more pollution decrease but stay positive until the marginal benefits of polluting curve hits the horizontal axis, at 16,600 tons. At this point, the power plant no longer benefits from emitting; if it pollutes any more, it will hurt itself more than it will benefit.

In this example, the plant faces a standard that limits emissions to 5,000 tons. If it complies completely with the standard, its emissions will need to drop from 16,600 to 5,000 tons. The cost to the power plant for complete compliance is the forgone benefits of those 11,600 tons, approximately $5.9 million, measured as the area under the marginal benefits curve between 5,000 and 16,600 tons. If the plant does not face a penalty for violating the standard, it is unlikely to reduce its emissions because its profits will be $5.9 million higher if it pollutes up to 16,600 tons. Pollution reductions, then, require some form of penalty in the case of noncompliance. The penalty can take many forms—a financial penalty or jail terms for those responsible, for example. The existence of the penalty provides the motivation for sources to reduce their emissions.

If the source is willing to risk these penalties, it still has to decide how much to emit. The most likely criterion for its decision is that it will seek to maximize profits while taking into account the possibility of the penalty. In other words, it seeks to balance the profits it might earn from noncompliance with the costs it will suffer if its noncompliance is discovered.

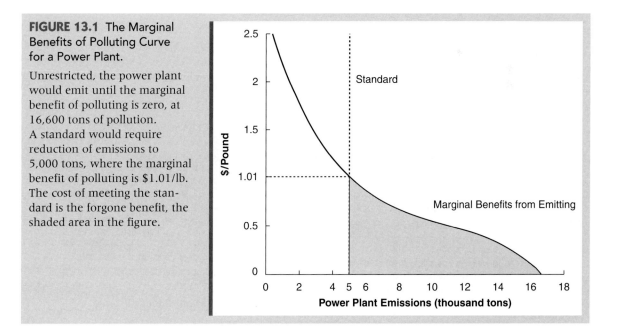

FIGURE 13.1 The Marginal Benefits of Polluting Curve for a Power Plant.

Unrestricted, the power plant would emit until the marginal benefit of polluting is zero, at 16,600 tons of pollution. A standard would require reduction of emissions to 5,000 tons, where the marginal benefit of polluting is $1.01/lb. The cost of meeting the standard is the forgone benefit, the shaded area in the figure.

Figure 13.2 shows the costs the regulator could impose on the source. Those costs are zero if the source is in compliance—that is, if emissions are no greater than the amount allowed by the standard or permit. If emissions are greater than the allowable amount, the penalties, or costs of violation, become positive. In the figure, the penalty that the source expects to face is $1.50 per pound, which would be multiplied by the excess emissions, 16,600 − 5,000 tons, for a total penalty of ($1.50/pound) * (2,000 pounds/ton) * (11,600 tons) = $34.8 million. This is much greater than the $5.9 million benefits of further emissions. Another way to see this result is that the penalty per unit, $1.50/pound, exceeds the marginal benefit of polluting, $1.01/pound, at the level of the standard. Because it is cheaper to abate than to emit and be fined, the firm will abide by its permits and emit 5,000 tons of NO_x pollution.

The penalty line reflects two aspects of the problem—the amount of penalty a source will have to pay if caught and the likelihood that a source will get caught. The usual way of modeling the penalty is the **expected penalty** or **average penalty**, which is the value of the penalty multiplied by the probability that the source will have to pay the penalty. If a source does not believe that it will ever be caught in violation, then the penalty is meaningless. If, on the other hand, the source is sure that a regulator will require the source to pay the penalty if its emissions exceed the standard, then the penalty is a certainty to the source. A 50 percent probability of detection means that, half the time that the source is in violation, it will have to pay the penalty; the other half of the time, it will not have to pay. On average, then, the source pays the penalty half the time, which is equivalent to its paying half the penalty all the time. If the penalty is $1.50 and likely to be detected half

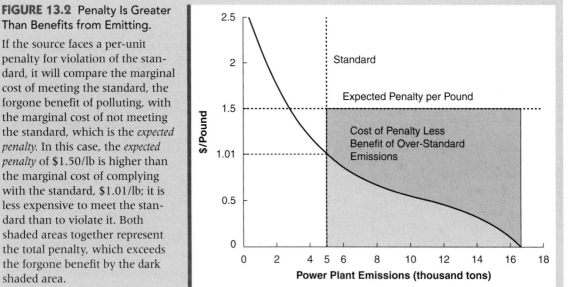

FIGURE 13.2 Penalty Is Greater Than Benefits from Emitting.

If the source faces a per-unit penalty for violation of the standard, it will compare the marginal cost of meeting the standard, the forgone benefit of polluting, with the marginal cost of not meeting the standard, which is the *expected penalty*. In this case, the *expected penalty* of $1.50/lb is higher than the marginal cost of complying with the standard, $1.01/lb; it is less expensive to meet the standard than to violate it. Both shaded areas together represent the total penalty, which exceeds the forgone benefit by the dark shaded area.

the time, the cost of violating the standard is $0.75 for every unit of pollution above the allowed amount. So the expected penalty is the same if it is $0.75 detected 100 percent of the time or $1.50 detected half the time.

Figure 13.3 shows the case where the expected penalty is $0.75/lb. Now the firm emits where its marginal benefits from emitting are equal to the expected penalty, at 7,000 tons. The expected penalty is now ($0.75/pound) * (2,000 pounds/ton) * (7,000 − 5,000 tons) = $3 million, while the benefit of additional polluting—the area under the marginal benefit of polluting curve between 5,000 and 7,000 tons—is about $3.26 million; it is larger by the roughly triangular area between the marginal benefit from emitting line and the expected penalty line. If emissions were lower, increasing emissions would increase profits as long as the marginal benefits from emitting exceeded the expected penalty. If it emitted more, it would expect to pay more in penalties than it costs to abate the pollution. Therefore, 7,000 tons of emissions, 2,000 tons more than the standard, maximizes its profits.

In the diesel case, some of the companies were charged with evading emissions requirements for as long as 10 years. Suppose, for example, they knew that they would face a penalty of $1.1 billion if they were caught and convicted. If there is no doubt that they would be found in violation, the probability of getting caught is 100 percent (or 1.0), and the expected penalty is 1 * $1.1 billion = $1.1 billion, plus the costs to them of the lawsuit. In that case, they might have stayed in compliance. On the other hand, if the probability of having to pay that penalty was only 1 in 100 (1 percent, or 0.01), then the expected penalty is 0.01 * $1.1 billion = $11 million. In other words, a $1.1 billion fine with a 1 percent probability of detection has the

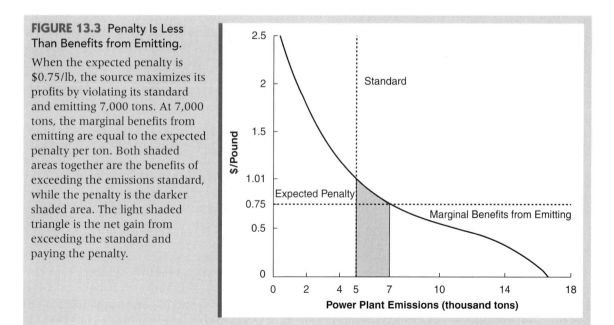

FIGURE 13.3 Penalty Is Less Than Benefits from Emitting.

When the expected penalty is $0.75/lb, the source maximizes its profits by violating its standard and emitting 7,000 tons. At 7,000 tons, the marginal benefits from emitting are equal to the expected penalty per ton. Both shaded areas together are the benefits of exceeding the emissions standard, while the penalty is the darker shaded area. The light shaded triangle is the net gain from exceeding the standard and paying the penalty.

same expected penalty as an $11 million fine with a 100 percent chance of being responsible for payment. If the diesel engine manufacturers believed that the likelihood of being detected and convicted was very low, and if profits from their way of making the engines exceeded their expected penalty, then their manufacturing plan may have appeared to be financially sensible—until the EPA sought penalties against them.

Penalties can be set in different ways. In this example, the source pays the same fine per pound of emissions. In other cases, the expected penalty per unit increases with the size of the violation. An upward slope suggests either a higher chance of getting caught as the violation increases, or a higher penalty as the size of the violation grows, or both. Where emissions are to air or water, a larger effluent stream is more obvious and so more likely to be reported. It is also possible that the penalty could be constant for any violation of the standard: a small violation is treated the same as a large one. For example, polluters might be fined $5,000 regardless whether they spilled 1,000 gallons or 1,000,000 gallons of effluent. Sources faced with penalties that ignore the magnitude of the damages will either comply or ignore the standard completely. In the example of a $5,000-per-incident fine, for instance, a penalty for a 1,000-gallon spill is $5/gallon, a serious deterrent, but the cost for violation for a big spill would be only $0.005/gallon. Even with a 100 percent probability of getting caught, a large polluter with a substantial probability of a large spill may decide to pay the fine rather than undertake any effort to avoid spills; in contrast, small polluters may be very cautious even in the face of low probabilities of being caught. Thus, a penalty that ignores the degree of damages affects small polluters more than large ones and leads to less protection against large spills than against small ones.

If the expected penalty is very high, the source has an incentive to comply with the standard; if the expected penalty is very low, then it is more likely to violate the standard. For these reasons, the amount of resources that an environmental agency can devote to enforcement has a significant effect on the amount of abatement that actually occurs.

THE REGULATOR'S DECISION

In our study of pollution policies in Chapter 12, the regulator imposed a policy, sources complied, and the environment improved. In fact, though, regulatory agencies have a number of roles to play. They have to decide on priorities for the range of programs in their jurisdiction. For instance, they may choose between studying an industry further in order to learn more about abatement costs and regulating the industry despite incomplete information. The agency may also choose whether to put more budget and personnel into monitoring and enforcing some regulations while allocating fewer resources to other regulations. Depending on the laws under which it operates, the agency may have the ability to choose the penalties that a polluter may face. In other words, the regulator may be able to determine the expected penalty that a polluter faces. If the regulator puts more effort into monitoring and enforcement, or if it increases the penalty for a violation, the expected penalty line shifts upward. In response to an increase in the expected penalty, the polluter will reduce its violation; if the expected penalty is high enough, the polluter will comply with the standard.

Many regulators are not blind to the economic consequences of their enforcement actions. For example, spray painting furniture produces considerable reactive organic effluents into the air, and it is not considered essential to the economy of Southern California. As a result, this activity has been regulated to the point where spray painting furniture is no longer done in the Los Angeles air basin. On the other hand, dry cleaning also causes emissions, but for economic reasons dry cleaners have not been so tightly regulated as to cause firms to leave the industry. In China, hundreds of thousands of deaths per year may be due to air pollution, and hundreds of millions lack access to safe drinking water, due to the drive to industrialize the country. Even though China has laws restricting pollution, enforcement is often lax. Polluters seek to avoid cleanup costs, and local officials may be reluctant to enforce actions that would impose costs on their neighbors. At the legislative and political level, there is always consideration of the tradeoff between a cleaner environment and the costs of cleaning up.

BOX 13.2

Who Are Regulators?

In the United States, regulatory agencies are part of the executive branch of government. Congress or state legislatures adopt environmental legislation, but regulatory agencies, under the direction of the president or state governors, do the day-to-day work of regulation and compliance. The U.S. Environmental Protection Agency, the Army Corps of Engineers, and the Fish and Wildlife Service are all important U.S. regulatory agencies.

The first step in regulation is to write detailed rules to implement the general goals that are set out in legislation; that's where environmental lawyers, scientists, and economists work out the details of how the laws will work. After the rules are finalized, the next steps include informing businesses of their obligations, helping with voluntary compliance, and enforcing the rules against those who don't comply. The process of enforcement often includes a hearing in front of an administrative law judge (an attorney who works for the agency, not for a court), subject to review by a court.

Most agency employees are selected through a civil service process based on their education and training. The highest positions in regulatory agencies, such as the agency head, may be political appointments. Political considerations can come into play when agency employees seek promotions to policy-making positions and when an agency decides on budget priorities. Regulators, then, range from career civil servants to political appointees; their roles range from calculating the costs and benefits of regulations to developing broad budget and policy priorities.

In theory, then, it is possible for the regulator to achieve perfect compliance in all cases by some combination of putting enough money into enforcement and setting the per-unit penalty high enough. Indeed, if the regulator sets an extremely high penalty even for small violations—hundreds of billions of dollars, for instance—then it would need to spend almost no effort on enforcement to get perfect compliance. In fact, though, as the diesel case hints, the expected penalty may not always ensure compliance. In this case, the engine manufacturers may have believed either that they were operating legally when they manufactured the engines or that the behavior was worth the expected penalty. Why isn't the expected penalty high enough for complete compliance at all times?

There are several possible answers. The ways that the regulator can affect expected penalties include choosing the size of the penalty, choosing the amount of enforcement (which affects the probability that a source in violation will get caught), and choosing the size of the violation that leads to enforcement action. Each of these may be limited in some way.

First, there may be legal or practical limits on the size of the penalty. If a law limits the size of the penalty that the regulator can recover, then the regulator clearly cannot set the penalty higher. Often of more importance, if a polluter's total assets—the value of everything belonging to the polluter, such as the value of the company—are smaller than the penalty, then the polluter may choose to violate the law and enjoy the benefits until caught, and then go into bankruptcy rather than pay the fine. A regulator or a court may also be unwilling to impose a penalty so high that the violator will go out of business because a polluting facility may employ many people and provide tax revenues to the community in which it is located. Driving such a producer out of business may be very unpopular for those in the community, especially if they are not directly affected by the damages. A large penalty, then, may not always be possible or desirable in practice.

Second, enforcement may be costly enough for the regulator that the probability of a source being caught in violation is small. For instance, many small businesses pollute. Dry cleaners are just one example. The wonderful smells that bakeries emit into the air include hydrocarbons that can contribute to smog and ground-level ozone. Auto painting facilities also may emit hydrocarbons. Visiting every dry cleaner, bakery, and auto painting company to monitor its emissions would be extremely costly for a regulator; as a result, the probability of any one source being caught in a violation of laws may be very small. Indeed, some environmental laws include exemptions for small producers, partly on the basis that any one small source may not pollute very much (although cumulatively their effects may be large), and partly because of the practical matter that monitoring them is infeasible.

Small businesses, at least, are **stationary sources**: they don't move. Enforcement is much harder with vehicles, which are **mobile sources**. Because detecting on-the-road emissions from vehicles is vastly more difficult than observing the results of laboratory tests, it may be surprising that the EPA did detect the differences in emissions, which it did when it conducted additional engine testing in the diesel case.

Third, industry lobbying is a common part of the legislative process. Lobbying means that people with political agendas, including representatives of industry and public interests, argue to lawmakers for legislation to support their agendas. At its best, lobbying means that elected officials get useful information about both the cost of abatement to industry and the benefits of abatement to consumers. At its worst, lobbying means that representatives of better-financed interest groups, or people with better access, persuade lawmakers to change abatement goals, penalties for polluters, and enforcement budgets of regulatory agencies for their own private purposes.

Finally, even if the environmental goal is set in law, if the regulator thinks that the standard is too stringent, one way of easing the standard is for the regulator not to enforce the standard unless there is a violation larger than some other level that it sets. A regulator may want to be more generous to pollution sources for several reasons. Perhaps a legislative body adopted an environmental law with environmental and public health goals in mind, but the regulator brings additional understanding about the difficulties and high cost of abatement. On the other hand, the *captive regulation* hypothesis argues that regulators are often very sympathetic to those they regulate, and they may in fact act to benefit the polluters rather than the public at large. The regulated industry may exert political pressure on the regulator by means of campaign contributions or even outright corruption. **Captive regulation**, or **capture**, occurs when the regulator does the bidding of the regulated industry. With capture, the regulator may choose not to enforce a requirement as rigorously as the public interest might demand. Capture of local officials by industry appears to contribute to China's environmental problems.

All these arguments suggest that the behavior of regulators will not lead to perfect compliance. Other factors, though, argue that a regulator may want to over-regulate or may have ways of regulating beyond the simple expected penalty formula. Let's look at some of those.

Sometimes regulators get to keep the money that they raise in penalties. They may be able to use this money for more enforcement actions, for other programs in the agency, or, as in the diesel case, for cleanup projects. In these cases, the regulator becomes interested in both the level of compliance and the amount of the money raised. Increased monitoring then has two benefits: compliance and cash. This view assumes that the regulator is less interested in the well-being of those it regulates and is more interested either in ensuring that laws are enforced or in keeping its budget large.

Regulators may also have more sophisticated enforcement approaches than occasional monitoring. One tool to increase compliance is to over-monitor sources that have been previously caught. Because those sources probably had a reason for not complying, they may be more likely than other sources to violate requirements again. The regulator can use the evidence of previous noncompliance as a signal of which sources are more likely not to be in compliance in the future, and she can focus her efforts where they are most likely to improve environmental performance. In this case, if the polluters know in advance that being caught in violation will result in closer monitoring, there are two penalties to being caught a

BOX 13.3

Captive Fishery Regulators

Fisheries are regulated by Fisheries Management Councils, made up of representatives from the fishing and processing industries, plus public representatives. As a result, the councils are guaranteed to represent the fishing interests when they make decisions on how to maintain fish stocks. Here is one view of how well it works to let the regulated do the regulating:

> The Commission's investigation has identified no other publicly owned American natural resource managed through a process that allows resource users to decide how much of the public resource can be taken for private benefit. In the majority of fisheries examined by the Commission, this system has created nearly insurmountable obstacles to managing the resource for sustainable catches and for the broad public benefit over the long term. ("America's Living Oceans: Charting a Course for Sea Change." *PEW Charitable Trusts* 2006, p. 45)

In January 2007, President Bush signed the Magnuson-Stevens Reauthorization Act of 2006, which required measures to end overfishing. It required, at section 109-479, that:

> (6) [the Council] develop annual catch limits for each of its managed fisheries that may not exceed the fishing level recommendations of its scientific and statistical committee or the peer review process established under subsection (g).

This is a large change: it is now the scientific and statistical committee that limits the catch. Time will tell if the new version of the act has really shifted the balance of decision-making authority from the industry to an independent technical committee.

first time: they must pay a fine, and they will be monitored more frequently. As a result, the expected penalty to polluting increases without an increase either in monitoring or in the penalty, and sources are more likely to comply than if the regulator did not focus attention on violators.

EQUILIBRIUM IN THE COMPLIANCE MARKET

Polluters decide whether to comply, or how much to violate a requirement, based on the expected penalty that they face. A regulator, expecting that polluters will make this decision based on the expected penalty, may decide how much monitoring to conduct, whom to monitor, whether to seek penalties in case of a violation, and what penalties to impose. Putting all these factors together creates the expected penalty that the polluters face. The polluters then decide how much they will actually pollute, and the regulators decide how much enforcement action to take and against whom. This is the **equilibrium level of pollution**: the amount of pollution that will result from the regulatory and source decisions. If the expected penalty is greater than or equal to the cost of compliance, the equilibrium level of pollution is the amount required under the standard, since sources prefer to comply rather than face the expected penalty. Figure 13.2 is an example of an equilibrium level of pollution equal to the amount of pollution allowed under the standard. This equilibrium is complete compliance. However, if the expected penalty is not high enough to result in complete compliance, the equilibrium level of pollution is where the cost of compliance (or forgone benefit of polluting) equals the cost of violation (the expected penalty). This is the case in Figure 13.3.

In practice, most polluters seek to be in compliance with environmental laws. While the expected penalty provides a strong incentive for compliance, polluters may also be motivated by a desire to be law-abiding or good public citizens. They may also want to avoid the adverse publicity that would come from being found in violation. When these nonmonetary incentives are taken into account, many of the firms depicted in Figure 13.3, which would profit from emitting more than they should under the standard, may choose to comply.

On the other hand, some firms use public relations campaigns to promote a better environmental image than is warranted by their actual compliance. Another strategy is to lobby captive regulators to adopt weak regulations that are not costly to firms; then the firms can truthfully state that they are in full compliance.

Many violations are accidental or unintentional; in those cases, regulatory agencies often prefer to seek compliance without penalties, to encourage good future behavior. Without monitoring and penalties, though, it is likely that violations of environmental laws would be more common and contribute to serious environmental problems.

IN SUMMARY

- When pollution sources decide how much to comply with environmental regulations, they are likely to consider both the penalty that they will face if caught in violation and the likelihood that they will be caught. The expected penalty is the product of the probability of getting caught and the penalty. Higher expected penalties should lead to greater compliance.
- Regulators usually have some choice over both the frequency of monitoring sources and the penalties that they impose if a source is found in violation of a standard. In other words, regulators may be able to choose the expected penalty that sources face. They may not set the expected penalty high enough to ensure complete compliance if they feel the regulation is too stringent, or if they support the industry that they regulate.
- The equilibrium level of pollution is the amount required under the standard if the expected penalty is greater than or equal to the cost of compliance. If the expected penalty is lower than the cost of compliance, the equilibrium level of pollution is where the marginal cost of compliance (or forgone benefit of polluting) equals the marginal cost of violation (the expected per-unit penalty).

Political Economy

Under a benefit-cost approach to public policy issues, it is desirable to undertake all projects as long as the benefits outweigh the costs, and to expand all activities only as long as the marginal benefits outweigh the marginal costs. This approach has the property of ensuring the greatest total net benefits. Is this the rule that policy makers actually use in deciding, for instance, ambient pollution standards, or how much wilderness to set aside, or what agricultural policies to implement?

Because environmental economics generally involves public policy issues, and because government intervention is often required to achieve environmental goals, it is useful to think about how policy goals are set in practice. **Political economy** is the area where political science and economics overlap. It seeks to describe how policy makers actually decide issues. What drives policy makers? Do they seek the greatest net benefits, or do they have other objectives? Let's consider two aspects of the problem: what is likely to happen when a majority vote decides the outcome and what is likely to happen when a political figure decides the outcome.

In some locales, a popular vote may decide whether the community will tax itself to buy a park, or improve its water treatment system, or otherwise enact an environmental improvement. In the simplest political-economic world, the views of the voter in the middle (the median voter) determine the outcome because the median voter casts the deciding vote. Many environmental projects have wide-spread benefits and concentrated costs; that is, many people gain a little from the policy (such as cleaner air from reduced truck emissions), while a small number of people (trucking companies, for instance) bear very high costs. Most people believe that the costs will accrue only to those who have to do the cleaning up, though it is likely that many of the costs will be passed along to consumers over time. If these policies are submitted to a vote, it is likely that the majority of people will believe that they gain more from environmental protection than they will suffer from higher costs for goods whose availability may be reduced (due to, for example, higher trucking costs). In other words, the median voter, who does not represent either the environmentalist or the industrialist extreme, will be the decisive voter. As a result, voters would probably support stringent environmental policies, even if, in some cases, the costs of the project exceed the benefits.

On the other hand, small groups with strong vested interests, such as the truckers, may be more motivated to campaign and to vote than many citizens. Elections may be won or lost based purely on turnout. If the general public is not interested enough to vote, then a small motivated group can win despite being in the minority.

In many other cases, public officials decide on the level of environmental protection. What factors are these political figures likely to consider when deciding on that level of protection? Among the major goals of most public officials is to stay in office by being re-elected or elected to a new position. As a result, it is likely that they will seek policies that will help them continue in their positions. That objective can lead to very different policies from those that seek maximum net benefit.

For instance, for many years and in many places, the U.S. Forest Service, which manages the national forests of the United States, has sold the rights to logging on its land for less than it costs to conduct the sales—costs such as administering the sales and building roads for logging trucks. These "sales below cost" impose financial costs on the Forest Service, and, to the extent that logging in the forests is ecologically damaging, this approach contributes further to ecological disruption. Why would the Forest Service allow logging in areas that lose money for it?

The lesson from political economy is that a small group with an intense interest can often get its will done. The majority of Americans who probably would have preferred less logging to losing money on timber sales were unlikely to pay any attention to each sale that the Forest Service conducted; people in Massachusetts, for instance, would not monitor forest sales in Montana. In contrast, the logging companies near each national forest, and the local communities in which the loggers lived, would pay very close attention and would solicit greater timber sales from the Forest Service.

The small, motivated group will spend a great deal of personal time and energy in persuading public officials to support their goals. In contrast, the large group is likely to be more concerned with other issues; they will not, for instance, put much effort into opposing public officials who support timber sales. As a result, the will of the small, motivated group is more influential than that of the larger group. Again, in such cases, net benefits are unlikely to be a decisive factor in the policy maker's mind.

BOX 13.4

Local Monitoring Can Get Results

Environmental organizations that concentrate on reducing the exposure of poorer citizens to harmful emissions are part of the environmental justice movement. The West County Toxics Coalition in Richmond, California, works for a cleaner environment in a neighborhood wedged between railroads, freeways, a chemical plant, and two large refineries. The coalition's activities have included lobbying local air quality authorities to study emissions, to get a monitor for the highly toxic compound dioxin, and to shut down an incinerator that emitted toxics.

What makes the coalition different from most lobbying groups is its emphasis on monitoring as a first step to enforcement. The West County Toxics Coalition is one of many organizations using bucket brigades. A bucket is a portable air-sampling device that can be built for about $125; the sample is analyzed at a laboratory. Bucket brigades are local citizens who live near emissions sources and who independently monitor the local air. The results of sampling are used to pressure the emitter and the local air authority to clean up the air. Dara O'Rourke and Gregg Macey examined the effectiveness of "bucket brigades." These programs gave communities near toxic facilities a greater sense of empowerment and a means, independent of regulatory agencies and polluting facilities, to monitor their air quality. At the same time, it was unclear at the time of the study whether the monitoring efforts reduced the number of accidental toxic releases.

One of the methods that a small group will use to influence decisions is to contribute money to political figures. Winning elections takes both support from voters and the money to earn that support. According to www.opensecrets.org, "The forestry industry donated $3.3 million to federal candidates and campaigns in 2006, with a generous 80 percent given to Republicans. Weyerhaeuser Co., International Paper and the Hardwood Federation were top industry contributors in 2006." The contributions peaked at $5 million in 2008, the presidential election year. They lobbied on a broad collection of issues including immigration, illegal logging, and biofuels. Industry money does flow to politicians.

A political figure could, for instance, vote for increased logging for biofuels, accept campaign contributions from timber companies, and use those contributions to advertise her position in support of clean air or other issues important to constituents. The net perception of the voters might well be that the politician, though a logging fan, was pro-environment. Even if damages that the voters experienced from the logging exceeded the gains to the logging supporters, the politician's calculation was that she would lose few votes while gaining resources necessary for the campaign. The financial power of money from small, organized groups therefore makes them disproportionately powerful in the political process.

Political scientists argue that the influence of small, motivated groups is only one factor in public officials' decision processes. Their personal ideologies, their views of the public good, the process of trading favorable votes with other decision makers, and the views of their constituents are all likely to play roles in addition to those of special interest groups. As they contemplate all these factors, note that the public good is, at best, only one of the factors that public officials consider. A benefit-cost approach is, in practice, likely to be balanced against political and personal gains and losses as the policy maker decides.

IN SUMMARY

- Environmental policies in practice are the outcome of public processes. Public processes often consider the results of benefit-cost analysis, but rarely are decisions based entirely on those results. As a consequence, policy decisions are not always efficient.
- In cases where people vote on a policy, the median, or middle, voter ends up casting the deciding ballot. In many environmental policies, it is likely that the majority of people believe that the benefits they will get from environmental improvements outweigh the costs that they will bear because they may believe that the costs imposed on polluters will not be passed along to them. As a result, the majority of people may vote for environmental policies, even if the total costs outweigh the total benefits. On the other hand, because small, financially oriented groups have a strong incentive to organize and motivate voters, they may be successful because many in the general public may not turn out to vote.
- In cases where public officials decide policies, it is important to consider the objectives of those decision makers. They are likely to focus on whatever

keeps them in their positions of power, and they are likely to support those who will help them. While many people will benefit from programs (such as pollution reduction), the costs of those programs often fall disproportionately on small groups (such as pollution sources). The groups that will be most directly affected have a large incentive to be politically active, while the majority who feel the effects less strongly are not likely to express their views. As a result, these small, focused groups are likely to have disproportionate influence on public officials, and the public officials will put less weight on the views of the general public.

Voluntary Environmental Improvements

As environmental awareness has increased in the general public, businesses have been trying to find ways to make "green" behavior profitable. If sources pollute because polluting is less expensive than abating, why would sources even consider reducing their emissions without government regulation?

The EPA makes public a Toxics Release Inventory (TRI), a list of emissions of toxic substances from every source in the United States over a certain size. The TRI itself carries no requirement to reduce emissions; any obligations that exist are under other laws. Nevertheless, studies have found that sources with relatively high emissions in the TRI reduce their emissions more than other sources.

Why would sources voluntarily reduce their emissions? In some cases, sources have found that they were using chemicals inefficiently, and they were able to reduce their costs by cleaning up. In other cases, sources wanted either to avoid bad publicity or to create good publicity by becoming greener. If consumers show a preference for a company that is more environmentally friendly, then reducing emissions might be another way that being environmentally friendly can help profits. A third, more strategic possibility is that doing some cleanup voluntarily might postpone regulation. While it is unlikely that most environmental improvements will directly increase business profits, the heightened attention to environmental problems from both the public and businesses has led many businesses to reconsider their polluting ways.

CHAPTER SUMMARY

Here are the key lessons from this chapter:

- Environmental policy in practice is different from environmental policy in theory. While economic theory can help identify the levels of environmental quality that will lead to the greatest net gains, and the ways to achieve those gains, policy makers and regulators have many other considerations in their actual activities.

- Compliance with environmental policies requires regulators to monitor pollution sources, bring enforcement actions when violations are present, and impose penalties as disincentives for violations.
- In deciding how much to comply with requirements, pollution sources respond not only to the threat of a penalty but also to the likelihood that their violations will be found. The expected penalty, the product of the penalty and the probability of getting caught, signals the average penalty that a source will face over time. A high expected penalty, which results from a combination of a high penalty and a high probability, will induce more compliance than a low expected penalty.
- Regulators typically have choice over their monitoring (and thus the probability of catching a violation) and the penalty that a violator faces. They may choose not to set the expected penalty high enough to get all sources to comply, either because it is too costly to monitor all sources, or because they may believe the regulation is too stringent, or because they support the industry that they regulate.
- The equilibrium level of pollution is the amount required under the standard if the expected penalty is greater than or equal to the cost of compliance. If the expected penalty is lower than the cost of compliance, the equilibrium level of pollution is where the cost of compliance (or forgone benefit of polluting) equals the cost of violation (the expected penalty).
- The equilibrium level of pollution may not be complete compliance with environmental requirements, but many sources comply anyway, for reasons ranging from eagerness for a positive public image to a desire to be a good citizen.
- Efficiency is only one factor that influences the development of environmental policies. The distribution of the benefits and costs among different groups of people also plays a large role in influencing both individual and group decisions on public policies.
- Majority votes are decided by the median, or middle, voter. If the general public believes that it will benefit from a policy more than a concentrated few will suffer, a policy may pass even if its costs outweigh its benefits. If the concentrated few are more motivated than the majority, they may pass a policy even if its costs outweigh its benefits.
- Concentrated interests are more likely to influence policy makers than the general public because the general public feels much less direct effect. As a result, public officials may respond disproportionately to the concentrated interests than to the general public.
- These simple models of economic agents are only the starting points in political and economic analysis. Explaining all the interactions between regulators and the industries that they regulate, or between interest groups and public officials, can involve many factors beyond those discussed here. These simple models nevertheless highlight that positive net benefits may not be the only guiding principle for environmental policy.

KEY TERMS

average penalty *(p. 310)*
captive regulation *(p. 315)*
capture *(p. 315)*
compliance *(p. 306)*
equilibrium level of pollution *(p. 317)*

expected penalty *(p. 310)*
mobile sources *(p. 314)*
political economy *(p. 318)*
stationary sources *(p. 314)*

NOTES

The story of the diesel truck engines can be found in John H. Cushman, "Record Penalty Likely Against Diesel Makers," *New York Times*, October 22, 1998, p. A1; Joby Warrick, "Diesel Manufacturers Settle Suit With EPA; Will Pay $1.1 Billion," *Washington Post*, October 23, 1998, p. 3; and U. S. Environmental Protection Agency, "DOJ, EPA Announce One Billion Dollar Settlement with Diesel Engine Industry for Clean Air Violations," October 22, 1998, at http://yosemite.epa. gov/opa/admpress.nsf/b1ab9f485b098972852562e7004dc686/93e9e651adeed6b7 852566a60069ad2e?OpenDocument, accessed on May 25, 2009.

The smog test fraud story is from a press release of the San Francisco District Attorney's office, "DA Harris Cracks Down on Environmental Crime: Man Convicted and Sentenced for Issuing False Smog Certificates," at www.sfdistrictattorney.org, accessed on April 20, 2009.

The figure of approximately $3.4 billion for fines, cleanup, and damages following the Exxon Valdez spill comes from totaling the numbers given by the U.S. Supreme Court for cleanup, criminal fines, restitution, restoration, settlements, and the damage award from a civil lawsuit. The source is the court's opinion in *Exxon Shipping Company* v. *Baker* (June 25, 2008), 128 Supreme Court Reporter 2605, which reduced the punitive damage award to $507 million.

Figures 13.1 and 13.2 were constructed from the marginal cost of abating NO_x curve for power plants from Chapter 12. We divided the quantity by the approximate number of large power plants, 600, and then converted the curve into its mirror image, the marginal benefit of polluting curve.

China's environmental problems are described in Joseph Kahn and Jim Yardley, "As China Roars, Pollution Reaches Deadly Extremes," *New York Times* August 26, 2007, at http://www.nytimes.com/2007/08/26/world/asia/26china. html, accessed October 19, 2009.

The theory that regulators act to benefit the regulated industry is spelled out in George J. Stigler, "The Theory of Economic Regulation," *Bell Journal of Economics and Management Science* 2 (Spring 1971): 3–21 and in Sam Peltzman, "Toward a More General Theory of Regulation," *Journal of Law and Economics* 19(2) (August 1976): 211–240.

The website of the West County Toxics Coalition is www.westcountytoxic scoalition.org. The study of the effectiveness of bucket brigades is by Dara O'Rouke and Gregg P. Macey, "Community Environmental Policing: Assessing New Strategies of Public Participation in Environmental Regulation," *Journal of Policy Analysis and Management* 22(3) (2003): 383–414.

Research on responses to the Toxics Release Inventory include Shameek Konar and Mark Cohen, "Information as Regulation: The Effect of Community Right to Know Laws on Toxic Emissions," *Journal of Environmental Economics and Management* 32(1) (January 1997): 109–124 and Madhu Khanna, Wilma Quimio, and Dora Bojilova, "Toxics Release Information: A Policy Tool for Environmental Protection," *Journal of Environmental Economics and Management* 36(3) (November 1998): 243–266.

Information on industry contributions to members of Congress comes from http://www.opensecrets.org/industries/background.php?cycle=2010&ind=A10. This site, accessed on October 19, 2009, provides data from the public reports of candidates.

EXERCISES

1. What is the response of a potential polluter in a marketable permit system? To answer these questions, it will help to look back at Figures 13.2 and 13.3.
   - (a) What happens to the emissions standard the firm must meet if it buys a permit?
   - (b) Suppose that the firm is compliant, as in Figure 13.2, and it is offered the right to buy or sell one unit of pollution (move its standard by one unit). If the market rate for permits is less than the expected penalty, what will it do and why?
   - (c) Suppose that the market rate is higher than the expected penalty. Now what does it do?
   - (d) Now suppose the firm is noncompliant, as in Figure 13.3. If the market price of permits is $1.04, what will the firm do?
   - (e) Instead the market price is $0.50. What does the firm do?

2. Explain why Congress might pass laws against pollution and then not fund the agencies sufficiently to enforce them. Does it surprise you that a pro-business administration might choose to shift agency effort away from enforcement activity to other agency obligations? Keep in mind that some but not all voters are passionate about the environment, and others are more concerned with the economic outcome.

3. Use the Echo system, http://www.epa-echo.gov/echo/index.html, to locate the firms that have permits for emissions in your zip code. What is the ratio of large to small firms? What is the ratio of "notice of violations" (NOV) to other enforcement actions? Who are the biggest polluters? Look at http://www.peri.umass.edu/Toxic-100-Table.265.0.html for one compilation of results from the Toxics Release Inventory. Are these also the largest industrial firms in the United States? Which entries do you find surprising?

4. Use the arguments in the political economy section to explain why the United States almost decided to finance the Gravina Island Bridge (which became

known to its opponents as the Bridge to Nowhere), a $385 million bridge to an island with a population of 50 and an airport.

5. Under some pollution control laws, if a pollution source is found to be in violation of the standard it faces, it must pay a penalty equal to the gains that it earned by being in violation. Under what conditions will this policy lead to 100 percent compliance with the standards?

6. The profits associated with producing Q for Nash Enterprises are $\pi = 20Q - Q^2$, and marginal benefits are $MB = 20 - 2Q$. Pollution damages (costs) associated with its production are $D = 10Q$; the marginal damages are $MD = 10$.

(a) In the absence of any pollution regulation, how much will Nash produce? What will its profits be if it produces that amount? What will be the net benefits (that is, profits less damages)?

(b) What is the efficient level of production for Nash Enterprises—that is, the level that leads marginal benefits to equal marginal damages? What will its profits be if Nash Enterprises produces the efficient amount? What will be the net benefits (that is, profits less damages)?

(c) Will net benefits be higher under efficient production than under profit-maximizing production? (They should be!)

(d) Describe one policy that, if adequately enforced, will lead to Nash producing the efficient quantity.

(e) The environmental regulator imposes a standard that restricts Nash's production to $Q = 5$ every year, but, because of the costs of enforcement, it monitors Nash's production only one year out of every two (and Nash knows the monitoring schedule). If it is found in violation of the standard, it must pay $10 for each unit when it exceeds the standard. If Nash is a strict profit maximizer, how much do you expect it to produce in the years when it is not monitored? In the years when it is monitored? What is the two-year average for how much it will produce? What are the two-year average profits and average net benefits?

(f) Now, suppose the penalty in (d) is set at $20 for each unit when it exceeds the standard. If Nash is a strict profit maximizer, how much do you expect it to produce in the years when it is not monitored? In the years when it is monitored? What is the two-year average for how much it will produce? What are the two-year average profits and average net benefits?

(g) The regulator has a limited budget for enforcement. Would it get better compliance from Nash if it set a higher penalty (for instance, $40/unit) for noncompliance but monitored once every four years, on a known schedule? What is the average over four years for how much it will produce? What are the average profits and average net benefits?

(h) Now, suppose that the regulator monitors randomly, so that Nash doesn't know in any year whether it will be penalized or not. The probability of getting monitored is 50 percent, and the payment if found in violation is $20/unit. What is the expected or average penalty that it will pay per unit? How much will it produce if it faces this expected penalty? What are the resulting profits and net benefits?

(i) Is society better off in this case with Nash facing an uncertain monitoring schedule or a certain one, if the penalty is $20/unit and the probability of getting monitored is 50 percent? With which schedule is Nash better off?

7. A paper recycling facility is proposed for a town. Because of the bleaches and other chemicals used in paper recycling, there are concerns about the air and water pollution from the plant. A team of economists has studied the facility. The total benefits associated with the facility (including the benefits of not using virgin forests for paper) are estimated to be $10 million; the total costs (including environmental costs) are estimated to be $5 million. Let's consider different scenarios for examining whether the plant is likely to be built.

   (a) Is it efficient to build this facility? Why or why not?

   (b) Suppose that the plant is located inside the town, which expects to bear all the benefits and costs (which are evenly distributed across the population). If there were a vote on whether to build the plant, would you expect it to be built? Why or why not?

   (c) Suppose that the plant is located inside the town, which expects to bear all the benefits and costs. Now the benefits all go to a small group in the town, while the costs are spread among the majority. If there were a vote on whether to build the plant, would you expect it to be built? Why or why not?

   (d) Suppose that the plant is located inside the town, which expects to bear all the benefits and costs. The benefits all go to a small group in the town, while the costs are spread among the majority. Now one city manager decides on the project. Under what conditions might the plant be built? Under what conditions might the plant not be built?

   (e) Suppose that the plant is located just outside the town. While the people in the town will disproportionately bear the costs of the facility, those who will decide whether it should be built are in the rural area outside of town. Would you expect the plant to be built? Why or why not?

8. There are different theories in political science to explain the behavior of people who work in government agencies. Some argue that agencies are inherently conservative: that is, they continue to make decisions as they have in the past. Others argue that agencies want to maximize their budgets: that is, they operate in ways that bring more money to the agency because more money to spend gives them greater power. A third theory says that agencies get "captured" by the industries they regulate: because they work so closely with these industries, they become supportive of them. Yet a fourth theory suggests that agencies act in the public interest.

   Consider the case of below-cost sales of wood from Forest Service lands described earlier in this chapter. Which, if any, of the theories cited here might support the Forest Service allowing these sales? Does this practice contradict any of these theories? What kind of additional evidence might you want in order to understand whether the behavior of the Forest Service fits any of these models?

The Time Factor
Discounting

Energy conservation often requires a significant expenditure in the present in order to reduce energy costs in the future. For example, insulation and expensive light bulbs will reduce heating and electricity bills, but the benefits will appear some time after the costs are incurred. How do we decide whether to make those purchases? Consider a choice between two small refrigerators of the sort that fit in a dorm room or office. If one model claimed to save $5 per month in electricity compared with the other model, would it be worth spending an additional $100 for the energy-efficient model? As a general principle, how do we view benefits and costs that occur at different times than the present? This chapter highlights how economists model the process of making decisions about the future. This chapter will examine:

- The relationship between money in the present and money in the future: *interest* and *discounting*;
- The way that *interest rates* affect the values of goods in the future;
- Why there are many different *interest rates* in the economy;
- The appropriate *discount rate* for analyzing public projects involving the future;
- Energy conservation investment decisions in practice.

Investing in Energy Conservation

A kilowatt of energy conserved is a kilowatt of energy not produced. Most energy is produced by plants that burn fossil fuel or use nuclear power and produce externalities such as emissions or nuclear waste. Reducing energy production through conservation reduces these external effects. Conservation measures, such as installing attic insulation and thermally efficient windows, are often undertaken by individual consumers. How, then, do consumers decide how much to invest in energy conservation?

The Home Energy Saver website (http://hes.lbl.gov) allows people in the United States to calculate ways of conserving energy in their own homes. Some simple and inexpensive actions could both save money and reduce production of greenhouse gases and other pollutants. Other suggestions are more involved or costly, but they pay for themselves in the long run. One of the simpler conservation tools is a programmable thermostat that reduces the temperature in the house when people are in bed or not home. It costs about $70. For a consumer who lives in a cold climate, buying and using this device saves about $45 per year. Is this a good deal for consumers?

For more extensive investments in energy conservation, major home renovations provide excellent opportunities. For instance, energy-saving decisions could include not just a thermostat but also double-paned windows, wall insulation, and energy-saving appliances. These cost an additional $4,047. In exchange, utility bills would drop about $744 per year, and releases of carbon dioxide would be about 11,803 pounds lower every year. Is making such an investment a good deal for consumers?

The Time Value of Money

How do we decide whether to invest in energy savings when there are large up-front costs and benefits only over time? If we gain the benefits from burning fossil fuels now but must face the costs due to warming of the planet in the future, how do we balance current benefits against future costs? Answering that question requires examining the opportunity cost of money.

Let's consider the household deciding whether to invest $4,047 now in order to save $744 per year on heating. What else might someone do with $4,047 instead of investing in energy conservation measures? One possibility that would also earn money is to put it in a bank.

Suppose that a consumer is trying to decide between making these energy conservation investments and depositing the $4,047 in a savings account. The original deposit is called **principal**. The deposit is a loan of money to the bank. This is an **investment**: the use of money to earn more money in the future. In exchange for the loan, the bank pays *interest*. An **interest payment**, often simply called **interest**, is the amount of money repaid to the lender in excess of principal. Interest is the cost to the bank of borrowing money from the consumer, and it is the benefit to the consumer of lending money to the bank. If a consumer decides to spend that money on energy conservation measures in her home instead of putting the money in the bank, she gives up the opportunity to earn interest. The interest payment, then, is the opportunity cost of spending a sum of money instead of investing it.

We hear more about *interest rates* than interest payments in daily life. The **interest rate**, often abbreviated r, is the interest payment (usually per year) divided by the principal. This quantity is usually multiplied by 100, to make it a percentage. The interest payment, then, is r multiplied by the principal. If a principal of $50 will earn an interest payment of $2.50, that means that the interest rate is $2.5/50 = 0.05$, or 5 percent. An interest rate of 5 percent, then, implies that an investment of $50 yields $52.50 a year from now.

Let's look at how interest works by considering the relationship between the *present value* and *future value* of money. The **future value (FV)** of an investment is the total value that the principal will produce at a defined future time when invested at rate r. It is the sum of the principal (e.g., $50) plus the interest payment (e.g., $2.50) accumulated during the defined time period (one year). **Present value (PV)** is the amount that, if invested at rate r, will produce the future value after the defined length of time.

How does present value relate to future value? Money now is worth more than money later. "A bird in the hand is worth two in the bush." If a consumer isn't going to end up with more money in the future, he isn't likely to give up the utility from consumption in the present.

Let's consider an investment that lasts one year, our defined future time. Principal will produce $(1 + r)$ times itself in one year. So the future value is $(1 + r)$ times the principal. The present value of this investment is the principal itself because it is the principal that was invested for one year to produce the future value.

In mathematical terms, the interest payment equals r times PV. To get the future value, we add PV to $r * PV$. Thus, $FV = PV + r * PV$, or $FV = (1 + r) * PV$. With an initial investment of $50 and an interest rate of 5 percent, $r * PV = \$2.50$, and $FV = (1.05) * 50 = \$52.50$. Let's call the value in year 1 FV_1 and the value in year 2 FV_2. If the investment is left to earn additional interest at rate r for another year, then the value in year 2, FV_2, is $(1 + r) * FV_1$, or $FV_2 = (1 + r) * (1 + r) * PV$, or $FV_2 = (1 + r)^2 * PV$. In the example, $FV = (1.05)^2 * 50 = \$55.13$. If the investment continues to earn r until year t, then it is easy to continue this logic to find that $FV_t = (1 + r)^t * PV$. In other words, the future value at time t is equivalent to the principal today invested at rate r.

Principal can grow into a large future value over a time because the interest rate is multiplied by a larger number each year. Starting with a principal of $50 and a 5 percent interest rate, the interest payment is $2.50 in year 1, increases to $2.63 in year 2, and increases at an accelerated pace every year. This process of interest payments increasing exponentially, with value after t years increased by $(1 + r)^t$, is called **compounding**.

DISCOUNTING

While compounding tells us the future value of a present investment, **discounting** describes how much money a person must invest now to achieve a specific value in the future. In other words, discounting is the reverse of compounding. The interest rate used in discounting is called the **discount rate**, though economists often use the term "interest rate" for the discount rate.

In our example, the present value of $52.50 next year is $50 today; the present value of $55.13 in two years is $50. More generally, if $FV_t = (1 + r)^t * PV$, then

$$PV = \frac{FV_t}{(1 + r)^t}$$

Discounting, then, converts an amount in the future into its present value. Using this information in decision making requires one more step: comparing the present value of a future benefit to the amount of money needed to invest right now to achieve that future benefit. If the present value of a future benefit exceeds the cost—the current investment—then the project, such as the home improvement, is worth doing.

For instance, suppose that it costs $1,000 to plant a forest that can be harvested in 30 years; at that time, it will produce $FV_{30} = \$5,000$ worth of wood. Is this investment a good idea? The present value of that $5,000 with an interest rate of 5 percent is $PV = \$5,000/(1.05)^{30} = \$1,157$. The present value of the forest in 30 years exceeds the cost of planting that forest in the present; investing in trees produces more money than investing that $1,000 in the bank. The **net present value (NPV)** of this investment (also called the **present net value**, or **PNV**) is the present value of the benefits less the present value of the costs. Here, the net present value is $NPV = PV(\text{Benefits}) - PV(\text{Costs}) = \$1,157 - \$1,000 = \$157$.

This formula is based on the situation where there is a value at only one time in the future. If, instead, there are amounts V_1 through V_t in years 1 through t, then the present value of these payments is the sum of the present value of each of the payments:

$$PV = V_0 + \frac{V_1}{(1 + r)^1} + \frac{V_2}{(1 + r)^2} + \ldots + \frac{V_t}{(1 + r)^t}$$

For instance, perhaps there would be a thinning of the forest in year 15 that would produce $1,000 of value, though it would reduce the value of the future harvest to $4,000. The present value now is $PV = \dfrac{\$1000}{(1.05)^{15}} + \dfrac{\$4000}{(1.05)^{30}} = \$1,407$. Conducting the thinning increases net present value by allowing some revenue closer to the present. Getting money sooner is desirable because there is the opportunity to earn interest on it from the time it is received.

There are a few more formulas that are useful for determining present values. First, suppose that the same payment is made every year for t years starting in one year's time, so that $V_1 = V_2 = \ldots = V_t$. This amount is called an annual value (AV), or *annuity*. An **annuity** is a payment that is made every year for a specified period. For instance, a lottery winner who gets $2 million usually is offered

$100,000 per year for 20 years. Is this amount in fact worth $2 million? The formula for the present value of t payments starting next year is:

$$PV = \frac{(1 + r)^t - 1}{r(1 + r)^t} * AV$$

Box 14.1 presents the derivation of this formula. At a 5 percent interest rate, the present value of the lottery prize is $PV = 100,000 * \dfrac{(1.05)^{20} - 1}{(0.05)(1.05)^{20}} = \$1,246,221$. This is the amount that, if invested in the bank at 5 percent for 20 years, would allow a person to withdraw $100,000 every year for 20 years before the account ran out. Clearly, this amount is much less than the $2 million advertised. As the fine print on the lottery ticket explains, the lucky winner can choose between the annual payment and a one-time payment that will produce annual payments that sum to $2 million if it's wisely invested.

If the annual value extends from a year from now until infinity, this formula becomes:

$$PV = \frac{AV}{r}$$

BOX 14.1

The Math of Present-Value Formulas

When the same payment, AV, is made in every year, there are formulas for calculating the present value both for a perpetuity and for an annuity.

For a perpetuity starting in a year from the present, the formula $PV = \dfrac{AV}{r}$ comes from finding the sum of an infinite series:

$$PV = \frac{AV}{1 + r} + \frac{AV}{(1 + r)^2} + \ldots + \frac{AV}{(1 + r)^t} + \ldots$$

Multiplying both sides of the PV equation by $(1 + r)$ gives:

$$(1 + r)PV = AV + \frac{AV}{1 + r} + \frac{AV}{(1 + r)^2} + \ldots + \frac{AV}{(1 + r)^t} + \ldots$$

(Continued)

BOX 14.1

(continued)

Notice that the terms starting with $\dfrac{AV}{1 + r}$ are exactly PV! We can substitute PV for these terms, which produces $(1 + r) * PV = AV + PV$, which simplifies to:

$$PV = \frac{AV}{r}$$

To get the value of an annuity that lasts until t, let's start with the value of a stream of payments starting in year 1 (that is, there is no payment in the present):

$$PV = \frac{AV}{1 + r} + \frac{AV}{(1 + r)^2} + \frac{AV}{(1 + r)^3} + \ldots + \frac{AV}{(1 + r)^t}$$

The trick to simplifying this formula is to find a way to reduce the number of terms, which we'll do with some manipulation of the equation. First, multiply the equation by $(1 + r)$ to get:

$$(1 + r) * PV = AV + \frac{AV}{1 + r} + \frac{AV}{(1 + r)^2} + \frac{AV}{(1 + r)^3} + \ldots + \frac{AV}{(1 + r)^{t-1}}$$

Subtracting the first equation from the second gives:

$$(1 + r) * PV - PV = AV - \frac{AV}{(1 + r)^t}$$

because the intermediate terms cancel out. Some collecting of terms produces:

$$r * PV = AV \frac{(1 + r)^t - 1}{(1 + r)^t}$$

Dividing through by r gives:

$$PV = AV \frac{(1 + r)^t - 1}{r(1 + r)^t}$$

A **perpetuity** is an investment that pays a fixed annual amount forever. Perpetuities can be purchased for a present value based on this formula. For instance, a payment of $100,00 a year forever at 5 percent is worth PV $=$ $100,000/0.05 $=$ $2 million: it would be necessary to get the annual lottery payment, not just for 20 years, but forever, to get the equivalent of $2 million at 5 percent interest.

Note that the present value of $100,000 for 20 years is $1,246,221, while the present value of $100,000 forever is $2 million. The difference between these two values gives the present value of $100,000 per year forever, if we waited 20 years from now to start counting toward forever. This difference, $753,779, is worth very much less than the simple sum of $100,000 forever, which is infinity; it is also worth much less than having that infinite stream of money starting now. Values in the future are worth less than values today because having them today provides the opportunity to invest and earn interest.

The purpose of all these formulas is to estimate what people consider the present equivalent of something in the future. In each of these cases, a person has to choose between alternative activities, one in the present and one in the future. The lottery winner has to decide whether to take a lump sum now or receive annual payments. The forester has to decide whether to harvest trees now or later. And the homeowner has to decide whether to buy insulation or put money in the bank. The present value of future money signals the opportunity cost associated with investing in a project, since the money could always be invested in a bank instead. If a project produces a higher present value, then the project produces more value than money invested in the bank and thus is more valuable; if the present value of the project is less than the money available at the beginning, money in the bank provides greater earnings.

In our energy conservation example, a homeowner could invest $4,047 today in home improvements and earn $744 per year in reduced electricity bills, starting next year when the construction is done and continuing as long as the house is standing. If we can approximate this time frame by infinity, then the annual savings are equivalent to PV = AV/r = $744/0.05 = $14,880, and the present net value is $14,880 − $4,047 = $10,833. In this case, it is definitely more profitable to invest in energy conservation than in the bank. On the other hand, if the homeowner only expects to live in the house another five years before moving, the present value is PV = $744 * $\dfrac{(1.05)^5 - 1}{(0.05)(1.05)^5}$ = $3,221, for a NPV = −$826; he won't be in the house long enough to make the investment worthwhile from a purely financial standpoint.

However, the homeowner needs to think about more than just his yearly energy savings on the house. Might higher energy conservation also increase the value of the house when it is sold? If it did, by even $1,000, then the investment would be worthwhile. A new homeowner would be willing to pay that amount if he expected to stay in the house for at least two years, since the energy savings (PV = $744/1.05 + 744/1.05^2 = $1,383) exceed the additional cost. If the investment costs can be included in the house value, the investment in energy conservation is financially worthwhile over time.

Because people are willing to pay a bonus to have something in the present rather than in the future, the otherwise identical good in the future is worth less than the good right now. Discounting future values estimates the present-value worth of those future goods.

SAVING, BORROWING, AND MARKET INTEREST RATES

A person who has a sum of money can either save it or use it for current consumption. A person who does not have a sum of money but wants to buy something now can borrow the money—if he is willing to make an interest payment. Interest exists because some people are willing to pay a price to get money in the present rather than wait for it in the future. Banks have money available to make loans because some people are willing to delay consumption—to save—in order to get the interest payment.

Savers are producers of loans. Borrowers are consumers of loans. The interest rate on loans is the price that the bank pays to borrow money from a saver, and it is the price that a borrower pays to borrow money from the bank. People decide how much to save or to borrow based on the interest rate. The **market interest rate** is the rate that equates the quantity of savings—the supply of money available for borrowing—with the quantity of money that people borrow—the demand for loans. The market interest rate serves as the market-clearing price in the market for moving money between the present and the future.

When people decide whether to save or to borrow, they consider the money available to them now, the money available in the future, the interest that they can earn if they save, and the interest that they will have to pay if they borrow. Consider a person deciding how much to consume now and next year. He has income, Y, which is the present value of all of his income during the two-year period. Borrowing and saving allow him to reallocate the money between this year and next. He spends C_1 in the first year, leaving him savings of $Y - C_1$ to spend next year. Because he earns interest on his savings, his consumption next year is $C_2 = (1 + r) * (Y - C_1)$. Solving for Y gives the budget constraint $Y = C_1 + \frac{1}{1 + r} C_2$. If the price of consumption now is 1, the price of consumption in the future is $1/(1 + r)$: the consumer has greater buying power next year because of the interest he has earned. Put another way, there is an opportunity cost to spending money now: the ability to get more in the future. An important insight is that the consumer can shift money between now and the future via the ability to borrow or to save, regardless when his income arrives.

As with any good, the consumer makes decisions based not only on price—the interest rate—but also based on individual preference. How much the consumer consumes now compared with next year depends on his preferences—his indifference curves—for present consumption compared with future consumption. Each consumer has individual preferences about the value of current consumption relative to future consumption. The **personal rate of time preference** is a personal discount rate that measures how much a person values utility in the future relative to utility in the present. A person with a high personal rate of time preference will borrow more and live more expensively than a person with the same access to money but a lower personal rate. With a high enough personal rate of time preference, a college student could choose to live in the same style as he will as an employed graduate, by taking out loans that he will repay when he gets a job; of course, to repay the loans, his lifestyle once he has the job will not be as luxurious as if he did not have the loans. If his personal rate of time preference is low, though, he may choose to live frugally now to avoid the interest costs of moving future money to the present. Depending on his personal rate of time preference, then, a consumer will move future income to the present by borrowing, or move present money to the future by saving.

Not all borrowing is for the purpose of consumption. Some borrowing is for the purpose of investing in a *capital good*. **Capital goods** provide a stream of services in the future in exchange for a cost today. Both consumers and firms invest in capital goods. A consumer may borrow money to install insulation in a home; a firm may borrow money to install production equipment in a factory.

The amount that can be earned in the future by investing in capital goods is known as the **return on investment**. For instance, power plants are built because the present value of selling the power, less the operating costs, is greater than the cost of building the plant, including the interest payment on the money borrowed to build the plant. Consumers can borrow money from a bank to invest in home insulation that leads to lower energy costs over time. Education is an investment; the return on that investment is the higher income of a college graduate than a person without a college degree.

The savings necessary to provide loans come from people who prefer earning interest to spending more money now. They may have a low personal rate of time preference, or they may be planning ahead for expenses in the future, such as buying a house or paying for additional schooling. In either case, those savings provide banks with the means to lend money to businesses and individuals for capital investments.

Both borrowing and saving decisions depend on the interest rate. With a lower interest rate, the price of borrowing goes down; because the cost of investment is lower, more people want to borrow more money for either investment or current consumption. On the other hand, a lower interest rate provides less incentive for people to save, and therefore less money is available to borrowers. A higher interest rate leads to more people saving but fewer people willing to borrow and pay them interest. In a market equilibrium, the interest rate will adjust to make the quantity of savings equal to the quantity that people want to borrow.

IN SUMMARY

- Interest is the opportunity cost of spending a sum of money instead of investing it. The interest rate is the interest payment divided by the principal. The future value of an investment is the total value that the principal will produce at a defined future time when invested at a specific interest rate. Present value is the amount that, if invested at a specific interest rate, will produce the future value after the defined length of time.
- Compounding interest payments over time provides estimates of the future value of an investment in the present. Discounting reverses this process to

calculate the present value of an amount of money in the future: that is, the present value of future money is the amount that would produce that future amount if it is invested in the present with compound interest.

- The net present value (NPV) is the present value of benefits minus the present value of costs for an activity with benefits and costs over time. If the NPV is positive, then the activity will produce more net benefits than if the money for the project were invested in the bank; if the NPV is negative, the bank is a better investment opportunity.

- Saving and borrowing are mechanisms for moving money between the present and future. People have individual rates of time preference that determine their preferences for consumption now relative to consumption later.

- Capital goods provide a stream of services in the future in exchange for a cost today. The return on investment is the amount that can be earned in the future by investing in capital goods.

- Higher interest rates lead to more saving and less investing. Lower interest rates lead to less saving and more investing. The market interest rate is the equilibrium price that equates the amounts of saving and borrowing.

The Effects of Different Discount Rates

The discount rate can have a significant effect on the present value of an amount. Let's return to the example of our homeowner and consider the energy conservation investment for seven years, the average amount of time that a person lives in one place in the United States. At a 5 percent discount rate, the benefits over seven years are $\text{PV} = \$744 * \dfrac{1.05^7 - 1}{0.05 * (1.05)^7} = \$4,305$, more than the initial cost of $4,047. Suppose that the homeowner, instead of earning a 5 percent interest rate, could now earn a 10 percent interest rate at the bank. Over the seven years she intends to stay in the house, the present value of $744 per year with that 10 percent opportunity cost is $\text{PV} = \dfrac{1.1^7 - 1}{0.1 * (1.1)^7} * 744 = \$3,622$. Now the homeowner is better off putting the money in the bank than spending it on energy conservation.

Why does a higher interest rate change the decision to invest in energy savings? The market interest rate reflects the opportunity cost of that investment; the opportunity cost is the forgone interest that the homeowner could have earned by putting money in the bank. If the opportunity cost is relatively high, such as 10 percent, then people are getting a strong signal to put their money in a bank, rather than in energy savings. Investments that yield a lower return than the bank are not worth doing, even though they will provide returns for years to come. As a result, when the interest rate is high, activities that provide benefits in the future appear less worthwhile because the benefits over time are low in relation to the immediate cost.

A low interest rate, in contrast, makes investment that pays off in the future more attractive. At an interest rate of 2 percent, for instance, the present value of seven years of energy savings is PV = $744 * $\dfrac{1.02^7 - 1}{0.02 * (1.02)^7}$ = $4,815: the advantage of energy savings over the bank is even greater than at an interest rate of 5 percent. Two extreme interest rates demonstrate this effect. An interest rate of 0 percent represents no discounting of the future at all: people are indifferent between the present and the future. The present value of energy savings in this case is

$$PV = \$744 * [\dfrac{1}{1 + r} + \dfrac{1}{(1 + r)^2} + \dots + \dfrac{1}{(1 + r)^7} = \$744 * (1 + 1 + 1 + 1 +$$

1 + 1 + 1)] = $744 * 7 = $5,208. It makes no difference to the homeowner whether energy savings come immediately or in seven years; the present value is the simple sum of the benefits each year. At the other extreme, an interest rate of infinity means that anything after today is worthless. With an infinitely high interest rate, $\dfrac{1}{1 + r}$ is effectively zero, and any amount in the future is unimportant. Infinite discounting is equivalent to "Eat, drink, and be merry, for tomorrow we die." While very few people discount the future infinitely, some people do borrow on credit cards at high interest rates, or from lenders of last resort (such as pawnshops), when money in the present is truly important to them.

Figure 14.1 shows the effects of different interest rates on the present value of energy savings. The present value of the energy investment is highest when the

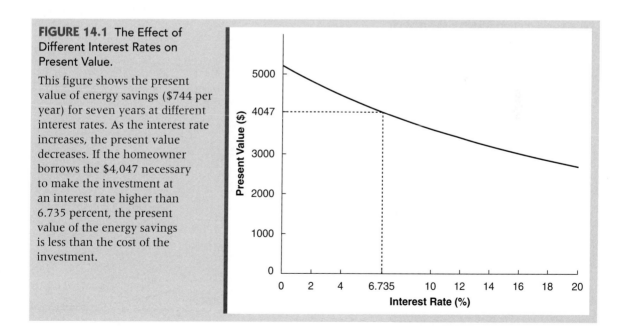

FIGURE 14.1 The Effect of Different Interest Rates on Present Value.

This figure shows the present value of energy savings ($744 per year) for seven years at different interest rates. As the interest rate increases, the present value decreases. If the homeowner borrows the $4,047 necessary to make the investment at an interest rate higher than 6.735 percent, the present value of the energy savings is less than the cost of the investment.

interest rate is zero, and it falls off steadily as the interest rate increases. The present value of the energy savings exceeds the cost of the initial energy investment, $4,047, as long as the interest rate is less than 6.74 percent. The interest rate that makes the present value of benefits equal to the present value of costs is called the **internal rate of return**. If a consumer knows the internal rate of return on an investment, he can compare that value with the rate of return on other investments and easily see which are more profitable.

The time period over which discounting occurs has a huge effect on the present value of an amount. Figure 14.2 shows the present value of $1,000 for periods up to 100 years, for 2 percent, 5 percent, and 8 percent interest rates. The present values fall off more quickly with a high interest rate than with a low interest rate, but all of them drop rapidly over time. The present value is less than half the original value after less than 10 years using an 8 percent discount rate, but that same reduction in value takes 35 years with a 2 percent discount rate. Almost regardless of the interest rate, values in the very distant future become very small when they are discounted. For example, at a 2 percent discount rate, $1,000 in 100 years is worth only $138, and it is worth $0.45 with an 8 percent discount rate. In other words, benefits and costs in the distant future that are discounted to a present value are relatively unimportant to benefit-cost comparisons.

FIGURE 14.2 The Effect of Time on $1,000 in Future Value.

This figure shows the effect of time on $1,000 in future value using three different interest rates. In all three cases, the value falls rapidly; it falls much more rapidly with higher interest rates. Values in the very distant future are worth little in present-value terms.

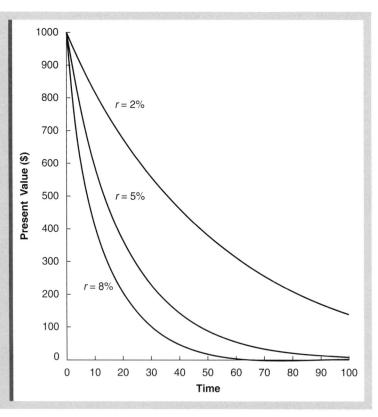

Whether the distant future deserves so little value in our decisions is a very important and unresolved policy and ethical question. Chapter 7 discussed the option value that some people place on environmental resources. The option value is the benefit of leaving open the possibilities of both use and preservation of natural resources for future generations, or even for the current generation at a future date. The American pioneers who transformed the prairie into a farming region in the nineteenth century made a decision that, for good and ill, reduced preservation options for their descendants. Similarly, fishers and fishery managers today are making decisions that will affect fish stocks for their grandchildren. High discount rates make preserving options for the future look relatively unimportant. Understanding the role of the market interest rate provides insights into why people make these decisions and the environmental impacts of those decisions.

BOX 14.2

How Much Fuel Economy?

How much fuel gets saved if a car's fuel economy increases? The answer is that it depends on the car's existing fuel economy.

Consider a car that gets 10 miles per gallon (mpg) and is driven 12,000 miles per year. It will use $12,000/10 = 1,200$ gallons of gasoline a year. Suppose the auto company offered an optional technology that increases efficiency by 1 mpg, to 11 mpg. In that case, the car will use $12,000/11 = 1,091$ gallons per year, 109 fewer.

Suppose, though, that the model without the technology gets 35 mpg, and the more efficient model gets 36 mpg. In this case, the additional 1 mpg will save only 9.5 gallons—less than 10 percent of the fuel savings gained when switching from the 10 mpg car to the 11 mpg car.

Is the extra cost worth it? Let's suppose the owner will drive it the same 12,000 miles per year for the vehicle's lifetime, about 15 years. For the choice between 10 and 11 mpg, the present value of the fuel savings from that additional 1 mpg, using a 5 percent interest rate, is $PV = \dfrac{(1.05)^{15} - 1}{0.05 * (1.05)^{15}} * 109 \text{ gallons} * \text{fuel price}$. If gasoline costs \$3/gallon, PV = \$3,396. If additional technology to improve fuel economy costs less than \$3,396, the added technology would pay for itself over the vehicle lifetime. For the driver choosing between 35 and 36 mpg, the present value of fuel savings is $PV = \dfrac{(1.05)^{15} - 1}{0.05 * (1.05)^{15}} * 9.5 \text{ gallons} * \$3/\text{gallon} = \$341$.

These values are sensitive to the interest rate, the price of fuel, and to the years used in the calculation. For the 10 mpg vehicle, if the interest rate is 7 percent, the 1 mpg improvement provides \$2,981 in fuel savings. If gasoline costs only \$1.50/gallon, the fuel savings are worth \$1,698 (using the 5 percent interest rate). And, if the consumer only plans to own the car for seven years and ignores the

(Continued)

BOX 14.2

(*continued*)

effect of improved fuel economy on resale values, the savings are only worth
$$PV = \frac{(1.05)^5 - 1}{0.05 * (1.05)^5} * 109 \text{gal} * \$3/\text{gal} = \$1,415.$$

If these calculations seem confusing, consider the plight of an actual vehicle buyer. Do people buy the most cost-effective amount of fuel economy—that is, the amount that recovers their fuel savings? Thomas Turrentine and Kenneth Kurani found, in a survey of 54 households, that no household did a systematic analysis of its fuel savings. Molly Espey and Santosh Nair, on the other hand, found that consumers' fuel economy purchases reflected the value of their fuel savings over the lifetime of the vehicle with reasonable interest rates.

IN SUMMARY

- Present values of future goods are lower when interest rates are higher. Present values are higher when interest rates are lower. Higher interest rates mean that the interest payment would be high if people put money in a bank; the forgone interest is the opportunity cost of investing in the future. Higher rates imply that people "discount" the future more: the opportunity costs of investing in a project are relatively high and discourage investment. Lower rates imply that people don't discount the future very much; because the interest payment from a bank would be low, the opportunity costs of investing in the future are relatively low. Thus, lower interest rates encourage investment.

- The internal rate of return is the interest rate at which the present value of benefits equals the present value of costs. The rate of return provides an easy way to compare the net benefits of activities. If the rate of return on one project exceeds that of an alternative investment, the first project provides greater net benefits.

- Discounting makes values in the very distant future worth little in present value. Whether effects in the very distant future should receive so little weight in our present decisions is an important policy and ethical question.

Different Market Interest Rates

Any look at the advertising for a bank shows that there are, in fact, many market interest rates. Interest rates differ by whether the rates are real or nominal, whether a person is investing or borrowing, the time commitment of the investment or loan, and the riskiness of the investment. Let's consider these one at a time.

INFLATION

Three generations ago, an American family could buy an entire house for the cost of a renovation today. This is because of *inflation*. **Inflation** is an overall increase in the prices of goods and services. In its simplest form, inflation is like changing from euros to dollars, or from any one currency to another: it does not change the price of one good compared with another, but the actual prices are measured differently. Suppose that the prices of all goods and services in the economy increase by 5 percent in a year. Inflation is 5 percent in this case. A dollar buys 5 percent less than it did. If a person put a dollar in the bank and earned 5 percent interest, and inflation was 5 percent, at the end of the year, he would be able to buy exactly what he could have bought at the beginning of the year. The 5 percent increase was not a real increase in value.

Because inflation does not itself affect the actual value of goods, it is important to distinguish between interest rates adjusted for inflation and unadjusted interest rates. Interest rates adjusted for inflation are called **real interest rates**. **Nominal interest rates**, on the other hand, are interest rates not adjusted for inflation. The difference between these is the rate of inflation. The nominal interest rate is the rate "named" by the bank; it is the interest actually paid. Suppose that inflation is 5 percent per year and that a bank account pays 7 percent interest: 7 percent is the nominal rate. An investment of $1,000 would provide $1,070 to spend in a year. What would $1,070 buy, though? Because prices went up by 5 percent, the amount that $1,070 would buy will go down by 5 percent. Purchasing power will be $1,000 * (1.07/1.05) = $1,019$: the real interest rate is 1.9 percent. The real interest rate, the nominal rate adjusted for inflation, shows what the consumer can "really" buy.

Now let's consider the relationship between the real and nominal rate. If i is the rate of inflation and r is the interest rate, then the real interest rate, the interest rate when inflation is considered, is $(1 + r)/(1 + i) - 1$, or 1.9 percent in this example. A good approximation of the real interest rate is the nominal interest rate minus the inflation rate, $r - i$. Because of inflation, a homeowner considering paying 5 percent interest on a loan should consider that the nominal rate of 5 percent will cost him less than 5 percent in real interest over time.

Should present value analysis be done using nominal or real interest rates? It doesn't matter, as long as all values are consistently either nominal or real. One way to value the $1,000 saved, for instance, is to use the real interest rate and say that it would earn $19 real. Another way is to use the nominal interest rate, find the nominal payoff of $70, and then divide that by the increase in the price level to get $19 real again. In other words, the real return is the same whether it is calculated using a real interest rate or a nominal rate adjusted for inflation.

In our energy conservation analysis, the $744 in savings every year is a real value. If energy prices increase over time at the same rate as inflation, the savings will be higher in nominal terms, but the real savings are the same every year. In this case, the present-value analysis should use only the real interest rate because the energy savings are also in real terms. Because it is often at least as difficult to predict inflation as it is to predict energy savings or other future values, conducting analyses in real terms is frequently more practical than conducting them in nominal terms.

BORROWING VS. SAVING

Perhaps our homeowner wants energy conservation in both his home and his car. He decides to use his savings for home improvements, instead of leaving them in the bank at 5 percent interest. He also decides to borrow money to buy a new fuel-efficient car. At this point, he will notice that the interest rate to borrow money is higher than 5 percent. The interest rate is the price for money; a person who deposits money in the bank is a seller of money, and a person who borrows is a buyer of money. The equilibrium price for money, like any other good, is the price that leads to an equal amount of money saved and money borrowed. In a simple equilibrium model with no transactions costs, the interest rate should be the same for both borrowers and sellers.

In fact, though, a person seeking to borrow money from a bank will face a higher interest rate than someone saving at the bank. The difference is due to the costs that the bank faces in bringing together the loans and the savings. The bank evaluates borrowers, keeps cash available for people cashing checks, collects payments from borrowers, keeps track of all the accounts, and ensures that interest payments get to the investors. These transaction costs provide a gap between the interest rates for borrowing and saving.

DURATION

The length of time that money will be saved or borrowed also affects interest rates. To examine the effect of the duration of an investment, let's consider a *bond.* A **bond** is a form of borrowing in which a company or a government borrows money from investors for a fixed duration at a fixed interest rate. The amount of the loan is the purchase price that the investors, called **bond-holders**, give to the company or government, the **bond-issuer**. The bond-issuer receives the purchase price in exchange for paying back the principal with interest over a fixed period of time. Some bonds are for short periods of time, such as three months; others may be for 10 or 20 years. The interest rate for a bond tends to increase as the **term**, or the duration of the bond, increases. Most bonds commit the borrower to pay the same nominal interest rate for a fixed period of time. Because the nominal rate of interest is fixed and the rate of future inflation is unknown, the real interest rate is unknown. As the duration of the bond increases, so does the uncertainty of the real return. More generally, there is likely to be more risk associated with investments over longer periods of time because more unexpected things can happen in a longer period, and greater risk leads to higher interest rates (as will be discussed shortly).

Bonds are a popular way for governments to raise money for public works because they give the government money immediately and spread out the repayment by taxpayers over time. For instance, California voters in 2008 decided to allow the state government to issue bonds to pay for a high-speed rail system. Selling the bonds gives the state the money to invest immediately in the project, and taxpayers will pay back the costs in principal and interest payments over the life of the bonds.

RISK

Governments borrow money by issuing bonds. Because the U.S. government is expected always to meet its obligations, its bonds, called Treasury bonds, are considered the safest form of investment. An individual seeking to borrow money to buy a car, on the other hand, may not always pay the required amount on time. If a bank were deciding to whom to lend money, with both the U.S. government and the car owner offering the same interest rate, it is hard to imagine that the bank would lend money to the car owner. How, then, can the car owner borrow money? By paying a higher interest rate.

A risky investment is one where there is some likelihood that the loan may not be repaid because the person who borrowed the money does not earn enough to keep up with payments or because the project to be undertaken with the loan may not produce the expected benefits. Investors demand a **risk premium**, an extra payment to compensate for the possibility that the loan will not be repaid, if they lend money to a borrower undertaking a risky investment. The risk premium is the interest rate on the risky investment less the rate on a safe asset, such as a Treasury bond. The higher interest rate for riskier investments acts to discourage people from undertaking risky activities and to encourage investors to lend money for those activities. If investors manage their portfolios carefully, the extra compensation from those who do repay the loans will exceed the losses from those who default on their loans.

Risk can come into play in another way, through the relationship of the return on one investment to the return on another. For instance, suppose our homeowner decided to buy energy improvements for his home but to continue driving his older, less fuel-efficient car. The savings of $744 per year from home energy savings is an estimate based on current prices; if the price of energy increases unexpectedly, these savings will increase, and the investment will be even more profitable than originally predicted. On the other hand, if the cost of commuting goes up as part of the increase in energy prices, the net benefit of owning the other energy-intensive good—the car—will go down when the price of energy increases. Of course, the reverse happens when energy prices drop: the net benefits from the home renovation are lower, but the net benefits from the old car are higher. Because the energy savings from home conservation increase when the benefits of an old car decrease, and vice versa, the consumer's net energy benefits will be more stable over time, and the risk associated with energy expenditures will be smaller with both of these goods than if the consumer had only one of these goods. In other words, the cautious consumer might choose one energy investment at a time—car or home— because of the risk of unpredictable energy prices.

If the benefits associated with two goods tend to move in the same direction in response to unforeseen events, then having both of the goods increases the risk associated with the two goods. On the other hand, if the benefits associated with the two goods move in opposite directions, as with home improvements and an old car, then having both of them reduces risk. If one good responds differently than most other goods to unexpected events, that good may be especially desirable when owned in combination with the other goods, even if it is risky when considered alone. Holding assets whose benefits respond differently to unforeseen events as a way to reduce risk is called **diversification**. Diversification is a highly recommended financial strategy.

There are two types of risk. Risk that falls on all firms—for instance, the risk that the economy might go into recession—cannot be diversified away; it is called systematic risk. Other risk is specific to a particular business: its product might not appeal to consumers during good or bad times. Investors can diversify away that risk by holding a portfolio with lots of unrelated stocks whose price movements are independent of each other; this is called idiosyncratic risk. Because the idiosyncratic risks can be diversified away, only the systematic risk matters for pricing stocks. Shares of firms are priced based on how much systematic risk they carry.

IN SUMMARY

- There are many different market interest rates in the economy, due to consideration of inflation, transactions costs for banks, the duration of the investment, and risk.
- Inflation refers to a general change in the level of prices in an economy. If all prices and wages change by the same proportion, then there is no real change in purchasing power, but the nominal amount needed to conduct a transaction changes. Nominal prices and interest rates include inflation; real prices and interest rates adjust for inflation. Present value analyses can be done with either form of interest rate, as long as nominal prices are associated with nominal interest rates, and real interest rates are used with real prices.
- Interest rates for borrowing exceed those for saving so that the intermediary (typically a bank) gets paid for its role in the transaction.
- Rates of return on investments often vary with the duration of the investment. Usually investments over a long period of time involve higher returns than those over a shorter period of time, due to expectations about inflation and higher uncertainty about the future.
- When one investment is riskier than another investment, the riskier investment must offer a higher return in order to attract investors. Investors must decide whether they are willing to accept a greater risk of not getting paid back in exchange for more money if they are paid back.
- Investors can reduce their risk by diversifying their investments to include goods that respond differently to unexpected events. If an unexpected event, such as an energy price change, occurs, then having one investment that increases in value from that event along with an investment that decreases in value because of the event will reduce the investor's total risk.

BOX 14.3

Socially Responsible Investing

A mutual fund is a collection of stocks, which are small shares of ownership in a company. Buying a share in a mutual fund has the same effect as buying a small amount of each of the companies that the mutual fund includes. Mutual funds make diversification easy.

However, not all investors are happy owning all types of investments. Many mutual funds own parts of defense contractors, utilities using coal and nuclear power, tobacco companies, casinos, or other activities of which some people disapprove. Some investors wish to signal their disapproval by avoiding financial involvement with those companies. There are special funds for investors who wish to narrow the types of stocks they own to only those in companies that meet their ethical screens. The investment manager for these funds needs to construct a list of social "screens," a list of criteria that companies must meet to have their shares in the fund. Examples of screens include no tobacco companies or no companies that invest in countries with identified human rights violations. A social fund then chooses a diversified portfolio from among the companies that pass the social screens. An environmental screen could rule out utilities that have been caught exceeding their permitted emissions, but it would allow stocks from power producers that have complied with the Clean Air Act. A fund with a "green" focus could diversify by buying stock in two energy companies, one using solar power and one using wind to produce electricity, and it could further diversify by going beyond electricity production to invest in a company making electric-powered cars.

From a purely financial point of view, social funds have two disadvantages. First, because it takes more work to screen stocks for social issues, the funds may have to charge investors a higher fee. The second disadvantage is that a social fund is less diversified. By design, it gives up some diversification and thus gives up the chance that some polluting industries might make the most money.

Companies that sell social funds argue that social responsibility is good business practice because it leads to fewer fines and lawsuits. The response to this argument is that, in the long run, companies that incur fines and lawsuits may be less profitable, so social screens are not needed to encourage green behavior. The counterargument is the problem of imperfect enforcement, which allows companies to pollute without facing costs in some cases.

Some environmentally conscious investors put their money into mutual funds that include "dirty" companies. There are two reasons for this decision. First, if these investors believe that unscreened funds or polluting companies will provide higher returns, the investors can plan to use the higher returns they have earned for "green" causes. Second, the investors may try to change the companies' behaviors as part-owners of these companies.

Although less diversified than a traditional fund, a socially responsible fund still pursues diversification within its screening criteria.

Interest Rates for Public Projects

Present-value calculations are so common that they are designated buttons on many business calculators. Businesses use them any time that they are deciding whether to make investments in new facilities. Businesses use the interest rate that is the most direct reflection of the firm's opportunity costs—either the rate at which it would borrow money or the rate of return it would receive if it invested the money in an alternative project. Using a rate that reflects the return on the next best alternative provides the business with information on which activity is most profitable.

Environmental agencies also compare the benefits and costs over time of their activities. For instance, in deciding whether to fund such development activities as dams, the World Bank—which provides funding for international development projects—compares the benefits of the dam over time, such as clean electricity and irrigation water for crops, with the costs of building the dam, including environmental costs and the disruptions to communities that would be flooded by the reservoir. What interest rate should be used in these calculations?

For private investment decisions, the choice of an interest rate for calculating a present value is simple: it is the market interest rate at which the borrower can take out a loan. For instance, a homeowner evaluating whether to borrow $4,047 to invest in energy conservation would estimate the present value of the energy savings using the interest rate on the loan. Similarly, a business that is deciding whether to build a new factory will compare the present value of the profits from that factory with the costs of building it, using the interest rate at which it borrows the money.

Businesses, if they are to stay in operation, must recover their costs of operation, including their loan costs. As a result, they can't stay in business in the long run if the present value of their net benefits falls below zero. Governments, on the other hand, have the ability to raise money through taxation. They are not obligated to earn profits; many government activities, such as providing parks or national defense, provide huge benefits but not necessarily profits. For these situations, the estimated values of nonmarketed benefits should be included in the benefits and costs over time. The question remains, though, what rate the government should use for its present-value calculations.

One consideration is that the effective interest rate to borrowers is different from the effective interest rate to savers, due to taxation. In the supply and demand for investment money, lenders have an upward-sloping supply curve for savings, which provide the money for investment. Businesses, which use investment money to undertake projects, undertake fewer projects as the interest rate gets higher; they have a downward-sloping demand curve for money for investment. Without taxation, one interest rate would bring them to equilibrium. But investment earnings are taxed, both with corporate income tax and with a personal income tax on dividends. As a result, the interest rate to lenders is less than that to businesses. A $1 million project that that returns $70,000/year to investors forever—a 7 percent return—will provide less—perhaps $30,000, a 3 percent return—to the lenders. Which of these rates reflects the return on the investment? The return on this investment represents the opportunity cost of the money if the government uses it for a project and thus should determine the government discount rate.

There are a variety of ways to approach this question. In one approach, the interest rate for the public sector is a weighted average of the consumer and business interest rates, with the weights given by the proportion of the funds given up by the two groups. Another approach says that the investment interest rate reflects the returns that would be made if the government did not "crowd out" the investment spending and thus represents the true opportunity cost. Yet a third approach argues that the consumption rate is the correct rate because ultimately consumers bear all the costs as the ultimate owners of businesses and payers of taxes. The U.S. Environmental Protection Agency's *Guidelines for Preparing Economic Analyses* discusses these and other methods for determining the public discount rate.

Some argue that, in certain cases, the public sector should use a social discount rate that is lower than the private interest rate because of a market failure in the borrowing and saving decisions that determine market interest rates. In our daily life, we focus too much on the short term, and we want our public sector to avoid making this error. For instance, many Americans who drive, keep their houses well air-conditioned, and otherwise do activities that produce high levels of greenhouse gases, were disappointed that their government did not sign the Kyoto Protocol on climate change, which would have required reductions in those emissions. Similarly, corporations have been criticized for focusing too much on short-term profits and not planning ahead for the well-being of their company in the long run. A social interest rate would lead the public sector to put relatively more money into investments that produce net benefits in the future (such as parks, roads, or other infrastructure) than into activities that produce net benefits in the present (such as unemployment compensation payments). A lower, social discount rate, combined with the government's ability to raise money by taxation, would, in essence, take money from the present and give it to the future.

For what projects might the social discount rate be appropriate? The discussion centers on activities that the private sector is unlikely to conduct, primarily those involving correcting market failures, such as providing public goods. Some argue that the only rate to use is the market interest rate because it reflects the opportunity cost—the other things government could do with the money. Others argue that, if asked, people would like their public representatives to put more weight on the future than they do as individuals. The 2006 Stern Review on the Economics of Climate Change argues that "it is hard to see any ethical justification" for putting less value on the welfare of future generations than on present ones.

The practical result of these debates is that different government agencies use different interest rates. The U.S. Office of Management and Budget, which reviews the proposed activities of government agencies for the president, recommends using a 7 percent discount rate as the approximate rate of return on private investment. The Congressional Budget Office recommends 2 percent as representing the real cost of borrowing for the federal government. The U.S. Forest Service has used 4 percent, and the U. S. Environmental Protection Agency has used 3 percent and 7 percent.

Because there is wide disagreement, one practical approach is to use a range of discount rates, as the U.S. Environmental Protection Agency has done, to see if the results of the analysis are sensitive to the interest rate used. If the net present value stays positive (or negative) over a reasonable range of interest rates, then the basic result—whether the benefits outweigh the costs—does not depend on the choice of interest rate. In our energy conservation example, any interest rate below 6.73 percent justifies the investments in energy savings over seven years. With a longer time span for receiving benefits, the interest rate at which the investment is worthwhile—the rate of return—would increase.

IN SUMMARY

- The private sector, when it conducts present-value analyses, uses either the rate at which it would borrow money or the rate at which it would invest the money in an alternative investment.
- Some argue that the public sector should always use a market interest rate in its present-value analyses because the market rate reflects the government's opportunity cost—the other things government could do with the money. Others argue that the public sector should use a lower social discount rate in its analyses because the public sector should put more emphasis on the future than the private sector does.

Valuing Energy-Conserving Investments in Practice

In our homeowner example, if the present value of energy savings outweighs the present value of costs, then the investment is worth undertaking, and we would expect people to undertake these investments. When economists have studied whether people actually do make these purchases, though, it turns out that people often ignore energy savings that are financially worthwhile.

For instance, an energy-efficient refrigerator requires a higher initial expenditure than a less-efficient refrigerator, but it lowers electricity bills for the life of the machine, about 10 years. People who discount the future a great deal will feel that the present value of the savings in electricity is less than the additional cost of the more-efficient refrigerator and will buy the less-efficient one. People with low discount rates will care more about the long-run electricity savings and will buy the more expensive, more efficient one.

Observing how many efficient refrigerators are bought, and how many inefficient ones, permits us to estimate what interest rate consumers used in the present value calculation. Four different studies on consumer purchases of energy-efficient appliances came up with interest rates of 40 to 60 percent. In other words, even though these consumers would have been better off financially using a credit card with a 21 percent interest rate to buy the more energy-efficient appliances, consumers placed much greater value on saving money in the present than saving money in the future. Studies of other energy measures, such as those to increase the thermal integrity of a house, suggest that people discount at somewhat more normal interest rates of 10 to 30 percent. It is still a research topic to explain the size of these interest rates. Possible answers include that the buyer doesn't believe the energy savings claims; that the buyer doesn't intend to keep the appliance for very long; that estimating the savings with the information provided is very difficult; that the buyer is not able to borrow the money to cover the higher initial costs; that the buyer expects a better appliance to be available at a later date; or that the energy-efficient appliance may be less attractive, less convenient, or have other undesirable effects.

These apparently high discount rates mean that new energy-saving technologies often do not get adopted, even when they will save consumers money. Should governments require minimum energy efficiency standards, to impose these requirements on people against their own inclinations? Economists typically assume that consumers are the best judges of what is best for them, but they also argue that market failures, such as prices of electricity that do not include the full cost of the environmental damages associated with electricity, need to be corrected.

IN SUMMARY

- Even when energy conservation produces positive present net benefits with any plausible interest rate, people often do not buy energy-efficient products.
- Some possible reasons for this financially inefficient behavior are that consumers are skeptical of the benefits, that consumers do not plan on owning the appliances long enough to earn back the benefits, or that the appliances may have other undesirable characteristics.

Discounting Human Lives

Consider two programs to reduce pollution. One would save 100 people immediately. The other would save 200 lives 25 years from now. They cost the same amount of money, but there is only enough money to do one of them. Which program is better?

Maureen Cropper, Sema Aydede, and Paul Portney asked this and similar questions in a survey of 3,000 households. They wanted to see if people discounted in contexts other than money; and, if so, what discount rates they used. They varied the number of lives saved at different times, to see if people used the same discount rate for short periods as for longer periods. They also asked about monetary tradeoffs to see if people discounted lives in the same way that they discounted money. Finally, they asked about saving the lives of younger people versus older people.

The findings were broadly consistent with other studies of how people discount. Short-term discount rates are higher than long-term discount rates: while the average discount rate is 16.8 percent per year over a five-year period, it drops to 3.4 percent over 100 years. The rate is similar to that for discounting money (20 percent over a five-year period, similar to results in the energy conservation studies). Finally, saving one 20-year-old was deemed equivalent to saving eight 60-year-olds.

When people were asked why they preferred to protect lives in the present rather than lives in the future, the most common responses were: "(1) that it is better to live for today, to solve today's problems; (2) that improvements in technology will allow future lives to be saved more cheaply than lives today; and (3) that the future is uncertain." The first and last are clearly indications of a positive personal rate of time preference. Nevertheless, about 10 percent of respondents had negative discount rates because they felt a responsibility toward future generations. Discounting the future, then, appears to represent people's behavior toward the future in realms beyond the financial.

CHAPTER SUMMARY

Here are the key lessons from this chapter:

- Whenever a decision involves benefits and costs over time, future benefits and costs must be discounted to a present value before they can be compared. Any value in the future has the opportunity cost of an investment in an interest-bearing account, such as a savings account. Discounting future values, the inverse of compounding interest on an investment, is a way to take into account that opportunity cost.
- Interest rates reflect the fact that people generally prefer things now to later, as well as the fact that investments now can lead to future benefits that are higher over time. People are willing to pay a premium (interest payments) to borrow money and have it now, and people must be paid a premium (again, interest payments) to save their money and make it available for investment. The investments provide more in the future in exchange for present investment.
- Higher interest rates reflect greater overall impatience; things in the future are worth less than things now. At the extreme, a zero interest rate means that a value many years in the future is worth the same as that value now; an infinite discount rate, in contrast, means that anything after this moment is worthless.
- There are many market interest rates in the economy, reflecting inflation, banking costs, the duration of investments, and the risk associated with investments.
- When the private sector conducts present-value analyses, profit maximization requires that it use the market interest rate at which it would either borrow or invest the money.

• The public sector does not need to maximize profits. The public sector may want to use the same rate as the private sector when it makes investments like those in the private sector. Some argue that the public sector should always use market interest rates, which reflect the government's opportunity cost. Others argue that the public sector should use a lower discount rate because it should put more weight on the future than the private sector does.

KEY TERMS

annuity *(p. 330)*

bond *(p. 342)*

bond-holders *(p. 342)*

bond-issuer *(p. 342)*

capital goods *(p. 335)*

compounding *(p. 329)*

discount rate *(p. 329)*

discounting *(p. 329)*

diversification *(p. 344)*

future value (FV) *(p. 329)*

inflation *(p. 341)*

interest *(p. 328)*

interest payment *(p. 328)*

interest rate *(p. 328)*

internal rate of return *(p. 338)*

investment *(p. 328)*

market interest rate *(p. 334)*

net present value (NPV) *(p. 330)*

nominal interest rates *(p. 341)*

perpetuity *(p. 332)*

personal rate of time preference *(p. 334)*

present net value (PNV) *(p. 330)*

present value (PV) *(p. 329)*

principal *(p. 328)*

real interest rates *(p. 341)*

return on investment *(p. 335)*

risk premium *(p. 343)*

term *(p. 342)*

NOTES

Consumers' perceptions of fuel economy are discussed in Thomas Turrentine and Kenneth Kurani, "Car Buyers and Fuel Economy?" *Energy Policy* 35(2) (February 2007): 1213–1223 and Molly Espey and Santosh Nair, "Automobile Fuel Economy: What Is It Worth?" *Contemporary Economic Policy* 23(3) (July 2005): 317–323.

There is a very readable survey of consumer's energy conservation decisions in Ken Train, "Discount Rates in Consumer's Energy Related Decisions: A Review of the Literature," *Energy* 10 (1985): 1243–1253.

For a discussion of the debates about which interest rates government agencies should use, see http://www.cbo.gov/showdoc.cfm?index=601&sequence=0, Box 2. The U.S. Environmental Protection Agency's *Guidelines for Preparing Economic Analyses* discuss discounting in Chapter 6, at http://yosemite.epa.gov/ee/epa/eed. nsf/webpages/Guidelines.html.

The Stern Review on the Economics of Climate Change was published on October 30, 2006, under the direction of Nicholas Stern, who was then head of the Government Economic Service of the United Kingdom. More information about it, including a link to the report itself, is at http://www.occ.gov.uk/activities/stern. htm. The quote is from p. 31.

Maureen L. Cropper, Sema K. Aydede, and Paul R. Portney, "Preferences for Life Saving Programs: How the Public Discounts Time and Age," *Journal of Risk and Uncertainty* 8 (1994): 243–265 describes the study of people's preferences for saving lives in the present and future.

EXERCISES

1. An activity to improve the well-being of some impoverished people will provide benefits of $1 million right now, but it will obliterate the earth in 200 years. The world's value in 200 years is projected at 10^{12}. There are no costs or benefits between these two dates.
   (a) Is it worth avoiding the world's destruction in 200 years at a 10 percent discount rate?
   (b) Is it worth avoiding the world's destruction in 200 years at a 6 percent discount rate?
   (c) If 10 percent is the interest rate in the private sector, what are some of the arguments for using a 10 percent discount rate?
   (d) What are some of the arguments for a lower discount rate?
   (e) Do you think discounting and benefit-cost analysis are appropriate ways to handle this problem? Why or why not?

2. Mining is proposed for Wonderful Wilderness. This area provides two benefits: recreation (it is known for its remarkable backpacking opportunities) and biodiversity (it is a unique habitat for endangered wildlife and plants). The mining is expected to reduce backpacking visits from its current level of 10,000 recreation visitor-days (RVDs, a measure of recreational use) per year to 4,000 RVDs/year for the next 10 years; after that time, recreational use would partially rebound to 7,000 RVDs/year into perpetuity. If the mine is not opened, recreational use is expected to continue at current levels into perpetuity. Mining is expected to bring profits of $1 million/year for the 10 years of the mining operation.
   (a) What is the present value of mining in the area (excluding effects on recreation) if the interest rate is 6 percent? If it is 3 percent?
   (b) If one RVD of backpacking is worth $P, what is the present value of recreation in the area if it is mined? If it is not mined? (*Hint*: your answer will be $P times some number.) Again, do the calculation using both a 6 percent and a 3 percent discount rate.
   (c) How much would an RVD of backpacking have to be worth (i.e., what is P) to make the benefits of mining worth less than the benefits of not mining, considering only the benefits and costs of mining and recreation, not biodiversity? Do the calculation for both 6 percent and at 3 percent.
   (d) Suppose that travel cost studies determined that an RVD of backpacking in Wonderful Wilderness is worth $80/RVD. Would preservation be the efficient solution, considering only the benefits and costs of recreation and mining, at 6 percent? At 3 percent? If so, under what conditions, if any,

might mining nevertheless be the efficient solution? If not, how much would the area's value for habitat have to be worth in present value to make mining not worthwhile?

(e) Which interest rate makes the best case for mining? Why?

(f) One option for the area is to delay mining for 10 years. If an RVD of backpacking is worth $80, what is the present value of this alternative? How does it compare with the present value of mining the area in the present?

3. The benefit of cutting down a forest is $1 million now. The environmental cost of that harvest is $10/year forever.

(a) At a 0 percent discount rate, are the benefits of harvesting greater than the costs? Why or why not?

(b) The private market discount rate is 4 percent, but the government has decided to use a social discount rate of 0 percent. What is the opportunity cost associated with using the social discount rate in this situation? Explain.

4. What is the value of a piece of land? Consider the following scenarios.

(a) Suppose that you own a farm run by tenants. You can keep it and earn $100,000 per year. How much is that worth to you in present value, if the interest rate is 4 percent? Note: you'll need to decide how long a time to use in the present value calculation. Why have you decided on that time?

(b) Someone proposes to buy the farm from you for $1 million. Would you make more by selling the farm or keeping it? Why?

(c) At what price would you be indifferent between selling the farm and continuing to get the earnings from it?

(d) If $100,000 per year is the maximum that the farm is likely to produce, what is the maximum price that a purchaser is likely to offer? Why?

(e) Is the maximum price that a purchaser might offer greater than, equal to, or less than the amount at which you would be willing to sell? Explain.

(f) Suppose that your personal rate of time preference is higher than 4 percent. Would you be more or less likely to sell? Why?

(g) A developer proposes to turn the farm into a subdivision. Why might the developer be willing to pay a higher price than the previous offerers?

5. In the early 2000s, as a way to diversify risk, financial institutions bundled mortgages from many people into one investment. The underlying concept was that, if one person defaulted on a mortgage, the effect on the overall investment—the value of real estate—would be small because the other mortgages would continue to provide returns.

(a) If this approach succeeded in reducing risk, would the interest rate for mortgages go higher or lower? Why?

(b) If the interest rate for mortgages did as you said in (a), would the number of people seeking to buy houses increase or decrease? Why?

(c) What would you expect to happen to housing prices in response to your answer to (b)? Why?

(d) There were many reasons why housing prices increased during the 2001–2008 period, including government policies by both Presidents Clinton and Bush that made home ownership easier. Given that people observed this upward trend in prices, would people want to buy a house in the present or wait until the future, when they expected houses to be more expensive? Can an increasing price lead to more buyers? Why?

(e) What happens when the market runs out of buyers? By 2007 there weren't many new buyers left: they already had houses. Would prices continue to increase then?

(f) In 2008 and 2009, many people found themselves holding mortgages requiring them to pay far more than they could recover if they sold the houses. A number of people, as a result, defaulted on their mortgages. In that case, what happens to prices? And what happens to the desire to buy a house as a "good investment"?

(g) Was risk in fact diversified? That is, was the likelihood of default by one borrower unrelated to the likelihood of default by others?

Benefit-Cost Analysis

Under the Clean Air Act, the U.S. Environmental Protection Agency (EPA) sets the National Ambient Air Quality Standards based on protecting public health, including a margin of safety. What should the EPA do if there is no safe level of a pollutant? Ground-level ozone, a very common pollutant, occurs naturally in some places, and studies to date have not identified any levels below which there are no health effects. Avoiding all human-generated ozone might involve eliminating all driving and fossil fuel–fired electricity generation and perhaps regulating emissions from bakeries and backyard barbeques. Should the EPA prevent all possible effects on human health by extreme control measures, or should it take a more nuanced approach that balances the cost to human health against the benefits of economic activities?

An environmental regulation increases efficiency if the benefits are greater than the costs. Benefit-cost analysis is a measure of the efficiency of a proposed action. Government and international agencies, such as the World Bank, regularly require agencies to conduct benefit-cost analyses of their proposed actions. How these analyses are conducted and how they are used in the decision-making process attract a great deal of controversy. This chapter will examine:

- Benefit-cost analysis as a way of understanding the efficiency of public activities;
- The elements of a benefit-cost analysis;
- The use of benefit-cost analysis in practice.

The Tellico Dam and the Snail Darter

Dating back to a law from 1936, federal projects for flood control in the United States have been required to undergo a comparison of their benefits and costs before they could be built. The law says:

> destructive floods…constitute a menace to national welfare….[T]he Federal Government should improve…navigable waters…for flood-control purposes if the benefits to whomsoever they may accrue are in excess of the estimated costs….

The benefits of these projects do not need to come only from flood control. Many projects also provide benefits to navigation, irrigation, or electricity generation. However, they can also have significant social and environmental consequences. A flood control dam turns a river into a lake, which leads to major changes in water temperature, species mixes, and recreational opportunities. Large areas of land go under water, while new areas become shoreline property. Because of the potentially enormous and usually negative ecological effects, many of the largest environmental battles of the twentieth century involved opposition to dams.

The Tennessee Valley Authority (TVA) first proposed building the Tellico Dam in 1936 on the Little Tennessee River, a tributary of the Tennessee River. The TVA's purposes, from its origins in the Great Depression, included shoreline and other economic development. According to the TVA, benefits would include "flood control, power production, and improved navigation" as well as "significantly increase[ed] commercial barge operations in the Valley." According to the TVA's calculation, the present value of these benefits exceeded the present value of the costs.

Dam construction finally began in 1967—31 years after the project's proposal— and faced stiff opposition. The environmental community fought vigorously against this project. The reservoir behind the dam would be 33 miles long and submerge 15,560 acres. Significant historical sites, both of the Cherokee nation and early colonial settlements, as well as surrounding valuable farmland, would be inundated.

The TVA was able to defeat a series of legal actions claiming that the TVA did not conform to the requirements of the National Environmental Policy Act (NEPA), but the 1973 discovery of the snail darter, a new species of fish, in the area in question changed the situation entirely.

The Endangered Species Act (ESA) of 1973 required federal agencies to ensure that their activities would not "jeopardize the continued existence of any endangered species or threatened species or result in the destruction or adverse modification of habitat of such species...." Because the site of the Tellico Dam was the only known location of the snail darter, the court ordered that the dam not be finished, even though it was more than 90 percent complete, because its completion would extinguish the species.

Congress, which had appropriated $116 million to build this dam, wanted this outcome reconsidered. It amended the ESA to create the Endangered Species Committee, which could permit actions that would eliminate a species. This committee is sometimes called the God Squad because it holds the power of life and death over entire species. On February 8, 1979, the committee found that the dam should *not* be completed. The dam, they said, had no economic benefits whatsoever. One member reported:

> It does not pay. The costs clearly outweigh the benefits. It would have cost $35 million to complete it and we would be inundating $40 million worth of land. You would lose important Indian archeological sites, scenic values and the river in its natural state. (*Washington Post*, January 24, 1979)

Despite the Supreme Court decision and the decision of the Endangered Species Committee, the Congressional delegation from Tennessee still wanted the

BOX 15.1

The National Environmental Policy Act

The U.S. National Environmental Policy Act (NEPA) was signed into law by President Nixon in 1970. NEPA requires major projects funded or controlled by the federal government, such as highways or dams, to consider their environmental impact. Control includes the issuance of federal permits, such as permits that allow incidental harm to a species covered by the ESA, or permits for dredging sediments from water bodies under the Clean Water Act. NEPA requires the production of an **environmental impact statement (EIS)** that examines the environmental impact of the project and considers ways to mitigate environmental impacts, including alternatives to the project. NEPA allows private parties to challenge the adequacy of an EIS in court. Many environmental lawsuits are based on the inadequacy of the EIS, which is distinct from the underlying issue of the extent of environmental damage: as long as an agency adequately considers the harm and alternatives to it, it can impose environmental damages. In contrast to U.S. law, Swedish law both requires an assessment of impact and permits litigation related to the reasonableness of the damage relative to the benefits obtained from the project. Because federal funding and control extend to many state, local, and even private projects, the preparation of an EIS that can withstand public and legal scrutiny is an important job for environmental scientists and economists.

project completed. Senator Howard Baker of Tennessee was able to pass further legislation making the dam exempt from the Endangered Species Act. The dam was finished in 1979.

The snail darter was found in other rivers.

Today, the only developments on the shores of the lake are small retirement communities. There has been little of the economic development originally envisioned as the rationale for the project.

The good farmland and the Cherokee villages sit at the bottom of the reservoir.

Should the Tellico Dam ever have been built? Both environmentalists and economists thought not. The TVA and the Endangered Species Committee came to opposite conclusions as to whether the costs outweighed the benefits. How does benefit-cost analysis work, and how does it influence public policy?

Benefit-Cost Analysis Defined

Benefit-cost analysis (BCA) identifies whether the benefits of an activity are larger than the costs. As the Flood Control Act of 1936 implies, the roots of BCA in the United States are in water projects. Today, BCA is used for a wide range of

BOX 15.2

Benefit-Cost Analysis for Ethanol

As concern about carbon dioxide emissions has grown, there has been a great deal of interest in biofuels—fuels made from living plants, rather than fossil fuels. Lawmakers representing farming regions in the United States seized on this enthusiasm to promote federal tax credits for ethanol as a substitute for gasoline. In the United States, ethanol is commonly made from corn. For each gallon of ethanol blended into gasoline, the government pays 45 cents. In addition, the Energy Policy Act of 2005 requires that 7.5 billion gallons of biofuels be produced by 2012. The 7.5 billion gallons of ethanol will displace about 5 billion gallons (120 million barrels) of gasoline. Does this subsidy and mandate policy have more benefits than costs?

The key elements in a BCA of ethanol are (1) the benefits to reducing gasoline use; (2) changes in pollution, including greenhouse gas emissions; (3) the cost of making biofuels; (4) the changes in producer surplus and consumer surplus because of higher grain prices; and (5) the deadweight loss of the taxation needed to pay for the subsidy.

Let's start with reducing gasoline consumption; because gasoline is refined from oil, that means reducing oil consumption. The United States benefits from having to buy less oil; at $60 per barrel, that is approximately a $7.2 billion benefit. In addition, when the United States consumes 120 million barrels less oil, the demand curve for oil shifts downward and the world price falls. A reasonable estimate is that the price falls by $8 a barrel. Because the United States imports about 3.5 billion barrels of oil a year, a price drop of $8/barrel could reduce costs by as much as $28 billion a year!

As for the effect of ethanol on pollution, there is no agreement. There is some not yet conclusive evidence of slightly less toxic emissions, slightly more criteria pollutant emissions, and slightly less greenhouse gas emissions. While ethanol's

government activities in many countries, from road and dam construction to endangered species protection and health and safety regulations.

Let's look more closely at the elements of a benefit-cost analysis. These are the benefits, the costs, the comparison of the benefits and costs of the proposed project against alternatives, and the discount rate. In principle, these are simple things; in practice, they can be difficult to estimate.

ESTIMATING BENEFITS

The benefits of a project are the values of the outputs of the project. For instance, the Tellico Dam was intended to enhance flood control, power production, and navigation in the Tennessee Valley. Other dams provide water supplies for agriculture or appeal has been the hope that it can reduce greenhouse gases, the effect on GHG appears to be modest at best because significant inputs of fossil fuels are needed to grow corn and turn it into ethanol.

The third element is the cost of making ethanol, for which estimates point to perhaps $60 per barrel gasoline equivalent with current grain prices. In other words, ethanol production costs about the same as gasoline production for the same amount of driving.

The fourth element is the effect on corn prices. A program to use ethanol increases the price of corn by $1 or more per bushel. The major effect for the United States is an increase in earnings per bushel on exported corn. With exports around 2 billion bushels, the United States earns about $2 billion more in export revenue. As for the change in consumer surplus, it is felt most sharply outside the United States. Because corn is a staple food in Latin America, rising corn prices have caused misery for poor people in Mexico and Central and South America. Nevertheless, rising corn prices also increase grocery prices in North America.

Finally, the deadweight loss due to subsidizing 7.5 billion gallons of ethanol at 45 cents/gallon is $1.1 billion.

Robert Hahn and Caroline Cecot argue that the cost of increasing ethanol production to almost 10 billion gallons a year is likely to exceed the benefits by about $3 billion annually. They suggest that earlier attempts at promoting ethanol would likely have failed a benefit-cost test and that the U.S. Congress should consider repealing ethanol incentives.

Current biofuels research aims to make ethanol from cellulose at much lower cost than today's ethanol from corn. These new processes may well pass the benefit-cost test. In the meantime, the 2007 Energy Independence and Security Act increased the requirement for use of biofuels to 36 billion gallons by 2022.

for urban uses. Many of these benefits, such as increased agricultural production, are marketed goods; in other cases, the benefits are nonmarket environmental goods. For example, the city of Ann Arbor, Michigan, is considering removing the Argo Dam on the Huron River to provide the benefits of improved aquatic habitat and river-based recreational opportunities. Reducing air pollution gives the benefits of a decrease in deaths and illnesses and improvements in views from lessened smog. Building a new road can reduce the amount of time that people spend commuting, with the added benefit of reduced carbon emissions on a more direct route. These are the direct, primary benefits to be included in a benefit-cost analysis.

The most important aspect of estimating the benefits of an activity or project is listing all the benefits. Some benefits, such as the market value of increased electricity production, are quantified in monetary units by estimating the consumer surplus associated with their production. For other benefits, such as the effects of turning river-based recreation into lake-based recreation, it is more difficult to estimate both the quantities involved and how much those quantities are worth. Even if it is not possible to express all the benefits of a project with a quantitative or monetary measure, though, identifying all the benefits is critical. Because the primary purpose of a benefit-cost analysis is to provide useful information to a decision maker, the decision maker needs to know *all* the benefits of a project, not just those that can be estimated in monetary units.

The first step in estimating benefits is to determine the quantities of the outputs that the project is expected to produce. An important principle is that the benefits are the *change* due to the project relative to the world without the project. If, for instance, electricity production would have gone up even in the absence of the Tellico Dam's construction, then the benefit of electricity from Tellico would only be the increase over and above that already increased production. Otherwise, there would be benefits assigned to Tellico that are, in fact, unaffected by Tellico's existence. The same is true for the change in the price of electricity that is expected if production of electricity increases.

The estimates for quantities of benefits may come from a variety of sources. Engineering studies may provide some quantities—for instance, the electricity output of the dam. Estimates of recreational changes require the use of stated or revealed preference methods. The number of premature deaths avoided by air pollution reductions comes from public health studies. Changes in driving time due to road expansion require estimates not only of the increased capacity of a road but also of the changes in driving patterns—such as people switching from mass transit to cars—associated with an expanded road. These estimates often require the skills of experts in many fields.

Turning these quantity estimates into monetary units involves multiplying the quantities by prices. Prices for marketed goods, such as electricity, are the market prices of the goods. Multiplying quantity by price is a good method if the change in the quantity is small enough that prices are not likely to change. If prices change too, then it is necessary to use a benefit measure such as consumer surplus, compensating variation, or equivalent variation. These effects can be substantial: in Mexico, for instance, there was a proposal to build a dam to irrigate fields to produce string beans. Ultimately the project was not built, in part because a BCA showed that the world price for string beans would drop precipitously if that much additional land was dedicated to string beans.

Estimates of changes in price in nonmarket goods, such as recreation, are likely to come from nonmarket valuation methods, either from an original study or by using the results of an existing study.

ESTIMATING COSTS

The costs of a project are due to the inputs required to perform it. Inputs include the materials, machinery, labor, energy, and any other goods or services required to undertake the project. As with estimating benefits, many of these input requirements come from engineering studies.

As with the benefits, *all* the costs of the project need to be included. The environmental damage from a project—for instance, the loss of the snail darter and archeological sites in the case of the Tellico Dam—are part of the costs. Sometimes it is unclear whether environmental damage is a cost or whether it is a benefit reduction. For instance, if one of the benefits is improving air quality, and this involves taking a pollutant out of the air and disposing of it in a landfill, the damages caused by placing the pollutant in the landfill could be considered either a cost or a reduction in the benefits. It is important to include this effect; whether it is an increase in cost or a reduction in benefits is unimportant except for the magnitude of the ratio of benefits to costs, which we will discuss soon.

As with benefits, only the costs specifically associated with the project should be included as costs. Construction equipment, for instance, rarely is used for only one project. Therefore, charging the full cost of the equipment to the project overstates the cost. On the other hand, not including these costs is also incorrect because there are opportunity costs associated with using the equipment on a project. The cost of renting the equipment for the period of the project is one way to estimate the specific project expense.

The principle that costs are opportunity costs extends to labor costs. Labor is often the single largest cost of a project. What would someone building the Tellico Dam be doing if she were not working on that project? It is likely that she would have another construction job; if not, she is still likely to be employed elsewhere, creating some valuable output. The opportunity cost of using that worker at Tellico, then, is the value of the output that she would otherwise produce, measured as the wage that she would get in that alternative job. If, on the other hand, a person employed at Tellico would otherwise be unemployed, she would not be creating something of value to be included in the opportunity costs. The cost of her labor should be zero in the BCA, regardless of what pay she receives. The opportunity cost argument, then, is that labor is a cost, to be valued at the wage a worker would earn in the next-best alternative job.

Public projects built during times of high unemployment have opportunity costs of labor that may be very different from wages. For instance, when President Franklin D. Roosevelt took office in 1933, during the Great Depression, the U.S. unemployment rate was 25 percent. FDR set up an agency called the Works Progress Administration, which hired thousands of people to build public works project, including bridges, trails, parks, and buildings. Many of these—for example, a beautiful ski lodge on Oregon's Mount Hood—are still in use. Because of the very high unemployment rate, it was not very likely that the workers on these projects would be otherwise employed. So, although their wages were most of the cost of the project, the opportunity cost of their labor was very low. A benefit-cost analysis of building these public works would have been overwhelmingly positive because the opportunity cost of the labor input, by far the largest input, was near zero. This same logic applies today to public programs that employ young adults who would otherwise face very high unemployment rates. For instance, the AmeriCorps program employs young adults in jobs ranging from trail maintenance to tutoring. Because the opportunity cost of their labor is very low, projects like AmeriCorps pass benefit-cost tests.

BOX 15.3

Jobs and Timber-Dependent Communities

In the western United States, large areas of land are owned by the U.S. government, much of it in national forests. Unlike national parks, which are dedicated to preservation of ecosystems and providing recreational opportunities, national forests are also available for extractive uses such as timber harvesting. Many small communities surrounded by national forests exist primarily because of job opportunities in the wood products industry. If timber harvesting in the area is reduced or eliminated, not only these jobs, but the communities themselves, may no longer have a reason to exist. As a result, people in these communities often protest strongly against wilderness designations or endangered species decisions that limit or stop harvesting.

There is no question that reducing or eliminating these jobs is highly disruptive to the individuals and communities affected by these decisions. It is also clear that, in many of these situations, large environmental gains result from environmental protection. From a purely benefit-cost perspective, if the environmental gains outweigh the forgone profits from timber harvesting, then the people in these communities would provide greater net benefits by taking different jobs, most likely in different places. The American West has many "ghost towns" that prospered during periods of heavy resource extraction, such as gold rushes, and subsequently closed down as people moved away. For some timber-dependent communities, their choice is to find new ways to make money that do not rely on timber harvests, such as recreation services, or to follow the miners of old to new jobs in new places.

What about the effects of a public project on business revenues and profits? Most public works projects are built using government contracts with construction companies. The government agencies make payments to the construction companies. These payments are a cost to the government, but they also could be viewed as a benefit to the construction companies. Of course, this logic would make all projects pass a BCA test! What is missing from this logic is that a construction company, as a producer of roads or dams, incurs costs for inputs such as labor and materials. If the revenue to the company is included in a BCA as a benefit, the cost to the company, including the opportunity costs of capital, must be included as well. So including the company in the benefit-cost analysis adds revenue and subtracts costs. Revenue minus costs equals economic profits. In the long-run equilibrium, economic profits are zero. So, for a construction industry in equilibrium, revenues and costs would offset each other, and counting the construction company's benefits and costs in a BCA would give the same result as omitting them.

However, politicians see the world through the lens of reelection, a very different perspective from benefit-cost analysis. From that perspective, a project that provides jobs and business revenues in their districts, yet imposes most of the costs on people outside the district, is a desirable project. Because the constituents don't have to pay the cost of getting these jobs and revenues, for them the benefits outweigh the costs. The supporters of Tellico Dam, the representatives and senators from Tennessee, provided for their constituents all the economic activity and other benefits from the dam, while people from the other 49 states bore most of the costs. From a politician's point of view, jobs are perhaps the major benefit of a project: jobs, not net benefits, provide votes. Business revenues and accounting profits are also important, as they translate into campaign contributions, local tax revenues for local services, and business owners who vote for the politician. The logic of BCA and the logic of reelection are very different things.

USING BCA TO CHOOSE AMONG ALTERNATIVE POLICIES

Whether a project represents the best choice according to a BCA depends on the possible alternatives. Historically, for many water project proposals, the only alternative to building a project was no project. If a dam was proposed and the benefits for that dam were greater than the costs, then the dam could be built. This approach may not, though, produce the best social outcome.

Projects compete with other projects for the same site. It may well be that, though a project has greater benefits than costs, another project may have an even greater excess of benefits over costs. A "dry dam"—a dam that did not block water flow most of the time but could hold water in case of a flood—may have been a better choice for the Tellico Dam site than filling the reservoir. If the TVA did not consider any alternative besides building or not building the specific dam it had in mind, it may have proposed too large or small a project, or the wrong kind of project.

Projects compete with other projects for the same funding. If an organization has limited funds and cannot undertake all activities that have positive net benefits, it will best serve its purposes by looking for the project that produces the most net benefits per dollar spent.

Finally, projects compete with the same project undertaken at other times. While undertaking a project ends the opportunity of not doing it, not undertaking a project keeps open the possibility of doing it later—its option value. For instance, the TVA could have delayed the filling of the reservoir until there were indications that it was needed, or to see whether the snail darter might exist elsewhere, or to explore local community development possibilities without the reservoir. There are two parts to this argument. The first relates to knowledge of future conditions. If, for instance, the TVA were transplanting the snail darters to another local river, it could have delayed the project until the darters were established. While there would have been a loss of the benefits of having the reservoir sooner, there would have been fewer costs associated with losing the snail darter. The second argument relates to uncertainty about future conditions. If local community development might happen without the reservoir, the TVA could have waited to see if that development occurred. If it did, the reservoir would have been less necessary; if development did not happen, the reservoir option would have continued to exist, though the local development would have been delayed. Waiting would have allowed the TVA to avoid flooding the area unnecessarily. For this reason, if there is a choice about when to build a project, the net gains may be greater by waiting for more information.

THE DISCOUNT RATE

For a project with benefits and costs over time, choice of the discount rate is extremely important for the outcome of a BCA. The discount rate determines the present value of both costs and benefits. An agency often chooses one discount rate that it will use in evaluating all its projects. The purpose of choosing a discount rate is to ensure consistency in analyses, to facilitate comparisons across projects.

Benefits in the distant future that appear large when using a low discount rate become very small with use of a high discount rate. Shortly before the battle over the Tellico Dam, President Jimmy Carter created a huge political firestorm when he asked analysts to re-evaluate the net benefits of a number of water projects that were justified years earlier with very low discount rates. Water projects, as with many capital investments, involve large initial costs for benefits spread over time into the future. Using a higher discount rate meant that the net benefits of many projects went from positive to negative. Because, however, the politicians whose districts benefited from those projects nevertheless wanted them built, President Carter's "hit list" of water projects created major political difficulties that continued throughout his presidency.

The choice of discount rate involves assessing factors such as the riskiness of an activity, the role of inflation, and public attitudes toward public investments for the future. In most cases, removing inflation by conducting all analyses with real (not nominal) values simplifies the analysis. At that point, many government agencies advise use of specific discount rates that they have chosen for all their activities. Evaluating, for instance, different alternative uses of the same site is much easier if the net benefits calculations for all alternatives use the same discount rate. Using a range of discount rates provides more information than using a single rate. If a project has positive (or negative) net benefits regardless of the discount rate, then the evidence is quite strong on the net benefits of the project.

IN SUMMARY

- Conducting a benefit-cost analysis requires having the best available estimates of the benefits and costs of an activity compared with the baseline of not conducting the activity, the range of possible alternatives, the timing of the benefits and costs, and the decision on the discount rate(s) to be used.
- The benefits estimates require the quantities and prices of the expected outputs of the activity. Where the change in output for marketed goods is small enough that price is not likely to change, these estimates involve multiplying price times quantity. If market price may change, it is necessary to estimate

the welfare change—consumers' surplus is often sufficient. Changes affecting nonmarketed goods are likely to require methods of nonmarket valuation. Even if it is not feasible to get good estimates of the monetary value of all benefits, it is extremely important to list and include in the analysis all benefits associated with a project.

- Costs come from the inputs to the project. As with the benefits, all costs need to be considered in a BCA, even nonmarket costs.
- Although jobs are often discussed in public debates as benefits of a project, in a BCA labor is an input and therefore a cost. Labor should be charged at its opportunity cost, which may be different from the wage if the worker would otherwise be unemployed. Even for the workers themselves, jobs are a means to the end of having income and producing valuable outputs. If the project is not worth undertaking, then the jobs it might create would be more valuable going toward other projects.
- The profits of businesses that will be paid to build the project are part of the costs of a project because the profits are part of the payments that the public agency makes to these businesses.
- A BCA should consider a wide range of alternatives. Projects compete with other activities in space, in time, and for resources. Sometimes waiting for new information may be more desirable than undertaking a project immediately; waiting provides an option value. Searching among alternatives may identify ways to achieve greater net benefits.
- The discount rate can have a major effect on the outcome of a BCA when the benefits and costs are spread over time. Using a range of discount rates can provide a useful sensitivity analysis on a BCA. If changing the discount rate does not affect whether the benefits outweigh the costs, then a policy maker can have more confidence in the result of the BCA.

Methods to Compare Benefits and Costs

Now let's consider three different ways to compare benefits and costs: the net present value, the *benefit-cost ratio,* and the *internal rate of return.* While all indicate whether benefits exceed costs, each is properly used for slightly different purposes.

NET PRESENT VALUE AND BENEFIT-COST RATIO

BCA seeks to maximize net present value. The net present value (NPV) is the difference between the present value of benefits and the present value of costs. That is, if B is the present value of benefits, and C is the present value of costs, then $NPV = B - C$. If NPV is positive, benefits are bigger than costs. The reverse is true if the NPV is negative. Suppose that building a dam costs $10 million and has a present value of benefits of $20 million. Then NPV is $10 million.

The **benefit-cost ratio (BCR)** is the present value of benefits divided by the present value of costs: BCR = *B/C*. If the NPV is greater than zero, then the BCR is greater than one.

If we are evaluating only one project, NPV and BCR give the same information; the only difference is whether it is expressed as a ratio or a dollar amount. For instance, for the dam with $20 million of present value and $10 million of costs, the BCR is $20 million/$10 million, or 2. With either measure, the benefits exceed the costs.

Now let's consider some of the more complicated decisions that a government agency might face. In some cases, an agency may face a choice between two or more mutually exclusive projects. In that case, NPV is a better way to decide among projects than the BCR. In other cases, an agency may have to choose which of a list of proposed projects should be built with a fixed amount of money. In that situation, the BCR provides more useful information. To see why, let's continue with our dam example.

When there are two or more alternative projects for the same site, and the amount of money to be spent has not been fixed in advance, the efficiency criterion argues for the project that provides the greatest amount of net benefits. Ranking the projects by their NPVs identifies the most efficient among them. For instance, floods can be controlled by reinforcing levees or by building a dam. Once one project is done, there is no reason to do the other. Table 15.1 shows why this decision should be based on NPV rather than BCR.

Because the ultimate objective is to get the highest NPV, the greatest gain in benefits over costs, using the NPV criteria will do just that. In the example, the dam has a NPV of $15 million and the levee a NPV of only $10 million. This is the case even though the dam has a smaller BCR.

Another way to see this result is to compare the marginal benefits and marginal costs of changing from the levee to the dam. The marginal costs of changing from the levee to the dam are $10 million (costs of $20 million for the dam less costs of $10 million for the levee), but the marginal benefits of changing from the levee to the dam are $15 million (benefit of $35 million for the dam less benefits of $20 million for the levee). Because the marginal benefits are greater than the marginal costs, net benefits increase by building the dam.

TABLE 15.1   Comparing Net Present Value and Benefit-Cost Ratio.

This table shows the benefits and costs (in $ million) of a hypothetical project. The NPV of the dam exceeds the NPV of the levee, but the levee has a higher BCR.

	PROJECT BENEFITS	PROJECT COSTS	NPV	BCR
LEVEE	$20	$10	$10	2
DAM	$35	$20	$15	1.75

Under one set of circumstances, though, the BCR can maximize net benefits better than ranking NPV. It is where several projects are possible and are not mutually exclusive, but there is a fixed total amount of money available for all projects. That is, the objective is to get the most possible benefits for a limited cost. In Table 15.1, suppose that exactly $20 million is available to protect from floods and that many places need levees and dams. This $20 million can be used to build either two sets of levees or one dam. Levees have a BCR of 2, while the dam has a BCR of 1.75; ranking by BCR suggests building two levees. Two levees give a combined NPV of $20 million, larger than the NPV of $15 million for a dam. So building the projects with the highest BCRs until the money runs out provides the greatest NPV for all projects combined.

California issued bonds for improving water delivery. Cities and water districts submitted the benefits and costs of projects that they would like funded. The state chose the projects in the order of BCR until it exhausted its funds. To see that this solution maximizes NPV, consider removing a high BCR project from the list of projects accepted and replacing it with a lower BCR project. The costs stay the same because the total expenditure is fixed, but the sum of the benefits from the projects now falls. So, if the funds for projects are limited, ordering projects by BCR will provide the highest NPV from the collection of projects. If, on the other hand, funding is available but doing one project rules out doing another project, then NPV maximizes net benefits.

INTERNAL RATE OF RETURN

The final method of benefit-cost analysis is a comparison of rates of return. The **internal rate of return (IRR)** of a project is the interest rate that makes the project's NPV equal zero. Equivalently, the IRR is the interest rate that makes the present value of costs equal the present value of benefits. Internal rate of return is used by firms that seek to carry out projects that have positive NPV at the interest rate the firm must pay to obtain funds. The internal rate of return for a project is compared with the *hurdle rate*. The **hurdle rate** is the opportunity cost of funds to the firm. If the IRR exceeds the hurdle rate, the project has benefits greater than costs.

A public agency, like a private firm, sometimes borrows funds. This is commonly done by selling bonds—the proceeds from the sale provide the needed money—and paying interest to the bondholders. For a public agency, IRR can help determine whether it is a good idea to issue bonds for a particular project such as water treatment or flood control.

Let's see how to find the internal rate of return for a project that has up-front costs and benefits that occur later in time. The internal rate of return, IRR, is the interest rate that solves the equation:

$$\text{Benefits}/(1 + \text{IRR})^t - \text{Costs} = 0$$

The left-hand side of this equation is also the net present value of the project, if the NPV is evaluated using the IRR as the discount rate. Because costs in this example occur in the present, they are not discounted.

Let's look at a project with immediate costs of $10 million and benefits of $20 million in 10 years. We set up the equation for IRR as:

$$\$20 \text{ million} = \$10 \text{ million} * (1 + IRR)^{10}$$

Solving for IRR yields 7.18 percent. If the hurdle rate is 6 percent, the project clears the hurdle; if the hurdle rate is 8 percent, the project does not clear the hurdle, and its net present value is negative.

Now let's see how IRR relates to NPV. Consider two projects with immediate costs of $10 million. Project A produces benefits of $20 million in 10 years, while Project B produces benefits of $30 million in 20 years. Figure 15.1 shows how the NPV varies with the interest rate for both projects. Both projects are worth doing if the hurdle rate is 3 percent; only Project A is worth doing if the hurdle rate is 7 percent.

If we had to choose between the two projects, though, which criterion identifies the project with greater net benefits? The answer is NPV. Project A has the higher IRR; it surpasses more hurdle rates than Project B. However, if the discount rate is below 4.14 percent, Project B has a higher NPV. At or above a discount rate of 4.14 percent, project A has the higher NPV. The discount rate is a fixed value, determined either by the cost of borrowing for private companies or as a policy variable for government agencies. For a given discount rate, then, only one of these projects will produce more net benefits.

IRR, unlike NPV, does not resolve the choice between mutually exclusive projects. Further, IRR does not add information about which projects should go

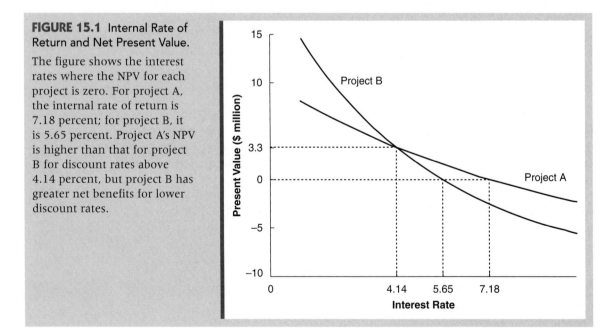

FIGURE 15.1 Internal Rate of Return and Net Present Value.

The figure shows the interest rates where the NPV for each project is zero. For project A, the internal rate of return is 7.18 percent; for project B, it is 5.65 percent. Project A's NPV is higher than that for project B for discount rates above 4.14 percent, but project B has greater net benefits for lower discount rates.

BOX 15.4

Distinguishing a Cost from a Benefit Under Three BCA Methods

The three BCA approaches provide different tools for deciding whether environmental damage is a cost or a benefit reduction. Earlier we discussed the situation where improving air quality involves taking a pollutant out of the air and disposing of it in a landfill. Should the damages from the landfill compounds be considered either a cost or a reduction in benefits? For the NPV or IRR calculations, there is no difference mathematically. If B is the benefit, C is the cost, and D is the landfill damage, then the NPV is either $(B - D) - C$, or $B - (C + D)$; in either case, the answer is the same. For IRR, the interest rate where $B = C + D$ should be the same as the interest rate where $B - D = C$.

This difference will affect the magnitude of a benefit-cost ratio, though: the BCR could be either $(B - D)/C$ or $B/(C + D)$. If $B - C - D > 0$ (that is, if the project has a positive NPV), then both ways of calculating the BCR will be greater than one, but the specific values will be different. For BCR to be used to rank projects, C must be a defined fixed sum, as it was in the case of the bond funds used to finance water saving projects. Otherwise, BCR can be manipulated by moving D into different places.

---

forward if there is a fixed amount of funds available. In that case, BCR should be used. IRR does, however, provide a bottom line: if a project does not clear a hurdle rate, it should not be built.

IN SUMMARY

- Net present value is the difference between the present value of benefits and the present value of costs. If the NPV is positive, a project increases net benefits. A benefit-cost ratio is the ratio of benefits to costs. A BCR greater than one signals that a project has positive net benefits. The internal rate of return for a project is an interest rate that makes the present value of the cost of a project equal to the present value of the benefits of the project. If the IRR exceeds the hurdle rate (the discount rate reflecting the next-best alternative investment possibility), the project has positive net benefits.
- To evaluate whether a single project is worth doing, analysts can use NPV, BCR, or IRR. In the case of two or more mutually exclusive projects, ranking projects by NPV is a better criterion than BCR or IRR because choosing a project with higher net benefits produces more net benefits. In the case where a number of projects can be built with a fixed sum of money, ranking projects by BCR and doing them until the money runs out gives the greatest net benefits. The IRR is not a good way of comparing the returns on two different projects.

Use of Benefit-Cost Analysis in Practice

The principle of benefit-cost analysis seems straightforward: a project should have positive net benefits if it is to be undertaken. If the benefits outweigh the costs, then society gains from the project. If the costs are larger, then the project creates a loss of social welfare. In practice, decision makers must realize that no BCA can provide perfect information, must exercise judgment in the face of conflicting analyses, must consider who will enjoy the benefits and who will bear the costs, and must confront the distributional issues of the effect of a policy.

BCA is not an exact science. The choice of discount rate is a matter of judgment; predictions about the future are inevitably uncertain; and data may be incomplete. No BCA can provide perfect information. If analyses of competing alternatives are conducted with consistent methodologies and data, though, then BCA can still give useful information about the relative desirability of the alternatives. At the least, the BCA can provide insight into what is known about a project and its expected consequences.

If the public policy process is open and democratic, then the process of review and discussion can reduce mistakes and biases in BCA. In the case of the Tellico Dam, the original BCA did not consider the value of the land to be drowned. As part of the interagency process, this flaw in the BCA was found and corrected. The debate over decreasing CO_2 emissions for cars saw evidence that the reduction could be achieved for as little as $1,000 per car or as much as $3,000 per car, magnitudes that affected the net benefits of the policy. A federal court heard the evidence and concluded that the regulation should be permitted. A BCA provides an accepted framework to organize evidence about the desirability of a project, but it does not guarantee that different parties to a regulatory matter will bring the same evidence. Ultimately, there must be a choice among the competing evidence and a decision.

Just because a project provides positive benefits under a BCA does not mean that everyone will be better off. Efficiency and Pareto improvement are not the same. Under a Pareto improvement, no one is made worse off, while all or some benefit.

Environmental policies are seldom Pareto improving, even if they are efficient: even if there are net benefits, someone is usually worse off. Opposition to many public policies that pass benefit-cost tests shows that some believe that these policies will make them worse off, even though the sum of the benefits exceeds the costs for the total population. The BCA criterion permits actions that are not Pareto improving. BCA is designed to measure the excess of benefits over costs, "to whomever they accrue." While a BCA can identify which groups receive benefits and which pay costs, the BCA itself takes no position on whether this distribution of costs and benefits is desirable. For instance, the oil refineries around Richmond, California, emit regulated amounts of pollutants into the air and water in order to produce gasoline and other fuels. The benefits of the fuel production exceed the costs of the emissions. The people who live near the refinery, though, disproportionately suffer the costs of pollution from refining. This kind of disproportionate impact, especially to lower-income and minority communities, has been termed an environmental injustice. Environmental agencies have begun evaluating environmental justice as part of the regulatory process to understand better who bears environmental burdens. This evaluation is not part of a BCA but adds a consideration of the distribution of costs in addition to the information provided by the BCA.

An additional factor in public projects are the transactions costs. Though some funding comes from user fees, money for public projects most commonly comes from taxes. Collecting tax money is expensive: Martin Feldstein estimated that, for the United States, the cost of raising federal funds, termed the deadweight loss of taxation, is 30 percent. Therefore, even projects that merely redistribute tax funds, like general assistance welfare programs, are likely to fail a BCA test. Many people nevertheless support these programs for their beneficial effects on distribution of income.

It is also important to note that many projects, such as the Tellico Dam or ethanol subsidies, receive strong support even if they fail a benefit-cost test. Some people will get benefits, though they come at the expense of others. BCA can point out the opportunity costs of the activity, but a BCA does not by itself determine which activities occur; policy makers can use their own criteria. While BCA can be a powerful consideration in the policy arena, rarely, if ever, is it the only factor in public decision making.

BOX 15.5

The BCA of Nuclear Power

Does construction of new nuclear power plants pass a BCA analysis? A team at MIT has done a BCA of nuclear power from the point of view of a private firm considering building a new power plant. The timing of the costs and benefits of a nuclear plant make a big difference as to the result.

Let's start with the present value of the costs. The present value is calculated in the year that the plant is completed, called year zero. Based on experience in the nuclear power industry, the MIT analysis assumes that it takes five years and costs, including accumulated interest, of $5.46 billion to build a 1,000-megawatt (MW) plant. The plant begins production in year one and lasts until decommissioning—taking the plant out of production—in year 40. Decommissioning costs $1.816 billion in year 40. With a discount rate of 10 percent, the present value of the decommissioning cost is $40 million $= 1.816$ billion$/(1 + 0.1)^{40}$. The after-tax fuel costs in year zero would be $40.17 million if the reactor were open in that year. The rate of inflation is 3 percent, and the real cost of fuel goes up each year at 0.5 percent, so the nominal price of fuel increases by $1.0352 = 1.03 * 1.005$ each year. Each year, then, the (constant) price of fuel gets multiplied by 1.0352 and is discounted by 1.10. To use the formula for the present value of n payments all the same, we need to make $1.0352/1.1$, the cost-inflation rate divided by the

(Continued)

BOX 15.5

(continued)

discount rate, into one factor that looks like an interest rate. The r that makes $1/(1 + r) = 1.0352/1.1$ is 6.26 percent. Now we use our formula to get the present value: fuel costs (40 years) $= \dfrac{1.0626^{40} - 1}{0.0626 * 1.0626} * 63.76$ billion $= \$0.58$ billion. Finally, there are some miscellaneous costs with a present value of about \$320 million. The present value of costs, then, is:

Construction	\$5.46 billion
Decommissioning	\$0.04 billion
Fuel	\$0.58 billion
Other	\$0.32 billion
Total	\$6.41 billion

Now let's look at the benefits. The plant has a capacity of 1,000 MW/year, but it is expected to run at 85 percent capacity. Thus, it will produce 1,000 MW/year * 0.85 = 850 MW. If each MW earned \$0.10/kilowatt-hour (KWH), the annual revenue would be \$0.10/KWH * 850,000 KWH/year * 365.25 days/year * 24 hours/day = \$745 million. Taxes are 37 percent of the revenue, so what is left for the operator of the plant is \$469 million. The inflation rate is again 3 percent, but there is no price increase for electricity beyond inflation. The after-inflation interest rate, then, is $1/(1 + r) = 1.03/1.1$, or $r = 6.8$ percent. The present value to year zero of after-tax revenues is:

$$\text{After-tax revenue} = \frac{1.068^{40} - 1}{0.068 * 1.068^{40}} * 469 \text{ billion} = \$6.41 \text{ billion}$$

The price for electricity that exactly pays for the plant, \$0.10/KWH, is called the levelized cost. It is the break-even point, where costs equal benefits. So it is a good business decision to build the plant if investors believe that the price of electricity will be at least \$0.10/kwh.

The authors performed the same exercise for a power plant fueled by natural gas and found a levelized cost of \$0.078/KWH. That is, a natural gas plant will break even at a lower price of electricity than a nuclear plant.

For North America, then, apart from considerations of safety and climate, natural gas is the more profitable fuel. Nuclear power poses safety risks, while natural gas is a fossil fuel that produces carbon dioxide. Neither of these external costs is included in the benefit-cost analysis, for the simple reason that is an analysis of a private investment decision.

Suppose that there is a cost for emitting carbon. At a cost of \$50/ton of CO_2, nuclear power and gas-fired plants both cost the same per KWH. So nuclear power becomes the more profitable method of providing electricity, apart from accidents, when carbon is priced above $50/tCO_2$.

Remaining unpriced in this analysis, but important to consider, is the risk of accident, the risk of nuclear proliferation, and the full cost of spent fuel disposal. The latter is accounted for by a government fee that may not be sufficient to pay the full cost.

The authors vary the parts of their formula that they believe might change a lot and see what that does to their answer; this is known as sensitivity analysis. Because the major cost of gas-fired plants is the gas, a 20 percent increase in gas prices would make nuclear more profitable. Nuclear, on the other hand, has construction as its major cost. If construction costs return to their 2003 levels and stay there, then nuclear becomes cheaper. A more cautious conclusion is that, given the uncertainty in energy prices, carbon prices, and capital costs, nuclear power is not very different in its costs over its expected plant life than natural gas.

From the point of view of private investors, the BCA does not rule out one or the other type of power. Public policies such as taxing carbon emissions or requiring insurance against nuclear accidents can influence these choices. While this BCA would benefit from inclusion of monetized environmental effects, it at least does acknowledge those benefits.

IN SUMMARY

- Benefit-cost analysis depends on data, which can be incomplete, and on predictions about the future, which cannot be made with certainty. The regulatory decision maker needs to exercise judgment to choose between competing analyses.
- Even if net benefits are positive, most projects have winners and losers. The distributional effects of the projects may determine their outcome at least as much as the BCA does.
- Collecting money for government projects through taxation is itself costly and can add substantially to the costs of a project.
- Projects with benefits less than costs often get enacted because decision makers want to provide benefits to a group, even if others bear greater costs.

BCA in the EPA

A number of agencies in the U.S. government play a role in environmental protection. The Department of the Interior has jurisdiction over the national parks and other public lands, as well as threatened and endangered species. The Department of Agriculture manages uses of the national forests and many wilderness areas, and it assists farmers in reducing soil erosion and protecting wetlands. The Department of Commerce supervises coastal zone management and oil spill prevention. The National Aeronautical and Space Administration conducts studies of climate change. Nevertheless, the government agency probably most associated with the environment is the U.S. Environmental Protection Agency (EPA).

The EPA has primary responsibility in the United States for controlling air and water pollution, pesticide use, toxic substances, and hazardous waste. The role of economic analysis in its activities is often confusing. In some cases, such as pesticide use, the EPA is required by law to conduct a benefit-cost analysis as part of its regulatory activities. In other cases, such as deciding on the appropriate level of ambient air quality, the EPA is required by law to consider only public health, not costs. Nevertheless, a number of presidents have issued executive orders that require the EPA to conduct benefit-cost analyses of its rules, even when the ultimate decision is not based on the results of that analysis.

The BCAs can serve a number of purposes. If the benefits outweigh the costs, it may be politically easier to enact a rule. In 2007, the President's Office of Management and Budget reported that the benefits of EPA regulations over a 10-year period were in the range of $98.5 *billion* to $483.6 *billion*, while the costs over that period were between $39.2 *million* and $46.2 *million*. In fact, if the marginal benefits are a good deal larger than the marginal costs, the BCA may point out that a proposed rule is not strong enough. Lower costs of environmental improvements imply that higher levels of environmental quality are socially desirable. By making the EPA and others more aware of the costs and benefits of the rules, BCA can encourage them to design regulations that provide more net benefits than alternatives.

Because many of EPA's rules deal with complex environmental settings, the BCAs are often very costly in time, money, and human effort. Some have suggested that the requirements for BCA are a form of "paralysis by analysis," a way of delaying rulemaking and the associated costs to polluters. To reduce the costs of the analysis, and to coordinate efforts across EPA's regulatory programs, the EPA has issued *Guidelines for Preparing Economic Analyses.* These guidelines include EPA policy on such issues as the discount rate to use, the baseline for comparison of alternatives, and sources of values for nonmarketed goods. The issues in this textbook are not just academic; as a look at the guidelines will demonstrate, they play a significant role in the public policy process.

CHAPTER SUMMARY

Here are the key lessons from this chapter:

- Benefit-cost analysis involves a comparison of the benefits and costs of a project over time. Three commonly used metrics for it are the net present value, benefit-cost ratio, and internal rate of return. Ranking projects by net present value provides the best way to compare mutually exclusive projects, while BCR is best for ranking priorities from a large set of potential projects. IRR uses a discount rate, called a hurdle rate, to determine whether a project is worth doing. Undertaking a project with a negative NPV or BCR less than one requires justification on grounds other than net benefits to society.

- A benefit-cost analysis requires estimating the benefits and costs of a project over time, discounting those benefits and costs with an appropriate discount rate, and considering an appropriate range of alternatives. While no BCA is likely to account fully for all benefits and costs, it should include as much information as possible, even if not measured in monetary terms, about these factors to avoid biased analysis.
- Benefits come from project outputs; costs come from project inputs. Estimates of benefits values are likely to include consumers' surplus and nonmarket valuation methods. Cost estimates require estimates of the labor, materials, and other expenses of undertaking the activity.
- Benefit-cost analysis is not an exact science. As with any prediction of the future, it likely has errors because of changes in circumstances and erroneous forecasts. An honest BCA will avoid systematic biasing of estimates to produce a desired outcome.
- BCA is an efficiency tool. While it can provide information on the distribution of benefits and costs, it takes no position on what a good or bad distribution is. Decisions on public projects almost always include considering who gains and who loses from an activity, not just the net benefits.

KEY TERMS

benefit-cost ratio (BCR) *(p. 366)*
environmental impact
  statement (EIS) *(p. 357)*

hurdle rate *(p. 367)*
internal rate of return
  (IRR) *(p. 367)*

NOTES

The 1936 Flood Control Act is Title 33 of the United States Codes. The declaration of policy is Section 701a. The TVA's information about the Tellico Dam can be found at http://www.tva.gov/sites/tellico.htm. The history of the snail darter is told by Chief Justice Warren Burger in *TVA v. Hill*, 437 United States Supreme Court Reports 153 (1978), at http://caselaw.lp.findlaw.com/scripts/getcase.pl?court=us&vol=437&invol=153#f7. The Endangered Species Act is Title 16, Chapter 5 of the United States Codes, beginning with Section 1531. The language quoted in this chapter is from Section 1536(2), found at http://www.law.cornell.edu/uscode/html/uscode16/usc_sec_16_00001536----000-.html. The reasoning of the Endangered Species Committee was reported in Margot Hornblower, "Panel Junks TVA Dam; Cites Cost, Not Snail Darter," *Washington Post* (January 24, 1979), p. A12. For a discussion of the effects of Tellico Dam 25 years after its completion, see Jack Neely, "Tellico Dam Revisited," *Metro Pulse*, 14, No. 50 (December 9, 2004).

    The National Environmental Policy Act is found in Title 42 of the United States Codes, beginning with section 4321. There is a thorough discussion in Daniel R. Mandelker, *NEPA Law and Litigation* (Thomson Reuters/West, 2nd ed., updated July 2008), accessed on October 2, 2008, at www.westlaw.com.

"The Benefits and Costs of Ethanol: An Evaluation of the Government's Analysis" is by Robert Hahn and Caroline Cecot, *Journal of Regulatory Economics* 35 (2009): 275–295.

Information about the Works Progress Administration during the Great Depression is at http://livingnewdeal.berkeley.edu.

"Tax Avoidance and the Deadweight Loss of the Income Tax" is by Martin Feldstein, *The Review of Economics and Statistics* 81(4) (1999): 674–680.

The discussion of the benefits and costs of nuclear power is based on Yangbo Du and John E. Parsons, *Update on the Cost of Nuclear Power*, Center for Energy and Environmental Policy Research, MIT (May 2009).

The costs and benefits of regulations by the EPA and other federal agencies can be reviewed on page 4 of the report at http://www.whitehouse.gov/omb/inforeg/2007_cb/2007_cb_final_report.pdf.

The EPA *Guidelines for Preparing Economic Analyses* can be found at http://yosemite.epa.gov/ee/epa/eed.nsf/webpages/Guidelines.html.

EXERCISES

1. You are analyzing various programs to reduce water pollution from food-processing plants. In consultation with your staff, you have developed the following matrix of effects (where PV = Present Value):

	STANDARD A	STANDARD B	STANDARD C	POLLUTION TAX
PV TOTAL COST ($ MILLION) (EXCLUDES TAX)	50	70	225	80
ANNUAL PLANT COSTS ($ MILLION) (INCLUDES TAX)	5	7	22.5	15
FOOD PROCESSING JOBS LOST	1,400	1,750	2,200	1,500
TONS OF BOD REDUCED (MILLIONS)	0.8	1.0	1.5	1.2
$/TON OF BOD REMOVED	$63	$70	$150	$67
PV TOTAL BENEFITS ($ MILLION)	75	115	150	130

(a) What is the present net value of each alternative? Which alternative has the highest net benefits?

(b) Calculate the benefit-cost ratio for each alternative. Which alternative has the highest benefit-cost ratio?

(c) Which alternative gives the "biggest bang for the buck"—that is, has the lowest cost per ton of pollution removed?

(d) Based on your answers to (a)–(c), which alternative is the most efficient?

(e) Which alternative do you expect (i) labor unions, (ii) environmentalists, and (iii) food processors to support, if one of these will be enacted? Why?

(f) Who, if anyone, do you expect to support the efficient alternative? Why?

2. The Environmental Protection Agency (EPA) is conducting a study on the efficiency of its expenditures on environmental protection programs. You have been hired to work on the analysis. You are presented with the following information:

   (i) The $10 million spent to reduce ozone air pollution is estimated to save one person from death and 500 from illness during episodes when ozone exposures are particularly high per year; once ozone levels are reduced, there are no lasting effects. Those affected are primarily those with lung problems, such as asthma, who can be of any age.

   (ii) The $20 million spent to reduce children's exposure to asbestos in schools is estimated to save 10 children per year from getting cancer when they are middle-aged. Of those 10 cancer cases, four are expected to result in death, and six in survival after treatment.

   (iii) The $5 million spent to reduce lead in household drinking water is estimated to save 10 people from death and 500 from other complications (learning and behavioral problems) per year from lead exposure. Of those affected, 70 percent are children.

   (iv) Spending $2 million to encourage people to wear seat belts is expected to save 50 people from death and 200 from other injuries per year. People of all ages are affected.

   The study is designed to determine if money should be reallocated among programs. *Getting increased funding is not an option.*

   (a) If the value of a human life is estimated at $3 million, and the value of avoiding a serious injury or illness as $50,000, which, if any, of these programs has positive net benefits?

   (b) If the criterion for funding a program is maximizing the lives saved per dollar spent, regardless of illnesses, which program best meets this criterion? Why?

   (c) If the criterion for funding is maximizing the number of healthy years that people will have per dollar spent, which program is likely to provide the greatest benefit? Why?

   (d) If a major criterion for public funding is that a public good is involved, in contrast to a risk over which individuals have control, which program is most likely to merit funding? Why?

   (e) Would you reallocate funding among these programs? If so, in what way? Why have you chosen the reallocation that you have? If you have not reallocated funding, why have you decided to stay with the current funding?

3. Redwood National Park in northern California contains the tallest known redwood tree, as well as a remnant of the coastal redwood ecotype that once dominated coastal California. It does not receive many visitors: it has been

estimated that no more than 5,000 visitors go each year, each spending an average of three days, for a total of 15,000 recreation visitor-days (RVDs) per year. When Redwood National Park was acquired by the federal government from private timber companies (who intended to manage it for redwood lumber), it cost approximately $600 million. That $600 million can be viewed as the present value of an annual stream of future costs.

(a) What is the annual cost of Redwood National Park if the interest rate is 10 percent?

(b) What is the opportunity cost of the establishment of the park, in terms of use of the land?

(c) Why is it useful to calculate the *annual* cost of the park in this example? (*Hint*: we are about to compare benefits to costs.)

(d) What would the benefits per RVD have to be if recreational use were the *only* justification for Redwood National Park, and if the net present value of the park were to be nonnegative? If recreation were the *only* justification for the park, do you think that purchasing the park was efficient?

(e) What other justifications might exist for establishing Redwood National Park?

(f) There are approximately 100 million households in the United States. How high would average annual household willingness to pay for Redwood National Park have to be to justify it?

4. What decision maker would use benefit-cost analysis as a decision rule? That is, identify a decision maker whose only interest is the total net benefits to society of an activity, not the distribution of those benefits. If you identify one (or more), explain why distribution is not important to them. If you cannot identify one, explain why benefit-cost analysis may not be a decision rule, and discuss whether a benefit-cost analysis might nevertheless be useful.

Nonrenewable Resource Management

Oil, minerals, coal, and many other resources exist in finite supply. Every time one of these resources is used, there is less of it for the future. Untapped sources are increasingly difficult to find, and the new finds are often much more costly to extract than the old finds. Because using the resource now decreases the quantity left to use later, these resources are called *nonrenewable*.

Energy resources and metals are classic examples of *nonrenewable resources*, but they are not the only examples. Some resources that initially appear to be renewable in fact cannot be reproduced in any time frame relevant to current generations. For instance, forests are generally renewable: if they are cut down, they can grow back. However, the ancient redwood forests of California are unique ecosystems that took hundreds, if not thousands, of years to develop, and they produce wood with qualities unavailable from younger redwoods. Once these trees are harvested, they are gone, unavailable for multiple generations to come. If using the resource is depleting it, how should it be used? How to manage the resource, how to decide how much to use, and how the market does and should allocate the resource are central questions in natural resource economics. This chapter will examine:

- The role of opportunity cost in allocating *nonrenewable resources* between the present and the future;
- Other factors that affect producers' decisions about extracting those resources;
- How producers and consumers adapt to the possibility of running out of a *nonrenewable resource*;
- The complex realities of *nonrenewable resource* theory when applied to oil.

Old-Growth Redwoods: A Nonrenewable Resource

Old-growth redwoods, found in the coastal mountains of California, are majestic trees. They can rise more than 100 meters (300 feet) into the air, with unique ecosystems in their upper reaches that have barely been explored. The oldest trees, many of which are preserved in parks, are more than 2,000 years old. If cut, reproducing these trees and their ecosystem would take the better part of a millennium.

Resources for which the supply cannot increase—for which there is a fixed amount that will only decrease with use—are **nonrenewable resources**. Old-growth redwood meets this definition because stands of these trees no longer increase their net volume, and reproducing them is effectively impossible. Petroleum meets the definition even better: it takes millions of years for decayed plant material to turn into oil. Mineral deposits are nonrenewable; some minerals go back to the origins of the planet. Once extracted, some nonrenewable resources, such as oil, are used up with their first use. Others, such as iron, may last many years and then be recycled. Ultimately, though, all these resources will be used up.

In the early years of redwood exploitation, most people were not very interested in preserving redwood forests. Redwoods were simply a commodity. Old-growth redwood was and continues to be prized for the beauty of its grain. The rich color and light weight of the wood make it highly valued for decorative housing material and furniture, far more than the wood from young redwoods.

As the old-growth redwood forests were reduced by logging, public appreciation of their beauty and ecological significance increased, and many old-growth redwoods were preserved in parks. This reduced the quantity left for harvest. With less old growth available for harvest, the price of the remaining old growth went up. Indeed, when the timber companies that owned the old-growth sold it for parks, they got a bonus: the price of all their remaining old-growth trees went up!

Now, few old-growth redwoods are available for harvest: they either have been cut down or are in the redwood parks. This chapter uses the story of old-growth redwoods, from relative abundance to depletion, to explore the economics of nonrenewable resource extraction.

Opportunity Cost and Resource Pricing

While producers of manufactured goods think about production costs and price when deciding how much to sell, producers of nonrenewable resources have to think about an additional factor: time. They must decide when to sell their product, knowing that eventually they will have no more to sell.

THE PRODUCER'S DECISION: THE ROLE OF INTEREST

How does a nonrenewable resource producer maximize profits? To answer that question, let's look at his choices. He has a *stock* of the resource. The **stock** at a given time is the total quantity of the resource at that time. One choice is to sell the resource, which would give him a sum of money. He could then earn interest by putting the money in a bank. Another choice is to keep the resource. He would then have the option of selling the resource at a future time, but he would give up having money now. A third choice is to sell some of the resource now and save some of it for the future. How will he decide?

A producer wants the option that maximizes the present value of his profits. Let's look at his choices in the simplest setting: he knows the stock of the resource, the interest rate, and the current market price for the resource. How much he should sell now depends on what the price will be in future years. There are three possibilities: price might increase at a rate lower than the rate of interest, price might increase a rate greater than the rate of interest, or price might increase at the rate of interest. We will work through these three possibilities.

Our model begins with a resource that is sold before it is extracted, such as old-growth redwoods, which are sold while still in the ground, "standing up." Because the resource is sold before extraction, the producer bears no extraction costs.

If the producer sells some of the resource now, he will get the market price P_0 (where the 0 indicates price at the current time) for each unit he sells. If he waits until next year to sell, he will get P_1, the price one year in the future. With r as the interest rate, the present value of next year's price is $P_1/(1 + r)$. If $P_0 > P_1/(1 + r)$, then the price now is higher than the present value of price next year; the producer is better off selling the resource now and putting the money in the bank. On the other hand, if $P_0 < P_1/(1 + r)$, then he is better off waiting to sell the resource because the price he could get for the resource is rising faster than the interest that he could earn. If $P_1 = P_0(1 + r)$, the present value of price in both periods is the same, and he will be indifferent between selling the resource now and selling it next year. Thus, the only way a producer will sell some of the resource now and some of the resource next year is if the price goes up at the rate of interest.

Another way to describe the same decision is as a problem of opportunity cost. Selling in the next period has gain of P_1 per unit but comes at an opportunity cost of $(1 + r)P_0$, the value of selling now and banking the proceeds. The producer only sells in the next period if the next period price exceeds or is equal to the opportunity cost.

Now let's look at the producer's decision over many time periods. The producer only extracts in those periods where the present value price is highest because he can choose when to harvest. The per-unit value of the resource when sold at the time that gives the highest present value price is the called the **user cost** because it represents the opportunity cost of selling the resource at any other time. The producer extracts only in the periods in which the present value price is equal to the user cost. So a producer who extracts in every period must face a present value price that is always equal to the user cost. The price of the resource at time t, P_t, is called the **rental rate**. Both user cost and rental rate refer to the price of the resource before extraction.

What does this mean for prices over time? If the producer sells some now and some next year, the price next year is $P_1 = P_0(1 + r)$. The producer faces the same decision looking ahead to the second year. At the end of that second year, then, the price is $P_2 = P_1(1 + r) = P_0(1 + r)(1 + r) = P_0(1 + r)^2$. Because this decision will be the same every year, then, after t years, the price of a resource must be $P_t = (1 + r)^t P_0$. A series of prices over time is called the **price path**.

The rule that prices must increase at the rate of interest if producers are to sell some of the resource in every time period is called the **Hotelling rule**. It was discovered by Harold Hotelling, the same economist who originated the travel cost method. Hotelling's observation is of great importance in allocating a resource between present and future generations.

The dots in Figure 16.1 show the actual prices for old-growth redwood for the years 1953–1983. Because old growth is sold standing up, the owners have no extraction costs. Let's set 1953 as year zero. To find the "price goes up at the rate of interest" function, $P_t = (1 + r)^t P_0$, that fits these price data, we have to find the values of r and P_0. Regression analysis by Peter Berck and William Bentley provides the values of r and P_0 that give a curve that most closely fits the price data: $r = 13.1$ percent, and the starting price, P_0, is \$14.20. The solid line in Figure 16.1, then, graphs the function $P_t = (1 + 0.131)^t P_0$.

FIGURE 16.1 Redwood Prices Over Time.

The dots indicate the actual prices for old-growth redwood in the years 1953 (year 0) to 1983. The solid line graphs the "price goes up at the rate of interest" function, $P_t = (1 + r)^t P_0$, with the values of the interest rate, r, and the starting price, P_0, that best fit these price data. These values are $r = 13.1$ percent and $P_0 = \$14.20$. All values are current dollars, so 13.1 percent is the nominal interest rate. Thus, the solid line in this diagram is a graph of the function $P_t = (1 + 0.131)^t P_0$.

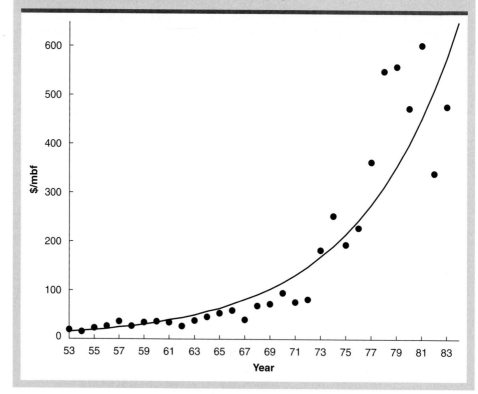

BOX 16.1

Headwaters Forest Reserve

The Headwaters Forest in Northern California was the scene of an intense public debate over preserving an old-growth redwood ecosystem that included habitat for a rare seabird, the marbled murrelet. The forest was owned by Pacific Lumber Company, which was bought by Maxxam Corporation in 1986. Pacific Lumber then more than doubled the rate of harvesting to pay off money that Maxxam had borrowed to finance the purchase of the lumber company. The higher rate of harvesting, in addition to being necessary to pay the interest charged on the borrowed money, was typical for other lumber companies. However, because Headwaters was one of the last privately held stands of old growth, these events provoked a bitter conflict between the logging industry and environmentalists. Loggers feared for their jobs if timber harvesting slowed, while members of a group calling itself "Earth First" chained themselves to trees to stop their harvest.

In 1999, Pacific Lumber sold the 10,000-acre Headwaters Forest to the public for $480 million in state and federal funds; the Headwaters Forest Reserve is now managed by the U.S. Bureau of Land Management. The hefty price tag is a signal of the value to legislators of protecting the environmental values of this area. The deal included a habitat conservation plan that allowed Pacific Lumber to log its remaining 200,000 acres, subject to restrictions designed to protect wildlife and streams. In 2007, Pacific Lumber declared bankruptcy, claiming that additional government restrictions on harvesting made the business unprofitable; in 2008, the bankruptcy court approved the sale of the remaining timber land to the Mendocino Redwood Company. Satisfying the conditions of the Hotelling rule may lead to profit maximization, but it may not satisfy social goals for environmental protection.

Unlike makers of manufactured goods, then, producers will not be willing to charge the same price every year because there is an additional opportunity cost associated with the resource: selling a unit now means that it will not be possible to sell that unit in the future. The price path resulting from the Hotelling rule makes producers indifferent between selling now and in the future. The next step in determining the amount that is actually sold requires consumers, who decide how much of the resource to buy.

THE CONSUMER'S DECISION AND QUANTITY SUPPLIED IN EQUILIBRIUM

As with all other goods, consumers have demand curves for nonrenewable resources that indicate how much they will buy at different prices. Also, as with all other goods, a market equilibrium requires finding a price–quantity combination that brings together quantity supplied and quantity demanded. The Hotelling rule makes producers willing to sell any amount in a year, as long as price increases with the interest rate each year. The specific price–quantity combination, then, is determined by consumer demand.

Figure 16.2 shows a linear approximation of the actual demand for old-growth redwood. At the highest price on the demand curve, $650 per thousand board foot (mbf), the quantity demanded is zero. This is the **choke price,** the price at which the quantity demanded is zero. When the price reaches the choke price, demand is "choked off," and consumers will stop buying old-growth redwood and use other decorative materials instead.

In a market equilibrium, the quantity supplied is equal to the quantity demanded. This must hold true in each period of time. Producers will sell in every time period only if the price goes up at the rate of interest; once the price in year zero is set, future prices are determined by that first price: $P_t = (1 + 0.131)^t P_0$. Because the Hotelling rule maximizes profits for producers, consumers determine the quantity by responding to price. As the price increases every year, consumers buy less every year.

Figure 16.3 shows this interaction. The left-hand part of the figure is the line from Figure 16.1 that shows price going up at the rate of interest. For instance, the dashed lines show that the price in 1961 was $38/mbf, and the price in 1980 was $400/mbf. The right-hand part of the figure is the demand curve from Figure 16.2. Continuing to follow the dotted line from $38 to the demand curve, and then down to 1.39 billion, shows that, in 1961, the price was $38 and the quantity demanded was 1.39 billion board feet (bbf). In 1980, the price was $400/mbf and the quantity demanded was 0.57 bbf. This combined figure shows how to find the quantity for each year. This relationship between quantity and time is the **extraction path.**

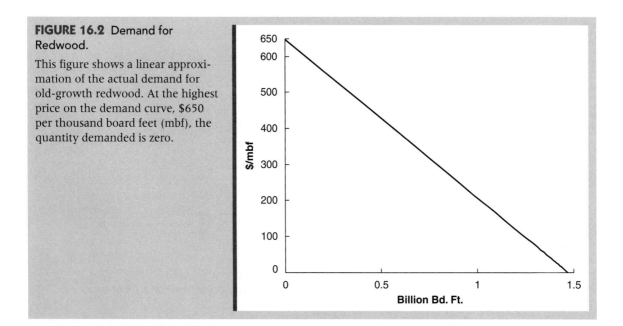

FIGURE 16.2 Demand for Redwood.

This figure shows a linear approximation of the actual demand for old-growth redwood. At the highest price on the demand curve, $650 per thousand board feet (mbf), the quantity demanded is zero.

FIGURE 16.3 Finding Redwood Quantity Used in Each Year: The Extraction Path.

The left-hand part of this figure is the line from Figure 16.1 that shows price going up at the rate of interest. For instance, the price in 1961 was $38/mbf, and the price in 1980 was $400/mbf. The right-hand part of the figure is the demand curve from Figure 16.2. Following the dotted line from 1961 to $38/mbf on the price path, over to the demand curve, and down to 1.39 billion, shows that, in 1961, when the price was $38/mbf, the quantity demanded was 1.39 billion board feet (bbf). In 1980, the price was $400/mbf and the quantity demanded was 0.57 bbf. This combined figure shows how to find the quantity for each year.

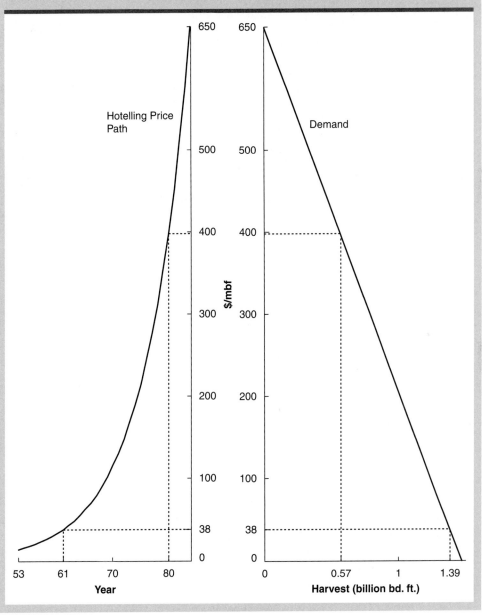

Notice that the quantity consumed decreases each year. Unlike makers of manufactured goods, whose cost of production does not necessarily change every year, producers of nonrenewable resources require price increases; as a result, consumers buy less each year. As the resource gets used up, the higher price encourages conservation: people are more sparing in their use of an increasingly scarce and expensive resource.

Notice that, once there is an initial price P_0, the prices and quantities for future years are determined by the interaction of producers' and consumers' behaviors. The final step, then, is to understand what value P_0 should take.

USING UP ALL OF THE STOCK OVER TIME

As long as people find a good desirable, they will want to use all of it. Producers will want to sell all of the resource because it provides no economic value to them unless it is sold. So the Hotelling theory predicts that the entire stock eventually will be used up.

The key to finding the initial price starts with the expectation that the stock of the resource eventually will be used up. The initial price determines the price path, and the price path determines how much of the resource is bought every year. Because all of the stock eventually will be used, then the total stock of the resource must equal the sum of the quantities sold in each year. Let's call the total stock of the resource X, the time at which it will be used up T, and the quantity produced in year t Q_t. The total stock of the resource, X, must equal the sum of the quantities sold every year through T:

$$X = Q_0 + Q_1 + \ldots + Q_T$$

Let's call demand D. Then, the quantity that consumers will buy at price P_t depends on price, or $D = D(P_t)$. Because the quantity sold equals the quantity purchased in any year, then $Q_t = D(P_t)$. Making this substitution in our equation for the exhaustion of the resource produces:

$$X = D(P_0) + D(P_1) + \ldots + D(P_T)$$

Because price goes up at the rate of interest, all the prices in fact are simple functions of the first price, $P_t = (1 + r)^t P_0$.

$$X = D(P_0) + D[(1 + r)P_0] + \ldots + D[(1 + r)^t P_0] + \ldots + D[(1 + r)^T P_0]$$

This equation shows that the total amount produced is equal to the stock. It is the sum of the quantities demanded at all the times until the resource is exhausted at time T. If we know the demand curve, we know everything in this equation but the initial price, P_0. Getting to P_0 involves one more behavior: the producers will not want to run out until consumer demand is choked off. Otherwise, they could continue to profit from keeping the resource another year.

Let's see how this works in our redwood example. Suppose that a producer has the world's last board-foot of old-growth redwood. The demand curve indicates that, if the price gets as high as $650/mbf, nobody will want to buy it; the quantity will be zero. The producer will sell that last board-foot for just under $650/mbf. Because the price had to rise at 13.1 percent per year, the previous year's price had to be $650/1.131 = $575/mbf. The demand curve indicates that, at that price, consumers would buy about 0.17 bbf, for a total in those two years of about 0.17 bbf. The previous year, price would be $575/1.131 = $508/mbf, resulting in consumer purchase of 0.32 bbf, for a total of 0.49 bbf sold in those three years.

The producer can continue to calculate backward in this way, finding the price in the previous year and the quantity sold that year, and adding up those quantities, until he reaches the total amount of old-growth redwood. In this example, there is a total of about 34.6 billion board feet of old-growth redwood in 1953. By continuing to work backward with the demand curve and the price path, it is possible to estimate that, on this price path, it will take until about 1984 to use up all the redwood. The initial price to make the path work smoothly is about $14.20/mbf.

Getting the right initial price is critical for making sure that the producer runs out of the resource only when people no longer want to buy it. If P_0 is very low, then the quantity demanded in each period would be very high, and the sum of the quantities would be greater than the available stock, X, before price gets to the choke price. If P_0 is very high, then the quantity demanded in each period would be very low, and there would be stock left over when people no longer want to buy the good. There is only one P_0 that makes the total quantity demanded over time for the resource equal the initial stock while the price path satisfies producers.

We can show this equilibrium by adding two more graphs to Figure 16.3. Let's start by showing the two new graphs by themselves, and then we will combine all four graphs. Figure 16.4 shows billions of board feet of old-growth redwood sold. This figure has two pieces. The right-hand part has quantity on both axes and a 45° line. It does nothing but translate numbers on the horizontal axis to the same number on the vertical axis. The left-hand graph has quantity (increasing downward) on the vertical axis and the year on the horizontal axis. It shows how much redwood was purchased in each year: the extraction path. For 1961, for instance, the quantity consumed was 1.39 billion; in 1980, quantity was down to 0.57 billion.

Now we put the four quadrants together in Figure 16.5 on page 389 and read them in a clockwise direction. In the top-left box, price is on the vertical axis, and the year increases from left to right. Time zero is 1953, t is the number of years since 1953, and r is 13.1 percent. The upward-sloping curve shows the price going up at the rate of interest, $P_t = (1 + r)^t P_0$. The upper right-hand quadrant, where the vertical axis is price, P, and the horizontal axis is quantity, Q_t, shows the demand curve. The lower-right box translates quantity from the horizontal to the vertical axis. The lower-left box shows the quantity sold in each year, the extraction path.

Let's follow the dotted lines for our two example years to see the quantity bought and sold in each year. For 1961, start in the upper left-hand quadrant and trace the horizontal dotted line up to the $P_t = (1 + r)^t P_0$ curve and then over to the vertical axis to see that, in 1961, the price for a thousand board feet of redwood

FIGURE 16.4 Drawing the Curve for Quantity Consumed Per Year.

This figure shows sales of old-growth redwood. The right-hand part has quantity on both axes and translates numbers on the horizontal axis to the same number on the vertical axis. On the horizontal axis, the quantity of redwood sold increases to the right; on the vertical axis, quantity increases downward. The left-hand graph has quantity (increasing downward) on the vertical axis and time on the horizontal axis. It shows how much redwood was purchased in each year. In 1961, the quantity consumed was 1.39 billion. In 1980, the quantity consumed was 0.57 billion.

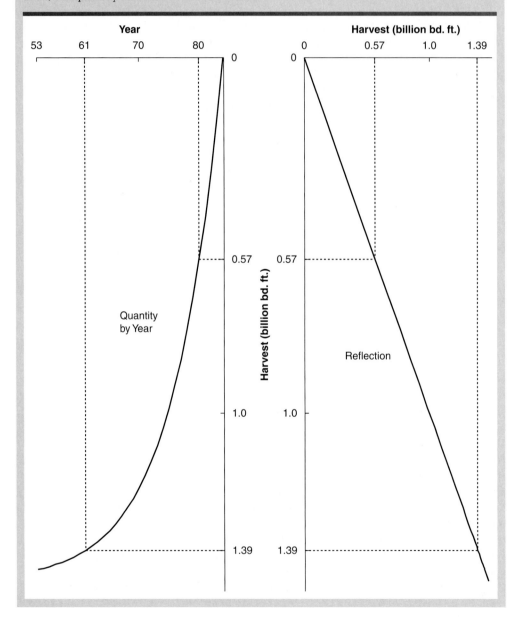

FIGURE 16.5 Quantity and Year for Old-Growth Redwood: The Complete Diagram.

We read these diagrams in a clockwise direction. For example, for 1961, follow the dotted line up to the price path at $38/mbf, over to demand at 1.39 billion bf, down and over in the third quadrant to 1.39 billion bf, and finally over to the point on the extraction path, which shows that 1.39 billion bf were harvested in 1961.

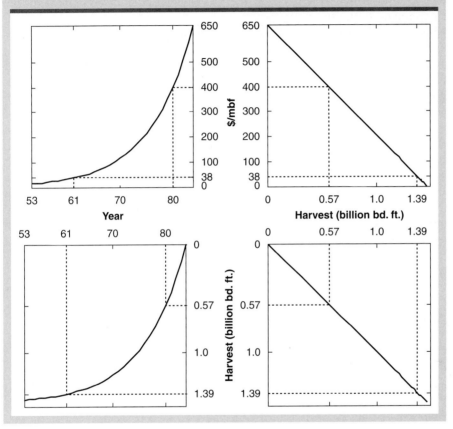

was $38/mbf. Now follow the same line to the demand curve in the upper right quadrant; there, follow the vertical dotted line down to the quantity of 1.39 billion board feet. The third quadrant transfers that quantity to the vertical axis in the third quadrant. The last step is to connect the quantity sold, 1.39 bbf, to year 1961 in the lower left quadrant.

Now let's repeat the process for 1980, using the set of dotted lines. In the top left quadrant, the price of redwood in 1980 was $400/mbf. In the top right quadrant, the quantity of redwood produced in 1980 was 0.57 billion board feet. The bottom right quadrant transfers the quantity to the vertical axis. The bottom left quadrant shows the resulting point (1980, 0.57 billion).

As the diagram is drawn, the price in 1984 is \$650/mbf and its quantity is zero. So the last year of old-growth redwood production is 1984, 31 years after we began counting, at $T = 31$. In algebra, choke price $= (1 + r)^T P_0$. As the initial price increased at an interest rate of 13.1 percent, the price finally reached a level at which demand was choked off. As the model predicts, most of the stock of old-growth redwood was in fact used up by the 1980s. That is one reason that the remaining stand in Headwaters Forest was so valuable to its owners and so prized by environmental activists.

Now that we have constructed the extraction path, we can add up the quantities for each year and check to see if they add up to the stock available. For this purpose, we have enlarged the lower left quadrant as Figure 16.6. The shaded area between the curve and the horizontal axis in Figure 16.6 represents the total volume consumed. For each shaded rectangle, the height of the rectangle is equal to the quantity of redwood produced for one year, and the width of the rectangle is equal to one year. The sum of the areas of all these rectangles is the total amount of old-growth redwood used between 1953 and 1983. The amount used over those years sums to the amount of the original stock available for harvest, about 34.6 billion board feet.

What would happen if there was a different initial price? In these diagrams, the starting price in 1953 was \$14.20/mbf. If P_0 were lower than \$14.20/mbf, the prices in each year would be lower. Because lower prices lead to a higher quantity demanded, the quantities produced each year would be higher. If the quantities produced each year were higher, consumers would demand more of this finite resource each year. If they demanded more in every time period, they would run out sooner than they would if $P_0 = \$14.20$, and before the price hit \$650/mbf. Because consumers have a

FIGURE 16.6 Total Quantity of Redwood Used.

The shaded area between the curve and the horizontal axis represents the total volume consumed. For each shaded rectangle, the height is the quantity of redwood produced for one year, and the width of the rectangle is one year. The sum of the areas of all these rectangles is the total amount of old-growth redwood used between 1953 and 1983. It sums to the amount of the original stock, about 34.6 billion board feet.

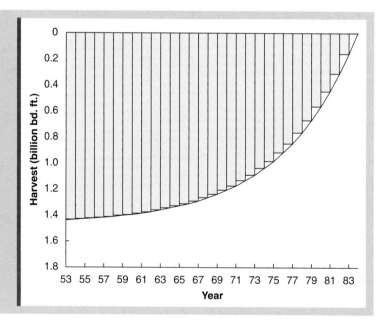

positive demand at prices less than the choke price, quantity demanded would be positive, while quantity supplied would be zero: quantity supplied would not equal quantity demanded, and the market would not be in equilibrium.

The argument is similar for a higher initial price. If the initial price were higher than $14.20/mbf, then there would be leftover redwood when price reached the choke price. Producers would still want to sell the wood, but consumers would not buy it. Again, this would not be in equilibrium.

Our four-quadrant diagram illustrates all the rules for equilibrium for a nonrenewable resource:

1. Prices go up at the rate of interest, in the upper left quadrant.
2. The quantity produced is equal to the quantity demanded, in the upper right quadrant.
3. The sum of the quantities demanded is the amount of the original stock, in the bottom left quadrant.
4. The last harvest date, T, is the date when demand is zero, in the combination of the left quadrants.

PROFIT

Have you noticed that, despite the zero harvest costs associated with redwoods, there is a positive price? There is a gap between price and marginal cost, the user cost, which represents the opportunity cost of selling the resource now instead of holding it for the future. As a result, the resource owner earns profits.

Profit arises because the resource is in finite supply. Because the redwoods are nonrenewable, if their owner set price equal to (zero) marginal cost, people would use up the resource very quickly, and it would not be available for the future. The user cost, which is pure profit to the owner, serves the important role of providing him with an incentive to save the redwoods for future use.

Many people have gotten rich by claiming nonrenewable resources before other people. Gold and land are but two of the resources that people have rushed to claim in order to get rich quick. Even if getting the resource is free, it will have a positive price, and earn profit, that will serve the function of rationing use over time.

IN SUMMARY

- The Hotelling model of a nonrenewable resource involves three factors: getting producers to provide some of the resource both in the present and future; matching the quantity produced in each period with consumer demand; and using up all of the resource only at the time that people will no longer buy it.
- The price of a nonrenewable resource should go up at the rate of interest because the interest rate represents the opportunity cost of holding the resource. This condition makes a producer indifferent between selling the resource now and selling it in the future. Otherwise, a producer would either sell it all now (if he would make more money by investing the revenues in a bank account)

or sell none now (if the price is rising so fast that he would prefer to save it to sell in the future).

- As price goes up, the quantity that consumers want of the good decreases: the price provides an incentive for conservation of the increasingly scarce resource.
- If the market is in equilibrium, producers will run out of the resource at the same time that the price gets high enough that consumers will no longer buy the resource.
- Owners of nonrenewable resources earn profits. If the price equals the marginal cost of zero, the resource will be depleted while people still want to buy it. The profit provides an incentive to allocate the resource over time, so that it is depleted only when people are no longer willing to pay for it.

Adjustments to the Hotelling Model

Figure 16.1 shows the prices of redwood from 1953 to 1983. The dots are the actual prices observed, and the solid line shows the closest fitting exponential curve to these data points. The Hotelling theory argues that this price path should follow a smooth exponential increase. In the picture, however, the dots are close to the line but not actually on it. The data do not exactly fit the prediction. Why not?

The Hotelling model presented so far is a simplification. It focuses on the role of the interest rate in the price path for a nonrenewable resource, without considering other factors that influence the price. Indeed, even the interest rate may not be a constant. Let's look at the different factors that combine to influence the price path of nonrenewable resources.

THE INTEREST RATE

Interest rates fluctuate due to a variety of factors, including the productivity of resource use in the economy, inflation, money supply, and people's attitudes toward saving for the future. Even if we remove inflation from the problem by using a real interest rate, interest rates change. How do these changes affect nonrenewable resource extraction?

The interest rate reflects the opportunity cost of not extracting the resource. If the resource were extracted, the profit could be put in the bank and earn interest. Just as changing the discount rate has a major effect on the present value of a future amount, changing the interest rate affects the opportunity cost of not extracting the resource. The interest rate will also have other effects on a natural resource market because of its effect on demand. For simplicity, though, let's use Figure 16.7 to trace the effects of a change in interest rate with demand unchanging.

Figure 16.7 has the starting price at its original value of \$14.20/mbf with the addition of a line for an interest rate of 20 percent. The price path in the top left quadrant shows price going up at the rate of interest. Because price increases faster

FIGURE 16.7 Higher Interest Rate with Original Initial Price.

The starting price is at its original value of $14.20/mbf. In the top left quadrant, the interest rate is 13.1 percent for the solid line and 20 percent for the dashed line. Because the new interest rate is higher, the dashed price path is everywhere above the solid price path. Following the dotted lines for 1970 around the diagram shows the higher price path translated into the lower quantity path in the bottom left quadrant. Because quantity is lower in every year, stock is not exhausted.

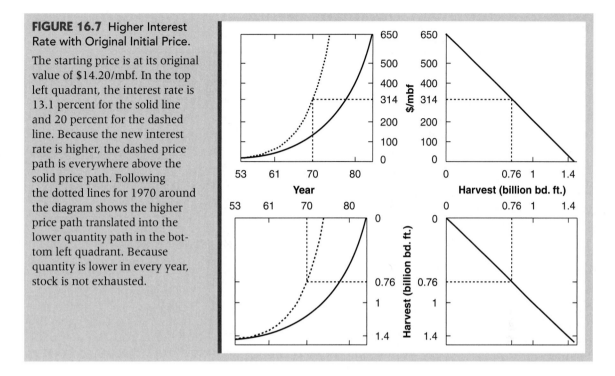

at 20 percent interest, the price in all time periods after the first period is higher with the new interest rate (the higher, dashed line) than with the old one.

The top right quadrant shows the demand curve that goes with each year. Because the price is higher, the quantity must be lower. The bottom two quadrants develop the new curve, showing quantity used by year, the dashed line in the bottom left quadrant. Because price is higher in every year, the quantity consumed is lower every year, and the dashed line shows less resource use each year at the higher interest rate.

The area inside the curve showing quantity by year is the sum of all the quantities that consumers buy. In the original example, the total quantity used was equal to the total stock that was available at the beginning. Because the new dashed quantity-per-year curve reflects a lower quantity at every point, less of the resource is used in total. With a higher interest rate and the same initial price, the resource is not used up. Because producers still have stock they would like to sell when price chokes off demand, the market is not in equilibrium.

Suppose, instead, that the initial price is lower. If so, price will be lower every year, and quantity demanded will be higher every year, than with the initial price of $14.20/mbf. In Figure 16.8, the solid line reflects the original price of $14.20/mbf and interest rate of 13.1 percent, and the dashed line is based on a new initial price of $4/mbf and the new interest rate of 20 percent. Now the new dashed price path, in the top left quadrant, starts below the original path. With the higher

FIGURE 16.8 Equilibrium with a Lower Price and a Higher Interest Rate.

The solid line reflects the original price of $14.20/mbf and interest rate of 13.1 percent, and the dashed line is based on a new initial price of $4/mbf and the new interest rate of 20 percent. Following the dotted lines around the diagram, the lower left quadrant shows the new and old quantity paths. The dashed year-quantity curve is initially outside the original curve and then inside the original curve after 1978. The area between the year-quantity curves and the axis is the same for both original and new curves, so they both exactly exhaust the resource.

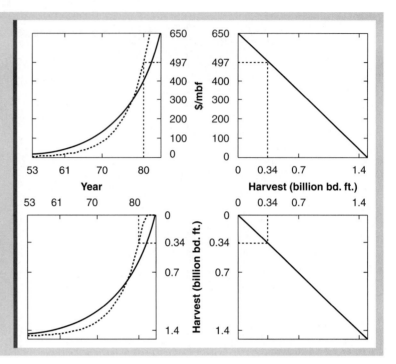

interest rate and lower initial price, the price grows faster because it has a higher interest rate. In about 1978, it crosses above the old path and is subsequently higher than the old price path.

Next, let's look at the relationship between price and quantity. Before 1978, the price is lower than in the original example, so the quantity consumed is higher. In 1978, because the price is the same as in the original example, the quantity consumed is also the same. After 1978, the higher price with the higher interest rate leads to a lower quantity consumed. This is shown in the bottom left quadrant, where the year-quantity curve is outside the original curve for 1953 and inside the original curve after 1978.

In Figure 16.8, both combinations exactly exhaust the resource. The combination of higher interest rate and lower starting price, however, exhausts the resource sooner. Under the original scenario, price reaches the choke price and consumption goes to zero in 1984. With the new combination, the resource is exhausted in 1980. Still, it is an equilibrium in which quantity demanded equals the stock, and the resource is used up only when people are no longer willing to pay for it.

Why does a higher interest rate make extraction happen faster? The higher interest rate increases the opportunity cost that the resource owner faces; the bank is offering a higher return on the money he can earn if he sells the resource now. This higher return gives him an incentive to sell the resource faster. Because a higher interest rate indicates less weight on future values than on present values, the equilibrium with a higher interest rate gives more of the resource to present consumers, who are less concerned with ensuring that the resource is available in the future. At the extreme of an infinite interest rate, people will use up the resource instantly and leave none for the future. A high interest rate makes holding onto the resource unappealing compared with having the profits from it immediately.

A lower interest rate, which does not discount the future as much, leads to flatter price and consumption paths. As people put similar weight on the future as they do on the present, they are more inclined to ensure that some of the resource is available for the future. At the extreme of a 0 percent discount rate, with a constant demand curve, producers will sell the same amount every period to consumers, who in turn want the same amount every period.

SHIFTING CONSUMER DEMAND

The demand curve for nonrenewable resources can shift over time. In the case of old-growth redwood, the demand curve shifted up during the twentieth century as a result of increased income in the United States: people could afford to spend more to decorate their homes. In the case of oil, another nonrenewable resource, the upward shift of the demand curve is in part a result of increased income in India and China that has led to more people having cars in recent years.

The demand curve for a resource could shift down as well, due to increased availability of substitutes or improved technologies. For instance, if a substitute for oil, such as ethanol, becomes cheaper, or if people shift to more fuel-efficient cars, the demand curve for oil will shift down. How do changes in demand affect the extraction path of nonrenewable resources?

Suppose that there was an unexpected increase in the demand for redwood in 1965; perhaps Americans' income grew faster than forecasted, and the demand curve for redwood shifted up. Let's compare the extraction path with and without the demand shift. With the initial price, P_0, and the demand shift, a larger quantity would be demanded at every time. Because the quantity demanded in every time period would be larger, the total quantity demanded over all the time periods, until price choked off demand, would be greater than the stock! For the total quantity consumed to equal the stock, the quantity used each year has to be lower. To make this happen, the price in 1965 and subsequent years would have to be higher. Price would jump at the time of the unexpected demand shift. Once the demand shift takes place, though, the price would once again go up at the rate of interest, though from a higher starting place. Producers would still expect price to increase with the interest rate, to keep them indifferent between extracting now and later. The increased price would compensate for the upward shift in demand, and the total quantity demanded over time would again equal the resource stock.

We can reverse this logic in the event of an unexpected decrease in the demand for redwood, perhaps due to a decrease in the price of a substitute building material. Then the demand curve for redwood would shift down. In that case, a smaller quantity would be consumed each year. Because the quantity in every time period would be smaller, the stock would not be used up when the price rose to the choke price. Now, for the total quantity to equal the stock, consumers must be persuaded to increase the quantity used each year. To make this happen, the price in 1965 and subsequent years would have to be lower. Just as in the case of an upward shift in demand, once the price drops in 1965, the price would again go up at the rate of interest. Just as in the case of an upward shift in demand, the change in price would compensate for the shift in demand, and total quantity demanded would equal the resource stock.

What would happen if, in 1953, it were known that demand would shift in 1965? Producers, aware of the change, could start to prepare for it right away: for an increase in demand, for instance, they could start hoarding the resource, so that they would have more available when the price increased; for a decrease in demand, they could increase their sales, so that they would not have more around than consumers would want to buy. Once this initial change took place, though, the producers would expect price to increase smoothly with the interest rate. An anticipated future change in demand, then, leads to a change in present behavior. Because the present and the future are all part of the equilibrium for the redwood market, changes in one period immediately affect all other periods, both in price and quantity. This immediate feedback between the present and the future leads to the resource being available when people want it and to the resource running out only when demand is choked off.

EXTRACTION COSTS

Most nonrenewable resources are extracted—taken from the earth—before they are sold. Oil producers must pump the oil out of the ground before they can sell it. Copper producers must mine and smelt copper before they can sell ingots (bars of metal). Extraction costs are production costs. What is the price path of a product, like ingots or ready-to-ship oil, that is made from a nonrenewable resource?

To see how the product price behaves, think of two firms. One firm owns the redwood grove and sells it at a price of $R/mbf. The other firm buys the redwoods for $R/mbf and incurs harvest costs $MC/mbf. The owner-firm has no production costs, and the price of the resource in the ground goes up at the rate of interest. The firm that harvests the resource and brings it to market for $P/mbf has two costs: the cost of buying the resource and the costs of harvesting and bringing it to market. The current (not present value) cost of buying the resource in the ground is the rental rate. Therefore, the harvester's marginal costs are the sum of the marginal cost of harvesting, MC, and the cost of buying the resource in the ground, R, for a total marginal cost of $MC + R$. As a profit-maximizing firm, the harvester will operate where price equals his marginal costs, so $P = MC + R$. Put another way, price equals marginal extraction cost plus rental rate.

The rental rate, the price of the unextracted resource, goes up at the rate of interest: that is, $R_{t+1} = (1 + r)R_t$. If we substitute $R = P - MC$ into our Hotelling price rule, we get a more general form of the Hotelling rule, $(P_{t+1} - MC_{t+1}) = (1 + r)(P_t - MC_t)$. Rearranging this equation gives $P_{t+1} = (1 + r)P_t + [MC_{t+1} - (1 + r)MC_t]$. This equation says that the product price P generally does not rise with the rate of interest, even though the rental rate does, because the cost of extraction does not necessarily go up at the rate of interest. If there are constant marginal costs of extraction, so that $MC_t = c$, the price increase of the product is $P_{t+1} = (1 + r)P_t - r * c$, and the product price P goes up slower than the rate of interest.

Another way to look at this equation is to ask how much of the price is based on the marginal cost of extraction and how much is based on the rental rate. Because product price rises more slowly than the interest rate if extraction costs remain constant, then product price rises very slowly in the case where extraction costs remain constant and are a large fraction of the product price. In that situation, the rental rate is a relatively small share of the price. For example, lead is plentiful; most of its price comes from the costs of mining and smelting, and the price does not rise very fast. In contrast, for finished redwood lumber, about half the price was the rental rate, and half was the cost of logging and processing by producers that bought the standing trees from the redwood owners. If a good is abundant, the rental rate is a small fraction of the product price, and marginal cost dominates the price. In other words, the price of a more abundant good approaches the pattern for the price of a manufactured good, with price almost equal to marginal cost.

BACKSTOP TECHNOLOGY

What happens when we run out of a nonrenewable resource? Usually, we find something else to substitute for it. In the case of old-growth redwood, other woods and perhaps other materials can serve redwood's purposes. In the case of oil, some combination of nuclear power, coal, natural gas, and renewable sources will provide energy. Whatever substitutes for the exhausted resource is called a **backstop technology**, named after the backstop that blocks loose balls in a baseball game.

How does the existence of a backstop technology affect our model? Let's suppose that it is 1980, and the price of redwood is $400/mbf. Suppose that a backstop technology becomes available: for instance, walnut paneling can be produced renewably for $400/mbf. If the redwood owner tries to save some redwood for next year to get a higher price, he will not succeed: consumers will buy walnut paneling instead. Thus, the price cannot increase above $400/mbf.

Remember that a redwood owner will save some of the resource for the future only if he expects the marginal profit to increase in the future. The redwood owner no longer has any incentive to save redwood for next year, and he will sell it all. After the redwood is gone, people will happily buy renewable walnut paneling for $400/mbf instead of redwood.

Now, let's suppose it's 1961, and the price of redwood is $38, when news arrives that walnut paneling can be a perfect substitute for redwood but only at a price of $400/mbf. Smart redwood owners would instantly realize that the price of redwood cannot increase above $400/mbf; otherwise, everyone will buy the backstop, and nobody will buy redwood. As a result, the owners will want to sell all of the nonrenewable resource by the time its price reaches the price of the backstop technology. To make this happen, the owners will sell more redwood now, so that it runs out when the price hits the cost of the backstop technology.

BOX 16.2

The Valuation Principle

How much is the stock of a natural resource worth? Suppose the government wants to buy a grove of old-growth trees, or a company wants to buy another company that owns oil wells. What is the right value for the resource?

The Hotelling theory implies that the value of a resource stock is the price today times the stock, or P_0X. Why? Let's think about the extraction of the resource over time. If the amount extracted in year t is Q_t and the price is P_t, the present value of all quantities extracted until the resource is used up at time T is:

$$\text{Present Value} = P_0Q_0 + \ldots P_t\,Q_t/(1+r)^t + \ldots + P_TQ_T/(1+r)^T$$

The Hotelling price rule is that prices go up at the rate of interest, so that $P_t = P_0(1+r)^t$. When we substitute in this price rule for price, we get:

$$\text{Present Value} = P_0Q_0 + \ldots P_0Q_t + \ldots + P_0Q_T$$

Because the sum of the quantities extracted, Q, is the stock, X, we get:

$$\text{Present Value} = P_0(Q_0 + \ldots + Q_t + \ldots + Q_T) = P_0X$$

The Hotelling valuation principle is that the value of the resource stock is simply its current price times the stock. If the resource has extraction costs, the valuation principle is that the rental rate multiplied by the stock equals the value.

Miller and Upton tested this rule for a sample of 39 oil-producing firms using the stock market value of the firms and the quantity of their reserves (stock) of oil and gas. They multiplied the number of barrels of reserves of oil and gas by the then-current price of oil and gas and summed up the total value of reserves. They found that the total value of reserves, P_0X, was a good predictor of the stock market value of the firm.

The valuation principle played a major role in determining the price that the United States paid when acquiring private land for Redwood National Park in Northern California. The timber owners argued successfully that the price per board foot of small parcels of redwood that were bought and sold voluntarily should be used as the price per board foot of the very large property that was to be the park. Their argument was that the large property, if not taken for the park, would be sold a little at a time over many years. Because the present value of price each year should be the same, it would not matter how much was sold each year; the price per board foot of a little "dab" would be the same as the price per board foot of the much larger parcel.

The increased quantity sold in the present will cause the price to drop. Then the rental rate, the price for unharvested redwood, once again will increase at the rate of interest, to keep producers selling some now and some later. Because the price of redwood has dropped, though, the increase in redwood price at the rate of interest is now starting from a lower point. As a result, it will take longer for the redwood price to reach \$400/mbf, and it may take longer before the backstop enters the market, so that all the redwoods can be sold at a price below \$400/mbf.

Running out of a nonrenewable resource is much less important to consumers if there is a good alternative to it. If we have adequate substitutes for redwood products, then losing the old-growth stock to complete depletion, or locking it away in national parks, will have little effect on consumers, as the backstop eases the resource scarcity. Similarly, having renewable alternatives for energy resources means that using up fossil fuels is much less important to our energy future—other than the environmental consequences of using those fossil fuels.

EXPLORATION

For many resources, our knowledge about remaining stocks is imperfect at best. New oil deposits, for example, are discovered occasionally. What is the effect of exploration on resource management?

When a producer finds a new deposit of a nonrenewable resource, suddenly the stock increases, even if that deposit will not be used for many years. As a result, it is possible for consumers to have more of the resource both now and in the future: the resource has become less scarce. If the resource stays at the current price, though, consumers will not buy more. To induce consumers to purchase more, the price must drop immediately, even if the new deposit will not be extracted for some time. The discovery expands the stock, decreases scarcity, and lowers price.

Exploration, however, can be very costly. Why would producers spend the money to find new deposits? In the hope of making profits, of course. Remember that a nonrenewable resource produces profits because of its scarcity. Those profits not only help to allocate the resource over time, but they also provide the incentive for explorers to seek new deposits. Because finding a new oil deposit will allow the finder to sell the oil at the market price, people will search for oil. In fact, explorers will spend up to the expected amount of the profits to find these new deposits.

The Hotelling rule says that the rental rate, which is equal to price less marginal extraction costs, increases over time. A very important effect of the rental rate increasing over time is that it provides an increasing incentive for new discoveries. As rental rates increase, people are willing to spend more money to find more of the resource. When they are successful, the new discoveries then reduce price and ease resource scarcity, making consumers happier. Because price drops, rental rates drop, which reduces the incentive to explore—but only immediately after the new discovery has happened. When rental rate again increases, producers will explore again and, with luck, increase the stock again.

For many years, people have predicted the imminent depletion of many resources, such as oil: predictions from around 1950 estimated that the world only had about 20 years of oil left for use. This prediction has not proven very accurate. The cycle of increasing scarcity leading to greater exploration, which leads to new discoveries and reduced scarcity, means that we have continued to use many nonrenewable resources well past the times previously predicted for their exhaustion.

◢ IN SUMMARY

- The extraction and use of nonrenewable resources depends on a number of factors, including the interest rate in the economy, consumer demand shifts, extraction costs, development of backstop technologies, and exploration.
- A higher interest rate, all other things constant, leads to faster present extraction because the opportunity cost of saving the resource for the future is higher. Conversely, a lower interest rate results in more of the resource in the future.
- An expected change in future consumer demand will lead to immediate effects on the current market, as price adjusts to account for those future shifts. An expected increase in future demand will increase both the present and the future price, which will lead to less of the resource being sold now so that more is available when people want it in the future. In contrast, an expectation that future demand will shrink will lead to a drop in price and to the producer selling the resource while the demand is still high.
- If there are constant marginal costs of extraction, the Hotelling rule implies that price increases at less than the rate of interest. When the marginal costs of extraction are constant and account for a large fraction of the product price, the product price will increase only very slowly.
- Both the existence of a backstop technology and discovery of new resource deposits reduce the importance of holding onto existing stocks of the nonrenewable resource. As a result, the introduction of either of these scenarios will lead to increased production of the resource in the present, even if the new resource is not immediately available, and an associated reduction in price.
- The increasing rental rate of a resource provides an incentive for exploration and for development of backstop technologies. That new discovery will reduce the rental rate, and thus the incentive to find alternatives, until the rental rate again increases sufficiently that producers will once again seek ways to increase the stock of a resource.

Running Out of Resources vs. Running Out of Environment

How important are concerns about running out of nonrenewable resources? Are there market failures involved in our use of nonrenewable resources that cause inefficiency? Should we avoid use of nonrenewable resources, since our dependence on them will only bring problems when we use them up? Or should we take advantage of them while they exist and hope that alternatives will come along before we run out?

Concern over depletion of nonrenewable resources encourages individual producers and whole societies to look for the new deposits or technologies that will substitute for the resource and ease scarcity. This concern also persuades consumers to conserve the resources so that we only run out when we have alternatives. Understanding that a resource is finite will help ensure that we use it more wisely. At the same time, if the resource is managed efficiently, it will be available for consumers as long as they want the good. They will only run out when a high price or availability of alternatives chokes off demand. Using resources in the meantime provides current benefits, while the concern over running out ensures conservation and the hunt for substitutes.

In other words, the fact that nonrenewable resources are available only in finite supply is a manageable problem. While we would be better off with greater abundance, we can manage the resources wisely. The limited supply of nonrenewable resources need not lead to crisis.

There is an extremely important warning that must accompany this hopeful view of resource scarcity: the problems that arise due to market failures, especially externalities. Extraction of nonrenewable resources often leads to environmental and ecological damages. Harvesting old-growth redwoods destroys ecosystems in the upper branches that ecologists have only recently begun to study. Mining coal, oil, or minerals can cause major harm to landscapes and rivers. If resource extractors are not responsible for these environmental costs, then the equilibrium quantity produced is not efficient. As in the case of gasoline consumption, the quantity consumed would be lower if external costs were included in marginal cost and therefore in price. Ignoring these costs leads to more rapid depletion, and more environmental damage, than if the extractors had to face these costs and consumers had to face the increase in product price.

In the case of two nonrenewable fossil fuel resources—oil and coal—exhaustion of resources is likely to be a much less serious problem than the environmental effects of using the resources at the current rate. People can adapt to resource depletion with energy efficiency and backstop technology, but the pollution produced from oil and coal pose immediate and ongoing threats.

The lessons about externalities apply equally to the use of nonrenewable resources as they do to other goods: these external costs impose real damages to society, and the price of the resources should reflect the full damages associated with those goods. In the absence of including these costs, the price of the resource will be lower than the efficient level. As a result, the resource will be used more and faster, and the damages will be higher, than if its price reflected its full cost.

IN SUMMARY

- Completely depleting a nonrenewable resource need not be a serious concern if the resource is managed by the Hotelling rule. Increases in the rental rate give signals to consumers to conserve the resource, and to producers to

BOX 16.3

Coal, Climate Change, and Cancer

One recent estimate is that the world has 200 years of coal left. Relatively cheap and plentiful coal has helped millions of people in China and India escape poverty through electrification and industrialization. But there is a high price, both to the climate and to human health, from using coal.

Coal emits more greenhouse gases than oil per unit of energy. As developing nations, China and India are exempt from the limits on carbon emissions in the 1997 climate change treaty known as the Kyoto Protocol. China recently surpassed the United States in total greenhouse gas emissions per year. If the developing nations do not start to limit these emissions, controlling climate change becomes almost impossible.

In addition, coal produces black soot as well as particles too small to be seen. Particle pollution is linked to lung cancer, asthma, and heart disease. In China, air pollution kills hundreds of thousands of people each year; pollution-related cancers of all sorts are the leading cause of death. While "clean" coal technology reduces particle pollution, it does not affect production of greenhouse gases.

Even though coal is a nonrenewable fossil fuel, running out is the least of humanity's problems with this resource.

find new deposits and good substitutes. The resource will be depleted only when price is high enough that nobody will want to buy it anyway.

- Environmental damages are a cost of doing business that resource extractors usually do not consider adequately. Ignoring these costs leads to excessive environmental damages and overly rapid resource depletion.
- Including all external damages in the extractors' calculations of costs, and therefore in the price to consumers, is necessary for efficient management of nonrenewable resources.

Oil

Oil is the nonrenewable resource that occupies most of the world's attention. How well does it fit our theory of a nonrenewable resource? Not as well as theorists would like! The differences between theory and reality for oil show both how difficult it is to predict the future of a resource and how the theory still has explanatory power.

Let's start by looking at the price of oil over time. Figure 16.9 shows the price of oil as a dashed line and the price of oil adjusted for inflation (the real price) as a solid line. The price graph does not look much like the neatly rising trend that we

FIGURE 16.9 Nominal and Real Price of Oil Over Time.

The dashed line is the nominal price (that is, the price not adjusted for inflation) of oil. The solid line is the real price of oil, the nominal price divided by the Consumer Price Index, a measure of inflation, set so that both prices are the same in the third quarter of 2008.

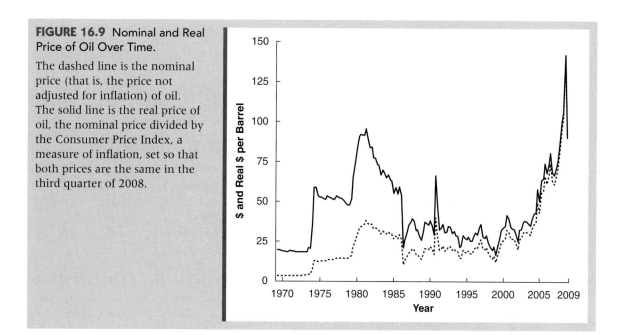

saw with redwood. Understanding this price path requires examining some of the major features of oil price history.

First, petroleum is not traded in a perfectly competitive market. The Organization of Petroleum Exporting Countries (OPEC) has, with some success at times, managed to manipulate the price of oil by withholding its supplies from the market. This market power, combined with oil deposits lying in politically volatile regions, has contributed to the swings in oil prices.

The first success of OPEC came a year after Colonel Qaddafi's seizure of power in Libya in 1969, when OPEC was able to raise its price by 20 cents a barrel. In the aftermath of the Arab–Israeli Yom Kippur War in 1973, OPEC attempted an embargo on oil sales to the United States and other supporters of Israel; in addition, Saudi Arabia, the world's biggest oil producer, cut its production by 35 percent. These actions were responsible for the 1973 price increase on the graph. Between 1978 and 1981, prices rose again due to OPEC production controls, the overthrow of the government of Iran, and war between Iraq and Iran.

The high prices engineered by OPEC during the 1970s led to an increase in output by non-OPEC nations, such as Norway's production from the North Sea, as well as conservation. As a result, prices slid all the way to a nominal price of $12.51/barrel in 1986. With Iraq's invasion of the major oil producer Kuwait in 1989 and the ensuing first Gulf War in 1990, prices increased briefly but then subsided to $10.87/barrel. So, if this graph stopped in 1999, it would look like oil prices had been decreasing or steady for quite some time, not at all the increasing price path that the theory predicts.

From 1999 to 2008, however, prices increased dramatically, peaking at $142/barrel before sliding to $50 in the third quarter of 2008. The 2008 price spike is believed to stem from an increase in demand from the rapidly developing economies of India and China. The decrease in late 2008 was due in part to a slowdown in the economy of the United States, which affected industrial activity in other parts of the world as well. Thus, market power and world events play a major role in the price path for oil.

Yet another factor influencing the price of oil is the behavior of **speculators**, financiers who bet on the future prices of goods. During price peaks, speculators bought oil. The speculators were not planning to use the oil; instead, they were betting that its price would continue rising, and they wanted to be able to sell the oil at those higher prices, as our theory would predict. When the price began to fall, they sold the oil they had bought, again as our theory would predict. When price was rising, they made prices go higher by adding to the quantity demanded, and when price fell they made prices go lower by adding to the quantity supplied.

With all these shocks pushing the price of oil around, it is hard to see any clear Hotelling effects. Indeed, James Hamilton's recent estimate of the price path of oil is that it is just as likely that oil price will go up as it will go down!

If oil is a nonrenewable resource, then we should be running out of oil. Indeed, there is no doubt that the amount of oil left in the earth is going down. However, because we don't know all possible deposits of oil, we can't measure how much is left. Instead, Table 16.1 shows *proven reserves*. **Proven reserves** are the oil reserves that we have currently located and that can be extracted at current prices.

The table shows that reserves have increased—in fact, nearly doubled—since 1980, despite substantial production of oil. If we looked at the 1980 proven reserves and subtracted all the production since then (about 23 billion barrels per

TABLE 16.1 Proven Reserves of Oil and Production in Selected Countries.

The top part of this table shows proven reserves, in billions of barrels per year, in three major oil-producing countries and in the whole world. The bottom line of the chart shows production for the whole world.

YEAR/PLACE	1980	1990	2000	2008
RESERVES				
CANADA	6.8	6.1	5	175
VENEZUELA	17.9	58.5	77	87
SAUDI ARABIA	166	258	264	267
WORLD	645	1,002	1,017	1,332
PRODUCTION				
WORLD	23	24	28	31

Source: Energy Information Administration, U.S. Department of Energy.

year), we would conclude that by 2010 there would be no oil left. To the contrary, proven reserves are higher than they were before.

Proven reserves are an uncertain measure of oil in the ground. Reserves are self-reported by countries and may be wildly inaccurate. Even if they are accurate, not all proven reserves are available for production and consumption, due to cost or technological or legal restrictions on their use. Additionally, there is no economic incentive for a firm to spend money now to find oil that it is going to use in 20 years. Because of the lack of incentives to find and verify reserves for use in the distant future, the proven reserves are limited to about a dozen years of extraction. As a result, there may be new deposits of oil that people have not yet tried to identify.

A way to estimate how much oil is left in producing fields is to look at production. When a field is first opened to production, the oil is under pressure that pushes the oil out. As the field is produced, the oil and gas in the field decrease, and so does the pressure. Because pressure decreases in a field over time, the amount extracted decreases over time. Extrapolating what production to expect from existing fields, based on how long they have been producing and what they have produced, gives a much lower estimate of how much oil is left in existing fields. This analysis is called the **peak oil** approach because it assumes that the productivity of existing fields has already reached its peak and is going to decline. It is, however, based on production in fields that are currently under production, not total oil.

Another reasonable measure of oil scarcity involves looking at the cost of extraction for newly found oil. Saudi crude oil cost about a dollar per barrel (in today's dollars) to extract in 1950, but the tar sands that were added to the Canadian reserves in 2002 have an extraction cost of more than \$15/barrel. The new additions to reserves are more expensive than older additions to reserves. If we are not running out of oil, at least we are running out of cheap oil.

There are many possible energy sources other than oil. These constitute backstop technologies. In the United States, nuclear energy is under consideration after years of neglect, which was due to its high cost and to a long-running scientific and public debate about its safety. There is now also extensive exploration and development of natural gas, with huge potential reserves. Electricity from wind and solar is becoming more common. For vehicles, ethanol and other more renewable fuels are getting increased attention. Conservation, from increased energy efficiency and less energy use in many sectors of the economy, is another highly effective backstop technology. All of these sources substitute for oil in some uses. So running out of oil, or at least oil that is cheap to extract, may not be catastrophic.

IN SUMMARY

- Oil is a nonrenewable resource on which the world depends heavily. Its price path does not follow the smooth Hotelling path that theory predicts. A closer look at the details of the oil market identify other factors that economic theory suggests should lead to a jumpy price path.
- World events lead to shifts in either the supply of or demand for oil. When the Organization of Petroleum Exporting Countries (OPEC) reduces its

production, supply drops, and price jumps; when OPEC is not coordinated, supply increases, and price drops. Expansion or contraction of economic activity can lead to shifts inward or outward in the demand for oil.

- Although the world appetite for oil continues to increase, and oil is nonrenewable, reserves of oil have *increased*. This apparent contradiction is due in part to the difficulty in measuring new reserves, in part to new discoveries, and in part to development of backstop technologies.

Hotelling's Theory and Redwood National Park

The U.S. government has the power of **eminent domain**, also called **taking**: the government can take private property for a public purpose, as long as the owner is fairly compensated. In 1968, the government used this power to take privately owned old-growth timberland and created Redwood National Park; in 1978, it expanded the park. These two takings transferred a considerable fraction of remaining old-growth from the harvestable stock to public protection: 3.1 million mbf of timber was taken, leaving 7.2 million mbf in private hands.

At the second taking, the forest industry claimed that the economy of the redwood region would be ruined. For loggers, these concerns had merit: old-growth logging jobs were lost when old-growth was placed in parks. However, because the stock of a nonrenewable resource is used up eventually, it was only a question of when the jobs would disappear.

For the owners, however, placing the redwoods in the park actually made them better off. First, the owners were paid for the timber that was taken. Next, the old-growth remaining in private hands became even more valuable because the finite supply became even smaller. The increased value of the remaining stock as a result of a taking is called **enhancement.** Although the law permits enhancement to reduce the compensation paid for a taking, there was little use of enhancement to reduce the compensation paid to the owners in the Redwood National Park case. Later, a calculation of enhancement using the Hotelling model resulted in an estimate that the value of the enhancement was 85 percent of the value of the compensation paid. In effect, the redwood owners (as a group) were paid nearly twice for the park.

In the end, not only environmentalists, but also the owners of old-growth redwoods, became better off from the expansions of the protected redwood parks.

CHAPTER SUMMARY

Here are the key lessons from this chapter:

- In equilibrium, (1) the present value price of the unextracted resource, the user cost, is the same in every year in which the resource is extracted; (2) the demand curve determines the quantity extracted at a given time; and (3) the sum of the quantities extracted over time equals the initial stock.

- Unlike the case of perfect competition, profits exist for nonrenewable resources. These profits provide the incentive for a producer to save some of the resource for the future, instead of running out of the resource rapidly.
- If the interest rate increases, producers will extract the resource more quickly. A drop in the interest rate leads to slower extraction.
- Anticipated future demand shifts affect price immediately. If resource owners expect that the demand curve will shift up sometime in the future, they respond by saving more of the resource for that time. To keep equilibrium in the present, the present price will rise. On the other hand, a predicted future downward shift in demand leads to an immediate drop in price, as producers try to sell more of the good while people still want it.
- Both backstop technologies and discoveries of new deposits of a resource reduce the scarcity of the resource. As a result, even if the alternative is not presently available, the prospect of an alternative immediately causes a drop in price. The reduced price allows consumers to use more of the resource in the present and still have the alternative in the future.
- The profits from a nonrenewable resource provide the incentive for exploration and for developing new technologies. These profits help ensure that these alternatives become available before the present stock is used up.
- If the nonrenewable resource is not subject to market failures, then running out of the resource will happen only when people no longer want the good, either because the price is too high or because alternatives are cheaper. One common market failure is environmental degradation associated with resource extraction. Failure to include environmental costs in the marginal cost of producing a resource leads to extraction more rapid than if these market failures did not exist.
- The price paths of oil and other nonrenewable resources often do not follow the smooth Hotelling line. Demand shifts, new discoveries, political events, and market manipulations lead to jumps in the price paths.

KEY TERMS

backstop technology *(p. 397)*
choke price *(p. 384)*
eminent domain *(p. 406)*
enhancement *(p. 406)*
extraction path *(p. 384)*
Hotelling rule *(p. 381)*
nonrenewable
  resources *(p. 380)*

peak oil *(p. 405)*
price path *(p. 381)*
proven reserves *(p. 404)*
rental rate *(p. 381)*
speculators *(p. 404)*
stock *(p. 380)*
taking *(p. 406)*
user cost *(p. 381)*

NOTES

The Hotelling rule was first described in Harold Hotelling, "The Economics of Exhaustible Resources," *The Journal of Political Economy* 39 (April 1931): 137–175.

The Headwaters story is told in several news articles: Jane Kay, "North Coast remembers 'great leader' Judi Bari; 1,000 attend rites for activist who fought to save old-growth forests," *San Francisco Examiner*, March 10, 1997, Section A; Glen Martin and Jonathan Curiel, "Last-minute Headwaters deal OK'd; stands of ancient redwoods preserved in landmark sale," *San Francisco Chronicle*, March 2, 1999, A-1; "A hard-won deal to save headwaters," *San Francisco Chronicle*, March 3, 1999, A-18; Tom Abate, "Pacific Lumber leans—company in Headwaters deal files for bankruptcy, citing logging restrictions," *San Francisco Chronicle*, January 20, 2007, C-1; Kelly Zito, "Gap founders win approval to take over Pacific Lumber," *San Francisco Chronicle*, June 7, 2008; Bruce Weber, "John Campbell dies; led Pacific Lumber in '90s," *San Francisco Chronicle*, October 27, 2008, C-3. These articles can be found in the combined *Chronicle* and *Examiner* archives at http://www.sfgate.com.

The Redwood National Park takings and the price path example are from Peter Berck and William R. Bentley, "Hotelling's Theory, Enhancement, and the Taking of the Redwood National Park," *American Journal of Agricultural Economics* 79 (May 1997): 287–298.

In Figure 16.9, the oil price graph, real price is the nominal price divided by the Consumer Price Index (CPI). The CPI is a commonly used measure of inflation in the United States; it is based on the rise in prices of a bundle of consumer goods such as food, fuel, and housing. For this diagram, the CPI has been used so that all prices are measured in dollars equivalent to those in 2008, quarter 3.

The proved reserves and production of oil in Table 16.1 are from the Energy Information Administration, U.S. Department of Energy, http://www.eia.doe.gov/emeu/international/oilreserves.html and http://www.eia.doe.gov/emeu/international/oilproduction.html.

Sources for the discussion of coal, climate change, and cancer include Philip J. Hilts, "Study Pinpoints Death Risk From Small-Particle Pollution," *New York Times*, March 10, 1995; Joseph Kahn and Jim Yardley, "As China Roars, Pollution Reaches Deadly Extremes," *New York Times*, August 26, 2007; and Elisabeth Rosenthal, "Europe Turns Back to Coal, Raising Climate Fears," *New York Times*, April 23, 2008. These stories may be located at www.nytimes.com.

EXERCISES

1. Congratulations! You just won a million-barrel oil well! You are now trying to manage your asset. The previous owner pumped all the oil out of the well and put it into storage tanks; it will cost you nothing to sell it. Oil now sells for $15/barrel. Interest rates are 1 percent per month. With your well comes membership in the Good Resource Extraction and Sale Enterprise, an organization for well owners to exchange information, socialize, and get cheap drinks.

    (a) At a party, Dr. Rig (head of the Enterprise) announces that oil prices will double next month. How much oil will you sell this month, before the price increase?

    (b) Dr. Rig then announces that the price will also double the following month. How much oil will you sell next month, before the following month's price increase?

(c) Dr. Rig then says that, in the fourth month (the current month is the first), oil prices will drop to \$10/barrel and will stay that low for years. How much oil do you decide to sell in the third month, before the fourth month's price drop?

Someone you know and trust comes to tell you a few minutes later that Dr. Rig has been celebrating a bit too much and is making up all this information. Instead, your friend tells you, prices should follow the trend that economists have promised all along.

(d) What is that trend for prices?

(e) Given that trend, will the Enterprise as a whole sell more oil in the next month than in the current month, or less?

(f) How do you expect this price trend to affect the incentives for Enterprise members to explore for new oil deposits?

2. You still own the oil from exercise 1, which has a price of \$15/barrel, and the interest rate is 1 percent/month. The Enterprise now faces competition: the Synthetic Lubricant Industrial Manufacturing Effort says that it can make synthetic oil, every bit as good as your oil, from used plastics and leftover food, at a price of \$20/barrel. Once the Effort gets going, there will be a perfect substitute for your oil.

(a) Assuming that anyone who wants to can make synthetic oil through the Effort's process, and that we are in no danger of running out of either used plastic or leftover food, what will be the price trend of oil after the Effort comes into production?

(b) Are you concerned about this threat? How long do you have until competition from this industry will knock you out of business, with the price trend you've predicted in part (a)?

(c) How much oil will you wish to have on hand at the time the Effort goes into production? Will you speed up or slow down your sales of oil, relative to your sales plan before you knew about the Effort?

(d) If everyone uses your strategy, what will happen to the current price of oil?

(e) If the current price of oil does as you say in (d), what will happen to the time period before the synthetic oil becomes economical?

3. You learn that new regulations are about to be imposed on your well to reduce the vile odors that come from it. These regulations will make extraction costly (i.e., there will be positive costs).

(a) Compared to a case where the regulations did not exist, do you expect to extract your oil more quickly or more slowly? Why?

(b) Compared to a case where the regulations did not exist, do you expect the value of your oil well to be higher or lower? Why?

4. You learn that your oil deposit is in the Amazingly Naturally Wonderful Region. Extracting your oil will harm the region's scenery and ecosystems.

(a) If you are interested only in your monetary earnings, will the fact that your deposit is in this region affect how you develop the oil? Why or why not?

(b) From an efficiency perspective, should the fact that your deposit is in this region affect how you develop the oil? If yes, how should it affect your oil development? If not, why not?

5. Let's see how the demand curve, combined with the Hotelling rule, can define the market equilibrium. There are two periods, now and later. The demand curve in each period (t = now or later) is $Q_t = 10 - P_t$. The stock of the resource is 10 units, with zero extraction costs. The interest rate is 4 percent.

   (a) A market equilibrium requires identifying price and quantity at all times. What are the four variables for which we need to find numerical values to find the equilibria?

   (b) To find four unknowns, we need four equations. These equations are (i) the two demand curves, (ii) the Hotelling price path, and (iii) a summing-up condition that says that the quantity used in both periods sums to the stock. Write down these four equations.

   (c) Solve the four equations by substitution: first, use the summing-up condition to eliminate Q_{now} from the Q_{now} demand curve; second, use the Hotelling price path to eliminate P_{now} from the Q_{now} demand curve; finally, use the now-modified Q_{now} demand curve with the Q_{later} demand curve to solve for P_{later}. Once you've solved for P_{later}, use the previous relationships to solve for all the other variables.

   (d) Does price rise with the interest rate? Does quantity demanded increase or decrease between the two periods? Does the producer make profit? How much?

   (e) There are many ways to elaborate on this simple model, to examine other effects studied in this chapter. Using the same process outlined previously, consider:

   (i) What happens when the interest rate increases to 10 percent?

   (ii) What happens when demand later increases to $Q_{later} = 15 - P_{later}$?

   (iii) What happens when demand later decreases to $Q_{later} = 5 - P_{later}$?

   (iv) What happens if the stock is expected to increase by 5 later, due to new discoveries? (Hint: If you know about the increase now, will the producer want to adjust his behavior now?)

6. Many people are concerned that production of petroleum has peaked; people will have less petroleum available to them from now on.

   (a) If everyone has perfect knowledge of world petroleum stocks, and production has indeed peaked, what do you expect to happen to the price of petroleum over time, if demand stays constant or increases?

   (b) How do you expect people to respond to the price trend you identified in (a)? Will this response make future oil scarcities more or less of a problem?

   (c) In fact, people do not have perfect knowledge of world petroleum stocks. It is possible that more oil exists than is currently known; it is also possible that some known stocks may not be developed, due to costs or environmental problems. How might these uncertainties affect the responses you discussed in (b)?

Renewable Resource Management

R enewable resources have always played a role in human well-being, as we grow crops and forests and manage animal populations for food, shelter, clothing, transportation, and other purposes. While people have domesticated many varieties and created new ones, we have also depleted the populations of many species, and we have driven many others to extinction. Why do we drive some species to extinction? How should we manage *renewable resources* to provide benefits to present and future generations? This chapter will examine:

- The dynamics of *renewable resources*: how populations of these species change in response to human activity;
- Exploitation of *renewable resources* when harvest is unrestricted;
- The principles underlying efficient *renewable resource* management;
- The risk of extinction, both when harvest is unrestricted and when harvest is managed efficiently;
- Methods to restrict the harvest of *renewable resources*.

Overfishing Herring in the North Sea

Herring is an important part of the world's food supply, both directly and indirectly. This fish was once a vital source of protein for poor people in Europe. It is still a staple food in Scandinavia and is now a delicacy for the North American descendants of poor immigrants from Europe. Herring is also used for animal feed, pet food, fish bait, and fertilizer.

The part of the Atlantic Ocean north of Scotland and west of Norway is called the North Sea. In the North Sea, the herring population was quite large in 1963: the stock was about 2 million metric tons of herring. In 1963, only eight Norwegian purse seine vessels were harvesting these fish. A purse seine is a fish net that wraps around a school of fish from below and closes at the top, just like a net purse. These eight boats were quite successful. The next year, 121 boats fished herring. They too were successful. By 1968, 352 vessels were in the fishery. By this time, there weren't enough fish for all the boats. By 1977, the stock of fish was down to 166,000 metric tons, and only 24 vessels were fishing. At that point, the Norwegian government and the European Economic Community (predecessor to the EU) stepped in and closed the fishery to further exploitation.

The tale of the herring is hardly an isolated tale. Many fisheries in the developed world have been overexploited. In response, government agencies often step in to regulate the fisheries, though often without success. U.S. fisheries regulation is such a case.

Modern fishery regulation in the United States began with the Magnuson-Stevens Fishery Conservation Act, originally passed in 1976 and most recently amended in 2006. This act accomplished two major purposes. The first was to declare American economic control over the waters within 200 miles of the United States, now called the exclusive economic zone. Because the United States includes the states of Hawaii and Alaska and holds territories in the Pacific, this is a significant portion of the Pacific Ocean. In the exclusive economic zone, the United States has limited or eliminated fishing by foreign vessels. America is hardly unique in this; other countries have also declared exclusive economic zones.

The second purpose of the Magnuson-Stevens Act was to regulate the fisheries within the exclusive economic zone that were not within control of any of the individual states. In order to regulate these fisheries, the United States set up eight fishery management councils charged with making fishery regulations to be approved by the Secretary of Commerce. These councils in practice were dominated by people with an interest in the business of fishing. Here is one view of what happened:

> About 30% of the world's fisheries are considered today to be overfished. The U.S. fisheries are some of the most highly regulated fisheries in the world, characterized by substantial investment in science, management plans, monitoring, and enforcement. Yet 40% of U.S. fisheries are considered overfished. When the Magnuson Act was passed in 1976, the federal government listed 14 overfished species in U.S. waters. Today, there are 81. The 25-year history to date of federal management of fisheries in the United States does not include the story of a single rebuilt marine fish stock. The Northeast Atlantic fisheries managed by the European Union are in even worse condition: 64% are classified as over-exploited, seriously over-exploited, or collapsed. (Josh Eagle and Barton Thompson)

There is debate about who is to blame for the collapse of the U.S. fisheries. One view is that the councils put political objectives like immediate employment above the advice of their biological experts. In response to the record of overfishing, Congress has recently required the Fishery Management Councils to pay closer attention to the findings of their scientific committees. Whether the new legislative language forces a change in regulatory behavior is yet to be seen.

Renewable Resources

Renewable resources are goods that are produced by natural processes, not by manufacture. Plants and animals, of course, reproduce. Fish, trees, and any unmanaged crop, like wild blackberries or range grasses, are renewable. When they are left to themselves, they increase within ecological limits. Trees grow in volume, and new trees sprout. Grasses grow taller and seed bare spots. Fish spawn, and young fish grow in size.

A less obvious example of renewable resources is the capacity of rivers and the air to clean up pollution. When moderate amounts of fecal matter enter a river, they are consumed by bacteria, and the river becomes clean again. When CO_2 goes into the air, plants take some of it out again. Economists use the concept of renewal to refer to any natural process that increases the quantity of a good, be it the cleanliness of the air or the size of fish stocks.

Renewable resources are, however, subject to biological limits on the potential *growth* or renewal of these resources. Despite the *growth* potential of renewable resources, it is possible to extinguish them. Wooly mammoths were renewable resources, and now they are extinct. In these respects, renewable resources are different from manufactured goods.

GROWTH

The stock of a resource is the amount of the resource at a particular time. The **growth** of the resource is the change in stock in a defined period of time due to natural causes. The growth accounts for the growth of individuals in the population and their birth and natural death. Growth depends on the size of the stock. With a small stock, reproduction is also small, and this limits growth. With a large stock, competition for food or habitat limits growth. Therefore, growth first rises and then falls as stock rises.

Trond Bjornal and Jon Conrad studied the North Sea herring; this discussion is based on their findings. Figure 17.1 shows an approximation to the *growth function* for North Sea herring. The **growth function**, abbreviated $G(S)$, provides the growth for different levels of the stock, S. On the horizontal axis is the size of the herring stock in million metric tons (mmt). On the vertical axis is the yearly growth in the stock, in thousand metric tons (kmt). The figure shows that there is no growth when there are no herring; the fish cannot reproduce when none exist. In addition, there is no growth when there are 3.2 mmt of herring, due to such factors as limits on habitat range and food availability. So 3.2 mmt is the maximum possible stock. The highest point on the graph, at a stock 1.6 mmt, shows where the growth is largest; at this point, the growth is 64 kmt per year.

Let's follow the dynamics of this resource to understand fishery growth. Suppose that the current stock is 1.6 mmt. In the absence of any harvesting or other disruption, the growth will be 64 kmt. As a result, next year the population will be $1.6 + 0.064 = 1.664$ mmt. Because this increase is small, the growth the following year will be similar. The stock in two years, then, will be approximately $1.664 + 0.064 = 1.728$ mmt. At that stock, growth is slightly smaller, about 63 kmt, leading to stock in the third year of $1.728 + 0.063 = 1.791$ mmt. If we skip ahead a few years, at year nine, with a population of about 2 mmt, growth is about 57 kmt. By year 40, population has grown to about 3 mmt, but growth is down to 10 kmt. After 110 years, the population is at its maximum, and growth is 0. If left to itself, a

FIGURE 17.1 The Growth Function.

The growth depends on the stock for the North Sea herring. The estimate of the growth function is $G = 0.08 * S * \{1 - [S/(3.2 * 10^6)]\}$. *Carrying capacity* is 3.2 mmt. *Maximum sustained yield stock* is 1.6 mmt, and *maximum sustained yield* is 64 kmt.

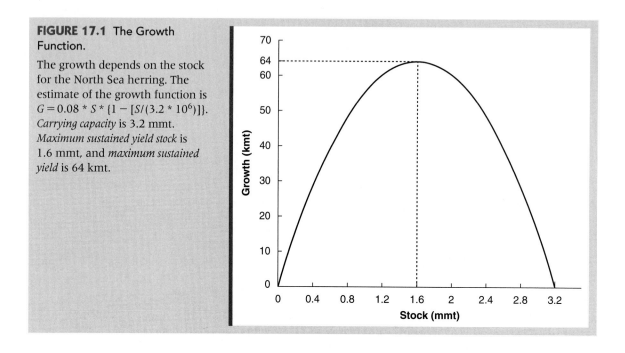

population will tend to grow to its maximum, called the **carrying capacity**, the largest population that an area can support. At that point, the growth is zero.

When the stock of herring changes from 1.664 mmt to 1.728 mmt, for instance, the growth changes from 64 kmt per year (0.064 mmt) to 63 kmt (0.063 mmt) per year. The change in growth divided by the change in stock at this level of stock is $(0.063 - 0.064)/(1.728 - 1.664) = -0.016$. This **marginal growth** is the slope of the growth curve, the change in growth as a result of a change in stock. If the growth curve is $G(S)$, and a small increase in stock is x, then marginal growth is approximated by $[G(S + x) - G(S)]/x$. In our previous example, x was $1.664 - 1.728 = -0.064$ mmt.

Table 17.1 shows the growth and marginal growth for several values of fish stock. Notice that, when the stock is low, the growth—measured along the vertical axis of Figure 17.1—is increasing as the stock increases. The slope—the marginal growth—is positive because an increase in stock leads to an increase in growth. When the stock is higher, on the other hand, increasing the stock leads to *lower* growth, as the species competes for scarce food or habitat. In this situation, the growth curve slopes down. Growth itself is positive, but marginal growth is negative.

CATCH AND SUSTAINED YIELD

The North Sea herring population has hardly been left to itself. The change in stock comes not just from natural causes but also from harvesting. With high enough

TABLE 17.1 Growth and Marginal Growth.

The growth changes as the stock changes. At low stock levels, there are few fish to reproduce. More fish reproduce more rapidly, until habitat and food constraints limit reproduction. Marginal growth, which measures how growth changes with changes in the stock, is the slope of the growth function.

STOCK (MMT)	GROWTH (KMT)	MARGINAL GROWTH
0	0	0.0775
0.1	7.75	0.0725
0.2	15.00	0.0675
0.3	21.75	0.0625
0.4	28.00	0.0575
0.5	33.75	0.0525
0.6	39.00	0.0475
0.7	43.75	0.0425
0.8	48.00	0.0375
0.9	51.75	0.0325
1.0	55.00	0.0275
1.1	57.75	0.0225
1.2	60.00	0.0175
1.3	61.75	0.0125
1.4	63.00	0.0075
1.5	63.75	0.0025
1.6	64.00	−0.0025
1.7	63.75	−0.0075

harvesting, the species can be depleted or even exhausted. Let's see how harvesting affects the stock-growth dynamic.

Let's use H_t to describe the catch (the amount that is harvested) at time t, and S_t to describe the stock in a particular year, t. The stock next year, $t + 1$, is the stock this year, S_t, plus growth, G, less catch, H_t.

$$S_{t+1} = S_t + G(S_t) - H_t$$

If a fishery is managed or regulated, the most important decision is to limit the size of the harvest, also called the yield or catch. One option is to choose a yield that keeps stock constant. If yield equals growth, the stock will stay constant. Mathematically, if $S_{t+1} = S_t$, then $G(S_t) = H_t$.

Let's go back to our starting point of 1.6 mmt of herring. Now, suppose that, instead of letting the stock grow, the fishing industry harvested 64 kmt. Because the industry harvested exactly the growth in the herring stock, the stock itself would be unchanged. It would be possible to continue this harvest year after year without affecting the stock. In other words, when the stock is 1.6 mmt, 64 kmt is the annual **sustainable yield** or **sustained yield**, the amount that can be caught each year without changing the stock level.

Are there other possible sustained yield levels? Suppose that, instead, the stock were about 1 mmt. Table 17.1 indicates that the growth at 1 mmt is about 55 kmt. At a stock of 1 mmt, then, 55 kmt is the sustained yield. It is also possible to have sustained yield when the stock is high enough that fish are competing for food and the marginal growth is negative. Look at Figure 17.1, on the downward-sloping side of the curve. At a stock of 3 mmt, 10 kmt is the sustained yield. Any point on the growth curve, then, represents a volume of harvest that can be sustained forever because the stock stays constant. If the stock stays constant, the growth remains constant, and the harvest can therefore be constant.

The harvest of 64 kmt, however, is unique. It is not the only sustained yield, but it is the largest amount that the industry can harvest sustainably, year after year, without depleting the stock. This harvest is called the **maximum sustained yield (MSY)**. The stock (1.6 mmt) that leads to the MSY harvest is called the **maximum sustained yield (MSY) stock.** There is no economic reason to choose the MSY stock as a policy goal because it does not account for costs of fishing or when the resource is harvested. It is, however, often cited as a goal of biological management.

Figure 17.1 is not only a graph of growth; it is also a graph of sustained yield. Changing the label on the vertical axis from "growth" to "yield" would show a sustained yield curve instead of a growth curve. That is because growth and yield are identical when the catch is equal to a sustained yield.

The growth curve pictured in Figure 17.1 is a good starting point for population dynamics, but it is only a starting point. More sophisticated models account for such things as water temperature, competing species, and the age and size distribution of the fish. For larger animals, like elephants and tigers, the growth curve would incorporate *minimum viable population*. The **minimum viable population**, the smallest size of the population that can be sustained, is much greater than zero for most species. A large minimum viable population makes a species vulnerable to extinction from overharvesting; we will discuss extinction later in this chapter.

IN SUMMARY

- Renewable resources differ from nonrenewable resources in that they can reproduce. They are different from manufactured goods in that their rate of reproduction is biologically limited. Within these limits, human management can influence the amount of reproduction—for instance, through choosing the size of the harvest.

- The stock-growth curve summarizes the population dynamics of a renewable resource. The growth—the increase in the population in a year—depends on the stock. Usually growth is low when population is low because there are very few existing of the resource to reproduce. Growth is also low when population is high, as other resource constraints, such as nutrition and habitat, limit the population. The highest growth is termed maximum sustained yield; the stock that produces this amount is the maximum sustained yield stock. The carrying capacity is the maximum population of the resource that an ecosystem can support.

- If harvest is less than growth, the stock of the resource will increase. If, instead, harvest exceeds growth, the stock shrinks. If a harvester takes exactly the amount of growth every year, then the stock of the resource stays constant. Harvesting exactly the growth is called a sustained-yield harvest. It can occur at any level of the stock where growth is positive.

- The marginal growth of the resource is the slope of the stock-growth curve. It is the change in growth as a result of a change in stock. To the left side of the MSY stock, the marginal growth is positive; increasing the stock increases the growth. To the right of the MSY stock, the marginal growth is negative, as growth slows with a stock increase. At the MSY stock, marginal growth is zero.

Open Access

Until 1977, the North Sea herring fishery was completely unregulated. Anyone could take a boat and catch fish without a license or any legal restrictions. Unregulated or poorly regulated fisheries are an example of *open access*. When anyone, without restriction, can take a good, then there is **open access** for that good. Open access is a market failure caused by the absence of clear ownership rights. The failure of open access is the failure of excludability. Other examples of open access include effectively unregulated harvest of elephants, rhinoceroses, and other big game; gathering of forest products and wood without limit; and the unregulated grazing of range lands before they were fenced.

Let's compare an open access fishery to a redwood forest. The redwood forest had an owner. The owner decided when to harvest her trees. She chose the time to harvest her trees to maximize profit. She recognized that she had an opportunity cost of harvesting immediately: whatever she harvested immediately would not be available for harvest in the future. In contrast, an open access fishery has no owner. Anyone can come and harvest the fish. The fisher has an opportunity cost of zero for harvesting immediately. If the fisher does not harvest now, some other fisher will, and the fish not harvested will not be available to that fisher next period. Open access is fundamentally a failure to have secure property rights.

To understand how lack of property rights leads to mismanagement of these resources, let's compare three cases of management in the long run, the period long enough so that all entry has already happened: (1) a competitively produced manufactured good, (2) a fully owned natural resource, and (3) an open access resource.

The competitive producer of a manufactured good makes zero profits in the long run because of the entry of other firms. If the producer were making profits in the short run, other producers would enter the industry, driving the short-run supply curve outwards and the price downwards. This process would continue until profits were zero. New producers can enter because nothing limits their entry: nothing is scarce in the long run. In the absence of externalities, the long-run competitive equilibrium is efficient: it maximizes the sum of producer surplus plus consumer surplus.

A fully owned natural resource differs from the competitive industry because there is an underlying scarce resource. In contrast to manufacturing, there are no new entrants to drive down prices because all of the resource is already owned by the existing firms. Because there can be no entry even in the long run, natural resource firms earn positive profits. Also in contrast to manufacturing, natural resource firms have to decide how much of the resource to harvest in different time periods. For every unit sold in one time period, a firm faces an opportunity cost, the money it could have earned by holding onto the resource and selling it later. This opportunity cost, the user cost, is the price per unit of the resource when sold at the time that gives the highest present value price. Because the resource is scarce, the user cost is greater than zero—there is a positive opportunity cost to selling a unit of the resource. As with competitively produced manufactured goods, natural resource firms choose their production quantities to maximize profits. In the absence of externalities, the long-run competitive equilibrium for fully owned resources is efficient: it maximizes the sum of producer surplus plus consumer surplus exactly as with manufactured goods.

Like the fully owned resource, the open access resource is also limited in size or reproducibility. Unlike the fully owned resource, though, there is no restriction on the entry of new producers. Anyone who wishes to come and harvest the resource may do so. Therefore, there is entry into the open access resource market until profits are zero: that is, until the resource price equals its average cost of extraction. This is the same rule as for a manufactured good in long-run competitive equilibrium. What is not the same as the competitive model is replicability of the resource. In the competitive model, entry would lead to more of the good; in the resources world, it leads to more, and more immediate, extraction, but at the expense of availability of the resource for the future. Because the resource is unowned, a typical harvester reasons that someone will take whatever she does not harvest. From the harvester's point of view, the opportunity cost to leave the resource untouched until later is zero; in other words, there is no user cost. So the open access harvester chooses a quantity where the marginal cost of extracting the resource equals price. Because the individual harvester sees a user cost of zero, her costs are too low, and she harvests too much. This is a market failure because it does not lead to maximizing consumer and producer surplus. Without opportunity cost as a signal to save some of the resource for the future, extraction is too fast, the stock of the resource is depleted, and too little of the resource is available for consumers in the future.

Common property is a less extreme form of property ownership in which many people jointly own the resource, and entry of new people is limited. For instance, a village commons, a pasture used by all the residents of the village, or a fishery in a small area can all be managed by the local community. Some communities operate cooperatively and act to maximize net benefits for the community over time. Often they use social sanctions to limit harvest and efficiently manage the resource. In other cases, communities have managed the resource so poorly that it is virtually indistinguishable from an open access resource.

Because an open access resource has no restrictions on entry, a harvester will seek to extract a resource as long as she believes that she can make money from it. If, on the other hand, she believes she will lose money from harvesting the resource, she leaves it alone. To understand the effects of open access management on renewable resource populations, we need to examine the relationship between dynamics of the renewable resource and the profits of harvesters.

BOX 17.1

Grazing

Rangelands that can be grazed by any rancher are an example of an open access resource. Before barbed wire and federal regulation, the American Great Plains were open access rangeland. Due to speculators who were attracted to the impressive profits of ranching, and a seemingly unlimited supply of free grazing on federal lands, livestock herds grew rapidly on the public rangelands. In 1870, there were 4.1 million beef cattle and 4.8 million sheep in the 17 western states. In 1900, there were 19.6 million beef cattle and 25.1 million sheep. The lands could not support herds this large and became severely degraded.

Cattle on the open range do not mix well with other forms of wildlife. Some species, such as bison and prairie dogs, compete with cattle for food; predatory species, like wolves, eat them. The ranching community has sought to limit or eliminate some of these species to protect their operations.

In response to the degradation of the Great Plains due to overgrazing, the federal government in 1934 turned this open access resource into a managed resource. The Taylor Grazing Act (and its successor, the Federal Land Policy and Management Act of 1976) required grazing permits that limited the number of animals on land owned by the U.S. government. While the open access problem was reduced by the permitting process, the conflict between grazing and other uses of the range lands remain.

THE CATCH FUNCTION

Finding the profits for a fisher starts with finding how much a boat harvests per fishing season. Fishing **effort** is a measure of how much fishing equipment is in the water and for how long. One measure of effort is a **boat-year**, the use of a boat in a fishery full time for a year. For instance, 6.1 boat-years could mean six boats for the whole season and one boat for a tenth of the season. How many fish does a boat catch in a boat-year?

It is easier to catch fish when the stock of fish is high than when it is low, for two reasons. First, a net placed in an ocean full of fish will catch more fish than in an ocean whose stock is very low. Second, it is easier to find fish when there are more of them. One common assumption is that the relationship between the stock of fish and the catch is linear: a stock twice as high leads to a harvest twice as high.

The **harvest function** mathematically measures the harvest that results for specified levels of stock and effort. Harvest, H, is the product of effort, E; stock, S; and a constant, k: $H = E * S * k$. The constant k, called the **catchability constant**, is the amount that one boat-year would catch if there were 1 mmt of fish in the sea. If E is specified, the resulting line, which relates the stock of the resource to the harvest, is called a **harvest line**.

Figure 17.2 shows the relationship among stock, effort, and yield in the North Sea herring fishery. It shows the growth curve from Figure 17.1. Added to the figure are three dashed harvest lines labeled E, which represent yield at three different levels of effort, measured in boat-years.

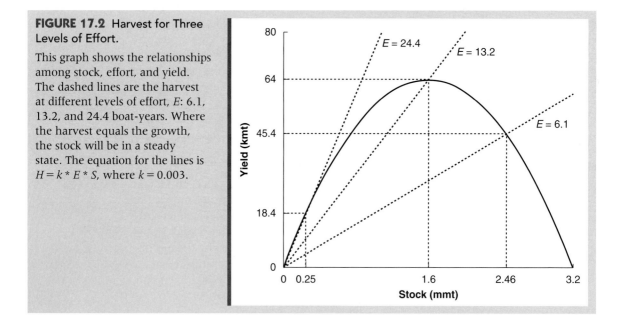

FIGURE 17.2 Harvest for Three Levels of Effort.

This graph shows the relationships among stock, effort, and yield. The dashed lines are the harvest at different levels of effort, E: 6.1, 13.2, and 24.4 boat-years. Where the harvest equals the growth, the stock will be in a steady state. The equation for the lines is $H = k * E * S$, where $k = 0.003$.

Let's first look at the line labeled E = 6.1. It shows how much fish 6.1 boat-years of effort would catch for different levels of fish stock. The assumption that the relationship between stock and catch is linear means that it is a straight line from the origin.

The harvest line for E = 6.1 boat-years intersects the stock-growth curve at a stock of 2.46 mmt and a harvest of 45 kmt. If the initial stock in the fishery is higher than 2.46 mmt—for instance, if the herring is at its carrying capacity of 3.2 mmt—then the harvest line indicates that harvest will exceed growth, and the stock of herring will fall in response to 6.1 boat-years of fishing. If, on the other hand, the initial stock of the resource is lower than 2.46 mmt—for instance, at 1 mmt—the harvest is less than the growth, and the stock of the resource will continue to increase. However, it will grow less slowly with harvest than if there is no harvest. At the point where the harvest line intersects the stock-growth curve, the boats are harvesting exactly the growth, and they can harvest sustainably at this level forever.

What happens if more boats enter the fishery? The harvest will be higher if there are more boats than if there are fewer boats, for any initial stock. The new harvest line will be steeper than the first line because more effort for a specified stock means more harvest. Because more fish are harvested, the new sustained-yield harvest has a stock level lower than the stock associated with fewer boats. Thus, while the initial effort of 6.1 boat-years has a stock of 2.46 mmt associated with its sustained-yield harvest of 45.4 kmt/year, 24.4 boat-years results in a stock of only 0.25 mmt at a sustained-yield harvest of 18.4 kmt/year. If there are 13.2 boat-years of fishing, then the sustained-yield harvest is the maximum sustained yield of 64 kmt, with a stock of 1.6 mmt.

While the stock-growth curve is important for the biology of the system, a different graph is more useful for the economics of the system. Figure 17.3 illustrates the **effort-yield curve**. This curve shows the relationship between the amount of effort (the number of boat-years, along the horizontal axis) and the harvest, or yield (along the vertical axis). This curve comes from Figure 17.2. With an effort of 6.1 boat-years, the stock-growth curve indicates a sustained-yield harvest of 45.4 kmt/year, represented by point A on Figure 17.3. Point B shows the MSY harvest of 64 kmt/year with 13.2 boat-years, and point C shows that 24.4 boat-years will have a sustained-yield harvest of 18.4 kmt/year. The figure shows that, as effort increases, the sustained-yield harvest first increases and then decreases.

PROFITS

The effort-yield curve gives the physical relationship between effort and harvest. Harvesters, of course, are less concerned with this physical relationship than they are with profits. Getting to profits requires comparing revenue—price times quantity—to cost.

At the time these herring figures were recorded, the price of a ton of herring was about 735 Norwegian kronor (abbreviated NOK and worth $73.50 USD). If we multiply every value on the curve in Figure 17.3 by 735 NOK, the curve now represents the total revenue associated with different levels of effort. Figure 17.4 on page 423

FIGURE 17.3 The Effort-Yield Curve.

This curve shows the sustained-yield harvests associated with different levels of effort. Low levels of effort have low sustained-yield harvests but high stock levels. As effort increases, harvests initially increase and then decrease as the stock is depleted.

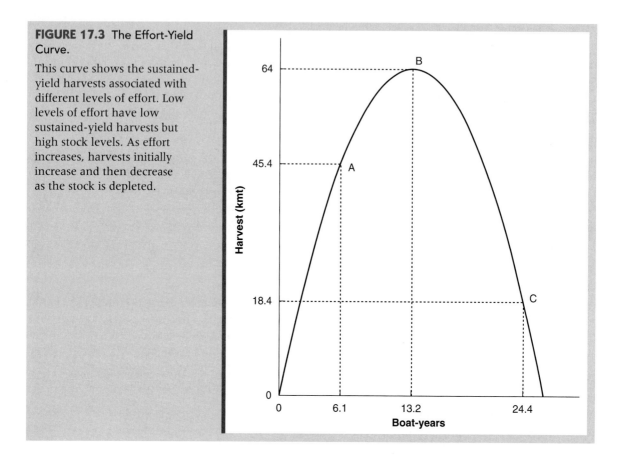

shows this conversion of quantities of herring caught into money. While the horizontal axis still measures effort, the vertical axis measures the monetary value of harvest.

To calculate profits, the next step is to calculate total costs. The costs of operating a boat for a year in the herring fishery are 557,000 NOK. For each level of effort, then, the costs associated with that harvest are 557,000 NOK times that level of effort. The straight line in Figure 17.4 is the effort times 557,000 NOK. The diagram shows both total revenue and total cost for different levels of effort. The gap between revenues and costs for any level of effort is the profit associated with that level of effort.

An open access renewable resource industry is in equilibrium if two conditions are met: growth equals harvest, and profits are zero. When both fish stock and effort are unchanging, the system is in a steady state. So an open access equilibrium is a steady state. If growth equals harvest, the yield of fish will be the same year after year. If profits equal zero, the number of boat-years will be the same each year; new fishers will not enter the fishery, and current fishers will not exit the fishery or change their effort. The stock associated with these two conditions is called the **open access stock**. What levels of effort lead to the open access equilibrium?

FIGURE 17.4 The Effort-Revenue and Effort-Cost Curves.

Multiplying price times harvest turns the effort-yield curve into an effort-revenue curve, with the vertical axis measuring Norwegian kronor. The effort-cost curve shows the total cost as a function of effort.

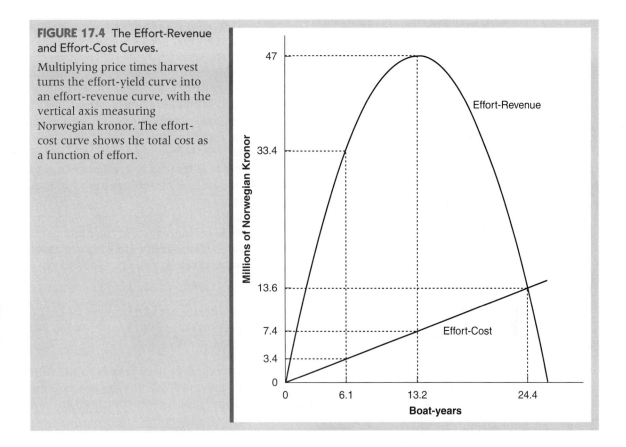

Suppose that effort is 6.1 boat-years. Those boats would harvest 45 kmt/year, for total revenue of (45 kmt) * 735 NOK/ton = about 33 million NOK. Total costs would be (557,000 NOK/boat) * 6.1 boat-years = about 3.3 million NOK. Thus, total profits would be about 29.7 million NOK, almost 5 million NOK per boat, or approximately $500,000 USD per boat.

In an open access fishery, just as in a competitive industry, entry will occur as long as there are positive profits to be made. The appeal of 5 million NOK per boat would be a major attraction, and new boats will enter the fishery.

Total revenues increase up to the point where there are 13.2 boat-years of effort. As more boats can catch more fish, total costs increase too. Total revenue with 13.2 boat years is 64 kmt * 735 NOK/ton = 47 million NOK, with costs of (557,000 NOK/boat) * 13.2 boat-years = 7.2 million NOK, for total profits of about 39.8 million NOK. Again there are positive profits, although, per boat, they are now down to about 3 million NOK. So if there were 13.2 boat-years, more boats would want to enter the fishery.

Beyond 13.2 boat-years, total revenues start to decrease while costs continue to increase. The stock of fish drops below the MSY stock, and the sustained-yield harvest falls from the peak. At 24.4 boat-years of effort, revenues equal costs, and profits equal zero. A look back to Figure 17.2 reveals that the 24.4 boat-years leads to a stock of only 0.25 mmt and a yield of 18.4 kmt/year. Because profits equal zero with 24.4 boat-years, this is an open access equilibrium.

From the point of view of protecting fish populations or maintaining the ecological system of which fish are part, the open access equilibrium is not desirable. In this example, the fish stock is reduced to less than one-tenth of the no-fishing stock. A stock this low may have considerable consequences for other fish stocks that feed on the target stock. Depending on the growth curve for a particular fish, it is possible for the open access equilibrium to occur at extremely small or even zero stocks: zero stocks means zero profit too! Because no boats and no fish is an open access equilibrium, open access can lead to extinction.

Open access is also economically undesirable. Notice that, at either point with lower effort, harvests, profits per boat, and total profits were larger than in the open access equilibrium. Everyone—consumers, harvesters, and environmentalists who care about the ecosystem—would be better off if it were possible to restrict entry into the fishery.

BOX 17.2

Dynamics of Open Access

The open access equilibrium is the outcome after the fish stock adjusts to the fishing effort and the fishing effort adjusts to the fish stock. What does the process look like during the adjustment process? The adjustment process is controlled by two equations. First is our growth equation for fish:

$$S_{t+1} = S_t + G(S_t) - kES_t$$

The number of fish next year (S_{t+1}) is the number now (S_t) plus the growth $G(S_t)$ less the harvest, where harvest is the catchability constant (k) times the effort (E), times the fish stock, our catch function.

The second equation gives the change in effort:

$$E_{t+1} = E_t + m(pkS_t - c)$$

The amount of effort next year (E_{t+1}) is the amount now (E_t) plus new entrants. Let's assume that entry increases faster when profit per boat is higher. Each boat catches kS_t fish and thus has revenue of pkS_t, where p is the price of fish. With c the cost per boat, profit per boat is $pkS - c$. The number m is the constant of proportionality that measures how much new entry there will be for each unit of profit per boat. Figure 17.5 shows how fish stock and effort evolve.

In the figure, the stock (measured on the horizontal axis) starts at 0.75 mmt, and effort (measured on the vertical axis) begins at 15 boat-years at point A. With so much stock, harvesting is profitable. The curve goes up and to the left, as the number of boats is increasing and stock is decreasing. At a stock of 0.25 mmt, the open access stock, harvesting becomes unprofitable (point B), leading to a decrease in the number of boats. Eventually the number of boats falls far enough so that the stock begins growing again. For instance, effort hits a minimum around 4 boats at a stock of 0.25 mmt (point C). With so few boats, stock starts to increase, making fishing profitable again, leading to more effort, and the cycle starts again. The result is an inward spiral with its center at the open access equilibrium. In this case, the open access equilibrium keeps the species alive. Not all species are so lucky.

FIGURE 17.5 Evolution of the Fishery.

When the stock is high at point A, profits per boat are high, and many boats enter. The high number of boats reduces the stock, and boats drop out of the fishery at point B. As the fishery recovers, profits increase again, boats enter again, and the cycle repeats.

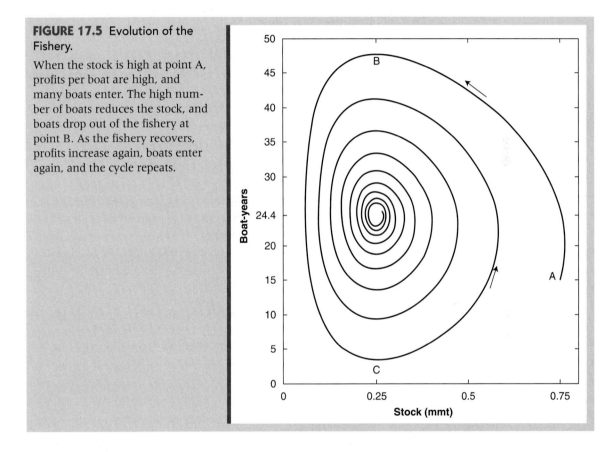

IN SUMMARY

- Well-defined property rights are necessary for efficient management of both renewable and nonrenewable resources. If it is impossible to exclude people from the resource, the resource is termed open access. People will enter and extract the resource until profits are zero.

- Open access does not have conditions that allow people to save the resource for the future. As a result, extraction is too fast, and the stock of the resource is depleted. Consumers get too much of the resource in the present, and too little in the future. Unlike the case of perfect competition, zero profit in a resource market signals inefficient management.
- Common property is a form of property ownership in which many people jointly own the resource, and entry of new people can be limited. Some common property resources have been managed well for centuries; others operate very closely to being open access.
- In an open access resource, harvesters will enter and exploit the resource as long as total revenue exceeds total cost. Although smaller levels of effort would be more profitable for the harvesters in the long run, the inability to restrict harvest drives profits to zero. The high levels of harvest under open access lead to great reductions of the stock and cause significant ecological damage. While some open access resources can achieve a steady state, others may lead to extinction of the resource.

Efficient Renewable Resource Management

If open access is inefficient, what does efficient management of a renewable resource involve? If a resource is privately owned, the owner can control access to the resource and, thus, the amount and timing of harvest. Sometimes the resource manager is a government regulator. For instance, the European Union and Norway together now manage the North Sea herring fishery.

Efficient management of a renewable resource involves identifying the stock and the sustained-yield harvest level associated with that stock that maximize profits. We'll consider here two of the major factors that determine the efficient management of a nonrenewable resource. Costs are important because they affect the profitability of harvesting. Opportunity costs matter because leaving fish in the sea is an investment in the future. Because the interaction of these two effects is complex, we will discuss them separately and then discuss how they affect the efficient stock level.

HARVEST COSTS

Looking at the role of costs involves looking at effort. Figure 17.6 shows how profits vary with effort. The top panel repeats Figure 17.4, while the bottom panel just subtracts the costs from the revenues. Profits are positive for all levels of effort less than 24.4 boat-years. Between 24.4 and 12.2 boat-years of effort, the gap between revenue and cost—profit—increases as effort decreases, for two reasons. First, reducing the number of boats saves the expense of those boats. Second, because reducing effort allows stock to increase, the growth of the species, and thus the sustained-yield harvest, increases. Reducing effort continues to increase profits until the profit-maximizing effort of 12.2 boat-years, the top of the profit-effort curve in the figure.

FIGURE 17.6 Profits in the Steady State.

Subtracting total costs from total revenues in the top panel results in the profit-effort curve in the lower panel. Profits reach their maximum at an effort level of 12.2 boat-years. In open access, profits are zero with effort of 24.4 boat-years and a much lower stock.

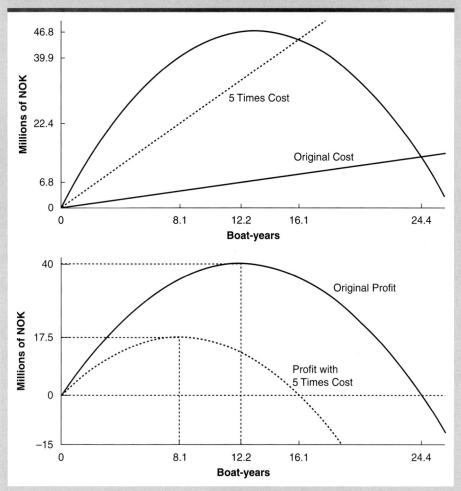

A comparison of the top and bottom panels shows that revenue and profits do not peak at the same level of effort. The peak of revenue is the level of effort associated with MSY, 13.2 boat-years. Because costs fall faster than revenue between 13.2 and 12.2 boat-years, the profits increase by reducing effort. At 12.2 boat-years, profit is at its maximum. At the profit maximum, the harvest is 63.6 kmt/year, resulting in a stock of 1.725 mmt and profits of 40 million NOK/year.

Because high effort is associated with low stock, and vice versa, maximizing profits in the managed fishery results in a much higher stock than does open access. In fact, the stock that maximizes profits is higher than the MSY stock.

In general, higher costs reduce effort and allow the stock to increase. The dashed lines in the figure show the effects of five times higher costs per boat. Higher costs lead to a steeper effort-cost line, which leads to a lower profit-maximizing effort. In the example, the profit-maximizing effort is only 8.1 boat-years. Lower effort in turn leads to more stock in steady state.

In a managed resource, then, the profit-maximizing effort is less, much less, than the open access effort because the resource manager is able to prevent entry; profits do not have to be driven to zero. Less effort leads to greater stocks. Moreover, increasing cost leads to decreasing effort and increasing stock.

THE INTEREST RATE AND OPPORTUNITY COST

Why should there be profits in a managed fishery if there are no profits in the long run in a competitive industry? When an industry makes zero profits in long-run competitive equilibrium, profits include all of the costs, including opportunity cost. A fishery makes profits in the long run only if that calculation does not include the value or opportunity cost of the fish; it is as though the fish were free. Let's see what happens when we account for the value of this resource.

Because the manager controlling a renewable resource can limit entry, she can choose how much of the resource to harvest in each time period in order to maximize the present value of profits. Let's assume she has perfect foresight about prices and profits. How much should the manager harvest each year?

Let's say that the initial stock is 1.6 mmt, the maximum sustained-yield stock, and there are no costs associated with harvesting the fish. The manager has the options of harvesting 64 kmt forever, harvesting less than 64 kmt, or harvesting more than 64 kmt. If she chooses the last of these options, the fish stock will go below 1.6 mmt. Suppose that the manager decides to reduce the harvest this year by one ton. Doing so reduces revenue from that one ton of fish by the price, 735 NOK. What does she get in exchange for that reduction?

Because there is one less ton of fish harvest, there will be one more ton of stock next year. As a result, the growth next year, $G(S_{t+1})$, will be different from the growth this year, $G(S_t)$, because the stock is larger. A one-unit change in stock, then, leads to a change in growth of $[G(S_{t+1}) - G(S_t)]$. Marginal growth, the slope of the growth curve, is the change in growth divided by the change in stock; let's call it MG. Now the extra ton saved results in 1 + MG extra tons added to the stock next period. The profit next year associated with saving that ton of fish for next year, then, is (1 + MG) * 735 NOK/ton. Because the profit will not come until next year, that amount must be discounted: after all, the fisher could sell that ton and earn interest by investing at a rate r. The present value of that profit next year is (1 + MG) * 735/(1 + r). Whether it makes sense for the manager to delay harvesting that ton by a year depends on which is higher, the 735 given up this year, or (1 + MG) * 735/(1 + r) to be gained next year. More generally, the tradeoff with a constant price is between getting profit, π, this year or $\pi * (1 + MG)/(1 + r)$ next year. Note that asking whether $\pi > \pi(1 + MG)/(1 + r)$ is the same as asking whether $r > MG$. If $r > MG$, it is better to harvest this year and not wait until next year. When $MG > r$, profits are higher next year. When $MG = r$, the fisher has found the right balance between harvesting this year and next year.

The interest rate represents the opportunity cost of keeping the resource. The resource manager has the choice of letting the fish stock increase, of depleting the stock and investing the profit from the sale, or of keeping the stock constant and harvesting only the growth. If the fish stock is growing faster than money in the bank—that is, if marginal growth is higher than the interest rate r—the manager will increase profits for fishers by letting the fish grow. On the other hand, when the interest rate is higher than marginal growth, the fishers are better off converting some of the stock to money and getting that higher return at the bank. When the marginal growth equals the interest rate, the fisher is getting the same return by letting fish grow as she is by investing money in the bank; she cannot increase her profits by moving money between the bank account and the fishery.

On the growth curve in Figure 17.1, the slope G is steep for low levels of stock. As the stock increases, marginal growth decreases. It reaches zero at the MSY stock, and it is negative for higher stocks. Because interest rates are almost always positive, maximizing profit in a costless fishery by setting $MG = r$ means that the slope of the growth curve will be positive, which means that stock will be lower than the MSY stock.

Why is the profit-maximizing stock lower than the MSY stock? MSY is at the top of the growth curve; increasing or decreasing stock cannot make growth higher. If the fisher reduces the stock, she gets an immediate amount of cash, but she gives up some annual growth. For small stock reductions, the effect on annual growth is very small. The gains from that initial sale outweigh the future reductions in harvest. For larger reductions in stock, though, the effect on growth, and thus future harvests, is large; the species will reproduce faster than money will increase at the bank. The fisher will stop adjusting the stock and conduct a sustained-yield harvest when the fishery grows at the same rate as money in the bank.

Table 17.2 demonstrates the relation of the $MG = r$ rule to profits for North Sea herring. The first column lists different possible harvest levels, starting with a current stock of 1.6 mmt. The manager can allow harvest of none, all 1.6 mmt, or an intermediate level. The second column shows the stock that will remain, equal to 1.6 mmt less the harvest now. The third column shows the growth that would occur if the stock is at that level. The fourth column shows the remaining stock plus the growth, which is what is available for harvest next year. The fifth column gives the present value of profits with a 5 percent interest rate: 735 NOK * (Harvest Now + Harvest Next Year/1.05). Finally, the sixth column lists the marginal growth associated with the stock. Notice that the marginal growth equals the interest rate at a stock around 0.6 mmt, which also happens to be the stock where profits are at their maximum.

When the resource manager wants the industry to maximize profits, a positive interest rate leads the manager to reduce the stock below the MSY stock. Unless the

TABLE 17.2   How Much to Harvest Now?

The initial stock is 1.6 mmt. The fisher can harvest any amount up to that level. For any initial harvest, the stock that remains determines both the growth, which determines the harvest available the following year, and the marginal growth. The present value of profits is the value of the initial harvest plus the value of the next year's harvest, discounted at 5 percent. Maximum profit occurs when marginal growth equals the interest rate, with an initial harvest of about 1.1 mmt.

HARVEST NOW	STOCK (MMT)	GROWTH (KMT)	HARVEST NEXT YEAR	PRESENT VALUE OF PROFITS	MARGINAL GROWTH
1.6	0	0	0	1176	0.0775
1.5	0.1	7.75	0.10775	1177.925	0.0725
1.4	0.2	15	0.215	1179.5	0.0675
1.3	0.3	21.75	0.32175	1180.725	0.0625
1.2	0.4	28	0.428	1181.6	0.0575
1.1	0.5	33.75	0.53375	1182.125	0.0525
1	0.6	39	0.639	1182.3	0.0475
0.9	0.7	43.75	0.74375	1182.125	0.0425
0.8	0.8	48	0.848	1181.6	0.0375
0.7	0.9	51.75	0.95175	1180.725	0.0325
0.6	1	55	1.055	1179.5	0.0275
0.5	1.1	57.75	1.15775	1177.925	0.0225
0.4	1.2	60	1.26	1176	0.0175
0.3	1.3	61.75	1.36175	1173.725	0.0125
0.2	1.4	63	1.463	1171.1	0.0075
0.1	1.5	63.75	1.56375	1168.125	0.0025
0	1.6	64	1.664	1164.8	−0.0025

marginal growth for a species is very low at low population levels, however, this interest rate effect will not induce the manager to choose complete depletion of the stock.

Now we have examined the effect of the interest rate in a model with no harvest costs, and we have also studied the role of harvest costs in a model with no interest rate. Combining these two effects is generally done with complex mathematical methods that we will not discuss here. The key lesson, though, is that these effects operate in different directions. The interest rate effect pushes the efficient stock below the MSY stock, while harvest costs push the efficient stock above the MSY stock. The profit-maximizing level of stock depends on the specific values of all these factors.

DEMAND SHIFTS, MANAGEMENT COSTS, AND ECOLOGICAL FACTORS

Renewable resources, even more than most nonrenewable resources, play complex roles in both human societies and ecological systems. The role of costs and interest rates are two major factors in efficient management, but a number of other factors play a role. Here we give brief mention to these.

BOX 17.3

Forests: The Other Renewable Resource

Forests, like fisheries, are renewable resources. Harvesting forests provides many goods that people appreciate, including housing materials, paper, and firewood. Forests can regenerate when harvested. Forests can also be overharvested, leading to ecological damages in addition to the loss of wood products. Like fisheries, the amount of wood available in a forest depends on biological processes that limit their availability. The economics of forests and fisheries management appear different in one important dimension, though: while the stock of fish in the future depends on the population of the fish now, the stock of wood available in a forest depends primarily on the time since it started growing. Put another way, the stock of fish is mostly measured by the number of fish; the stock of wood in a forest is mostly measured by the size of the trees, which depends on the trees' age.

In many managed forests, the forest is divided into a number of plots. Within each plot, the trees are all planted at the same time, so that they are all the same age, and they will be harvested at the same time. The plots are planted at different times, so that the harvesters always have trees available to harvest, while other trees are growing. For instance, a 5,000-acre forest might be divided into 100 50-acre plots. If one plot is harvested each year, then the landowner can harvest a plot, replant it, and let it regrow for 100 years while she harvests the other stands in order of their ages. After 100 years, she will come back to the first plot, which now has 100-year-old trees on it. This form of management is known as rotation forestry, where a rotation is the length of time the trees grow before they are harvested.

The optimal management of this kind of even-aged forest (trees all the same age) was first described by Martin Faustmann in 1849. The key forestry question is, How old should a stand of trees be when it is harvested?

(Continued)

BOX 17.3

(continued)

The first two columns of Table 17.3 show the age and yield for Douglas-fir trees in five-year increments. The yield, $F(t)$, is the quantity of wood per acre that would be sold at the age t shown. The next column shows what $1 t years from now is worth today; it is a discount factor, $1/(1+r)^t$, for $r = 2$ percent. The trees are sold for $200 per thousand board foot (mbf). The next column shows the present value of the wood when sold, $200 * discount factor * yield. The present value-maximizing time to harvest the trees is at age 85, if there is no further value from the land after harvest.

But there is further value. Once the trees are cut, there will be another stand of trees that will start growing, and then they will be cut, and then another stand, and so on. The value of the land, the **soil expectation value (SEV),** is the sum of the present values of all harvest from the land. If the trees are harvested at age L,

$$\text{SEV} = P\left[\frac{F(t)}{(1+r)^t} + \frac{F(t)}{(1+r)^{2t}} + \ldots + \frac{F(t)}{(1+r)^{2t}} + \ldots\right] = \frac{PF(t)}{(1+r)^t - 1}.$$

TABLE 17.3   Age and Yield (in thousand board feet, mbf) for Douglas-fir Trees.

AGE	YIELD (MBF)	DISCOUNT FACTOR	VALUE OF FIRST STAND ($)	VALUE OF ALL STANDS ($)
30	0.30	0.552	33	74
35	1.99	0.500	199	398
40	4.50	0.453	408	745
45	7.93	0.410	651	1,104
50	12.40	0.372	921	1,466
55	17.87	0.337	1,203	1,813
60	23.80	0.305	1,451	2,087
65	29.60	0.276	1,635	2,258
70	35.20	0.250	1,760	2,347
75	40.57	0.226	1,838	2,376
80	45.70	0.205	1,875	2,358
85	50.53	0.186	1,877	2,306
90	55.00	0.168	1,851	2,225

The last column of the table shows the SEV. The present value-maximizing cutting age is 75. When all the rotations are considered, the present value-maximizing rotation age is younger than the age if there were only one rotation, so that it is possible to get the future wood a little sooner than the one-harvest-only calculation. A higher discount rate reduces the rotation age to get profits even sooner. Figure 17.7 shows the SEV as a function of the rotation age for two different interest rates, the 2 percent rate used previously and 7 percent. The higher interest rate makes the SEV much lower and also lowers the rotation age.

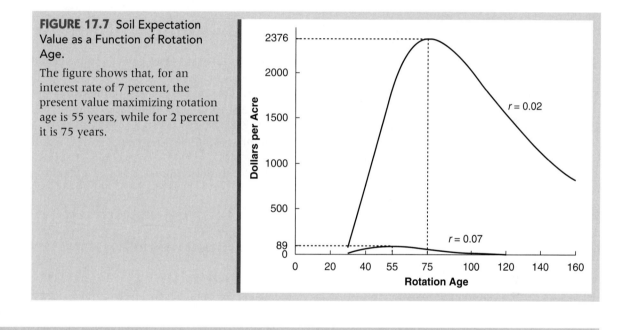

FIGURE 17.7 Soil Expectation Value as a Function of Rotation Age.

The figure shows that, for an interest rate of 7 percent, the present value maximizing rotation age is 55 years, while for 2 percent it is 75 years.

First, people's desires for resources change over time. If demands change, the price of a resource will change. Because resource adjustments take time, though, only trends in resource prices affect resource management. For instance, if people gradually become more convinced of the health benefits of eating fish, then the price of fish will increase over time. Because having fish in the future will become more profitable, a resource manager will want the stock to grow; for the stock to grow, she must reduce current harvest. Once the demand for fish stabilizes, though, the price of fish in the future will no longer increase. In that case, she will seek a stock level that accounts for costs and the interest rate but not price changes. If there are no trends but only sudden changes—for instance, if the price of fish doubles overnight—then there is no time for the stock to grow, and the resource manager will not change her stock.

Second, while higher harvest costs lead to increased stock levels, costs of keeping or growing the resource—management costs—reduce stocks. While growing herring in the North Sea costs nothing, growing salmon in fish farms, cattle, or plantation forests can involve significant costs—for land, feed, fertilizer, or other forms of tending to the resource. Any of these costs will lead to lower stocks than in the absence of these costs.

Third, renewable resources interact with the ecosystems in which they live. Droughts, changes in temperature, fires, floods, pollution, introduction of competitor or predator species, and other ecological shifts can change the stock of a resource or the carrying capacity of the place where it lives. A resource manager must be sensitive to these changes to achieve efficient management.

IN SUMMARY

- Efficient management of a renewable resource involves consideration of the harvest costs and interest rate, among other factors.
- Costs of harvest discourage harvesting. Because less harvesting increases the stock, the presence of harvest costs leads to the efficient stock being higher than the efficient stock in the absence of these costs.
- For a fishery without costs, the rule for an optimal stock is that the marginal growth equals the interest rate.
- Other factors, including changes in consumer demand, costs of managing the resource, or ecological changes can also affect the efficient stock of a resource.

Extinction

Although renewable resources have the ability to replenish themselves, they can be depleted completely. Renewable resources are not necessarily renewed. Historically, people have harvested a number of species to extinction. Passenger pigeons, for instance, were once the most common bird in North America. They are now extinct, due to massive hunting of them in the nineteenth century for inexpensive meat and sport.

Biological characteristics contribute to the probability that a species might become extinct. Some species have low marginal growth even at low population levels; if their numbers are depleted, it is difficult for the population to recover. Because passenger pigeons lived in flocks, it was easy for hunters to shoot many of them at once. One biological characteristic that predisposes a species to extinction is a minimum viable population greater than zero. When a population gets too low, it loses genetic diversity, and every member becomes susceptible to the same diseases. Small populations can also find it difficult to find mates. Human preferences and economic factors, though, can also play a very large role in which species face extinction.

In particular, while open access is more likely to lead to extinction, private owner-ship is nevertheless not a guarantor of species survival. In the open access fishery model, extinction will occur if entry is profitable for stock levels below the mini-mum viable population. Entry will be profitable as long as price * harvest – costs > 0. Because harvest H is the catchability constant multiplied by effort and stock, $k * E * S$, multiplying harvest by price and subtracting costs, $P * k * E * S - c * E$, is profit. Solving this equation for the stock where profit is zero yields $S_{profit=0} = c/(P * k)$. For the herring fishery, $S_{profit=0} = 250$ mt in open access. To demonstrate the dy-namics of extinction, Figure 17.8 shifts the herring growth curve downwards so that its minimum viable population is 430 mt; below this level, while the stock is still positive, growth is negative.

As long as stock is larger than 250 mt, profits will be positive, and effort will increase. Eventually the effort will be so large that stock will reach the minimum viable population size, at 430 mt. Then growth will be negative, and the stock will decline to zero.

Extinction can happen in a privately managed resource as well, due to lack of incentives to protect a species. There are many species for which market incentives for their protection are weak or nonexistent. These include many plants and ani-mals for which people have no direct use and whose role in ecosystems are not well understood or appreciated. For instance, a higher profit for agriculture than for forestry will cause landowners to remove forests and extinguish whatever endemic creatures live in them. Biodiversity is a public good; destruction of these species

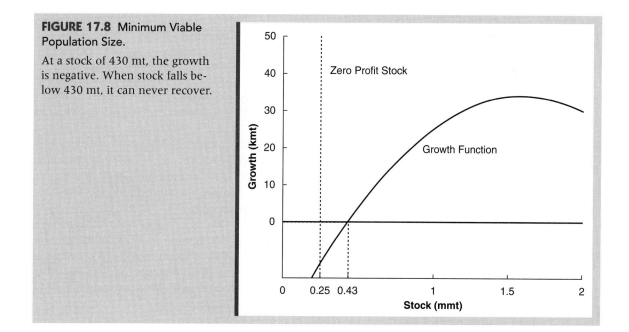

FIGURE 17.8 Minimum Viable Population Size.

At a stock of 430 mt, the growth is negative. When stock falls be-low 430 mt, it can never recover.

through loss of habitat is an example of the market failure of underproviding public goods. If the benefits of biodiversity are greater than the producer and consumer surplus from clearing land, then clearing the land is not efficient. In other cases, species are harmed by externalities, such as water pollutants. Because our understanding of the role of any one species in the web of life is incomplete, we cannot assess the full benefits of maintaining that species now and in the future. Therefore, it is very unlikely that extinguishing a species can ever be efficient.

IN SUMMARY

- Extinction of a species results from a combination of biological characteristics and human behaviors. Open access contributes to the depletion of a resource. The absence of restrictions on access leads to excessive harvest, which reduces the stocks.
- Other market failures, such as externalities and the underproviding of public goods, can lead to extinction even if a resource is fully owned.

Regulating Renewable Resources

If the management of renewable resources were left entirely to private markets, there would be both the externality problems inherent in producing other types of goods and potentially the open access externality that characterizes many fisheries and much big game management. To reduce these market failures, many governments regulate the use of these resources by means of both standards and market-based incentives. In some cases, instead of regulating private use of resources, governments directly own the resource.

Managing a renewable resource efficiently leads to dramatically different outcomes than leaving it as open access. First, the stock level under open access will be much lower than the stock under efficient management, quite possibly so low that the resource stock cannot survive. Second, efficient resource management will lead to greater profits than under open access. Though consumers in the short run would pay a lower price for the resource under open access than they would under efficient management, over time the reduced stock of the resource under open access will lead to scarcity and thus higher prices. For this reason, resource regulators, such as departments of fish and wildlife, game wardens, and forest rangers, have long sought ways to protect the stocks of renewable resources.

A common way to regulate a renewable resource, especially a fishery, is through standards that make it harder to harvest. Typical fishing regulations, for instance, involve standards that make fishing more difficult and costly. Limits are set on harvest (called allowable catch), on methods of harvesting (for instance, types of nets or kinds of boats), or season length. For example, there is a season length of just one day to catch crab in Humboldt Bay, California. Many governments have forest practices acts that, for instance, restrict how many trees can be harvested from a site or prohibit harvest near rivers to reduce ecological damage. All these regulations increase the costs of harvesting and thus reduce the level of effort.

These standards raise harvesting costs. As in Figure 17.6, higher costs lead to an open access equilibrium with less effort and higher stock, but still with zero profits. In practice, the stock is driven closer to MSY. Therefore, the yearly harvest increases. Increase in yearly harvest provides more of the resource for consumers and more sustainable work for harvesters and processors in the long run. In the short run, though, harvesters see less employment because there is less effort.

Improved technologies reduce the effectiveness of standards in keeping costs high. Fish finders and stronger engines have reduced the costs of fishing considerably. The lower costs led to even lower open access stocks in the EU and the United States. Helicopter logging has allowed forests to be logged in more remote and steeper areas than in the past. In order to rebuild these stocks, regulators would need to impose even more restrictions to make harvesting even more costly, which in turn would reduce the profits from harvesting. Regulators have faced extreme political pressure to allow continued harvest, even in the face of resource depletion. As a result, many regulated fisheries have been so overfished that they must be closed, and large swaths of land have been deforested.

Because the traditional methods of regulation have not worked in practice, market-based regulations have been proposed. One alternative is to increase costs by taxing harvests. If the tax is equal to the user cost, the harvester is made to face the opportunity cost of taking the resource. The government would act as owner and collect the rents from the resource. In effect, there would no longer be a lack of ownership or a market failure. A tax would increase the cost of harvesting, reduce harvest, and increase stock. It is preferable to standards because, instead of increasing costs by requiring inefficient methods, it would raise money that could be used for public activities. However, harvesters' incomes would decrease. For this reason, taxing harvests, like taxing pollution, is politically unattractive. No U.S. or EU fisheries are managed this way.

A relatively new policy to regulate fisheries is *individual transferable quotas*, which are used extensively in New Zealand. An **individual transferable quota (ITQ)**, sometimes called an **individual fishing quota (IFQ)**, is a right to catch a fixed fraction of the allowable catch of fish of a given species. Just as in a marketable permit system for pollutants, the right to harvest fish can be bought and sold. The regulator must still set a total allowable catch. ITQs are efficient for the same reason that a tax would be efficient: it limits harvest, and fishers will not have to spend money on inefficient equipment. Because the permits are transferrable, more efficient fishers will buy permits from less efficient ones. The cost of buying an additional ITQ is an additional cost of harvest, just like a tax would be. Unlike the tax, however, harvesters usually receive the ITQs for free. As a result, they can profit either by harvesting or by selling their ITQs. Because a large harvest, allowed with high numbers of ITQs, lower the value of the ITQs, fishers are no longer advocates for unrealistically high total allowable catch. The ITQs change the fishers into owners of the fishery.

Although New Zealand fishers are happy with the use of ITQs, this system has met resistance in the United States and the European Union. Because more efficient harvesting is likely to reduce the number of boats, it is likely to reduce the number of fishers as well as the number of ports that boats will use. Many small fishing communities are concerned that, although the fishers may be financially secure, their towns may suffer from the reduced use of the ports.

BOX 17.4

Poaching Ivory

The unlawful harvest of animals is called poaching. Poaching large animals like the African elephant can lead to their extinction. The economic story is the standard open access model. There is free entry for poachers. All they need to enter are a gun and a truck. Because elephants are big and easy to find, low elephant numbers do not make poaching much more expensive than high elephant numbers. The benefit to poaching elephants is selling their tusks for ivory. As long as the quantity killed plus the quantity that die naturally is greater than the number of elephants born, the number of elephants will decline.

The population numbers for the African elephant are not known with any certainty. Approximately 500,000 elephants are alive today. Perhaps as many 3 million to 5 million were alive at the start of the twentieth century. The low point of the population was in the 1980s with about 400,000 elephants.

Many policies were undertaken to stem the decline of the elephant. In 1989, the African elephant was protected by the Convention on International Trade in Endangered Species of Wild Fauna and Flora (CITES). The convention, backed up by laws in many importing countries, made international trade in new ivory illegal. As a result, the demand curve for new ivory shifted inward, and the quantity of ivory purchased and the number of elephants killed went down.

Many African countries, with the help of the international community, increased their anti-poaching efforts. This raises the cost of killing elephants and so decreases the harvest.

There is also considerable effort in Africa to preserve land that serves as elephant habitat, for instance, in game parks. However, the meaning of a park is not as clear in Africa as it is in the European Union and the United States. People live in many of the African parks or on their borders. It is vital to the health of the parks and the elephants that the human inhabitants see it in their interest to preserve the elephants. The tourism business in the parks can serve that function.

Despite these international and national actions, not all is well for elephants. In Central Africa, poaching is continuing unabated. The resurgence of the elephant population in the southern part of Africa is not matched in other places.

With Africa's human population near doubling in 25 years' time and the world demand for food and fuel crops vastly increased, the tussle for land between elephants and people will surely continue.

IN SUMMARY

- Efficient resource management increases the stock of the resource as well as profits for harvesters. Compared with open access, efficient resource management provides greater assurance of stock protection for both species preservation and future consumption.
- Resource managers have long used a variety of methods to restrict harvests and protect resource stocks. Methods such as gear restrictions and season limits increase the costs of harvest, and thus decrease harvest, but they require use of inefficient harvest methods. Market-based incentive approaches like those used for pollution policy—taxing harvests or using individual transferable quotas—can achieve the same goal of reducing harvest at lower cost than gear or season restrictions.

Fish Stocks Today

The North Sea herring fishery was so depleted by open access in the 1970s that the fishery was completely closed for a period to allow stocks to recover. Although regulations were put in place to protect the fishery, it once again drew near collapse in the 1990s. Norway and the European Union currently have agreements on joint management of the fishery that specify ways of setting harvest quotas. The herring stocks have once again recovered, almost to levels of the early 1960s. In the meantime, levels of cod in the North Sea declined 76 percent between 1963 and 2001.

Fish populations in many parts of the world are in continuing danger of collapse. The potential losses to human well-being and ecology are huge. The principles of efficient management provide tools for the sustainable use of fish stocks and other renewable resources, but getting them implemented has proven politically difficult.

CHAPTER SUMMARY

Here are the key lessons from this chapter:

- Renewable resources differ from nonrenewable resources in their ability to reproduce. They differ from manufactured goods because their biology limits their reproduction. While people have, at best, limited ability to increase the growth of a species in a short period of time, they can reduce the species population by harvest. If harvest exactly equals growth, the stock will be constant, and the harvest will be a sustained yield.
- An open access resource is available to anyone who wants to harvest it. The lack of restriction on entry leads to harvesters exploiting the resource until nobody is making any profits. Open access leads to high levels of harvesting effort and to levels of stock below the maximum sustained yield (MSY) stock.
- Efficient resource management requires an ability to restrict access to the resource. A resource manager will reduce harvest and the effort associated

with harvest; both the stock of the resource and the profits from the resource increase. Efficient management takes into account the costs of harvest (higher costs increase the stock), the interest rate (a higher interest rate decreases the stock), demand shifts (higher future demand increases the stock), and management costs (higher management costs decrease the stock).

- Efficient management benefits consumers over time by providing for the availability of the resource in the future as well as the present. It also benefits producers, who get higher profits in both the present and future, and it benefits the resource stock and its ecological role because it reduces stock depletion. Efficient management nevertheless can be difficult to accomplish because some harvesters and associated industries may suffer from the loss of resource access if those who gain do not compensate them.

- Extinction occurs for a renewable resource when harvests exceed growth until the stock is below minimum viable population. Under open access, extinction can and has occurred when harvest costs are low. Under private ownership, low harvest costs, low marginal growth even at low population levels, and inadequate incentives to protect the public good of biodiversity all can contribute to species extinction.

- Resource managers have long tried to reduce open access overharvesting by measures such as gear or season restrictions that increase harvest costs. These methods lead to heavy investment in unproductive technologies. Alternatives that avoid these excess investments include taxing harvest or transferable harvest quotas.

KEY TERMS

boat-year *(p. 420)*
carrying capacity *(p. 414)*
catchability constant *(p. 420)*
common property *(p. 419)*
effort *(p. 420)*
effort-yield curve *(p. 421)*
growth *(p. 413)*
growth function *(p. 413)*
harvest function *(p. 420)*
harvest line *(p. 420)*
individual fishing quota (IFQ) *(p. 437)*
individual transferable
   quota (ITQ) *(p. 437)*

marginal growth *(p. 414)*
maximum sustained yield
   (MSY) *(p. 416)*
maximum sustained yield (MSY)
   stock *(p. 416)*
minimum viable population *(p. 416)*
open access *(p. 417)*
open access stock *(p. 422)*
renewable resources *(p. 412)*
soil expectation value
   (SEV) *(p. 432)*
sustainable yield *(p. 416)*
sustained yield *(p. 416)*

NOTES

The quote about overfishing despite regulation is from Josh Eagle and Barton H. Thompson, Jr., "Answering Lord Perry's Question: Dissecting Regulatory Overfishing," *Ocean & Coastal Management* 46 (2003): 649–679.

The North Sea herring example is from Trond Bjornal and Jon M. Conrad, "The Dynamics of an Open Access Fishery," *The Canadian Journal of Economics* 20(1) (February 1987): 74–85. We simplified the model a bit for this chapter. The most recent information on herring and cod stocks comes from the United Kingdom Office of National Statistics, at http://www.statistics.gov.uk/cci/nugget.asp?id=367.

The discussion of efficient forest management comes from an 1849 article by Martin Faustmann, "On the Calculation of the Value Which Forest Lands and Immature Forests Possess for Forestry," republished in *Journal of Forestry Economics* 1 (1995): 7–44.

Information about elephant poaching is from the World Wildlife Federation Species Action Plan for the African Elephant for 2007–2011, http://assets.panda.org/downloads/wwf_sap_african_elephants_final_june_2007v1_1.pdf.

Information on grazing on Western range land is from John H. Cushman, Jr., "Administration Gives Up on Raising Grazing Fees," *New York Times*, December 22, 1994.

EXERCISES

1. You inherit a ranch from someone named Hardin, and you are learning how to manage sheep there. In research on range sustainability, you find these relationships between stock and sheep weight (in pounds, lbs.):

POPULATION	0	5	10	15	20	25	30	35	40	45	50	55	60
Stock Now	0	250	650	1,150	1,700	2,275	2,850	3,400	3,900	4,300	4,550	4,600	4,650
Stock Next Year		0	500	1,050	1,650	2,250	2,850	3,425	3,950	4,400	4,700	4,800	4,650	4,650

The current stock is 40 sheep, 3,900 pounds. The sheep come when called, making their harvest costless. The interest rate is 10 percent, and sheep sell for $1/lb.

(a) Calculate growth for different stocks. (Growth is the change in stock between this and next year for current stock.) Graph the stock-growth curve (both axes should measure weight, *not* population). Label minimum viable population, maximum sustained yield, and carrying capacity.

(b) Next, calculate the *change* in growth, which is the change in growth between two stock levels. For instance, growth for a stock level of 0 is 0, while it is 250 for a stock of 250. The change in growth *associated with the 0 stock level* is Growth(stock = 250), 250, – Growth(stock = 0), 0, = 250. *There will be no value for population = 60.*

(c) The *marginal growth* is the change in growth over the change in stock for a specified stock. Calculate the marginal growth for this parcel. *There is no finite value for population = 0.*

You are now deciding the profit-maximizing stock. For parts (d)–(g), calculate: (i) pounds of sheep you will sell to get to that stock and profits associated with that sale; (ii) sustained-yield harvest and the annual profits that will come from that stock; (iii) the present value of that annual stream of profits; (iv) the total value of your management for that population [the sums of (i) and (iii)].

(d) What is the value of the herd if you keep it at its present size?

(e) If, instead, you sold all 40 sheep (3,900 lbs), what is your profit?

(f) You contemplate operating the herd at 25 animals, 2,275 pounds. What, if anything, is special about this herd size?

(g) Your economics professor told you another rule for profit-maximizing herd size. What is that rule and the stock associated with it? (Choose the closest value in the table if a precise point is not an option. Do not extrapolate between levels.)

(h) At which stock is the present value of profits highest? Was your professor right?

(i) What is the minimum price at which you would be willing to sell your ranch? If you sell it, will you make economic profits on the sale? Why or why not?

(j) While you still have 40 sheep, a rumor arises that the interest rate might drop to 5 percent. If so, (i) at which point would you now expect maximum profits? (Choose the closest value if a precise point is not an option. Do not extrapolate between levels.) (ii) What would annual profits be at that point? (iii) What is the present value of that annual stream of profits? (iv) If you are not now at that level, calculate your profits or costs to achieve it. (v) Find total present value (the values of adjusting the stock plus the income stream).

(k) You are considering selling your ranch or using it as collateral in taking out a loan. Do you as a businessperson prefer a high or a low interest rate? Why?

(l) The interest rate stays at 10 percent. The sheep become ornery and refuse to come when called; you now hire sheepherders to harvest them. How will this affect your decision from (h) on the profit-maximizing stock? (A numerical answer is not possible. The question is whether stock size should be higher or lower.)

2. You have moved to a small village in a developing country. The people in this village rely on the nearby forest for the wood they use for cooking. The forest officially is a park and should not be harvested, but there are very few park rangers, and most of them have family reliant on wood products from the forest.

(a) If people in the village work closely together on forest management, in what condition do you expect to find the forest? Why?

(b) Harvesting wood from the forest damages the quality of the water that people in the village drink. If people in the village work closely together, do you expect them to manage the water quality problem well? Why or why not?

(c) You observe that, in fact, the forest is being rapidly depleted. Why might this problem arise?

(d) If the forest is being rapidly depleted, do you expect the water quality problem to be managed better or not as well as in (b)? Why?

(e) You survey the area and discover that several other communities rely on the forest for their wood. You wish to help them have increased and sustainable harvest levels. What might be necessary to achieve that goal? Develop a plan, think about the objections that you might get from area residents, and adjust your plan to address those objections.

3. The factors that influence efficient renewable resource management are the same as the factors that affect nonrenewable resource management: the demand for the resource, the initial stock, the costs of extraction, and the discount rate. In contrast to nonrenewable resources, of course, the growth rate of the renewable resource also plays a role. Let's compare and contrast the role of these factors for the two kinds of resources.

(a) How does a higher discount rate affect the immediate harvest of a renewable and a nonrenewable resource? Does a higher interest rate have the same or different qualitative effect?

(b) How does an increase in the initial stock affect the immediate harvest of a renewable and a nonrenewable resource? Does it have the same or different qualitative effect?

(c) How does an increase in costs of extraction affect the immediate harvest of a renewable and a nonrenewable resource? Does it have the same or different qualitative effect?

(d) Suppose that demand for a renewable resource is expected to increase in the future. Would resource managers prefer to have more or less of the resource available then? How can they arrange to have their preferred stock at that time? What effect will that arrangement have on current harvest of the renewable resource? Is this effect qualitatively the same as or different from the effect of future increased demand for a nonrenewable resource?

(e) Unlike for a nonrenewable resource, it is possible to have a sustained-yield harvest of a renewable resource. Is a sustained yield harvest always desirable? Provide an example of a situation where an unsustainable harvest may nevertheless be efficient.

(f) Nonrenewable resources, such as aquifers (underground pools of water) can also be open access resources. Do you expect that open access will pose the same problems for nonrenewable resources that they do for renewable resources? Why or why not?

CHAPTER 18

Economic Growth and the Environment

The Industrial Revolution of the eighteenth and nineteenth centuries led to great increases in production and income. Technological innovation led to greatly increased output at reduced cost. As mass production made goods such as cloth and clothing less expensive, individuals began to purchase goods that they previously made entirely themselves. Interdependence began to overtake individual self-sufficiency, and social structures changed. Standards of living increased greatly. This great industrial expansion also led to air pollution, contamination of water bodies, and unsafe disposal of toxic substances that are not yet cleaned up. *Economic growth* provides tremendous benefits in wealth, improved educational attainment, and better health; it can also lead to great environmental damage. Is this a necessary connection? Does environmental protection harm *economic growth* in a country? Opposition to environmental regulation often arises because of the costs that it imposes. At the same time, the benefits of environmental protection are real and contribute substantially to human well-being. This chapter will examine:

- The relationships among *economic growth*, human welfare, and environmental protection;
- How national income accounts measure *economic growth* and how those measures can be "greener";
- Whether environmental regulations harm industry;
- The *environmental Kuznets curve* and the demand for environmental quality as income increases;
- Climate change, market failures, and income.

Climate Change, Market Failures, and Economic Growth

Perhaps the biggest environmental issue that humans have ever faced is the change in our climate due primarily to the burning of fossil fuels. The Intergovernmental Panel on Climate Change (IPCC), an intergovernmental body composed of scientists, provides a consensus of the scientific literature on climate change. The panel has concluded that the climate is getting warmer, that human-caused emissions are largely responsible, and that, without a change in human behavior, the change in climate will exceed the ability of humans and ecosystems to adapt. The IPCC and former Vice President Albert Gore won the 2007 Nobel Peace Prize for their work on climate change.

IPCC expects a warmer climate to affect people through its impacts on food, water, ecosystems, coasts, and health. The impacts to health, ecosystems, and coasts are all expected to be negative. Health problems come from higher temperatures and the spread of diseases. Ecosystem effects arise from the difficulties species are likely to face in adapting to new climates. Coastlines will move inland as melting glaciers and icecaps raise sea levels. For other impacts of climate change, there could be winners as well as losers. Water is projected to be more available in the tropics and the high latitudes but less available in the middle latitudes. For small changes of temperature, agricultural production is projected to increase in middle latitudes, though it will decrease in low latitudes. The projected increase in agricultural output for mid-latitude countries like the United States could be an important positive impact of climate change, and it has attracted considerable additional research. However, some newer findings suggest that, once irrigation is included in the analysis, there is no positive impact of warming even in middle latitudes. While there is consensus that global warming will impose large social costs, there is still vigorous debate about the size of the effects. In addition, the most significant contributors to climate problems may not bear the largest proportions of the costs.

The first major international action plan in response to climate change was the Kyoto Protocol, adopted in 1997. The Kyoto Protocol sets binding targets for 37 industrialized countries and the European Union to reduce GHG emissions by an average of 5 percent from 1990 levels by 2012, though emissions reduction targets vary by country. Developing countries, including China and India, were not required to reduce their emissions, so that they could pursue *economic growth* without costly restrictions. They argue that they are responsible for almost none of the GHG currently in the atmosphere. China has since become the world's largest emitter of GHGs.

The European Union, a signatory to Kyoto, is not certain to reach its targets for 2012. Fifteen of the EU countries have accomplished a 2.7 percent reduction in GHG and need a further 5.3 percent decrease to meet their 2012 goal. The United States did not ratify the Kyoto Protocol, but the government under President Obama has promised to participate in future climate treaties. Countries that are not signatories, most notably China, India, and the United States, have been increasing GHG emissions.

Developing countries, as well as some developed countries, have resisted calls to reduce their GHG emissions due to concerns that their economies would suffer. How significant is the effect of environmental regulation on economic development? And how is it possible to measure these effects?

National Income Accounts and Human Welfare

The first step in examining economic well-being is to examine how it is measured. The most common method is the **National Income and Product Accounts (NIPA)**, often shortened to **national accounts**, which keep track of how much countries produce and consume. National accounts are a type of **economic indicator**: a measure of economic well-being. Table 18.1 shows part of the national accounts for the United States in 2008.

If it seems odd to you to measure the well-being of a country through accounting of consumption and production, you are not alone. Robert Kennedy, attorney general during his brother President John F. Kennedy's administration, made this point while running for president himself in 1968:

> Too much and too long, we seem to have surrendered community excellence and community values in the mere accumulation of material things. Our gross national product...if we should judge America by that—counts air pollution and cigarette

TABLE 18.1   U.S. National Income and Product Accounts for 2008 (in billions of dollars).

This table shows the relationship between gross national product and other national income accounts.

Gross domestic product	14,420.5
Plus: Income receipts from the rest of the world	805.8
Less: Income payments to the rest of the world	688.4
Equals: **Gross national product**	14,538.0
Less: Consumption of fixed capital	1,899.7
Equals: **Net national product**	12,638.3
Less: Statistical discrepancy	160.5
Less: Corporate profits, capital consumption adjustments, taxes, Social Security contributions, and other adjustments	4,258.1
Plus: Personal income receipts on assets and personal current transfer receipts	3,921.2
Equals: **Personal income**	12,156.8
Less: Personal taxes	1,473.5
Equals: **Personal disposable income**	10,683.3
Less: Personal savings	115.7
Equals: **Personal outlay**	10,567.6

advertising, and ambulances to clear our highways of carnage. It counts special locks for our doors and the jails for those who break them. It counts the destruction of our redwoods and the loss of our natural wonder in chaotic sprawl. It counts napalm and the cost of a nuclear warhead, and armored cars for police who fight riots in our streets. It counts Whitman's rifle and Speck's knife, and the television programs which glorify violence in order to sell toys to our children.

Yet the gross national product does not allow for the health of our children, the quality of their education, or the joy of their play. It does not include the beauty of our poetry or the strength of our marriages; the intelligence of our public debate or the integrity of our public officials. It measures neither our wit nor our courage; neither our wisdom nor our learning; neither our compassion nor our devotion to our country; it measures everything, in short, except that which makes life worthwhile.

Let's look at traditional national accounting and how it is being enlarged to include environmental and other considerations in a process known as greening the national accounts. or **green accounting**.

MEASURING PRODUCTION, CONSUMPTION, AND WELL-BEING

The most watched economic indicator is the *GDP* of a nation. **Gross domestic product (GDP)** is the value of all *final goods and services* produced by labor and property located in a country. Thus, it is the "domestic" product. An equivalent definition of GDP is that it is the sum of the value of private consumption, government spending, investment, and net exports. The two definitions of GDP are equivalent because GDP is output, and output has to go somewhere.

Individual consumers get utility from goods. A country, if viewed as the sum of its citizens, gets well-being from the sum of the goods consumed. For that reason, GDP is one rough approximation of the economic well-being of a nation. GDP includes factors that do not go directly into the utility of individual consumers, though, such as equipment in factories. In addition, for purposes of measuring the sustainability of production, it can be useful to measure whether a country is increasing or drawing down its capital investments. Therefore, the national accounts include other components.

Closely related to GDP is *GNP*. **Gross national product (GNP)** is the market value of goods and services that the nationals (residents and citizens) of a nation produce. The difference between GDP and GNP is that GDP measures output only inside a nation's borders, while GNP adds the output of a nation's citizens and property located outside the nation. Thus, in Table 18.1, GNP comes from adding to GDP the income that U.S. citizens earn from production abroad, and subtracting the U.S. income that people from outside the United States own. For most countries, GDP and GNP are so similar that either can be used for most purposes. In the United States in 2008, for example, GDP differed from GNP by 0.8 percent.

Both GDP and GNP measure *final output*, not *intermediate goods and services*. **Intermediate goods and services** are used in producing other goods. For instance, this book is a *final good*, but the paper used to print this book is an intermediate good. If the sale of the paper to the publishing company counted as part of GNP, then it would be counted twice: once when the publishing company bought it as paper, and once when the consumer purchased it in the form of a book. **Final goods and services** are all those goods and services that are not intermediate.

Economic growth is the percentage change in GNP or GDP. The United States, the countries of the European Union, Canada, Australia, and other relatively wealthy countries, called developed countries, have experienced reasonably steady economic growth over time. Some developing countries, such as China, India, and Brazil, in recent years have economic growth greater than that of the developed world, though their per-capita GDP is still low. If their economic growth continues to remain high, they may in the future move into the ranks of developed countries. The poorest developing countries, such as Haiti and Chad, have trouble sustaining economic growth.

The next step in national accounting is to adjust GNP from gross product to net product. GNP is "gross" because it measures output before deducting the consumption of fixed capital. Using a piece of machinery in a factory wears it down, and the machine eventually wears out. The gradual loss of usefulness of machinery is called **depreciation.** Deducting the consumption of fixed capital from GNP produces **net national product (NNP)**. NNP is the amount of output left over for consumption if investment were just sufficient to keep the capital stock constant. The two lines below GNP in Table 18.1 show capital consumption subtracted from GNP in order to arrive at NNP.

Having looked at net output, let's turn to consumer expenditures. Moving down Table 18.1 leads to *personal disposable income.* **Personal disposable income** is the amount of money consumers can choose to spend or save. Getting from NNP to personal disposable income involves a number of adjustments. For instance, corporate profits are taken out, while the part of corporate profits that is distributed to households is put back, to exclude that part of corporate profits retained by firms. The part of personal disposable income that people save is subtracted from personal disposable income to get *personal outlay.* **Personal outlay** is the amount of income that people actually spend. **Personal consumption expenditure (PCE)**, also the amount of income that people actually spend, differs from personal outlay only in how it is measured. Personal outlay is calculated as we have just seen, and PCE, not in the table, is based on surveys of actual consumer expenditures. The two methods produce very similar results.

These different national income accounts have in common that they are ways of measuring the income of a country and its citizens. They are sums of all the income in a country. They do not consider how the income is divided among the country's residents: in some countries, for instance, the vast majority of wealth is in the hands of a small number of people. They differ in focus: GDP looks at all the goods produced, while personal outlay focuses on what people consume.

WHAT GDP AND NNP DO AND DO NOT MEASURE

Although GDP only measures final goods, many studies have found correlations between the GDP of a country and other measures of well-being. For instance, Diener and Diener found that higher GDP is associated with greater income equality and longer life expectancy. In 101 rich and poor countries, 26 out of 32 indicators of social well-being (categorized as affecting biological needs, social interactions, and group welfare) were positively associated with GDP. Boarini and colleagues studied the 30 middle- and upper-income countries belonging to the Organization for Economic Cooperation and Development. For those countries, higher GDP is associated with greater income equality and life expectancy. So countries with high GDPs also tend to have higher levels of health and other indicators of well-being.

Although GDP is correlated with many measures of well-being, it has flaws as a measure of well-being. Consider the example of cigarette production. Producing cigarettes adds to GDP because it is a final product that many consumers buy. Providing health care for the people who smoked the cigarettes also adds to GDP because it too is a final product that many smokers need. Are cigarettes and their contributions to cancer and heart disease therefore good for a country, since both increase GDP? GDP measures output; as Kennedy said, it does not directly measure well-being.

GDP measures only marketed final goods and services. It does not measure nonmarketed environmental goods, services provided by unpaid labor, or depletion of natural capital stocks. Let's consider these one at a time.

Clean air and water, wilderness protection, and environmental services are final goods, but, because they are not market goods, their production yields no increase to GDP. However, to produce the increase in environmental services, the firm will need to incur costs. It will buy intermediate goods. For instance, a coal-fired power plant could buy a scrubber, an intermediate good that reduces air pollution. To be counted in GDP, the purchase of the scrubber would need to cause an increase in the value of the final good, electricity sold. In the model of identical competitive firms in the long run, the increase in average costs from building the scrubber would result in a price increase. If the price increases more than the quantity demanded drops due to the price increase, the value of electricity sold, and thus GDP, go up. On the other hand, if the quantity demanded drops more than the price increases, then the value of electricity sold drops, and GDP goes down. Finally, suppose the scrubber is installed by a plant grandfathered under the Clean Air Act long after other firms have entered the power industry. The intersection of long-run supply and demand, determined by the newer firms, doesn't change. (See Figure 19.3.) Now electricity price and quantity stay the same, and nothing happens to GDP. As the examples show, an increase in environmental quality can lead to an increase, decrease, or no change in GDP.

GDP also leaves out the value of unpaid, or nonmarket, labor, including volunteer work and work at home. People who volunteer in hospitals, schools, or homeless shelters, or people who take care of their homes and children, provide tremendous benefits, but they do not show up in GDP. On the other hand, substitutes for work at home and volunteer work, such as paid nursing assistants, cleaning services, convenience foods, and childcare, do contribute to GDP because they provide final goods and services. The contributions of volunteers and homemakers greatly improve the quality of life in communities, but GDP does not include those benefits. GDP measures marketed final goods; neither nonmarketed labor nor environmental services are included in the tally.

Women's Labor and Economic Growth

To look at the opportunity cost of labor, let's go back to 1959, a world without DVDs, cell phones, or microwave ovens, and with less computing power in the whole world than an average laptop has now. There were few convenience foods; most meals were prepared at home.

In 1959, 37 percent of American women worked outside the home. In 2004, that figure was 66 percent, a big change in the amount of marketed labor supplied. And, of course, that change in labor force participation led to an increase in GDP. While the increase in the GDP is quite real, it does not tell the whole story. The increase in the GDP came at the expense of time spent in other activities. Whether that activity was childcare, housework, volunteer work, gardening for food, or even leisure, an activity not contributing to GDP was given up in order to spend more time in the labor force. So the GDP increase tells only one side of the story: the value of the additional marketed work performed. It leaves out the other side of the story: the value of the nonmarket activities given up.

Another way to say that the GDP does not account for nonmarket labor is to say that it treats nonmarket labor as having an opportunity cost of zero. Few home-makers or volunteers would agree that the value of the time they spend in uncompensated work activities is indeed zero.

NNP is also an incomplete accounting measure. The difference between NNP and GNP is capital consumption. Capital consumption accounts for the wearing out of machinery and buildings and thus accounts for the ability of manufacturing services to continue their production. However, capital consumption does not include the depletion of natural resources. Natural resources, such as soils, forests, and minerals, are capital stocks; extracting them reduces their future availability in the same way that capital consumption affects capital equipment and buildings. However, the national income accounts do not subtract the depreciation of natural resource stocks from GDP. When agriculture leads to soil erosion, or oil production reduces future oil reserves, the agricultural and oil production become part of GDP, but NNP is not adjusted to reflect the soil and oil depletion. Similarly, when power production releases greenhouse gases, decreasing the atmosphere's ability to radiate heat, this depreciation of the atmosphere is not subtracted. As a result of the non-accounting for natural resource depletion, using natural resources leads to higher measures of NNP than use of factories and buildings. When developing countries feel pressure to improve their economic growth, exploiting natural resources is an inaccurately inexpensive way to improve their national accounts.

"GREENING" NATIONAL INCOME ACCOUNTS

Economists have known of these problems with the national income accounts for many years. In response, various researchers have sought to revise the national income accounts to correct for these omissions. **Greening GDP** is the process of adjusting the national income accounts to include environmental and other missing factors that affect social well-being. If these factors were easy to measure, GDP would have been "green" from the beginning. Measuring nonmarket goods and their values is challenging for small quantities, much less for all the nonmarket goods in the economy. Nevertheless, economists and other social scientists have used a number of ways to improve estimates of a society's well-being.

One effort comes from Redefining Progress, a U.S. nongovernmental organization dedicated to measuring all the factors that the American national accounts omit. It has produced a "Genuine Progress Indicator" that includes more than 20 different adjustments to the national accounts. For instance, since 1989, Americans have been working more hours. Redefining Progress estimates the opportunity cost of that time at $400 million in 2004. Depletion of resources such as oil and forests accounted for $1.7 trillion, depletion of the protective stratospheric ozone layer $479 billion, carbon dioxide emissions $1.182 trillion, conventional air pollution $40 billion, and water pollution $120 billion. These adjustments, a total $3.5 trillion, indicate a significant overstatement of a GDP of $12 trillion and of PCE of $7.6 trillion for 2004. After making all adjustments, the Genuine Progress Indicator (GPI) concludes that income has not increased by 3.81 percent each year from 1950 to 2004, as GDP would indicate, but rather has been stagnant since 1978!

The World Bank publishes adjusted net savings statistics for many countries. Net savings is approximately a country's investment less its capital consumption—in other words, net savings is the money spent for new machinery and buildings and excludes the money spent for replacement machinery and buildings; it is the increment to physical capital. If an economy has too little net savings, its GDP and people's incomes will fall. Adjusted net savings adds three additional factors to net savings: depreciation of natural resources, pollution damage, and investment of human capital, also known as educating people. As with the first two factors, the national accounts do not include education, a major form of investment.

Figure 18.1 on page 453 shows adjusted net savings and its components for four countries. India and Sweden have high net savings before any adjustments. In Sweden's case, pollution is low and education is 7.3 percent of GNP; adjusted net savings come out just under 20 percent. India has higher net savings, lower education, higher pollution, and adjusted net savings of just over 20 percent. Ethiopia and Brazil start with lower net savings than the other two countries, have moderate educational expenditures and pollution, and end up with low net savings for Brazil and negative net savings for Ethiopia. These adjustments may signal different investment patterns than the standard measures in the national accounts.

Other indices move away from the national accounts perspective as they try to measure well-being. The Human Development Index (HDI), calculated by the United Nations Development Program, combines data on life expectancy, education,

BOX 18.2

The Genuine Progress Indicator

How does the GPI come up with its estimates? The GPI begins with personal consumption expenditure, since consumption is a better measure of consumer welfare than wealth (even if consumption is not a good measure). Redefining Progress (RP) then makes a number of adjustments. For instance, to include the value of household labor, RP took estimates of the number of hours of household work from surveys, and it multiplied that value by the hourly wage of people who performed that work for wages.

The amount that households spend on defensive pollution abatement, such as air and water filters, comes from an extrapolation of data collected by the U.S. Bureau of Economic Analysis. Rather than being an addition to GDP, though, it is a cost because it is considered an expenditure to compensate for a reduction in environmental quality.

The cost of water quality damage involves a number of extrapolations. The value begins with several estimates from 1972 of the damages of water quality, $12.0 billion in 1972 dollars; the value is $39.7 billion in 2000 dollars. Between 1972 and 1992, the researchers assume that these damages increase in the same proportion as per-capita expenditures on water pollution abatement. After 1992, because the expenditures on water pollution were no longer available, they assumed the value of damages increased at 3 percent per year.

The air pollution costs also begin with a 1972 estimate of the damages. For air pollution, though, the damages are scaled based on the proportion of air pollutants relative to 1972 levels. Because sulfur oxides and particulate matter have decreased greatly since then, the damages from air pollution are estimated to be less than half the 1972 levels.

The GPI makes these kinds of adjustments for 26 categories of effects. As these examples indicate, they are often rough approximations based on old data and strong assumptions. An advantage of the national income accounts is that they have standard methods for data collection. Improving the data available for "greening GDP" may help to increase its acceptance in policy circles.

and national income into one index. Figure 18.2 (on page 454) shows the HDI for Sweden, Brazil, India, and Ethiopia. While all show increases between 1975 and 2005, the indices also suggest the large disparities in welfare across different countries. For less developed countries in particular, the HDI does a better job of measuring welfare for the general population than GDP, which measures only aggregate wealth. The HDI sub-indices measure many dimensions of human welfare that are not necessarily coincident with income in less developed countries.

All these measures indicate that measuring a country's well-being via GDP is an inaccurate process at best. Some of GDP is borrowing from the environment without

FIGURE 18.1 Adjusted Net Savings and Its Components.

Each set of bars is a component of adjusted net national savings. The components are net savings, education, pollution and depletion, and adjusted net savings for 2006. Within each set of bars, each bar represents a country: Brazil, Ethiopia, India, and Sweden.

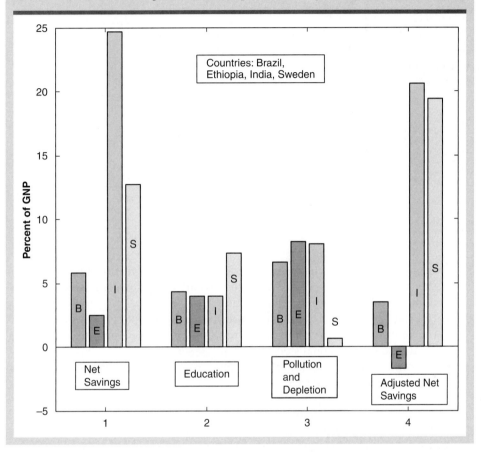

acknowledging the depreciation, some of it is offset by the omitted effects of pollution, and some of it is the result of more work at the expense of nonmarket activities. People are not getting rich nearly as fast as they might think based only upon GDP growth. GDP does have the tremendous advantage of being measured reasonably consistently around the world and over time. In contrast, the alternative attempts to measure GDP vary greatly in method, content, and results.

▶ IN SUMMARY

- Gross domestic product (GDP) measures output, not well-being. It is the value of all final goods and services produced in a country. GDP equals the sum of private consumption, government spending, investment, and net exports.

FIGURE 18.2 Human
Development Index for Sweden,
Brazil, Ethiopia, and India.

The Human Development Index
combines information on a country's life expectancy, education,
and national income. These figures
show increases for developing
countries but also wide disparities
between developed and developing
countries.

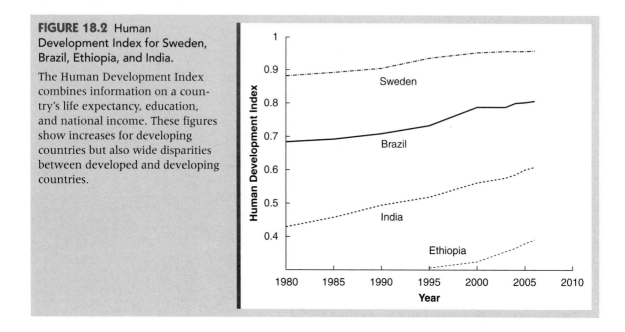

Economic growth is change in GDP. Gross national product (GNP) is GDP plus
the value of overseas production for a country's nationals, less the value of
domestic production of non-nationals.

- Net national product (NNP) measures output less capital consumption. It is
  the amount of output left over for consumption if investment were just sufficient to keep the capital stock constant.
- Personal outlay and personal consumption expenditure measure what consumers spend after taxes, savings, and other adjustments.
- GDP does not count value of nonmarket goods such as environmental goods.
  It also fails to count nonmarket work at its opportunity cost. NNP does not
  include the depreciation of natural resources.
- Because national income accounts exclude a number of factors that are important to people, these accounts overstate well-being and economic growth. Green
  accounting considers the opportunity cost of time, the value of nonmarket
  goods, and the depreciation of stocks of natural resources, including change in
  stocks of stock pollutants. Other measures of national well-being move away
  from the national accounts to look directly at measures of human welfare.

Do Environmental Regulations Harm Economic Growth?

What is the effect of environmental regulation on "the economy"? A common
voice of opposition to environmental regulation is the regulated industries. Firms
that are facing regulation fear that their costs will increase; if they face competition

internationally, those domestic cost increases provide an advantage to overseas competitors who may not be regulated. Because the GDP of a country is determined by the output of its firms, a competitive disadvantage for a country's firms will lower its GDP.

Our model of an industry in the long and short run (Chapter 9) can help to see whether this concern is justified. When a country, state, or province considers adopting an environmental regulation, industries fear that there will be two types of firms, those with lower average cost curves and those with higher average cost curves. The regulated firms would have higher cost curves due to the regulation. The unregulated firms would have lower cost curves. If the industry were in long-run competitive equilibrium when the regulation was adopted, then the newly high-cost firms would be making negative profits and would exit the industry.

An initial question is whether abatement adds enough to the costs of production to have a significant effect on industrial competitiveness or on GDP. The U.S. government's Pollution Abatement Costs and Expenditure (PACE) survey in April 2005 put the cost at $5.9 billion, about one-twentieth of 1 percent of $11.7 trillion GDP in 2004. To economists, that seems like too small an amount to make a very large difference in national output.

On the other hand, a study by Michael Greenstone found that counties in the United States that were subject to stringent air quality requirements lost about $75 billion in manufacturing output and 590,000 jobs between 1972 and 1987 relative to counties that were not subject to the same requirements. The study distinguished between "attainment" counties that had already attained their air quality goals and "non-attainment counties" that were subject to strict oversight under the Clean Air Act because they had not met these goals. His study controls for industry, county, and time and makes use of the change in regulations in 1972. He sought to rule out other causes of the decreased output and estimate how much was attributable to the attainment status of the county. While acknowledging the public health benefits of the Clean Air Act, the paper shows that environmental regulation can disproportionately affect the areas facing the strongest regulation.

The **pollution haven hypothesis** states that businesses will move from areas with costly environmental regulation to places with more lax regulation. In the Los Angeles area, for example, furniture factories left for Mexico, partly to get away from stringent regulations on spray finishes. If it is possible to make the goods in an unregulated location and then to return to the regulated location to sell them, then an environmental regulation will place local firms at a competitive disadvantage. If, on the other hand, a regulation affects what is sold in a jurisdiction, not just what is produced there, the pollution haven effect is not as great. For instance, fuel economy standards apply to all cars sold in the United States, so the place of manufacture confers no competitive advantage.

Measuring these effects is very difficult. When a new industry opens in a developing country, is it due to the pollution haven effect or to increasing economic growth in the country? In the international context, a survey of the literature by Jaffee et al. from 1995 found inconclusive evidence that pollution-intensive industries were systematically leaving regulated places. The decision to move a factory involves many factors beyond environmental regulation, including access to raw materials, labor and other costs, and the costs of shipping final goods to their ultimate consumers; it is difficult to disentangle the effects of environmental regulation from these other factors.

TURNING REGULATIONS INTO ADVANTAGES: THE PORTER HYPOTHESIS

Can an environmental regulation actually provide a competitive advantage for some regulated firms? If environmental regulation encourages technological innovation, the innovations may lead to new products that are superior to the older, more polluting versions. If so, then the regulated businesses may have the advantage of owning and patenting new, improved products that unregulated businesses did not pursue. Consider protection of the stratospheric ozone layer (not to be confused with ground-level ozone pollution), a part of the atmosphere that provides protection against harmful solar radiation. In the 1970s, scientists discovered that the industrial chemicals called chlorofluorocarbons (CFCs), used for refrigeration and other industrial needs, were damaging the ozone layer. The treaty to protect the ozone layer, the Montreal Protocol, required developed countries to stop using CFCs by 1996. China was allowed to continue its use until 2010. After 1996, China became the largest producer of CFCs and shipped refrigerators with CFCs in them to developed countries. Because CFCs were a cheaper means of producing refrigeration, producers in developed countries were at a competitive disadvantage. China then phased out CFCs and did so earlier than its treaty obligations.

Did China end up with a competitive advantage? Michael E. Porter proposed that manufacturers like the Chinese refrigerator manufacturers are in fact now at a disadvantage. Because manufacturers in the developed world have had 20 years more experience producing refrigeration without CFCs, they have likely learned cheaper ways to produce refrigeration. So the countries that adopt new technology first have an advantage over the later adopters of the new technology. California used the "Porter hypothesis" to justify its adoption of greenhouse gas emissions standards for automobiles more stringent than those of other states and the European Union. If other places adopt similar regulations in the near future, those auto makers that develop cars for California now might inherit a cost advantage in the wider market from their longer experience, after the wider market also becomes regulated.

In practice, the evidence on the Porter hypothesis is mixed. Most studies of environmental regulation find that production costs go up after regulation. On the other hand, a study of the Japanese automobile industry found that firms responded to regulations on emissions with technological innovations and increased output per unit of labor, benefits for all production activities.

THE EFFECT OF REGULATIONS ON GDP AND JOBS

A regulation that changes the cost of production has effects that spread out into the whole economy of a country, affecting the prices and quantities of output not only for the regulated good but also for substitute and complement goods, the quantity of goods imported and exported, employment in the regulated industry and related industries, and so on. Some of these changes will have positive effects on GDP, and some will have negative effects. How does an environmental regulation affect the quantity of output and thus affect GDP?

Consider regulations on cars. In 1999, the U.S. Environmental Protection Agency required vehicles to reduce their emissions of nitrogen oxides, at an added cost of about $100 for cars and $200 for light-duty trucks. Consumers may buy fewer cars because the price is higher. Did the value of car output go down or up? That depends on how many fewer cars people bought. The elasticity of demand for cars is about −1; that is, a 10 percent increase in price of all car models, not just one model of car, leads to a 10 percent decrease in the number of cars sold. If the number of cars goes down by 10 percent, while the price per car goes up by 10 percent, then the value of automobile output will remain the same. In essence, the same amount of machinery is being produced; all that has changed is that it is packaged into fewer cars. As a result, GDP is unlikely to be much affected by such a regulation.

More generally, the effect of an increased cost on producers depends on whether price goes up more than quantity goes down, and on the degree of competition that an industry faces. If a regulation makes new entry into an industry difficult, such as when new producers face stricter regulations than old producers, then the old producers may profit from regulation.

Another effect occurs when the higher price of the regulated good leads consumers to buy substitute goods. When regulations lead to lower sales, the money not spent on the regulated good is spent on other goods, so that aggregate output may not go down. For instance, a consumer might respond to higher automobile prices by buying a bicycle, a transit pass, walking shoes, and tennis lessons and would have money left over to buy additional goods. All of these substitute goods contribute to GDP. Depending on the price and quantity of substitute goods purchased, total output may be the same, higher, or lower than it was before the regulation.

The effect of environmental regulation on employment is also uncertain. Regulated industries may cut back on employment due to the reduction in output. Some forms of regulation, however, can require hiring of new workers. Installing insulation in homes to reduce energy demand for heating and cooling uses more workers than increased energy production, which relies more on machinery. Increasing energy prices to reduce environmental impacts may have either a positive or negative effect on employment, as people switch from wanting energy to wanting insulation.

GDP and jobs may increase or decrease due to regulation. Neither of these indicators, though, by itself indicates whether net social benefits increase. Because neither of these measures includes the value of external effects, a requirement that reduces GDP may nevertheless have positive net benefits.

IN SUMMARY

- Industries that are regulated are placed at a competitive disadvantage if other industries are able to produce goods in a location that is not regulated. The

BOX 18.3

Green Jobs

As of 2009, the United States is experiencing a **recession**, a period of negative economic growth. This recession includes extensive job losses, business failures, and other disruptions in the United States and the rest of the world. President Barack Obama has proposed stimulating economic activity and creating jobs by investing public money in energy efficiency and alternative energy. He hopes to address three problems—unemployment, building domestic green technology, and climate change—by promoting output of goods and services that reduce greenhouse gases.

---

pollution haven hypothesis states that businesses will move from areas with costly environmental regulation to places with more lax regulation. Regulators can reduce this effect by restricting the sale as well as the production of goods in the location under their control.

- The Porter hypothesis argues that regulated firms, by being forced to develop improved technologies, will be better off than unregulated firms. The evidence is mixed on this effect.
- Regulations can leave GDP unchanged, lower, or even increased. Regulation increases the cost of production and thus the price of goods. Even if fewer units are sold, each unit will be sold for a higher price. When regulations lead to lower sales, the money not spent on the regulated good is spent on other goods. Depending on the price and quantity of the substitute goods purchased, GDP may not go down.
- Regulation may either increase or decrease employment, depending on the labor needs as industries respond to the regulation.

The Environmental Kuznets Curve and Demand for Environmental Quality

How is GDP related to changes in environmental quality? On the one hand, avoiding pollution often increases production costs, placing regulated firms at a competitive disadvantage, and sometimes leads to lower output. For that reason, it seems reasonable to expect that stronger environmental safeguards would be at the expense of GDP. If so, environmental quality and GDP should move in opposite directions. On the other hand, if environmental quality is a normal good—one for which demand increases as income increases—then, as a country's income grows, its citizenry is likely to demand higher environmental quality. In that case, environmental quality and GDP should increase together. In other words, either a negative or a positive relationship could exist between GDP and environmental quality. Which prediction do the data support?

One way to approach this question is to borrow a theory that explores the relationship between GDP and income equality. Simon Kuznets argued that, as GDP per capita (per person) increases in a country, the country's distribution of income initially becomes less equitable—some get higher incomes while others do not. With further growth, though, the higher income starts to reach the poor, and inequality decreases. As a result, a graph with income inequality on the vertical axis and GDP per capita on the horizontal axis shows an inverse U shape, as inequality first increases and then decreases.

A number of economists have sought to apply Kuznet's observations to environmental quality. The **environmental Kuznets curve (EKC)** graphs the relationship between GDP per capita and some measure of pollution. Figure 18.3 shows a sample EKC, with an estimate of the correspondence between sulfur oxides (SO_x) emissions, measured on the vertical axis, and the GNP (not GDP in this case) per capita of a number of countries, measured on the horizontal axis. The data show an inverse U-shaped pattern, similar to the original Kuznets curve. As per-capita GNP increases, SO_x emissions increase until GDP per capita is about $3,000, and then steadily decrease as GNP per capita continues to grow. Other studies have shown similar results for some other measures of pollution.

The EKC can be viewed as the summary of several effects of a country's growth. First, as a country grows, its economic activity increases; this scale effect suggests that pollution increases with growth. Secondly, as a country grows, the composition of its economy may change—for instance, from manufacturing to services. The

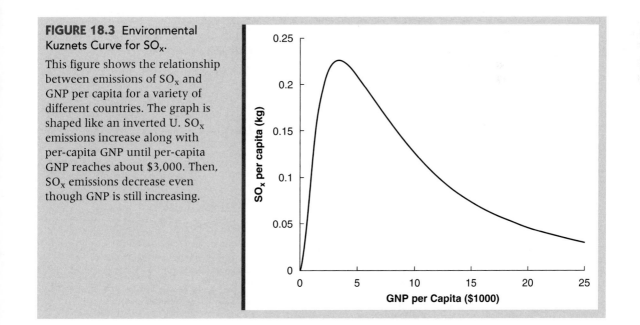

FIGURE 18.3 Environmental Kuznets Curve for SO_x.

This figure shows the relationship between emissions of SO_x and GNP per capita for a variety of different countries. The graph is shaped like an inverted U. SO_x emissions increase along with per-capita GNP until per-capita GNP reaches about $3,000. Then, SO_x emissions decrease even though GNP is still increasing.

composition effect may either increase or decrease pollution. Finally, a wealthier country can afford to use more environmentally friendly techniques—the technique effect.

The inverse-U pattern is not always obvious. Greenhouse gas emissions are a global pollutant. Meaningful abatement requires cooperation from counties at many different levels of income. How much the United States is willing to abate depends on how much China will abate, which depends on income in China. So the need for international cooperation breaks the presumed link between national income and abatement. Figure 18.4 plots U.S. emissions of carbon dioxide (CO_2) against U.S. per-capita GDP. Unlike SO_x, GHG emissions continue to increase with GDP through 2010. Many authors have extrapolated the GHG emissions into the future using regression models and argued that there will be a turning point in the future. As yet, the jury is out on whether increased income will go along with decreased GHG emissions.

The EKC summarizes the past relationship of environmental quality and GDP per capita. The common inverse-U shape suggests that, once a country reaches a threshold level of GDP per capita, its environmental quality will switch from deterioration to improvement. In a review of the EKC literature, Kriström and Lundgren found that a common view of the EKC is that countries can grow their way out of environmental problems: all that is necessary for environmental improvement is an increase in per-capita income.

The EKC is not, however, a guarantee that all countries will get cleaner as their GDP goes up. First, as the example of greenhouse gases measured as CO_2 equivalent shows, the EKC may not hold for all environmental problems; some environmental

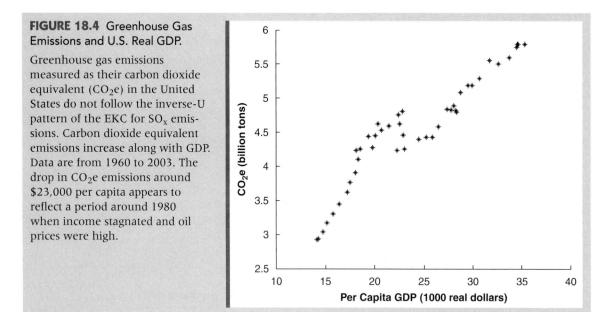

FIGURE 18.4 Greenhouse Gas Emissions and U.S. Real GDP.

Greenhouse gas emissions measured as their carbon dioxide equivalent (CO_2e) in the United States do not follow the inverse-U pattern of the EKC for SO_x emissions. Carbon dioxide equivalent emissions increase along with GDP. Data are from 1960 to 2003. The drop in CO_2e emissions around $23,000 per capita appears to reflect a period around 1980 when income stagnated and oil prices were high.

problems may continually get worse, and others may continually improve, with increasing income. Secondly, a country's environmental quality depends on many factors other than its GDP per capita, including the political structure and social norms. If it is political pressure that leads to lower pollution, then form of government should matter. Democratic countries tend to be less polluted than autocratic countries. So developing autocratic countries may not "grow out" of their pollution problems. Thirdly, current developed countries have grown large nonpolluting service sectors, such as information technology. This is the composition effect: not all economic sectors grow at the same rate. Currently developing countries may not grow in this same pattern, especially if their growth involves mineral extraction for export to developed countries. Nevertheless, it is noteworthy that environmental quality and economic growth have occurred together. Improving the environment does not always require a loss of income.

▰▰ IN SUMMARY

- An environmental Kuznets curve is a graph of an environmental quality indicator, such as SO_x emissions, and GDP per capita. For many pollutants, it reveals an inverse-U shape: pollution increases for low levels of per-capita GDP and decreases at high levels of per-capita GDP. One possible explanation is that, when countries are poor, higher income causes environmental harm but is more important than environmental quality, while wealthier countries are willing to invest in achieving a better environment.
- Greenhouse gases (GHG) have been increasing along with GDP, with no sign of downturn. Perhaps this will change now that climate change is a major concern, or perhaps GHG emissions do not follow the EKC.
- The EKC indicates, but does not guarantee, that a country can have increasing GDP per capita with increasing environmental quality.

Trade, Development, and Climate Change

If GDP is a measure (albeit imperfect) of a country's well-being, and if environmental regulation hurts GDP, then it is quite understandable why developing countries put less emphasis on environmental protection than the developed world. Many developing countries have rightly noted that the existing volumes of human-generated greenhouse gases (GHGs) come from the wealthy nations of the world. They argue that, therefore, the burden for reducing GHG emissions should fall on the developed countries, and several developing countries have not accepted mandatory restrictions on their emissions.

The fact that some countries do not participate in the Kyoto treaty creates special difficulties in a world where many goods are traded internationally. Countries that do not participate in the treaty are likely to have lower costs for energy because they do not have to avoid GHG-intensive energy production. Several developing

BOX 18.4

IPAT

Environmental issues grew to national and international prominence in the late 1960s. As environmental scientists sought to understand environmental problems, one of the lead contenders for root cause was population. A growing population that consumed the same amount per person as the rest of the population would lead to increased environmental impact. Another way of considering the links between economic development and environmental impact came from Paul Ehrlich, who became famous for his book *The Population Bomb*, which predicted famine and ecological destruction due to population growth. Along with John Holdren, Ehrlich proposed the equation: Environmental impact (I) = Population * Consumption/Person * Impact/Consumption. With consumption per person called "affluence," and impact per unit of consumption called "technology," this equation became known as IPAT.

IPAT breaks environmental impact into the three components of population, affluence, and technology. Both population and consumption per person (in the form of personal consumption expenditure, or another national income account) are reasonably well measured. Technology can be measured as a leftover: if the impact (such as emissions of a pollutant) is known, and both population and affluence are known, then impact per dollar of consumption is, by definition, $T = I/(P * A)$.

Population and affluence are analogous to the scale effect for the EKC: environmental impacts increase directly with either population or affluence. The technique effect is related to the technology variable, which can increase or reduce impacts. For instance, impact per dollar of consumption may decrease if more effort goes into pollution abatement, or it may increase for environmentally damaging forms of consumption. The simplest version of IPAT does not directly consider the composition effect.

How useful is IPAT as an explanation of the causes of environmental problems? IPAT is an identity: because the technology variable is calculated from the others, it will always be true. From a policy perspective, Ehrlich and Holdren wanted to emphasize the importance of population as a driver of environmental problems. Others have focused on the technology variable: if we find more environmentally sound ways to consume, then we can maintain our population and our standard of living without increased damage. Missing from it, though, is consideration of the human motivation underlying any of these variables. The contribution of social scientists, including but not limited to economists, is to understand better the reasons that people seek to multiply (P) and thrive (A), and to identify ways to steer them toward more environmentally sound ways (T) of achieving their goals.

countries, including China and India, produce the same types of goods the United States produces and are significant contributors to GHG emissions. It is possible that the developing countries could produce all these goods and ship them to the European Union and the United States, at the expense of jobs and GDP in those countries, while producing as much or more pollution. **Leakage** is the term for pollution reduction that does not take place because environmental regulation in one area causes the pollution to move to a new area, as the pollution haven hypothesis predicts.

The inability of negotiators to bring the developing world into the treaty reduces the success of the treaty. In addition, the problem of leakage leaves firms in the regulated location at a competitive disadvantage. Indeed, the United States did not ratify the Kyoto treaty because the developing world did not face the same incentives to reduce their emissions as the developed world, and the United States feared a competitive disadvantage. The challenge for the successor treaty to Kyoto is how to restrict emissions in the less-developed countries as well as the developed ones. The Copenhagen Conference in 2010 produced no binding accords at all, although the big developing countries, China, Brazil, and India, did agree to a statement of principle.

The drafters of the Kyoto Protocol sought ways to include the developing world, even if those countries were not under the same obligations as the developed world. Under the **Clean Development Mechanism** (**CDM**), developed countries obliged to reduce their GHG emissions can instead pay developing countries to reduce their emissions. Developing countries have many potential projects that reduce emissions at low cost. Cleaning up their emissions often helps their development. By allowing the developed world to pay for these reductions, the CDM creates a market for GHG abatement in the developing world. The CDM thus fosters development and at the same time cleans up the environment at lower cost than if the developed countries lacked this option.

CDM projects often involve private firms in both the developed and developing world. For example, through the Beijing Building Material Group (BBMG) project, businesses in the United Kingdom provide financing to factories in China so that the Chinese factories can reduce their emissions by 74,350 tons. The businesses in the United Kingdom receive permits for those 74,350 tons of carbon emissions that they can use domestically. This CDM project will recover waste gas and heat from two cement factories to produce 72,170 megawatt-hours of electricity. These will replace some of the electricity those plants purchased from the North China Power Grid, which relies heavily on coal. Because the effects of GHG are global, removing 74,350 tons of GHG emissions in China has the same effect on global climate as removing the same amount in the United Kingdom.

The CDM increases efficiency by allowing developed countries to achieve the same carbon reduction at lower cost. CDM expands the number of options for reducing GHG emissions for the entire world. In addition, a project to generate electricity in China without using coal provides benefits beyond GHG reduction. The BBMG project will reduce the devastating health effects that the Chinese people have suffered from breathing polluted air, and it will do so without depriving China of the economic benefits of the two cement plants.

To ensure that a CDM project results in a net reduction of GHG, the project sponsors must demonstrate that the abatement project would not have been done without CDM financing, a requirement called **additionality**. Additionality can be a very difficult concept to demonstrate and to enforce: how is it possible to know whether emissions would have occurred in the absence of the project? The BBMG project had to consider whether a private investor would have been likely to finance the waste heat recovery system. The analysis determined the net present value of the project and compared the internal rate of return to the 12 percent hurdle rate generally used in China's cement industry. With an internal rate of return of 7.04 percent at one factory and 7.44 percent at the other, the project was considered unattractive to private investors, so the CDM arrangement met the additionality test.

Because the CDM is also a development program, projects must contribute to increasing the welfare of the host country, called co-benefits. Finally, GHG outputs under the CDM must be verifiable: the payment under the CDM is made only once the reductions have been proved to have happened.

Recently, United Nations climate experts have been making plans to allow forestry projects to earn credits in the CDM scheme under projects called Reducing Emissions from Deforestation and Forest Degradation, REDD. Because forests store (sequester) carbon, increasing forest volume means less carbon in the atmosphere. In addition, both replanting areas that were previously harvested and protecting forests from harvest in the first place provide many benefits beyond carbon sequestration. The forest plants and animals are preserved; the trees protect hillsides from erosion that harms land productivity and silts up rivers; and indigenous forest peoples can continue their ways of life. REDD has the potential to sequester a lot of carbon. However, forests can burn or be logged illegally, which reduces sequestration. In addition, because it may be impossible to know whether an area would have been logged in the absence of a project, additionality may not occur in practice. While sequestration has great potential, enforcement and additionality issues remain.

Both CDM and REDD provide means for developed countries, in essence, to pay developing countries to reduce GHG emissions. This approach has the potential to reduce damages from climate change while allowing developing countries to get wealthier. For these programs to be successful, though, there must be ways of ensuring that emissions reductions do in fact take place. The ability to monitor emissions reductions in the developing world was a major issue in the Copenhagen round of climate negotiations in 2009.

IN SUMMARY

- The Kyoto treaty imposes restrictions on the GHG emissions of developed countries that have joined the treaty. The omission of developing countries from it creates the possibility of leakage, as some production moves from treaty members to nonparticipants.
- Developing countries can participate through the Clean Development Mechanism, in which developed countries pay them to abate their GHG emissions instead of abating their own emissions. The CDM increases efficiency both by providing an incentive for developing countries to reduce their GHG

emissions and by reducing the costs for the developed world of achieving reductions. Concerns exist about whether emissions reductions from the developing world are in addition to reductions they would have made without the CDM.

Paying Developing Countries to Preserve Forests

Brazil is home to 60 percent of the Amazon rainforest. Even before climate change caught the world's attention, efforts were under way to protect the diversity of plants, animals, and indigenous cultures in this area as large as half of Europe. One effort is the Amazon Region Protected Area (ARPA) program, a project of the World Bank, World Wildlife Fund, Brazilian government, and others. The long-term goal of ARPA is to protect 60 million hectares (148 million acres) of rainforest, with some completely protected and some open to sustainable use.

One incentive to reduce deforestation is a debt-for-nature swap. Many developing countries borrowed money and then could not pay those loans back. Because they were not paying their loans back, the loans were worth less than face value; for example, a developing country's promise to pay $5 million could be bought for $1 million. In a debt-for-nature swap, developed countries and environmental protection organizations buy the discounted debt of a developing country in exchange for protection of ecologically important land in that country. The developing country gets $5 million worth of debt forgiveness at a cost of only $1 million to the purchasing organization. In 2006, for instance, the United States, Guatemala, and two environmental organizations arranged more than $20 million in debt forgiveness in exchange for tropical forest preservation. Developed countries benefit from these programs because they get protection of forests, with their myriad environmental benefits. Developing countries get financial relief that assists them in developing. Debt-for-nature swaps thus can make all parties better off, an example of Coasian bargaining.

CHAPTER SUMMARY

Here are the key lessons from this chapter:

- GDP and GNP measure the value of final goods and services. GDP does not measure well-being, although many measures of well-being increase when GDP increases.
- GDP omits nonmarket goods, including environmental goods, nonmarketed labor, and natural capital. Their exclusion from GDP and the other national accounts means that these accounts may not accurately reflect a country's well-being.
- By some measurements, the omissions in GDP and NNP are so large that they account for nearly all GDP growth: GDP growth is coming at the expense of nonmarket labor and environmental goods and stocks. Adjusting GDP for omitted nonmarket goods is called green accounting. A number of alternatives to GDP have been developed to measure a country's well-being.

- Environmental regulations cause regulated firms to have higher costs and place them at a disadvantage relative to nonregulated firms. Regulations increase the cost of producing goods, thus increasing the price and decreasing the quantity sold of the regulated good. However, because GDP measures the monetary value of output, GDP will not necessarily change when people buy a smaller quantity of the good at higher prices.
- The Porter hypothesis states that those regulated first will learn about regulation and have an advantage over those regulated later. The evidence is mixed as to whether this holds true.
- To study the relationship between environmental quality and economic growth, economists have compared GDP per capita to various measures of pollution in the environmental Kuznets curve. A comparison of countries from least to most developed finds that, for some pollutants, pollution first increases and then decreases. It may increase because an increase in industrial activity, absent regulation, increases pollution. It may decrease if countries with high enough GDP per capita choose to reduce pollution. The EKC is not a guarantee that growth will solve pollution problems. Nevertheless, it indicates that environmental quality and economic growth can go together.
- Developing countries have resisted many environmental regulations, including participation in the Kyoto Treaty to reduce GHG emissions, in part because of concerns that participation will reduce their economic growth. If some polluting activities move from the developed world to the developing world, some emissions may change location rather than be abated.
- Clean Development Mechanisms allow developed countries to finance greenhouse gas abatement projects in developing countries. While these mechanisms create the possibility for both emissions reductions and continued economic development in poorer countries, ensuring that emissions reductions actually take place is a difficult challenge.

KEY TERMS

additionality *(p. 464)*
Clean Development Mechanism (CDM) *(p. 463)*
depreciation *(p. 448)*
economic growth *(p. 448)*
economic indicator *(p. 446)*
environmental Kuznets curve (EKC) *(p. 459)*
final goods and services *(p. 448)*
gross domestic product (GDP) *(p. 447)*
gross national product (GNP) *(p. 447)*
green accounting *(p. 447)*
greening GDP *(p. 451)*

intermediate goods and services *(p. 447)*
leakage *(p. 463)*
national accounts *(p. 446)*
National Income and Product Accounts (NIPA) *(p. 446)*
net national product (NNP) *(p. 448)*
personal consumption expenditure (PCE) *(p. 448)*
personal disposable income *(p. 448)*
personal outlay *(p. 448)*
pollution haven hypothesis *(p. 455)*
recession *(p. 458)*

NOTES

Robert Kennedy's speech about GNP was given at the University of Kansas, Lawrence, Kansas, on March 18, 1968. It can be found at http://www.jfklibrary.org/Historical+ Resources/Archives/Reference+Desk/Quotations+of+Robert+F.+Kennedy.htm.

The sources for the relationship between quality of life and GNP or GDP are from the following: Romina Boarini, Asa Johansson, and Marco Mira d'Ercole, "Alternative Measures of Well-being," *OECD Observer* 11 (May 2006), http://www. oecd.org/dataoecd/26/61/36967254.pdf, and Ed Diener and Carol Diener, "The Wealth of Nations Revisited: Income and Quality of Life," *Social Indicators Research* 36 (November 1995): 275–286.

The figures for GDP and GNP in the United States are the initial estimates for 2008 quarter 3 at annual rates, found in Tables B26 and B27 and B30 of the *Economic Report of the President*, U.S. Government Printing Office, Washington, D.C. (February 2009). For the definitions of National Income and Product Accounts, see http://www.bea.gov/national/pdf/nipaguid.pdf.

Abatement costs are from the *Pollution Abatement Costs and Expenditures Survey*, United States Bureau of the Census (April 2005).

Information about women's labor force participation is from the annual *Economic Report of the President*, February 2005, U.S. Government Printing Office, Washington, D.C. (2005), www.gpoaccess.gov/eop/2005/2005_erp.pdf. GDP is on p. 204. Labor force statistics, on p. 257, are from the U.S. Department of Labor, Bureau of Labor Statistics.

The Genuine Progress Indicators can be found at: John Talberth, Clifford Cobb, and Noah Slattery, "The Genuine Progress Indicator 2006: A Tool for Sustainable Development." San Francisco: Redefining Progress, 2007, http://www.rprogress.org/publications/2007/GPI%202006.pdf.

The Human Development Index is calculated by the United Nations Development Programme. The data presented here were taken from http://hdrstats.undp.org/indicators, accessed February 7, 2008.

The debate about the Porter hypothesis can be followed in several sources, including Michael E. Porter, *The Competitive Advantage of Nations* (London: MacMillan, 1990); Runar Brännlund, Lauri Hetemäki, Bengt Kriström, and Erik Romstad, *Command and Control with a Gentle Hand: The Nordic Experience*, Nordic Environmental Research Program, Sveriges Lantbruksuniversitet, Report #115 (Umea, Sweden, 1996); and Akira Hibiki, Toshi H. Arimura, and Naoto Takeba, "An empirical study of the effects of the exhaust gas regulation on R&D and the productivity of the Japanese auto industry," Paper presented at INRA, Paris, May 7, 2007.

The experiences of attainment and nonattainment counties is documented in Michael Greenstone, "The Impacts of Environmental Regulations on Industrial Activity: Evidence from the 1970 and 1977 Clean Air Act Amendments and the Census of Manufactures," *Journal of Political Economy* 110 (2002): 1175–1213, 1219.

Figure 18.3, on the environmental Kuznets curve, is drawn from a formula given in Theodore Panayotou, 1993, "Empirical Tests and Policy Analysis of Environmental Degradation at Different Stages of Economic Development," Working Paper,

Technology and Environment Program, International Labour Office, Geneva. Later work by this author and others makes it clear that it is very difficult to be certain what level of GNP leads to the highest emissions.

Figure 18.4, on the relationship between GDP and carbon emissions in the United States, is based on the *World Development Indicators*, World Bank, Washington, D.C. 2008. The IPCC conclusions are found in the Fourth Assessment Report of the Intergovernmental Panel on Climate Change, Synthesis Report, 2007, www.ipcc.ch.

The discussion of scale, composition, and technique effects comes from Arik Levinson, "Environmental Kuznets Curve," entry in *New Palgrave Dictionary of Economics,* 2nd ed., 2008, accessed at http://www9.georgetown.edu/faculty/aml6/pdfs&zips/PalgraveEKC.pdf, June 23, 2009.

The IPAT formula is a continuing topic for research and discussion. One relatively recent article with background information is by Courtland L. Smith, "Assessing the Limits to Growth," *Bioscience* 45(7) (July/August 1995): 478–483.

Information on the Beijing Building Materials Group is from the United Nations Framework Convention on Climate Change website, at http://cdm.unfccc.int/Projects/DB/SGS-UKL1193135464.43/view and http://cdm.unfccc.int/UserManagement/FileStorage/A7EIFDFI0K5NT52KKU06RVMAXPAORN.

Two reports on deforestation are: Stephan Schwartzman, Daniel Nepstad, and Paulo Moutinho, "Getting REDD Right: Reducing Emissions from Deforestation and Forest Degradation (REDD) in the United Nations Framework Convention on Climate Change (UNFCCC)," http://www.whrc.org/resources/published_literature/pdf/SchwartzmanetalREDD.WHRC.07.pdf, and Federal Ministry for Economic Cooperation and Development, "Reducing Emissions from Deforestation in Developing Countries: The Way Forward," Eschborn, Germany, April 2007, http://www.gtz.de/de/dokumente/en-climate-reducing-emissions.pdf.

Information on the Amazon Region Protected Area program is from the World Bank (http://go.worldbank.org/UIIX9GFRX0) and the World Wildlife Fund (www.wwf.org), both accessed November 19, 2008.

The debt-for-nature swap was reported in Marc Lacey, "U.S. to Cut Guatemala's Debt for Not Cutting Trees," *New York Times*, October 2, 2006.

EXERCISES

1. Compute the discount factor $1/(1 + r)^t$ for $r = 1$, 5, or 10 percent interest rates and $t = 30$ and 50 years. Remember that 1 percent is .01. Based on your computation, is the choice of discount factor important for deciding whether to do something about global warming today? Why or why not?

2. If global warming caused a 2-meter rise in worldwide sea level, what would happen to the price of land? How would that result affect your calculation of the benefits of slowing climate change?

3. What decisions made in the United States might depend upon GDP? Do you think that change in GDP influences the results of elections? Why? What use would GDP predictions be to firms? To the government?

4. What do you think the green measures of national income would look like for a heavily oil-dependent nation like Saudi Arabia or Venezuela? What might these countries do to offset their resource depletion?

5. (a) Why might there be a negative relationship between gross domestic product (GDP) and environmental quality for a country? Why might there be a positive relationship between GDP and environmental quality?

   (b) Do you expect all pollutants for one country to have the same shape of the environmental Kuznets curve? If so, what shape do you expect? If not, does the EKC always imply that a country can grow its way out of polluting?

   (c) If increased GNP is associated with improved environmental quality, does this relationship mean that a cleaner environment comes at no cost—actually at positive benefit—to GNP? If so, why is environmental regulation so often opposed? If not, what explanation exists for this relationship?

CHAPTER 19

Sustainability

I n 1983, the United Nations commissioned a report to address concerns over environmental degradation and its present and future effects on human welfare. Several years later, in 1987, the World Commission on Environment and Development, chaired by Gro Brundtland (prime minister of Norway), defined **sustainable development** as "development that meets the needs of the present without compromising the ability of future generations to meet their own needs." Because human needs require both economic development and environmental protection, sustainable development and environmental economics should be able to inform each other. This chapter will examine:

- The relationship among sustainability, welfare, and equity;
- The role of substitute goods in sustaining consumption and production;
- Sustainability as a societal goal;
- Ways of measuring sustainability.

Multiple-Use Management and the U.S. Forest Service

The tradition of managing forests on a sustainable basis goes back to Faustmann in 1849 and long predates the modern interest in sustainability. The law that controls the 190-million-acre National Forest System in the United States is the Multiple Use-Sustained Yield Act of 1960. It defined sustained yield as "the achievement and maintenance in perpetuity of a high-level output of the various renewable resources of the national forests without impairment of the productivity of the land." The U.S. Forest Service manages these lands. Like national parks, national forests provide recreational opportunities and include wilderness set aside for ecological protection. Unlike national parks, non-wilderness national forest lands are also used for resource extraction, including harvesting wood products, grazing for livestock, and mining. Since World War II, the increase in the demand for housing has put great pressure on the Forest Service to increase wood production.

A forest is being harvested for a sustainable yield when the annual harvest is the same as the annual growth. As a result, the volume of trees on the land remains unchanged. In the largest wood-producing region in the national forests, located in western Oregon and Washington, timber harvesting in the 1960s was not sustainable. Because many of the trees were old growth, meaning that they had grown to just about their maximum size, their growth was very slow. The Forest Service aimed to achieve sustained-yield harvests by reducing the stocks of old growth and replanting with young, fast-growing trees. After such a stock adjustment, the forest could be harvested sustainably. In those years, though, harvests exceeded growth, as Figure 19.1 shows.

The cutting of the old-growth forests had a second problem with sustainability: the ecological character of the forests changed dramatically. Harvesting forests, if not done carefully, can lead to significant soil erosion that harms aquatic systems. Converting old-growth forests to new growth, possibly of different species, alters the ecosystem, including the wildlife. In the early 1990s, concerns over loss of old-growth forests in the Northwest centered on the northern spotted owl, a species dependent on these forests for habitat; its numbers were dropping as old-growth habitat was harvested. The U.S. Fish and Wildlife Service declared it a threatened species under the Endangered Species Act. This declaration led to a halt in national forest timber harvests in the area and triggered an enormous controversy: was it more important to sustain the owl or to sustain timber harvests and jobs?

The compromise between the timber industry and environmentalists, brokered by President Clinton in 1994, led to greatly reduced timber harvests in the national forests,

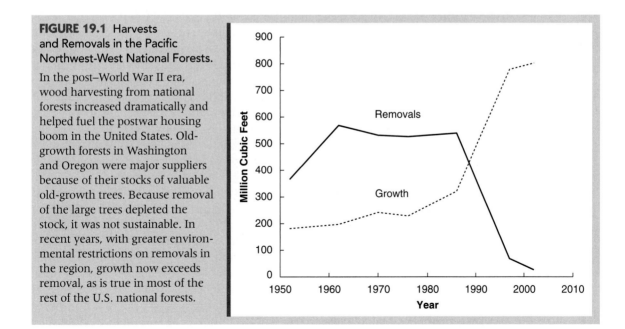

FIGURE 19.1 Harvests and Removals in the Pacific Northwest-West National Forests.

In the post–World War II era, wood harvesting from national forests increased dramatically and helped fuel the postwar housing boom in the United States. Old-growth forests in Washington and Oregon were major suppliers because of their stocks of valuable old-growth trees. Because removal of the large trees depleted the stock, it was not sustainable. In recent years, with greater environmental restrictions on removals in the region, growth now exceeds removal, as is true in most of the rest of the U.S. national forests.

a new emphasis on ecosystem management, and funds for retraining displaced workers and for economic development. As Figure 19.1 shows, timber harvests have since been substantially below growth in the region. As a result, the volume of timber in the forests is increasing. Forest industry jobs dropped after the plan was implemented. However, because of a boom in high-technology jobs in the Northwest during that time, overall unemployment in the affected region dropped, rather than increased. *The New York Times* reported that "…[at] the nation's largest center for retraining displaced woodworkers, nearly 9 of every 10 people…have found new jobs." In the years since the forest plan was enacted, the population of the northern spotted owl has continued to decline. If sustainability is our goal, what is it that we want to sustain—individual species? Ecosystems? Lumber production? Forest industry jobs? In a world that is constantly changing, what does sustainability mean?

Sustainability, Welfare, and Equity

Sustainability is rapidly entering the goals of a wide number of institutions, including universities, businesses, cities, and countries. For sustainability to be meaningful, though, it is necessary to define it in practical, measurable terms. What exactly must be sustained? From an economist's point of view, the purpose of an economic system is to provide human welfare. Thus, one possible criterion is to sustain human welfare. Indeed, the definition from the Brundtland report focuses on the well-being of people. Under this view, a community has achieved sustainability if human welfare does not decrease over time.

People's welfare depends on many goods. In the national forest example, well-being comes from wood products' harvests, employment in the forest industry, the population of the northern spotted owl, recreational opportunities, and old-growth ecosystems. For some of these goods, substitutes exist if the national forests do not provide them. For instance, we can get wood products from old-growth trees, from plantation forests, or from multiple-use forests. Indeed, for housing products, even more substitution possibilities become available, such as stone, brick, or steel. Forest industry jobs could change from harvest-based activities to tourism-based activities, or workers could move into entirely new industries. Welfare may be sustainable even if the national forests no longer provide those goods, as long as other goods can substitute for them.

Not all people will agree, though, how to measure sustainability. Is human welfare sustainable if the northern spotted owl or old-growth ecosystems are diminished? Some people have no special feelings for either of these; their welfare is sustainable even with the loss of these, as long as they receive more of substitute goods. For others, though, an ecosystem or a species is unique, without a good substitute. If nothing can compensate for the loss of the owl or the ecosystem, ensuring sustainable levels of those is necessary for welfare sustainability. This difference in attitude leads to political disagreements about endangered species and ecosystem management. In addition, these forests provide a number of ecosystem services, such as water purification and storage of carbon dioxide, that are public goods; protecting these forests involves the usual problems of providing public goods.

If sustainability of human welfare is a desirable societal goal, human ability to find substitutes for desirable goods has great influence on how easy it is to sustain well-being. Even if the present generation does not provide old-growth forests from which future generations can get their wood supplies, providing them with other forests and building materials will offer the same homebuilding services. If, instead, the present generation gets utility from old-growth forests because of the ecological or biodiversity services they provide, and if we are not willing to accept substitutes for those forests, then sustaining welfare will require maintaining those particular resources.

Because people differ on their notions of utility, how does society measure the overall well-being of people and determine whether it is sustainable? Economists' opinions differ. Efficiency adds up individual well-being, as measured by consumer surplus, equivalent variation, or compensating variation; this measure ignores who gains and who loses, with the goal of achieving the greatest total welfare. Other measures focus on the well-being of those worst off in society, based on the idea that the well-being of a society is best measured by the status of the least fortunate. This contrast between efficiency and distributional effects shows up in almost all political debates: how should financial gains be distributed? Should programs that lose money continue because the beneficiaries are politically popular?

Not everyone defines sustainability in terms of maintaining and improving human welfare. Ecologists focus on protecting ecosystems; anthropologists emphasize protecting cultures and languages; others, based on ethics, argue for values for all species independent of human welfare. Because economics focuses on people and their behaviors, focusing on sustaining and improving human welfare is a logical extension of the economic perspective, but it is only one perspective.

As Robert Solow has pointed out, at its heart, sustainability focuses on distributional equity across time. Sustainability seeks to ensure that the well-being of those in the future is at least as great as our well-being now. While working out criteria for deciding whether an action is sustainable, many policy makers have argued that greater equality in the present generation should be one of those criteria. If equity across generations is important, they reason, then so is equity in the present generation. After all, if we care about the well-being of other people in the future, shouldn't we also be concerned about the well-being of other people now? When the distribution of wealth in society is extremely unequal, then the society may not be politically stable or morally just. If equity in the present and future is an important consideration for sustainability, then measuring social well-being may need special attention to the factors that improve the welfare of those currently worst off.

IN SUMMARY

- The Brundtland Commission report on environment and development defines sustainable development as "ensur[ing] that it [development] meets the needs of the present without compromising the ability of future generations to meet

BOX 19.1

Climate Change Hits Poor Countries Hardest

Climate change is a question of sustainability: it raises the issue whether we can sustain both output of consumption goods, c, and a livable climate, which is part of green goods, g. The Stern Report on the Economics of Climate Change came up with a wide range of possible losses in global welfare. At the high end of the projected temperature increase, 5–6°C, the losses range from 5 to 20 percent of GDP. The estimate of losses is higher if environmental goods are included. Another factor that influences the level of the losses is how the effect on the poorest countries is included in the analysis. "[A] disproportionate share of the climate change burden falls on poor regions of the world," states the report. "If we weight this unequal burden appropriately, the estimated global cost of climate change at 5–6°C warming could be more than one-quarter higher than without such weights." In other words, taking equity into account changes the magnitude of the effects of climate change significantly.

their own needs." This definition is similar to the economic perspective in its emphasis on human welfare. Others define sustainability as the maintenance of ecosystems or even individual species, or in reference to yet other goods.

- Humans get utility from many different goods, and those goods are produced in many different ways. When there are many substitutes for goods, or for ways to produce goods, then it is easier to maintain and improve human welfare. If people are not willing to accept substitutes for some unique and scarce goods, such as individual species or ecosystems, then protecting those specific resources becomes more important.
- Sustainability focuses on distributional equity across time. One implication is that distributional equity in the present should also be a concern.

The Role of Substitute Goods in Sustaining Consumption and Production

What exactly do we hope to sustain? Let's define sustainability using two familiar concepts: utility and production.

SUSTAINING UTILITY

Because consumers get utility from goods, a reasonable place to start is with consumption of marketed goods. Personal consumption expenditure (PCE) is personal disposable income less savings. Per-capita PCE is the average amount that people in a given nation spend each year on marketed goods. Thus, it is a measure of consumption in a country.

Just as GDP is not a complete measure of human welfare, neither is PCE a complete measure of utility. PCE only measures consumption of marketed goods. A complete measure of utility should account for time used for leisure and noncompensated activities plus the value of environmental goods to individuals.

For simplicity, let's focus on a single representative member of society and see if she has a sustainable level of utility. All the consumption goods that she purchases—including the wood products made from national forest timber—are grouped into a composite consumption good; let's call that consumption good c. All of the environmental goods that contribute to her utility, including the spotted owl and old-growth habitat, are grouped into another composite good, g, for green. Her bundle of goods is the amounts of c and g, as these are the only two goods.

The utility of our representative at time t is $U_t(c_t, g_t)$: that is, our representative gets utility as a function of both c and g at time t. At future time $t + 1$, the consumer sustains utility if $U_{t+1}(c_{t+1}, g_{t+1}) > U_t(c_t, g_t)$: that is, if utility does not decrease over time.

Let's graph these relationships using indifference curves. Figure 19.2 shows two indifference curves and four consumption bundles, A, B, C, and D. The consumer's bundle at time t is bundle A_t. The other bundles B_{t+1}, C_{t+1}, and D_{t+1}, are possible bundles at time $t + 1$. Utility is sustained if the consumer's bundle in $t + 1$ is B_{t+1} or C_{t+1}. Bundle B_{t+1} is on a higher indifference curve and so utility has increased. Bundle C_{t+1} is on the same indifference curve, so utility is constant. In contrast, because D_{t+1} is on a lower indifference curve, that bundle does not sustain utility.

FIGURE 19.2 Sustained Utility.

The figure shows three indifference curves and four consumption bundles. The bundle at time t is A. Utility is sustained when the bundle at time $t + 1$ is B or C but not D.

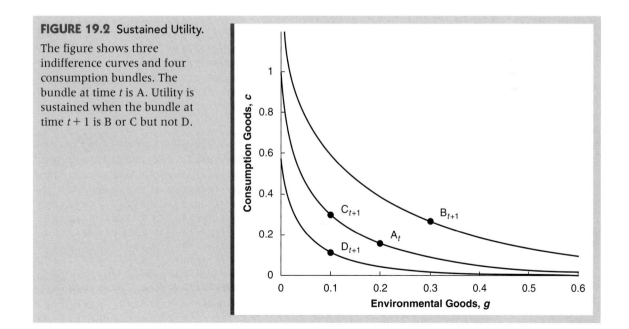

The easiest way to sustain utility is if both consumption goods and environmental goods are constant or growing over time, as in the move from bundle A_t to B_{t+1}. The move from A_t to C_{t+1} also sustains utility, but it does so by decreasing environmental goods and increasing consumption goods. So sustaining utility does not require sustaining the benefit that people get from the environment. Under the **strong sustainability** criterion, both utility and the quantity of environmental goods must not decrease. In contrast, under the **weak sustainability** criterion, only utility must be sustained; the quantity of environmental goods may decrease. Moving from A to B, or even staying at A, is an example of strongly sustainable utility. Moving from A to C is an example of weakly sustainable utility. Weakly sustained utility describes a person in a developing country who suffers from increased air pollution due to economic development but benefits from better nutrition that comes with development. If her utility has increased, she has weakly sustained utility. The reason to make the distinction is that some believe that a decrease in environmental goods is a failure of sustainability. To them, sustaining consumption without sustaining environmental goods is not as good as sustaining consumption and sustaining environmental goods. Sustaining each environmental good is a very strong requirement on an economy. Unlike our single dimensional g, the list of environmental goods to be sustained is very long: services of the atmosphere, existence value of every plant and creature, services of prairies and forests, ecological services such as those provided by wild bees. The list itself is daunting.

In Figure 19.2, going from A to C sustained utility because both bundles were on the same indifference curve. With a different shape to the indifference curves, the move from A to C might not sustain utility. The shape of indifference curves depends on whether one of the goods in the bundle can substitute for the other. Usually, indifference curves are shaped like a crescent moon. The crescent shape means that the goods on each axis are somewhat substitutable for each other. In that case, utility can increase even if the amount of one good decreases, as long as there is a sufficient increase in the other good. For instance, if growth in the consumption of electronic gadgets increased a person's utility more than lost wilderness decreased utility, then that person's utility would increase despite a reduced quantity of environmental goods. The indifference curves in Figure 19.2 have this typical crescent shape.

In many cases, though, one good does not substitute easily or completely for another. Better nutrition is not a complete substitute for breathable air, and most people want some combination of electronic gadgets and outdoor recreation. In the extreme case, there is no substitutability between the goods. In Figure 19.3, the indifference curve takes an L shape instead of a crescent when there is no possibility for substitution. In that case, only an increase in both goods will sustain utility in the second time period.

Points A and C are shown again in Figure 19.3, but this time the indifference curves are L-shaped. Point C shows an increase in consumer goods and a decreased quantity of environmental goods compared with point A. The indifference curve through C is lower than the indifference curve through A, reflecting less utility at time $t+1$ than at time t. In this extreme case, there is no substitutability between

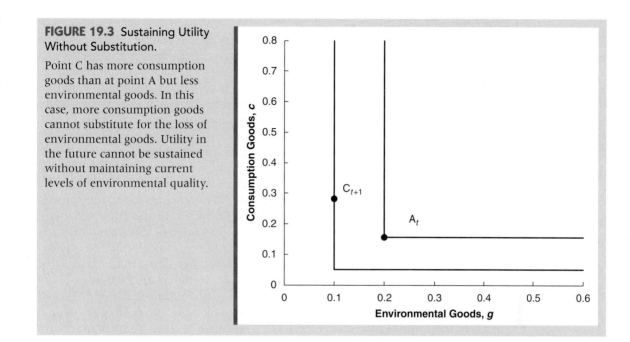

FIGURE 19.3 Sustaining Utility Without Substitution.

Point C has more consumption goods than at point A but less environmental goods. In this case, more consumption goods cannot substitute for the loss of environmental goods. Utility in the future cannot be sustained without maintaining current levels of environmental quality.

consumer goods and environmental goods; any loss of the environmental good diminishes the consumer's utility, even if she gets more consumption goods. Consider, for example, people who have lived in old-growth trees for months at a time to prevent loggers from cutting them down. The "tree sitters" could have spent that time enjoying consumer comforts on the ground, but, for them, no amount of consumer goods could substitute for this particular environmental good.

Sustaining utility depends on people's willingness to substitute between consumption goods and environmental goods. If it is possible to substitute increasingly abundant consumption goods for less available environmental goods, then sustainability may not be difficult to maintain. However, for people who demand specific environmental goods, such a solution would not fit their definition of sustainability.

SUSTAINING PRODUCTION

Sustaining production over time requires the ability to maintain or increase quantities; with t still representing time, $c_{t+1} \geq c_t$, and $g_{t+1} \geq g_t$. To sustain all production, as in strong sustainability, c and g must both be sustained. Sustaining utility, however, does not necessarily require sustaining both c and g. Utility may allow for substitution between c and g; one could go up and the other could go down. Sustaining production, however, requires that neither c nor g can go down. Therefore, it is harder to sustain production than to sustain welfare.

To see how to sustain production, let's examine how goods are made. Consumption goods are made from labor, capital, and other inputs. Some of the other inputs are nonrenewable resources, such as oil. Others are renewable resources, such as wood, but using them to produce consumption goods reduces the quantity of environmental goods, such as habitat and clean air. For either renewable or nonrenewable resources, using them to produce c may decrease the stock of natural resources that contribute to g. So, producing more c makes sustaining production of g difficult, unless there is a way to produce more g to replace the g that is used up. To see whether that is possible, let's consider how labor, capital, and other inputs are used to produce c and g.

Labor is very important in the production of consumption goods. It accounts for about two-thirds of the value of GDP. It is possible to increase the quantities of some environmental goods by using labor. For instance, labor is often used to replant forests and to reduce soil erosion. Other environmental goods, such as wild species or native ecosystems, are much more difficult to increase through use of labor. Human labor has a great deal more ability to increase consumption goods than to increase environmental goods.

Capital is also required to make final output. The remaining third of the value of GDP comes from capital. Capital can both come from nature, such as stocks of minerals or forests, and be made by people, such as buildings and factories. Capital that comes from nature is called *natural capital*, which the UN defines as "natural assets in their role of providing natural resource inputs and environmental services for economic production." Some environmental goods can be increased in quantity through use of capital as well as labor. For instance, a scrubber is a large piece of capital equipment that helps keep the air clean by "scrubbing" pollutants from exhaust gas. For other environmental goods, however, like wild species and native ecosystems, human-made capital is of little use in increasing their quantity.

Because capital is essential to increase c, and can increase some forms of g, let's take a moment to think about it. Capital comes from investment, the process of setting aside some current output to make more goods for the future. Some capital stocks, such as metals, cannot be increased because they are nonrenewable; others, such as renewable resources and human-made capital, will grow with investment. Because output can be consumed right away, investing requires giving up some current consumption. Replanting trees in the national forests or in the Dominican Republic, for instance, requires spending money that could be used for other purposes, such as providing health care to forest workers. Reducing current consumption to invest in the future can, in turn, be used to make more consumer goods, environmental goods, inputs to production, or capital. Sustaining capital plays a major role in sustainability. Allowing the deterioration of capital leads, over time, to a reduction in the consumption goods that capital can provide. Investing the profits from capital into new, productive capital can ensure a sustainable future by protecting our ability to produce in the future. For these reasons, maintaining and enhancing capital plays a critical role in sustaining future consumption. At the same time, because investment comes at the expense of current consumption, people—especially impoverished people—are not always willing or able to protect capital stocks.

The last category consists of the other variable inputs. Some of these inputs are themselves manufactured; greater availability of labor and capital make the quantities of these goods easy to expand. Some variable inputs, such as oil, come from drawing down nonrenewable capital stock. Because the quantity of oil is limited, then so ultimately would be the quantities of final goods that require oil, and not substitutes for oil, for their production. However, while gasoline is difficult to make other than from oil, there are other transportation fuels. For instance, cars can be made to run on ethanol, which is made from renewable resources. When oil becomes less plentiful and pricier, use of gasoline may not be sustainable, but use of cars may be able to continue by switching to new fuels. The sustainability of production can be made difficult by dependence on exhaustible resources. The availability of inexpensive substitutes for the exhaustible resource makes it easier to sustain output.

There is one last consideration for production sustainability: technical progress, which allows more output with the same quantity of inputs, or the same output with different, less scarce inputs. For example, improved sawmill methods mean that it is possible to get more wood products out of a log than in the past; it may be possible to sustain wood products production while harvesting fewer trees. Research into biofuels holds the possibility of biofuels that use less land to make the same amount of ethanol per acre as is made now. Technical progress, which can provide more and better goods more cheaply, is an important source of increased output, an ingredient in sustainability. Technical progress can also be very important in reducing energy use and sustaining the carbon dioxide concentration in the atmosphere. New types of cars and lights, new types of insulating windows, and many more innovations reduce energy use. However, some environmental resources do not get much benefit from technical progress. Maintaining intact natural ecosystems, like the Amazon, still is mostly a matter of not disturbing them, which is not amenable to technical progress. Technical progress is a very important part of sustainability, but many natural systems do not directly benefit from technical progress.

Sustaining production is possible due to three growth factors: (1) maintaining or enhancing labor and capital inputs; (2) ability to substitute away from natural resource inputs that are in limited supply; and (3) technical progress. Some environmental goods respond exactly as consumption goods to these growth factors. Clean air, for instance, depends on abatement equipment that requires labor and capital and benefits from technical progress. Clean air is also provided by substitution, for instance, away from use of coal and toward other energy sources. However, not all environmental goods benefit from these growth factors. Labor and capital are not big factors in producing habitat, nor are there substitutes for the land necessary for habitat. Finally, technical progress is not applicable to wilderness. The outputs that will be hardest to sustain are those least susceptible to the three growth factors.

▨ IN SUMMARY

- Sustainable utility means that utility should not decrease over time. The ability to sustain utility is affected by our willingness to substitute among the goods that contribute to our well-being. If people will accept, for instance, more consumption goods in exchange for fewer environmental goods, then sustaining utility is easier than if it is necessary to sustain or improve both consumption and environmental quality over time. Strong sustainability refers to maintaining or enhancing environmental goods instead of allowing

BOX 19.2

Investment and Sustainability

Let's use a mathematical model to look more formally at the role of investment in sustainability. We start with two types of capital stocks: natural, N, such as land, oil, or forests; and human-made, K, such as machinery or factories. These capital stocks plus labor, L, are used to make our consumption good, c. For instance, land, seed, machinery, plus labor produce agricultural goods. A mathematical function that indicates the level of output associated with different amounts of inputs is called a production function. In this case, a generic production function for the consumption good is $c = F(N, K, L)$. It is often true that increasing any one input, while increasing or holding the others constant, increases output. For instance, more food can result from improved machinery that can harvest better, more workers who can harvest when the crop is most ripe, or more land planted to the crop. If output is held constant, then increasing one input while decreasing another input provides the isoquant discussed in Chapter 8.

Once c is produced, people can consume it, which we will call $c_{consumed}$, or they can invest it to make more capital, which we'll call I. Farmers for millennia have saved some of the crops they have harvested to plant the next year; they can also save some of the money from selling the crops to buy more machinery. Mathematically, $c_{consumed} = F(N, K, L) - I$. This equation indicates that a society that invests more reduces its current consumption.

The investment is used in part to replace human-made capital stock that is worn out or used up (depreciation), and in part to increase that capital stock. We assume that a fixed percentage, δ, of the capital stock is used up each year. Let's call this year's human-made capital stock K_t and next year's capital stock K_{t+1}. The effect of investment and capital consumption on next year's capital stock is $K_{t+1} = K_t + I_t - \delta K_t$. This equation indicates that, while consuming less, the society that invests more will have a higher capital stock tomorrow. The higher capital stock results in more goods tomorrow, through the production function. Hence, reduced consumption now can increase consumption for the future. Notice that net savings = investment less depreciation = $I_t - \delta K_t$ plays a crucial role in increasing output: investment must exceed depreciation for capital to grow.

Natural capital differs from human-made capital in the low importance of K and L in its production. People can extract or use the resources, but there are limited opportunities for people to increase the resource stock. In the simplest case of an exhaustible resource, such as an oil deposit or a wilderness area, there is no way to increase the capital stock by investment; $N_{t+1} = N_t - c_{consumed}$. In the fishery model, the natural net growth, $F_N(N)$, depends only on the current stock of the resource. In this case, $N_{t+1} = N_t + F_N(N_t) - c_{consumed}$. Saving fish stocks results in higher future stocks both through the savings itself and through growth. Soil productivity is a case where people can, to some extent, substitute chemical fertilizers for the natural capital; if fertilizer were a perfect substitute, then $N_{t+1} = N_t + I_t - \delta N_t$. Fertilizers are not perfect substitutes, though, and often cause deterioration of water resources.

For both types of capital, maintaining stocks is important for maintaining production. The lesson for human-made capital is that investment, even if it decreases current consumption, is necessary to maintain the stock; without investment, either the natural capital or labor must substitute for human-made capital as inputs, or production will drop. The lessons for natural capital are more complex. First, the human ability to increase it is not guaranteed; in some cases, humans may be capable only of reducing the stocks. Therefore, reliance on natural capital for production requires careful consideration of the depletion of the resource, as discussed in Chapters 16 and 17; otherwise, production will decrease. Next, as discussed in Chapter 18, the national income accounts do not take into account the depletion of natural capital; this omission hides the problem of natural capital depletion. Finally, note that the sustainability of production will depend either on maintaining natural capital or on finding ways to substitute other goods for it in the production process.

consumption goods to substitute for them, while weak sustainability would allow for consumption goods to take the place of environmental goods.
- Sustaining production requires that production not decrease over time. Sustaining production is not required to sustain utility, if people are willing to accept some more abundant goods for less available goods.
- Sustaining production relies on maintaining or enhancing capital and labor, the ability to substitute away from increasingly scarce resources, and technical progress that finds new ways of getting the same output with less or less expensive inputs. If these factors are less effective in producing environmental goods than consumption goods, then sustaining production of consumption goods may be easier than sustaining environmental goods.

Sustainability and Intergenerational Equity

Why would people choose an unsustainable development path? The underlying question is whether we are always willing to postpone gains today so that the future is better off. Are there circumstances where we might want to be better off now than in the future?

Consider forest management. If a forest has had its chance to grow without human interference, then it may achieve a condition where the new growth equals the volume of trees that die; the forest has reached its carrying capacity. In this situation, there is no sustained-yield harvest because the forest is no longer growing. If people harvest some of these trees, the initial harvest is not sustainable. Reducing the stock to a lower level, such as the maximum sustained-yield level, is a one-time harvest. Once the stock is reduced, though, the net growth goes from zero in the original steady state to positive, and it is possible to have a sustained-yield harvest. In this case, the only way to get any wood products from the forest is an unsustainable initial harvest. Should a sustainability criterion stop these harvests?

Nonrenewable resources pose an even harder case. Any use of them is not strongly sustainable: it is not possible to maintain the same level of availability forever. Even if a material, such as steel or aluminum, is recyclable, at very best we can keep supplies constant; more likely, losses will occur over time. Should we therefore not use any nonrenewable resources because we will eventually deplete them?

One possible answer to these questions is that we may be willing to have more now, even if welfare levels in the future are not as high. People have different personal rates of time preference; many are willing to accept reductions in welfare in the future in exchange for more now, especially if the future seems far away or beyond their expected life spans. Others may ask why we emphasize protecting the welfare of people in the future when many people in the present face starvation, disease, oppression, and other crises; perhaps, instead of investing resources for the future, we should address today's problems.

Another, more hopeful, answer is that we may be able to have some now and more later, through wise investment of the gains we get from these resources. As John Hartwick pointed out, if we take the proceeds from using nonrenewable resources or harvesting renewable resources unsustainably, and we invest those proceeds in productive capital, then we can convert those unsustainable gains into different but sustainable gains. Hartwick's rule for nonrenewable resources is that, if the entirety of the resource rent is invested in new capital, then production can remain constant. The resource rent is the price of the resource product less the cost of producing the product. For instance, the resource rent for oil in the Canadian tar sands is the price of oil (about \$60/barrel) less the cost of producing it, about \$15/barrel; Hartwick's rule calls for the difference, \$45/barrel, to be invested.

Hartwick considered a simple good's production; the only inputs that change from period to period are capital and the extraction of the nonrenewable resource. According to the Hotelling theory of nonrenewable resources, the resource rent goes up at the rate of interest; that increase in value balances the desirability of using the resource now with an incentive to save some of the resource for the future. As the rent goes up, so does the price of the extracted resource, which increases the price of the produced good. Because these price increases reduce the quantity demanded, both extraction per period of production and production go down. Hartwick found that, if all the resource rent was used to buy new capital to substitute for the nonrenewable resource, then the added capital would make production go up by exactly as much as the lower use of the extracted resource made it go down. So the Hartwick rule for sustainability is to invest all the resource rents in a substitute form of capital, in compliance with weak sustainability.

For instance, if we invest some of the gains from using oil into developing ways to make fuels and plastics from renewable resources, or into completely different materials that provide us with transportation and materials, we can enjoy benefits now and in the future. Even if oil is not sustainable, this investment in alternatives can sustain or improve human welfare. These investments in future welfare nevertheless come at the expense of present consumption. Sustained improvements in welfare in this case depend on our ability to convert the benefits from unsustainable activities into other things that provide utility to people in the future.

BOX 19.3
Sustainable Development in the Dominican Republic

Plan Sierra began in 1979 as a program to reduce rural poverty and soil erosion, as well as to provide sustainable development, around the Cibao Valley in the Dominican Republic. Initially funded primarily by the Dominican government, it also received support from the W. K. Kellogg Foundation. Plan Sierra proposed alternatives to the existing practices of cutting down native forests and choosing land uses that provided immediate income. Many of these land uses, such as burning off the forests to grow food crops, called "slash and burn," produced tremendous soil erosion. The soil that ran off from the land ended up in the reservoirs of electricity-generating dams and shortened the life span of the dams. Alternative land uses, such as coffee growing or managed forests, produced much less soil erosion, but they were not as profitable as the slash-and-burn food plots.

Alain De Janvry, Elisabeth Sadoulet, and Blas Santos suggested three criteria by which to measure the effects of Plan Sierra: it should improve the well-being of the land users (which they called acceptability); have positive net benefits, including the external effects of soil erosion on the dams (feasibility); and have greater benefits for both farmers and electricity production in the future than in the present (sustainability). If a project is acceptable, then current land users are less likely to resist it. If it is feasible, then it is possible to achieve distributional goals by transferring money from gainers to losers. Sustainability implies that the well-being of the area will increase over time.

The traditional activity of slash-and-burn food plots scored highly on acceptability and feasibility, but it failed on sustainability. Many of the feasible activities that Plan Sierra recommended, such as better-managed food plots and coffee production, were acceptable and sustainable for the farmers but not for the dams. Nevertheless, the damage to the dams was much lower for these practices than for the traditional practices. Planting trees, one of Plan Sierra's recommended activities, was feasible and sustainable but only at a cost to current farmers. If, however, it were possible for current farmers to take out loans to plant trees, then they could avoid those costs, and the loans could be paid back with revenues in the future.

Plan Sierra provided education to regional farmers about the effects of different crops and land-management practices. In addition, it provided financial management skills, access to health care, and vocational training. As Fermin Rodriguez, the executive director of Plan Sierra, has said, "For any ecosystem to be truly sustainable, you have to focus on the individual who is part of that ecosystem. If that man, that woman, that family is not fully involved in the conservation, the preservation of the ecosystem will never be sustainable."

As a result of Plan Sierra, farmers are not only terracing the steep hillsides—a way to reduce soil erosion—but also replanting trees. Between 1981 and 1991, the area of forested land in the watershed increased from 22 to 36 percent. Through

(Continued)

BOX 19.3

(continued)

more careful and longer-term planning, both the productivity of the land and community profits have increased.

Many activities designed to improve the welfare of poor people nevertheless have adverse consequences on the environment and on the future; other activities designed to protect the environment and future generations leave the present generation impoverished. Identifying projects that are feasible means that gains outweigh losses. With imaginative use of loans, taxes, and subsidies, it may be possible to make a feasible project both acceptable and sustainable, as Plan Sierra showed.

IN SUMMARY

- Investing for the future involves reducing current consumption. Ensuring welfare or other forms of sustainability for our society involves a tradeoff with providing for those in need now.
- Under weak sustainability, human welfare can be sustained even if our use of some resources is not sustainable. If we take the benefits from use of those resources and invest them to provide future benefits, then even exhaustible resources can contribute to a sustainable society.

Measuring Sustainability

How can we tell how sustainable a society is? This discussion suggests several principles for measurement. First, a measure oriented toward utility better represents sustainability—at least in the sense of the Brundtland Commission—than a measure oriented toward production or capital. Second, a measure must include environmental and other nonmarketed values, not just marketed goods. Third, one measure may not be adequate. If some goods that contribute to sustainability do not have substitutes, then it is necessary to monitor how well those specific goods are doing.

Implicit in this discussion is the question of aggregates, or averages, compared with individual measures. Is it important, for instance, for each country to be sustainable? Or can some countries operate unsustainably if other countries compensate for those losses? How important is equity? If we operate sustainably on average, but some people or goods are much worse off than others, are we proceeding in a satisfactory way?

Averages can be misleading. If the richest person in the world walks into a room, the average wealth of people in the room will increase tremendously, although nobody actually becomes better off. If sustainability requires some measure of equity, then a measure that focuses on the worst-off people or goods, or a measure of that inequity, provides better insight into the sustainability of our actions. If, though, sustainability does not require that everyone or everything be sustainable, then an aggregate or average measure may be sufficient.

Another difficulty is that people's preferences differ and sometimes conflict. For instance, some people would feel an irreplaceable loss if old-growth forests were logged; others would prefer to have the unique wood products from those ecosystems. In some remote parts of the Amazon, some indigenous people are worried that development will destroy their way of life; other indigenous people perceive advantages in modernity and want to bring it to their community. If nobody is willing to accept a substitute for the disputed resource, then economic principles cannot provide a simple solution to the conflict; moral and political factors will instead determine the outcome.

Chapter 18 reviewed some economic and social measures of sustainability. Let's look now at some ecological measures.

When some species, ecosystems, or other contributors to planetary welfare do not have good substitutes, then strong sustainability requires their protection. A difficulty with achieving this goal is that species and ecosystems have evolved since the beginning of life. A species may go extinct due to forces of natural selection, for instance. Some species have lost most of their native habitats and may only survive in zoos or through captive breeding programs. Invasive species, such as the Asian carp that threatens to outcompete other fish in the Great Lakes ecosystem, may lead to greatly changed ecosystems. Is the survival of each species a critical component of a sustainable world, or might some of these losses reflect the evolution of life on earth?

Many ecological factors contribute to our welfare; this section presents a sampling. Some people will not insist on the need to protect these resources, if receiving consumption goods will compensate for their loss; for other people, losses of some of these goods may be irreplaceable.

Figure 19.4 shows the change in forest cover in Brazil, Sweden, and India. While India has relatively little forested land, its forest cover has increased in recent

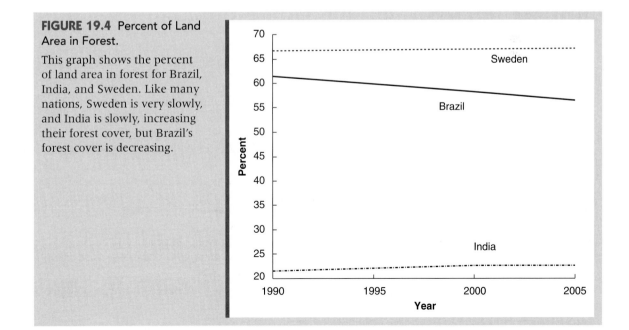

FIGURE 19.4 Percent of Land Area in Forest.

This graph shows the percent of land area in forest for Brazil, India, and Sweden. Like many nations, Sweden is very slowly, and India is slowly, increasing their forest cover, but Brazil's forest cover is decreasing.

years. Forest cover has also increased in Sweden, a country with abundant forests. Brazil, in contrast, shows a decline in its forested areas.

Figure 19.5 shows the change in the numbers of threatened mammal, fish, and plant species in the world. The numbers of threatened plant and fish species especially appear to have increased greatly in recent years.

Carbon dioxide emissions, an enormous factor in climate change, vary greatly by country, due to factors such as population and stage of development. Figure 19.6 shows carbon dioxide emissions from the United States, China, Ethiopia, Brazil, Sweden, and India. While Sweden, a developed country, shows stable emissions, emissions from India, which is developing, are growing very rapidly. Ethiopia, a much less developed country than India, remains too poor to have high levels of carbon dioxide emissions. Large emissions from the developed world have been the major contributors to carbon dioxide buildup in the atmosphere. The 30 countries, mostly developed, that make up the Organization for Economic Cooperation and Development emitted 48 percent of the world's carbon dioxide in 2005; the United States alone produced 21 percent of world emissions. Nevertheless, emissions from developing countries are increasing rapidly. In 2005, China produced 19 percent of world carbon dioxide, almost as much as the United States. By 2008, China had surpassed the United States as the largest carbon emitter. Figure 19.7 (on page 488) shows a per-capita distribution of carbon dioxide emissions from these countries.

As these figures suggest, some ecological indicators, such as forest cover in India and Sweden, show improvements, while others, such as the numbers of threatened species and carbon dioxide emissions, show increasing problems. These and other indicators vary by location and by what is measured.

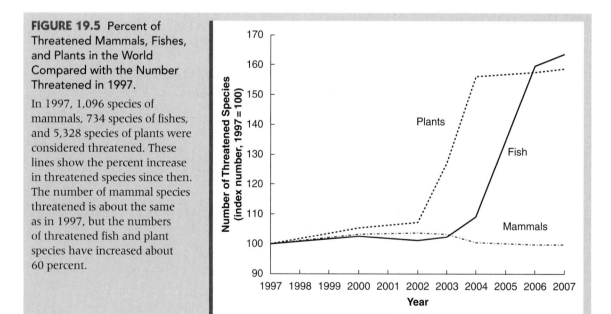

FIGURE 19.5 Percent of Threatened Mammals, Fishes, and Plants in the World Compared with the Number Threatened in 1997.

In 1997, 1,096 species of mammals, 734 species of fishes, and 5,328 species of plants were considered threatened. These lines show the percent increase in threatened species since then. The number of mammal species threatened is about the same as in 1997, but the numbers of threatened fish and plant species have increased about 60 percent.

FIGURE 19.6 Carbon Dioxide Emissions in the United States, China, Brazil, India, and Sweden.

This graph shows carbon dioxide emissions. Sweden has decreased its carbon emissions by making increasing use of forest byproducts and even garbage as biofuels. India emits increasing amounts of carbon dioxide as it develops. The United States and China emit the most.

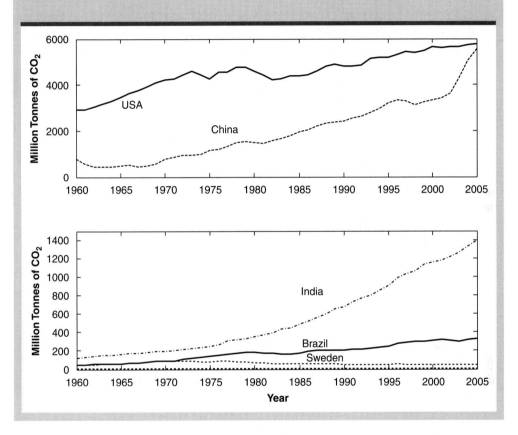

 IN SUMMARY

- There is no single, commonly accepted way of measuring sustainability. Any one index is an aggregate or average and will not reveal the status of individual components. Numerous measures analyze different aspects of the problem.
- Because some goods important for sustainability do not have good substitutes, it is important to look at trends in those specific indices as well. Some measures in some places show improvement over time; other measures reveal increasing problems.

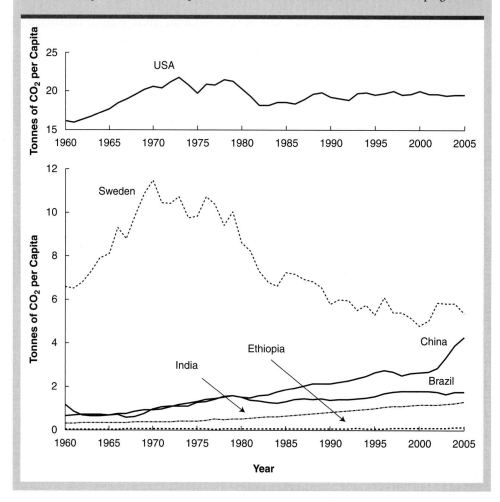

FIGURE 19.7 Per-Capita CO$_2$ Emissions.

While the total emissions in Figure 19.6 give the best information on the sustainability of atmospheric services, the per-capita emissions show that, while the United States has stabilized and Sweden has lowered its per-capita emissions, both countries emit far more per person than the developing countries. The developing countries cite these disparities as a reason for deep cuts in the developed world rather than limitations in the developing world.

Consumption Now or a Sustainable Climate?

How much money should be spent over the next 30 years to reduce GHG emissions? When should it be spent? The economic problem comes down to deciding how much to reduce consumption now in order to avoid climate change and therefore have higher consumption later. The efficient solution is to seek a policy that maximizes net present value benefits—the present value of benefits in the future minus costs in the present.

Because the costs of reducing GHG come now and the benefits of avoiding climate change come later, the discount rate will make quite a difference in the analysis. If the discount rate used in this benefit-cost analysis is high, it will not place much weight on the future, and the benefit of future climate stability must be very large—or the cost of abatement right now must be very small—in order to justify GHG reduction. If the discount rate is low, it places great weight on future climate effects and favors spending money now to obtain these benefits in the future. Economists do not agree on what discount rate to use.

William Nordhaus argues that the best policy is to take only steps that are very cheap or free today and to steadily increase the effort over time. He uses standard assumptions about the long-run interest rate, the size of the damages, and the size of the costs, thus treating climate change as a standard benefit-cost problem. While abatement will be costly, the costs will come much closer in time to the benefits from reducing global warming. Abating climate change a small amount now with increasing stringency in the future reduces the burden on the present generation.

In contrast, the Stern Review on the Economics of Climate Change, produced by Sir Nicholas Stern, head of the Government Economic Service of the United Kingdom, concludes that immediate, strong action is necessary. The review estimates that the expected damages from climate change will cost about 5 percent of world GDP now and forever, and that these damages could be as high as 20 percent of global GDP. The costs of mitigating these effects, in contrast, are on the order of 1 percent of global GDP each year. These magnitudes and a low discount rate imply that strong action now is well worth the costs.

The Stern Review differs from other studies, like those of Nordhaus, in its use of a very low discount rate, 1 percent. The lost GDP due to climate change does not come for very many years, while the costs of prevention are immediate, but the low discount rate means that great weight is placed on the future. This increases the present value of the damage and leads to the conclusion that a high level of abatement right now is the efficient solution. A higher discount rate, such as the rate used by Nordhaus, reduces the present value of the damages, so that the efficient level of current abatement is smaller. Indeed, the major effect of the Stern Review was an outpouring of articles either taking issue with the assumed low interest rate or giving other reasons for the act-now conclusions.

One argument, from Martin Weitzman, was that the expected damages could be much larger than the damage at the expected temperature change. The report of the Intergovernmental Panel on Climate Change (IPCC) gives a range of possible temperature increases; most are a couple of degrees, but there is some chance of an increase of 6°C or higher, which would lead to catastrophic changes, resulting in a 20 percent decrease in GDP. Weitzman argues that avoiding climate damages is, in effect, an insurance problem. People are often willing to pay some amount of money every year to avoid major costs of serious problems. Health insurance pays for care if something happens; automobile insurance provides coverage in case of an accident; and homeowner insurance compensates for loss due to theft or fire. In all these cases, the present value of the premiums is more than the expected value of the damage. People prefer to pay small amounts with certainty to avoid a chance of having to pay a much larger amount. In Weitzman's analysis, fast action on climate is insurance against the worst-case outcomes. Because these worst-case outcomes have very large damages to human society, it is these outcomes that should dominate the analysis.

Thomas Sterner presents a simpler reason to abate today. As temperature goes up, some goods, like cereal grains, become harder to grow. Because there will be less of them, their prices will be higher. As a result, the damages from climate change should incorporate the new higher prices for goods affected by climate. In his view, the damage estimates are too small because they do not account for the increased scarcity of many commodities. In this benefit-cost analysis, the decisive factor is not the discount rate, but the magnitude of the damages. For any given discount rate, a greater degree of harm in the future justifies spending more money now to avoid the harm.

Even if greenhouse gas abatement does not reduce GDP very much, there is still considerable resistance to greenhouse gas reduction policies. Much of the change in lifestyle has to happen in the developed countries that are at relatively low risk from climate change. Many people do not want to live with smaller vehicles, less driving, less electricity use, and costly investments in energy conservation. After all, most of the benefits of those changes will go to others—those in the future and those in areas most severely harmed by climate change. The personal and political obstacles to reducing climate damages are very large—large enough that it is somewhat surprising that any climate policies have been enacted.

Faith in Ingenuity?

My faith in the future rests squarely on the belief that man, if he doesn't first destroy himself, will find new answers in the universe, new technologies, new disciplines, which will contribute to a vastly different and better world in the twenty-first century.

—Barry Goldwater, *With No Apologies*, 1979

Arizona Senator Barry Goldwater, the 1964 Republican nominee for president, was a staunch conservative, a believer in free enterprise. The tenor of his remarks suggests an absolute faith that technical progress will be the engine that propels mankind through this century. He believed that, if humans avoided nuclear war, sustaining human welfare depended on what people invented and discovered. In Senator Goldwater's lifetime, horrible diseases like polio were eliminated, man had landed on the moon, hybrid corn had greatly increased yields, and the coming atomic age still seemed promising. Ingenuity had accomplished a huge increase of human well-being. Does this mean that sustainability only concerns people without enough faith in human ingenuity?

The promise of ingenuity is gain without pain. We can continue to consume as we always have because, as we run out of some goods, we will find alternatives for them. This promise relies on substitution possibilities: renewable and nuclear energy will replace coal, cleaner vehicles will replace dirtier ones, plantation forests will replace old-growth forests, and so on. At the same time, ecologists and environmental scientists warn of the losses of genetic and biological diversity and ecosystem services that result from thoughtless human progress. In the words of Aldo Leopold, "To keep every cog and wheel is the first precaution of intelligent tinkering." While ingenuity has greatly increased human quality of life and is critical for addressing some of the most important problems of our world, our ability to understand the full implications of our new technologies is almost inevitably incomplete. Whether the world is sustained in its current condition, or how it evolves, depends on human choices, the fundamental topic of economics.

CHAPTER SUMMARY

Here are the key lessons from this chapter:

- Sustainability is often, but not universally, defined as development that allows those in the future to be at least as well off as the current generation. This concept emphasizes intergenerational equity: protecting the welfare of those in the future is an important role for those in the present. Its relationship to equity in the current generation is less clear. If people in the present care about other people in the future, it seems logical that current people should care about other people in the present as well. However, providing more resources for the future, through investment, reduces wealth that could be used now to address current problems, such as poverty and access to health care.
- The ability to substitute some goods for others greatly increases the ability to maintain or improve welfare. If there are substitutes for goods that may be depleted, such as fossil fuels, or if technological advances allow us to substitute abundant resources for depleted ones, then we can improve our welfare even while running out of some goods. If, though, there are no adequate substitutes for goods that give us utility, such as biodiversity, then strong sustainability implies that we must maintain those specific elements to sustain our welfare.
- Sustaining consumption does not require sustaining production, as long as substitutes are available for goods no longer produced.
- Investing to provide more for the future requires reducing current consumption, and some people prefer to use resources now rather than bequeath them to the future. On the other hand, investment provides greater returns in the future; the reductions to ensure future welfare may not need to be large, if we invest wisely.
- There is no one commonly accepted measure for sustainability. An aggregate or average index does not provide information on its individual components, such as the welfare of the poorest people. Goods that lack adequate substitutes must individually be sustainable for social welfare to be sustained. Available indicators give mixed evidence on whether our activities are sustainable: some show improvements, while others show increasing problems.

KEY TERMS

strong sustainability *(p. 476)*   weak sustainability *(p. 476)*
sustainable development *(p. 470)*

NOTES

Much of the discussion of sustainability here owes an intellectual debt to two articles by Robert Solow, "An Almost Practical Step Toward Sustainability," *Resources Policy* 19(3) (September 1993): 162–172, and "Sustainability—An Economist's Perspective," *National Geographic Research and Exploration* 8(1) (1992): 3–6.

The New York Times of October 11, 1994, discusses employment after the Clinton Forest Plan, "Oregon, Foiling Forecasters, Thrives as it Protects Owls," pp. A1 and A16.

Figure 19.1, "Harvests and Removals in the Pacific Northwest-West National Forests," is from http://www.fs.fed.us/pnw/publications/gtr699/pnw-gtr699c.pdf.

The Plan Sierra example comes from Alain de Janvry, Elisabeth Sadoulet, and Blas Santos, "Project Evaluation for Sustainable Rural Development: Plan Sierra in the Dominican Republic," *Journal of Environmental Economics and Management* 28(2) (March 1995): 135–154, and the W. K. Kellogg Foundation, "People Preserve their Ecosystem with Plan Sierra," http://www.wkkf.org/default.aspx?tabid=55&CID= 145&ProjCID=323&ProjID=11&NID=28&LanguageID=0, accessed July 2, 2009.

John Hartwick analyzed the role of capital investment in a sustainable future in 1977, in "Intergenerational Equity and the Investing of Rents from Exhaustible Resources," *American Economic Review* 67(5) (December 1977): 972–974.

One discussion of sustainability indicators is in Peter Bartelmus and Graham Douglas, "Indicators of Sustainable Development," in Cutler J. Cleveland (ed.), *Encyclopedia of Earth* (Washington, D.C., Environmental Information Coalition, National Council for Science and the Environment, 2007). Published in the *Encyclopedia of Earth* April 25, 2007; retrieved February 6, 2008, http://www.eoearth. org/article/Indicators_of_sustainable_development.

The quote on weighting income loss to reflect equity concerns is from "The Stern Review on the Economics of Climate Change," Executive Summary, p. x., http://www.hm-treasury.gov.uk/independent_reviews/stern_review_economics_ climate_change/stern_review_report.cfm. The estimate of 5–20 percent reduction of global consumption is in the Executive Summary, p. x.

Data on threatened species come from the United National Environmental Programme Global Environment Outlook (GEO) Database, http://geodata.grid. unep.ch/index.php, accessed February 8, 2008.

Data on carbon dioxide emissions come from the U.S. Department of Energy, Energy Information Administration, "Emissions of Greenhouse Gases Report," http://www.eia.doe.gov/oiaf/1605/ggrpt/, accessed January 31, 2009. The report that China has surpassed the United States as the largest emitter of carbon dioxide is from Andrew C. Revkin, "China Pulls Ahead in the Great Carbon Race," *New York*

Times, June 14 (2008), http://dotearth.blogs.nytimes.com/2008/06/14/china-pulls-ahead-in-the-great-carbon-race.

The UN definition of natural capital is found at *Glossary of Environment Statistics, Studies in Methods*, Series F, No. 67, United Nations, New York, 1997.

The source of the quote for Aldo Leopold is the *Sand County Almanac*.

EXERCISES

1. Efficiency over time involves maximizing the present value of net benefits. What is the relationship between sustainability and efficiency? Is an efficient society likely to be sustainable? If so, what about efficiency leads it to sustainability? If not, can an efficient society be made sustainable? Is a sustainable society likely to be efficient? Why or why not?

2. Economist John Maynard Keynes proposed, in response to the Great Depression of the 1930s, that countries tax their citizens when the economy is strong and save it to have available when the economy is weak. When the economy is weak, Keynes encouraged governments to spend (even to go into debt) to stimulate economic activity. This policy of "counter-cyclical" government expenditures would dampen the good times in the hopes of reducing the pain of the bad times.

   (a) Describe a way that a government could spend its money in bad times that would primarily increase current well-being. Also describe a way that a government could spend money to increase future well-being.

   (b) Keynes originated the saying, "In the long run, we're all dead." He meant in this statement that, if conditions are bad enough in the short run, people might not survive to reach the long run. Does this statement suggest that Keynes would focus government expenditures in bad times on ways to increase current wealth or on ways to increase future well-being?

   (c) Would Keynes advocate for spending to increase future wealth rather than current consumption when the economy is strong or when the economy is weak? Why?

   (d) What might go wrong with Keynesian counter-cyclical spending if the timing is wrong? That is, suppose that a government is slow to enact its spending in the face of economic difficulties and it instead encourages growth when the economy is already recovering. In that case, government spending may compete with private spending for labor and materials. What is likely to happen to prices in the economy? Will this price effect help or hurt the economy?

   (e) Governments are also often reluctant to increase taxes, even when economies are doing well. What problems might arise from failure to raise government funds?

   (f) If Keynesian counter-cyclical spending worked as Keynes sought, would human well-being be more or less sustainable than in the absence of the policy? If Keynesian counter-cyclical spending instead often suffered from the problem of bad timing, would human well-being be more or less sustainable than in the absence of the policy?

3. Consider the following possible development paths.
   (i) We use many nonrenewable resources and eventually exhaust them; at that time, we shift to renewable resources. The gains from using those resources are great enough that current generations can and do achieve very high standards of living. Because the gains from those resources are spent on improving the well-being of current generations, future generations will be worse off.
   (ii) We use many nonrenewable resources and eventually exhaust them; at that time, we shift to renewable resources. Unlike scenario (i), though, much of the gains from using those resources are invested in finding better ways of using renewable resources, such as improving technologies. Current generations do not live as well as in (i), but future generations have a better standard of living than in (i).
   (iii) We cease our use of nonrenewable resources quickly and use renewable resources. Though we face an immediate reduction in well-being—our living standard is the lowest of these three scenarios—our well-being gradually increases.
   (a) Which of these scenarios would be considered sustainable? Why? In answering this question, be explicit about what you mean by sustainability.
   (b) Which of these scenarios is likely to be most efficient? Why?
   (c) Which development path do you think best describes our current behavior?
   (d) Which development path do you think we should choose? Why?
   (e) If your answers to (c) and (d) are different, why are they different? In what ways are our markets, political systems, or personal choices leading us down the wrong path? If your answers to (c) and (d) are the same, are our markets, political systems, and personal choices all operating in the best way that they can, or is there room for improvement?
   (f) In the 1800s and early 1900s, much wood products harvesting in the United States was described as "cut and run": loggers would strip an area of its most valuable trees, without regard for the environmental damage left behind, and leave for the next place with valuable stands of trees. Which policy listed previously is most analogous to cut-and-run forestry?
   (g) Environmentalists sought "nondeclining even flow" as policy for wood harvests from national forests. Under this policy, harvests would only increase over time; it would not be permitted to have high initial harvests with smaller harvests in the future. Which policy listed previously is most analogous to nondeclining even flow?

Index

Well-being. *See also* Human welfare
  GDP as measurement for, 447, 449,
    452–453, 461
  national accounts/human welfare and
    measuring, 447–448
West County Toxics Coalition, 319
Wheat
  marketing loan program, 29–30
  supply and demand (1960), 29
Willig, Robert, 100
Willingness to accept (WTA). *See* WTA
    (willingness to accept)
Willingness to pay (WTP). *See* WTP
    (willingness to pay)

Wolves
  demand curves for, 89–90
  existence as a good, 41
  markets and, 36–37, 45
  protection, 51
  utility change and, 95, 97
Women's labor, and economic growth, 450
World Bank, 451, 465
World Commission on Environment and
    Development (1987), 470
WTA (willingness to accept)
  definition, 97
  utility change and, 97
  WTP differences with, 105

WTP (willingness to pay)
  definition, 95, 97
  marginal, 83–84, 89–90
  for public goods, 89
  total. *See* TWTP (total willingness to pay)
  utility change and, 97
  WTA differences with, 105

X

Yield, 416. *See also* Catch; Effort-yield
    curve
  North Sea herring stock/effort and,
    420–421